Jesuit Saints
&
Martyrs

Jesuit Saints & Martyrs

*Short Biographies of the Saints,
Blessed, Venerables, and
Servants of God
of the Society of Jesus*

Joseph N. Tylenda, S.J.

Second Edition

an imprint of
Loyola Press

Chicago

an imprint of
Loyola Press

**3441 North Ashland Avenue
Chicago, Illinois 60657
1-800-621-1008**

Cover design by Anne Bruns
Interior design by Carol Sawyer

Library of Congress Cataloging-in-Publication Data
Tylenda, Joseph N.
   Jesuit saints & martyrs : short biographies of the saints, blessed, venerables, and servants of God of the Society of Jesus / Joseph N. Tylenda. — 2nd ed.
        p.   cm.
   Includes bibliographical references and index.
   ISBN 0-8294-1074-0
   1. Jesuits—Biography. 2. Christian saints—Biography. 3. Christian martyrs —Biography. 4. Blessed—Biography. I. Title.
BX3755.T94   1998
271'.53022
[B]—DC21
                                                                          97-49656
                                                                              CIP
                                                                              r98

98 99 00 01 02 / 10 9 8 7 6 5 4 3 2 1

IOANNI PAVLO SECVNDO AVCTOR

PIETATE ET OBOEDIENTIA MOTVS

SOCIETATIS SEMPER PROPRIA IESV

IGNATIANIS AB INITIIS ATQVE

HISCE VITAE NARRATIONIBVS

MIRANDVM COLLVSTRATA IN
EXEMPLVM

OBSERVANTER DICAT AMANTER

SCRIPTIONEM SVAM

PETRI SVCCESSORI

Table of Contents

March

April

May

June

July

October

November

December

Appendices

List of Illustrations

Introduction

This is a book about Jesuit Saints, Blessed, Venerables, and Servants of God, and it is intended for my fellow Jesuits interested in becoming more familiar with those predecessors of ours who had eminently lived their vocation and achieved holiness. It is also intended for our many friends who would like to know more about us for a variety of reasons—because they have attended a Jesuit school or worship in a Jesuit church, or because they have a relative in the order or have participated in or generously supported our apostolates in this country and abroad. Since these friends enjoy reading about us, these brief biographies may show them what it means to be a Jesuit.

There is a total of 179 entries dealing with 347 Jesuits. The date assigned to each entry is usually that of the individual's death, and in some cases it coincides with the date of his liturgical celebration in the Society of Jesus. If two or more have died on the same date, that date is given to the one of higher rank; for example, a Servant of God yields to a Blessed, and the one of lower rank is assigned a date as near as possible to the date of his death.

The Jesuits whose sketches follow are (1) those Saints and Blessed who appear in the General Liturgical Calendar of the Society of Jesus, (2) those whose causes for beatification are on file in Rome with the Congregation for the Causes of the Saints, and (3) those whose causes are being prepared for submission to that same congregation. Those of the first category may be found in Appendix I; those of the second category in *Index ac Status Causarum* (Rome, 1985), and those of the third in the *Acta Romana Societatis Iesu,* the annual publication from Jesuit headquarters in Rome.

The titles of Servant of God, Venerable, and Blessed are given to individuals whose causes are still in progress, whereas the title of Saint indicates that the process has come to its desired completion. Servant of God is given in the first stages of the process. After the death of a person who was known for holiness of life and whose intercessory power with God has been experienced by a great number of the faithful, the bishop of the diocese where the Servant of God had lived and/or died, formally initiates the cause by meticulously investigating that person's life and by seeking the testimony of witnesses who had known him or her. The bishop also collects that person's writings and seeks the assurance that no public cult or veneration has been accorded the individual. In the case of a martyr, the process is somewhat less complicated since the principal objective need be only to prove that he or she had died for the faith. If the outcome of these early investigations is affirmative, the bishop then submits his findings to the Congregation for the Causes of the Saints in Rome.

When a cause arrives and is accepted in Rome, a Postulator is appointed, whose principal task is to represent the petitioner. The work done under the bishop's supervision is there scrutinized and the Servant of God's writings are examined for orthodoxy. In the case of one not a martyr, the *Positio* (something similar to a position paper) is prepared. Basically this document is a biography of the individual, demonstrating the Servant of God's holiness by showing that he or she had lived the Catholic faith to an extraordinary or exemplary degree, especially as manifested by the exercise of the theological virtues (faith, hope, charity) as well as the cardinal virtues (justice, prudence, temperance, fortitude). Once a panel of theologians studying the case votes affirmatively on the *Positio,* the case is presented to the pope who, on approving the work done up to this point, declares that the Servant of God has in fact lived a life of heroic virtue, and the person is thereafter known as Venerable.

To advance to the next step, which is beatification, one miracle, clinically recorded and accepted by a team of physicians as well as theologians, is required for the purpose of attesting to the Venerable's intercessory power with God in heaven. When the miracle has been formally accepted, the Venerable is beatified. In the case of martyrs the required miracle may be waived. With beatification the new Blessed is permitted public veneration for the first time, but it is limited to a definite geographic area, that is, a country or a province where the Blessed had lived, or to the religious order of which he or she had been a member. After another miracle has been approved, the Blessed is canonized a Saint and proposed to the universal Church for public veneration. Readers who are interested in more extensive coverage of these processes will find it in Kenneth L. Woodward's *Making Saints: How the Catholic Church Determines Who Becomes a Saint, Who Doesn't, and Why* (New York: Simon & Schuster, 1990).

In the present volume we list 44 Jesuit Saints, 140 Blessed, 36 Venerables, and 127 Servants of God. Among these 347 there are 4 bishops, 235 priests, 44 scholastics, 62 brothers, and 2 candidates. To view them from another perspective, 265 (76 percent) are martyrs and 83 (24 percent) confessors. Although it is certainly not any "better" to be a martyr than a confessor, clearly the process leading to beatification /canonization is more simple. Postulators of the cause of a confessor must establish that the potential saint lived a holy life, while the cause of the martyr depends only on establishing that the person was killed for the faith.

World history has had a significant effect on the circumstances under which these Jesuits achieved their places in the calendar, as well as their nationality. The great number of martyrs reflects the persecutions that the Church had to endure in various countries, e.g., in England, Japan, France (during the French Revolution), and Spain (during the Spanish Civil War). Among the 21 countries these Jesuits represent, Spain can claim the greatest number, 98, followed by Portugal with 66, France 58, Britain 33, Italy 30, Japan 24, Germany and Mexico 6 each, Poland 5, Lebanon 4, Belgium, Chile, Holland, Hungary, Ireland, and Korea 2 each, Croatia, Peru, Switzerland, Syria, and the United States 1 each.

In the second half of the sixteenth century, Spain and Portugal supplied the most missionaries because both nations had colonies abroad and hence sent native sons—not only Jesuits but Franciscans and Dominicans as well—to foreign shores. England was Protestant and hence had no Catholic missionary effort abroad. When Englishmen entered the Society, their desire was to return to England to convert their countrymen. To cover all of the events in four-and-a-half centuries of Jesuit missionary history would take much more space than is afforded by this introduction, but generalizations like these should serve to answer some of the most obvious questions.

Cultural differences also have an influence on population statistics in the calendar. Since causes begin at the diocesan level, Continental nationals have no better access to the process than anyone else, but Latins (Italians, Spanish, etc.) do exhibit a more effusive piety than their Anglo-Saxon neighbors. When a person renowned for holiness dies (or in some cases even before death) Latins are very much inclined to invoke that person's intercession in their behalf. As a result that individual's cause progresses somewhat quickly, because his or her compatriots continually bombard heaven with their petitions and eventually miracles do happen. Applying a relic to a sick person's body in hopes of a miracle seems only natural to them, whereas it would not be so for many Americans.

This second edition is a revision of *Jesuit Saints and Martyrs* first published in 1984. Since that time the Society has 6 new Saints, 12 new Blessed, and 4 new Venerables. In some cases these additions have resulted in a change of dates for some entries. All told, there are 19 new entries dealing with 24 additional Jesuits.

This volume has seen completion only because of the kindness of many brother Jesuits throughout the world who most graciously responded to my requests for information. To these, I am in debt.

May 16, 1997
Feast of St. Andrew Bobola

January

January 1

Solemnity of Mary, Mother of God and of the Giving of the Holy Name of Jesus

Titular Feast of the Society of Jesus

On the eighth day after the Child's birth in Bethlehem, he was, according to Luke 2:21, circumcised and given the name Jesus. Since the Society of Jesus bears that same holy name, it regards January 1 as its titular feast.

St. Ignatius of Loyola and his companions were not always known as the Society of Jesus; they only chose this name after several years of close companionship and much prayer. Between the years 1530 and 1535, when Ignatius was recruiting his first companions in Paris, his group was without a name. In 1537, when they were in Venice awaiting the arrival of the pilgrim ship, which was to take them to the Holy Land, they kept busy by working in two of Venice's hospitals. They still had no name for themselves, but the Venetians called them Iniguists after Ignatius' baptismal name, Iñigo. This name was not of their choosing.

Due to the threat of war between Venice and the Turks, the chances of the group's going to Jerusalem were greatly diminished; hence, toward the end of September or in early October 1537, Ignatius and his companions gathered in Vicenza, a day's journey from Venice, to discuss their future plans. One of the questions they discussed was, When anyone shall ask us who we are, what name shall we give them? This was an eminently practical question, and to arrive at a fitting answer Ignatius suggested that they pray over it. When the discussion was resumed, everyone acknowledged that, since no one among them was their head, but only Jesus Christ, and since it was Jesus whom they desired to serve, they ought to carry his name. Thus they chose to be known as the Society of Jesus, that is, an association of friends or companions of Jesus.

It is not known who among the group first proposed the name; if it was not Ignatius, it was certainly in line with his thinking. Following his conversion at Loyola, he had given himself entirely to his Master. His pilgrimage to the Holy Land in 1523 was his response to his meditative reading of Ludolph of Saxony's *Life of Christ,* and while Ignatius walked the streets of Jerusalem he tried to visualize Christ walking the very same streets. He even had to check in which direction Christ's feet were pointed when he ascended into heaven! After Ignatius' ordination to the priesthood on June 24, 1537, and while preparing to celebrate his first Mass, his daily prayer to our Lady was that she would place him next to her Son. Ignatius wanted to be with Jesus, to walk in his footsteps, to think his thoughts, and to live his life. For him the Society of Jesus was the only name for his group.

Not long after the gathering in Vicenza, Ignatius experienced a spiritual vision in which he believed God was confirming the Society in its choice of a name. It was sometime in mid-November 1537, when he and two companions, Peter Favre and James Laínez, were heading for Rome to offer their services to Pope Paul III, that they stopped to enter a tiny chapel on the Via Cassia, in the small village of La Storta, about eight miles north of Rome. As soon as Ignatius entered the chapel he felt a sudden change come over him, and while in prayer he had a remarkable vision. He saw God the Father together with Jesus, who was carrying his cross. Both Father and Son looked kindly upon him, and he heard the Father say to the Son: "I wish you to take him as your servant." Jesus then directed his words to the kneeling pilgrim and said: "It is my will that you serve us." This was what Ignatius had always wanted. The Father then added, "I will be favorable to you in Rome."

The vision at La Storta was God's response to Ignatius' constant prayer, for it was in that small chapel outside Rome that he was placed next to Mary's Son. In Ignatius' mind God was confirming the Society's name. He and his companions were now Jesus' servants. Once Ignatius had this divine approval, he would not hear of having the name changed. So important was this name to him that he included it at the very beginning of the summary description he drew up, when he sought papal approval for his new order. It is true that no order before this time had ever taken the name of Jesus. This was not presumption on the part of the first Jesuits; all they meant to do was to indicate their desire to grow more and more in the service of Christ for the good of the Church.

By carrying the name of Jesus, the Society defines its way of life; namely, that Jesus is its sole model. The members of the Society must not only know him and love him, they must also follow him, even in poverty and humiliation. The name Society of Jesus is a reminder that Jesuits must live Jesus.

It was an angel that gave Jesus his name, and though the name of the Society of Jesus was not given to the first Jesuits by an angel from heaven, nevertheless, Ignatius and his followers believed that God had indeed approved their carrying his Son's holy name.

Prayer

Lord God, you gave the name of Jesus to your eternal Word, born of your hand-maid, the Virgin Mary. Open our minds and hearts to receive in our own day the word you speak to us in your Son, our Lord Jesus Christ, who lives and reigns with you and the Holy Spirit, one God, for ever and ever.

January 5

S. G. Ignatius Arámburu 1852–1935

Fr. Ignatius Arámburu spent forty-three years of his life in the ancient Spanish city of Burgos and so greatly did the people value his priestly ministry among them that they named him "Apostle of Burgos." He was born in northern Spain, in the town of Segura, in the Basque region of Guipúzcoa, on January 31, 1852, and was named after the martyred bishop St. Ignatius of Antioch. After attending the local schools, Ignatius entered the novitiate of the exiled Spanish Jesuits at Poyanne, in southern France, on July 2, 1871. He was then nineteen years old. During his two years as a novice he learned what it was to be a Jesuit and to what he was being called, and then on July 31, 1873, he pronounced his three vows of religion. Ignatius remained in France for the next five years, studying the humanities for two years and pursuing courses in philosophy for three. When in 1878 it was possible for the Spanish Jesuits to return to their homeland, Ignatius went to teach at the college at La Guardia, and after three years in the classroom he went to Oña, in 1881, for his theological training. The theologate at Oña, a former Benedictine monastery, had only recently been acquired by the Jesuits and was used as their house of studies. It was in the monastery's chapel that the thirty-two-year-old Ignatius was ordained to the priesthood on July 27, 1884.

In 1886 Fr. Arámburu's first assignment, after completing his years of training, was to write for and edit the Spanish edition of *The Messenger of the Sacred Heart*. The writing came easily since he was filled with devotion to the Sacred Heart of Jesus. When Fr. Arámburu's health began to fail, his superiors thought the climate of Burgos, a city more to the south, would be better for him, and in September 1891 he moved to his new assignment. From the date of his coming to the date of his death—forty-three years later—the names of Arámburu and Burgos became so closely associated that they were almost inseparable.

Assigned to the Jesuit residence in Burgos, Fr. Arámburu viewed the entire city as his parish. Knowing that the working people were for the most part uneducated and in need of instruction in the faith, he arranged classes for them. He chose exemplary Catholics as his catechists and together they offered weekly classes, which hundreds of people regularly attended. He also formed societies to promote frequent Communion and devotion to our Lord in the Blessed Sacrament. The youth of the city were, perhaps, Fr. Arámburu's special joy, and these he gathered about him and formed into sodalities of our Lady, training them to be responsible in living their faith. He likewise founded residences and shelters where the poor and needy could prepare for future employment. Fr. Arámburu's concerns also extended to those in prison, whom he often visited, and to the sick and dying, whom he attended in their homes. So frequently did he walk the streets of Burgos to anoint a dying person that it was said that there was not a single house in the city he had not visited. In addition, he spent many hours in the confessional giving instruction and spiritual direction. Fr. Arámburu loved Burgos and once said: "I am very happy, very happy among the people of Burgos. Among them I have no enemies and everyone is my friend and brother." The Burgalese thought the same of him.

The country's religious climate started to change in the 1930s. Masonic Lodges sought to curtail the Society's apostolic work in Spain and they began their attack by publishing lies and false reports about the Society and by having Jesuits insulted as they walked through the city. The Masons succeeded and on January 23, 1932, the atheistic republican government decreed the Society's dissolution and confiscated its property. The Jesuits were sent into exile, but Fr. Arámburu, who was now in his eighties, and another elderly Jesuit were permitted to remain in Burgos. The government expected no harm to come from two old men. Fr. Arámburu was deeply distressed by the blow given the Society, and in one of his last letters he signed himself as "Servant of Christ, an exile in his own country, without citizenship after having served Spain for eighty years, and now living on alms in a strange house. Ignatius Mary Arámburu."

Toward the end of October 1934, Fr. Arámburu suffered a pulmonary infection and was put to bed. His health steadily deteriorated and he died on January 5, 1935. The news of his death quickly spread through the city, and within hours of his going to God his many friends gathered at his room to express their love for him. His friends quietly passed by his body, touching it with rosaries and medals. Among these were the sodalists—the boys whom he had taken off the streets and given a home—and the workers, who had learned religion in his classes. They all remembered him.

Fr. Arámburu was buried in the cemetery of St. Joseph, but his remains were later transferred to *La Merced*, the Jesuit church in Burgos. Because of the people's love for their apostle and because they recognized his holiness while he was among them, they prayed to him after his death, seeking his intercession with God. When so great a number of prayers were answered, it was decided that Fr. Arámburu's cause should be introduced in Rome.

S. G. Peter Joseph de Clorivière 1735–1820

Fr. Peter de Clorivière is the historical link that joins the old and the restored Society in France. He was born at Saint-Malo, Brittany, on June 29, 1735, and was educated at the English Benedictine school in Douai, 1749–1753. At age eighteen he tried the sailor's life for a year, but since it was not to his liking he went to Paris in 1754 to begin the study of law. There he met a diocesan priest, who suggested that he make a retreat. It was during those prayerful days that he experienced what he called his conversion—a growing interest in prayer, an increased love of God, first thoughts about the priesthood, and an overwhelming desire to receive Holy Communion daily, something unheard of during the eighteenth century.

The only contact Peter had with the Jesuits in Paris was when he sometimes attended Mass at the church attached to their novitiate. On February 23, 1756, as he was leaving the church, a lady, whom he did not know, said to him: "God is calling you under the protection of St. Ignatius and St. Francis Xavier. This is the novitiate. Enter it." Peter retraced his steps into the church and spent more time in prayer. When he rose to leave he felt certain that God wanted him to be a Jesuit.

Peter entered the novitiate on August 14, 1756, pronounced his vows on August 17, 1758, and then began his study of philosophy. Because he had a stuttering problem, he was afraid that he would never be able to teach or preach as a priest should. He decided, therefore, that he should be a brother instead. His superiors insisted, however, that he continue his studies for the priesthood. He taught at Compiègne from 1759 until April 1, 1762, when the government closed all Jesuit schools in France and ordered the expulsion of all Jesuits. Peter then went to the English College in Liège, Belgium, to study theology. Ordained on October 2, 1763, he remained there to complete his studies.

After his years of Jesuit training, Fr. Clorivière's first assignment was in London, where he arrived in July 1766. Shortly after his arrival he became mysteriously ill with a sickness that lasted six months. Since his health was poor, his superiors thought it better for him to go to Ghent, Belgium, as assistant to the master of novices—an important position but one not so demanding on the body.

In 1770 he was assigned to be spiritual director of the English Benedictine nuns in Brussels. Three years later on July 21, 1773, Pope Clement XIV, who had been pressured by various European monarchs to suppress the Society of Jesus, acquiesced to their demands and signed the brief that brought about the Society's dissolution. With the brief's promulgation, Fr. Clorivière was no longer a Jesuit, nevertheless, he continued at the Brussels monastery until 1775, when it became unlawful for a subject of another nation (in this case France) to be the director of a Belgian monastery. Fr. Clorivière thus returned to his native land and assumed the directorship of another monastery at Jarcy, near Paris, and in 1779 became pastor at Paramé on the Breton coast. Fr. Clorivière's stuttering was a torment and a humiliation, but he did not allow this to keep him from doing his duty in the pulpit. He stormed heaven with prayers asking for a cure, and one Sunday morning in 1780, when he awoke, he felt somehow different. It was only when he began his sermon that day that he knew that his prayers had been answered. His stuttering had disappeared. He remained at this parish until 1786, when the bishop made him director of the diocesan school at Dinan.

The coming of the French Revolution brought persecution to the Church, and since his priestly ministry was now curtailed at home, Fr. Clorivière wrote in 1790 to Bishop John Carroll of Baltimore, Maryland, asking to work in his diocese. While a student in Liège, he had met Carroll, who had also been a student there. Fr. Clorivière thought that he could, perhaps, work to restore the Society of Jesus in the United States of America, and it appears that he would have gone to Maryland if Providence had not had him change his mind. If he could labor for the Society's restoration abroad, he reflected, then why not work for it during these difficult times in his native France. With this conviction in mind, he remained at home and initiated the work that was to become his special apostolate. He founded the Society of Daughters of the Heart of Mary in 1790 and the Society of the Heart of Jesus in 1791. Both congregations had the aims and goals of the Society of Jesus, but because of the times during which they were founded, neither society lived in community. Fr. Clorivière devoted his life and efforts to these groups—he instructed the members in the principles of the religious life and wrote their rules.

On learning that the Society of Jesus still existed and was active in White Russia (today's Belarus)—Catherine the Great had forbidden the publication of the papal brief of suppression—Fr. Clorivière wrote to the Russian superior asking for readmission into the Society. But before he could act upon the favorable reply he received, he was arrested on May 5, 1804, and cast into a Paris prison on suspicion that he had been involved in the Cadoudal conspiracy on Napoleon's life in December 1800. He was totally innocent but the authorities had confused him with his nephew who bore the same name. The nephew, who seems to have been implicated in the conspiracy, left France rather suddenly and set out for Savannah, Georgia. Fr. Clorivière's greatest affliction during imprisonment was his inability to celebrate Mass, but he did have the consolation of keeping the Blessed Sacrament, which was brought to him whenever friends came to visit. Even in prison his zeal could not lie dormant; he continued to guide his two societies, instruct converts, and write commentaries on various books of the Old and New Testaments. Finally set free on April 11, 1809, when he was seventy-four years old, Fr. Clorivière again wrote to the Jesuits in White Russia about readmission. This time the superior advised him to remain in France and continue his efforts there for the Society.

On August 7, 1814, to every Jesuit's joy, Pope Pius VII restored the Society throughout the Church. The immediate response to this decree was overwhelming and by the end of 1814 Fr. Clorivière had sixty novices. A good number of these were priests who had been members of the Society of Faith during the revolution. Together with their superior, Fr. Joseph Varin, they had sought admission into the Society of Jesus. Within three years Fr. Clorivière's group numbered 144 men, with two residences and five colleges. The Society in France was growing, but Fr. Clorivière, who was now beginning to show his age, asked in 1818 to be relieved of the burdens of superior in order to prepare himself for death. He continued to live a simple life (attending community functions, meals, and recreation) and to be an inspiration to everyone. On January 9, 1820, he woke up, as he regularly did, at 2:45 A.M. and spent the next hour meditating in his cold room. At four he went to the chapel to make his usual half-hour of adoration, kneeling at the communion rail. When the community came in at 4:30, the Jesuits discovered that their beloved father had died in prayer at his place before the Blessed Sacrament.

Fr. Clorivière, who worked tirelessly for the restoration of the Society of Jesus in France, died in his eighty-fifth year, a worthy son of the Society and of its founder St. Ignatius. His cause is presently under consideration in Rome.

January 10

S. G. Paul Ginhac 1824–1895

Fr. Paul Ginhac spent his entire priestly ministry as spiritual guide to younger Jesuits. He was born on May 31, 1824, at Mazel-Serverette, Languedoc, France, the seventh of twelve children. In 1836, when he was twelve years old, he entered the Mende Academy, but in 1839 his father enrolled him in the Chirac Seminary, in the hope that discipline would cool his son's exuberant spirit. The son complained bitterly about the school: there was no freedom; he was reduced to slavery; the diet was monotonous. After a year his father withdrew him and he returned to Mende to graduate two years later. Paul had an independent spirit and planned to go to Paris to pursue a career in business, though his parents objected. When he related his plans to his sister, a Visitation nun in Mende, she asked him to talk his plans over with a priest who lived nearby. He did as she requested and the priest, in turn, asked him to go with him to a mission that a Jesuit was then giving in one of the local churches.

Unable to say no without giving offense, Paul agreed to go. His heart was unexpectedly touched by the sermon and he continued the mission to its end. On the mission's last day a procession was organized to walk through the city's streets, and when Paul came upon it, he saw a large crucifix carried by young men. He looked upon our Lord's figure and it seemed to him that rays of light came from the face and penetrated his whole being. Trembling all over, he said in a loud voice: "From this moment I will belong to God alone." From that hour Paul Ginhac was dead to self and lived only for God.

Paul entered the Jesuit novitiate in Avignon on January 4, 1843, determined always to be faithful to the Society's rules and to make his life an uninterrupted exercise of union with God. Before completing his novitiate training he was sent to Ben-Aknoun in Algeria as prefect in charge of orphans. In 1848 he returned to France, to Vals-près-Le Puy, to begin his studies for the priesthood. He was ordained on December 18, 1852, somewhat earlier than the other members of his class because he was appointed assistant to the master of novices. In 1855 Fr. Ginhac became master at Vals and took on the task of fashioning the young men who entered the Society, teaching them the principles of the spiritual life and introducing them to prayer and mortification. Fr. Ginhac was rather young for this important task—he was only thirty-one years old—but his virtue and good judgment made up for his lack of experience. He successfully fulfilled this office for the next fourteen years. In 1860 when the novitiate moved from Vals to Toulouse, he also became rector of the community. He spent eight years in Toulouse, and in addition to guiding Jesuits, he was the director of some chosen souls in that great city. Among these were two outstanding individuals, namely, Blessed Mother Mary of Jesus (Emilie d'Oultremont), foundress of the Society of Mary Reparatrix, and Blessed Marie-Thérèse de Soubiran, foundress of the Society of Mary Auxiliatrix.

In 1869 Fr. Ginhac became instructor of tertians at Castres, a position similar to that of master of novices but of greater responsibility, since the tertians were mature, ordained priests and not mere youths. He was their spiritual guide, but rather than instructing them in the rudiments of the spiritual life, his task was to instill in his tertians the spirit of St. Ignatius and stimulate them in the pursuit of perfection. During the years from 1877 to 1880 he was instructor at Paray-le-Monial, living in the same house where St. Claude La Colombière had lived and near the monastery where our Lord revealed the treasures of his Sacred Heart to St. Margaret Mary Alacoque.

In 1880, when the anticlerical government of France closed the Society's churches, schools, and residences, the Jesuit scholastics left the country to complete their studies and training elsewhere. Through the generosity of the Countess de Vilèle, however, the tertianship moved to her château at Mourvilles, and Fr. Ginhac continued his work there until 1890, when the tertianship returned to Castres.

While giving a retreat to Carmelite Sisters in Paris during the summer of 1894, the wound in Fr. Ginhac's leg opened and caused him much pain. He continued the retreats he had scheduled for the summer and when he returned to

Castres his wound was worse. When the infirmarian suggested that he go to bed to permit the wound to heal, he would not hear of it. After Christmas he caught a cold and one of his lungs became congested. He was subsequently confined to bed with a fever and a rash of large spots soon appeared on his body. Because of the intolerable itching, his sleepless nights were spent in continual tossing. Yet throughout his sufferings he repeated: "May God be praised!" By the morning of January 10 it was clear that he could not survive. After being anointed, he blessed the community gathered in his room, bade them goodbye, and patiently waited for the end to come. At 10:30 that evening this model Jesuit died, giving his soul to God in return for the love that God had given him. Fr. Ginhac was seventy-one years old and had been a Jesuit for fifty-two years. His cause was introduced in Rome on February 27, 1924.

January 12

S. G. Bartholomew Álvares 1706–1737
S. G. Emmanuel de Abreu 1708–1737
S. G. Vincent da Cunha 1708–1737
S. G. John Caspar Kratz 1698–1737

Martyrs of Vietnam

During the first half of the eighteenth century the Christian missions in Tonkin (part of modern day Vietnam) periodically suffered persecution. In 1735, the new king was somewhat tolerant, unlike his father, and Jesuit superiors at mission headquarters in Macao thought that, despite some dangers, new missionaries could be sent into that region. Five priests were assigned: Bartholomew Álvares, Emmanuel de Abreu, John Caspar Kratz, Christopher da Sampayo, and Emmanuel Carvalho. All were Portuguese except Kratz, who was German.

Fr. Álvares was born in Parâmio on August 10, 1706, and entered the Society in Coimbra in 1723. He went to India in 1730 and during the following year transferred to Macao. Fr. Abreu, born on October 14, 1708, in the Aveiro district of Portugal, became a Jesuit in 1724; he arrived in Goa, India, in 1733 and went to Macao the following year. Since the other two Portuguese Jesuits, Frs. Sampayo and Carvalho, did not die as martyrs, they are only peripherally connected with this narrative.

Fr. Kratz was an adventurer from his youth. He was born in Golzheim bei Düren (between Aachen and Cologne) on September 14, 1698. He attended the Jesuit gymnasium in Düsseldorf, and after completing his studies (1721) left home and spent the next five years traveling through Italy, Spain, Portugal, and France. He returned to Germany, but travel was in his blood and the mysterious East beckoned. He went to Amsterdam and there enlisted as an officer in the colonial army of the Dutch East India Company. He sailed during the summer of 1727 and after a seven-month voyage disembarked (January 1728) at Batavia (today's Djakarta, Indonesia). Since the citizenry there were almost all Dutch Calvinists, John had to keep his Catholicism to himself. Whenever a Portuguese vessel from Macao came to port, or a Spanish galleon from Manila, he boarded it in search of a priest so that he could receive the sacraments and attend Mass. Then in May 1730 the Jesuit Philip Sibin came to Batavia. John met him and discussed his desires with him, and when the vessel returned to Macao in June both Fr. Sibin and John were aboard. In Macao, John, now thirty-two years of age, entered the Society (October 27, 1730) and after noviceship spent two years studying theology. He was ordained shortly before Christmas 1734, and in early 1735 he too was appointed to the Tonkin mission.

These five missionaries departed Macao on April 13, 1735. After a few days of good sailing, and having passed Hainan Island, they were stopped by Chinese coastal guards and arrested. Their attempt to purchase their freedom was unsuccessful and, hence, they were taken to Nao-Cheu and imprisoned. When their superior in Macao heard of their detention, he sent an emissary to Nao-Cheu to negotiate a release. The five were given their freedom in November on condition that they return whence they had come. Thus the five missionaries were back in Macao on December 24, 1735.

Though their first attempt to reach Tonkin proved abortive, they did not abandon their plan. To the five already assigned, another was added, namely, Fr. Vincent da Cunha. He too was Portuguese, born in Lisbon on February 2, 1708; he had been a Jesuit since 1726 and had gone to Macao in 1734. The six missionaries, now dressed as Chinese merchants, left Macao on March 10, 1736. Avoiding sea travel, they and their guide followed a land route through China's Guangdong province which brought them to Lienchow, on the northeastern shore of today's Gulf of Tonkin. From there the group sailed the short distance to Lofeu, a Tonkin mission station, located near the border of both kingdoms.

At Lofeu their guide left them to return to Macao. After a much needed rest among the Tonkinese Christians, the missionaries were eager to go inland. Fr. Sampayo, however, because he had fallen ill, was unable to travel, and so Fr. Carvalho stayed behind to care for him. Thus four Jesuits together with two Tonkinese catechists, Mark Trí and Vincent Nghiem, sailed for Batxa, where a prominent Christian gave them hospitality for two days.

The news of their presence in Batxa, however, was not kept a total secret and some non-Christians, hearing of the priests' arrival, planned to waylay them after they had left the city. This happened on April 12, when the missionaries were ambushed and robbed. With chains on arms and feet, they were taken to the local mandarin, who on finding a crucifix on one of the missionaries' chests, exclaimed: "There is no doubt that these are teachers of that religion which has often been forbidden in these states, and under grave penalties." After heavy, wooden yokes were placed about each one's neck, they were led to prison. On the 18th they were handed over to the district governor who kept them until the 26th, when he sent them, in cages, to the capital, Ketcho (today's Hanoi).

The trip under the hot sun lasted three days and by the time they arrived the four missionaries and two catechists suffered acutely from hunger and thirst. At the royal palace mandarins interrogated both catechists, while the missionaries were invited to tread upon a crucifix placed on the ground before them. Rather than profane their religion, each knelt down and kissed the crucifix. In response to their being kicked and goaded, the missionaries expressed willingness to lose life and limb, but they would not apostatize. Unsuccessful in their attempt, the mandarins ordered the six to be incarcerated until the king's wishes were known.

Days later the prisoners were taken before the supreme tribunal, and the catechists were again interrogated. Because they courageously continued to profess their faith, Mark was given fifteen hammer blows to his knees and Vincent five. Recalled the following day and once more subjected to questioning, they responded as they had done the previous day. At the moment that they were about to receive more hammer blows, one of the judges stood up and spoke: "This one," pointing to Mark, "deserves, without any further examination, to be quartered, because he led these teachers of a proscribed religion here. This companion of his should also be beheaded because he is his accomplice. The same should be done to the four teachers of that religion; though forbidden, they dared to come here with no other reason than to teach it."

The mandarins then ordered the prisoners to be taken to the prison known as "the Hell of the East." This prison deserved its name because it was sweltering hot—it was exposed all day to the beating sun, with thin walls, without light, and the only air was what entered through several narrow wall slits. The air was always fetid, and the stench from decaying bodies was so overpowering that prisoners sometimes became delirious. Chains never left their feet and the bare ground served as their beds. Mosquitoes so abounded that not long after arrival their bodies were swollen from bites. In addition, meals were sparse and the bread they received was hard and stale.

Executions, by custom, were carried out on the twelfth day after the last moon, which in 1737 was January 12. On the 7th of that month a government functionary came to the prison to make official recognition of the prisoners (the missionaries as well as other malefactors). Two days later a catechist named Benedict came to see the Jesuits: "You should give me a tip for I bring you good news. You are now half-martyrs, but within days you will be beheaded for Jesus Christ."

Amid their expressions of thanksgiving to God, they answered Benedict: "We will repay you with love, the coin used in heaven." On the 10th a mandarin arrived to read them their sentence of death and assigned an executioner to each.

Before dawn on the 12th, Christians gathered near the prison entrance, and with the coming of dawn soldiers also arrived. The prisoners had their arms bound behind them and the procession began its long way to the place of execution. Each was escorted by a soldier on one side and an executioner on the other. Fr. Álvares led the procession, then came Frs. Abreu, Kratz, and Cunha. Afterwards came the felons. When they arrived at the royal palace, a mandarin appeared and read out the sentences. To the missionaries he said: "At the king's command, you four foreigners are to be beheaded, for having come to this kingdom to preach the prohibited religion of the Portuguese."

The place of execution was a large field, in whose center were wooden posts, waist high. Each was led to a post. Kneeling down, with backs to the post, each was tightly bound. When the king's uncle, standing in a nearby pavilion, gave the signal with his fan, the executioners raised their sabres and struck their victims. Frs. Álvares and Kratz were beheaded with one stroke each, while Fr. Abreu's head hung on his chest. Fr. Cunha's executioner's first blow landed on one of the martyr's arms, the second also failed, and a third was needed.

After the execution the Christians, who had witnessed the martyrdoms, took the bodies of the missionaries to their villages to be buried, until they could later be transferred to Macao. As for the two catechists, Vincent had died in prison on June 30, 1736, as a result of maltreatment, and Mark had been sent into exile. He had asked to die with the missionaries, but this was denied him. He died sometime in June 1737.

January 19

Bl. James Salès 1556–1593

Bl. William Saultemouche 1557–1593

Martyrs of Aubenas

Fr. James Salès and Br. William Saultemouche were martyred in France for their defense of Christ's real presence in the Eucharist.

James Salès was born at Lezoux in the Auvergne on March 21, 1556. He attended the Jesuit school at Billom from 1568 to 1572, and in his early teens became especially devoted to our Lord in the Blessed Sacrament. During his last year at Billom, he felt that God was calling him to be a Jesuit priest, but as his parents' only son, he knew he was needed at home. When he moved on to Clermont College in Paris, his desire to become a Jesuit increased and often he knelt before the Blessed Sacrament asking our Lord to remove the obstacles keeping him from entering the Society. The following year his father granted him permission, and on November 1, 1573, James entered the Jesuit novitiate at Verdun.

After a two-year noviceship he went, in October 1575, to the University of Pont-à-Mousson, to pursue his philosophical and theological studies. In 1580 his course in theology was interrupted when his superiors asked him to teach philosophy at the university, thus postponing ordination. This teaching experience lasted three years. He then went to Clermont College to complete his theology and was ordained there on April 20, 1585. He was now twenty-nine years of age and was again assigned to Pont-à-Mousson, this time to teach theology.

In January 1587 Fr. Salès wrote to Fr. Claudio Acquaviva, general of the Society in Rome, expressing his interest and willingness to go to any mission in America, China, or Japan. The response was, at first, disappointing—he was told there was mission work to be done at home. He studied the general's letter and understood what he meant—France itself was mission territory, especially since it was being torn apart by the Wars of Religion. Since 1562 the Huguenots, or French Calvinists, had sought to force their heterodox views on Catholics. Thus, Fr. Salès resolved to make France his mission field to confirm the Catholics in their faith and to demonstrate the errors of the Calvinists.

Fr. Salès remained at Pont-à-Mousson until 1589, teaching in the university with intermittent excursions to nearby towns to preach missions to the faithful. One such visit was to Metz, a hotbed of Calvinism, and there he put his theology to excellent use. The Huguenots of Metz also attended his sermons, and whenever the Catholics listened intently to the arguments of Fr. Salès, the Huguenots tried to break up the meetings by causing a disturbance and heckling the preacher. No matter how they tried to disrupt the mission, the end result was that the Catholics were strengthened in their faith.

In 1590 Fr. Salès was appointed to the chair of "controversial" theology at Tournon. It was his task to draw up a program of studies specifically designed to treat the religious controversies of the day; that is, to show the truth of the Catholic teaching and to respond to the objections of the Protestants. In addition to his regular classes he found time to continue his mission preaching, and as an aid for himself as well as for others, he wrote several short booklets explaining the Catholic faith. One of these was on the Eucharist. When his provincial learned of the quality of these booklets, he suggested that they be printed so that others could also benefit from them. But before anything could come of this suggestion, Fr. Salès was sent to Aubenas on his final mission.

In 1587 the Catholic people of Aubenas had overthrown the Huguenots, who had control of the city for several years. Thereafter the baron of Montréal, governor of Aubenas, annually requested a Jesuit to give the Advent and Lenten series of sermons. In 1592 he again made the request; this time he wanted not merely a preacher who would confirm the Catholics in their beliefs, but one who could also refute the Calvinist ministers, whose boldness was increasing day by day. Because this was precisely the work that Fr. Salès had been involved in at Tournon, he was well-suited for the task. When he heard that he had been chosen for Aubenas it was the happiest news he could receive, and in thanksgiving he kissed the relic of the martyred Edmund Campion, which he wore next to his heart, for having obtained this great favor for him.

As his companion to the Aubenas mission, Fr. Salès was given Br. William Saultemouche, who had recently arrived in Tournon. Br. Saultemouche was born in late 1557 at Saint-Germain-l'Herm and entered the Society as a brother in 1579 at Verdun. He served as porter at Pont-à-Mousson and was known for his simplicity, gentleness of character, and obedience. He was commonly referred to as "an angel come down from heaven in human form." He was transferred to Paris, then to Lyons, and, in the autumn of 1592, to Tournon, just in time to join Fr. Salès on the Aubenas mission.

When Fr. Salès left Tournon he knew that he would not return. He had told a fellow Jesuit: "Adieu, pray for us. We are going to our death." Fr. Salès opened his Advent sermons in Aubenas on November 29 and in his talks he kept to a clear exposition of Catholic teaching together with its proof. Never did he engage in insults or recriminations against Protestants. When the series came to an end, he visited other towns in the province, but since the tension between Catholics and Huguenots was increasing in Aubenas, he felt he had to return there. When offered shelter from the inevitable Huguenot attack, he replied: "As for death, I have been thinking of martyrdom for the past fifteen years, and I desire to sacrifice my life for God. If I am struck down in hatred of the Catholic faith, then blessed is the hand that gives that deathblow."

The two Jesuit missionaries returned to Aubenas, and on the evening of February 5, 1593, while Fr. Salès was instructing a Calvinist family, he heard an unusual uproar outside. Recognizing it for what it was, his first thought was to save the Blessed Sacrament from Huguenot profanation. He rushed to the church where he found Br. Saultemouche and together they offered their lives to God. They then went home and spent the night in prayer.

Early on Saturday, February 6, cries of "Death! Death!" were heard in the streets and within minutes three soldiers forced their way into the Jesuit residence to find their victims at prayer. Fr. Salès and Br. Saultemouche were taken to Huguenot headquarters, where a few Calvinist ministers were gathered to interrogate them. The examination, led by the Calvinist minister Labat, began with a discussion of various Catholic practices: fasting, followed by a discussion of free will, and ending with the sacraments, but with emphasis on the Eucharist. Throughout the inquiry Fr. Salès defended Christ's real presence, which the Huguenots rejected as idolatry. Thinking they could get the Jesuits to deny their faith by heaping insults upon them, the ministers called them false prophets, impostors, unbelievers, seducers, and so forth. Because they kept Fr. Salès from responding to questions by constant interruption, he told them to read what he himself had written on the Eucharist. Having his booklet in his cassock pocket, he handed it over to Labat to study. Though Br. Saultemouche was not subject to such questioning, he was witness to the abuses suffered by his companion and prayed for him in silence.

Without food all day Saturday, and after spending the night in a damp cell, both Jesuits were returned to headquarters on Sunday morning, where the interrogation continued. Once more the subject was the Eucharist, and though Fr. Salès was suffering from fatigue, he never broke under Labat's relentless examination. Labat then left the session to deliver his regular Sunday sermon, but instead of speaking of God or of Christ, it was a diatribe against the Jesuits, calling them Antichrist and worse than Antichrist.

When Labat later learned that Fr. Salès still had not succumbed to the rigors of the interrogation, he determined that the priest had to die. As the soldiers were taking Fr. Salès outside, Br. Saultemouche insisted on going with him. If his companion was to be martyred, he wanted to receive the same crown.

Outside the residence in an open square, Labat once more asked Fr. Salès to abjure his belief in Christ's real presence in the Blessed Sacrament. When the priest refused, a shot was fired into his back and he fell to the ground, saying the names "Jesus, Mary!" A soldier then drove a sword through his breast. As Br. Saultemouche bent down and threw his arms around his martyred companion, someone thrust a sword into his side and stabbed him until he too lay dead at the feet of his murderers. It was early afternoon, February 7, 1593. Fr. Salès was thirty-seven years old, and Br. Saultemouche thirty-six.

In their hatred for the Jesuits, the Calvinists had the bodies of their victims dragged like dead animals through the streets of Aubenas and for six days they were left without burial. The ministers then ordered the bodies taken outside the town to the ruins of an old church, which served as a dumping place for debris. That night, under cover of darkness, two brave Catholics found the bodies and buried them in a corner of a nearby garden.

Fr. James Salès and Br. William Saultemouche were beatified by Pope Pius XI on June 6, 1926, and their memorial is liturgically celebrated on January 19.

Prayer

Lord God, you honored these brothers of ours, Blessed James Salès and Blessed William Saultemouche, by making them one with your Son, Jesus, in the shedding of their blood. Hear their prayers, and gather into perfect unity all who believe in him. We ask this through our Lord Jesus Christ, your Son, who lives and reigns with you and the Holy Spirit, one God, for ever and ever.

Bl. William Ireland 1636–1679

Martyr of England

Fr. William Ireland was the first Jesuit martyr of the infamous Titus Oates plot. William was born in Lincolnshire in 1636, the eldest son of William Ireland of Crofton Hall in Yorkshire. He was educated at the English College at Saint-Omer, Flanders (1647–1655), and on September 7, 1655, at age nineteen, entered the English Jesuit novitiate at Watten, also in Flanders. He did his theological studies at Liège and was ordained in 1667. During the next decade he taught at Saint-Omer and was confessor to the Poor Clares at Gravelines. His chance to return to his homeland came in June 1677.

Fr. Ireland was appointed procurator of the English Province. He was stationed in London and used the alias "Ironmonger," but his apostolate at home lasted only a bit more than a year. Between July and September 1678, a certain Titus Oates, a renegade Anglican minister, out of hatred for the Society of Jesus, concocted a nefarious story with Israel Tonge, also a minister, in which they accused the English Jesuits of planning the assassination of King Charles II, of overthrowing the government and its established religion, and of reinstating the Catholic Church. This fabricated plot, which eventually came to be known as the "Popish Plot," roused the fury of the nation and renewed the persecution of Catholics. On September 28, Frs. Ireland, John Fenwick, and Mr. John Grove, their lay assistant, were arrested in the dead of night, at their residence on Wild Street in Covent Garden. They were imprisoned in the Newgate, where they suffered much from the loathsomeness of the prison and the heavy chains that rubbed the flesh raw on their legs. After nearly three months of incarceration, Fr. Ireland and his companions were brought to trial on December 17. Together with them were Fr. Thomas Whitbread and the Benedictine brother, Thomas Pickering.

During the trial, Oates falsely testified that he had been present at a special meeting of Jesuits held in April of that year, when plans were supposedly made for the king's murder. He further testified that Frs. Ireland, Fenwick, and Whitbread were present. As for Br. Pickering and Mr. Grove, he claimed they were assigned to carry out the assassination. Oates also declared that Fr. Ireland had been seen loitering about the royal residence during the month of August and that the assassination would have taken place but that on three occasions Br. Pickering's pistol failed to fire. The second witness was a certain William Bedloe, who agreed with Oates in most matters, except that he only had on hearsay that Frs. Whitbread and Fenwick had been present at the April meeting.

Fr. Ireland maintained that he was absent from London at the time he was supposed to have been loitering about the royal palace, and was able to produce witnesses to prove that he had been in the Midlands and North Wales at that time. Instead, Oates brought forth a young maid, bribed to say that she had seen the priest in London during that same period. On the basis of this false testimony, Fr. Ireland, Br. Pickering, and Mr. Grove were found guilty of high treason and ordered to be hanged, drawn, and quartered. When Fr. Ireland returned to his cell, he recorded his actions between August 3 and September 14, listing the cities he had visited and the persons with whom he had conversed.

The execution was postponed for a month by royal order. Charles II never believed that the Jesuits were involved in a plot against him, but when Oates produced more disreputable witnesses, the king, fearing the people's anger, allowed the executions to take place.

On Friday, January 24, 1679, Fr. Ireland and Mr. Grove were taken to Tyburn, the place of execution. Br. Pickering was given a reprieve, but was later executed on May 9. As Fr. Ireland and Mr. Grove were dragged to Tyburn, the London populace abused them and pelted them with stones. When they arrived at the gallows, Fr. Ireland spoke for both of them, and following the custom of the day, professed their innocence and denied any complicity against the king's life. He then added: "I beg God Almighty to shower down a thousand and a thousand blessings upon his Majesty . . . and all the royal family, and also on the whole kingdom. As for the Catholics that are here, we desire their prayers for a happy passage into a better world, and that God would be merciful to all Christian souls . . . and so I beseech all good people to pray for us and with us." On completing these words, the priest and his assistant recollected themselves in prayer. The cart was drawn from under them and they remained hanging until they were dead. The bodies were then cut down and quartered. Fr. Ireland was forty-three years old and had been a Jesuit for twenty-four years.

Fr. William Ireland and Mr. John Grove were beatified by Pope Pius XI on December 15, 1929. Fr. Ireland's memorial is celebrated by his Jesuit brethren on December 1.

Prayer

Almighty, eternal God, you chose from the people of England and Wales Blessed William Ireland and his companions to be made like Christ, who died to save the world. Listen to their prayers; strengthen your Church by the same faith and love that strengthened them, and bless it always with your gift of unity. We ask this through our Lord Jesus Christ, your Son, who lives and reigns with you and the Holy Spirit, one God, for ever and ever.

Bl. Julian Maunoir 1606–1683

To his beloved Bretons, Fr. Julian Maunoir was always and everywhere known as "Good Father." He was born in the tiny hamlet of Saint-Georges-de-Reintembault, in the diocese of Rennes, Brittany, on October 1, 1606. The local parish priest introduced him to the elements of Latin and then in 1620, when he was fourteen, he entered upon his studies at the Jesuit college in Rennes. There he enrolled in the sodality and when his Jesuit teachers noticed his attraction for the spiritual life, they instructed him in mental prayer and often spoke to him about the Jesuit missionaries in China, Japan, and Canada. It was with the Canadian mission in mind that Julian entered the Society in Paris on September 16, 1625, at age nineteen. After he pronounced his three vows as a Jesuit on September 17, 1627, he went to study philosophy at La Flèche, where one of his companions was the future martyr Isaac Jogues.

In 1630 Julian was assigned to the College of Saint-Ives at Quimper, Brittany, where he taught Latin and Greek. One day, while leading his students on a pilgrimage to the local shrine of *Ty-Mamm-Doue* (The House of the Mother of God), Julian resolved to begin studying the difficult Breton language so that he could teach the faith to the neglected Breton peasants. This, he decided, was to be his life's work. He set himself studying this tongue and within the incredibly short period of two months was sufficiently fluent to be able to preach in it. Julian always attributed his success in learning the language to our Lady's help. He spent each Sunday either at Quimper, preaching somewhere in the city, or in some nearby hamlet, and continued this practice until 1633 when he went to Tours. The following year he moved to Bourges to begin his theological training prior to ordination.

A frequent topic of discussion among the theological students at Bourges was the Canadian mission. Three of Julian's companions in that old cathedral city did get to serve in Canada, and one of these was the martyr Gabriel Lalemant. Julian himself was torn between two mission fields: was it to be Canada or Brittany? He entered the Society to go to Canada, yet he felt that God was especially calling him to Brittany. The solution came when he was at the point of death. In mid-December 1636 he contracted a fever. His left arm became inflamed and gangrene set in. Death seemed certain and on Christmas Eve, as Julian received Viaticum, he was moved to make a vow: if his health was restored he would devote his life to preaching God's salvation to the Bretons. The infection ceased, the swelling receded, and within days he left his bed. There was no doubt what God was asking of him. Julian was ordained on June 6, 1637, and remained another year at Bourges to complete his studies.

Fr. Maunoir returned to Brittany in August 1640, once more assigned to Quimper. He had a mission to fulfill but did not know how to begin it. He met with Fr. Michael Le Nobletz, the onetime itinerant missionary of Lower Brittany, now retired because of poor health, and decided to use the same methods that Fr. Le Nobletz had used among the poor, hardworking peasants and fisherfolk of the peninsula.

From 1640 to 1654 Fr. Maunoir's companion was Fr. Pierre Bernard. They visited the cities and towns of the mainland as well as the offshore islands, some of which had not seen a priest for many years. Their work was preaching and hearing confessions. A good number of the Bretons were ignorant of their faith, only because there was no one to teach them. Fr. Maunoir insisted on giving them a good basis in Christian doctrine. His missions usually lasted four to five weeks and he preached on God, the purpose of life, the commandments, the sacraments, and the four last things. As visual aids in catechizing the people, he made use of charts depicting the life of Christ, the seven deadly sins, hell, and so on. Some of the more symbolical charts—he had received about forty of these from Fr. Le Nobletz—demanded detailed explanations. He also learned from the veteran missionary the need for instructional hymns to teach the faith and moral values. Some of these hymns he inherited from Fr. Le Nobletz, but he composed most of them himself, setting them to well-known tunes. The people memorized the hymns during the mission and months later they sang them to recall the truths they had learned.

Fr. Maunoir's missions bore great fruit and his audiences were not always limited to single parishes. Often several parishes came together, totalling some 10,000 to 30,000 individuals. On these occasions he asked the parish priests, whose parishioners were attending the mission, to help in hearing confessions, catechizing, and distributing Holy Communion. When these priests saw the fruit resulting from these missions, seven of them asked their bishop's permission to join "Good Father." Fr. Maunoir was jubilant at the news and immediately began training his assistants. In 1651 there were seven; by 1665 there were 300, and by 1683 almost 1,000. Fr. Maunoir organized them into the "Breton Missionaries," who then carried on the work after his death.

Fr. Maunoir gave forty-three years of his life to the Breton people, to whom he gave some 400 missions—an average of ten a year. He took off one month per year in which to rest and write spiritual books. During his final years, 1681 and 1682, because of declining health, he gave only six missions a year. Toward the end of 1682, having just completed a mission at Scrignac, he was on his way to the next town when he sensed that death was near. He asked his companion to return to Plévin with him. When the two Jesuits arrived at Plévin, Fr. Maunoir was so exhausted that he had to go to bed. In his worn-out condition he contracted pneumonia, and though his Jesuit brethren tried to have him brought to Quimper for better care, "Good Father" preferred to remain where he was. After weeks of pain this "Apostle of Brittany," who had spent his life crossing and recrossing the peninsula, returned his soul to the God who had given him life. It was 8:00 P.M., January 28, 1683.

The bishop of Quimper arranged for Fr. Maunoir to be buried in the cathedral, but the people of Plévin had different plans. When the bishop threatened them with excommunication, they still would not give up the saint who chose to die among them. The bishop finally acquiesced and "Good Father" was buried in the Plévin parish church.

Fr. Julian Maunoir was beatified by Pope Pius XII on May 20, 1951, and his memorial is liturgically celebrated in the Society on July 2.

Prayer

O God, through the work of Blessed Julian Maunoir you restored faith to the hearts of rural people. Hear his prayers for us and grant that we may firmly profess this same faith and may all our actions reflect what we believe. We ask this through our Lord Jesus Christ, your Son, who lives and reigns with you and the Holy Spirit, one God, for ever and ever.

January 30

S. G. Thomas Esteban 1879–1934

On December 16, 1931, Fr. Thomas Esteban heard the distressing news that communist soldiers were encamped but a short distance from his residence in Wuyuan and were sure to take the village. All through that night he heard gunfire on the surrounding mountains; the Chinese nationalists were trying to stem the advance of the communists. Before dawn on the 17th, not knowing what was to become of him or of his Christians, Fr. Esteban rose and celebrated Mass. Shortly before daybreak his faithful servant, Lao Mei, came to urge him to flee. The communists were already in the village. But the missionary would not flee, because flight would indicate a lack of faith in God and would be a mark of cowardice. No, he would remain in his residence and wait.

Not long after he had made his decision to remain, he heard soldiers marching outside and then a loud knock on his door. When he answered it, he faced three armed men with some twenty coolies standing outside. The armed men pushed their way into his home, made a hasty search and took his two mules with them. A bit later there was another banging, this time a group of eighteen entered and asked for money. Having only twenty yuan—that was all there was in the house—Fr. Esteban gave them to the group's leader and they too left. Finally, later in the day, a third group arrived and demanded 10,000 yuan. The request was absurd and the priest's answer was that they were asking for a fortune from one who did not even have a single yuan. In return, the leader ordered his men to search the priest and the house. Finding nothing they put a halter around his neck and led him through the streets of Wuyuan to their headquarters in the south.

Fr. Esteban was born in the small village of Sesma in Navarre, Spain, on September 23, 1879. He first attended the local school, but in 1891, when he was twelve, he transferred to the school operated by the Piarist Fathers at Irache. Three years later (1894) he went to the minor seminary in Pamplona, and the following year he advanced to Pamplona's Saint Francis Xavier Seminary for his philosophical studies and to begin his course in theology. For his final year in 1902 he went to the seminary of Saints Valero and Braulio in Saragossa. He was ordained in Pamplona on September 21, 1904, and celebrated his first Mass on October 9 in his home parish in Sesma.

Since Fr. Esteban was a diocesan priest, his bishop first assigned him as an assistant in Mélida and after a few months transferred him to Mendigorría. For some years he had thought about the Society of Jesus and had known many Jesuits at the seminary in Pamplona. Then in early 1909 a Jesuit came to his parish to give a mission, and shortly after it ended he resolved to enter the Society. With his bishop's permission he left the diocese and on April 16, 1909, began his novitiate training at Loyola. He was then thirty years old. His two years as a novice were no different from that of any seventeen-year-old novice. Though a priest, he still had to serve table, work in the laundry, kitchen, and so on. He pronounced his vows on April 17, 1911, and spent the next year at Burgos refreshing his knowledge of the classics. In 1912 he went to Oña to review philosophy and theology.

In 1913 the Jesuit province of Castile, to which Fr. Esteban belonged, was given China as its mission and, thus, he began to think of going to the Orient. When he was an infant, his mother dedicated him to St. Francis Xavier, who was also a Navarrese. He now hoped to make that offering complete by becoming a missionary. Thinking of China, he took as his motto: "To save many souls and to give my blood and life for him." Fr. Esteban wrote to his superiors volunteering for the mission, but before he could receive a response he was assigned to teach Latin at the minor seminary in Durango. He taught there for two years, but his thoughts and desires were in China. He wrote in his diary: "I keep thinking of, and asking the same thing of our Lord, to work, suffer, and to die for him on the Chinese mission, saving many souls." During the summer of 1916 his request was finally honored and in September he went to Manresa for tertianship. On August 24, 1917, together with five other missionaries, he departed Barcelona and set out for the East. Since the Suez Canal was then closed to maritime traffic, the missionaries had to go via the Atlantic. They arrived in New York City on

September 6, traveled across the United States, and sailed from San Francisco on September 29. By October 31 they were in Shanghai. Once on Chinese soil they set out for mission headquarters at Wuhu, in the province of Anhui, arriving there on November 12.

Missionaries in China usually need at least two years of intensive language study. But a few months after Fr. Esteban's arrival, with his Chinese still in poor shape, he was sent to Yingshan to assist a French Jesuit missionary. Yingshan was mostly Catholic, so he was able to continue his language study while he served the people as their priest. During his five years there, he was known for his kindness, simplicity, and amiability. Then in 1922 he was given the mission of Wuyuan. This was a difficult mission. There were some 400 Christian families in that district, but they had not had a visit from a priest for decades. Moreover, they spoke a dialect altogether different from the Mandarin, which Fr. Esteban had learned. But missionaries are accustomed to facing challenges, and with a courageous heart he left Yingshan for Wuyuan. The area of his new district was vast and mountainous, which made trips to the outlying villages difficult. With the aid of loyal catechists, however, he regularly visited his Christians—sometimes having to cross five mountain ranges to reach them.

By 1927 the Chinese communists were beginning to gain ground, and when General Chiang-Kai-shek took over the government in 1928, he set himself to fight the growing communist menace. Unfortunately, the reds had a good foothold in the south, where Fr. Esteban had his mission; their power grew and they took over the village of Wuyuan on December 17, 1931.

After Fr. Esteban had been arrested by the communists, they led him on a five-day walk to their headquarters in Geyuan, in Jiangxi province. Because his captors were badly in need of money, they intended to use their prisoner as a pawn setting a high ransom on his life. From prison Fr. Esteban wrote letters, some of them obviously dictated by his captors, which were addressed to the Jesuit superiors in Wuhu, to the French consul in Nanjing, and to the Spanish minister in Beijing. He informed them that the price of his freedom was set at 100,000 yuan. The Jesuits, consul, and minister tried every diplomatic means available to secure the priest's release, but without success. The communists did not want diplomacy, they wanted money.

Since the demanded 100,000 yuan were not forthcoming, the communists, now desperate, reduced the ransom to 20,000, then to 10,000, and finally told Fr. Esteban to write his superiors that it would only cost the mission 2,000. In a letter to his bishop, dated March 31, 1932, he wrote: "Three times I was placed on public display and once without my clothes, I had to endure the people's ridicule; hatred abounds around me; three times I thought my end had come. I fear nothing. Either live in order to work for Jesus, or die to reign with him."

Since diplomacy had failed, the Jesuits now sought to negotiate directly with the communists. Lao Mei, Fr. Esteban's former servant, and another Chinese named Wuyulai served as intermediaries. Wuyulai was known to the communists and thus was able to secure passports to enter communist-held territory. Wuyulai made his first attempt at negotiations in July 1932, when the price set for the priest's freedom was 30,000 yuan. But Fr. Esteban told him to warn the Jesuits against sending money to the communists. After several weeks of silence, Wuyulai appeared with a letter in which the ransom was lowered to 2,000. The intermediary had seen Fr. Esteban during his visit and reported that his arms and body were covered with sores. On February 2, 1933, Lao Mei, with 2,000 yuan hidden in his ragged jacket, set out together with Wuyulai for the prison in Geyuan. About a mile from the city they came upon the house where the priest was kept prisoner. When Lao Mei entered he saw the priest leaning against a wretched bed, which he shared with a fellow prisoner. At first the missionary did not recognize his former servant dressed in such ragged clothing, but when he heard the familiar voice he was assured that a friend had come.

After they had exchanged greetings and news, the two intermediaries went to the communist chief's office and there paid him the 2,000 yuan. The leader was happy at the sight of the money, but when Lao Mei asked for a passport so that Fr. Esteban could leave with them, the leader remarked: "You can't buy a European's life with only 2,000 yuan!" The asking price was now 20,000. Sorrowfully the intermediaries left and on February 11 the Jesuits in Wuhu received the telegram: "We are deceived; Esteban is not returning."

The Jesuits never gave up hope. In April Wuyulai again went to the prison and told Fr. Esteban that he brought Holy Communion for him in his jacket. There in the dirty room, after having been deprived of Holy Communion for fifteen months, he received his Lord. In July the ransom price came down to 3,000, a sure sign, the Jesuits thought, that the prisoner was in poor health. Wuyulai once more visited the prison toward the end of 1933, but Fr. Esteban was no longer there. It was later learned from his prison companion that the missionary had been taken to a hospital. In January 1934 Wuyulai again set out hoping to gather further information about him, but nothing was ever heard from Wuyulai, nor about him. He simply disappeared and negotiations came to an end.

The date of Fr. Esteban's death in unknown. Perhaps it was in December 1933, or perhaps, as late as June 1934, as some think. We have here chosen the date of January 30 because it was in January when all hope to save Fr. Esteban came to an end. Perhaps Wuyulai did reach the prison, and because the missionary was already dead, the communists may have caused the intermediary to disappear.

Some few years later, after the communists had abandoned the Jiangxi province, the Jesuits sent out a party to search for Fr. Esteban's remains. They arrived at Geyuan, found the town's grave digger and persuaded him to lead them to where the priest had been buried. He pointed out a grave between two trenches and there they found a half-covered worm-eaten coffin. The remains, identified as those of Fr. Esteban by an examination of the teeth, were taken to mission headquarters in Wuhu, where they were buried.

Fr. Thomas Esteban's cause was initiated within a few years of his death; but because of subsequent problems in China, the cause has not been able to advance.

January 31

S. G. Peter John Cayron 1672–1754

Peter Cayron was born in Rodez, in southern France, on January 13, 1672. When he was ten years old he began his studies at the Jesuit school in his native city, and when he was fifteen he decided to enter the Society. His parents, however, were opposed to his leaving home. Thinking they could change his mind, they forbade him contact with his Jesuit teachers, other than that which was absolutely necessary for class work; they also kept him from attending weekday Mass. Peter endured these restrictions for a year, but he never weakened in his resolve. His friend, Anthony Delmas, who entered the Jesuits in 1687, had all the novices praying for Peter. These prayers were answered. Peter's parents saw that it was useless to oppose what they now regarded as God's will, and with their permission Peter entered the novitiate in Toulouse on December 7, 1687.

When Peter completed his two years of noviceship he pronounced his three vows of religion on December 8, 1689, and remained in Toulouse to do his philosophy. He spent the years from the fall of 1691 to the summer of 1698 teaching—first at Montpellier and then from 1695 at Tournon, where Fr. John Francis Regis had once been a student. From his youth Peter was attracted to the saintly Fr. Regis, and this attraction remained with him throughout his years in the Society. After Tournon, Peter taught for short periods at Béziers, Le Puy, and finally Albi. He then returned to Toulouse in September 1698 to begin theology in preparation for ordination. This took place at Rodez on September 21, 1700. Fr. Cayron then completed his theological studies, and during tertianship wrote the first of seven letters to the general of the Society volunteering for the foreign missions. In answer to each of these letters, Fr. Cayron was told to remain at the disposal of his provincial.

Fr. Cayron's first assignment after his long training was to teach philosophy at Carcassone. Because he was living in the district sanctified by the ministry of Fr. Regis, he was asked, besides his regular duties, to promote Fr. Regis's beatification cause among the faithful. This he did most willingly. In 1708 he returned to Tournon to teach philosophy to young Jesuits and while there, very much in the spirit of Fr. Regis, began an apostolate among the poor. He collected alms from the wealthy and distributed them to the needy. Having made friends with those he had helped, he gathered them for instruction, and within a short time he had them receiving Holy Communion once a month. When class was not in session, he went into the countryside, again in imitation of Fr. Regis, to preach missions and retreats.

Toward the end of 1708 he was transferred to Rodez, where he continued to teach young Jesuits, but his mind was still set on the foreign missions. It was at Rodez that he finally discovered his vocation within the Society. One day in prayer he received the grace to understand that he could help souls immeasurably by teaching and training others to be priests and missionaries. It was not necessary for him to go to the missions, but by training others to be apostles he would have a share in their work. For the rest of his life Fr. Cayron fulfilled this mission.

At the end of 1711, he was named assistant to the master of novices in Toulouse, and then in February 1713 became both master and rector of the community, a position he retained until the end of 1729. He was also named vice-postulator of Fr. Regis's cause. To Fr. Cayron's joy Fr. Regis was beatified on May 8, 1716, and he saw that the event was properly celebrated in the novitiate.

After directing novices for sixteen years, Fr. Cayron became, at the end of 1729, rector of the college in Toulouse. When Fr. Michelangelo Tamburini, the Jesuit general, died in February 1730, Fr. Cayron was chosen to be one of the electors of the new general. He spent the months between October 1730 and February 1731 in the Eternal City and returned to Toulouse the following April. The new general, Fr. Francis Retz, asked him to resume his former position as novice master and in 1733 Fr. Cayron returned to the novitiate for five more years. In 1738, now in his sixty-sixth year, he was appointed rector of the Jesuit residence in the city. Since Blessed John Francis Regis had been canonized on June 16, 1737, Fr. Cayron, as rector of the church in Toulouse, held an eight-day celebration in honor of the new saint.

In 1745, when he was seventy-three years old, an age when most men have retired from active work, Fr. Cayron returned to the novitiate in Toulouse to take on the task of being instructor of tertians. He did this until 1752. Fr. Cayron's love for the saints of the Society did not end with canonization of St. John Francis Regis. Now he began to promote the cause of the Jesuit martyrs of Aubenas and that of the great missionary of Brittany, Fr. Julian Maunoir.

Fr. Cayron was now in his eighties and after a life of prayer, of self-abnegation and mortification, his body grew weak. By January 1754 he was somewhat feeble, though he still managed to get around. The night of January 20 was unusually cold in Toulouse and no matter how Fr. Cayron tried, he could not get warm. He realized this was the beginning of the end. The next morning he celebrated Mass, but only with great effort. It was his last Mass. A week before his death he asked the brother infirmarian whose feast was celebrated on January 31. When he learned it was that of St. Peter Nolasco, he smiled, for he knew that it was to be the day on which he would die. His strength slowly left him and on the thirtieth he suffered a severe asthma attack. Then on Thursday, January 31, with his Jesuit brethren at his side, Fr. Cayron went through his last agony and rendered his soul to the God whom he loved above all else.

During his life Fr. Cayron was known for his charity, prayerfulness, and love of the poor and the sick. When he died he was acknowledged by Jesuits and the faithful as a saint. His cause is now under study.

February

February 1

St. Henry Morse 1595–1645
Martyr of England

In 1612 the seventeen-year-old Henry Morse left Corpus Christi College, Cambridge, to begin his study of law at Barnard's Inn, London. While pursuing these studies he grew progressively uncomfortable with the established religion. Born of Protestant parents in the village of Broome, Suffolk, in 1595, he became more and more convinced of the truth of the Catholic faith. Hence in May 1614 he crossed over to the English College at Douai, Flanders, and was there received into the Catholic Church on June 5. His older brother, William, had become a Catholic the year before and at that time was a seminarian at Douai. Shortly after his conversion, Henry returned to England to complete plans for his entrance into the seminary that autumn. When he landed, however, port authorities put Henry's faith to the test by requesting him to take the oath of allegiance that acknowledged the king's supremacy in all religious matters. A Catholic of only a few weeks, he resolutely refused and as a result was committed to New Prison in Southwark. The young convert, who had so admirably manifested his allegiance to Christ and his Church, endured imprisonment for four years. In 1618 the king, ridding his prisons of religious dissenters, released hundreds of them, including many priests, and banished them to the shores of France. As one of those banished, Henry made his way in August 1618 to Douai, where he intended to enter the seminary. The college, however, had more students than it could comfortably handle and Henry was sent to the English College in Rome, where he was ordained in 1623.

After ordination Fr. Morse was to return to England, but before leaving Rome he visited the Jesuit general and requested to be admitted into the Society of Jesus. The general told him that he was indeed welcome, but that he should enter the Society after he had returned to England. The general, in the meantime, wrote to the Jesuit superior in England instructing him to accept Fr. Morse upon his arrival. Fr. Morse thus probably joined the Jesuits in 1624. He was assigned to the Newcastle area and lived in the Lawson residence known as St. Anthony's. After eighteen months of visiting station after station in northern England, it was time for him to conclude his novitiate by making his thirty-day retreat in Watten, Flanders. The ship he was sailing on was unexpectedly halted on April 12, 1626, before it left the Tyne River. Soldiers boarded it in search of a priest, possibly disguised as a foreign merchant. They found Fr. Morse instead and arrested him, but since he carried only a rosary, they were unable to prove he was a priest. Nevertheless, he was committed to Newcastle's Newgate Prison.

On the first of May, Fr. John Robinson was also brought to the prison on suspicion of being a priest. He had been apprehended the day before when his boat docked at Newcastle where he had come to replace Fr. Morse at St. Anthony's. When both priests met in prison it was a reunion of old friends, for they ·had been fellow students in Rome. Together they were transferred to York Castle where they both carried on their ministry by aiding Catholic and non-Catholic alike. Since Fr. Robinson had been a Jesuit for six years, he directed Fr. Morse through his thirty-day retreat and the completion of his Jesuit training.

After three years in York Castle, Fr. Morse was released, probably in March 1630, and banished from the land. Fr. Robinson, on the other hand, had to endure eleven more years of prison life. Fr. Morse went to Watten and became chaplain to the English soldiers serving in the Spanish army quartered in Flanders. He continued in this ministry until his health broke, at which time he became assistant to the rector at the Watten novitiate. Then in 1633 he was directed to return to England to replace Fr. Andrew White, who in November 1633 had accompanied the first Catholic settlers to southern Maryland, where he became the founder of the Church in the American colonies.

Fr. Morse was appointed to work in the parish of St. Giles, a poor district outside London. During the four years he worked there, the city was ravaged by a plague. In late 1635 several isolated cases were discovered, but by April 1636 London was in alarm—the city and suburbs were overcome by the dread disease and the populace was in panic. Fr. Morse was assigned to work full time among the plague-stricken; he went about hearing confessions, securing medicine for the sick, taking Viaticum to the dying, and preparing the dead for burial. Then on February 27, 1638, as he was returning from the bedside of a victim, he was recognized by priest-hunters and arrested. He was charged with being a priest and of persuading Protestants to leave their faith for the Catholic Church. On March 28 he was moved to Newgate Prison and his case came to trial on April 22. He ably defended himself and, though the jury found him guilty, sentence was never passed. Finally on June 17 he was released through the gracious intervention of Queen Henrietta Marie, in recognition of his admirable work among the plague victims. He returned to his priestly ministry in and around

London, but because he could no longer work unmolested, in early 1641 he went to the Continent, where he again became chaplain to English soldiers in the Spanish army.

In 1643 Fr. Morse was instructed to return to England, but since he was too well known in London, he was assigned to serve in the Cumberland area. One night, eighteen months later, as he was returning from a sick call, he accidentally walked into a party of soldiers on their way to Durham. They suspected he was a priest because he was travelling alone at night and unarmed. They arrested him and he was forced to spend the night with them at the house of a local official. It turned out that the official's wife was Catholic and with her help he escaped. He enjoyed his freedom for six weeks, but then one day he and his guide, having lost their way in the countryside, innocently knocked on the door of a house to ask directions. The gentleman who answered happened to be one of the soldiers who had apprehended him six weeks before. Arrested once more, Fr. Morse spent several weeks in the Durham jail, then was transferred to that of Newcastle and in January 1645 was sent to London, where he was kept in Newgate Prison. Toward the end of the month he was tried in Old Bailey, but the proceedings were brief since he had already been convicted of being a priest several years previously. His very presence before the judge proved that he had violated the law by returning to England after he had been banished. He was found guilty of high treason and condemned to death.

During the four days between sentencing and execution, many visitors came to his cell seeking his prayers or asking for a keepsake. Among them were ambassadors from the Catholic countries who wished to show their solidarity with the Catholics of England. At 4:00 A.M. on the first of February, Fr. Morse celebrated his last Mass, visited other condemned prisoners, and patiently waited for the sheriff to arrive. At 9:00 A.M. the sheriff appeared and Fr. Morse was dragged to Tyburn, the place of execution outside London. At Tyburn he mounted the cart beneath the gallows and placed the noose about his neck. He turned to the people and addressed them: "I am come hither to die for my religion. . . . I have a secret which highly concerns His Majesty and Parliament to know. The kingdom of England will never be truly blessed until it returns to the Catholic faith and its subjects are all united in one belief under the Bishop of Rome." He ended by saying: "I pray that my death may be some kind of atonement for the sins of this kingdom." The sheriff then ordered him to say his prayers, and after he had recollected himself he asked that the cap be pulled over his eyes; at that moment he beat his breast three times, giving the signal to a priest in the crowd to impart absolution. He then said: "Into your hands, O Lord, I commend my spirit." The cart was then drawn away from under him and he was left hanging until dead. His body was torn open, his heart removed, the entrails burned, and his body quartered. In accordance with the custom that followed executions, his head was exposed on London Bridge and his quartered body mounted on the city's four gates.

Fr. Henry Morse was fifty years old at the time of his martyrdom and had been a Jesuit for twenty years. He was beatified by Pope Pius XI on December 15, 1929, and canonized by Pope Paul VI on October 25, 1970. His memorial is celebrated on December 1, together with the other Jesuits who suffered martyrdom for their faith in England and Wales.

Prayer

Almighty, eternal God, you chose from the people of England and Wales Saint Henry Morse and his companions to be made like Christ, who died to save the world. Listen to their prayers; strengthen your Church by the same faith and love that strengthened them, and bless it always with your gift of unity. We ask this through our Lord Jesus Christ, your Son, who lives and reigns with you and the Holy Spirit, one God, for ever and ever.

February 3

Bl. John Nelson 1535–1578

Martyr of England

Fr. John Nelson, about to be executed at Tyburn, London, for his faith, looked upon those standing near the gallows and said: "I die in the unity of the Catholic Church; and for that unity do now most willingly suffer my blood to be shed; therefore, I beseech God . . . to make you, and all others that are not such already, true Catholic men, and both to live and die in the unity of our Holy Mother, the Catholic Roman Church." Fr. Nelson's enthusiasm for his faith was no greater at the moment of his death than it had been when he lived in Skelton, near York, England.

Born in Yorkshire about 1535, the son of Sir Nicholas Nelson, John had always been known for his intense practice of the faith. Though Queen Elizabeth's government was unfavorable toward Catholics and spies abounded, John never feared to demonstrate his adherence to Catholicism. He deplored the weakness of those who yielded under governmental threats and attended Protestant services merely to escape the penalties imposed upon recusant Catholics. John was convinced that it was only by the shedding of blood that England could again be restored to the faith, and it was this firm conviction that led him in 1573, when he was approaching forty years of age, to go to Flanders and matriculate at the

English College in Douai. To his joy, his younger brothers, Martin and Thomas, followed him to Douai in 1574 and 1575, respectively. John was ordained a priest on June 11, 1576, at Bynche, and on the following November 7, he and four other newly ordained priests left the Continent for their native land.

Fr. Nelson had only one year to exercise his priestly ministry and not much is known about his apostolate, but it must have been similar to that of other Catholic priests in England who were forced to celebrate Mass secretly in Catholic households. On Saturday, December 1, 1577, as he sat in a London residence reading his breviary in the evening, the priest-hunters surprised him. They arrested him on suspicion of being a Catholic priest and took him to London's Newgate Prison. Within a week of his arrest he was brought before the queen's high commissioners, where he adamantly refused to recognize the queen's authority over the Church. When asked who then was the head of the Church, he unequivocally answered that it was the pope. When asked how he would then describe the queen's position, he boldly declared that she was a schismatic, a heretic, and that the religion practiced in the land was of her own making. He was thereupon returned to Newgate to await trial. The trial, such as it was, took place on February 1, 1578, and during it he repeated the remarks he had previously made to the high commissioners. In view of his constancy in refusing to take the oath acknowledging the queen's supremacy in religious matters, he was found guilty of high treason and condemned to be executed as a traitor—to be hanged, drawn, and quartered.

During his last two days of life he was kept in a dark, damp, vermin-infested dungeon, where he spent his time fasting, praying, and preparing for death. On the morning of February 3, he was brought to the prison's upper level and dragged to Tyburn for execution. After he had been placed in position for hanging, he asked the Catholics present to pray with him, and aloud he recited the Creed, the Our Father, and the Hail Mary, all in Latin. He then went on to encourage the bystanders to adhere to the Catholic faith, asked forgiveness of all whom he might have offended, and asked God to forgive his enemies and executioners as he himself had done. As he was finishing these words he was hanged. He was cut down while still alive so that he could further suffer disembowelment. His head was severed from his body after the executioner's third attempt and his body was quartered. The martyr's head was then displayed on London Bridge, and portions of his body were exhibited at each of the city's four gates.

Fr. Nelson had been an admirer of the Jesuits since he had met them in France, but there was no Jesuit mission in England until 1580, two years after his death. He had, however, written to the French Jesuits during his imprisonment for permission to be admitted into the Society. They were happy to accept one who was about to be martyred for Christ.

Fr. John Nelson was beatified by Pope Leo XIII on December 9, 1886, and his memorial is celebrated on December 1, together with that of other Jesuits who had been slain for Christ in England and Wales.

Prayer

Almighty, eternal God, you chose from the people of England and Wales Blessed John Nelson and his companions to be made like Christ, who died to save the world. Listen to their prayers; strengthen your Church by the same faith and love that strengthened them, and bless it always with your gift of unity. We ask this through our Lord Jesus Christ, your Son, who lives and reigns with you and the Holy Spirit, one God, for ever and ever.

February 4

St. John de Brito 1647–1693

Martyr of India

John de Brito was born in Lisbon on March 1, 1647. Since his parents were members of the Portuguese aristocracy—his father was governor of Rio de Janeiro—John became, at age nine, a member of the royal court and served as page and companion to the young prince, who in time became Peter II. At age eleven, John fell critically ill and when the physicians lost all hope of his recovery, his mother turned to St. Francis Xavier and promised that if her son recovered, he would wear the Jesuit cassock for a year in thanksgiving. St. Francis heard her appeal and within a few days her son was out of bed. When John next went to court he appeared as a miniature Jesuit. At the end of the stipulated period he removed the cassock, but he had already thought of becoming a Jesuit in fact. Though the king and prince tried to persuade him to remain at court, he was, nevertheless, determined to follow what he saw to be God's will.

John entered the Jesuit novitiate in Lisbon on December 17, 1662. The new novice was only fifteen years old. After he took his vows in 1664, he went to study the classics at the college in Évora, but because of health problems he transferred to the University of Coimbra. There he began his course in philosophy (1666) and while pursuing these studies his interest in St. Francis Xavier and India began to shape his outlook. In 1668 he wrote to Fr. General Gian Paolo Oliva, requesting to be sent to the East as a missionary. That mission would one day be his, but first he had to finish his studies for the priesthood. Completing his philosophy in 1669, he taught grammar at the College of St. Anthony in Lisbon and in 1670 returned to the university for his theology. He was ordained in 1673, most probably on February 5.

Now that he was a priest, Fr. Brito prepared to go to India. His mother had tried to keep him from leaving, but God's will prevailed and he left Lisbon in mid-March 1673, arriving at Goa, India, the following September 4. There he completed his theology, and because he had been an exceptional student his superiors thought of having him teach philosophy in the seminary. But his reply was: "I came to India not to seek the laurels of science but martyrdom."

Fr. Brito's mission was in Madura and he focused his activity in the regions of Kolei and Tattuvanchery. He familiarized himself with the Indian caste system and its complicated procedures and discovered that most Christians belonged to the lowest and the most despised caste. For Christianity to have a lasting influence, he knew that members of the higher caste would also have to be converted. Since Indian ascetics, *pandaraswamis,* were permitted to approach individuals of all castes, Fr. Brito established himself as one of these and lived as they lived. He ate only a few handfuls of rice a day and used a floor mat as his bed. He dressed as they did in a red cloak and turban and set up small retreats in the wilderness, similar to hermitages, where interested Indians could visit him. In time he was accepted as a *pandaraswami* and as his reputation grew so did his conversions. While living out the role of an Indian ascetic, he also continued his visits to his mission stations in the kingdoms of Tanjore and Gingi.

In 1685, after eleven years on the mission, he was made superior in Madura, but because he was successful in converting many to Catholicism, the Brahmans, the highest Indian caste, sought to kill him. They almost succeeded in 1686 when their soldiers apprehended him and his catechists and fettered them with heavy chains. Several times the soldiers threatened to kill them and each time Fr. Brito responded by offering them his neck. At the last minute, however, the soldiers always withdrew. After a month of prison and torture, they were unexpectedly released in August 1686 and the group returned to its mission.

Upon Fr. Brito's return, he was appointed to go to Portugal to report on the status of the mission and Church in India. He left Goa on December 15, 1686, and reached Lisbon on September 8, 1687. His return to Portugal after an absence of fourteen years was like the return of a hero. He visited the universities and colleges, describing to his fellow Jesuits and their students the adventurous life of an Indian missionary. When he visited the royal court, King Peter II noticed that his friend and former companion was now thin, stooped, worn out, and bore the marks of torture. He asked the priest to remain at home and be tutor to his two sons, but the missionary declined the royal offer, citing India's needs as being the greater.

Fr. Brito left Portugal on March 19, 1690, and after a seven-month voyage arrived in Goa on November 2, and immediately returned to his mission in Madura. Though seas separated him from his king, the latter, still feeling the need to manifest his appreciation for his old friend, decided to appoint him an archbishop. Fr. Brito, however, did not want to give up his chance for martyrdom, and thus he chose to continue his work of catechizing and baptizing, visiting missions and founding new ones.

Though the raja of Marava had threatened in 1686 to kill Fr. Brito if he ever returned to his territory, the missionary, nevertheless, felt compelled to revisit his Marava Christians. He did so by traveling at night to each station, where he would celebrate Mass and baptize neophytes.

Near Muni, where Fr. Brito was staying, lived Prince Tadaya Theva. The prince was interested in Christianity and had a catechist instruct him in the faith, but when he fell sick he asked Fr. Brito to come and baptize him. To be sure that the prince had the proper dispositions, the missionary sent one of his catechists to interrogate him. When the catechist arrived he found the prince dying, so together they recited the Apostles' Creed. The catechist then read a Gospel passage over him and the prince immediately felt better and was soon cured. The prince attributed his recovery to his decision to become a Christian and again invited Fr. Brito to perform the ceremony. The priest went to him in early January 1693, but on learning that the prince had several wives, he informed him that he would have to choose the first to be his only wife and let the others go. The prince willingly did this and was baptized on January 6.

One of the prince's wives, however, was the niece of the raja of Marava. Insulted that his niece had been repudiated, the raja sought vengeance on Fr. Brito. On January 8, he sent his soldiers to arrest the missionary and to take him to a prison in Ramnad. On January 28 the raja called the missionary before him; Fr. Brito had disobeyed his earlier command not to return to his territory or to preach the Christian faith, so the raja ordered the priest to be exiled to Oriyur. It was the raja's intention, however, to have Fr. Brito executed there. In a letter to his brother, whose province included Oriyur, he gave instructions to carry out the execution.

Fr. Brito was taken to Oriyur on January 31 and was kept in prison until February 4. On that day, about noon, he was led to a peaceful knoll overlooking the river. Reaching the spot that had been selected for his martyrdom, the priest knelt down in prayer. The raja's order was publicly read, and when the executioner hesitated to do his job, Fr. Brito encouraged him: "My friend, I have prayed to God. On my part, I have done what I should do. Now do your part. Carry out the order you have received."

The executioner approached and noticed a reliquary hanging around Fr. Brito's neck. Thinking it might be a talisman that could bring him bad luck, he slashed at it. He separated it from Fr. Brito's neck, but he also inflicted a wound on the priest's breast and one of his shoulders. The next swing was directed at the martyr's neck, and as the scimitar came down the victim's head fell into the sand. The executioner next cut off the martyr's hands and feet, bound them to the torso and placed it on a stake, where it was left as food for the birds and animals.

Fr. John de Brito was beatified by Pope Pius IX on May 18, 1852, and canonized by Pope Pius XII on June 22, 1947. His Jesuit brethren celebrate his memorial on February 4.

Prayer

Lord God, you sent your martyr, Saint John de Brito, to preach the gospel by word and example. Grant a rich harvest of grace to those who are fearless in proclaiming the word of our Lord Jesus Christ, your Son, who lives and reigns with you and the Holy Spirit, one God, for ever and ever.

February 5

S. G. Pedro Arrupe 1907–1991

Fr. Pedro Arrupe was the Society's twenty-eighth superior general. He was a Basque, as was St. Ignatius, and was born on November 14, 1907, in Bilbao, Spain. His father was an architect, whose staunch faith led him to help establish one of Spain's first Catholic daily newspapers, *La Gaceta del Norte*. Pedro's early education was in his native city under the Piarist Fathers, but when he decided on medicine as a career in 1922, he first went to Valladolid and later to Madrid's Central University. Without waiting to complete his degree, however, he entered the Society of Jesus at Loyola on January 15, 1927. After noviceship and juniorate studies, he moved in 1931 to Oña near Burgos, to begin his philosophical course, but his stay there was brief. In October of that year, the Society in Spain was dissolved by governmental decree, and the young Jesuit students had to go abroad to continue their training. Thus Pedro and his Jesuit companions travelled to Marneffe, Belgium, where they completed their philosophy. The next step was theology and for this Pedro went in 1933 to Valkenburg, Netherlands. He was ordained there on July 30, 1936.

Less than two months later, Fr. Arrupe sailed from Antwerp, Belgium, to the United States. His final destination was St. Mary's College in Kansas. There he completed his theology and made tertianship at St. Stanislaus Novitiate in Cleveland, Ohio. It was in June 1938, toward the end of tertianship, that he received his assignment to the Japan mission. Years earlier, while still a junior, he had written to Fr. General Ledóchowski volunteering for the missions, but it was only now that he received an affirmative response.

Fr. Arrupe sailed from Seattle, Washington, on September 30, 1938, and arrived at Yokohama, Tokyo, on October 15. He immediately immersed himself in studying the Japanese language at Nagatsuka, near Hiroshima, and by 1940 he was in charge of a rural parish in the Yamaguchi mission. On the day that

Japan declared war on the United States, December 8, 1941, Fr. Arrupe's residence was searched. He was suspected of being a spy for Western powers. The next thirty-three days were spent in solitary confinement in an unheated Yamaguchi military prison, and after thirty-six hours of continued interrogation he was released on January 12, 1942. On leaving prison he thanked his jailer for his "gift," that is, the opportunity to suffer for Christ. In later years, referring to this period of imprisonment in his *One Jesuit's Spiritual Journey,* he remarked: "Many were the things I learned during this time: the science of silence, of solitude, of severe and austere poverty, of inner dialogue with the 'guest of my soul.' I believe this was the most instructive month of my entire life."

Two months after regaining his freedom, Fr. Arrupe was named, on March 9, 1942, master of novices at the Nagatsuka novitiate, and a few days later he became vice-rector of the novitiate-theologate complex. Then on the morning of August 6, 1945, the first atomic bomb fell on Hiroshima. From the Jesuit residence at Nagatsuka, some six miles away, Fr. Arrupe saw the blinding light and heard the deafening explosion. Hiroshima was enveloped in flames. He and several of his fellow Jesuits directly set out for the city to see what assistance they could give. Their advance, however, was halted by the flames encircling the city and the thousands of wounded in flight. They would have to turn back, and as Fr. Arrupe looked upon the tragic scene about him, he came to realize that the best help he could offer his fellow Japanese was to put his past medical training to immediate use. Consequently, he converted the novitiate into an emergency hospital with himself as chief medical officer and his young novices as nurses and orderlies. The one-time novitiate accommodated more than 200 of the injured. Finally, some twelve hours after the explosion, Fr. Arrupe was able to enter devastated Hiroshima. He was in search of the five Jesuits who resided there. He found them alive but injured and with the assistance of his novices, he took them to Nagatsuka. The novitiate served as an improvised hospital for the next six months.

Fr. Arrupe was master of novices until November 1954, when he was named vice-provincial of Japan. Shortly after his appointment he set out for an eleven-month recruiting and fund-raising tour of Latin America, the United States, and Europe. The Japan mission had expanded greatly after the war and since new departments were being added to the Jesuit-operated Sophia University in Tokyo, new missionaries were constantly in need. Then when the vice-province became a province in October 1958, Fr. Arrupe was its first provincial. Among his accomplishments as provincial were a new high school in Hiroshima and the shrine to the Japanese martyrs in Nagasaki, dedicated in 1962.

With the death of Fr. General John Baptist Janssens on October 5, 1964, a general congregation, the thirty-first, was called to elect his successor. Fr. Arrupe went to Rome. The congregation opened on May 7, 1965, and on the 22nd, Fr. Arrupe was elected superior general, the twenty-seventh successor to St. Ignatius. As general he not only had to promote the renewal of Jesuit life in accordance with the teachings of the gospel and the *Spiritual Exercises* of its founder, but also to see to the Society's authentic implementation of the directives given by the Second Vatican Council.

During Fr. Arrupe's years in office, he attended the final session of the council and participated in five international synods of bishops. He likewise attended the meetings of the Latin American bishops in Medellín, Colombia (1968), and in Puebla, Mexico (1979). He traveled extensively, and through his meetings and speaking with countless Jesuits, he became aware of the world's major needs and of the new opportunities being offered to the Church. Because of this international experience, he early perceived that the center of worldwide Christianity was gravitating toward Africa and Asia. He expressed the opinion that future missionaries will have to adapt the Christian message and the ways of the Church to these diverse cultures. In his travels he also encountered the ravages of world poverty and became convinced that religious faith, as expounded in the gospel, has to oppose oppression and injustice, and to alleviate poverty and eradicate racial discrimination. He was likewise among the first to be alerted to the world refugee problem and in 1980 launched a program to meet the needs of the millions of refugees, especially in Asia and Africa.

Fr. Arrupe's years as general were not totally troublefree. The Society's membership diminished and certain tensions arose within it. Nevertheless, throughout these years he manifested himself as a man of God and a man of the Church, possessed of extraordinary simplicity and understanding. He was so highly esteemed by his peers that for five consecutive terms he was elected president of the Union of Superior Generals in Rome.

During the summer of 1981, Fr. Arrupe visited the Philippines on the occasion of the 400th anniversary of the arrival of the Jesuits in that country. He left the Philippines on August 5 and spent the following day in Bangkok visiting Jesuits working among refugees. He returned to Rome's Fiumicino Airport early on August 7, but before he could leave the terminal he suffered a cerebral thrombosis. This man of great energy and activity was now reduced to helplessness. In view of Fr. Arrupe's health and his inability to govern, Pope John Paul II, in his usual concern for the Society, appointed Fr. Paolo Dezza on October 5 of that year as his personal delegate to oversee the Society's everyday government and to prepare the way for a future general congregation. When the congregation did meet in Rome, Fr. Arrupe formally submitted his resignation to the assembled delegates on September 3, 1983. In his valedictory address he shared with his fellow Jesuits his view of his illness. "More than ever, I now find myself in the hands of God. It is what I have wanted all my life, from my youth. And this is still the one thing I want. But now there is a difference: the initiative is entirely with God. It is indeed a profound spiritual experience to know and feel myself so totally in his hands." Then on September 13, the congregation elected Fr. Peter-Hans Kolvenbach as Fr. Arrupe's successor.

Fr. Arrupe's illness lasted for almost ten years. While in the Society's infirmary in Rome, he concelebrated Mass daily until autumn 1987, when he suffered a severe setback. His speech became difficult and more limited. Now confined to his room, Mass was celebrated there each day with the other infirmary patients attending. Throughout his last years he suffered with great patience, serenity of soul, and full abandonment to the Lord's will. Then in his final weeks he fell into a coma and was anointed on Friday evening, January 25, 1991. On the following Sunday, when Fr. Arrupe's condition deteriorated still further, Fr. Kolvenbach requested the Holy Father's blessing on the former general. The Holy Father, however, chose to impart his blessing personally and that evening he arrived at Fr. Arrupe's bedside and prayed silently. Before leaving he asked the Jesuits assembled in the room to recite the *Alma Redemptoris Mater* with him. Fr. Arrupe never regained consciousness. During the next several days, the generals and superiors of the other orders and religious congregations came to pray at the bedside of their revered colleague.

Fr. Arrupe died on February 5, 1991, at 7:45 P.M. In Japan it was already the 6th, the feast of the Japanese martyrs. Fr. Arrupe was eighty-four years old and had been a Jesuit for sixty-four years, a missionary for twenty-seven, and superior general for eighteen. His funeral was held on February 9 in the Society's Church of the Gesù in Rome, and according to the Society's custom, the liturgy was presided by Fr. Damian Aloysius Byrne, Master General of the Order of Preachers. Rev. Fr. Kolvenbach assisted with some 500 concelebrants.

In response to a request made by the Jesuit delegates attending the 34th General Congregation (1995), Fr. Arrupe's cause is now under consideration.

February 6

St. Paul Miki 1564–1597

St. John de Goto 1578–1597

St. James Kisai 1533–1597

Martyrs of Japan

During the forty-one years after the coming of Fr. Francis Xavier to Japan in 1549, Christianity experienced a rapid growth. By 1590 the number of Christians had grown to 200,000, most of whom lived either on the southern island of Kyushu or in central Japan. Because several influential political leaders had become converts, and because Toyotomi Hideyoshi had been for several years favorably disposed to Christianity, the Jesuit mission prospered. In 1587, however,

Hideyoshi's attitude changed, and by a decree of July 25 he ordered all foreign missionaries out of Japan. The reason for this edict may have been due to some Japanese leaders who were Buddhists and feared that the increase of Christians was but a preliminary move on the part of the Spaniards to conquer Japan, as they had done to the Philippines. Some Jesuits obeyed the edict and left the country; but most remained and went undercover so as to continue caring for their people. The edict, however, was never enforced with full vigor, so the missionaries were somewhat free to evangelize though they were never totally free from the threat of persecution.

A new crisis was precipitated when the Spanish vessel, *San Felipe,* on its way to Mexico from Manila, met disaster off the Japanese coast on October 19, 1596. While its cargo was being confiscated, it is said that an unfortunate remark by one of the ship's officers was interpreted to mean that the Spaniards aboard had come with the intention of subduing Japan. Hideyoshi and his non-Christian counselors made the most of the incident and ordered the arrest of all Spanish Franciscans, who had come to Japan from the Philippines in 1593. In rounding up the Franciscans, the police also arrested the Jesuit scholastics Paul Miki and John de Goto, together with James Kisai, a Jesuit brother.

Paul Miki was born in 1564 of well-to-do parents in Setsu no Kuni, near Osaka, and his family became Christian when he was about four or five years old. At twenty, he entered the Jesuit-operated seminary located in Azuchi and two years later, in August 1586, entered the Society. Though still a student he proved himself an excellent disputant with Buddhist leaders and won several non-believers to Christianity. Among the Christians of Arima and Omura Paul was acknowledged as an eloquent speaker, so much so that he had been asked to preach in several cities. On December 9, 1596, just a few months before he would have been ordained, he was arrested with his two companions in Osaka, at the house where the Jesuits resided.

John de Goto was born of Christian parents in 1578 on one of the islands of the Goto archipelago. When the *daimyo,* or prince, of Goto began a persecution against Christians, John's family along with many others, crossed over to Nagasaki so that they could practice their faith in freedom. When John was fifteen he sought entrance into the Society, but before being accepted the Jesuits asked him to assist their missionaries as a catechist. At this time he was living with the Jesuits in Osaka and may have already been accepted as a scholastic for the Society.

James Kisai was born in 1533 of a pagan family, in the village of Haga, near Okayama. He received his early education from a Buddhist bonze but was later baptized. He married a Christian convert who bore him a son. His wife, however, returned to her former Buddhist beliefs and unable to talk her out of her decision James separated from her and entrusted his son to a Christian family to ensure the child's upbringing in the faith. He then went to Osaka and found employment with the Jesuits. At times he helped about the house and for a period was house porter and cared for the guests who came to the residence. When the Jesuits saw how well he knew his faith, they made him a catechist. He most probably became a brother sometime in 1596. Thus, on December 9, Paul Miki, John de Goto, and James Kisai happened to be under the same roof when the police arrested them.

The three were held under house arrest from December 9 until January 1, 1597, when they were taken to Miyako (today's Kyoto), the capital, and imprisoned with six Franciscans and their fifteen tertiaries. On January 3 the twenty-four prisoners were led into the public square where sentence of death by crucifixion was passed upon them. As a mark of shame the lobe of each man's left ear was cut off. On the following day, with hands tied behind them, the martyrs left Miyako on the long arduous walk to Nagasaki. As the prisoners passed through various villages on the way, the populace ridiculed and derided them, but the Christians who saw their brothers going to death gained strength from their witness. Both Paul Miki and the Franciscan Fr. Peter Baptist frequently preached to the bystanders. Finally on February 5, after four weary weeks the procession of prisoners reached Urakami, a small Christian village about a mile outside Nagasaki. Two Jesuit priests met them and as Fr. Rodríguez went among the prisoners hearing confessions, Fr. Pasio took the three Jesuits into the chapel at St. Lazarus Hospital and there Paul Miki renewed his vows, while John de Goto and James Kisai pronounced their religious vows for the first time.

That same morning the twenty-four were led to the hill where the execution was to take place. Along the road two Christians who tried to comfort the prisoners were added to those who were to die. At their destination the martyrs saw lying on the ground the crosses on which they were to meet death; seeing these instruments of their salvation they spontaneously burst forth singing the Church's traditional hymn of thanksgiving, *Te Deum*. Looking forward to union with God, the martyrs rushed to their crosses, embraced them, placed themselves upon them and waited for their executioners to fasten their bodies with ropes. Around their necks they had metal bands placed to keep their heads erect. As the crosses were lifted into the holes, John de Goto noticed his father in the crowd and spoke to him: "Father, remember the soul's salvation is to be preferred to everything else." The father answered: "My son, I thank you for your words of exhortation. Face death with joy because you are undergoing it for our holy faith. Your mother and I are also ready to die for the same cause."

While Paul Miki was hanging on his cross, he found the strength to speak to the crowd and the words of his last sermon invited the onlookers to embrace the Christianity for which he was glad to offer his life. He ended by forgiving his executioner for what he was about to do. At a given signal the soldiers standing at each cross thrust a lance into each martyr's breast. At the moment that Paul Miki's executioner transfixed him, he said: "Into your hands, O Lord, I commend my spirit." Thus, at age thirty-three Paul became the first Jesuit and first Japanese religious to be martyred in Japan. John de Goto was nineteen years old and James Kisai sixty-four.

The hill on which these twenty-six martyrs met God became known as "Martyrs' Hill," and in time a Jesuit residence was erected near it. These martyrs were beatified by Pope Urban VIII on September 14 and 15, 1627, and canonized by Pope Pius IX on June 8, 1862. The members of the Society of Jesus celebrate the memorial of these brothers of theirs on February 6.

Prayer

God our Father, source of strength for all your saints, you led Paul Miki, John de Goto, and James Kisai through the suffering of the cross to the joy of eternal life. May their prayers give us the courage to be loyal until death in professing our faith. We ask this through our Lord Jesus Christ, your Son, who lives and reigns with you and the Holy Spirit, one God, for ever and ever.

February 8

Ven. Philip Jeningen 1642–1704

Philip Jeningen was born in Eichstätt (Bavaria), Germany, on January 5, 1642. He was the second son of the town's mayor. Philip attended the Jesuit school in his native city and at sixteen wanted to become a Jesuit, but because of his parents' opposition he waited five more years. He received his master's degree from the University of Ingolstadt and then entered the Society at Landsberg on January 19, 1663. Philip subsequently did his philosophical and theological studies at Ingolstadt as well and was ordained on June 11, 1672.

During Fr. Jeningen's years of study, he had written to Fr. General in Rome requesting permission to go to the missions. After a grave illness in 1670, from which he said he was cured by St. Francis Xavier, his requests for the missions became more frequent. His missionary work, however, was not to be abroad but at home. After completing his Jesuit training, he was sent to Mindelheim and Dillingen to teach. Seven years later he was sent in 1680 to Ellwangen to give retreats and parish missions. This apostolate, traversing the dioceses of Augsburg, Eichstätt, and Würzburg lasted two dozen years. That he was successful was primarily due to the fact that he was a living example of what he preached. The basis of his success, he claimed, was mortification, prayer, and humility—all of which he practiced to an eminent degree.

Fr. Jeningen's primary concern during his missions was to bring the lost sheep back to the fold and to make lax Catholics more fervent. He at the same time visited the sick and the poor as well as those in prison. He always enjoyed being with small children and adolescents, and to these he never tired of speaking about God.

During his life Fr. Jeningen had to endure persecution and calumny, but this did not dishearten him; it gave him, in fact, greater strength to continue preaching God's truth. Throughout his religious life he enjoyed special graces, such as visions and interior revelations. These are now known only because his superiors had ordered him to write an autobiographical account of his spiritual life. On February 13, 1681, after he had celebrated Mass, and during a time when he was especially depressed, our Lord and our Lady appeared to him. Our Lord gave him his right hand and said: "I will show you that I am a father to you," and our Lady added: "I will show you that I am your mother." The visit restored his confidence and from then on neither detractors nor calumniators could disturb his inner peace. On another occasion our Lord appeared and said to him: "I love you, my dear Philip, and I will love you eternally."

While saying Mass sometime in 1674 God gave him the light to understand that he had but thirty years in which to live and work, and in 1694 another revelation was granted him—he had but ten years left. Then in January 1704 while visiting the villages around Ellwangen, he came upon a farmer, who, when he saw the priest, broke out into a rage and began blaspheming God. Fr. Jeningen tried to calm him, but the more he tried the more enraged the man became. The priest was so disturbed by this outburst of irreverence that he became ill. Knowing that he was to die in 1704, he viewed this as the illness that would take him to his Lord. Others felt the illness was something slight and insignificant, but Fr. Jeningen knew differently. He decided that the best preparation to meet the Lord—would be to make the Spiritual Exercises of St. Ignatius. On the sixth day of his retreat, January 28, he became worse and could hardly walk. When he ended the retreat on January 30, his strength was gone and he had to take to his bed. He asked to be anointed on February 2 and spent his few remaining days prayerfully, in close contact with God.

Fr. Jeningen had no anxieties about death; his soul was filled with such great peace and joy that he said he felt that he had already begun to participate in the vision of God. On the morning of February 8, it became clear to his superiors that death was imminent. As evening approached, Fr. Jeningen asked the members of his community for forgiveness, if he had ever offended them, thanked them for their kindness to him, and asked to be remembered at the altar. That evening the sixty-two-year-old Fr. Jeningen quietly offered his soul to his Beloved, who once told him: "my dear Philip, I will love you eternally."

When the news spread through the city and surrounding region that "the holy man" had died, crowds came to the Jesuit residence to pay their final respects. He was buried on February 9 in the cloisters attached to the Jesuit church in Ellwangen. Fr. Philip Jeningen's cause was introduced in Rome on March 23, 1945, and the decree confirming his heroic practice of virtue was issued December 21, 1989.

February 9

Fr. Saturninus Ibarguren was a Basque, who exercised his apostolic ministry in three countries: Spain, Cuba, and Colombia. He was born at Villareal de Ur- retxu, in the province of Guipúzcoa, Spain, on February 11, 1856. After he com- pleted his education in his hometown, he was called, at eighteen years of age, to serve in the army, which at that time was involved in the Carlist war. During his two years as a soldier (1874 and 1875), Saturninus' vocation matured, and when his term of duty was over he entered the Jesuit novitiate in Poyanne, France, on March 31, 1876. From his earliest days as a religious, Saturninus was known for his faithful observance of the rules and for his practice of mortification. The penances he had set for himself as a young religious remained with him for the rest of his life, as did his love of prayer. Saturninus pronounced his three reli- gious vows in 1878, and began a two-year course in the humanities, also at Poy- anne. He returned to Spain for his philosophical studies (1880–1883) and spent one year at Carrión de los Condes and two at Oña. From 1883 to 1887 he taught—one year at Carrión de los Condes and three at La Guardia—and then went to Oña for theology. He was ordained to the priesthood on July 27, 1890.

The young Fr. Ibarguren was assigned in 1891 to Loyola as assistant to the novice master. After his province had decided to establish a Jesuit house at Xavier castle in Navarre, he was chosen in December 1893 to be its first supe- rior. For eleven years he labored in Navarre, where he not only established the Jesuit residence, but also supervised the construction of the basilica dedicated to St. Francis Xavier, and founded an apostolic school for young boys. In addi- tion to overseeing these projects, he also went into the surrounding towns and villages, always walking from one to the other, preaching tridua, retreats, and missions.

A wealthy Cuban lady residing in San Sebastián, Spain, desired to estab- lish a Jesuit college and mission center at Sagua la Grande, in northern Cuba, and asked Fr. Ibarguren to be the founder. Obedient to his superiors' wishes, he embarked for Cuba on April 20, 1906. The college at Sagua opened toward the end of 1908, and at the beginning of 1909 the Jesuit church opened its doors for worship. Fr. Ibarguren's work was not confined to the college; he also visited several of Cuba's dioceses to preach missions and retreats. During the winters of 1907 and 1908 he went to Puerto Rico to give retreats to priests and religious communities.

Because Fr. Ibarguren's zeal for souls and his success in the pulpit had be- come well known, the bishop of Pinar del Río asked the Jesuit superior to assign him to his diocese as a missionary. The request was granted in May 1909 and the priest spent ten years traversing that diocese as an itinerant preacher, catechizing children and adults, baptizing converts, and regularizing marriages. The diocese may have had its bishop and priests, but it was Fr. Ibarguren's powerful sermons that brought the faith back to countless Cubans. Then, toward the end of July 1919, he was sent to Cartagena, Colombia.

When he arrived in Cartagena in his sixty-third year he set about imitating the example of St. Peter Claver. Like his predecessor, he went to work among the blacks, comforting them in their sorrow while he taught them the rudiments of the Catholic faith. He regularly visited the city's hospitals as well as the nearby leprosarium. By the end of 1925 he began to suffer from a prostate disorder, but refused to see a physician until he could no longer endure the pain. He was taken to the hospital in March 1926 and after several weeks of suffering he recovered enough to return home in August. Two months later he was ill once more and in the middle of October was again hospitalized and remained there until January 1927. The physicians decided that an operation was necessary; he was transferred to Barranquilla at the end of January and the operation took place on February 8. As a result of the operation he was extremely weak and early the next morning he died peacefully in the Lord. He was buried in the crypt of the College of St. Joseph in Barranquilla, but later his remains were transferred to the crypt of the Sanctuary of St. Peter Claver in Cartagena.

Because Fr. Saturninus Ibarguren was known as a man of prayer, who lived a holy and virtuous life, and enjoyed closeness to God, the process leading to beatification has been initiated and is in progress.

February 15

St. Claude La Colombière 1641–1682

"I will send you my faithful servant and perfect friend." With these words our Lord described Fr. Claude La Colombière to Sr. Margaret Mary Alacoque; he was sending him to her so that both could make known the devotion to his Sacred Heart.

Claude was born on February 2, 1641, in Saint-Symphorien d'Ozon, in southern France, and before he reached his tenth birthday he was studying grammar at the Jesuit school in Lyons. Having completed grammar, he passed on to literature and following that he began philosophy. In 1658, when he was seventeen, he felt drawn to be a Jesuit and on October 25 entered the novitiate in Avignon. Claude pronounced the three Jesuit vows of poverty, chastity, and obedience on October 20, 1660, and remained in Avignon for another year to complete the philosophy course he had begun in Lyons. In 1661 he taught his first classes in grammar and literature at Trinity College in Avignon. This assignment lasted until 1666 when he was sent to the College of Clermont in Paris to begin theology. He was ordained a priest on April 6, 1669. In the summer of 1670 Fr. La Colombière returned to Lyons and again entered the classroom, this time to teach rhetoric for three years. In 1673 he was appointed preacher at the Jesuit church attached to the college and there, each Sunday and holy day, he instructed his congregation in the fundamentals of the Catholic faith.

After a year in the pulpit he began his tertianship: a year of solitude and prayer, very much like his years of novitiate. But as an older Jesuit he was now expected to advance in virtue and to intensify his prayer. Unknown to Fr. La Colombière, God was preparing him for a singular mission. For three years he had been thinking of vowing to God exact obedience to all the rules of the Society of Jesus, but since this was something extraordinary he reflected long and prayerfully upon it. In December 1674, during his long retreat as a tertian, he finally felt ready to offer Almighty God this vow of complete fidelity. When tertianship was over, he was assigned to be superior of a small residence in the town of Paray-le-Monial, but he was not aware why God was sending him there.

In the Visitation convent of Paray, Sr. Margaret Mary Alacoque was being especially blessed by our Lord, who was then revealing to her the secret treasures of his Sacred Heart. Because she was misunderstood by some in her convent, who looked upon her as someone deluded, she suffered greatly. It was during those sad days that our Lord told her that he was sending her his "faithful servant and perfect friend," who would not only understand her but would also guide her. Fr. La Colombière arrived at his new assignment at the end of February 1675, and within a few days went to visit the convent. At the moment that he was introduced to the community, Sr. Margaret Mary heard an interior voice speak to her, "This is he whom I have sent to you." In her conversations with Fr. La Colombière she opened her soul and narrated the supernatural events that had been taking place in her life, and with his deep spiritual insight he confirmed that these revelations were indeed from God. In time our Lord made his wishes more clearly known to him and prepared him for the great revelations that he was planning. One morning, while Fr. La Colombière was celebrating Mass in the convent, our Lord showed Sr. Margaret Mary his own heart—it was a burning furnace containing two other hearts—and our Lord said to her: "my pure love unites these three hearts forever."

The mission that brought Fr. La Colombière to Paray was made known to him in June 1675, when our Lord made an explicit request regarding the devotion to his Sacred Heart. In an apparition to Sr. Margaret Mary during the octave of Corpus Christi, Christ showed her his heart and asked her to establish the Friday following the octave of Corpus Christi as a special feast in reparation to his Sacred Heart. Explaining how she should accomplish this, our Lord continued: "Go to my servant Fr. Claude La Colombière and tell him from me to do all in his power to establish this devotion and give this pleasure to my heart." On the Friday following the Corpus Christi octave, June 21, 1675, Fr. La Colombière and Sr. Margaret Mary obeyed our Lord's injunction and privately celebrated their first feast of the Sacred Heart.

Fr. La Colombière's stay in Paray was only a brief eighteen months. He was next assigned to be preacher to the duchess of York in London, where he arrived in October 1676. The duke and duchess were Catholics and, by special privilege of the duke's brother, King Charles II, they were permitted to have a chapel in St. James Palace. Since England was officially a non-Catholic country, English priests were forbidden to officiate in their homeland; therefore the chaplain of the duchess had to come from the Continent. Fr. La Colombière's task was to preach each Sunday and during the seasons of Advent and Lent, and to act as spiritual advisor to the duchess. During his sermons at court, he preached on Christ's love for mankind, symbolized by his Sacred Heart. His preaching on Christ's heart remained with the duchess, and years later she was the first royal personage to request Pope Innocent XII to establish a solemn feast in honor of the Sacred Heart. It would be some time, however, before such a feast would be established, but it was Fr. La Colombière who was its first apostle.

England in the seventeenth century was not a safe place for Catholic priests. In November 1678 a Frenchman, whom Fr. La Colombière had befriended and helped while he was in London, forgot the kindness shown him and falsely denounced the priest to the government in order to gain the 100 pounds sterling promised to anyone who would betray a Jesuit. Fr. La Colombière was arrested in the early hours of November 14, 1678, and charged with traitorous speech against the king and parliament. He was then imprisoned in a cold dungeon. His health soon began to deteriorate and after he had suffered frequent hemorrhages, the prison officials thought it better to send him back to France. He was released in mid-December and by early January 1679, he was again in his native country.

Fr. La Colombière arrived in Paris on January 14, 1679, and slowly made his way southward, frequently stopping because of his poor health. He arrived in Lyons on March 11. Because he could no longer engage in the apostolates that had formerly been his, he served as spiritual father to the young Jesuits teaching at Trinity College, inflaming their hearts with love for the Sacred Heart. Inasmuch as his health did not improve, his superiors thought perhaps the air of Paray would be better for him. On August 1, 1681, he returned to that beloved town. He arrived in a very weakened state and needed help to get around, even to dress and undress. When he was finally able, he paid a visit to the convent and spoke with Sr. Margaret Mary. In early February 1682 he suffered an attack of fever, and on February 15, at 7:00 P.M., the forty-one-year-old Fr. La Colombière died, offering to God the very heart that Christ had once placed in his own Sacred Heart. He was buried the following day in the Jesuit chapel; his remains today lie in a church that was built in 1685 over the same spot.

Fr. Claude La Colombière was beatified by Pope Pius XI on June 16, 1929, and canonized by Pope John Paul II on May 31, 1992. His Jesuit brethren celebrate his memorial on February 15.

Prayer

Lord and Father of us all, you spoke to Saint Claude La Colombière, your faithful servant, in the silence of his heart, so that he might be a witness to the riches of your love. May your gifts of grace continue to enlighten and console your Church. We ask this through our Lord Jesus Christ, your Son, who lives and reigns with you and the Holy Spirit, one God, for ever and ever.

February 16

Ven. Louis de La Puente 1554–1624

Fr. Louis de La Puente was one of the most esteemed ascetical writers of the seventeenth and eighteenth centuries, and countless priests and religious learned about the spiritual life through his books. He was born at Valladolid, Spain, on November 11, 1554, and at age fourteen, after finishing his classical studies, he matriculated at the University of Valladolid to begin his study of philosophy. Having completed this course, he entered the Dominican College of St. Gregory in 1572 for theology, but at the same time attended lectures of Fr. Francis Suárez at the Jesuit College of St. Ambrose. Fr. Suárez, who became one of the most learned Jesuits of his age, was then beginning his teaching career. Inspired by Fr. Suárez' lectures and moved by the sermons of Fr. Gutiérrez, the rector of St. Ambrose, Louis set aside his inclination for the Dominicans and decided to enter the Society of Jesus. His two younger brothers, however, chose to become Dominicans. Louis entered the Jesuit novitiate at Medina del Campo on December 1, 1574.

Since he had completed two years of theology prior to his entrance into the Society, Louis was sent in 1576, while still a novice, to continue his studies at Valladolid. There he pronounced his religious vows on December 8, 1576, and completed his theology in 1578. He spent the two years before ordination

(March 25, 1580) at Oñate and Villagarcía. From 1581 to 1585 Fr. La Puente taught theology at Léon and Salamanca. In 1585 he was appointed master of novices and rector of the community at Villagarcía. For a good part of his priestly life, he was exclusively engaged in the spiritual formation of younger Jesuits, either as master of novices (Villagarcía 1585–1589, 1593–1594, 1599–1601; Medina del Campo 1592–1593), or as spiritual father (Valladolid 1589–1592, Salamanca 1597–1599). Through personal experience he learned how to direct souls, leading them in prayer and showing them how to seek virtue. As a result of having received from God extraordinary gifts of prayer, even to having visions, he was well prepared to lead others along the same path.

Fr. La Puente's health was never strong, and after having served as rector of St. Ambrose in Valladolid between 1601 and 1602, he was forced to give up the burdens of administration for the less demanding office of prefect of studies. It was during these years that he turned to writing and in 1605 published his *Meditations on the Mysteries of Our Faith.* This was a practical book, supplying material for meditative prayer on the end of man, the four last things, the life of Christ, and the divine attributes. Within a short time the book was translated into several languages and through the years it had over 300 editions. Rare must have been the priest or religious who, at one time or another, had not used these volumes for daily prayer.

In 1609 Fr. La Puente published his *Spiritual Guide,* a profound work on the contemplative and active lives, together with their various practices. This was a more important book than those for meditation, but it never had the popularity that the others achieved. There followed, during the years from 1612 to 1616, his four volumes *On Christian Perfection in the Different States of Life*— this was the first time that a spiritual treatise spoke of perfection in the various states that a Christian might find himself. All these books were the fruit of his experience in guiding others, as well as his own prayer, mortification, and abandonment to almighty God.

In 1615 Fr. La Puente published his biography of Fr. Baltasar Álvarez, whom he had had as tertian instructor, and finally in 1622, his commentary on *The Canticle of Canticles* appeared. He was then sixty-eight years old and his health was steadily declining; consequently he relinquished his position of prefect of studies and for the next two years lived in relative seclusion. Aware that death would soon come, he spent his time in prayer, with many hours in the community chapel at St. Ambrose. Shortly before his death, he asked to receive the last anointing and Viaticum, and on February 16, 1624, at half past ten in the evening, as his gaze was fixed on the crucifix in his room, and as his lips uttered the words, "Into your hands, O Lord, I commend my spirit," he peacefully breathed his last. So quiet and calm was his passing to God that the Jesuits in the room with him thought that he had fallen sleep.

Fr. Louis de La Puente's cause was introduced in Rome on October 4, 1667, and the decree recognizing his heroic virtue was published in 1759.

February 18

Fr. John Cardim was a Portuguese, born in Torre de Moncorvo on June 2, 1585, the oldest of ten children. His parents supervised their children's religious upbringing so well that nine of them entered religious life. By the time John reached his thirteenth year, he was already in the habit of reciting the rosary and the office of our Lady every day. His usual reading material was the lives of the saints. Whatever religious instruction he received in school, he tried to impart to others, so that several times a week he gathered the servants around him and taught them catechism. He first studied with the Jesuits at the College of St. Anthony, Lisbon, and in 1600, when he was fifteen, he went to the University of Coimbra. As soon as he arrived he asked to enter the Society. In wanting to be a Jesuit he was following in the footsteps of three of his uncles: two of his father's brothers and one of his mother's. John was so frail in appearance that the Jesuit superior had to tell him that he could not be admitted because of his poor health. While admiring John's desire, the superior encouraged him to continue his university studies.

The fact that John had failed in his first attempt to become a Jesuit did not put an end to his thinking about becoming a priest. At the university he pursued courses in canon and civil law, and did so well that his professors remarked that he was sure to emerge as one of the better canon lawyers. Though talented and successful in studies, he felt he would never be happy unless he were in religion. He placed his problem before our Lady and one day while asking her to allow him to become a Jesuit, heard her say that his prayer would be granted. With spirits brightened he presented himself once more before the Jesuit superior and asked for admission, but this time he requested to enter as a brother. Once again the superior expressed doubts about John's health and his being able to withstand the rigors of religious life, but to this the young man remarked: "No need to be afraid, God has given me a body that is sufficiently robust to endure such penances." As a matter of fact, John had, for several years, been practicing bodily penances to a degree over and above that demanded by religious orders. Perceiving the obvious disappointment in John's face, the superior finally acquiesced and suggested that, since he was not far from ordination, he should continue his studies and that he would be accepted afterwards.

Fr. Cardim's ordination took place in 1611 and immediately thereafter, on June 23, he entered the novitiate at Coimbra to begin his two-year probation. Two of his brothers also entered the Society. As a novice Fr. Cardim taught catechism twice a week to poor children, and when he finished the lesson he sat down among them to chat and eat. In 1612 he was sent to the college in Braga to review his philosophy.

While at Braga, Fr. Cardim became familiar with the city's hospitals and prisons. On his weekly holiday from studies, he visited them or went to the city's outlying districts to teach the peasants about God. The poor of Braga found a friend in him and he found friends in them. When he left the Jesuit residence on an errand, people often gathered about him and followed him wherever he was going. It was only by stopping in the middle of the street and preaching to them that they could be satisfied, and only then would they permit him to continue on his way. They tried to attend his Masses in the Jesuit church, and some attested that they had seen him raised off the floor in prayer. The people of Braga knew that they had a treasure in Fr. Cardim, but they were not to have that treasure for long.

After four short years as a Jesuit, Fr. Cardim knew that he was soon to go to heaven. He fell ill with pleurisy, and when his time came to leave this world he kissed the crucifix in his hand. At the moment of his death he appeared to his mother, who was miles away, and spoke to her: "Rejoice mother, for I am now on my way to enjoy the vision of God; I owe a great part of my present happiness to you for the holy lessons you taught me."

After Fr. Cardim's death on February 18, 1615, innumerable favors were received through his intercession and the Portuguese Jesuits began collecting material with a view of promoting his cause for beatification. Unfortunately they were halted in their efforts during the time of the Society's suppression (1773–1814); it was only in 1972 that the Portuguese bishops again revived interest in Fr. Cardim's cause.

February 19

S. G. John Sullivan 1861–1933

A young Protestant lawyer had spent several months at a monastery on Mount Athos in Greece—he had thoughts of becoming a monk. He felt very much drawn to a life of close union with God, but judging this not the right time to come to a decision he returned to his law practice in London. His parents were Edward Sullivan, Ireland's Lord Chancellor, and Elizabeth Baily. John was born in Dublin on May 8, 1861, and was brought up in his father's Protestant faith. His mother, however, was a Catholic and John always attributed his conversion to her incessant prayers. As a youth John entered the Portora Royal School at Enniskillen in 1873 and remained there six years. In 1879 he matriculated at

Dublin's Trinity College and earned a degree in classics in 1883. He next turned his attention to law. He began his law studies at Trinity, but in 1885 moved to Lincoln's Inn, London, whence he graduated in 1888.

John set himself up in London to practice law. During his professional years he was able to travel widely; he especially loved Greece and it was during this period that he stayed at the monastery on Mount Athos. Sometime after his return from Greece he decided to adopt his mother's religion and on December 21, 1896, was received into the Catholic Church by the Jesuits at Farm Street, London. With his conversion John adopted an entirely new way of life; though he once had been a dapper young lawyer, now he chose to dress simply and to live poorly. He stripped his rooms of unnecessary furniture and gave much of his wardrobe away. He spent his free time visiting the sick and orphans, taking them gifts, and helping a variety of charitable causes. Many convents were the recipients of his benefactions. In the months following his conversion he thought of becoming a priest. At first he was inclined to become a Franciscan, but some of his acquaintances convinced him that he was meant to be a Jesuit, and so he entered the Society in Ireland and began his novitiate at Tullabeg on September 7, 1900. He was then thirty-nine years old.

John pronounced his three religious vows on September 8, 1902, and went to Stonyhurst in England to do two years of philosophy (1902–1904). He returned to Dublin and attended Milltown Park for theology (1904 to 1907). Though he was older and more experienced than the young Jesuits with whom he was studying, he was, nevertheless, known for his unpretentiousness, which included a habit of depreciating himself and of making others feel more important than he was. During his theological studies he began visiting a nearby hospice for the dying and a hospital for incurables. This apostolate to the suffering remained one of his chief concerns during his priestly life. He was ordained at Milltown Park on July 28, 1907, and was sent to Clongowes Wood School, where he spent most of his priestly life. There he taught young boys Latin and Greek, and though he was never considered a brilliant teacher, he did captivate the young men, many of whom chose him as their confessor and spiritual director.

Fr. Sullivan's influence was equally felt outside the academic community, for he was constantly walking, or riding his bicycle, to visit someone who was ill or to help someone in need. The distance did not matter, nor did the weather; he went whenever and wherever he was needed. The faithful who attended the Jesuit church at Clongowes always asked him to visit their sick—his prayers and blessings were deemed more helpful than the physician's visit. Having once experienced the efficacy of his prayers, the people turned to him in greater numbers and with greater affection.

Though his clothes were patched beyond description and his shoes always in need of repair, he was, nevertheless, always clean. He had no gloves for winter; his overshoes always had holes, but he said he did not mind the cold. He was abstemious at meals and rarely ate meat; he slept but a few hours at night and spent most of it before the Blessed Sacrament. As austere as he was toward himself, that is how compassionate and understanding he was toward others. Fr. Sullivan literally forgot himself and lived only to bring Christ's consolation and love to others.

In July 1919 he was appointed rector of the juniorate and retreat house at Rathfarnham Castle. His duty there was to supervise the spiritual growth of some two dozen young Jesuits who had just finished their novitiate and were engaged in university studies in Dublin. His first concern was for these young men and he treated them with his usual kindness, but when time permitted, he continued his apostolate to the suffering. He also gave the Spiritual Exercises to religious communities of women. In 1924 he returned to Clongowes to take up where he had left off in 1919. There he worked untiringly among his people until a few weeks before his death.

On February 4, 1933, because of a swelling on his elbow, Fr. Sullivan asked to see a physician and a few days later the arm was lanced. He remained in the infirmary and the nurse in charge told how Fr. Sullivan spent his time in prayer with his gaze always fixed on the crucifix. On February 17, just when he seemed to be getting better, he suffered a sudden attack of severe pain in his abdomen and the attending physician referred the case to a surgeon. The surgeon, who had been a former student of his at Clongowes, diagnosed it as an obstruction and ordered that he be taken to a Dublin hospital, where he was operated on that afternoon. It was discovered that a mesenteric thrombosis was causing gangrene in a large section of the small intestine. The operation relieved him of much of the pain, but it could not save his life. He spent the next two days in prayer and then on Monday, February 19, at 11:00 P.M, the seventy-two-year-old Fr. Sullivan peacefully offered his suffering and his life to his Lord who had suffered and died for him. The funeral was held the following Wednesday at Clongowes. Many of his clients who came to see him for the last time touched their rosaries to his casket and took dirt from his grave. Fr. Sullivan's vocation was to help his fellowmen and to serve God, and it seems that God was satisfied with his humble service. The faithful in Dublin still ask him to intercede with God in their behalf. Fr. John Sullivan's cause is presently under consideration in Rome.

February 20

S. G. Peter Joseph Mary Chaumonot 1611–1693

Peter, the son of a vinegrower, was born in the small Burgundian village of Sainte-Colombe-sur-Seine, France, on March 9, 1611. Because his maternal grandfather was a school teacher, the child, though only six, was placed under his care so that he might learn to read and write. When twelve Peter studied Latin in preparation for college with an uncle of his, a priest living in Châtillon-sur-Seine. Among his student companions there was one interested in Church music and this lad talked Peter into running away with him to Beaune to study Gregorian chant with the Oratorians. Since Peter had no funds of his own, he waited until his uncle was engaged in church and then stole a hundred sols and hastily left town. He was seventeen years old.

While living in Beaune Peter's money disappeared more quickly than he had anticipated and he found himself a pauper. Since he could not face returning home and being branded a thief, he chose to become a vagabond and headed for Rome "to seek pardon." During the journey he usually tried to join other travellers. He lived by begging and spent his nights either in barns or in open fields. In this manner he crossed the Alps into Italy, walked through Lombardy, down to Ancona and finally to Loreto, on Italy's eastern shore. On his arrival he was without shoes and his clothes were in tatters; his scalp was scabby, purulent, and lousy.

Peter never forgot his first visit to the Holy House of Loreto. While kneeling in that narrow shrine, he poured out his heart to our Lady and prayed that she have pity on him in his affliction. Would that she lead him to someone who could relieve him of his present misery! As he was leaving the church, a young man approached and said: "What's wrong with your head? Let me work on it and help you." The two then went behind the church and the young man, whom Peter later was convinced must have been an angel, cut off Peter's hair and rubbed his scalp with a white cloth. When Peter replaced his hat, he found his scalp thoroughly clean, without trace of his former malady. He was certain that our Lady had worked a miracle in his behalf.

After three days he set out for Rome, but while passing through Terni an elderly gentleman hired him as his valet. One day, feeling the need to go to confession, Peter went to the local Jesuit church, but not knowing Italian sufficiently he made his confession in Latin. Impressed by the youth's knowledge of Latin, the confessor encouraged him to continue his studies and offered to help him enter the Jesuit school. Peter however declined; he feared that the priest was trying to turn him into a Jesuit. While in Terni, Peter, to better his Italian, read the lives of the saints and as a result of the readings decided that after Rome he would return to France and become a hermit.

Peter's visit to Rome was brief. On his homeward journey he once more stopped in Terni and was again engaged by his former employer. He now attended classes at the Jesuit college and one morning, while at Mass in the Jesuit church, he heard a sermon on the recently beatified Francis Borgia. So moved was he that he asked admission into the Society. On May 18, 1632, now twenty-one years of age, he entered the Roman novitiate of Sant'Andrea. He pronounced his first vows of religion on May 16, 1634, and then taught for two-and-a-half years in Fermo, only a dozen or so miles from Loreto, so Peter made a second pilgrimage to our Lady's shrine.

Subsequently Peter began his studies at the Roman College where he became acquainted with Fr. Antoine Poncet, a fellow Frenchman, who showed him a letter from Fr. John de Brébeuf describing missionary life among the Huron Indians in New France (Canada). When Fr. Poncet mentioned that he was being assigned to that same mission, Peter asked to join him and took his request to Fr. General Muzio Vitelleschi, who remarked that the would-be missionary had hardly begun his study of theology. Nevertheless, he acquiesced to the request. In October 1637 Fr. Poncet and Peter made a pilgrimage to Loreto, where both placed their coming voyage under the Virgin's care. Peter, in addition, promised to build a chapel in honor of Our Lady of Loreto and resolved to adopt the names of Joseph and Mary, the former because St. Joseph was the patron of New France, and the latter because of his love of the Virgin.

Peter was ordained in Rome on March 19, 1638, and the following October left with Fr. Poncet for France. On May 4, 1639, they sailed from Dieppe. Three ships left port that day and on them were nine missionaries: three Jesuits, three Hospitaller Sisters, and three Ursulines. Among the latter was Marie of the Incarnation.

After a two-and-a-half-month crossing, during which they weathered a fifteen-day storm and a frightful encounter with icebergs, the missionaries arrived in Quebec on August 1. Within days after the missionaries' arrival, the Huron Indians, who had come to the French settlement to trade, were ready to depart. Unwilling to wait another year for the traders to return, Frs. Chaumonot and Poncet joined them on their homeward trip to Huronia, some nine hundred miles away. The flotilla followed the St. Lawrence River to Montreal, where it entered the Ottawa, then into Lake Nipissing and finally into today's Georgian Bay. On September 10 the two priests were at the Jesuit missionary station of Sainte-Marie, where their religious brethren greeted them.

In October a small-pox epidemic broke out in the Huron villages and Fr. Chaumonot learned how arduous missionary life could be. He accompanied Fr. Paul Ragueneau to La Conception mission, but the only success they had was in baptizing dying infants and a few adults. After five months of frustration and threats, they were forced to leave. His next assignment was with Fr. Anthony Daniel, who also served as his tutor in the Huron tongue. Because of his great facility with languages, the new missionary had, within a remarkably short time, sufficient command so as to preach in it. Years later he compiled a Huron grammar and vocabulary, works that proved invaluable to new missionaries. During the several years prior to Huronia and the Huron nation being all but obliterated by the Iroquois, Fr. Chaumonot worked with veteran missionaries such as Frs. John de Brébeuf, François du Peron, and René Ménard. With them he visited the various villages and preached to those willing to listen. He likewise learned to endure rejection and insults and to expect martyrdom.

As the Iroquois' hatred of the Hurons increased, so did their determination to destroy them. Beginning in 1648 the Iroquois initiated surprise attacks on Huron villages, during which three Jesuits were martyred (Fr. Daniel in July 1648 and Frs. Brébeuf and Gabriel Lalemant in March 1649) and thousands of Hurons were massacred or taken into captivity. Of those who escaped death, many went to live among the neighboring Petuns and Neutrals, while others sought refuge at the Jesuit headquarters of Sainte-Marie. Since there was no way to halt the Iroquois' advance, the missionaries at Sainte-Marie burned their mission headquarters (May 15, 1649) and took the Huron remnant to Ile Saint-Joseph (today's Christian Island) in Georgian Bay. But the winter there was most difficult for them and because of the ever-present Iroquois threat (Frs. Charles Garnier and Noel Chabanel were martyred in December 1649), the Jesuits and some 300 Hurons, all under Fr. Chaumonot's leadership, left the island in June 1650 for Quebec. During the following March they settled on nearby Ile d'Orléans. From that time on Fr. Chaumonot devoted his time and energy in behalf of his homeless Hurons. When the new settlement became a thriving community, many of their nation, who had gone to the Petuns or the Neutrals, joined them in Quebec.

Since 1653 the Onondagas, one of the five Iroquois nations, sent ambassadors to Quebec requesting missionaries. Fr. Chaumonot was chosen to go to them because he alone had the best command of their tongue. His companion was the newly arrived Claude Dablon. Both missionaries departed in September 1655, but the Onondagas' insincerity soon became obvious; by inviting missionaries they thought the Huron community would follow them. After bearing months of vexatious treatment, the missionaries returned to Quebec in April 1658. Fr. Chaumonot went to his Hurons, who in the meantime had migrated to Quebec. Apart from a few trips to Montreal on government business, the missionary remained with his Huron community until his death. When that community moved, so did he—to Beauport in 1666, then to Sillery in 1667, and finally to Lorette in 1673.

Throughout his years in New France, Fr. Chaumonot worked for the spiritual good of those given to his care. To guarantee the Christian quality of family life among the French and native population, he founded the Confraternity of the Holy Family (July 31, 1663) and promoted it wherever he travelled. To propagate this association he wrote *Solid Devotion to the Holy Family of Jesus, Mary and Joseph,* as well as *The Catechism of the Holy Family.* While in Sillery he built a chapel honoring Notre-Dame de Foy. Then in 1671 he received from Fr. Poncet, visiting Italy at the time, a statue of Our Lady of Loreto together with the plans of the Holy House. Fr. Chaumonot's promise could now be fulfilled, a chapel in honor of Our Lady of Loreto. The chapel—an exact replica— was built after the Hurons had migrated to a place that Fr. Chaumonot named Lorette (today's Ancienne Lorette), and was dedicated on November 4, 1674. Within a short period that chapel became a place of pilgrimage for the native population as well as for the French. Fr. Chaumonot spent the next seventeen years of his life there, instructing his parishioners, visiting the sick, and praying for their needs.

On March 20, 1688, the seventy-seven-year-old priest celebrated the fiftieth anniversary of his ordination—the first priest to celebrate such an anniversary in the New World. That same year, at the request of his religious superior, Fr. Dablon, he wrote his autobiography. In view of his advancing years, he resigned his post in 1691. He subsequently fell ill and in October 1692 was transferred to the Jesuit college in Quebec. On February 21, 1693, after months of illness, he suddenly sat up in bed, gazed toward the foot of the bed, stretched out his arms and said "Jesus, Mary, Joseph." He breathed his last at about 1 P.M. Fr. Chaumonot, the most famous and most beloved Jesuit in New France, was eighty-two years old, had been a Jesuit for sixty and had spent fifty-three years on the mission.

His Jesuit contemporaries saw him as a man of peace and prayer, revered him for his holiness, and acknowledged that miracles were performed through his intercession. Among the Hurons he was considered another John de Brébeuf, equal to him in sanctity and courage. After that martyr's death, they changed Fr. Chaumonot's Indian name of *Aroniatiri* (Heaven-bearer) to that of *Echon*, the name by which the great Brébeuf was known among them.

February 21

St. Robert Southwell 1561–1595

Martyr of England

Fr. Robert Southwell, a missionary to England during the reign of Queen Elizabeth I, is one of that nation's more illustrious martyrs and one of its better poets. He was born of a well-to-do family at Horsham St. Faith, near Norwich, sometime between October and December 1561. Since all institutions of learning had become Protestant, Robert was sent (May 1576) to the English College at Douai, Flanders. For a time he also studied at the College of Clermont in Paris, where he came under the influence of the Jesuit Thomas Darbyshire. Months before his seventeenth birthday (early 1578), Robert applied for membership in the Society in Paris, but was told that he was too young and that the novitiate was temporarily closed because of military activity in that area. Determined to be a Jesuit, he walked to Rome. There he was accepted and began his novitiate at Sant'Andrea on October 17, 1578. He did his philosophical and theological studies at the Roman College and was ordained during the summer of 1584. He was then appointed prefect of studies at the English College in Rome, a seminary that trained priests for England. In 1586 his prayer was answered: he was assigned to the English mission and together with Fr. Henry Garnet left Rome on May 8, 1586.

P. Robertus Soulhuuellus. Nobili sanguine in Anglia natus, Soc. IESV.
pro Religione Catholica suspensus et sectus Londini. A. 1595. 3. Mar.
C. S. d.   M. K. f.

St. Robert Southwell

Fr. Southwell and Fr. Garnet knew that port authorities were on the watch for incoming priests, therefore, they landed on a secluded coast a mile east of Folkestone on July 17, and made their way separately to London. Fr. Southwell was assigned to minister in and about London, whereas Fr. Garnet was given the counties in the Midlands. Fr. Southwell's first base of operation was with the Vaux family in Hackney. His next, in 1587, was with the Countess of Arundel and Surrey, whose husband, Sir Philip Howard, was imprisoned in the Tower for his faith. Fr. Southwell helped priests who had just entered the country; he saw to it that they had housing and informed them which counties they could visit and which households they could use as their headquarters. He likewise visited the dozen or so prisons in the city and frequently ministered in the counties surrounding London. When Fr. Garnet became superior of the mission and settled in London, it then became possible for Fr. Southwell to visit the outlying counties, preaching and administering the sacraments to the faithful living there.

When Fr. Garnet established a secret press in London, Fr. Southwell helped direct the printing of Catholic catechisms and devotional books. This press was the sole source of religious literature for English Catholics. Because Fr. Southwell had enjoyed the hospitality of the Countess of Arundel, he wrote several letters to Sir Philip; he later revised and published them as *An Epistle of Comfort,* intended for all who were imprisoned for the faith. This Epistle is one of the finest prose works of the Elizabethan age.

Fr. Southwell's active ministry lasted six years, during which time he had several close escapes from determined priest-hunters. His ministry came to an end in June 1592 when he was betrayed by a Catholic girl, Anne Bellamy, whose family he had known. Because she had refused to attend Protestant services, Anne was incarcerated, and after three months was found with child, having been forced or seduced by Richard Topcliffe, the professional priest-torturer. Topcliffe promised her an honest marriage and full remission for all members of her family if she could convince Fr. Southwell to come to her family home on a certain day. When released from prison, Anne did not return to her parents in Uxenden, near Harrow, but wrote to the priest asking him to meet her there. Thinking that Anne wanted to receive the sacraments, Fr. Southwell went to the Bellamy residence on June 25, 1592. It was not Anne who came that evening, but Topcliffe and his men. Hearing the tumult outside, the Jesuit slipped into a concealed room, and when he heard what had happened and how he had been betrayed, he willingly gave himself up.

Topcliffe was jubilant over his catch. From Fr. Southwell, who was the greatest prize of his career, he expected to learn the names and locations of all priests working in England. Topcliffe led his prisoner, bound in chains, to his residence next to the Gatehouse Prison at Westminster, where he had his own private torture chamber. Satanically, he put Fr. Southwell through excruciating torments, having him hang by the wrists with his feet off the ground. After a couple of days of such torture Topcliffe only learned that his prisoner was a Jesuit priest who had come to England to preach the Catholic faith and was ready to die for that cause. Fr. Southwell never revealed a single name. Unsuccessful in obtaining the information he sought, Topcliffe moved the prisoner on June 28 to the Gatehouse Prison, where he underwent further torture. He is said to have been tortured thirteen times in all. He proved so courageous that the officials finally gave up and cast him among the paupers to face cold, hunger, and thirst.

It was at the paupers' prison that his father visited him, and when he saw his son covered with vermin and looking like a corpse, he sent a petition to the queen: if his son had done anything worthy of death, then let it be death; but if not, let him be treated as the gentleman he is. At the queen's request, Fr. Southwell was moved to the Tower, where his father supplied him with necessities. Fr. Garnet sent Fr. Southwell his breviary and Bible, and the countess sent him a copy of St. Bernard's sermons. During his years in prison, but especially during his earlier days when he had to live in hiding for long periods of time, Fr. Southwell expressed his thoughts and feelings in poems. These proved popular, and after his martyrdom they were collected and published as *St. Peter's Complaint*. The book was especially well received among Catholic readers.

After about two-and-a-half years in the Tower, without visitors and unable to write or receive letters, Fr. Southwell sent a message to Lord Burghley requesting that his case come to trial, or that he be permitted visitors, or be released. Lord Burghley responded by ordering his trial, and on February 18, 1595, Fr. Southwell was moved to Newgate Prison. The trial took place on February 20 in Westminster Hall. During the trial Fr. Southwell readily admitted that he was a priest and had come to England to administer the Catholic sacraments to those who desired them, but he denied all complicity in plots against the queen. He was, nevertheless, found guilty of high treason. On the morning of February 21, when informed that he was to be executed that day, he told the jailer that he could not have received more joyful news.

He was tied to a hurdle and dragged to Tyburn, a journey of three hours. With a noose about his neck, he was placed beneath the gallows and spoke to the bystanders affirming his respect for the queen, for whose welfare he had constantly prayed. As he was saying his final prayer, "Into your hands, O Lord, I commend my spirit," the cart was drawn from under him. The noose, however, was improperly placed and his neck did not break. He remained hanging in agony, and with hands tied he tried to make the sign of the cross. Discovering the difficulty, the hangman pulled him by the legs and brought his agony to an end. Fr. Southwell was in his thirty-fourth year. After he was hanged his head was cut off and placed on a bridge and his body quartered and exhibited on four city gates.

Fr. Southwell was beatified by Pope Pius XI on December 15, 1929, and was canonized by Pope Paul VI on October 25, 1970. His memorial is celebrated on December 1, the day when the Society commemorates all of its English and Welsh martyrs.

Prayer

Almighty, eternal God, you chose from the people of England and Wales Saint Robert Southwell and his companions to be made like Christ, who died to save the world. Listen to their prayers; strengthen your Church by the same faith and love that strengthened them, and bless it always with your gift of unity. We ask this through our Lord Jesus Christ, your Son, who lives and reigns with you and the Holy Spirit, one God, for ever and ever.

February 22

Bl. James Carvalho 1578–1624

Martyr of Japan

Fr. James Carvalho's death was unlike that of most of the other Japanese martyrs beatified in 1867. Most had suffered death by slow fire or beheading, but Fr. Carvalho was frozen to death on the banks of an icy river in mid-February.

Fr. Carvalho was born in Coimbra, Portugal, in 1578 and entered the Coimbra novitiate of the Jesuits on November 14, 1594. In 1600 he left Lisbon for Goa (India) and studied some philosophy while there. In 1601 he went to Macao to complete his philosophical and theological studies. He was ordained a priest in 1608. The following year he sailed to Japan, arriving on June 29, 1609, and found the Christian communities there thriving and enjoying great peace. He spent his first year learning the language, then two years of missionary work in Amakusa, and in 1612 he was transferred to the region of Miyako (today's Kyoto), where he evangelized without interference or fear. That peace was brutally shattered in 1614, after sixteen years of benevolent toleration, when Shogun Iyeyasu issued a decree banishing all foreign missionaries and ordered the closing or destruction of all Christian churches. Fr. Carvalho was deported with about one hundred other Jesuits, and was taken to Macao. During this period of enforced exile, he became the cofounder of the Japanese mission in Cochin China. But Japan was his mission and to Japan he wanted to return. He secretly reentered the country in 1616 and was active for a time in the vicinity of Omura. Later he joined Fr. Jerome De Angelis in northern Japan, caring for the refugees who had moved there to escape the persecution in the south.

Fr. Carvalho worked among the miners in the districts of Oshu and Dewa where silver mines had recently been discovered. Conversions among the miners proved easy, but living in those frigid northern climates did not. For shelter he had to be satisfied with caves, barns, and huts. Despite the hardship of the weather and the many miles he had to travel, he succeeded in visiting all the Christians in those districts and saw to it that their number increased. In 1620 he crossed over to Yezo (today Hokkiado) the northernmost island of Japan, and on August 5, 1620, celebrated Mass at Matsumae, the first Mass to be said on that island.

In December 1623 Masamune, the prince of Oshu, who until then had been favorably disposed toward Christians, became their persecutor. Following the harsh example of the emperor, he ordered the governor of Sendai, his capital, to ferret out all Christians and put to death everyone who refused to apostatize. Fr. Carvalho was then staying in Miwake with John de Goto, a fervent Catholic, and spent Christmas and Epiphany with him. Upon hearing of Masamune's order, the priest left the Goto residence so as not to compromise his host. He left none too soon. Two apostate Christians, having learned where Fr. Carvalho was staying, passed the information on to the governor, who sent soldiers in search of him. Shortly before the soldiers arrived Fr. Carvalho and some sixty Christians had gone into a deep valley to seek safety. Unfortunately, their tracks in the snow showed where they had gone and the soldiers soon came upon the group. Before the soldiers had a chance to ask for the priest, Fr. Carvalho encouraged his Christians to flee; he then walked up to his captors and introduced himself as the one they wanted. On that February 8, 1624, all but a dozen of his companions took the opportunity to leave.

While the soldiers huddled around a fire and ate, the prisoners were kept standing in the cold valley. After the meal the soldiers led the prisoners on the seven-day march to Sendai. When two Christians were unable to keep up with the group, they were beheaded and their bodies hacked to pieces. After the group reached Sendai, the prisoners were marched through the streets. They were then taken to prison where they remained for four weeks and were fed nothing but a few handfuls of boiled rice, just enough to keep them alive.

On February 18 the final testing began. Near the prison fortress flowed the Hirose, a fast-moving river of icy water. It was to this river's bank that the ten prisoners were taken. A hole measuring several square feet was filled with the river's icy water. The prisoners, stripped naked, were forced to enter the pit. The freezing water came up to their knees; they had to kneel in Japanese fashion, sitting on their heels. From this position they were told to rise and stand exposed to the cold wind. They repeated this exercise for three hours and when their bodies were numb they were taken from the pit and offered freedom if they would deny their religion. When none would do so, they were taken back to the fortress where two more died. On February 22 the torture was repeated. Fr. Carvalho was in the pit with seven others, and together, hour after hour, they alternately knelt and stood. As the day wore on, the winds began to blow and a snowstorm came. One by one the companions died, but Fr. Carvalho, the last of the group, endured his torture well into the night. His voice, always raised in prayer, grew weak. In the end he was only able to whisper the names of Jesus and Mary. He died in the icy water and the soldiers left his body in the pit. Two days later a Christian came and buried it.

Because of insufficient information about Fr. Carvalho's companions in martyrdom, they were not included in the decree of beatification issued by Pope Pius IX on May 7, 1867. Fr. James Carvalho's memorial is celebrated, with the other Jesuit martyrs of Japan, on February 4.

Prayer

Almighty God, grant that this remembrance of your martyr, Blessed James Carvalho, may bring us joy. May we who depend upon his prayers glory in his entry into heaven. We ask this through our Lord Jesus Christ, your Son, who lives and reigns with you and the Holy Spirit, one God, for ever and ever.

February 25

Ven. Francis Nevill 1595–1679

Fr. Francis Nevill's family name was Cotton and he was born in Hampshire in 1595. He attended the English College at Saint-Omer in Flanders and then went to the English College in Valladolid, Spain (1613–1616). At age twenty-one, he entered the novitiate of the English Jesuits at Watten, Flanders (1616), and after his training and ordination (1620) was sent on the English mission, perhaps as early as 1622. He spent more than fifty years on the mission and during that time he filled many offices, including that of superior of various districts. The core of Fr. Nevill's apostolate, however, was in South Wales. By nature he was affable, and all who met him commented on his extraordinary sanctity and holiness of life. During five decades of his active ministry, he had evaded the snares of the priest-hunters, but he was finally arrested at a time when the Jesuits were being persecuted for their alleged complicity in a plot to assassinate Charles II. The plot was a fiction created by a renegade Anglican, Titus Oates, who sought revenge on the Society of Jesus.

Sometime in February 1679, Fr. Nevill, while lodging at the house of a Catholic nobleman in Stafford, was betrayed by an apostate Catholic. When the priest-hunters arrived to arrest him Fr. Nevill hid in the garret, but the hunters were determined to find their prey. After a methodical search throughout the house, they finally came upon him. In their hatred, the hunters threw the aged priest down a flight of stairs. His captors intended to take him to the Stafford jail, but as the eighty-four-year-old Fr. Nevill was being helped to the conveyance, he collapsed from exhaustion. Fearing that the priest might die on the way to jail, the soldiers carried him back to his chamber. A few days after the brutal event, sometime toward the end of February, the holy Fr. Nevill went peacefully to the Lord. Some accounts say that he died in his room, while others seem to indicate that he died in prison. He was declared Venerable by Pope Leo XIII in 1886.

February 26

S. G. Richard Friedl 1847–1917

Fr. Richard Friedl was born in Spalato, Dalmatia (today's Split, Croatia) on September 16, 1847, the second of five children. In 1852 the family moved to Ragusa (today's Dubrovnik), and there, when Richard was nine, he began his studies at the Jesuit school. In the following year he became a member of our Lady's sodality. When the family returned to Spalato in 1859, Richard continued his education in the public schools. As the result of a retreat he made in October 1862, he decided to enter the Society of Jesus. He left home on November 5 and arrived at the novitiate in Verona, Italy, on November 10. Within the first week of his arrival, he wrote to his parents; his happiness was so great that he gave "from Paradise" as his return address.

Richard pronounced his three vows of religion on November 13, 1864, at age seventeen, and was eager to begin his study of the humanities. Because of the growing revolutionary-independence movement in Italy, the Jesuit house at Verona was closed and the community moved to Feldkirch, Austria, in July 1866. In the following year the community returned to Italy and settled in Bolzano. During Richard's annual retreat from September 24 to October 2, 1869, he was granted an insight into the meaning of Jesus' cross, an insight he preached for the remainder of his life. On October 5, 1869, he went to Bressanone, in the Alps of northern Italy, where he taught for six years and remained to study theology. However, in October 1876 the college was closed and he went to Laval, France, to finish his studies. He was ordained to the priesthood at Laval on September 9, 1877.

Fr. Friedl longed to go to the missions and finally received word that he was to go to Mangalore, India. To prepare himself for this new apostolate he spent several months during 1878 in England, perfecting his English. But before departing for India, he had to make his tertianship and, thus, he went to Paray-le-Monial, France, where the holy Fr. Paul Ginhac was tertian instructor. Fr. Friedl viewed these months in Paray as the time when he perceived the meaning of Jesus' cross with greater clarity and learned the true value of prayer.

When his period of tertianship was over, India, he sadly learned, was not for him. Instead, his superiors made him assistant to the novice master at Aux Alleux, near Laval, the novitiate of the exiled Italian Jesuits. In June 1880 the French government ordered the expulsion of these exiles and on July 3, Fr. Friedl and the novices set sail for Spain, arriving in Valencia ten days later. Fr. Friedl was not to remain long on Spanish soil; no sooner had he arrived than he was directed to go to the seminary in Zara (present-day Zadar, Croatia). For seven years he devoted his time not only to his classes and to directing the seminarians but also to an active apostolate among Zara's highlanders. Then in September 1887 he was appointed master of novices at Portoré (now Kraljevica), where his province had its novitiate since 1883. This appointment was the beginning of Fr. Friedl's thirty years of leadership—difficult years during which he was charged with the responsibility of guiding others to God. When the novitiate was transferred in September 1894 to Soresino, near Cremona, Italy, Fr. Friedl was made its rector. As a man for whom prayer was of tremendous importance, he told the members of his community how he intended to govern them: "Fathers, I pray, I pray a great deal, because I believe that the best means of governing is by prayer."

After serving as rector at Soresino, Fr. Friedl was made provincial in October 1896 of the Veneto Province of the Society of Jesus. Shortly after he took office, he wrote a warm letter to the novices he had left at Soresino. What he wrote is a terse description of what religious life should be: "Be happy in the Lord, and to keep yourselves happy never deny our Lord any sacrifice. No matter what he asks of you, do it happily."

After a successful term as provincial of his own province, he was named, in May 1899, provincial of the Turin province. When this term came to an end in December 1903, he was appointed rector and master of novices at Avigliana, the novitiate of the Turin Province. Then, in October 1905, he became tertian instructor and rector of the tertianship at Sartirana della Brianza (Como), which later moved to Florence in 1907. Fr. Friedl remained active as instructor of tertians until the events of World War I brought an interruption to his work in 1916.

Fr. Friedl remained in Florence. He was now seventy years old and the wound in his right leg had become cancerous. He felt ill on February 10, 1917, but on the following morning was able, nevertheless, to celebrate his last Mass. When the attending physician told him there was no chance of recovery, Fr. Friedl, always resigned to the Divine Will, raised his eyes to heaven, then lowered them and said, "The Lord's Will be done." On February 27, 1917, at 8:45 A.M., his breathing became more difficult, and resting his head on his right shoulder, he passed to heaven to receive the reward for a life well lived. His peaceful death reflected a statement he frequently repeated: "At the moment of death my consolation will be the remembrance of a life of perpetual sacrifice and of martyrdom because of the various offices I held."

In 1930 Fr. Richard Friedl's remains were brought to the Church of Good Counsel in Florence and his cause was introduced in Rome on December 10, 1943.

February 27

Bl. Roger Filcock 1570–1601

Martyr of England

Fr. Roger Filcock was a native of Sandwich, Kent, and was born about 1570. He studied (1588–1590) at the English College at Rheims, France, and was among the first students to go to St. Alban's Seminary (1590–1597) in Valladolid, Spain, where he was ordained about 1597. When he requested to enter the Society of Jesus in Spain, he was encouraged to return to England for a probationary period under Elizabeth's anti-Catholic government and then to apply again. He embarked at Bilbao, Spain, in December 1597, and headed for Calais, France. The ship on which he was a passenger was becalmed while entering the port on the night of December 13. The following morning one of the Dutch ships blockading the Calais harbor pursued the Spanish vessel. Rather than permitting themselves to be taken captive, many passengers jumped into the water and successfully made it to shore. Fr. Filcock, however, was captured. He later managed to escape and landed on the Kent shore of England in early 1598, where he assumed the alias of Arthur and began his priestly ministry. His desire to be a Jesuit never diminished and he wrote to the Jesuit superior in England, Fr. Henry Garnet, asking to be numbered among his men. His request was granted in 1600. It was while he was making plans to go to Flanders for his novitiate that he was apprehended (summer 1600), betrayed by a former fellow student at Valladolid and committed to Newgate Prison in London.

On February 23, 1601, Fr. Filcock was charged with being a priest, which he would neither admit nor deny because he insisted that witnesses and evidence be brought forth. None was forthcoming. He returned to court for trial on February 26 and heard the indictment against him. He claimed that he had never used the names listed in it and hence the charge did not touch him. In addition, he requested that he be given a trial without jury because he did not want the verdict, which he knew would be against him, to be on the jurors' consciences.

Disregarding Fr. Filcock's wishes, the indictment remained as it was and the judge directed the jury, though there was no evidence against him, to find the defendant guilty, which they dutifully did. Fr. Filcock was thus sentenced to the gallows for high treason.

A companion of his in prison was Fr. Mark Barkworth, a Benedictine; they had been fellow students at Valladolid and were to be companions in death. February 27 was the day set for their execution. The two priests were bound together, tied to a hurdle, and then dragged to Tyburn. They arrived just after the execution of Anne Line, who once had been Fr. Filcock's penitent. Seeing her body still hanging from the beam, Fr. Filcock kissed the hem of her garment and said: "Blessed Anne Line, a thousand times more blessed than I; you beat me in the contest and in winning the crown." Anne's heroism merited her a place among the forty martyrs of England and Wales canonized in 1970.

Immediately prior to Fr. Barkworth's martyrdom, he intoned the Latin antiphon, "This is the day the Lord has made," and Fr. Filcock sang out the response, "Let us rejoice and be glad." Fr. Filcock witnessed the hanging and butchering of his companion, but the horrid sight made him more firm in his willingness to die for Christ. When it was his turn to mount the gallows, the sheriff attempted to get him to admit his treason, but this he firmly denied. He said, quoting St. Paul: "I desire to be dissolved and to be with Christ," and added that he was dying because he was "a Catholic, a priest, and a member of the Society of Jesus." After a short prayer the cart on which he stood was drawn from under him. He was hanged, then cut down, disembowelled, and quartered.

Fr. Filcock was beatified by Pope John Paul II on November 22, 1987, and his memorial is liturgically celebrated by his Jesuit brethren on December 1.

Prayer

Almighty, eternal God, you chose from the people of England and Wales Blessed Roger Filcock and his companions to be made like Christ, who died to save the world. Listen to their prayers; strengthen your Church by the same faith and love that strengthened them, and bless it always with your gift of unity. We ask this through our Lord Jesus Christ, your Son, who lives and reigns with you and the Holy Spirit, one God, for ever and ever.

March 2

St. Nicholas Owen ?–1606

Martyr of England

Among the English martyrs of the sixteenth and seventeenth centuries, Br. Nicholas Owen is unique. He was a mason and carpenter by trade and wonderfully used these talents in the service of his persecuted Church. His ingenuity saved hundreds of priests from capture, and his cleverness provided them with safe refuge from those who persistently hunted them. Nicholas was born in Oxford on an unrecorded date. His father, Walter, was a carpenter, and Nicholas may have served his apprenticeship under his father's watchful eye. Of his three brothers, two became priests and one a printer of underground Catholic books. Nicholas' first association with the Jesuits was from 1580 to 1581, when he served as Fr. Edmund Campion's servant. After Fr. Campion's martyrdom, Owen spoke out on behalf of his former master's innocence, an action that led to his own arrest in 1582, but he was soon released.

When Fr. Henry Garnet, superior of the English Jesuits, thought of establishing a press in London, about 1587, he sought the advice of the printer Henry Owen, a brother of Nicholas. Through Henry, Nicholas made contact with Fr. Garnet and became his associate. In time the priest-hunters got to know Nicholas as Garnet's man, but to the priests with whom and for whom he worked, he was known as Little John, an affectionate reference to his size.

Fr. Garnet employed Nicholas to devise and construct hiding places in the various mansions used as priest-centers throughout England. It is not known when Nicholas began building his priest-holes, but it may have been as early as 1580, at the time of his connection with Fr. Campion, or as late as 1587, when he first met Fr. Garnet. During the day he worked on the interior or the exterior of the building, always in public view so that the servants would think him a hired carpenter. During the evening and night, however, he worked on his concealed room, digging deep into the earth or chipping through thick stone walls. He worked alone to ensure secrecy, and only he and the owner of the house knew the secret room's location. In the larger mansions, where priests sometimes gathered for meetings, some of the holes were large enough to accommodate six to ten people, and to deceive priest-hunters he sometimes devised a priest-hole within a concealed room. It was during the construction of these secret places that he suffered a hernia from lifting large stones and heavy beams. And later, when his horse reared and fell upon him, he broke his leg. He limped ever after.

On April 23, 1594, Nicholas was helping Fr. John Gerard in a London residence when both were arrested and taken to the Counter Prison. Nicholas was still unknown as the mastermind behind the hiding places and, thus, he was looked upon as but a small fish in the vast ocean of Catholic disobedience. He was released and immediately returned to his inventive labors after a Catholic gentleman had paid his ransom.

In a letter that Fr. Garnet wrote to Rome in 1588, he expressed hope that his carpenter, unnamed in the letter, might someday enter the Society. If this carpenter is Nicholas, then it was sometime after that date that he became a Jesuit. To be sure, there was no formal noviceship for him; he received his religious training in his intimate collaboration with his superior.

There is no record of how many concealed rooms Br. Owen constructed—a few of those sixteenth-century houses still exist, but most have been destroyed. He himself had to seek refuge in one of his concealed rooms after the government's discovery of the Gunpowder Plot. Because King James I had reneged on his promise to repeal the penal laws against Catholics, several overzealous individuals planned to blow up the Houses of Parliament on the occasion of the king's visit on November 5, 1605. The plot was discovered, and though the conspirators were apprehended, the government, because of its hatred of the Jesuits, sought to implicate the Jesuit superior. Hence, on November 24, Br. Owen and Fr. Garnet went to Hinlip Hall, near Worcester, where Fr. Edward Oldcorne resided, to hide until the crisis passed. The mansion was quite suitable as a refuge; it had numerous hiding places, many of them were of Br. Owen's design. The priest-hunters of Worcestershire were informed by a betrayer that a search of Hinlip Hall would definitely yield Fr. Oldcorne and possibly Fr. Garnet. The sheriff, with over a hundred armed men, arrived early Monday, January 20, 1606, and began an intensive search. While Frs. Oldcorne and Garnet went into one hole, Brs. Owen and Ralph Ashley went into another. Unfortunately, the hole the brothers chose had no provisions, and on the fourth day of the search, Thursday, January 23, the famished brothers were forced to leave their seclusion. They hoped to act as decoys, thinking the hunters would mistake them for the priests and end their search. Among the hunters, however, there was one capable of recognizing the priests and, hence, the brothers were taken into custody and the search continued until Monday, January 27, when the two priests, quite ill and weak, were discovered. During the eight days of careful investigation the sheriff found no less than a dozen hiding places.

The four Jesuits were taken to Worcester and on February 3 they were transferred to London. Br. Owen was detained in the Marshalsea Prison where he revealed nothing during the preliminary interrogations. He was moved to the Tower for torture. The king's men knew that they had Garnet's man, the only one familiar with the hiding places and the residences of all priests working in England. If they could get him to break under torture, the entire Catholic underground would be broken. Though the custom of the time exempted those with a hernia from torture, Br. Owen was a victim. The rackmaster inhumanly suspended him by his wrists and kept him in that position for five to seven hours a day, several days in succession. Br. Owen's silence only made his persecutors more angry, and to add to his agony they placed weights on his feet. Throughout this merciless treatment he only uttered the names of Jesus and Mary, and whatever information his torturers hoped to gain from him, he firmly kept within his breast. His torture went beyond limits and on March 1, while suspended, his abdomen burst open and his intestines gushed out. He lingered in pain that day, and in the early hours of March 2 he yielded his blameless soul to God. Since the rackmaster had exceeded the limits of torture and caused Br. Owen's death, he cowardly spread abroad the rumor that Garnet's man had committed suicide.

Br. Nicholas Owen, one of the more illustrious martyrs of England, was beatified by Pope Pius XI on December 15, 1929, and canonized by Pope Paul VI on October 25, 1970. His Jesuit brethren celebrate his memorial on December 1, the same day they commemorate the other Jesuits who died martyrs' deaths in England and Wales.

Prayer

Almighty, eternal God, you chose from the people of England and Wales Saint Nicholas Owen and his companions to be made like Christ, who died to save the world. Listen to their prayers; strengthen your Church by the same faith and love that strengthened them, and bless it always with your gift of unity. We ask this through our Lord Jesus Christ, your Son, who lives and reigns with you and the Holy Spirit, one God, for ever and ever.

S. G. Gonçalo da Silveira 1526–1561

Martyr of Monomotapa

The Society's first martyr on the African continent was Fr. Gonçalo da Silveira. He was born in Almeirim, near Lisbon, Portugal, on February 23, 1526, the tenth child of the Count of Sortelha, and was brought up to take a position in the royal court. His early studies were in Coimbra and he was a student at the university when Fr. Simon Rodrigues and his Jesuit companions came to Coimbra to establish a college. Gonçalo became acquainted with them and on June 9, 1543, he entered the Society of Jesus.

After his regular course of studies in the Society, Fr. Silveira received, in 1550, a doctorate in theology from the University of Gandía, and spent the next three years traveling through Portugal preaching and instructing the faithful. In 1553 Fr. Ignatius made him rector of the professed house in Lisbon, where he was also pastor of the church of São Roque. But Fr. Silveira was looking toward the missions. Familiar with the achievements of Fr. Francis Xavier, Fr. Silveira wanted to walk in his footsteps, and though he labored well in Lisbon—he was a renowned preacher—he would have preferred to take Christ's message to foreign lands and receive a martyr's death as the reward for preaching that message. When the news of Fr. Francis Xavier's death arrived in Portugal, it was Fr. Silveira who wrote (January 1, 1555) to Fr. Ignatius in Rome, informing him of the sad event. Fr. Xavier had been provincial of India and in 1556 Fr. Ignatius named Fr. Silveira as his successor.

Fr. Silveira sailed from Lisbon on March 30, 1556, and arrived in Goa, India, on September 6. As provincial he governed the mission for three years with great prudence. The mission prospered. In Goa alone the Jesuits added 7,000 new converts to the faith. In 1559 he relinquished his office and in 1560 was called to a new work. The son of a native chief, from one of the kingdoms of southeastern Africa, had become friendly with Portuguese traders in Mozambique and was converted. Upon the son's return home he convinced his father to request a Christian missionary for their country. Thus, Chief Gamba wrote to the Portuguese viceroy in Goa asking for a missionary; the viceroy, in turn, sent the letter to the Jesuit provincial; and because Fr. Silveira was unassigned after serving his term as provincial he was appointed to lead the new mission.

The little band of three, Fr. Silveira, another priest, and a brother, landed in northern Mozambique on February 5, 1560. They then sailed southward along the coast to Inhambane and from there they worked their way inland to Otongue (April 27), where Gamba lived. After minimal instruction the missionaries baptized Gamba, his court and others—nearly 500 individuals in all. Fr. Silveira now had dreams of converting southern and central Africa, and the easiest way would be to convert southern Africa's most powerful king. With the king's conversion, the missionary envisioned the conversion of the entire nation. The mysterious King Monomotapa, whose capital lay far up the Zambezi River, about 100 miles north of today's Harare (Zimbabwe), was rumored to be the strongest king and that his vast territory extended far inland. After success in Otongue, Fr. Silveira instructed his companions to remain and continue their evangelizing, while he went on to search out the great Monomotapa.

By August Fr. Silveira was again in Mozambique, preparing for his new mission. Setting out on September 18, 1560, he sailed southward and entered the Zambezi River, went as far north as Sena, then disembarked and did the rest on foot. His exact route is not known, but he may have approached the Monomotapa's capital from the south, which would have meant that he had probably walked some 500 miles before arriving at his destination. The Monomotapa's village was on the Musengezi River, downstream from where it is joined by the Kadzi River. At Chatucy, perhaps today's Chitako, and about fifty miles from his goal, the missionary met Antonio Caiado, a Portuguese, much trusted by the Monomotapa, and who had many times served as his intermediary with Portuguese traders. It was December 24, 1560. Caiado went to the king and requested permission for the missionary to visit him. Fr. Silveira arrived at the king's village on December 26 and saw a young man who had been chief but a year. His name was Chisamharu Nogomo. He was neither as powerful as had been believed, nor were his lands as extensive as had been thought. But because gold had been discovered in the territory, he was known as "the golden king" and his land "the golden empire." But Chisamharu was uncivilized and uncultured. Within three or four weeks of Fr. Silveira's arrival, the king and his mother were baptized, and shortly afterwards another 300 individuals.

Jealous of Fr. Silveira's success with the Monomotapa, the Moslem traders, who lived in nearby villages, feared that the Portuguese would now get all the trade and, hence, they set to work poisoning the king's mind. They made him believe that the missionary was a spy for the Portuguese, who planned to take over the country. In addition, they played on the king's ignorance, telling him that the missionary was a sorcerer, who had come to bring drought and famine to the land and that he would kill the chief and set his subjects at war with one another. Believing these absurdities, the recently baptized Chisamharu decided that Fr. Silveira had to die.

Fr. Silveira sensed the change in Chisamharu. When he mentioned this to Caiado, the trader could not believe it and, thus, went to see the king himself. When Caiado returned, he informed the priest of the king's plans and urged him to leave at once. This Fr. Silveira could not do. He now began to make his final preparations. On March 15, after he had instructed a group of fifty neophytes, he baptized them all. Later that afternoon, when the Portuguese, whom he had summoned, came, he heard their confessions and entrusted his Mass equipment to them, keeping only a crucifix for himself. That night when it was time to retire, he told Caiado: "I am more ready to die than the Moslems are to kill me. I forgive the king, who is young, and his mother, because they had been deceived." Caiado then instructed two of his servants to remain with Fr. Silveira through the night. The missionary first prayed before his crucifix and then fell asleep. Before midnight the murderers, who had been watching, rushed into the priest's hut. They threw Fr. Silveira on his face and then lifted him up by his hands and feet. They tied a rope around his neck and pulled from both sides until he was dead. They then dragged the body outside and cast it into the Musengezi River. This martyrdom brought an end to the Society's first mission in Monomotapa.

In 1905, 344 years after Fr. Gonçalo da Silveira's death, the official investigation was begun to establish his martyrdom and to open his cause.

March 15

S. G. Eusebio Francisco Kino 1645–1711

Fr. Eusebio Kino was an explorer and cartographer, a founder of towns and cities, a missionary, and a builder of churches. So widespread were his accomplishments in southern Arizona that that state chose him as one of its two representatives for the Statuary Hall in the United States Capitol in Washington.

Eusebio was born in the village of Segno, near Trent, in northern Italy. The family name was Chino. His baptism on August 10, 1645, indicated that his birth was probably that day or the previous day. He studied at the Jesuit school at Trent and won a scholarship to attend the college in Hall, near Innsbruck, Austria. During these years of study he became seriously ill, sometime in 1663, and promised God that if he recovered he would become a Jesuit and devote his life to the foreign missions as St. Francis Xavier had done. Eusebio recovered and in memory of God's goodness, he added Francis to his name.

Eusebio entered the Jesuits at Landsberg, Bavaria, on November 20, 1665, and after two years of novitiate went to Ingolstadt, where he spent three years studying philosophy and science. In 1670 he returned to Hall to teach literature and was again in Ingolstadt in 1673 to begin theology. While preparing for the priesthood, he also taught mathematics to other Jesuit students in his community and then went to the University of Freiburg for further studies. So competent was he in mathematics that in 1676 the duke of Bavaria offered him a full professorship at Ingolstadt, but Eusebio's heart was on the missions. He had several times asked Fr. General to send him to China or to some other mission.

Eusebio was ordained at Eichstätt on June 12, 1677, and during his final year of Jesuit training, his tertianship, Fr. General appointed him and another Jesuit to go to the missions, one to China and one to Mexico, but without indicating who was to go where. The missionaries-to-be made their choice by lots. Fr. Kino picked Mexico. Together with eighteen other Jesuits, he left Genoa, Italy, on June 12, 1678, for Spain, but by the time they arrived at Cádiz, the fleet had already sailed for the New World. The missionaries waited for two years and then on July 7, 1680, they set sail. But before they left the harbor the ship hit a sandbar and the passengers returned to Cádiz. It was only on January 29, 1681, that they finally set sail and after a three-month voyage arrived at Veracruz, Mexico, on May 3. Not long afterwards, they were in Mexico City. Fr. Kino was appointed chaplain for Admiral Atondo's expedition to Lower California; he was also its astronomer, surveyor, and cartographer. The expedition sailed in January 1683 and slowly made its way up the coast, but since they were unable to establish a permanent settlement, even after several attempts, they returned to Mexico at the end of 1685.

Fr. Kino now made his own plans: he would go to the Jesuit missions in northwestern Mexico, then proceed to the unconverted tribes beyond, work his way westward and return through Lower California. On November 20, 1586, he began his 1,500-mile trek to the Pimería Alta, a region that included northern Sonora and southern Arizona, that is, land west of the San Pedro River and as far north as the junction of the Gila and Colorado rivers.

Fr. Kino arrived at the Pimería Alta, the land of the Pima, in March 1687 and immediately began his missionary work. For the center of his activity he chose the village of Cosari and named it Dolores, after Our Lady of Sorrows, and set about building a chapel. From Dolores he and his associates gradually extended their labors by founding missions in the San Miguel, Magdalena, Altar, Sonóita, Santa Cruz, and San Pedro valleys. Wherever he went, he taught the native inhabitants how to plant wheat, beans, squash, and other crops. He also taught them how to build sturdy homes and care for cattle. In larger communities he founded schools for the children, taught them reading and writing, and gave them instruction in the Catholic faith. After establishing one mission he moved on to found another. By 1690 he had pushed his frontier into present-day Arizona and by 1700 he had established the cities of San Cayetano de Tumacácori, San Javier del Bac, San Cosmé de Tucson, and San Agustín de Oyaut.

While working among the Pima, Fr. Kino helped Fr. Juan María Salvatierra establish the first permanent mission in Lower California. From the abundance of food produced at his mission, he was able to supply the new missions in Lower California. Fr. Kino never forgot that it was missionary work that brought him to those regions, and thinking of the missionaries who would follow him, he carefully and accurately mapped the Sonora and southern Arizona area for their use. From his diaries we learn that he made some forty exploratory expeditions into new territory, always with a view to establishing missions. He likewise proved that Lower California was a peninsula, not an island as some had previously thought.

In March 1711, when he was sixty-six years old and had been thirty years in the New World, he received an invitation from Fr. Agustín de Campos to go to Magdalena to dedicate the new church in honor of St. Francis Xavier. Since the mission was one of the first that Fr. Kino had founded, and since the church was honoring his patron, he gladly accepted. On March 15, the day of the dedication, while Fr. Kino was singing High Mass he became ill. That night, near midnight, God chose to call this selfless and untiring missionary unto himself. Fr. Campos buried his friend beneath the altar. The body remained there until 1966 when the Mexican government appointed a group of archaeologists to search for and identify the remains. As a result of their success the remains have been enshrined. In memory of this "Apostle of the Sonora and Southern Arizona," the town changed its name to Magdalena de Kino. Fr. Eusebio Kino's cause is under consideration.

March 16

St. John de Brébeuf 1593–1649

Martyr of North America

John de Brébeuf was born at Condé-sur-Vire, in the diocese of Bayeux in Normandy, on March 25, 1593. At age twenty-four, having completed his university studies, he entered the Jesuit novitiate at Rouen on November 8, 1617. Feeling that he was better suited for humble tasks, he asked to be a brother, but his superior prevailed upon him to continue studies toward the priesthood. From 1619 to 1621 he taught young boys at the Jesuit college in Rouen. He was ordained on February 19, 1622, and in the same year was made treasurer of the college.

In 1624 the Franciscan Recollects, who had operated the Huron mission in New France (today's Canada) since 1615, appealed to other religious orders of France for priests and brothers to assist in the evangelization of the native population of North America. Among the first group of Jesuits to leave their homeland, in answer to this appeal, was the tall, rugged Fr. Brébeuf. Now thirty-two years old, he left Dieppe on April 24, 1625, in the company of four other Jesuits. After a voyage of two months they arrived at Quebec on June 19. The Recollects' mission was about 900 miles from Quebec, situated among the Huron, a nation whom the Franciscans thought would be most receptive to Christian teachings. Thus, Fr. Brébeuf's mission field was to be Huronia.

While waiting for the Huron Indians to come to the French settlements on their annual trading visit, Fr. Brébeuf set out on his first mission. In October he joined the Montagnais in a hunting expedition that lasted until the following March. Over a period of five months he learned much: how to endure fatigue without complaint, how to be satisfied with the tasteless mush his native companions took for meals, and how to sleep on the hard ground. He also learned that they were superstitious, deceitful and arrogant, vengeful and cruel.

When the news spread that the Hurons had come to do their bartering, Fr. Brébeuf, with another Jesuit and a Recollect, went to meet them at Cap de la Victoire. The Hurons, at first, did not wish to give them passage, but after the offering of many gifts they agreed to take Fr. Brébeuf's colleagues but not him. He was a great hulk of a man, who so towered over the Hurons that they feared to take him in their canoes. Avarice finally won out and he was given a place, but he had to sit still to keep the canoe from capsizing. Thus on July 26, 1626, Fr. Brébeuf began his journey to Huronia. The trip took about thirty days, mostly over water. Where cascades did not permit the fragile canoes to pass, the travelers went overland, carrying the canoes and their supplies. Because of his size and strength, Fr. Brébeuf was able to carry a tremendous load; he so amazed his native companions that they named him "Echon," or "the man-who-carries-the-load." The missionaries arrived in Huronia in late August and headed for Toanché, the village of the Bear Clan of the Huron nation.

Fr. Brébeuf's work of evangelization could not begin until he himself had mastered the language, so he spent the first two years learning the Huron tongue, studying their customs and beliefs, and planning how best to instruct them. He had a natural affinity for languages and during his stay among them he wrote a Huron grammar, compiled a phrase book, and translated a catechism. Though successful in learning the language, he had no success with adult converts. There was a drought during the summer of 1628 and because the Huron sorcerers were unable to get their Thunderbird god to send rain, they concluded that the cause of the drought was the red cross on Fr. Brébeuf's cabin. The missionary refused to remove it, but to prove who really sends the rain he asked everyone to gather at his cabin the following day. When the time came he recited some prayers and then asked each of them to reverence the crucifix by kissing it. The rains came and the crop was saved.

Fr. Brébeuf spent the winter of 1628 instructing the Hurons about God and visiting the sick in their cabins. He had won their ears, but made no adult converts; the only baptisms were of those who were dying. In May 1629 he learned from a French agent visiting Toanché that England and France were at war, and that English ships, stationed at the entrance to the St. Lawrence River, kept French ships and supplies from reaching Quebec. Consequently, the French at Quebec had spent the last winter on short rations and it appeared that famine would soon overwhelm them, unless Fr. Brébeuf could bring them grain from Huronia. With twenty loaded canoes he reached Quebec on July 17, 1629, but two days later the French capitulated to the English. All settlers and missionaries were sent back to France.

Again on French soil, Fr. Brébeuf was assigned as chaplain to the students at Rouen and in 1631 was made treasurer of the college at Eu. In March 1632, by a treaty with the English, Canada was restored to France and he was reassigned to the mission, reaching it May 23, 1633.

The usual summer flotilla of trading Hurons came in late July. Fr. Brébeuf hoped to depart with them, but an Ottawa captain talked the Hurons into refusing to take any of the Frenchmen unless an Ottawa, imprisoned for murder in Quebec, was released. When the Hurons returned the following summer in 1634, they arrived with only eleven canoes rather than the usual hundred or more. They had not fully recovered from an epidemic that had struck Huronia, and since they were still ill with fever, they did not wish to take any foreigners with cumbersome baggage on the return trip. In the end, however, they agreed to take Frs. Brébeuf and Anthony Daniel. The small flotilla departed from Three Rivers on July 7, but the missionaries lost sight of each other enroute, since they were in different canoes.

The natives carrying Fr. Brébeuf were so eager to get home that, when on August 5 they arrived at the bay near Toanché, they dumped him and his belongings on shore, comforting him with the words that someone would eventually find him. The stranded Black Robe presumed that Toanché would be deserted by now and a new village built, but he knew not where to look. Fortunately, after only a two-mile walk he stumbled upon it. When the bedraggled and worn-out priest appeared at the edge of Taendeuiata, for that was the new village's name, the Hurons welcomed him with great joy. Their Echon had returned to them as he had promised. Knowing that Fr. Daniel was on his way and that other missionaries would soon be coming, he set about constructing a cabin. It was located outside, but near the village, and was called Ihonatiria. By the end of September three priests and five lay helpers were living in it. Fr. Brébeuf was the only one of the group who knew the Huron tongue, so he began teaching the newcomers the language and customs of Huronia.

At the beginning of 1635, Frs. Brébeuf and Daniel began their missionary work in earnest. They gathered the children in their cabin and taught them prayers and how to sing. The adults were invited in the evening and were given instruction about God, Christ, and the commandments. After a year at Ihonatiria, the missionaries counted only twelve baptisms—four dying infants and eight dying adults. In late spring a drought hit the village. When the sorcerers' incantations failed to bring rain, they attributed the drought to the cross in front of the priests' cabin. Fr. Brébeuf refused to remove it and in a council meeting reminded his people that since there had been rain throughout the previous year, the cross could not then be blamed for its present lack. If they wanted rain, he told them, they should give up their superstitions and resolve to love God and repent for their sins. The missionary suggested a procession around the village for nine consecutive days, during which they would pray for rain. At the same time the priests offered a novena of Masses for the same intention. On June 13, the last day of the novena, while the procession was in progress, the heavens opened and everyone felt the answer to their prayers.

Two more priests came to Ihonatiria. Fr. Charles Garnier arrived in August 1636 and was followed in September by Fr. Isaac Jogues. With the arrival of Fr. Jogues a smallpox epidemic broke out among the Jesuits and their helpers, and then it spread among the Hurons. The contagion lasted throughout the winter and during this time the missionaries baptized more than a thousand individuals, all near death. Because those baptized had in fact died, the Hurons, always suspicious of the Black Robes, concluded that the Jesuits had caused the epidemic to deplete their number. The missionaries were very much aware that their lives were in danger but the epidemic fortunately passed and they were able to continue their ministry. In June 1637 Fr. Brébeuf started a mission at Ossossané, but because the epidemic still lingered there, a council of village chiefs decided on his death. Resigned to his fate, if it be God's will, he remained at the mission until June 1638, when he moved to Teanaustayé.

The possibility of martyrdom was ever increasing. In a council of the Huron nation, which met in March 1640, the assembled chiefs determined that the Black Robes were to die. The chiefs claimed that the troubles afflicting their people over the past five years had been due to the Jesuits and the sooner the land was rid of them, the sooner the misfortunes would pass. In view of this decision Fr. Brébeuf moved to Sainte-Marie, the new mission center for the Jesuits in Huronia. He then spent a disappointing four months among the Neutrals, whose minds had been poisoned against him by the Hurons. Then a truly dangerous situation arose. The accusation was made that while he was with the Neutrals, he had contacted the Seneca Clan of the Iroquois, the Hurons' most bitter foe, and had planned to betray them. Fr. Brébeuf had no choice but to leave until the rumor subsided. He arrived in Quebec in June 1641 and took over as agent for the mission, gathering supplies for the fourteen Jesuits and nineteen lay helpers in Huronia. He also took charge of the Algonquin reduction in Sillery, where he remained until August 1644, when he, Frs. Noel Chabanel and Leonard Garreau joined the fur-trading Hurons on their return journey home. With his companions, Fr. Brébeuf arrived at Sainte-Marie on September 7, 1644, and there resumed his labors.

The Iroquois danger, however, was constantly on the increase. Fr. Isaac Jogues had been martyred in October 1646 and Fr. Anthony Daniel met a martyr's death in July 1648. In September 1648 a new recruit came to Sainte-Marie, his name was Fr. Gabriel Lalemant. He spent his first few months in language study and then joined Fr. Brébeuf in his round of visits to the villages. On March 15, 1649, they left Sainte-Marie for their weekly tour and spent the night at Saint-Louis village. That night the Iroquois attacked Saint-Ignace, about four miles to the south; apprised of the attack, the leaders at Saint-Louis prepared for the worst. They sent the women and children into the forest and encouraged Frs. Brébeuf and Lalemant to go as well, but the priests would not forsake their flock.

At dawn on March 16 the Iroquois swarmed over the palisades. It was not long before Saint-Louis came under their control and the Hurons, who were mostly Christian, were taken prisoner. A renegade Huron among the attackers informed the Iroquois that they had finally captured the mighty Echon, the most powerful Black Robe sorcerer, and that he deserved the choicest torture they could imagine. Now in command, the Iroquois slaughtered the sick and aged in their cabins and set fire to the village. The missionaries were stripped, had their fingernails torn out and fingers chewed. Since the captors were leading their prisoners to Saint-Ignace, where another contingent of Iroquois awaited them, the prisoners were forced to run naked through the winter snow and endure the cold March winds.

On arrival at Saint-Ignace, the Iroquois were ready and had them run the gauntlet. Throughout, Fr. Brébeuf encouraged the captive Christians: "Let us lift our eyes to heaven at the height of our afflictions; let us remember that God is the witness of our suffering, and will soon be our exceeding great reward." Having run the gauntlet, Frs. Brébeuf and Lalemant were led to two posts which were to be their crosses of martyrdom. Both grasped the posts and prayed, while the Iroquois stabbed them with sharp instruments. The tormentors' cruelty was now revealed. They heated a half dozen or so iron hatchets until they were the color of fire, strung them to form a necklace, and placed them on Fr. Brébeuf's shoulders. No matter which way he turned a red-hot blade seared his flesh. Throughout, the missionary did not speak a word of complaint nor did he utter a single groan. His silence only increased the irritation of his tormentors, who longed to see their victim plead for mercy. In their wrath they wrapped his torso with resinous bark and set it afire until flames surrounded him. With unspeakable control he continued to exhort the Christians suffering with him to endure pain in exchange for heaven. To silence the missionary, his tormentors cut off his nose, tore off his lips, and gagged his mouth by forcing a hot iron down his throat. In imitation of baptism they poured kettles of scalding water over his head. Under such pain his body slumped down, and fearing that Echon was about to die, one brave scalped him, another cut off his feet, and others sliced strips of his seared flesh and ate them. Someone finally buried a hatchet in his jaw and severed it from his face. When his body fell to the ground, the crazed Iroquois pounced on it and cut open his breast to get at his heart, which they proceeded to eat, believing they would, in this way, have a share in his indomitable courage.

Thus, Fr. John de Brébeuf, the "Apostle to the Hurons," after spending twenty years in New France, died at about 4:00 P.M. on March 16, 1649, at age forty-six. He longed for a martyr's death and that grace was not denied him. His body, together with that of Fr. Gabriel Lalemant, was taken to Sainte-Marie, where both bodies remained buried until they were taken to Quebec in 1650.

On June 21, 1925, Pope Pius XI beatified Frs. John de Brébeuf, Gabriel Lalemant, and their six companions, martyred in North America. Their canonization took place on June 29, 1930, and their feast is celebrated on October 19.

Prayer

Father, you consecrated the first beginnings of the faith in North America by the preaching and martyrdom of Saint John de Brébeuf and his companions. By the help of their prayers may the Christian faith continue to grow throughout the world. We ask this through our Lord Jesus Christ, your Son, who lives and reigns with you and the Holy Spirit, one God, for ever and ever.

March 17

St. Gabriel Lalemant 1610–1649

Martyr of North America

Gabriel Lalemant's uncle Charles was a missionary among the native population in New France (today's Canada). Ever since his uncle had crossed the Atlantic, Gabriel's own heart burned with a desire for the same mission. Gabriel was born in Paris, October 10, 1610. He was educated at the College of Clermont and entered the Jesuit novitiate in Paris on March 24, 1630. When he pronounced his vows in the Society on March 25, 1632, he added a vow to devote himself to the foreign missions. When he completed his studies, his request to go to the missions still had not yet received an affirmative answer; thus, he spent the next seven years teaching. Each year he renewed his request, but each year his superior thought otherwise. These refusals were due to the fact that Fr. Lalemant's health was always considered poor, and it was thought that he could accomplish more for God in France than in the wilderness of New France.

Fr. Lalemant's prayer was finally answered in 1646 when his provincial appointed him to the Huron mission. This permission was granted, perhaps, because another of his uncles, Jerome, had been made superior of the mission.

Together with three other Jesuits, two priests and one brother, he sailed from La Rochelle on June 13, 1646, and reached Quebec on September 20. Being totally unfamiliar with the Huron tongue, he spent his first two years at Sillery learning the language and becoming knowledgeable in native customs. He left for Huronia in August 1648, with the Hurons who had come to the French settlements to trade furs, and arrived at Sainte-Marie, mission headquarters, in September.

Fr. Lalemant's first few months were devoted to language study. Sometime in early 1649 he became Fr. John de Brébeuf's companion in a weekly round of Indian villages. He had a first-rate teacher, but his work among the Hurons was to be of very short duration.

On March 15, 1649, only six months after his arrival, he and Fr. Brébeuf started out on their weekly tour of duty. They spent the night at the village of Saint-Louis. That same night the Iroquois stormed and overtook the village of Saint-Ignace, four miles south of them. The Saint-Louis settlement heard of the attack and knew that it would be next. On the morning of March 16, shrieking Iroquois climbed over the palisades and swiftly murdered all who tried to defend the village or themselves. Within a short time Saint-Louis was theirs, and Frs. Brébeuf and Lalemant were taken prisoner, as were many of the Hurons. The missionaries had their nails bitten out and their fingers chewed; they were forced to run naked through the winter snow and winds to Saint-Ignace, where more Iroquois were waiting to torment them. Upon arrival the prisoners had to run the gauntlet, during which they were struck on the head, face, and neck. After that Frs. Brébeuf and Lalemant were tied to stakes. Contemporary accounts seem to indicate that Fr. Lalemant witnessed the horrifying atrocities performed on his brother Jesuit before his own torture began at 6:00 P.M.

The hateful Iroquois started a fire at Fr. Lalemant's feet to make him dance, then seared his flesh with red-hot hatchets, poured scalding water over his head, cut off his hands, gouged out his eyes and placed hot coals in their sockets. Wanting to preserve their victim for another day of torture, they desisted that night and on the following morning renewed their torture by forcing fire brands into the missionary's mouth and slicing off his tongue. Fr. Lalemant proved as invincible as Fr. Brébeuf, for during his torture he made no appeal for pity; his prayer was the simple, "Jesus, have mercy on us!" The brutal tormentors cut slices of his flesh and ate them, then ripped off his scalp and dug a hatchet behind his left ear. Finally, they ripped out his heart and ate it to gain his courage. After fifteen hours of unbelievable torment, Fr. Gabriel Lalemant, age thirty-six, rendered his soul to God at 9:00 A.M., March 17, 1649. The bodies of Frs. Lalemant and Brébeuf were found by their fellow Jesuits and were taken to Sainte-Marie, where they were buried near the chapel door. In 1650 these sacred relics were taken to Quebec.

Fr. Lalemant had accompanied Fr. Brébeuf in death, and together with six other martyred Jesuits, they were beatified on June 21, 1925, by Pope Pius XI, and canonized by him on June 29, 1930. St. Gabriel Lalemant's feast, and that of the North American Martyrs, is liturgically celebrated on October 19.

Prayer

Father, you consecrated the first beginnings of the faith in North America by the preaching and martyrdom of Saint Gabriel Lalemant and his companions. By the help of their prayers may the Christian faith continue to grow throughout the world. We ask this through our Lord Jesus Christ, your Son, who lives and reigns with you and the Holy Spirit, one God, for ever and ever.

March 21

S. G. Igino Lega 1911–1951

The chaplain rushed into the commander's office, knelt down before him and pleaded with him to spare the lieutenant's life. "Father, army regulations are quite clear. The young man fell asleep on guard duty. He is to be shot. There is nothing I can do." The chaplain insisted: "He was tired and overworked. If you and I were in the same position, we too would have fallen asleep. He's still a young man and his family is awaiting his return." "Father, a rule is a rule; these I cannot change." The chaplain rose, looked at the commander and said: "I will be standing between the firing squad and the condemned man. They will first have to shoot me." As Fr. Igino Lega left the room, he heard the commander tear up the execution order.

Igino Lega was born in Brisighella, near Ravenna, Italy, on November 14, 1911, the third-last of eleven children. His was an old and noble family. His father was a prosperous lawyer; one of his uncles was Cardinal Michele Lega, Prefect of the Sacred Congregation of the Sacraments, and another, Antonio Lega, was Archbishop of Ravenna. His mother's father, Antonio Nardozzi, was a renowned Latin scholar and translator of Virgil.

After elementary studies in Brisighella, Igino was sent to the Jesuit school in Casentino, and when that closed in 1926, he transferred to the Society's Collegio Cesare Arici in Brescia. Then on November 9, 1928, he entered the novitiate in Gorizia and on finishing his juniorate began, in September 1932, his philosophy in Mantua, but completed the course back in Gorizia. In 1935 he started teaching grammar at the Apostolic School in Roncovero, near Piacenza, and in 1937 went to Chieri, near Turin, for theology.

War came to Europe in September 1939. Italy was still at peace, but the times were uncertain and, thus, Igino and his class were ordained to the priesthood on May 31, 1940, somewhat earlier than usual. Ten days later Italy entered the war. During Fr. Lega's final year of theology, his studies were twice interrupted in order to serve the fatherland, once at a field hospital near Trieste and then in Bologna. Despite these interruptions, he completed his studies and was subsequently sent to Roncovero where he taught Latin, French, and history. He was not there five months when summons arrived in early February that he was to be mobilized once more. Now a naval chaplain, he set sail on February 17, 1942, for the Dodecanese (then under Italy), with Leros as his destination. The island had one of Italy's largest naval and submarine bases.

When Fr. Lega arrived on February 24, he was the base's only military chaplain and his 5,000 men were spread over the entire island. His first task was to get to know them and, thus, he went from installation to installation to meet the men. Where his old dilapidated bicycle could not take him, he went on foot. It was nothing for him to walk the four or five miles between installations, and when he arrived, he was sweaty and covered with road dust. It was Fr. Lega's simplicity and sincerity that won him an opening with the men. As chaplain, his men came first. He spoke up for them, especially when they were to be disciplined. He did not think it an inconvenience to spend the night in the cells of those who had to undergo more severe punishment. He believed everyone was good and he treated everyone that way.

Life on Leros may have been busy for Fr. Lega, but it was relatively tranquil for nineteen months. With September 1943 war came to the island. Mussolini had fallen in late July and on September 8 Italy's armistice with the Anglo-American forces was announced. Days later English forces came to the island and on September 19 the Germans began their steady bombardment. In the first days the ships in the harbor were rendered useless and on land the men's barracks were annihilated. By October 31 the island had suffered 140 raids. Four raids a day were frequent and one day there were eleven. During the long siege Fr. Lega spent his days and nights with his men. He seemed not to notice the danger surrounding him nor did he hear or see the shells falling nearby. His only concern was to get to the dying so that they could die peacefully in the Lord. When told that he should seek shelter, his answer was that his men were in danger and he had to be with them.

The first six days of November were quiet days. The Germans, who had by now occupied the islands surrounding Leros, were preparing a massive offensive. Then between the 7th and the 11th the island suffered another forty raids. Fr. Lega was again on the move and though bombs exploded everywhere, he crawled from one battery to another. His presence brought encouragement, but it was his voice that reassured the men. On the 12th the Germans began their landing operations and by the 16th the island was theirs.

The Leros defenders were now prisoners of war and Fr. Lega was kept with the officers. In early December, when the men were beginning to be sent to prison camps, Fr. Lega asked the German commander if he could go to prison with his men. Thus he boarded a ship on December 5, 1943, that first took them to Athens and from there they were herded (December 23) into cattle cars to be transported to Germany. After several stopovers at various camps, Fr. Lega was assigned (February 10, 1944) to the Recklinghausen work camp. He spent his days in the mines with his fellow prisoners, but spent his evenings praying with and for them, visiting the sick, comforting the depressed, and rallying those thinking of suicide. Though food was scarce, he frequently gave his rations to others, and when winter came he gave his undergarments to those suffering from the cold. In late spring he received word from the Jesuit provincial that the Society was trying to get him repatriated. In answer he wrote to him on June 21, 1944: "If you want to know what I really want, it is this. Leave me here, a prisoner with my prisoners. Leave me here. The Sacred Heart helps me. You will see me; I shall return, but with my soldiers and my sailors." The following August he was transferred to the camp at Hemer, where he was permitted to serve as chaplain. The camp had about 30,000 prisoners from various nations (Russian, Dutch, French, Greek, Italian), and when winter came many died each day, mostly from tuberculosis.

Liberation came in early April 1945, and though given the opportunity to return home, Fr. Lega declined saying that he could not leave as long as one Italian prisoner was left in Germany. He finally departed in September and was in Padua by the end of the month. After a visit home in Brisighella, he went in mid-October to Trent for tertianship and in the following July 1946 was assigned to the retreat house in Bassano del Grappa. Retreats and preaching parish missions were now his apostolate, but while in Bassano he also visited the workers in the factories during their lunch hour. He was no sociologist seeking to better their working conditions, but a priest trying to bring them back to God and to the practice of their faith after years of war and negligence.

Fr. Lega's extraordinary dedication to his sailors during the enemy's fierce bombardment of Leros and the total giving of himself to Italian prisoners of war in Germany were never forgotten. When word came in May 1947 that he was to receive the nation's highest honor for heroism, the *medaglia d'oro,* he tried to avoid it. He said it should be given to the Sacred Heart, for it was our Lord, who, by preserving him from danger, enabled him to do his duty in serving the men. The medal was conferred on him at the Naval Academy in Livorno on November 17, 1947, and as soon as the ceremonies were over, he went to the chapel and pinned the medal on a banner of the Sacred Heart.

The former chaplain's apostolate now entered a different phase. He was transferred to Modena to see to the spiritual welfare of factory workers. In large part Modena's workers were communists and since tensions existed between the communists and the Church, his was not to be an easy task. It took time for him to break through the wall of distrust and hatred, but that he did. The Italian workers found it impossible to spurn Fr. Lega's natural goodness, sincerity, and charity. Then in 1949 he was moved to Gallarate to be chaplain at a textile mill of some 3,000 workers. As he had done in Modena, he identified himself with the poor; helped them bear their burdens and solve their problems. They came to him with all their troubles; whether it be employment, housing, or food. He was sensitive to all their needs and did his best for them.

On March 15, 1951, a worker informed him that he and his family were homeless. Was there anything that the priest could do for him? Fr. Lega said: "Let's go and look." They both got on the priest's motorbike and headed for Varese. They finally found an apartment and as they were on the return trip, negotiating a turn in the road, a motor coach, coming in the opposite direction, sideswiped them. Both riders were thrown to the side of the road. At the Varese hospital Fr. Lega was told that his left leg was fractured in several places, but all would be well after a few weeks of convalescence. When his superior from Gallarate came to visit him on March 20, he noticed that the patient had developed breathing problems and was eating with difficulty. In speaking to the superior, Fr. Lega said: "I can no longer continue in this life. You don't know what it is to be continually among those in need and not being able to help them. For anyone with a heart, it is enough to kill him." The superior decided to spend the night with him. The next morning, Fr. Lega was no better and the physicians could not explain such a sudden change in their patient. He grew progressively weaker. He was subsequently anointed and died ten minutes later.

The body was taken to the scholasticate in Gallarate, where Fr. Lega had lived, and there he was given a hero's funeral. The body was then transferred to Brisighella. In view of Fr. Lega's holiness of life, the cause for his beatification was initiated in 1973.

March 25

S. G. Felix Cappello 1879–1962

Felix, the tenth of eleven children, was born on October 9, 1879, in the small village of Caviola di Falcade, in the heart of Italy's Dolomites. He first attended the elementary school operated by his maternal uncle in a nearby village and then he and his brother Louis, his elder by two years, went to the pre-seminary school operated by parish priests in Forno di Canale. This meant a daily walk of three miles, regardless of sun, snow, or rain. Three years later, in 1895, the brothers began their studies at the interdiocesan seminary in Feltre, and after two years they passed on to the major seminary in Belluno for theology. Louis and Felix finished their priestly formation together; Louis was ordained on January 20, 1901, but Felix, because he was not yet of canonical age, had to wait until April 20, 1902.

Fr. Cappello's assignments as a diocesan priest were in two small towns and while involved in parish work, he continued his studies in private. Within a few years he earned three doctorates: in theology (1904) from the University of Bologna, in philosophy (1905) from the Angelicum in Rome, and in canon and civil law (1906) from Rome's Apollinare. In 1906 he was appointed to teach canon law at the Belluno seminary and taught there until 1909. During these years he also taught Hebrew and Scripture, wrote for the diocesan weekly, and published his first book on selected canonical questions.

When the seminary came under the control of the Stigmatine Fathers of Verona, Fr. Cappello gave up his post, and with a fresh manuscript in his bag went to Rome to see about its publication. He spent his time in Rome studying and writing, and supported himself by giving private instruction and holding repetitions and review sessions for seminarians. When two positions in the Vatican did not materialize—he felt confident that he had done well in the examinations—he decided to spend a few days at Lourdes. Late one evening after the candlelight procession, he returned to the deserted grotto and spent the night in prayer. When he left the following morning, he had decided to become a Jesuit.

Fr. Cappello entered the Jesuit novitiate in Rome on October 30, 1913. This thirty-four-year-old author, whose name was becoming known among Italian canonists, readily submitted to the humdrum regime of novitiate living. Before his first year of noviceship was over he was sent in the autumn of 1914 to teach moral theology and canon law at the Leonine College in Anagni. He remained there until 1920 when he was transferred to Rome's Gregorian University.

Fr. Cappello's teaching career at the Gregorian lasted thirty-nine years, until 1959, when he retired from the classroom. These were productive years: he taught moral theology and canon law, wrote articles and books, was consultor for several Sacred Congregations, advised religious congregations in preparing their constitutions, carried on a worldwide correspondence, and was spiritual director to many of Rome's clergy.

Fr. Cappello was greatly appreciated as a teacher, particularly for his clarity in explaining the Church's canons. He rarely brought books or notes into class; he knew the Code of Canon Law by heart and whenever he cited the opinions of other authors, he did so from memory. His memory was indeed phenomenal; he is said to have known Virgil's *Aeneid* and Dante's *Divine Comedy* also by heart. He is best remembered for instructing his students to be humane in their application of law. He urged: "Principles are principles, and they remain firm and are always to be defended. But all consciences are not the same. In applying principles to consciences, we must do it with great prudence, much common sense, and much goodness." And again: "In your opinions and decisions never be severe. The Lord does not want that. Be always just, but never severe. Give the solution that offers the soul some room in which to breathe."

Clergy and laity brought their problems to him, knowing that they would get an immediate answer. He was as short on words as he was in stature; he listened intently to the case presented, penetrated the problem, listed the points to be kept in mind, then gave the solution without explaining the reasons for it. He was equally appreciated as a confessor. Not only did he hear the confessions of his Jesuit brethren, but it was not unusual to see priests, bishops, and cardinals waiting their turn outside his room on a Saturday evening. For more than forty years he regularly heard confessions in St. Ignatius Church, a short walk from his residence at the Gregorian. The number of penitents continually grew, and some, to make sure that they would have the chance to go to confession, waited for him at the university's entrance and then walked to church with him. To the Romans St. Ignatius Church was known as "Fr. Cappello's church," and he in turn became "the confessor of Rome."

When Fr. Cappello retired from teaching in 1959 he did not retire from work. He continued his confessional apostolate and took on added tasks as a member of several commissions preparing drafts of documents for Vatican Council II.

On Tuesday, March 22, 1962, now in his eighty-third year, Fr. Cappello started to feel weak. The following morning, though he felt worse, he celebrated Mass, and later in the day he had periodic spells of vomiting. That night he was unable to sleep. The next morning, not wanting to miss celebrating Mass, he did so with great effort. That afternoon he got the chills and developed a fever; when the physician returned in the evening he suggested that his patient be anointed. During Fr. Cappello's last hours he frequently prayed: "Sweet Heart of Jesus." The prayers for the dying were recited and at ten minutes to one on the morning of March 25, the feast of our Lord's Incarnation, he, who brought much happiness to souls knew what happiness it was to be with God.

The funeral was held in St. Ignatius Church on March 28 with the faculty and students of the Gregorian in attendance, as well as many of Rome's faithful, clergy, religious, bishops, and cardinals. These were all his penitents. They came not only to say goodbye to their father confessor but also to ask his continued intercession in heaven. His remains have been brought back to St. Ignatius Church and placed near the spot where his confessional had been. Fr. Cappello's cause was initiated in the diocese of Rome in 1987.

April

April 3

Bl. Robert Middleton 1571–1601

Martyr of England

Robert Middleton was born in York, England, and though his family was Catholic it seems that as a young man he followed the religion of the Established Church. He later said that he had stopped because of his reading and his conscience. Perhaps the martyrdom in York of Margaret Clitherow on March 25, 1586, had something to do with his return. Margaret was born a Middleton and might possibly have been a relative. She was an enormously brave woman who had been arrested for harboring priests and was inhumanly pressed to death. Her heroism for the faith merited her a place among the forty martyrs of England and Wales canonized in 1970.

At about age eighteen Robert left York for London and Kingston-upon-Hull, and several years later, in 1594, when he was in his early twenties, went to study at the English College in Rheims, then he transferred to the college in Seville, and later went to the English College in Rome, arriving there on April 14, 1597. He was ordained to the priesthood on January 4, 1598, and on April 20 of that year left for his native land. He crossed the Channel in a Dutch ship, landed on England's southern shore, and slowly made his way to Lancaster, where he exercised his priestly ministry for little more than two years.

On September 30, 1600, as Fr. Middleton was riding from Preston to Fylde in Lancashire, he was apprehended by Sir Richard Houghton. While he was being led away, four men tried to rescue him; the attempt failed and one of the four, Fr. Thurstan Hunt, was captured. Both priests were subsequently imprisoned in Lancaster Castle and their interrogation only revealed that they were priests. When asked what they thought of Queen Elizabeth, Fr. Middleton boldly replied that he acknowledged her authority in temporal matters and prayed that God would one day make her a Catholic. On the first of October Sir

Richard wrote to Lord Cecil in London informing him of the capture and asked whether the prisoners should remain in Lancaster until the next sitting of the court, or be sent to London. By order of the Privy Council the priests were transferred to a London prison.

Sometime in 1599 Fr. Middleton had written to Fr. Henry Garnet, superior of the English Jesuits, requesting to enter the Society; but when permission was finally granted by Fr. General in Rome, Fr. Middleton was already in a London prison and Fr. Garnet never learned whether Fr. Middleton had received the letter informing him of his acceptance. In March 1601 Frs. Middleton and Hunt were taken back to Lancaster for trial and were condemned to death because they were priests who had been ordained overseas and had dared to exercise their priesthood in England. Fr. Hunt was the first to be hanged. Then it was Fr. Middleton's turn, and because he was cut down before he was fully dead, he was also beheaded. The execution took place the same day as the sentencing, most probably on April 3, 1601, though some accounts place the execution at the end of March.

Fr. Robert Middleton was beatified by Pope John Paul II on November 22, 1987, and his memorial is celebrated by his Jesuit brethren on December 1.

Prayer

Almighty, eternal God, you chose from the people of England and Wales Blessed Robert Middleton and his companions to be made like Christ, who died to save the world. Listen to their prayers; strengthen your Church by the same faith and love that strengthened them, and bless it always with your gift of unity. We ask this through our Lord Jesus Christ, your Son, who lives and reigns with you and the Holy Spirit, one God, for ever and ever.

April 7

St. Henry Walpole 1558–1595

Martyr of England

Among the bystanders attending the execution of Fr. Edmund Campion there was a twenty-three-year-old young man named Henry Walpole. For months he had been reflecting on the religious controversy in England, and though he was born Catholic and was inclined toward the Catholic faith, he still sought further confirmation for his belief. Since he had attended the imprisoned Fr. Campion's discussions with Anglican divines, he felt he had to be present when a martyr was being given to God. When Fr. Campion's quartered body was thrown into the boiling water, a drop of the martyr's blood fell upon Henry's clothing; so moved was he that he interpreted this as God calling him to follow in the martyr's footsteps. When he returned home that day, fledgling poet that he was, he wrote a narrative poem honoring the dead Jesuit. Because the poem was quite offensive to Queen Elizabeth's government, he wisely had it printed privately.

Henry was born at Docking, near Sandringham, Norfolk, in October 1558. He attended the Norwich grammar school from 1567 to 1574, then Peterhouse at Cambridge, and in 1578 moved to London to take chambers at Gray's Inn to begin his study of law. With Fr. Campion's martyrdom Henry's life took a different turn; he now set aside law as a profession and decided to become a priest. With this as his goal he entered the English College at Rheims, France, in July 1582; then moved to the English College in Rome in April 1583, and subsequently entered the Society of Jesus on February 4, 1584. For reasons of health he was sent to the Scots College at Pont-à-Mousson, France, and there completed his studies. He was ordained in Paris on December 17, 1588, and his first assignment was chaplain to English Catholic refugees serving in the Spanish army in the Low Countries. He was captured by Calvinists in 1589 and imprisoned at Flushing for about a year. Upon his release he was sent to the English seminary at Valladolid, Spain, and it was not until 1593 that his desire to return to England was fulfilled.

Because England's southern ports of entry were closed due to the plague, Fr. Walpole, together with his brother and an English soldier, secured passage on a French vessel going to Scotland. After ten days of rough sailing they were put ashore on the night of December 4, 1593, at Flamborough Head, Yorkshire. The group separated and Fr. Walpole went inland ten miles to Kelham on the road to York. While resting at an inn that night he was unexpectedly arrested on suspicion of being a priest. He had, in fact, been betrayed by a Scottish prisoner, who had been aboard the French vessel with him, and who had been put ashore three days earlier to earn money for his ransom. Fr. Walpole never had the opportunity to exercise his priestly ministry among his countrymen. His capture was sorely felt among the Jesuits in England, for it was hoped that he would continue Fr. Robert Southwell's work after the latter had been imprisoned.

During his first interrogation Fr. Walpole only admitted that he was a Jesuit priest and that he had come to convert the English to God. After three days he was transferred to the prison in York Castle and remained there until the end of February 1594. On several occasions he was permitted to leave the prison to dispute with Protestant ministers. Richard Topcliffe, the infamous priest-torturer, came to York to see if he could successfully force information from him, but Fr. Walpole stood the test well and revealed nothing. During his imprisonment he only had his breviary and Fr. Robert Bellarmine's *Controversies* to keep him company. He had time to write one short work, *Guard Yourselves against False Prophets,* and to begin another, *On Invoking the Saints.* On February 25, 1594, he was moved to the Tower of London, for Topcliffe was certain that he could accomplish with Fr. Walpole what he had failed to do with Fr. Southwell. Fr. Walpole was racked with unbelievable brutality and was often suspended by his wrists for hours at a time. To ensure that his victim would not die prematurely, Topcliffe extended the tortures over a period of a year. In all, Fr. Walpole was tortured fourteen times.

In the early part of 1595 the priest was returned to York to be tried in the district of his capture. On April 3 he was indicted under the law that made it high treason for an Englishman to return to his country after receiving Holy Orders abroad. Fr. Walpole spoke out in his own defense and reminded the judges that the law in question pertained only to priests who had not given themselves up to officials within three days of their landing. Having been ashore less than twenty hours when he was arrested, he had not, in fact, violated the law. Defeated in their initial attempt to find him guilty, the judges then demanded that he take the Oath of Supremacy acknowledging Elizabeth to be supreme in all religious matters. When he refused to take the oaths, he was convicted of high treason.

On April 7, together with the priest Alexander Rawlins, Fr. Walpole was dragged to Knavesmire, the place of execution outside York. Fr. Rawlins was the first to die and when his murderers showed his quartered body to Fr. Walpole and offered him life if he would conform to the new religion, the Jesuit vehemently rejected the offer and courageously climbed the ladder. From the gallows he asked those present to pray with him. He recited the Our Father, but because the executioner had not the patience to hear the Hail Mary, Fr. Walpole was pushed from the ladder. After being hanged, he was dismembered, and an eyewitness recorded that he saw tears in the eyes of many bystanders.

Fr. Henry Walpole was beatified by Pope Pius XI on December 15, 1929, and canonized by Pope Paul VI on October 25, 1970. The Jesuits celebrate his memorial on December 1, the day when the Jesuit martyrs of England and Wales are commemorated.

Prayer

Almighty, eternal God, you chose from the people of England and Wales Saint Henry Walpole and his companions to be made like Christ, who died to save the world. Listen to their prayers; strengthen your Church by the same faith and love that strengthened them, and bless it always with your gift of unity. We ask this through our Lord Jesus Christ, your Son, who lives and reigns with you and the Holy Spirit, one God, for ever and ever.

Bl. Edward Oldcorne 1561–1606

Martyr of England

After seventeen fruitful years as an active missionary in England, and after having successfully escaped the many snares laid for him by priest-hunters, Fr. Edward Oldcorne was finally apprehended in 1606 and falsely charged with complicity in the foiled Gunpowder Plot.

Edward Oldcorne was born in York in 1561 of a non-Catholic father and a Catholic mother, who, on several occasions, was imprisoned for her faith. Edward was raised in his mother's religion and, undoubtedly, it was her strong example that encouraged him to become a priest. Setting aside his medical studies, he went to the Continent in August 1581 to study at the English College in Rheims, France, and then in 1583 was sent to complete them at the English College in Rome, where he arrived in April of that year. He was ordained to the priesthood on August 23, 1587, and afterwards asked to be admitted into the Society of Jesus. Fr. General Claudio Acquaviva readily accepted him as a Jesuit on August 15, 1588. Because he was to return to England and labor under the difficult conditions of the Catholic persecution, his noviceship training at Sant' Andrea in Rome was greatly abbreviated.

Together with Fr. John Gerard, Fr. Oldcorne landed on a remote beach near Norfolk in November 1588. The priests then separated for greater safety; Fr. Oldcorne joined a group of sailors on their way to London. In London he met Fr. Henry Garnet, superior of the English Jesuits, and stayed with him for a few months. In March 1589 he was assigned to Hinlip Hall, a few miles from Worcester. The Hall was the property of Thomas Habington, an ardent Catholic, who always offered hospitality to priests. At this time, however, the owner was in prison and his sister Dorothy was in charge. Priests still found hospitality in the Hall, but Dorothy was a Protestant who for years had been at Elizabeth's court; she merely tolerated their presence. Over a period of years several priests tried to reconcile her to the Church without success. It was left to Fr. Oldcorne to find the way. She listened to his instructions and sermons, unconvinced; but when she learned that he had been fasting for days to bring about her conversion, she finally yielded to God's grace. Her conversion served as a sign, for with her many others in the shire returned to the Church of their ancestors. Fr. Oldcorne lived at the Hall for sixteen years, made it the base of his operations, and even used "Hall" as one of his aliases. It became the Catholic center in Worcestershire, where many came to receive the sacraments, hear Fr. Oldcorne's preaching, and seek his advice. His ministry also extended beyond the shire to the surrounding counties. So heavy was his work and so many the stations he had to visit, that within a few years of his coming he requested an assistant.

From the time Fr. Oldcorne had returned to England his health had been a problem. He suffered from anemia and cancer developed in his throat, which, if operated upon, would have left him without a voice. He endured this condition for a couple of years; his voice had a hoarse sound and his throat caused him pain, but this never kept him from preaching the word. About 1591 he made a pilgrimage to St. Winifred's shrine in Flintshire to seek a cure and, thanks to God, it was granted him, for he returned stronger and healthier than ever. His cancer was healed and his anemia had disappeared.

With the death of Elizabeth and the accession of James I on March 24, 1603, English Catholics looked forward to an end to persecution, and the king led them to believe that he would grant them greater toleration. But such was not to be; the persecution, in fact, became more intense. Angered at the king's refusal to keep his promise, several Catholic laymen formed a conspiracy to blow up the king and the Houses of Parliament on November 5, 1605. The plot, aptly called the "Gunpowder Plot," was discovered as was the powder in the cellars of the parliament building. This resulted in greater hatred toward the Catholics and a determination on the part of the government to implicate the Jesuits in the plot.

On November 24, 1605, Fr. Henry Garnet, the Jesuit superior, realizing that the government would try to involve him in the plot, sought refuge, together with Br. Nicholas Owen, at Hinlip Hall. The Hall was an ideal place for refuge; it was equipped with more hiding holes than any other mansion in England. The fact that Frs. Oldcorne and Garnet were eventually arrested, however, was due to the betrayal of a certain Humphrey Littleton, who had been seized for harboring Robert Wintour, one of the men connected with the plot. Thinking all would go well for him if he betrayed a priest, Littleton told his captors that they would find Fr. Oldcorne and possibly Fr. Garnet, at his cousin's mansion, Hinlip Hall.

The sheriff of Worcestershire appeared at the Hall on the morning of Monday, January 20, 1606, to begin his search. He had over 100 men with him. He stationed a man in each room of the house and ordered others to tap on the walls in the hope of locating concealed priest-holes. By the end of the third day they found eleven such hiding places, but no priests. On the fourth day, January 23, starvation and thirst forced Br. Ralph Ashley, Fr. Oldcorne's assistant, and Br. Owen to emerge from their hole. They hoped the sheriff would think that he had finally caught his prey and end the search, leaving the two priests in safety. But the sheriff was determined and his men continued their close examination of the house. Finally on the eighth day, January 27, Frs. Oldcorne and Garnet were discovered. They emerged white, ill, and weak. The four Jesuits were taken to Worcester. Frs. Oldcorne and Garnet were kept at the sheriff's residence because of their uncertain health, while Brs. Ashley and Owen were taken to the common jail. On February 3 the prisoners, under escort, were on their way to

London. The two priests were first sent to the Gatehouse Prison and the two brothers elsewhere, but eventually all were moved to the Tower of London.

The prison officials at the Tower arranged it that on certain days Frs. Oldcorne and Garnet would have contiguous cells and each was told, as if out of compassion, that there was a crack in the wall through which they could communicate with each other. Four such conferences took place, but as the priests spoke to each other through the wall, prison officials were eavesdropping and recording what was said. The government hoped to involve both of them in the plot, but the priests only engaged in chitchat, and when they went to confession, they used a very low whisper. As a result much of what was said was inaudible and what was audible was useless to the eavesdroppers. That stratagem having failed, the priests were then sent to the rack. For a period of five consecutive days Fr. Oldcorne was racked five hours a day. Throughout this torture the rackmaster was unable to get a single name from him or anything that could connect him with the plot.

After his experiences on the rack, Fr. Oldcorne, together with Br. Ashley, Humphrey Littleton their betrayer, and a certain John Wintour, was sent on March 21, 1606, to Worcester for trial. During the Lenten assizes Fr. Oldcorne was falsely charged with complicity in the Gunpowder Plot. He denied involvement so well that the charge against him was changed to his being a Jesuit who had gained many to the Catholic faith. Thus he was found guilty of high treason and ordered to be hanged on the gallows.

Of those to die on Monday of Holy Week, April 7, 1606, on Red Hill outside Worcester, Fr. Oldcorne was the first to mount the ladder. Littleton, about to be executed himself, publicly asked pardon of Fr. Oldcorne and admitted that the accusation he had brought against him was false. After forgiving his betrayer, Fr. Oldcorne proceeded to pray aloud for the king and royal family, for his accusers, the judges, and the jury that had condemned him. He prayed to St. Winifred and as he was protesting his innocence the hangman pushed him from the ladder. He was cut down before he was dead; his head was then cut off and his body quartered.

Fr. Edward Oldcorne, together with Br. Ralph Ashley, who died with him, was beatified by Pope Pius XI on December 15, 1929, and his memorial is celebrated on December 1, with the other Jesuit martyrs of England and Wales.

Prayer

Almighty, eternal God, you chose from the people of England and Wales Blessed Edward Oldcorne and his companions to be made like Christ, who died to save the world. Listen to their prayers; strengthen your Church by the same faith and love that strengthened them, and bless it always with your gift of unity. We ask this through our Lord Jesus Christ, your Son, who lives and reigns with you and the Holy Spirit, one God, for ever and ever.

April 9

Bl. Ralph Ashley ?–1606

Martyr of England

The date and place of Ralph Ashley's birth as well as the facts of his early life remain unknown. He was the cook at the English College at Rheims, France, and in April 1590 went to be the cook and baker at the newly founded English College in Valladolid, Spain. It was there that he entered the Jesuits as a brother. Because of poor health, however, he was urged to return to his native land. He arrived in London on March 9, 1598. For a time he worked with Fr. Henry Garnet, superior of the English Jesuits in London, and was later assigned to assist Fr. Edward Oldcorne at Hinlip Hall, Worcestershire. He did this for eight years and was Fr. Oldcorne's companion in martyrdom.

Br. Ashley was at Hinlip Hall when Fr. Garnet and Br. Nicholas Owen came to seek safety after the discovery of the Gunpowder Plot. When the sheriff came to search the Hall on January 20, 1606, Brs. Ashley and Owen went into a priest-hole, which was, unfortunately, without supplies. They were able to maintain themselves throughout three days of the search, but on January 23, the fourth day, because of starvation and acute thirst, they had to emerge. They hoped that the sheriff, pleased with having captured them, would give up the search. But the sheriff was not satisfied with the two brothers and continued the search until he discovered the two priests on January 27. The four Jesuits were taken to Worcester and Brs. Ashley and Owen were housed in the common jail, until they were transferred to the Tower of London on February 3. While in the Tower, there was no contact between Fr. Oldcorne and Br. Ashley. Both were subjected to torture on the rack and on March 21 they were returned to Worcester to stand trial. Whereas Fr. Oldcorne was found guilty of being a priest and ordered to die the death of a traitor, Br. Ashley was found guilty of assisting him in his treasonable work.

On the morning of April 7, Br. Ashley, together with Fr. Oldcorne and two others, was taken to Red Hill, near Worcester, to be executed. After Fr. Oldcorne had died, Br. Ashley kissed the feet of the hanging martyr and said: "Happy I am to follow in the steps of my sweet Father." The hangman then pushed him from the ladder and he remained hanging until dead.

Br. Ralph Ashley was beatified with Fr. Oldcorne on December 15, 1929, by Pope Pius XI, and his memorial is celebrated on December 1, with his Jesuit brothers, all martyred in England and Wales.

Prayer

Almighty, eternal God, you chose from the people of England and Wales Blessed Ralph Ashley and his companions to be made like Christ, who died to save the world. Listen to their prayers; strengthen your Church by the same faith and love that strengthened them, and bless it always with your gift of unity. We ask this through our Lord Jesus Christ, your Son, who lives and reigns with you and the Holy Spirit, one God, for ever and ever.

April 10

S. G. Ferdinand de Huidobro 1903–1937

Fr. Ferdinand de Huidobro Polanco died as a chaplain on the field of battle, serving the legionnaires of Spain's nationalist army during that country's civil war. He was the son of a mining engineer, the sixth of nine children, born at Santander, Spain, on March 10, 1903. In March 1908 the family moved to Melilla, North Africa, where the father was engaged in planning the city's new harbor. Because of political problems the family moved to Madrid in December 1911. In the Spanish capital young Ferdinand attended Holy Angel College from 1912 to 1918 and though not a member of the college's St. Stanislaus Kostka sodality, he joined its members during Lent 1918 in making a retreat. Ferdinand was about to graduate and he wished to know what God wanted him to do; the outcome was his decision to enter the Society of Jesus. Because he was only fifteen, his mother asked him to wait until he was older and more certain of his decision. Immediately after finishing his courses at Holy Angel College, Ferdinand began his study of law at "Areneros" in Madrid and after a year there he was more convinced than ever that he wanted to join the Jesuits. With his mother's permission he left home for the novitiate in Granada and arrived there on October 16, 1919.

Ferdinand's noviceship training lasted the usual two years, at the end of which he pronounced his three vows of religion on October 21, 1921. He remained in Granada for his studies in the humanities from 1921 to 1924, as well as for his course in philosophy from 1924 to 1927. His time, however, was not totally spent with his books. On holidays from class he taught catechism to gypsies in a nearby village and gathered the impoverished young olive pickers to tell them about God. The years from 1927 to 1930 were spent teaching young

Spanish lads; for the first two years he taught grammar at Aranjuez and during the third year literature at Chamartín. For his theology he went to Oña in October 1930.

Spain's political situation was beginning to change. The king had gone into exile and on April 12, 1931, the dictatorship was replaced by a republic. The processes then in motion were eventually to end in Spain's terrible civil war. The republican government moved against the Jesuits by burning their residence in Madrid, and on October 13 voting to dissolve the Society and nationalize its properties. Ferdinand, then a theology student at Oña, closely watched these developments and foresaw that persecution would soon follow. The order of dissolution was finally signed on January 23, 1932, and the Oña theologate had to close. In the first days of February Ferdinand and several other Jesuits were exiles on their way to Marneffe, Belgium, where they arrived on February 7. In September of that year he went to Valkenburg, the Netherlands, to continue his theological studies and was ordained there on August 27, 1933. He remained at Valkenburg until the summer of 1934 when he went to the University of Berlin to attend classes in philosophy and in the fall of 1934 to Braga, Portugal, for tertianship. On his return trip to Germany, Fr. Huidobro stopped at Madrid to take his examinations leading to his doctorate in philosophy. His plan was to get a double doctorate, one in Spain and another in Germany. On October 20, 1935, he was at Freiburg, where he began graduate studies under the renowned German philosopher, Martin Heidegger.

In July 1936 civil war broke out in Spain. Fr. Huidobro was always concerned about the spiritual welfare of others and now that his country was sorely divided, he wrote to Fr. General in Rome asking permission to serve as a chaplain in Spain's nationalist army against the reds with their communist leanings. Permission was readily granted and Fr. Huidobro, having set aside his philosophy texts, arrived in Spain. On September 8 he was made chaplain to the legion's Fourth Regiment.

Fr. Huidobro's career as army chaplain lasted a short six months but in that brief period he performed acts of genuine heroism. He was as much a legionnaire as any of his soldiers; he marched when they marched and shared all their hardships. When the Fourth Regiment encountered hostile forces on their drive toward Madrid in November 1936, Fr. Huidobro selflessly cared for the wounded. To protect the dying, he threw himself over their bodies to prevent them from receiving further injury. On the ninth of November he himself was wounded and had to be taken to the hospital at Talavera. Because this was not an army hospital, he made it known that he would have preferred being with his legionnaires and only after much petitioning did the physicians at Talavera release him.

Fr. Huidobro returned to his regiment's hospital clinic on November 15. He was now walking with a cane, or rather, he was dragging himself with the aid of a cane. He visited his men and embraced each as a brother. At the end of January 1937 the regiment was ordered to Toledo to prepare for a major offensive.

After seven days of rest the regiment was again on the march, this time headed for Jarama on the outskirts of Madrid. Fr. Huidobro's regiment had only 2,000 men and they were to face a force numbering 20,000. During that bloody encounter, the priest worked so heroically among the wounded caring for them and evacuating them, that the regiment recommended him for the Military Medal. That the regiment was able to withstand the reds was attributed by the legionnaires to God's protection and Fr. Huidobro's prayers.

During a short respite from army life, Fr. Huidobro went to Villafranca to pronounce his final vows as a Jesuit on April 5. The following morning he left to rejoin his regiment at Aravaca. The regiment was preparing to leave to participate in the siege of Madrid. The fighting began on April 8 and lasted until April 13; it was fierce and uninterrupted. From the moment it began Fr. Huidobro was in the front lines tending the dying and the wounded in the trenches without concern for the bullets passing over him. So dangerous was it that the commander asked him to go behind the lines and care for the wounded there. Fr. Huidobro obeyed and while working among those wounded, an enemy shell hit that area. He and several legionnaires were killed in the blast. The date was April 11, 1937; Fr. Huidobro was thirty-four years old.

It was Fr. Huidobro's deep love of God and his love of neighbor that drove him to sacrifice his life for the wounded in his regiment. But the love he so heroically exhibited on the field of battle was the same love he possessed during his many years of Jesuit training. It only took an extraordinary occasion to bring it into the open.

Fr. Ferdinand de Huidobro's body was first buried in Toledo. In November 1942 his remains were moved to the Jesuit novitiate in Aranjuez and from there they were transferred in November 1958 to the church of the Sacred Heart of Jesus and St. Francis Borgia in Madrid. His cause was initiated on November 19, 1947.

April 11

Ven. Francis del Castillo 1615–1673

Fr. Francis del Castillo's apostolate was exclusively devoted to the people of Lima, Peru, and so fruitful was it and so well remembered, that he is revered as the "Apostle of Lima." He was born in that city on February 9, 1615, and entered the Society of Jesus toward the end of 1632. After finishing his course in philosophy he taught grammar for a time to young boys at St. Paul's College in Lima. This was followed by a few years of theological studies. After ordination in 1642, he longed to work among the native peoples of Peru or Paraguay. But his health had never been strong so his superiors, who feared that the hardships and privations of missionary life would prove detrimental to his already weakened state, assigned him to teach grammar at the college in Callao. However, when the Marquis de Mancera, viceroy of Peru, was preparing an expedition to confront the Dutch pirates off the coast at Valdivia, Chile, Fr. Castillo was included as chaplain. This successful 1645 expedition lasted six months and upon its completion the priest was back teaching at the college in Lima.

Fr. Castillo began his special apostolate in 1648. A market was held each Sunday in a large public square named Baratillo and it brought a great number of people into the city's center. One Sunday, as he moved among the thousands of people milling about examining wares and haggling over prices, Fr. Castillo was inspired to preach to them. He borrowed a table, stood upon it, called the people toward him, and began to speak on the same theme that St. John the Baptist had used when he began his ministry, "Repent, the Kingdom of God is near at hand." After the people responded favorably and appeared interested in what he had said, he decided to try it again. Within a matter of weeks Fr. Castillo's Sunday sermon in the square became a regular event and it continued for the next twenty-five years. In 1653 he no longer had to use a table as a makeshift pulpit; some artisans built him a brick platform and covered it with colored tiles. Fr. Castillo's sermons became an integral part of the Sunday market and in them he systematically went through the topics of the catechism, inspiring his hearers to live according to Christian principles, to frequent the sacraments, and to live good moral lives. His sermons were neither polished nor filled with rhetoric, but being sincere they touched everyone's heart.

When Fr. Castillo preached he usually held a large cross, on the bottom of which was a picture of our Lady. After the sermon he regularly led the audience to Our Lady's Chapel, located nearby, and there he prayed with them before the Blessed Sacrament. Because he made such frequent use of that chapel, the diocese transferred it in 1658 to the care of the Jesuits and Fr. Castillo made it the center of his apostolic activity.

Like Fr. Peter Claver, Fr. Castillo had a special love for the blacks and the Indians of Lima. When the blacks gathered each morning in the square to hire themselves out for the day's labor, he was among them, instructing them, preparing them for baptism, giving them hope. He did the same for the native peoples, taking an interest in their spiritual needs, encouraging them in their faith, trying to integrate them into Lima's community.

Among all his clients he promoted sodalities that regularly met in the chapel for meetings and prayers. Each group had its special day for its monthly General Communion. The Spanish sodality was called "The School of Christ" and had as its purpose a firm foundation in the faith. They had weekly meetings with sermons and meditations. When the members were later assigned to the different cities throughout the vast expanse that was the Lima diocese, they took these principles with them and helped plant Christianity in the new settlements. For the city's poor boys, Fr. Castillo organized a school, and for wayward girls, he founded a hospice to help in their rehabilitation.

Fr. Francis del Castillo was an early social reformer and because of his deep charity for all human beings, he was a father to the poor and neglected. He died at St. Paul's College in Lima on April 11, 1673, at age fifty-eight. He had been a Jesuit for forty-one years. His cause was introduced in Rome on September 22, 1741.

April 12

Ven. Bruno Bruni 1590–1640

Ven. Louis Cardeira 1585–1640

Martyrs of Ethiopia

Frs. Bruno Bruni and Louis Cardeira were the last of the eight Martyrs of Ethiopia. In 1632 when Negus (Emperor) Susenyos allowed his country to revert to its former belief of only one nature in Christ, it meant the beginning of the end of the Jesuit mission in Ethiopia. After the accession of his son, Fasilidas, Jesuit missionary activity was curtailed and in 1633 the Jesuits were ordered to assemble at their headquarters at Fremona. In the following year Fasilidas decreed their expulsion, but not all left the country; seven remained behind and secretly continued their ministry. Fr. Bruni, together with Frs. Gaspar Pais and John Pereira, found refuge near the city of Assa. On April 25, 1635, as the priests were about to celebrate Mass, they were attacked; Fr. Pais died immediately, Fr. Pereira a few days later, and though Fr. Bruni had received no less than fifteen wounds and was left for dead, he survived the attack. (Further details will be found under the date April 25.)

Bruno Bruni was born in Civitella del Tronto, Italy, on November 7, 1590. He went to Rome in 1605 to begin his studies at the Roman College, and while in Rome he read the letters of Francis Xavier, whose exploits for God aroused him to become a missionary and a Jesuit. Bruno entered the novitiate of Sant' Andrea in Rome on August 14, 1608, and continued his philosophical course at the Roman College. He then spent three years teaching in Florence and returned to Rome for theology. During his years at the Roman College he came to know John Berchmans, and when the latter was on his deathbed Bruno often spent the night reading aloud to him the life of Aloysius Gonzaga. After the death of Berchmans, Bruno wrote the obituary notice that circulated throughout the Jesuit houses.

With his studies completed and now an ordained priest, Fr. Bruni left Lisbon, Portugal, on March 25, 1623, for India. He arrived in Goa in May 1624 and was in Fremona, Ethiopia, by July 1625. He immediately set himself to learning Amharic, the spoken language of the Ethiopians. After three years of apostolic work in Fremona, he went to Nebesse, in Gojam province, where he established a Jesuit house and rebuilt the church of our Lady. He served as architect and stonemason on the church project. During his years in Nebesse he helped reform three monasteries and had many conversions to the Church.

Though Fr. Bruni had been severely wounded when Fr. Pais was killed, the Catholics who found him gave him such care that he recovered completely. He then found protection under Za Mariam, governor of Temben, and lived and worked with Fr. Louis Cardeira in a refuge on top of Mt. Amba Salama. For almost five years both Jesuits carried on their priestly ministry of dispensing sacraments and preaching God's word. After the martyrdom of Bishop Apollinaris de Almeida and his two companions, Frs. Bruni and Cardeira were the only Jesuits left in Ethiopia.

Louis Cardeira was born in Beira, Portugal, in 1585, and after studying at the University of Évora entered the Society on December 25, 1600. With his noviceship completed he continued studies at the university in humanities, philosophy, music, and mathematics. On March 20, 1611, after two years of theology in Coimbra, he sailed from Lisbon for India, where he finished his studies and was ordained. He then worked for eight years in the missions of Cambay and Mogor, India, before arriving in Ethiopia in January 1624. He was a multitalented Jesuit: a good theologian and mathematician, exceptional in languages, a skilled designer, and an accomplished musician. He taught at the seminary in Fremona and once he mastered the Amharic language he translated devotional books for the faithful. In 1627 he was superior at Gorgora and between 1631 and 1632 he was at Gojam, where he continued his translation work. During his years in Ethiopia he also wrote a dictionary and a grammar to help other missionaries learn Amharic.

The life of the two missionaries at Mt. Amba Salama was primitive and full of privations, but they found joy in their service to the Catholics who came to them. After Za Mariam was killed in 1638, holding off the men of the negus from besieging the mount and capturing the missionaries, the two Jesuits remained relatively secure in their mountain refuge. Then in April 1640 they received a message from the emperor promising them his protection and a safe passage out of the country, should they come down the mountain. On Good Friday, April 6, they descended, and as they walked toward the sea, thinking they were on their way to India, the new governor of Temben had them arrested. The local schismatic monks claimed they had the order of the negus to execute the Jesuits; believing their word, the governor imprisoned the priests. On Easter Thursday, April 12, they were led to the marketplace in Temben, where a great number of people had gathered. When the priests saw the large tree before them, they knew what kind of martyrdom was to be theirs. Assured that they would now die for Christ, they encouraged and absolved each other. As Fr. Cardeira approached the tree and saw the ropes with which they were to be hanged, he said: "Lord God, bless these ropes and this land of Ethiopia, which is being made fertile by the blood of so many martyrs." The assassins then stripped them of their garments, tied their hands behind them, placed ropes about their necks, and hoisted them up. As the bodies hung in full view, the bystanders pelted them with stones. The bodies remained hanging for four days. They were finally removed but the Catholics never discovered what had happened to them.

The cause of Fr. Bruno Bruni and Fr. Louis Cardeira was introduced in Rome on June 19, 1902, together with that of their six Jesuit brothers, all of whom died in Ethiopia in witness for the faith.

April 13

S. G. Emmanuel García Nieto 1894–1974

Emmanuel, the youngest of nine children, was born in the small town of Macotera, in the Spanish province of Salamanca, on April 5, 1894. His early education was in the local public school. When he reached age fourteen he told his widowed mother that he would like to enter the diocesan seminary, where his brother Ramón was a student. Thinking of Emmanuel's fragile health and of the fact that she would be left alone (of her nine children five had died in infancy, and of those surviving two daughters became nuns and the other son a seminarian), she thought it better for him to wait a bit longer. The son's tears, however, overcame the mother's fears, and in 1908 he enrolled at the minor seminary, but was permitted to pursue his study of Latin while living at home. His tutor was Ruperto Bueno, a Latinist who had retired from teaching because of blindness.

The following September Emmanuel went to live at the Jesuit-directed diocesan seminary in Salamanca, and there, for the first time, came into contact with members of the Society. His third year of Latin (1910–1911) was also spent at home because of poor health. When Emmanuel returned to the seminary in September 1911, the Jesuits were no longer there. He spent the next nine years studying rhetoric, philosophy, and theology, and finally on May 16, 1920, he was ordained a priest for the Salamanca archdiocese.

Fr. García Nieto's first assignment was as an assistant pastor in the little parish of Cantalapiedra. After two years he was appointed pastor of Santa María de Sando, a rural parish some sixty miles west of Cantalapiedra. While performing his various parish duties, he kept his interest in Jesuit spirituality and read books on the Society. Some of his annual retreats during those years were also given by Jesuits. Thinking of possibly entering the Society, he spoke with the Jesuit Fr. Rafael Garrido and later went with him to the novitiate at Carrión de los Condes to make a retreat under his direction. The result was his decision to enter the Society.

The thirty-two-year-old priest arrived at Carrión de los Condes on July 26, 1926, and began his noviceship on the 30th. Then in early October the novitiate was transferred to Salamanca. Though there were some sixteen years difference between him and the other novices, he fitted in perfectly with the novitiate's rhythm of life. He took his turn working in the kitchen, cleaning corridors, teaching catechism to local children, etc. When his two years as a novice ended, he took his vows of religion on July 31, 1928. That summer he was sent to the scholasticate in Oña to review his theology, and after a year was assigned in September 1929 to be spiritual father of the youngest students at the Comillas seminary and college near Santander. He was to be their confessor, give conferences on prayer and the ascetical life, and points for meditation.

Life at the Comillas seminary ran smoothly and peacefully until the coming of Spain's Second Republic in 1931. News of the burning of convents arrived at Comillas on May 11, and Fr. García Nieto remarked: "What can the reds do to us? Cut off our heads? They can keep mine, I'm going to heaven." Then on January 23, 1932, the government dissolved the Society in Spain, confiscated its property, and forbade the Jesuits to live in community. Since the Comillas seminary was a pontifical institution, the Jesuits were permitted to continue teaching there, but they had to live in private houses, generously offered them by various families in Comillas. On January 29, 1932, Fr. García Nieto was made the spiritual director of the entire seminary and also took on the task of teaching pastoral as well as ascetical and mystical theology.

Revolution broke out on July 18, 1936. On August 12, at 7:30 in the morning, two dozen buses and trucks came to the seminary; militiamen blockaded all exits and ordered the 200 inside to get ready to go to Santander. Fr. García Nieto went through the corridors encouraging his students: "We are in the best of hands. Jesus and Mary won't let us down." Students and faculty were transported to Santander that day and detained in the Salesian college until the 19th, when they were released. Fr. García Nieto remained in Santander and found housing with a private family. While in the city he went about disguised, searching for his seminarians, making sure they had places to stay, and helping them in any way he could. He secretly celebrated Mass in private homes and took Communion to many. In January of the following year he moved to the outskirts of Bilbao. Then after Generalissimo Franco liberated Bilbao (June) and Comillas (August), Fr. García Nieto returned to the seminary.

The seminary reopened in October. He was once again spiritual director and professor. As the number of students gradually increased so did his labors, and when an assistant came in 1950 to help him, he restricted his own direction to the 240 theologians. Then with the changes in theological education and seminary life following Vatican Council II, Fr. García Nieto no longer felt adequate to the task of spiritual director. Referring to the modern seminarians, he said: "I don't understand them." Thus, when the seminary transferred to Madrid (1967), he moved into the Jesuit residence in Comillas and there served as the community's spiritual father. He was then seventy-three years old.

This new position was not full-time so Fr. García Nieto did pastoral work in the area, showed great interest in the poor, and continued to give retreats to seminarians, priests, and religious. With increasing age his health declined—he grew deaf and his eyesight began to fail—but he never gave up spiritual direction. Many were the priests that came to see him. During the winter of 1973–1974 he developed a severe case of bronchitis and heart trouble, and eventually had to move to the community's infirmary.

In early March 1974 he caught a bad cold and on April 1, because there was a rapid decline in his health, he was anointed. Whatever time he did not need for resting, he spent in the chapel. He celebrated his last Mass on Holy Thursday morning and spent the whole of the following day, Good Friday, before the tabernacle. That evening the infirmarian checked on him at 11:15 and all seemed well, but then he noticed that his patient began to shake as if he were cold. He covered him with blankets, but the shaking did not stop. Though the priest's breathing became more and more difficult, he kept on praying: "Whatever you wish, Lord; if you wish today, then today; if you wish tomorrow, then tomorrow; whenever you wish. Lord, forgive me my sins . . . I offer you my life, I offer you my death, my eternity. I offer these to you for the Church, the Society, for priests, and for the world." On Holy Saturday, April 13, at 2 A.M., he yielded his soul to its Maker.

Fr. García Nieto's entire priestly life was devoted to educating seminarians and fostering holiness in them. All who had come under his direction acknowledged his humility and holiness. The Archbishop of Oviedo, Gabino Díaz Merchán, wrote of him: "We have a saint in heaven and from there he will continue to assist Comillas, priests, Jesuits, the poor, and thus we hope—we who have received so much from him during his life. The death of a saint is an example for those who are still on pilgrimage. Will the Church canonize Fr. Nieto, or not? We who have known him over so many years cannot think otherwise; he was a saint and his entire life has been an example to us."

April 15

S. G. Peter Barbarić 1874–1897

Peter Barbarić was twenty-three years old when he died; he had been a Jesuit for less than two days. Peter was a Croatian, born on May 19, 1874. His parents lived in the small hamlet of Siljevista, near the village of Klobuk, located in the region of Bosnia-Herzogovina. Peter was one of nine children. His first teachers were his parents, who taught him not only the lessons of the catechism, but also gave him the foundations of a solid education. As a child he developed the same great love for the Sacred Heart of Jesus and for our Lady as his parents had. When he took his father's flock to pasture, he carried a staff in one hand and fingered his rosary in the other, so as not to waste time daydreaming. As a young boy approaching his teens, he enrolled in the recently opened school at Veljaci. The hour-and-a-half walk to and from school meant nothing to the young lad; it gave him time to review his lessons. Because of the training he received from his parents, he completed his studies in two years rather than the usual four. His father then got him a job as a clerk in a store in Vitina, where Peter lived for a bit more than a year. Providence was calling him to something else. His old schoolmaster from Veljaci had received a letter from the rector of the diocesan seminary in Travnik asking him to recommend candidates suitable for higher studies and for the priesthood. One day the schoolmaster met Peter and mentioned the letter to him. Immediately the youth's face filled with joy for this was what he wanted.

Peter, now fifteen, accompanied by his father, set out on horse on the three-day trip to Travnik, arriving there on August 27, 1889. The diocesan seminary was under the care of the Jesuits. Peter did well in his studies and in 1892 added Italian to his regular classes, and then French and German, thinking that one day he would use these languages in hearing confessions. During his stay at the seminary he joined the sodality and when he was an upper classman was elected its prefect. He encouraged his fellow classmates to receive Holy Communion on the First Friday of each month and promoted the Nine First Fridays. For years Peter had been thinking about the diocesan priesthood; it was only during the school retreat in 1896 that he gave thought to becoming a Jesuit.

It was customary at the seminary that the Tuesday after Easter was a holiday, when the seminarians went on their spring picnic. The morning of April 7, 1896, was sunny, clear, and cheerful. A good day to be outside with one's friends. It was so warm a day that the students were dressed only in light clothing. The weather, however, suddenly changed. It clouded over and the students were caught in a great downpour. By the time they returned home they were soaked and chilled. The result of this for Peter was that he caught a cold, ran a high fever, and developed a frightful cough. On April 26 he was admitted to the infirmary, and though not confined to bed he was confined to his room for weeks.

When summer vacation came, the school physician recommended that he return home to enjoy his native air, in the hope that the air of Siljevista would do for him what medicine could not. Peter spent that summer with his family, but while living happily with those whom he loved he was, at the same time, developing tuberculosis.

On his return to school, which he had to take in stages because of his health, he stopped for a time at the seminary in Sarajevo and there the school physician chanced to examine him. The diagnosis was that Peter was tubercular; so affected were his lungs that, in the physician's judgment, there was no hope for the young man. Peter remained unaware of this diagnosis; all the while he continued to hope that he would regain his health, complete his studies and be ordained. In early 1897 his weakness became more and more pronounced and he found that he had to drop some of his courses. Eventually he had to stop going to class altogether and stay in the infirmary. Throughout March he grew weaker and had to use a cane to get about his room. On March 11 he told his confessor, "I've been making a novena to St. Francis Xavier asking to recover, but tomorrow I will begin a novena to St. Joseph and ask for a happy death." During the following month his health was in such rapid decline that he was anointed on April 10.

Peter's confessor knew that Peter wanted to be a Jesuit and that he would certainly have entered the novitiate, if he had not wanted to wait until he had graduated. On one of his visits to Peter's room the confessor asked him would he want, if permission were granted, to take Jesuit vows and die as a member of the Society. Peter responded that he himself had thought of this, but hesitated to request such a special favor. The confessor then informed the rector of Peter's desire, and the rector immediately sent a letter to the provincial requesting this privilege for Peter.

On Palm Sunday, April 11, Peter was taken to the seminary chapel for Mass and there he amazed everyone by standing throughout the long reading of Christ's passion. Each day Peter grew more feeble. He knew that his stay on earth was short and once said: "How nice it would be to celebrate Easter in heaven." On the afternoon of April 13, the provincial's telegram arrived granting the rector's request, informing him that he was accepting Peter into the Society, that Peter has permission to take vows of devotion, and that he may now wear the habit of the Society. Peter thought Holy Thursday, April 15, would be the perfect day to make this offering of himself and so planned on taking the vows after his Paschal Communion. His confessor doubted whether the young man would live to see Holy Thursday and therefore recommended that he take the vows that very day. At 9 P.M., in the presence of witnesses, Peter vowed poverty, chastity, and obedience, and promised to live in the Society for the rest of his life. The following day he spent in bed, totally exhausted, burning with fever. That evening his Jesuit brethren gathered in his room and recited the prayers for the dying. The next day, Holy Thursday, April 15, Peter was unable to eat and could hardly speak. In the early afternoon he asked for his crucifix, and when he had it in his hands he kissed it, and said "Jesus." Now he was calm and at peace. Minutes later he gave forth a deep sigh and at that moment, shortly after 2 P.M., Peter, after living a life of innocence and holiness, went to meet his Lord and God. He wore the Jesuit habit for the first time as his body lay in the coffin. He was buried on April 17, Holy Saturday, in the cemetery outside the city of Travnik.

Peter Barbarić had no secret way to holiness. His method was that of St. Stanislaus Kostka, St. Aloysius Gonzaga, and St. John Berchmans, and he described it in these words: "Of all the paths leading to heaven the shortest, the easiest, and the most reliable is the one a man takes by performing his everyday duties." His cause is presently under study.

April 19

S. G. Francis Gaetano 1568–1601

A young twenty-two-year-old nobleman, weary from hunting, returned to his country lodge for a short respite. In the quiet of his surroundings Francis Gaetano began to recite the rosary and while he prayed his mind became unexpectedly enlightened. He came to understand the brevity and fleeting character of this world's happiness and the longer he prayed the clearer did this realization become. By the time he came to the end of his prayer he had resolved to have nothing more to do with the world; he would change his way of life and devote himself to God's service.

Francis was the second son of the Count of Sortino and Cassaro, and was born on November 11, 1569, at Sortino, near Syracuse, in Sicily. In him flowed the blood of the most illustrious families of Spain and Sicily. He was trained as a knight and had learned those arts necessary for a nobleman to know. He was unsurpassed in horsemanship and was fond of hunting, dancing, and singing. Following the customs of the age, he excelled in the use of arms and successfully participated in jousts and tourneys. Thanks to his mother's careful teaching, he at the same time remained faithful to his Christian duties. He assisted at daily Mass, recited the rosary and our Lady's office each day, and was generous in almsgiving. He fasted on Fridays in honor of our Lord's Passion, and hoped to die on a Friday. This desire was eventually to be fulfilled.

As a consequence of his extraordinary religious experience in the hunting lodge in 1591, Francis made a general confession of his life and conceived such a hatred of himself that he took to wearing the garb of a penitent and visited the chapels and shrines in his area barefoot. In addition, he practiced bodily penances to an extreme degree.

In his desire to follow Christ, he thought of becoming a Capuchin, but then changed his mind and asked to be received into the Society of Jesus. He entered the Jesuit novitiate in Messina, Sicily, on April 21, 1593, and there met Fr. Bernard Colnago, a priest known for holiness of life. Fr. Colnago directed Francis during his early years as a Jesuit and it was he who ordered him to forgo many of the penances that he had been accustomed to perform, and to concentrate on interior mortification, which was more excellent in God's eyes. In obedience to his director's advice, Francis reduced his penances and strove for absolute detachment and total victory over self.

On completing his two years of noviceship training, Francis pronounced his religious vows and then spent the next two years studying the humanities. In 1597 he was sent to Palermo to teach Latin and returned to Messina the following year for his course in philosophy. Shortly after his return, his health failed and he suffered from hemorrhages and severe headaches. There was to be no recovery. About the middle of Lent in 1601, Francis grew more and more convinced that he would not live to see Easter, and so whenever guests came to visit him, he viewed the occasion as their last meeting on earth and took the opportunity to thank them for all they had done for him.

As Easter drew nearer, the sufferings of Francis increased. He was often heard saying this prayer: "My Lord Jesus, more suffering!" When Holy Thursday arrived, he received Holy Communion and afterwards grasped his crucifix in his hand and said: "My Lord, take me from this mortal life, and in your mercy grant me the joy of seeing you and your holy mother." Late on Good Friday, April 20, 1601, shortly before midnight, Francis Gaetano, after eight years in the Society, offered himself to his Lord and was accepted by him. His cause is in its preliminary stages.

April 20

Bl. Francis Page ?–1602

Martyr of England

On February 2, 1601, Fr. Francis Page was vested and about to begin Mass when the noises and shouts outside the house indicated that it was surrounded by priest-hunters. He had hardly taken off the vestments, hidden them, and taken a seat among the people who had come for Mass, when the hunters rushed in. Finding the room full of people seated before a prepared altar, the intruders were led to believe that the group was waiting for a priest to arrive. In the confusion that followed, the owner of the house, Anne Line, hustled Fr. Page away from the crowd into a concealed priest-hole. Fr. Page was safe, but on the evidence of a waiting congregation, Anne Line was arrested and later executed for harboring a priest. In 1970 she was canonized for her faith and courage.

Francis Page was born in Antwerp on an unknown date of well-to-do Protestant parents, who came from Harrow-on-the-Hill in Middlesex county. Young Francis decided on a lawyer's career and went to London to read law. In London he clerked for a noted Catholic lawyer. Francis fell in love with his employer's daughter, but she would not speak of marriage until Francis became a Catholic. His Catholic roommate had as his confessor, Fr. John Gerard, a Jesuit who was then in London's Clink Prison. So it was to Fr. Gerard that Francis went for instruction. While being taught in the faith, his soul was slowly drawn from the world toward Christ. Much to his fiancée's sorrow, Francis called off the marriage and began to think of the priesthood. When Fr. Gerard was transferred to the Tower of London he was no longer able to have visitors and Francis suffered greatly for not being able to talk with him. He missed seeing him so much that he daily loitered on the shore of the Thames near the Tower hoping to get a glimpse of his confessor at his prison window. One day Fr. Gerard noticed the young man outside; as Francis doffed his hat in respect, the priest blessed him. Young Francis thought his actions went unnoticed by prison officials so his coming for the blessing became a daily occurrence. He was finally apprehended, however, on suspicion of trying to communicate with a prisoner. After several days the police were unable to prove anything more against the young man and Francis was released.

There was no longer any doubt in his mind that he had to be a priest. He crossed the Channel to attend the English College at Rheims, France, and was ordained in 1600. Shortly afterwards he returned to England and was active in and around London. In February 1601, as mentioned above, he eluded the priest-hunters through the heroic actions of a woman, but fourteen months later he was betrayed by another. Since chances of recognition made it dangerous for priests to go about London during the day, they did most of their work in the evening. One night, in early April 1602, as Fr. Page left a London residence, he was recognized in the street by a woman who pretended to be a Catholic. It was known that she had already betrayed several priests for the monetary reward offered by the government. Fr. Page recognized her and quickened his step. The woman, hurrying after him, called out that she wanted to speak with him. Pretending not to hear her, Fr. Page rushed down a narrow alley. Careful not to enter the house of a Catholic family—he knew this was just what she wanted—he entered an inn where the door was left open. He locked the door behind him and asked the proprietor to let him out the back door, saying someone was following him whom he did not want to see. Before the priest had a chance to get to the rear entrance, the woman was furiously banging on the front door, screaming that there was a priest inside the inn. Her screeching brought the neighbors out and the Protestant proprietor took hold of Fr. Page and held him until the constables arrived.

Fr. Page's first examination in the Newgate Prison yielded no information. At his trial on April 19, 1602, he was accused of going overseas, of being ordained, and of returning to England as a priest. In his defense, Fr. Page noted that he did not come under that law because he was born in Antwerp not England. Nevertheless, he was found guilty of high treason and condemned to the gallows. He was then returned to prison, and when Fr. Henry Floyd, a Jesuit in a nearby cell, learned that Fr. Page had been condemned to death, he was greatly disturbed. Fr. Page consoled him, saying: "Share my joy in such a happy outcome, which opens up the way to unending happiness." On the eve of Fr. Page's execution, the jailer permitted him to visit with Fr. Floyd; the two priests spent the night in prayer and early the next morning, Fr. Floyd celebrated Mass.

Ever since Fr. Page had made friends with Fr. Gerard, he thought of becoming a Jesuit. After returning to England as a priest, he had contacted the Jesuit superior, Fr. Henry Garnet, about entering the Society, and was told that he would have to go to Flanders for his noviceship. Now that he was about to be executed, he wrote out the Jesuit vow formula and signed it in Fr. Floyd's presence. When morning came he was dragged to Tyburn, the place of execution outside London, with two priests, Frs. Thomas Tichborne and Robert Watkinson. At the gallows a minister tried to engage him in a discussion of religion, but he would not hear of it. Facing the people, he made a public profession of his Catholicism and expressed his happiness in dying for so good a cause as the faith and priesthood. He also announced that he had recently taken his vows as a member of the Society of Jesus. As he was pronouncing the name Jesus, the cart was drawn from under him and he remained hanging until dead. Then his body was dismembered.

Fr. Francis Page was beatified by Pope Pius XI on December 15, 1929, and his memorial is celebrated on December 1, with his brothers who also met martyrdom in England and Wales.

Prayer

Almighty, eternal God, you chose from the people of England and Wales Blessed Francis Page and his companions to be made like Christ, who died to save the world. Listen to their prayers; strengthen your Church by the same faith and love that strengthened them, and bless it always with your gift of unity. We ask this through our Lord Jesus Christ, your Son, who lives and reigns with you and the Holy Spirit, one God, for ever and ever.

April 22

The Blessed Virgin Mary

Mother of the Society of Jesus

At all important junctures in the life of St. Ignatius, our Lady had an important role to play. Ignatius' love and devotion to her was such that he placed himself and his Society under her protection and asked her to care for it as a mother cares for her children. The Society celebrates Mary's maternal protection on April 22, the date on which Ignatius and his companions pronounced their first vows as Jesuits.

Shortly after Ignatius accepted election as general of the Society of Jesus on April 19, 1541, he and his five companions in Rome made plans to pronounce their religious vows. On April 22, Friday of Easter week, having made a pilgrimage to the seven churches, they finally arrived at St. Paul Outside-the-Walls, where they confessed to each other. Ignatius as the newly elected general celebrated Mass at our Lady's altar.

At the moment of Communion, St. Ignatius held the consecrated Host and paten in his left hand and the formula of his profession in his right. Facing his kneeling companions, he said: "I, Ignatius of Loyola, promise to almighty God and the Sovereign Pontiff, his Vicar on earth, before the Virgin Mother and the entire court of heaven, and in the presence of the Society, perpetual poverty, chastity, and obedience, according to the manner of life contained in the bull of the Society of our Lord Jesus and in the Constitutions adopted and to be adopted. Moreover, I promise special obedience to the Sovereign Pontiff with regard to the missions as set forth in the bull. I likewise promise to undertake the instruction of children in the rudiments of the faith according to the bull and Constitutions." Then each of the other five recited his vows and at the end, St. Ignatius offered each Holy Communion. These were the first vows taken in the Society of Jesus.

St. Ignatius' love for our Lady did not begin with his convalescence at Loyola after his injury at Pamplona. As a Spaniard he was brought up to love our Lady, but it was at Loyola that the worldly courtier became an earnest pilgrim seeking to follow Christ. The adventurous lives of the saints, which he had been reading, so appealed to his chivalrous nature that he decided that he too could be another St. Dominic or another St. Francis of Assisi. Of great significance to him in this newly made resolve was the fact that our Lady and Child appeared to him one night in August or September 1521. Though he has not left us many details concerning his vision, St. Ignatius does tell us that was the night of his conversion. In speaking about the event many years later, in 1555, he notes that

110   Jesuit Saints & Martyrs

he "clearly saw the likeness of our Lady with the holy Child Jesus, and because of this vision he enjoyed an excess of consolation for a remarkably long time. He felt so great a loathsomeness for all his past life, especially for the deeds of the flesh, that it seemed to him that all the images that had been previously imprinted on his mind were now erased." Because of this night of transformation the wounded soldier pledged his allegiance to a new Captain.

St. Ignatius' "vigil of arms" before the Black Madonna of Montserrat, on the eve of the Annunciation, March 24–25, 1522, was his self-dedication to our Lady and her Son. That night he became our Lady's knight, and while he sought her patronage and that of her Son, he likewise professed his total commitment to them—a commitment he inviolably kept to the end of his life. As a pilgrim praying in the cold cave of Manresa during 1522 and 1523, God granted him many spiritual favors. Among these were frequent visits of our Lady to encourage him in his resolve. As a student in Paris, he and his companions chose to pronounce their private vows of chastity, of poverty, and of going to the Holy Land on our Lady's great feast of the Assumption, August 15, 1534.

After St. Ignatius' ordination and prior to celebrating his first Mass, his constant prayer was that his heavenly Mother should deign "to place him next to her Son." And when the time came for him to celebrate his first Mass in Rome, he did not choose to celebrate it at the tomb of St. Peter, but chose the altar of our Lady in the church of St. Mary Major. This was on December 25, 1538. And when he pronounced his vows as a Jesuit on April 22, 1541, again it was at our Lady's altar, "in the presence of the Virgin Mother."

That these events in St. Ignatius' life and in the life of the early Jesuits should be associated with our Lady is no coincidence. St. Ignatius deliberately chose those dates and those places because he recognized that he and his companions needed our Lady's continued protection. The early Jesuits followed their founder's footsteps in loving the Mother of God.

In 1966 the Thirty-first General Congregation of the Society urged its members to "trust in the patronage of the Blessed Virgin Mary in their assigned tasks and activities, and everywhere show more and more clearly the role of the mother of the Savior in the economy of salvation. For in holy Church and in our tradition the Virgin Mary 'holds a place which is the highest after Christ and yet very close to us.'"

Of all the Jesuits who have written about Mary, the words of St. Peter Canisius are among the most impressive. In an exhortation to his fellow Jesuits he told them: "All in our Society have had and ought to have, an outstanding devotion to Mary, our mother, our mistress, our patroness. . . . No one more pure in body and soul, or more innocent, or perfect; no one so filled with grace, or so near and united or more pleasing to God. No mother ever had more sons, no one was so blessed or showed more fidelity. None was ever so holy, beautiful, fair, so honored, and endowed with the gifts of the Holy Spirit. No mother ever had more love for her Son. . . . Mother of the living, full of grace, begetter of life, mother of God, our mother, who loves us and because of that love prays to God on our behalf and pleads for us. Mistress of the universe, queen of heaven and of the angels, mother of mercy, refuge of sinners, our advocate and gate of heaven."

Prayer

Almighty and everlasting God, you chose the Virgin Mary to be the mother of your eternal Word. Give us strength to be servants of that Word in the Society of Jesus, which is consecrated to your glory in the presence of Mary, our mother. We ask this through our Lord Jesus Christ, your Son, who lives and reigns with you and the Holy Spirit, one God, for ever and ever.

April 24

S. G. Adalbert Mary Baudiss 1842–1926

Adalbert Mary Baudiss was born in the town of Bojany na Bukowinie, in the Ukraine, on April 14, 1842. As a youth he studied at the Jesuit school in Lwów, and served Mass at the Jesuit church of Sts. Peter and Paul, where he quickly became friends with the brother sacristan. In their conversations he and the brother often spoke of religious matters and at times read from spiritual books, recited the rosary, or prayed before the Blessed Sacrament. In later years, Fr. Baudiss remembered this kind and humble brother and acknowledged that it was he who had first taught him how to pray. Because of this association, Adalbert began to think about entering the Society. At that time the Polish Jesuits of Galicia did not have their own novitiate. When Adalbert decided to enter, he was sent to the Austrian province's novitiate at Baumgartenberg, near Linz. He began his noviceship on September 12, 1856; he was only fourteen-and-a-half years old. His older brother, Clement, joined him at the novitiate the following year.

In 1858 Adalbert's province opened its own novitiate and scholasticate at Stara Wieś, and the Polish novices at Baumgartenberg returned home. Adalbert was not yet seventeen when he finished his two years of novitiate and had to wait until the spring of 1859 to pronounce his three religious vows. He remained at Stara Wieś to study the classics, and in 1861 began his course in philosophy. In 1864 he was sent to the Jesuit school at Tarnopol, where he helped prefect students, assisted the librarian, and taught French. In 1867 he added history,

Greek, and Latin to his teaching schedule. For his theological studies he went to Cracow in 1869 and was ordained to the priesthood on September 10, 1871, in the historic Wawel cathedral. Finally, he completed his long years of Jesuit training in 1873, when he was thirty-one years old.

Fr. Baudiss spent the next eleven years at the scholasticate in Stara Wieś. During his early years there his tasks were varied: he taught and heard examinations, was spiritual director for the young Jesuits, gave days of recollection and retreats, and was assistant to the master of novices. In 1878 he became master, one of the more important positions among Jesuits because it is the master's office to teach the novices the fundamentals of the religious life and to guide them in prayer. Fr. Baudiss fulfilled this office until 1884, when Providence called him to an even more important work, a task totally unexpected and delicate.

In the part of Poland known as Galicia there were fourteen Greek Catholic monasteries of St. Basil, but only sixty-one monks. Most of the monks were far advanced in age and for some time they had been living under relaxed rules. In some cases they lived in extreme poverty. For years they had no novices and it appeared that the congregation would soon become extinct. The archbishop of Lwów made a canonical visitation of the monasteries and was deeply distressed by the sad plight in which he found the Basilians. Not knowing what else to do, he turned to the Holy See. Pope Leo XIII studied the problem and agreed that the Basilian congregation had to be reorganized, but the provincial of the Basilians, who was himself elderly and in poor health, lacked the physical energy to carry out so radical a renewal. The pope then turned to the Polish Jesuits in Galicia for advice and help. Fr. Baudiss was chosen to assist the Basilians in their reorganization.

This was a difficult assignment but coming from the pope, he gladly accepted it. The pope had decided that the cradle of the reorganized congregation was to be the monastery at Dobromil and, thus, Fr. Baudiss was sent there in 1884. He was appointed assistant rector and assistant master of novices. It was inevitable that in the beginning there should be some friction, but it was not the result of what Fr. Baudiss did. He was a Roman Catholic who was being asked to reform Greek Catholics; a Pole who was being set to reorganize Ukrainians; a Jesuit who was to revive a congregation totally different from his own. His presence among the Basilians was viewed as the product of "Jesuit intrigue." Fr. Baudiss made it clear, however, that he was not interested in polonizing the Ukrainians, but that his concern was to revive their congregation and renew them in the spiritual life. He respected their Greek Catholic customs and traditions, learned Ukrainian so that he could give conferences to the monks, and thoroughly mastered their religious rule to better lead them. In a few years, the Basilian congregation began to live again.

In 1889 Fr. Baudiss was made superior of the monastery at Lawrów, but in 1892 returned to Dobromil to teach German and history. In the following year he became superior of the community and prefect of studies, and in 1896 novice master. by 1901, after Fr. Baudiss had been among the Basilians seventeen years, their common efforts in renewal bore phenomenal fruit: there were 67 priests, 40 scholastics, and 70 brothers, a total of 177. So greatly did the Basilians love him that they asked him to serve as provincial of their congregation, but in his humility Fr. Baudiss declined. Now that the members were of a new generation and brought up in their true spirit, it was time for them to continue on their own and in 1902 Fr. Baudiss left Dobromil for the Jesuit school at Chiróv.

In 1905 he was sent to Iasi in the Moldavian portion of Romania to be rector of the diocesan seminary, and with his usual prudence successfully smoothed out the difficulty that existed between the local bishop and the Society. With that task accomplished he was made provincial of Galicia in the fall of 1906, and when his term was completed, he became instructor of tertians at Tarnopol. From there he returned, during the early days of World War I, to Chiróv. In 1915, now seventy-three years of age, Fr. Baudiss was once more at Stara Wieś, where he remained until his death. He was spiritual father of the Jesuits and chaplain to a nearby convent of nuns.

One morning in the spring of 1923, as he got out of bed he felt dizzy and fell, injuring his hip. Through patient convalescence it mended somewhat and he was again able to get about. In time, however, his loss of hearing prevented him from hearing confessions. Then his feet gave out and he was no longer able to go to the sisters for Mass. Eventually, he had to give up saying Mass and was confined to bed.

After seventy years as a Jesuit, many of them in guiding younger Jesuits and Basilians in the way of holiness, Fr. Baudiss, on April 25, 1926, surrendered his soul to Jesus, his one and only love. The cause of Fr. Adalbert Baudiss is now under consideration.

April 25

Ven. Gaspar Pais 1593–1635
Ven. John Pereira 1601–1635
Martyrs of Ethiopia

The first Jesuit mission in Ethiopia, headed by Bishop Andrew de Oviedo during the mid-sixteenth century, proved a failure. It was not until Fr. Pedro Paez, a Spaniard by birth, went there in 1603 that the Jesuits began to meet with some success. By converting Negus (Emperor) Susenyos to Catholicism in 1622, Fr. Paez cleared the way for Patriarch Afonso Mendes to enter the country.

It was in 1624 that Fr. Gaspar Pais, a relative of Fr. Paez, arrived in Ethiopia. He was born in Covilhã, Portugal, in 1593, but when he was twelve his family moved to Goa, India. It was there that he entered the Society on November 23, 1607. He did all his Jesuit studies at St. Paul's College in Goa and after ordination requested to work in Ethiopia, now that missionaries were again welcomed there. The work of Fr. Pais among the Ethiopians in Fremona bore encouraging results. After a month's labor he converted more than 400 to Catholicism. Equally fruitful was his ministry among the Agau, a semi-subdued tribe in the north. His letters to the superior general in Rome, during the years 1625 and 1626, describe the missionaries' many activities. He notes in one of them that the Jesuits were busy translating the Bible and devotional books for popular use, and that the negus had subsidized their printing press.

Shortly before his death in 1632 Susenyos permitted the country to revert to its former beliefs, a change that was to bring much suffering to the missionaries. When his son Fasilidas came to the throne, he confiscated the Jesuit houses and properties—these had been given them by Susenyos—and in 1633 ordered the Jesuits all to assemble at their central headquarters in Fremona. They could be thus kept under surveillance. Before Fasilidas expelled them from the country in 1634, seven of the twenty Jesuits, then in Ethiopia, went underground. One of these was Fr. Pais. He found refuge with a certain Tecla Manuel, an Ethiopian sympathetic toward the missionaries and whose vast estate was near the town of Assa. On that estate Fr. Pais found a cave for a hiding place and from it he quietly moved among the Portuguese and other Catholics scattered in the vicinity. In time he was joined by Frs. John Pereira and Bruno Bruni.

Fr. Pereira was, like Fr. Pais, a Portuguese. He had been born in Cela, near Lisbon, in 1601, had entered the Society in Coimbra on March 12, 1619, and had come to Ethiopia as a missionary in 1628. Fr. Bruni was an Italian born near Rome in 1590. Because the three priests remained under Tecla Manuel's protection, they were able to exercise their ministry in relative safety. The negus, indignant because some Jesuits had outwitted him, gave orders that they were to be found and promised rewards to anyone delivering them into his hands. When Tecla Manuel's term as governor was over, he was succeeded by his brother Melcha Krestos, a rabid schismatic. Tecla informed the three Jesuits of his brother's hostility and urged them, since Melcha knew that the missionaries had been living on the estate, to separate and search for a safer area. The priests agreed to leave but not to separate. They found another remote spot which they thought suitable; it was in a deep valley protected by thick underbrush and surrounded by tree-covered hills.

The missionaries were at their new refuge only four days when they were discovered on the morning of April 25, 1635. Melcha Krestos arrived with more than a hundred armed men and remained under cover until dawn brightened the sky. Then Melcha alone walked toward the huts where the Jesuits and some

Catholic Ethiopians had gathered for Mass. Fr. Bruni noticed Melcha approaching, and thinking he was bringing them a message went out to greet him. At that moment the armed men ambushed him; he fell to the ground with fifteen spear wounds in his body. Hearing the cries outside, Fr. Pais, who was about to begin Mass, rushed out and he was instantly killed by a spear through the heart. The men next converged on Fr. Pereira and when the few Catholics there tried to surround and protect him, he forbade them to do so. Wounded in the lower chest and legs, he too collapsed to the ground. Presuming their victims dead, the assassins withdrew from the scene. The Catholics then went to the bodies and found Frs. Pereira and Bruni alive and carried them off to care for them. That afternoon they buried Fr. Pais.

Fr. Pereira never recovered from his wounds and on May 1, a week after the ambush, feeling that death was approaching asked to be taken to the cave that was their chapel. He spent the day there in prayer, and shortly before dying on May 2 said to those near him: "Do not weep for me; my blood is flowing for the glory of God." Fr. Bruni survived his wounds and lived to meet another martyrdom five years later. Fr. Bruni's letter (July 1639) to Fr. General Muzio Vitelleschi in Rome is his eye-witness account of how his two brother Jesuits had died.

The cause of these martyrs of Ethiopia, Frs. Gaspar Pais, John Pereira, Bp. Apollinaris de Almeida and five others was introduced in Rome on June 19, 1902.

April 27

St. Peter Canisius 1521–1597

Fr. Peter Canisius was a theologian, preacher, author, and administrator, who used his talents for the restoration of Catholicism in Germany and Austria. Peter Kanis (Canisius is the latinized form of his name) was born in Nijmegen, the Netherlands, on May 8, 1521, and his first introduction to education took place in his native city. In January 1536 he traveled to Germany, where he matriculated at the University of Cologne, and by May 1540 earned a master's degree. Thinking seriously about the priesthood, he decided to remain at the university for his theological studies. Word reached him of a new religious order calling itself the Society of Jesus, and eager to learn more about it he went to Mainz to meet Fr. Peter Favre, one of its founding members. After a long conversation,

P.Petrus Canisius S.I.Belga, perpetuus Hæreticorum malleus, appellatus Germaniæ Apostolus, & acerrimus Ecclesiæ defensor. Obijt Friburgi in Helvetia 21 Decemb: 1597. æt: 76.

St. Peter Canisius

Fr. Favre judged the young man a suitable candidate and guided him through the Spiritual Exercises of its founder. During the second week of the retreat, Peter came to the decision that he too must be a Jesuit and Fr. Favre accepted him as a novice. It was May 8, 1543, Peter's twenty-second birthday.

Peter returned to Cologne, finished his studies in theology and was ordained on June 12, 1546. For some months prior to his ordination he taught Scripture and while at Cologne he published new editions of texts of Cyril of Alexandria and Leo the Great. Between February and June 1547, he was the theological consultant of Cardinal Otto Truchsess at the Council of Trent. From there he went to Rome, where Fr. Ignatius assigned him to teach at the Society's first school in Messina, Sicily. He remained in Messina until recalled to Rome to undertake a new task. In September 1549 Pope Paul III asked him to return to Germany and defend the Catholic Church against the attacks of the Reformers. For twenty-five years the Church in Germany had suffered from the rise and spread of Protestantism. Fr. Canisius was asked to halt the defections among Catholics and to bring back those who had already strayed. This was an enormous task to assign to a single individual.

Fr. Canisius and companions arrived in Ingolstadt, Germany, on November 13, 1549, and immediately began teaching at the university. To his sadness he discovered that the Catholics were so in name only—they had not practiced their faith in years. He judged that it would only be by preaching that he could win them back, so whatever time he had free from his university duties he devoted to explaining from the pulpit the fundamental teachings of the Catholic faith. Within months of his arrival, the number of those attending Mass and instructions increased and for this he offered sincere thanks to God.

In February 1552 he was assigned to Vienna to accomplish there what he had done in Ingolstadt. In the Austrian capital he found churches that had small congregations and others that had been closed because of a lack of priests. He set about finding candidates for the priesthood and established a seminary next to the Jesuit college. Besides his duties as an educator, he was also appointed court preacher. Such was his success in Vienna that, when the city needed a new bishop, both pope and king thought of nominating the thirty-two-year-old Canisius to the post. He offered, instead, to serve as administrator of the diocese until a suitable candidate could be found.

During his years in Vienna, Fr. Canisius produced his most famous book, his Catechism. It became Germany' and Austria's most popular book because it satisfied a most urgent need. Written in Latin, the book appeared in April 1555 with the title *Summary of Christian Doctrine*. It contained questions and answers and was intended as a manual for college students. The topics not disputed by the Protestants received relatively short answers, but those under dispute were treated at great length. It was translated into German in 1556 and an adaptation was published for secondary schools, entitled *Shorter Catechism*. Another adaptation was published for children in their early years of religious instruction, called *Catholic Catechism*. These catechisms had some 200 printings during the lifetime of Fr. Canisius and continued to be reprinted until the nineteenth century. Throughout German-speaking lands the name Canisius became synonymous with catechism.

In July 1555 he went to Prague to open a college. Then in June 1556 he was appointed provincial superior of Germany, a province that took in Swabia, Bavaria, Bohemia, Austria, and Hungary. The office demanded that he visit the Jesuit houses under his jurisdiction, supervise expansion, and choose the cities for new colleges. Not only did he stimulate the Society's growth, but he made it a leading force in Germany's Counter Reformation.

During his term as provincial, Fr. Canisius represented the Church at ecumenical gatherings with Protestants at Regensburg (1556–1557) and at Worms (1557). From 1559 to 1566 he resided in Augsburg, where he was also cathedral preacher. He went to the Council of Trent in May 1562 as a theological expert, but returned sooner than he had planned. In his absence the Protestants again became active and the Catholics clamored for his return.

Fr. Canisius was provincial for fourteen years. Relieved of that burden in 1569, he went to Innsbruck, where he devoted his time to writing and preaching. He visited Rome in the spring of 1573 to discuss the German situation with the pope, and during these meetings he recommended more seminaries in Germany. He believed that the better the preparation of priests, the better the Catholics in the parishes. He returned to Innsbruck and resumed his writing and preaching.

In November 1580 he was asked to go to Fribourg, Switzerland, to open a new college. He had to collect the funds, select the site, and supervise the construction of the buildings. The school opened in 1582 and he named it after St. Michael, one of his favorite saints. Again he was occupied chiefly with preaching and weekly he ascended the pulpit in the church of St. Nicholas. He continued to preach until the spring of 1589, when poor health forced him to stop. He was now sixty-eight years old. Though he suffered a stroke in 1591 that forced him to use a cane, he continued to prepare manuscripts for the press. In September 1597 he was faced with additional physical problems. He became ill with dropsy, suffered from congestion of the lungs, and had ulcers in his throat. He could no longer say Mass. On December 21, 1597, in his seventy-sixth year, he died peacefully in the Lord. During his lifetime he founded eighteen colleges and authored thirty-seven books. His greatest achievement for the Church, however, was his preaching, and it was this apostolate that helped restore Catholicism in Germany and Austria.

Fr. Canisius was buried in Fribourg in the church of St. Nicholas. In 1625 his remains were transferred to the new church of St. Michael and were placed in the middle of the choir. Prior to his beatification by Pope Pius IX in 1864, his relics were placed beneath the altar in the chapel dedicated to the Sacred Heart of Jesus. Today that chapel is dedicated to him. He was canonized by Pope Pius

XI on May 21, 1925, and declared a Doctor of the Church in recognition of his writings in defense of the faith. The memorial of St. Peter Canisius is liturgically celebrated in the Society on April 27.

Prayer

God of patience and compassion, send us in our own day men of vision and wisdom like Saint Peter Canisius, to sow the good seed of your word among the peoples of the world, so that they may win them to you the living God, and to the one whom you sent, Jesus Christ, your Son, who lives and reigns with you and the Holy Spirit, one God, for ever and ever.

April 28

Ven. Emmanuel Padial 1661–1725

Emmanuel Padial was born on Good Friday, April 15, 1661, in Granada, Spain, the youngest of seven children. He attended the Jesuit college in his native city and at age twenty, when he completed his courses in philosophy and theology, he entered the Jesuit novitiate in Seville on May 5, 1681. During his early years as a Jesuit, God granted him the extraordinary gift of mystical prayer—a gift that remained with him throughout his life.

After Emmanuel pronounced his vows in the Society, he went to Carmona to review his studies in the humanities. But finding that the climate did not agree with him, he moved to Granada in August 1683. Except for his years as a novice and the three months at Carmona, his entire Jesuit life was spent in his home city. Once back in Granada he reviewed philosophy and theology and in 1687 was ordained. From 1687 to 1692 he taught grammar at the college, his alma mater. He was then advanced to the position of professor of philosophy and in 1698 appointed to the chair of theology. In 1708 he relinquished this last position to assume the office of rector of the college for three years. In 1711 he began his work as a parish priest, an apostolate he fulfilled until his death.

Fr. Padial's life was one of great contrasts: he was always jovial and outgoing when speaking with others, yet privately he led a severe and uncommonly mortified life. His dedication to Christ crucified led him to celebrate Fridays with special austerities. He used instruments of penance on his body, allowed himself little sleep at night, and fasted rigorously. On the feasts of the apostles and favorite saints, he went without food the entire day, and for feasts of our

Lord or of our Lady, he fasted for three days to prepare himself to celebrate it properly. When he did eat, he limited himself to scraps of bread and soup.

Just as Fr. Padial was given to penance and mortification, he was also given to prayer, and God responded generously with extraordinary gifts. He had great devotion to the Child Jesus and enthusiastically promoted this devotion among his clients. It was said that just a glance at a picture of the Christ Child was enough to transport him into ecstasy. He had a very scrupulous conscience and a great fear and hatred of sin, yet he was the city's favorite confessor and a much sought-after director of souls.

The last five years of Fr. Padial's life were an agony. In spring 1720 he began to suffer from rheumatism that caused pain in his legs and arms. He had difficulty in getting about, but with his strong will he managed to continue his parish work. By April 1722 he was confined to his bed for a prolonged period. Consequently, he developed abscesses, which demanded frequent lancing and brought him great discomfort. When he was a young priest, he had asked our Lord to grant him a share in his suffering; that prayer was now being answered. There was no remedy for his illness and the best the physician could do was to try to lessen the pain. During Fr. Padial's last four months all movement was impossible. So acute was the suffering that he remained immobile as if paralyzed. Throughout those many days and nights of suffering, he was clear headed and continued his jovial conversation with all who came to visit. When his friends were about to leave he asked them to remember him in their prayers, and to ask God to grant him the patience to bear his suffering. Finally, on April 28, 1725, at age sixty-four, after forty-four years in the Society, Fr. Padial yielded his soul to his crucified Lord. To the Jesuits who had lived with him, and to the faithful of Granada who had known him, Fr. Padial became the model of the heroic follower of Christ.

Fr. Emmanuel Padial's cause was introduced in Rome in 1749.

April 30

Ven. Abraham de Georgiis 1563–1595

Martyr of Ethiopia

Fr. Abraham de Georgiis was the first of the eight Jesuit martyrs of Ethiopia to die for Christ. He was a Maronite Christian, born in Aleppo, Syria, in 1563. He went to Rome for his studies and there entered the Jesuit novitiate of Sant'

Andrea on December 28, 1582. As a young Jesuit he studied in Florence and in Rome. After ordination, probably in the first half of 1591, he requested to go to the missions, and in July of that year, he left Rome for Lisbon, Portugal, to set sail for India. It was while in Lisbon that he learned, he said, through an internal experience, that he was to offer his blood as a sacrifice to the Lord.

Fr. de Georgiis arrived in Goa, India, in 1592, and worked among the St. Thomas Christians in that country's Malabar region. His labors there only lasted about a year, since he was recalled to Goa and in 1594 assigned to Ethiopia. The earlier mission of Patriarch Andrew de Oviedo to Ethiopia had been a failure and the country's rulers still refused to permit Catholic missionaries to evangelize the land. The only Jesuit in Ethiopia at the time was Fr. Francisco Lopes, a septuagenarian, residing alone in Fremona, and serving as pastor to the Portuguese families scattered there. Fr. de Georgiis was assigned to relieve the aging priest. He was well fitted for the task; he was fluent in Arabic, Hebrew, and Syriac and his features were such that he could easily pass the many Turkish checkpoints.

Fr. de Georgiis left Goa on January 6, 1595, for Diu, on India's northwest shore. He was disguised as an Armenian merchant, sporting a full beard and traveling with a servant, an Abyssinian youth. From Diu he took passage in March on an Indian merchant ship going to Massawa, an island off the Ethiopian coast, the country's main port of entry.

One day in April, not long after his arrival in Massawa, he judged it safe to go to the mainland and find his fellow Jesuit in Fremona. He requested permission of the island's Turkish governor and it was readily given. But before the boat was midway across the strait, the governor, because of suspicions raised against the priest, sent out a boat to overtake him. When Fr. de Georgiis was back on the island, the governor asked him whether he was a Moslem or a Christian. He answered that he was a Christian and was ready to die for the Christian faith. The governor tried to convince the priest to become a Moslem, assuring him that his goods would be returned and that he would be given safe passage to any port he chose. The missionary, however, would have nothing to do with these promises and retorted: "You will never get me to follow the laws of Mohammed. They are unworthy of men. I regard them in the same way that I regard the soles of my shoes." Confronted with such unshakable fortitude, the governor ordered him to be beheaded.

After some weeks in prison, Fr. de Georgiis was led outside the town and made to kneel while the executioner unsheathed his cutlass. Witnesses reported that the cutlass broke on the first attempt to behead the priest. On the next attempt the second cutlass also broke, though a slight wound was produced. The third was successful. It was April 30, 1595. The body was then taken to a nearby island and disposed of.

The cause of Fr. Abraham de Georgiis, together with that of seven other Jesuits martyred in Ethiopia, was introduced in Rome in 1902.

May

May 4

Bl. Joseph Mary Rubio 1864–1929

Fr. Joseph Mary Rubio Peralta was commonly known as the "Apostle of Madrid." He was born on July 22, 1864, at Dalías, in the province of Almería, southern Spain. In 1875 he went to the city of Almería, the provincial capital, to begin his studies, but because he wanted to be a priest he transferred the following year, when he was twelve, to the minor seminary in the same city. In 1879 he went to the major seminary in Granada and spent the next seven years studying philosophy, theology, and canon law. While in Granada he lived with Fr. Joachim Torres Asensio, a professor at the seminary, but when Fr. Torres was offered a position in the cathedral in Madrid in 1886, Joseph moved with him and there he finished his studies and was ordained on September 24, 1887.

Fr. Rubio was assistant pastor at Chinchón from 1887 to 1889, then became pastor in Estremera in 1889. In 1890 he was called to the seminary in Madrid where he taught Latin, philosophy, and pastoral theology for four years. He was drawn to the Jesuits and thought of entering the Society of Jesus, but because of the obligation of gratitude he felt toward Fr. Torres, who was now living with him, he was prevented from fulfilling that desire. Though he could not be a Jesuit in fact, he considered himself one in heart. In 1893 he became chaplain to a convent of Cistercian nuns, and there in the center of Madrid he began his unique pastoral ministry.

After the death of Fr. Torres in January 1906, there was now nothing to keep Fr. Rubio from becoming a Jesuit, thus he entered the Jesuit novitiate in Granada on October 11. He was forty-two years old and a priest with much experience. He pronounced his vows on October 12, 1908, spent the following year reviewing theology, and was assigned for a short time to the Jesuit residence in Seville. In 1911 he returned to Madrid and remained there for the next eighteen years.

Fr. Rubio exercised two important apostolates in Madrid, one in the confessional and the other in the pulpit. The lines standing outside his box were unusually long and among those waiting were aristocrats as well as simple folk. Masters and servants were equal when they met before Fr. Rubio's confessional, and the vast majority of them came to him more for spiritual direction than for absolution. As his fame grew so did the number of penitents. To be sure they would have a chance to speak with him, many came before the church doors were opened. He had similar appeal in the pulpit. Though Spain's best orators came to preach in the capital, the people preferred Fr. Rubio's simple and sincere sermons, which always touched their hearts. He helped prove that the simple sermon yields the best fruit. The people never tired of hearing him and he never tired of preaching to them about how they should love God, have devotion to the Blessed Sacrament or honor the Sacred Heart of Jesus.

Fr. Rubio's apostolate was not limited to the church building; he regularly visited the city's slums and there he preached to the homeless and the wretched. These unfortunates found a friend in him and weekly he was deluged with requests for help, ranging from someone in need of a place to sleep to some young girl's need of a dowry. All who came to him came because they knew he would help them.

Fr. Rubio organized an altar society called Marys of the Tabernacles, a group of some 6,000 women, who visited the hundreds of village churches in the suburbs and environs to see that the altars were properly appointed. For many of these churches the ladies provided the altar linens and Mass vestments. Fr. Rubio also directed a group which he called the Honor Guard of the Sacred Heart of Jesus. This group grew to a membership of over 5,000. Its prime purpose was to promote devotion to the Sacred Heart, but it was also active in the social apostolate. Its members provided scholarships and financial aid to schools, supplied dowries for poor girls, visited the sick and infirm, and organized parish missions and retreats.

No part of Madrid was untouched by Fr. Rubio's influence. It is said that during his forty-one years as a priest, he had helped 10,000 individuals along the road to perfection. He encouraged countless boys to enter the diocesan clergy and he sent many vocations to religious orders and congregations. During his last ten years he was spoken of as a miracle worker—such were the extraordinary events that were associated with him. The Madrilenians felt about him as the people of Ars felt toward their beloved curé, St. John Baptist Vianney.

While on a visit to the Jesuit novitiate at Aranjuez, where Fr. Rubio had gone for rest, he suffered an attack of angina on May 2, 1929, and died at 6:35 that evening. He was sixty-four years old and had been a Jesuit for twenty-three years. He was buried in the novitiate cemetery, but in 1953 his remains were taken to the professed house on Calle Maldonado in Madrid.

Fr. Joseph Mary Rubio was beatified by Pope John Paul II on October 6, 1985, and his memorial is liturgically celebrated on May 4.

Prayer

Father of mercies, who made Blessed Joseph your priest, a minister of reconciliation and a father of the poor, grant that we, filled with the same spirit, may manifest your love to all and undertake the care of those who are rejected. We ask this through our Lord Jesus Christ, your Son, who lives and reigns with you and the Holy Spirit, one God, for ever and ever.

May 8

S. G. John Philip Roothaan 1785–1853

Fr. John Philip Roothaan was the twenty-first general of the Society of Jesus. Since he had been elected fifteen years after the Society's restoration, a critical phase in its history, he had to see to its growth and development. So successful was he in guiding the Society during those years that Jesuits commonly refer to him as their second founder.

Pope Clement XIV, yielding to political pressure from several European rulers, had suppressed the Society in 1773, and when John was born in Amsterdam on November 23, 1785, the suppression was in its twelfth year. He received his elementary education in a classroom operated by Fr. Adam Beckers, a local parish priest who had been a Jesuit prior to the Society's suppression. From him John received the foundations of a good education as well as spiritual guidance. In 1796 he attended secondary school and mastered Latin and Greek, and then in 1800 entered Amsterdam's Athenaeum, where he studied philosophy and Hebrew. John was preparing for the seminary, but he was not yet certain where he should go. When he learned from Fr. Beckers that the Society of Jesus still existed in White Russia (today's Belarus) because Catherine the Great had refused to promulgate the papal brief of suppression, and that his priest-friend had recently been readmitted, John changed his mind about the diocesan clergy and planned to go to White Russia. He left Amsterdam on May 29, 1804, and traveled by ship to Riga, arriving on June 20, where Polish Jesuits met him. From there he went to Dunaburg (today's Daugavpils, Latvia), and arrived at the novitiate on June 30.

After two years as a novice, John pronounced his vows on June 21, 1806, and for the next three years taught at the Jesuit school in Dunaburg. In the fall of 1809 he went to Polotsk for theology and was ordained on January 27, 1812.

Because Napoleon's army was approaching Polotsk on its march to Moscow, the Jesuits there had to disband. Fr. Roothaan went to Pusza (Latvia), where a juniorate was temporarily set up in an old converted manor house, and there he taught Latin and Greek to young Jesuit scholastics. In August 1816 he was transferred to the college in Orsza, not far from Polotsk, and in 1818 was appointed preacher in the Jesuit church attached to the college. Though Napoleon had been defeated and Pope Pius VII had restored the Society on August 7, 1814, Fr. Roothaan remained in White Russia until the Jesuits were expelled from the country by Tsar Alexander I in 1820. After fourteen years with the Polish Jesuits, he left them in April 1820, and with a group of exiled scholastics arrived in Brig, Switzerland, on July 23.

At Brig Fr. Roothaan taught classics to the Jesuits still in training. Once he had mastered the German language (1822) he started giving missions in the rural parishes throughout the canton. In 1823 Fr. General Luigi Fortis appointed him to take over a college in Turin, Italy, which he did so successfully that during his six years as rector the school flourished; the student body grew from 30 in 1823 to 200 in 1829. In February 1829 he was called upon to take on a more important role. Fr. Fortis had just died and the Italian provincial Fr. Vincenzo Pavani was named vicar general. Since the latter had to guide the Society until a new general was elected, he appointed Fr. Roothaan vice-provincial of Italy. Fr. Roothaan considered himself insufficiently trained for his new task, but he obediently went to Rome, arriving on March 3, 1829. His one consolation was in knowing that this was a temporary assignment.

When the Society's delegates met in July to elect the new general, Fr. Roothaan was not yet forty-four years old, and was the second youngest in attendance. To his amazement, he was elected the Society's twenty-first general on July 9, 1829. For fifteen years, from 1814 to 1829, the Society had been trying to reestablish itself, and now with his election he was given the task of rebuilding the Society to the same status it had prior to its suppression.

During his twenty-four years as general, Fr. Roothaan placed great emphasis on the Spiritual Exercises of St. Ignatius as the basic means for reorganizing the Society. He published a new edition of the Exercises (1835) and wrote a commentary on them (1838). To help his Jesuit brethren gain the most from them, he wrote a booklet *On Meditation* (1836), which found great favor among Jesuits. To help strengthen the Jesuit school system, he revised its code of education, *Ratio Studiorum* (1832), and took an active part in the opening of several important colleges in the United States, for example, Fordham in the Bronx, Holy Cross in Worcester, St. Joseph's in Philadelphia, Loyola in Baltimore, and St. Louis University in St. Louis. When Bishop Simon Bruté of Vincennes asked him to take over a men's college in Notre Dame, Indiana, he declined, not only because of lack of manpower but also because he was not sure that a school in so remote a place could survive. He raised the Maryland mission into a province and made the St. Louis mission independent. He sent German Jesuits to open Marquette University in Milwaukee, Belgian Jesuits to work among the native peoples of America, and Italian Jesuits to open a mission in the Oregon Territory. In 1846, when Fr. Peter De Smet, the great Jesuit missionary among this country's native population, discovered a lake in northern Idaho, he respectfully named it Lake Roothaan. It is now known by the more popular name of Priest Lake.

Fr. Roothaan had equal concern for the work of the Society in other countries. He began a college in Calcutta, India, and sent missionaries to Algeria, Egypt, Australia, and Brazil.

After Fr. Roothaan guided the order for twenty-four years and supervised its expansion, the Society was well on its way to being what it once had been. By 1853 his strength, however, began to diminish. Now sixty-seven years old, he had slowed down considerably and began to walk with a stoop. On February 7 he suffered a cardiac affliction and for three months endured the agony of being almost constantly in pain. Throughout these days of torment, those attending him only heard words of resignation and surrender. On May 7 he again suffered severe pains in his heart and right side, and on the following day, when it was clear that he was dying, his Jesuit brethren gathered in his room to commend his soul to God. As he recited the invocations of his favorite prayer, *Soul of Christ,* he died peacefully in the hands of the Lord.

Fr. John Roothaan's cause has been introduced in Rome.

May 10

S. G. Stephen Le Fèvre 1597–1657

Fr. Stephen Le Fèvre was the first French Jesuit assigned to the Chinese mission and had been born in Mourières, near Avignon, on February 14, 1597. From a very early age he desired to be a priest, but his family was much too poor to give him an education. With his heart set on following Christ, young Stephen determined to work his way through school. He applied for a job at the Jesuit college in Avignon, and in exchange for his labor he asked only for room, board, and the privilege of attending class with the students. Thus he was given the classrooms to clean, allowing him to be free during the day to attend lectures. Stephen remained at the school for six years, and during that time he not only was a member of the sodality of our Lady but the sodalists elected him their prefect. Once he had become acquainted with the Jesuits and their manner of life, Stephen felt that he too was being called to be one of them, and on September 26, 1615, entered the novitiate in Avignon. Two years later he pronounced his vows and spent the following years teaching grammar. In 1623 he went to Lyons for two years of philosophy and in 1625 was again in Avignon studying theology in preparation for the priesthood.

During his second year of theology, Stephen's life took on an altogether unexpected course. In the summer of 1627, Fr. Sebastian Vieira, a missionary from Japan, stopped at Avignon on his way to Rome, where he was to inform the Jesuit general and the pope of the status of the Japanese mission. When Fr. Vieira spoke about Japan to the Jesuit seminarians, he touched Stephen's heart. On hearing the visitor speak of the sacrifices and the joys of missionary life, Stephen became convinced that this was what he ought to do and that very day he offered himself to Fr. Vieira for Japan. Stephen's provincial approved his decision and permitted him to be ordained early, after his second year of theology.

By January 1628 Fr. Le Fèvre was in Lisbon, Portugal, waiting for other missionaries to arrive, and in April, together with forty-three other Jesuits, set sail for Goa (India). Because the ship met contrary winds four months later they had to return to the port from which they had departed. This was a disappointment to the missionaries, but they were gladdened by the fact that there would be another sailing the following year. Sometime in early March 1629 the missionaries again gathered in Lisbon; this time the group was divided among nine ships. They set sail for Goa and arrived at their destination on October 21.

As soon as Fr. Le Fèvre landed in Goa he began his study of Japanese, and on April 6, 1630, sailed for Macao on the Chinese mainland. Upon arrival in September, he sadly learned that persecution was raging in Japan and that foreign missionaries were far from welcome. Japan was closed! China, however, was at peace, and since there was much work to be done there and many souls to be converted, Fr. Le Fèvre changed his field of labor. He devoted the next few weeks to learning Chinese and by the end of 1630 was on his way to Shanxi province.

Fr. Le Fèvre divided his labors between the Shanxi and Shaanxi provinces. His healthy constitution permitted him to imitate the poor Chinese in their simple diet of only vegetables and fruit. He learned their language and was soon preaching to them and instructing those who desired to become Christians. In 1635 he became superior of the Shaanxi mission and remained there until 1641, when he was sent to Peking (today's Beijing) to assist the Jesuit astronomer, Fr. Adam Schall. Fr. Schall had helped prepare the new Chinese calendar, and now with Fr. Le Fèvre's assistance, they translated several scientific books into Chinese.

While Fr. Le Fèvre was in Peking, his Christians in Shaanxi badgered the Jesuit superior for his return. After three years of hearing this same plea the superior finally yielded, and in 1644 Fr. Le Fèvre returned to them and spent the remaining thirteen years of his life with them.

Toward the end of 1656, when the missionary was in his sixtieth year, his health began to fail. After so many years of mortification his body was burnt out. Though weak and sick, he did not want to leave his faithful in Hanzhong. As the months passed he became weaker, and sometime in late April or early May 1657, Fr. Inacio da Costa, a Portuguese Jesuit stationed at nearby Xi'an, asked him to come and stay with him. Not only would he find some rest but in a larger city he could receive better medical treatment. Fr. Le Fèvre's Hanzhong Christians prepared a litter so that their priest could be transported to Fr. Costa's parish with the least discomfort. On May 10, Ascension Thursday morning, Fr. Le Fèvre, undoubtedly knowing that this was to be his last day on earth, told one of the Christians to go to Fr. Costa and thank him for his kindness, and to explain that he, Fr. Le Fèvre, no longer had any need of his assistance.

The priest then went to his room and penned his last letter to his priest-friend, to be delivered after his death. In it he told Fr. Costa that he was about to go to the Lord and after thanking him for all he had done for him over the years, he humbly asked forgiveness for his failures.

With great difficulty he then went to church to celebrate his last Mass. After removing his vestments he knelt before the altar to make his thanksgiving. Since the people remained in church with him, he picked up a small tree branch and holding it in his hand, turned and spoke to his parishioners for the last time. He encouraged them to remain steadfast in the faith and in the new life they had received in baptism. With the branch he slowly made the sign of the cross over his congregation, but the only words he was able to say were "Jesus, Mary." As he uttered these names, he peacefully closed his eyes and his body gently collapsed to the floor in front of the altar. It was noon and Fr. Le Fèvre was with God.

The Shaanxi Christians admired their missionary during life and looked upon him as a saint in death. He was equally beloved by the non-Christians, who honored him by erecting a pagoda in his memory. Fr. Stephen Le Fèvre's cause is under consideration.

May 11

St. Francis Jerome 1642–1716

Fr. Francis Jerome looked upon all of Naples as his parish and its 500,000 inhabitants as his parishioners. The first of eleven children, he was born in Grottaglie, near Taranto, in southern Italy, on December 17, 1642, of a family whose name was De Geronimo. His early education was in his native city, but when he was ten or eleven he went to live with the Theatine Fathers and in return for his room and board he served as sacristan in their church. The Theatines conducted missions in the neighboring towns and young Francis often accompanied them as catechist. In 1658, when he was sixteen, he received tonsure, indicating his intention to become a priest, and in 1659, with the recommendation of the Theatines, he went to the Jesuit school at Taranto to begin his classical and philosophical studies. In 1665 he transferred to the Jesuit college in Naples to study civil and church law, and in the following year, when the Jesuits were looking for some exemplary young priest to act as prefect for the sons of the Italian nobility attending the school, they offered the position to Francis. He accepted it and on March 20, 1666, he was ordained to the priesthood and began supervising the noble youths. After having known the Jesuits for more than ten years, Fr. Jerome was inclined to become one of them and, thus, he entered the novitiate on July 1, 1670, at age twenty-eight.

After only one year in the novitiate, he was sent to the diocese of Lecce to assist an experienced home missioner in giving retreats and missions. The years 1671 to 1674 were spent preaching in southern Italy. Little did he know that the remainder of his life was to follow this same pattern. He returned to Naples to refresh his knowledge of theology in preparation for his final examination, which he successfully passed in the spring of 1676. He was then assigned to his "Naples mission," and began a most fruitful apostolate that extended over the next forty years until his death.

Fr. Jerome's "Naples mission" involved a variety of tasks. For one, he was in charge of the sodality of artisans, which met for Mass and a sermon each Sunday in a chapel beneath the Gesù church. It was from this group that he chose assistants to help him in his apostolate in the city. Every Sunday and holy-day evening he preached in one of the city's public squares or busy thoroughfares, where the people could easily gather. He likewise promoted the monthly General Communion. It was the custom in the seventeenth century to receive Holy Communion only once a month, and at the Gesù this took place on the Third Sunday. Fr. Jerome spent the week before the designated day reminding the faithful that the coming Sunday was General Communion day and exhorting them to attend. He spent Monday and Saturday preaching in the streets of Naples, and Tuesday to Friday he preached in the suburbs. He sometimes gave up to forty short sermons in a single day. When the Third Sunday arrived no one was surprised to see that the Masses at the Gesù were crowded.

In addition to these duties there were others. Whenever a fleet of galleys came into Naples Bay, he visited the slaves and criminals chained to their places and tried to console and relieve their suffering in whatever way he could. At times he was successful in getting them to leave the ship and attend Mass in a nearby church.

Fr. Jerome knew there was no sinner who could not experience God's grace, so he ventured, accompanied by his sodalists, into those areas of Naples where vice predominated to preach God's forgiveness. Many were the sinners who were touched by his word and by God's grace to give up their sinful lives. When he had requested to go to the Indian or Japanese missions, the response he received from Fr. General was: "The Kingdom of Naples is to be your Indies and your Japan." And so it was.

Fr. Jerome also visited the sick, day and night. On these visitations he always carried a relic of St. Cyr, the Alexandrian physician martyred in the third century. Contemporaries attest that many a cure happened when Fr. Jerome prayed over the sick and blessed them with the relic, but to divert attention from himself, he always attributed the healings to St. Cyr.

During Fr. Jerome's first six years in Naples he met with signal success, but during the next six years, from 1688 to 1694, he met with humiliation and contradiction. Some ecclesiastics told the archbishop that they seriously doubted whether Fr. Jerome, who was occupied with street preaching and who was in constant contact with the worst kind of sinners, was suitable to give retreats to priests and nuns who were striving in virtue. As a result of this complaint, the archbishop placed restrictions on his labors. No longer allowed to preach in the city's streets, he spent his time in the confessional in the Gesù. If he could not go to his sheep, then the sheep would come to him. The archbishop eventually learned that the complaints against Fr. Jerome came from prejudiced and jealous individuals, and subsequently he apologized and reinstated him.

Then it was his own Jesuit superior who brought sorrow into his life. The provincial complained that Fr. Jerome's activities outside the Jesuit community were taking up so much of his time that he was not able to attend community functions. Henceforth, he had to ask permission for anything he desired to do in the city. Thereafter the humble Fr. Jerome asked for permission only to find that his requests were often denied, or, in some cases, that the provincial insisted on sending another priest in his place. Throughout these difficult years Fr. Jerome never yielded to depression; he viewed these as years of spiritual growth. In 1694 the provincial finally admitted his error and Fr. Jerome was again free to minister to his Neapolitans.

Fr. Jerome continued his labors in Naples and its suburbs until 1702, when he was asked to carry his mission outside Naples. From 1702 until his death in 1716, he gave six months of each year to Naples and during the remaining six months he was an itinerant preacher. The entire Kingdom of Naples heard about his prophecies and his healings and everyone considered him a distinguished preacher, not because his sermons were elegant according to classical standards, but because his language was simple and filled with earnestness and conviction of the truth. He gave his final mission in 1715 and his final sermon on the Third Sunday in March 1716, at that month's gathering for General Communion. In his last days he suffered from pleurisy, and when it was certain that his death was imminent his beloved Neapolitans gathered outside the Gesù inquiring about his health. He was anointed on May 9, and on the morning of May 11, 1716, between nine and ten o'clock, his Jesuit brethren at the Gesù gathered in his sickroom to commend his soul to God. When the tenth hour arrived, Fr. Jerome, the greatest missionary of Naples, breathed out his soul to God. He was seventy-four years old and had been a Jesuit for forty-six years.

Fr. Jerome was buried in the Gesù church and in 1736 his remains were moved to the chapel of St. Ignatius. When the French occupied the city in the early nineteenth century, the remains were removed for safekeeping and were returned to the Gesù when peace was restored in the city. After World War II they were taken to the Jesuit church in Grottaglie, Fr. Jerome's native city.

Fr. Francis Jerome was beatified by Pope Pius VII on May 2, 1806, and canonized by Pope Gregory XVI on May 26, 1839. His memorial is liturgically celebrated on July 2.

Prayer

O God, you made Saint Francis Jerome an outstanding herald of your message for the salvation of men. We ask you to hear his prayers and grant that we may always reflect with love upon the demands of your law and faithfully witness to them in our lives. We ask this through our Lord Jesus Christ, who lives and reigns with you and the Holy Spirit, one God, for ever and ever.

May 12

S. G. Matthew Ricci 1552–1610

Chinese Catholics look upon Fr. Matthew Ricci as the "Apostle of China," not because he converted thousands as St. Francis Xavier had done in India, but because he planted the seed of Christianity at a time when China had isolated itself and refused all cultural contact with foreigners. Today's Chinese Catholics are the spiritual descendants of those who had been fortunate to hear about Christ and his Church from the early Jesuit missionaries, but especially from him, whom the Chinese have reverently named "the wise man from the West."

Matthew Ricci was born in Macerata, Italy, on October 6, 1552. His was a prominent family and his father served as the city's governor. Matthew's first tutor was the local parish priest and when the Jesuits opened a school in Macerata in 1561, he was one of the first to enroll. He remained with the Jesuits until 1568, when it was time for him to advance to university studies. As the eldest son, it was expected that Matthew would succeed to the family honors and become a city magistrate as well. To prepare him for this future his father sent him to Rome's famous university.

Thus the sixteen-year-old Matthew matriculated at Rome's Sapienza and began his study of law. Since the university was not operated by the Jesuits, the young man sought them out at the Roman College, became acquainted with them, and there joined the sodality of our Lady. The result of this contact was his entering the Jesuit novitiate of Sant'Andrea in Rome on August 15, 1571. He studied rhetoric at the Roman College in 1572 and later advanced to philosophy in 1575. While at the college he was fortunate in having Fr. Christopher Clavius, the most brilliant mathematician of the age, as his instructor. Matthew was likewise interested in astronomy and while setting a thorough foundation for himself in these subjects, the young Jesuit was unaware that it would be his expertise in both these areas that would serve as the key to opening the great doors of China.

The foreign missions proved attractive to him and several times he requested of his superiors to go to India, but it was only in early spring 1577 that his requests resulted in an affirmative reply. He left Rome on May 18, traveled to Genoa and from there to Lisbon, Portugal, the usual point of departure for India. The next sailing would not be until the following spring so Matthew continued his theological studies at Coimbra. On March 24, 1578, together with thirteen other mission-bound Jesuits, he set sail for his foreign destination. He arrived in Goa, India, on September 13, and within days returned to the classroom to continue his theological course at St. Paul's College.

Because of poor health Matthew was sent southward, November 1579, to Cochin, India, to recuperate, and there he was ordained in July 1580. Shortly afterwards he returned to Goa to complete his studies. It was in his reading of St. Thomas Aquinas that he discovered the dictum that was to serve as the basis of his future method of evangelization, namely, "the infidel should be brought to the faith by persuasion, and not by coercion."

Word finally arrived that he was to go to Macao, the Portuguese colony off the coast of China to begin learning Chinese. There was no way for him to know whether he would ever get into China, since the country had been closed to foreigners for years. Only merchants and traders were permitted to enter, and these at specified times, and always under guard. If China should ever open its doors, he would be ready.

Fr. Ricci arrived in Macao on August 7, 1582, and began his study of Chinese. He was endowed with a remarkable memory, and the task of learning Chinese, usually difficult even for an intelligent student, proved relatively easy for him. After three months he surpassed those who had been studying it for three years.

With Fr. Ricci in Macao was a Fr. Michael Ruggieri, who had come there three years previously. Fr. Ruggieri had already made four short trips into China but was expelled after each one. On his most recent trip to Shuihing he let it be known that his companion in Macao was an accomplished mathematician and skilled in making maps, clocks, and spheres. In midsummer 1583 the unexpected happened. The two Jesuits were invited to Shuihing by the provincial governor. They arrived on September 10, 1583, with heads and beards shaved and dressed as Buddhist bonzes to let the Chinese know that they were men of God. On the land given them they built a house and chapel—the first Jesuit mission in China. In their residence they displayed the western clocks they had brought with them, as well as Venetian prisms, European paintings, and leather-bound books. These were items totally unknown in China and as a result the missionaries daily entertained a flow of visitors. In the case of some of the educated Chinese, their initial curiosity in the Jesuits gave way to genuine interest, and in due time Fr. Ricci numbered them among his friends. The Jesuits were especially respected for their exemplary lives and devotion to scholarship, qualities supremely admired by the Chinese. Still there were some who suspected them of being Portuguese agents, and some, when they heard the clocks chime the hours, were convinced that these foreigners were magicians.

Fr. Ricci never lost sight of the fact that he was in China to bring that nation to Christ. But before he could make Christianity acceptable he must first be accepted by them, and only then could he convincingly demonstrate the superiority of the Christian religion. His ultimate goal was to visit the emperor and convert him, but he would first have to be patient. During their six years in Shuihing the Jesuits made some seventy converts, but with the coming of a new governor to the province in 1589 the missionaries were asked to leave. Rather than return to Macao Fr. Ricci convinced the authorities to permit them to move to another province, and thus they went to Shaochow. They settled down (August 1589), built a residence and a chapel, and set to work once more among the graduate class or educated Chinese. During Fr. Ricci's six years there, he completed his translation of Confucius into Latin and designed the first system for romanizing the Chinese language. His eyes were still on the emperor in Peking (today's Beijing), and when the opportunity came for him to go further north, closer to Peking, he gladly accepted it. He also made an important decision; since Buddhist bonzes were little respected because of their lack of education, he determined to set aside his Buddhist robe and dress as a graduate. When he arrived in Nanchang on June 28, 1595, he wore the hat and purple garb of China's educated class.

Fr. Ricci was soon accepted among the literati of Nanchang and the number of his friends grew quickly. Here he wrote his first Chinese book, on friendship, which eventually became a Chinese classic. He rewrote his catechism and received permission for other "graduate preachers," that is, Jesuits, to join him in Nanchang. The Jesuit mission was progressing nicely. When the Nanking Minister of Rites asked Fr. Ricci to accompany him on a trip to Peking—the minister intended to introduce the missionary to the court so that it could take advantage of his knowledge of mathematics and astronomy and correct the Chinese calendar—Fr. Ricci jubilantly accepted. Anticipating meeting the emperor, he took with him some presents that would interest the emperor and perhaps induce him to give the priest leave to remain in Peking. The group arrived in the capital on September 7, 1598, but because China was then involved in a war with Japan the missionaries never saw the emperor. After months of idle waiting they returned south, this time to Nanking, the former capital, and arrived there on February 6, 1599.

Fr. Ricci was, by now, well known among China's intelligentsia. He had a reputation for being a prodigy of learning and his books made him one of the country's sages. As soon as he settled in Nanking many in the city came to meet him, and by popular request he began teaching them geometry and trigonometry. His stay there was short because in 1600 another opportunity came to visit Peking. With two other Jesuits he left Nanking and arrived in the capital on January 24, 1601. Through intermediaries he presented his gifts to the emperor, but in vain did he wait for an invitation to visit him. The emperor was delighted with the gifts and was especially enchanted by the western clocks, but never did he deign to call their donor into his august presence. Fr. Ricci and companions were given quarters in the city and the city's literati visited them, and Peking soon had its first Catholic converts. While residing in Peking, Fr. Ricci wrote and translated some scientific treatises into Chinese. Throughout his years in China, he produced some twenty books, and years later when the Great Encyclopedia of the Four Treasuries was completed in 1781, five of his scientific works were included in it.

Fr. Ricci's earnest desire had been to convert the emperor to Christianity, but after twenty-seven years in China and ten of them in Peking, he never succeeded in even getting a glimpse of Emperor Wan Li. In this regard Fr. Ricci was a failure, but by 1609, as a result of his and his companions' labors, there were some 2,500 Catholics living in China. This was the seed that was to grow and bloom, and subsequent prohibition, oppression, and persecution never succeeded in destroying it.

In 1609 Fr. Ricci began to feel the strain of his many years of activity and, thus, he began writing *The Coming of the Society of Jesus and Christianity to China*. This was an account of that country's history, the first book to offer accurate information on China to European readers. All earlier accounts were merely tales told by merchant travellers. On May 3, 1610, his heart began to cause him trouble and he gradually grew weaker and weaker. He was anointed on May 10, and on the 11th, after saying goodbye to his brother missionaries, and joining in the prayers for the dying, he rendered his courageous and magnanimous soul to the Father and Lord of all nations.

The Chinese have rightly honored Fr. Matthew Ricci as "the wise man from the West," and international historians have judged him to be the world's most outstanding cultural mediator between China and the West. In addition, his Jesuit brethren, who had lived with him and had known him, have all attested to his humility and holiness, and how he used his many talents solely for the glory of God and the spread of His kingdom. The Chinese bishops attending Vatican Council II in Rome in 1963 unanimously petitioned the pope to introduce Fr. Ricci's cause for beatification.

May 16

St. Andrew Bobola 1591–1657

Martyr of Poland

Fr. Andrew Bobola died a most painful and heroic death at the hands of fanatical Cossacks. He was born on November 30, 1591, in Strachocin in southern Poland. His family was part of the lesser nobility and was known for its devotion to the Catholic Church. In 1606 fifteen-year-old Andrew went to study at the Jesuit school in Braniewo, in the north of Poland. Five years later, on July 31, 1611, he entered the Society of Jesus. He pronounced his vows in Vilnius two years later, and spent the years 1613 to 1616 studying philosophy at the famous Vilnius Academy. He taught grammar for a year at Braniewo and for two years at Pultusk. He then returned to Vilnius in 1619 to pursue his courses in theology. He was ordained to the priesthood on March 12, 1622.

Fr. Bobola's first assignment was as pastor of the church connected with the Jesuit school at Nesvizh. During his years there he made many converts and gave missions in the suburbs. In 1624 he returned to Vilnius to St. Casimir's church, where he became an outstanding preacher and was in charge of the various sodalities of our Lady. It was from these sodalities that he recruited his assistants who helped him visit prisoners and the poor and assisted him in teaching catechism to children. During the two periods (1625 and 1629) when the plague struck Vilnius, he and his sodalists worked most zealously and tirelessly. Though other priests and many sodalists fell victim to the dreaded plague, Fr. Bobola was always spared. From Vilnius he went in 1630 to Bobruisk and proved himself an exemplary pastor. In that area of eastern Poland, he discovered that the majority of the people were of the Orthodox faith and that many who had been Catholics had joined the Orthodox Church, simply because they did not have their own priests and churches. Fr. Bobola built a church for them and offered all who wanted the opportunity to return to the Catholic faith.

He spent the years 1633 to 1655 in various towns and cities, e.g., Plock, Lomza, and Pinsk, and served in various capacities, sometimes as preacher, sometimes as prefect of studies in the school. He spent part of 1636 as preacher in the Jesuit church in Warsaw, and in 1642 he was again in Vilnius preaching a course of sermons on Holy Scripture. The years 1646 to 1652 were, because of poor health, years of reduced work in Vilnius.

When rumors reached him that animosity toward the Catholics and Jesuits was increasing, he sought to return to his former missions. According to the agreement of the Union of Brest-Litovsk, concluded in 1596, Roman and Russian churches were to coexist in peace. Some Orthodox, however, supported by Cossacks were eager to annul that union and rid those territories of Catholics and their churches. The leader of these Cossacks was the infamous Bogdan Chmielnicki, who did everything in his power to vitiate the union and expel the Catholics. By 1655 he had taken over large areas of White Russia (today's Belarus) for the schismatic cause.

Fr. Bobola was in Vilnius on August 8, 1655, when the tsar's army—Russia and Poland were then at war—marched into Vilnius and sacked the city. No longer able to continue his ministry there, he went to Pinsk to help the Catholics keep their faith and to encourage them to be steadfast in it, even under pressure from the marauding Cossacks. Everyone acknowledged Fr. Bobola's success. Two entire villages returned to the Catholic faith through his preaching. Thus, his enemies nicknamed him "soul-hunter," and grew to despise him more and more. Whenever he walked through town, adults urged street ruffians to throw mud and stones at him. But Fr. Bobola was about the Lord's work and such annoyances did not deter him from his main purpose. He must have sensed that his martyrdom was not far away.

In May 1657, when Pinsk was occupied by the Cossacks, the Poles and Catholics fled to the forests. On May 16 the Cossacks attacked Janów and massacred both Catholics and Jews. Fr. Bobola, however, was in Peredil at the time, but some schismatics informed the murdering Cossacks where to find him.

Unable to persuade the priest to embrace the Orthodox faith, the Cossacks threatened him with torture. Unmoved by these threats, Fr. Bobola remained steadfast in his resolve. Realizing they would never get him to apostatize, the Cossacks stripped him, tied him to a hedge and whipped him until the blood flowed. They placed a crown of twigs on his head, bound him between two horses and dragged him to a butcher's shop. There they stretched him on the butcher's table, and because he still would not renounce his Catholic faith, the angry Cossacks made him undergo one of the most cruel tortures that any of Christ's martyrs ever had to endure. Throughout Fr. Bobola was strengthened by divine grace for he withstood his torments without any sign of weakness. The Cossacks tore his skin from his hands and head, and in imitation of the chasuble worn by priests at Mass, they tore the skin from his chest and back. They then cut holes in the palms of his hands. After two hours of such torture, during which he continually prayed for his tormentors, they jabbed a butcher's awl into his chest near the heart. They then strung him up by his feet and finally gave him a blow with a sabre that mercifully brought his passion to an end.

At the moment that the martyr gave his soul to God, a band of Poles rushed into Janów to rescue him. Too late, they merely dispersed the Cossacks. The Catholics of Janów placed Fr. Bobola's body in their local church and later it was taken to the Jesuit church in Pinsk and placed in the crypt beneath the main altar. In 1808 the body was taken to Polotsk in White Russia, and in July 1922 the Bolsheviks, who were then in power, took it to a Moscow museum. In 1923 two American Jesuits, Frs. Edmund A. Walsh and Louis J. Gallagher, directors of the Vatican Relief Mission in Russia, requested the martyr's body in the name of Pope Pius XI. It was then taken to Rome, and after Fr. Bobola was canonized on April 17, 1938, it was returned to Poland. It is now venerated in the Jesuit church attached to the Jesuit theologate, the "Bobolanum," in Warsaw. St. Andrew Bobola's memorial is celebrated on May 16.

Prayer

Lord our God, your Son gave himself up to death to bring your scattered children into unity. Grant us perseverance in Christ's work of reconciliation for which Saint Andrew Bobola died a martyr's death. We ask this through our Lord Jesus Christ, your Son, who lives and reigns with you and the Holy Spirit, one God, for ever and ever.

May 19

Bl. Peter Wright 1603–1651

Martyr of England

Peter Wright was born in Slipton, Northamptonshire, England, in 1603, of poor parents. His father died when Peter was still young and because there were twelve children at home, Peter went to work for a local lawyer in Thrapston to help support the family. Through constant contact with Protestants visiting the law office and as a result of frequent religious discussions, Peter, little by little, lost the faith his parents had implanted in him. After ten years with the lawyer, he imprudently enlisted with the English forces in the Low Countries, but after a month he learned that loose military life was not to his liking, so he deserted and went to Brabant. He thought of making a pilgrimage to Rome, and while on a visit to Liège (Belgium), he went to the English Jesuits in that city and asked to be reconciled to the Catholic Church. From there he went in 1627 to Ghent, where he attended the college operated by Flemish Jesuits. In 1629 he decided to enter the Society of Jesus and that same year he entered the novitiate of the English Jesuits at Watten. He did his theological studies at Liège, was ordained there in 1639, and looked forward to being sent on the English mission. His superiors thought differently and sent him to serve at the English College in Saint-Omer in Flanders. They later appointed him chaplain to the English soldiers serving with the Spanish army in Flanders.

Fr. Wright was attached to Sir Henry Gage's regiment and returned to England with Sir Henry and the regiment in the spring of 1644, when the civil wars were still in progress. After Col. Gage was killed (January 13, 1645) during the siege of Abington, Fr. Wright became chaplain to the marquis of Winchester, first in Hampshire and later in London, and served him until February 2, 1651. The priest-hunters felt certain that Fr. Wright would be celebrating Mass at the marquis' residence on February 2, Candlemas Day, so they patiently waited for the hour when Mass would begin to surprise him. When the time came they rushed into the house, but the marquis successfully stopped them on the stairs, hoping to give the priest time to escape. Fr. Wright, who was about to begin Mass, heard the noise below; he hurriedly removed the Mass vestments and left the room through a window. He climbed to the roof to hide. When the soldiers entered the chapel and saw everything in readiness for Mass, they knew their prey was nearby. Seeing the open window, some of them climbed out and eventually found the priest. Fr. Wright was taken to Newgate Prison and put into a cell on suspicion of being a priest. His trial, however, was postponed until the prosecution could locate a special witness capable of identifying the prisoner as a priest. The witness was the unfortunate Thomas Gage, an apostate Dominican friar, and the brother of Col. Henry Gage. Thomas Gage knew Fr. Wright from the time the latter had served with his brother's regiment in Flanders.

The trial took place on Friday, May 16, 1651, and during it Gage testified that he knew the defendant to be a priest, a Jesuit, that he had often seen him celebrating Mass, and that he knew the defendant had seduced many Protestants to give up their religion for the Catholic faith. The jury brought in a verdict of guilty and hearing it Fr. Wright exclaimed: "God Almighty's holy name be blessed now and for evermore!" On the following day, May 17, he was sentenced to death—a sentence that brought him comfort, but affliction to his friends. The Spanish ambassador tried to save his life, but his efforts failed. Many friends and acquaintances came to visit him in his cell, asking him to remember them in his prayers and begging some little remembrance of him.

Fr. Wright spent the night prior to his execution in quiet prayer. On Monday morning, May 19, he awoke at five o'clock and celebrated his last Mass. When he heard the jailer's knock on his door, he answered: "I come, sweet Jesus, I come." He bade farewell to the other prisoners and let himself be bound to the hurdle that dragged him to the place of execution. The streets were lined with people, and it is said that when he arrived at Tyburn there was a crowd of 20,000 waiting to see a martyr go to God. That same day thirteen criminals were to die; while these were being hanged, Fr. Wright silently prayed.

When his time came, he mounted the cart beneath the gallows. After the noose was placed about his neck, he spoke to the bystanders: "Gentlemen, this is a short passage to eternity. . . . I was brought hither charged with no other crime but being a priest. I willingly confess I am a priest; I confess I am a Catholic; I confess I am a religious man of the Society of Jesus. . . . This is the cause for which I die; for this alone was I condemned and for propagating the Catholic faith. For this cause I most willingly sacrifice my life, and would die a thousand times for the same, if it were necessary." He then asked the people to join him in prayer and to pray for him, concluding with, "when I shall come to heaven I will do as much for you." He was left to hang until dead; his body was then cut down, beheaded, disembowelled, and quartered. His friends were permitted to take his butchered body away, and in due time it was taken to the Jesuit college in Liège, where it was given burial.

Fr. Peter Wright was forty-eight years old and spent twenty-two years in the Society of Jesus. He was beatified by Pope Pius XI on December 15, 1929, and his Jesuit brethren celebrate his memorial on December 1, the day when they liturgically commemorate all their brethren who died for the Catholic faith in England and Wales.

Prayer

Almighty, eternal God, you chose from the people of England and Wales Blessed Peter Wright and his companions to be made like Christ, who died to save the world. Listen to their prayers; strengthen your Church by the same faith and love that strengthened them, and bless it always with your gift of unity. We ask this through our Lord Jesus Christ, your Son, who lives and reigns with you and the Holy Spirit, one God, for ever and ever.

May 20

Ven. Adolph Petit 1822–1914

Fr. Adolph Petit was a Belgian, born in Ghent on May 22, 1822. His mother died when he was five and his father soon realized that he was unable to care for the family. Young Adolph was therefore adopted by his godfather. He attended a village school, but at age twelve had to leave to take a job with a piano maker. Adolph only knew poverty during his life, and though he wanted to be a priest he did not know how that could ever be; but he left that problem to our Lady, whom he had adopted as his mother. Adolph frequently visited our Lady's shrine in Ghent's cathedral and was often observed by a lady who was also in the habit of going there to pray. One day she stopped him and asked what he intended to do in life. The fourteen-year-old boy had no hesitation in replying that he wanted to be a priest. The lady then kindly arranged for a scholarship at the Jesuit school in Ghent, and in 1836 Adolph began his first instruction under the Jesuits. When he completed his course, he entered the Society's novitiate at

Drongen, three miles away, on September 25, 1842. He pronounced his religious vows of poverty, chastity, and obedience on September 26, 1844, and went to Namur for philosophy. He then spent four years teaching in Antwerp. In 1852 he went to Louvain for his theological course and was ordained on September 15, 1855. His final year of Jesuit training, tertianship, was spent at Drongen.

Fr. Petit's first assignment as a priest was to teach at St. Michael's College in Brussels. After three years in the capital, he moved in 1860 to Namur, where he became spiritual director for the young Jesuits studying there. In 1865, chosen to represent his province, he attended the beatification ceremonies of his countryman, John Berchmans, and on his return to the province, became instructor of tertians at Drongen. For twenty years he directed the newly-ordained Jesuit priests, instructing them how to deepen their prayer and strengthen their spiritual life. After he had completed his years as tertian instructor, he remained at Drongen to serve as spiritual director to the young Jesuits who had just arrived from the novitiate. Most of Fr. Petit's forty-nine years at the old abbey in Drongen were spent in the role of director of souls to one or another group of his Jesuit brethren. During this period he was also involved in another important apostolate. In 1866, shortly after his arrival at the old abbey, he initiated men's retreats and spent his summers traveling, giving retreats to sisters, brothers, and diocesan clergy. The retreat movement begun at Drongen flourished, and it was not long before retreat houses were built in other Belgian cities as well.

Fr. Petit's influence on others was not restricted to his retreats, for he had immeasurable influence on the diocesan clergy. He not only gave them their annual retreats but also gave them conferences during the year. Many priests chose him as their confessor and frequently came to seek his prudent advice. Among the clergy he promoted the *Apostolic Union,* an association whose purpose was to deepen the spiritual life of its members so that their ministry could bear more fruit for the Lord. After the *Union's* success in the diocese of Namur, he saw to its spread in other dioceses as well. Also to help priests in their pursuit of holiness, he wrote several volumes of meditations and conferences, inviting them to imitate the virtues of the Sacred Heart of Jesus. At the end of the nineteenth and the beginning of the twentieth century, there was hardly a priest in Belgium who had not read at least one of Fr. Petit's books.

By 1911, when he was eighty-nine years old, his health began to weaken. He slowed down, but he did not stop. As time passed he realized that his end was soon approaching, and he began to prepare to meet his Savior. With slow pace he continued to walk the abbey's cloisters with rosary in hand and a smile on his face, an inspiration to the young Jesuits living at Drongen. In May 1914 it became progressively more difficult for him to breathe, and on the 15th it became so difficult that he was confined to bed. The physician diagnosed the problem as bronchial pneumonia and informed his patient how serious it was. The humble priest only responded: "Thank you, doctor, God's will be done." In his last days Fr. Petit was in constant union with God, and the prayer most frequently heard coming from his lips was, "My Jesus, mercy. Lamb of God, who takes away the sins of the world, have mercy on me." He repeated this aspiration, for variety's sake, in Latin, then in French, and sometimes in Flemish. He was anointed but did not receive Viaticum, since he was unable to swallow. Finally, on the morning of May 20, at 2:20, the self-effacing Fr. Petit left this world to live forever with his God. He was buried on May 23 in the parish cemetery.

Fr. Adolph Petit's cause was introduced in Rome in 1937; he was declared Venerable in 1966 when, after a meticulous study, he was found to have lived a life of extraordinary virtue.

May 22

Bl. John Baptist Machado 1581–1617

Martyr of Japan

On July 7, 1867, Pope Pius IX solemnly beatified 205 martyrs, all of whom had died for the Catholic faith in Japan during the persecution under the shogun Tokugawa Iyeyasu, his son Hidetada, and grandson Iyemitsu. Of this number thirty-four were Jesuits, and the first to meet death during this Great Persecution was Fr. John Baptist Machado de Távora.

In 1598, after the death of Taikosama Toyotomi Hideyoshi, who had cruelly ordered the martyrdom of Paul Miki and his companions, the Christians again lived in peace and the years between 1598 and 1612 were years of great growth for the Church, so much so that they have been called the "golden age" of Christianity in old Japan. In 1612 a few provincial governors began to take action against the Christians, but in 1614 the persecution became much more extensive when Iyeyasu decreed the banishment of all missionaries, the destruction or closing of all churches, the confiscation of church property, and the proscription of the Christian faith. Many of the Jesuit missionaries departed for Manila or Macao, but a score or so remained behind to care for the Japanese Christians. One of those who stayed, at great risk to himself, was Fr. John Baptist Machado [Maciado].

He was a Portuguese, born, perhaps in 1581, at Angra on the island of Terceira, in the Azores. As a child he heard his mother tell stories about India and Japan—the letters of Fr. Francis Xavier had been recently published and were very popular in Portugal—and from these stories he developed a desire to walk in the footsteps of that great missionary. John studied with the Jesuits in Coimbra,

Portugal, and on April 10, 1597, he entered the Society. In 1601, two years after he had completed his novitiate, he left Lisbon for Goa, India, where he did his studies in philosophy. He then went to Macao to do theology and it was there that he was ordained a priest.

Fr. Machado arrived in Nagasaki, Japan, on June 29, 1609, and worked for five years among the Japanese Christians in and around the capital, Miyako (today's Kyoto), until the harsh edict of 1614 was promulgated. He was told by his superiors to leave Japan with some hundred Jesuits, but at his insistence he was permitted to remain. For the next three years he experienced the sadness of seeing many Christians give up their faith under threat of persecution, but he also had the sweetness of seeing countless Japanese remain steadfast in the faith they had adopted. During most of this period he stayed in Nagasaki and its environs, hidden during the day and traveling at night in disguise.

In April 1617 he made plans to go to the leper colony on one of the Goto islands, where there were many Catholics. His friends in Nagasaki tried to dissuade him; they knew that spies were stationed at the harbor and that everyone who came and went was checked. Nevertheless, Fr. Machado had to visit his Christians. He landed at the colony on April 21 and the Christians flocked to greet him. He visited their humble residences and celebrated Mass for them; but unknown to him, spies had followed him very closely. The next day, April 22, he was arrested, put into chains and taken back. He was first taken to Omura, north of Nagasaki, then transferred to the town of Kori, where a Franciscan priest, Peter of the Ascension, was held prisoner. Both were kept at the home of a minor official named Tomonaga, an apostate Christian and the brother of a Jesuit priest. Tomonaga not only permitted his prisoners to celebrate Mass daily, but also frequently visited and talked with them. After little more than three weeks of house arrest, a saddened Tomonaga came to them on May 22, Trinity Sunday, and with tears in his eyes informed them that they were to die that afternoon. While Tomonaga shed tears of sorrow, the priests sang hymns of joy and praise to God. Fr. Machado found a few minutes to scribble a final short note to his superior, in which he wrote: "I have just received the good news that I am going to die for love of my dear Lord. I make him the offering of my life and all my heart's love."

That afternoon Fr. Machado and Fr. Peter prayed together the litany of the saints and that of our Lady; then they were led to a wooded hill outside the town, each carrying a crucifix, their eyes fixed on the figure of our Lord. The executioner was prepared and waiting. After the priests heard each other's confession, Fr. Peter knelt down and placed his head on the block to receive the deadly blow. Then it was Fr. Machado's turn; three blows were needed to make him a martyr. At the time of his death he was thirty-seven years old and had been a Jesuit for twenty years. Within six months of this event, Tomonaga returned to the faith and died a martyr's death.

By his brief of May 7, 1867, Pope Pius IX beatified Fr. John Baptist Machado, Fr. Peter, and 204 other martyrs. Fr. Machado's memorial is celebrated by his Jesuit brothers on February 4.

Prayer

Almighty God, grant that remembrance of your holy martyr, Blessed John Baptist Machado, may bring us joy. May we who depend on his prayers glory in his entry into heaven. We ask this through our Lord Jesus Christ, your Son, who lives and reigns with you and the Holy Spirit, one God, for ever and ever.

May 24

The Blessed Virgin Mary, Our Lady of the Way

Jesuits have a special devotion to Our Lady of the Way, or Madonna della Strada, because the Roman church that bore that name was the Society's first church and it was there that St. Ignatius and the early Jesuits focused their apostolate.

Toward the end of 1538 St. Ignatius and his companions moved into an empty house on the Frangipani estate near the Torre del Melangolo, not too distant from the church of Our Lady of the Way. Because the church was near, they frequently celebrated Mass there, heard confessions, preached and taught catechism to the Roman children.

From December 1538 to well into May 1539, a severe cold gripped Rome and the outlying districts with the sad result that food became scarce. Romans were starving and it became more and more frequent to hear of people freezing to death during the cold nights. Amazed that little was being done to help these unfortunate victims of winter, St. Ignatius took them in by the hundreds and lodged them in different parts of the Frangipani house. The Jesuits then went among Rome's wealthy families and begged food for the hungry. During those terrible months St. Ignatius is said to have helped some 3,000 individuals.

Living in Rome at the time was a certain priest from Lodi, in northern Italy. Fr. Peter Codacio was a canon of the Lodi cathedral and a chamberlain in Pope Paul III's household. During that freezing winter he saw the flow of people seeking help and finding it at the house where the Jesuits lived. Moved by this example of charity, he became interested in them; this interest led him to make the Spiritual Exercises under St. Ignatius' direction, and this in turn led him to ask to become one of them. He was admitted into the Society in June 1539, and was appointed procurator, or community treasurer. Fr. Codacio is happily remembered for two things: he was the first Italian to become a Jesuit, and it was through him that the church of Our Lady of the Way came to the Society.

In 1540, when the holder of the benefice attached to the church of Our Lady of the Way relinquished it, the pope graciously granted it to Fr. Codacio on November 18, 1540. With Fr. Codacio now pastor, the Jesuits moved from the Frangipani estate and rented a house directly across from the church. On June 24, 1541, Fr. Codacio asked the pope to transfer the church, together with its property, to the general of the Society of Jesus so that it might become the Society's first church. The pope readily granted the request and offered the church to St. Ignatius, who accepted it on May 15, 1542.

The church was small and narrow, and even in St. Ignatius' day it was old and somewhat dilapidated. It's original name was Santa Maria degli Astalli, that is St. Mary's church built by the Astalli family; but in time the people came to call it Santa Maria della Strada. The origin of this change has not come down to us, but it is thought that it was because one walked directly into the church from the street, or *strada*. This church was greatly beloved by St. Ignatius and his followers. Countless Jesuits have prayed before the image of our Lady holding the Child, and it was at her altar that many of the early Jesuits pronounced their vows. Many a saint had knelt before it, and many a Jesuit went there to seek her patronage.

Now that the church was the center of the Jesuit apostolate in Rome, Fr. Codacio sold all his property—this was prior to his taking his vows in the Society—and used the money to erect a new residence for the Jesuits, adjacent to the church. The new building was ready for occupancy in September 1544 and was large enough to house all the Jesuits then living in Rome. The rooms that St. Ignatius used in that house remain today; they have been incorporated into the newer structure which eventually replaced the sixteenth-century edifice. These rooms are still visited by the faithful in Rome.

The church of our Lady soon proved too small for the crowds that came to hear the sermons of the Jesuits. St. Ignatius made additions to it, but these also proved inadequate. Frequently the people had to stand in the piazza and listen to the sermons. St. Ignatius thought of replacing the church, and when Francis Borgia came to visit him in 1550, plans for a new building were considered, but nothing much came of these early discussions.

When the early Jesuits died in Rome, they were buried in this church—among them were Blessed Peter Favre, who died on August 1, 1546, and Fr. Codacio who died on December 7, 1549. When it came time for St. Ignatius to return to God on July 31, 1556, he too was buried in the same church, in front of the main altar, where our Lady's image continued to look upon him.

In 1565 Francis Borgia became general of the Society, and with the financial assistance of Cardinal Alessandro Farnese he planned a new church to be called "The Holy Name of Jesus," or more popularly, the Gesù. The construction of the new church meant the tearing down of the old one, but from the very beginning a chapel was planned in the new edifice to house the famous image of Our Lady of the Way. While the new building was under construction, the image was transferred to the nearby church of San Marco, and there it remained for several years. In 1575 the image was returned to the Gesù and appropriately placed in a chapel immediately to the left of the main altar.

When the Gesù was completed, the remains of the first Jesuits were rein-terred within, but the body of St. Ignatius was placed near our Lady's chapel. After his beatification on July 27, 1609, the first Mass honoring him as one of the blessed in heaven was celebrated on July 31, 1609, in our Lady's chapel by the then general Fr. Claudio Acquaviva. An altar was erected in the left transept, next to our Lady's chapel, in time for his canonization on March 12, 1622.

The chapel of Our Lady of the Way is still a favorite shrine among Ro-mans, but it is especially beloved by Jesuits. Any Jesuit visiting Rome for the first time looks forward to celebrating Mass before that image of our Lady, in front of which so many other Jesuits, even saints and blessed, have offered the same sacrifice. The love that St. Ignatius had for Our Lady of the Way perdures in his sons, even after four hundred and fifty years.

Prayer

Lord, Holy Father, you revealed to us the way, the truth, and the life in your beloved Son. Grant that by faithfully following his example and teaching, and through the prayers of the Blessed Virgin Mary, we may be led in safety to you. We ask this through our Lord Jesus Christ, your Son, who lives and reigns with you and the Holy Spirit, one God, for ever and ever.

May 25

S. G. Leo Ducoudray 1827–1871

S. G. Alexis Clerc 1819–1871

Martyrs of the Paris Commune

During the terror-filled days of the Paris Commune, when revolutionaries had assumed control of the French capital, five Jesuits gave their lives as martyrs of the faith. Frs. Leo Ducoudray and Alexis Clerc died on May 24, 1871, and Frs. Peter Olivaint, John Caubert, and Anatole de Bengy died on May 26.

Leo Ducoudray was born in Laval on May 6, 1827. He first attended a minor seminary in Paris and then completed his studies at the College of Château-Gontier. After receiving his law degree, he entered the Society of Jesus at Angers on October 2, 1852, and pronounced his vows two years later. He pur-sued his philosophical studies at Laval for three years, after which he became as-sistant to the prefect of studies at St. Geneviève, a military school, in Paris. In

1861 he went to Lyons to begin his four years of theology and it was there that he was ordained in 1864. After he had completed the final year of his Jesuit training, that is, tertianship, he was named, on August 25, 1866, rector of St. Genevieve. It was there that Frs. Ducoudray and Clerc were arrested.

Alexis Clerc was born in Paris on December 11, 1819. Because his parents were indifferent about his early religious upbringing, he attended the College of Henry IV and the Polytechnic School of Paris. In 1841 he became a cadet and served in the navy for thirteen years. Through companionship with several sailors, who were practicing Catholics, Alexis returned to his faith in 1847, and while remaining in the navy he developed a deep spiritual life. In 1850, at the conclusion of a retreat he had made under the direction of the famous Jesuit preacher Fr. Gustave de Ravignan, he wanted to join the Jesuits, but his director urged him to wait. Alexis thus continued in the navy and went to sea. In 1854 he returned to Paris, where he was promoted to the rank of lieutenant with command over his own vessel. While in Paris he again visited Fr. de Ravignan and made another retreat, this time at the novitiate, and came to the decision that he would enter religious life. He resigned his commission and entered the Jesuit novitiate at Saint-Acheul on August 28, 1854. He was thirty-five years old. He pronounced his vows of religion on September 8, 1856, and spent the following year at the College of Vaugirard in Paris, where he studied philosophy and did some prefecting. In 1858 he was assigned to teach mathematics at St. Genevieve and there first met his future companion in martyrdom, Leo Ducoudray. In 1861 Alexis moved to Laval for theology and later returned to St. Genevieve. He spent part of 1870 making his tertianship at Laon, but after France had declared war on Prussia (July 1870), he went to Vaugirard to minister to the wounded and dying. As a member of a hospital corps, he cared for the injured brought in from the front. At the beginning of 1871 he returned to St. Genevieve.

The Germans kept Paris under siege for a long time. The possibility that the city might fall caused the government to move to Versailles. In its absence, socialist-minded anti-Catholic revolutionaries took command of the city on March 28, 1871, established a commune, restricted the activity of priests, and on April 3 announced the confiscation of properties owned by religious communities. Fr. Ducoudray, who was rector at St. Genevieve, had foreseen that this would happen and he had already relocated the students and Jesuit community outside Paris in the school's villa at Athis. He intended to join them, but a member of his community in Paris unexpectedly died on the morning of April 3; so he postponed his leaving. The Jesuits from Athis returned to Paris for the funeral, which was to be held on April 4. But as the 4th was just beginning—between midnight and 1:00 A.M.—the school was surrounded by armed communards. The banging on the residence door meant that the Jesuits would soon be under arrest. While the house was being invaded, one of the priests went to the chapel to consume the hosts in the tabernacle to prevent their profanation. The communards arrested Fr. Ducoudray and seven other priests, among them were Frs. Alexis Clerc and Anatole de Bengy; they also arrested four brothers and seven house servants. At 5:00 A.M., the nineteen prisoners were led to the Prefecture of Police. Fr. Ducoudray was put in the Conciergerie Prison while the other eighteen were put in a large room in the depot next to the prison with some thirty other prisoners.

Finding himself totally isolated, Fr. Ducoudray requested to have Fr. Clerc as a cellmate and to his surprise, the request was honored. On April 6 both priests were transferred to the Mazas Prison, and with them went Fr. de Bengy and several others from the depot's common room. Food was permitted to be brought in three times a week for the prisoners so their friends initiated a constant flow of provisions. Unknown to the officials, the Blessed Sacrament was usually concealed amid the food.

Life at Mazas was monotonous. The priests spent much time in prayer and in writing letters, not only to their Jesuit superiors but also to their families and friends. In the letters they noted that there was some suffering in prison life, but their greatest affliction was their inability to celebrate or attend Mass. In one of his letters to his brother, Fr. Clerc asked him to go to his room at St. Genevieve and bring him his mathematics books so that he could prepare his classes.

On April 13 two more Jesuits, Frs. Peter Olivaint and John Caubert, were added to the three at Mazas, but the other nine Jesuits and seven servants, who had been detained in the common room in the depot, were released without anyone learning why.

The commune was under pressure from the French government in Versailles and realized that it could not win in this conflict. On May 22 it ordered, as a reprisal, the massacre of all hostages in the Mazas Prison. Just as quickly as the order was given it was withdrawn, and the hostages were moved that night to La Roquette, a prison for condemned criminals. Earlier that day two elderly women somehow made their way into Mazas and gave each of the hostages a packet containing four consecrated hosts plus string and a tiny silk bag in which to carry the Blessed Sacrament around their necks. The fact that they were at La Roquette meant that death was imminent and on May 24, during their daily period of recreation outside their cells, each found time to go to confession. Having received word that the Versailles Army was marching against the Paris commune, the communards judged the greatest damage it could inflict upon the government would be to slay the hostages. Hence the order was given that sixty of them were to be put to death at 6:00 P.M. that day. Plans were again changed; they would only kill six of them, one-tenth the number. At 8:00 P.M., while the hostages were in their cells, a prison official broke into their peace and read out six names. These included George Darboy, the archbishop of Paris, Frs. Ducoudray and Clerc, two diocesan priests, and a city magistrate.

The six were marched outside the prison and were placed against the wall. To show his eagerness for martyrdom, Fr. Clerc opened the top of his cassock and bared his breast to the firing squad, while Fr. Ducoudray held his hand on his breast pointing where to hit. A volley of shots turned six hostages into six martyrs. When the shots were heard within the prison walls, the remaining hostages prepared for death. Their death, however, was not to come until May 26, and it was to be more brutal.

The bodies of the six martyrs were taken on the morning of May 25 to the nearby cemetery of Père Lachaise and buried without coffins in an open trench. After the commune fell on May 27, the bodies of Frs. Ducoudray and Clerc were recovered on May 29 and taken to the Jesuit church on Rue de Sèvres. Together with the bodies of their fellow martyrs, Frs. Olivaint, Caubert, and de Bengy, they were placed in the chapel of the Japanese martyrs and on May 31 they were buried in the cemetery of Mont-Parnasse. Two months later these sacred remains were returned to Rue de Sèvres and interred in the chapel of the martyrs.

The cause of Fr. Leo Ducoudray and Fr. Alexis Clerc, together with their three Jesuit brothers, who died on May 26, 1871, was introduced in Rome on February 17, 1937.

May 26

S. G. Peter Olivaint 1816–1871

S. G. John Caubert 1811–1871

S. G. Anatole de Bengy 1824–1871

Martyrs of the Paris Commune

Among the five Jesuits martyred during the frightful days of the Paris Commune were Frs. Peter Olivaint, John Caubert, and Anatole de Bengy.

Peter Olivaint was born in the French capital on February 22, 1816, the son of a retired military officer, who had served under Napoleon in Moscow. Though Peter's parents saw to it that he was baptized as an infant, they neglected to raise him as a Catholic. In 1828, at age twelve, he enrolled at the College of Charlemagne in Paris and there earned a bachelor's degree. In 1836 he received a scholarship to attend the renowned Normal School, where he specialized in history and graduated in 1839. It was from his classmates at school that he learned about the Catholic faith and developed an interest in religion. In 1835 he eagerly followed the sermons of the famous Dominican preacher Fr. Jean-Baptiste Lacordaire in Notre Dame cathedral in Paris. When, in 1836, Fr. Lacordaire yielded the pulpit to Fr. Gustave de Ravignan, a Jesuit, Peter continued to attend the weekly discourses with equal interest. So moved was he by these sermons that on

February 22, 1837, he went to speak with Fr. de Ravignan and made a general confession of his life. Peter always considered that date as the day of his conversion and his determination to lead a fervent spiritual life was strengthened by his companions, all young Catholic intellectuals, one of whom was the saintly Frederic Ozanam, with whom he helped promote the St. Vincent de Paul Society.

In 1839 Peter gave serious thought to becoming a Dominican. Fr. Lacordaire was about to reestablish the Dominican Order in France and was looking for recruits, but because of financial problems at home as a result of his father's death, Peter had to set aside his desire to be a priest until a later date. After graduating from the Normal School, he took, in 1839, the position of professor of history at Grenoble, but for health reasons returned in 1840 to Paris, where he taught at the College of Bourbon until 1841, at which time he became tutor to the young son of the duke of La Rochefoucauld-Liancourt.

When Peter's family's difficulties were resolved in 1845, he felt free to follow his call to serve God, but this time he chose to enter the Society of Jesus. He had known the Jesuits in Paris since his student days, appreciated their accomplishments and desired to share in their apostolate, especially since liberal voices were beginning to speak out against them. Peter entered the novitiate at Laval on May 2, 1845, but when it had to close its doors due to governmental pressure, the novices moved, in October 1845, to Vannes in Brittany. Peter remained in Vannes until September 1846, when he went to Brugelette, Belgium, to continue his novitiate and to teach history. He pronounced his vows on May 3, 1847, and returned to France that summer to study theology at Laval, where he was later ordained on September 21, 1850.

In October 1852 Fr. Olivaint went to Paris to teach at the College of Vaugirard, and except for the year he spent at Paray-le-Monial making his tertianship under Fr. Paul Ginhac, he remained there until 1865. In September 1857 he was named rector of the school, and during his term the school attained high standards and won the confidence and affection of the students and their parents. In 1856 he had established the Society of St. Francis Xavier, through which he sought to respond to the religious needs of the working man and in 1859 initiated the Work of the Christ Child, whose purpose was to prepare the many poor and homeless girls living in various hospices for their First Communion.

On August 11, 1865, Fr. Olivaint was transferred to the Jesuit residence on the Rue de Sèvres, thus exchanging the classroom and the academic training of students for a pulpit and the direction of souls. When the Franco-German War began in July 1870, the Jesuit residence was designated as an auxiliary hospital. He and other Jesuits gave selflessly in caring for the wounded and the dying who were brought to them during the long siege of Paris. Prior to the declaration of war, Fr. Olivaint observed a growing hatred among liberal thinkers toward the Jesuits and the Catholic Church. He predicted: "Persecution is at our doors and it will be terrible. We will have to go through a blood bath." Now that war was declared he was certain that hard times were imminent. When the French government transferred its headquarters to Versailles and the revolutionary element usurped municipal control on March 18, 1871, he moved his community outside the city. He too was about to leave when on the morning of April 4 he heard the distressing news that his brother Jesuits at the school of St. Genevieve had been arrested. As long as they were in prison he felt he could not leave, no matter what it might cost him.

With Fr. Olivaint was Fr. John Caubert. Fr. Caubert was born in Paris on July 20, 1811. He studied first at the College of Louis the Great and then went on for a law degree. After practicing law in Paris for seven years he entered the novitiate at Saint-Acheul on July 11, 1845, and took his vows on July 31, 1847, at age thirty-six. He spent a year studying philosophy and three years theology prior to ordination. Between 1851 and 1861 he spent three years as confessor to the seminarians at Blois and seven years as a teacher at St. Genevieve in Paris. In 1861 he took on the office of the province treasurer and made his residence at Rue de Sèvres, where he and Fr. Olivaint were arrested.

On the evening of April 4, 1871, about 6:00 P.M., a member of the commune, still grateful to Fr. Olivaint for a past kindness, came to urge him to leave the city, for he and Fr. Caubert were sure to be arrested that evening. The communards came on schedule, thoroughly searched the house, and took both priests as hostages to the Conciergerie Prison, where they placed them in separate cells to prevent contact between them. At the same prison there already were twelve Jesuit hostages from St. Genevieve, including Frs. Leo Ducoudray, Alexis Clerc, and Anatole de Bengy. Fr. de Bengy was born at Bourges on September 19, 1824, and after spending nine years at the Jesuit school in Brugelette, Belgium, went to Rome. He entered the Society at the Roman novitiate of Sant'Andrea on November 12, 1845, and pronounced his vows on November 13, 1847. He returned to Brugelette for four more years where he did some studying and more teaching. After ordination in 1854 he worked in several colleges in France, but in 1856 went as chaplain with the French army to the Crimea. When peace was restored, he returned to the classroom. At the outbreak of the Franco-German War he again volunteered to serve as chaplain. It was while he was at St. Genevieve in Paris tending the sick and wounded that he and eleven other Jesuits were arrested in the early hours of April 4.

On April 6 Frs. Ducoudray, Clerc, and de Bengy were moved to the Mazas Prison, but Frs. Olivaint and Caubert remained at the Conciergerie. Prison may not be the ideal place for making one's annual spiritual retreat, but not knowing what the future was to bring, Frs. Olivaint and Caubert began to make the Spiritual Exercises. Three times a week, when provisions were brought to the prison, the priests were glad to find that the Blessed Sacrament had been smuggled in with the food.

On April 13, Frs. Olivaint and Caubert were taken to the Mazas Prison, where they quietly continued their retreats and occasionally wrote letters to their religious superiors and families. Then on May 22 the group of hostages at Mazas were transferred to La Roquette, a prison for those condemned to die.

Two days later, realizing that death could come at any moment, the hostages, none of whom had yet been tried and convicted, went to confession during their recreation period.

The days of the Paris Commune were numbered and the communards finally came to realize that they could not win against the government. Hence, the punishment they could not inflict on the government they decided to inflict on the innocent hostages. On the evening of May 24, a prison official called out the names of six hostages, the first martyrs of the Paris Commune. These included two Jesuits, the archbishop of Paris, two diocesan priests, and a civil magistrate. After the six had been taken away, the remaining hostages knelt in prayer. It was not long before they heard a volley of shots in the courtyard.

Everyone in La Roquette was prepared for death. Nothing happened on the 25th, but then on the 26th, while the army from Versailles was marching against the commune, the communards chose to sacrifice more hostages. Prison officials came to where the hostages were enclosed and read out fifteen names; the first three to be called were Frs. Olivaint, Caubert, and de Bengy. When all fifteen names had been called, the prisoners were escorted outside and added to prisoners from other parts of the building. Their execution was to take place in the Belleville section of Paris, about one-and-a-half miles away. The prisoners began their last march at 4:00 P.M., and as they passed through the Paris streets, vagabonds, convicts, and deserters followed the group. As they advanced, the crowd grew in numbers, becoming more boisterous and more difficult to contain. Finally they arrived at Rue de Haxo about 6:00 P.M. The prisoners were herded into a courtyard called Cité-Vincennes and there the mob's brutality erupted. The wild mob attacked the defenseless prisoners with clubs and staves, guns and bayonets, and for an hour they killed, butchered, and massacred until there was no one left alive. At 7:00 P.M. fifty-two bodies were lying in the courtyard, all victims of human hatred.

On May 27 the French army arrived in Paris; unfortunately, a day too late. However, the infamous Paris Commune had come to its deserved end. The liberating forces emptied the prisons of all hostages and attended to the recovery of the bodies of the dead. Fr. Olivaint was found to have received a gunshot wound in his chest, Fr. Caubert was unrecognizable except for the crucifix he carried about his neck, and Fr. de Bengy was severely slashed by sabres and bayonets. The bodies of these three Jesuits, together with those of Frs. Ducoudray and Clerc, were taken to the residence on Rue de Sèvres and placed in the chapel of the Japanese martyrs. On May 31 they were buried in the cemetery at Mont-Parnasse. Two months later the bodies were brought back to the church on Rue de Sèvres and interred in the martyrs' chapel.

The cause of Frs. Peter Olivaint, John Caubert, and Anatole de Bengy, together with that of Frs. Leo Ducoudray and Alexis Clerc, was introduced in Rome on February 17, 1937.

S. G. Anthony Criminali 1520–1549

Martyr of India

The Society of Jesus has had many martyrs during its 450 years of existence, but it is especially fond of Fr. Anthony Criminali, the first of its members to shed his blood for Christ. He was born in Sissa, in the diocese of Parma, Italy, on February 7, 1520. After his early education with the local parish priest, he went to Parma to study for the priesthood and was ordained a subdeacon when he was eighteen. In 1539 Fr. Peter Favre came to Parma to preach parish missions and Anthony became acquainted with him. Under Fr. Favre's direction he made the Spiritual Exercises for thirty days, but did not enter the Society at this time, though some of his friends did. At the end of September 1541, he bade his parents goodbye and, dressed as a pilgrim, walked and begged his way to Rome. He arrived in November and immediately went to see Fr. Ignatius. In speaking to the founder of the Jesuits, Anthony, who was too humble to ask to be admitted as a candidate, merely requested to help the fathers by doing various chores about the house. Perceiving in him a young man ready to do God's will, Fr. Ignatius gladly took him in.

Shortly after Anthony's arrival in the Eternal City, he learned that his mother had died and that his father was deeply distressed and feared that he too would soon follow her to the grave. Sensitive to everyone's problems, Fr. Ignatius suggested to Anthony that he go home to comfort his father; at the same time he assured the young man that when he returned he would be accepted as a novice. As it turned out Anthony's visit to Sissa was not long. His father recovered from his depression and Anthony was soon again in Rome, where on April 9, 1542, he was admitted into the Society. On April 23 he left for Portugal to complete his studies at the University of Coimbra and was ordained there on January 6, 1544.

Assigned to the mission in India, Fr. Criminali left Coimbra for Lisbon in March 1544. He and a companion embarked on April 22, but because of a violent storm the ship was forced to return to port. It was not until March 29, 1545, that Fr. Criminali and his friend secured passage; they arrived in Goa, India, on September 2.

Fr. Francis Xavier assigned Fr. Criminali to work along the Fishery Coast, from Ramnad to Cape Comorin, an area that extended 130 miles. He began his labors toward the end of 1545 or the beginning of 1546. Fr. Criminali was young, only twenty-six years old, nevertheless, he was made mission superior. Throughout his three years in India he established mission stations and left a priest or a catechist in charge of each. Every month he visited each station on foot, disregarding the heat, cold, and rain. His gentleness of character was known to all, even to the non-Christians. In writing to Fr. Ignatius on January 14, 1549, Fr. Francis Xavier offered this description: "Anthony Criminali is at Cape Comorin, with six others of the Society. Indeed, he is a holy man, and seems to have been born to work in these lands. Men like him can achieve a good deal—I wish you would send us more of them. He is superior of those stationed at Cape Comorin and is beloved by native Christians, pagans, and Moslems. But the love that Ours have for him is beyond telling."

Sometime toward the end of May or in early June 1549, Fr. Criminali visited the mission at Vedalai. A bit north of the mission a road led to the place where Hindu pilgrims crossed over by boat to visit the sacred island of Rameswaram, a short distance from the mainland. The island was famous for its temple and, thus, many pilgrims traveled that road, especially on their feast days. The Portuguese, who ruled that part of India, unfortunately, had decided to take advantage of them and set up a tollgate on the pilgrim road. This greatly inconvenienced the pilgrims and they informed the Brahman priests at the temple that the foreigners were preventing them from coming to the shrine. The priests at the shrine took the problem to the Marava prince of Ramnad. Since such harassment had to stop, the prince contacted the Badaga, a fighting caste, and some 7,000 men were soon on their way to attack the Portuguese settlement.

When the Portuguese received word that an attack was imminent, they all hastened to the ships in the harbor, leaving the Indian Christians defenseless. Fr. Criminali scurried about the settlement trying to get the Christians to go to the ships as well. But the Badaga had already arrived and the priest saw one of them slay his catechist. They next surrounded him; he could neither advance nor retreat so he knelt down in their midst, raised his hands in prayer and waited for the blow to come. One of the Badaga jabbed him with a lance, while others tried to rip his cassock from him. They then left him. The missionary rose with blood streaming from his wound and tried to make his way to the chapel to die there, but he was once more surrounded. This time a lance was thrust into his breast. Again he tried to reach the chapel, and again a lance was directed toward him. It struck his right side and as he was falling to the ground a Badaga rode by and severed the head from the body.

The victorious Badaga carried away Fr. Criminali's head and cassock, and placed them as an offering on their shrine's altar. The Christians then took the priest's body and buried it in the sand. It was a very shallow grave because they had to bury it quickly, in fear that the Badaga would return and subject it to further indignities. Two days later they returned to the shore and buried the body deeper, waiting for the day when they would be able to place it in a fitting tomb. When the time came to transfer the body to the church, the Christians were unable to locate it. Many a hole was dug, but their every attempt proved unsuccessful. Either they forgot where the actual burial place had been or, more probably, the strong Monsoon winds, lashing furiously over the sandy beach had changed its contours so drastically that the Christians knew not where to search for the body.

At the time of his death, Fr. Anthony Criminali was but twenty-nine years old and had been a Jesuit for seven years. His cause was initiated in 1901.

Bl. Thomas Cottam 1549–1582

Martyr of England

Thomas Cottam was born in Lancashire, England, in 1549, of Protestant parents and was raised in the Established Church. He was educated at Brasenose College, Oxford, and earned his bachelor's degree in 1569. He then moved to London, where he obtained a schoolmaster's position and where he met Thomas Pound, an ardent Catholic. Through Pound's influence Thomas converted to Catholicism (about 1575), and as he matured in the faith Pound further encouraged him to become a priest. Thus in May 1577 Thomas left his teaching position and traveled to Flanders on the Continent to attend the English College at Douai. During 1578 he visited England (January to May), and on his return brought with him five young converts from Oxford. In his desire for a stricter way of life, he thought of becoming a Jesuit and in February 1579, after he had been ordained deacon, he left Douai for Rome, where he entered the novitiate of Sant' Andrea on April 8, 1579. Never expecting to return to his native England—the Jesuits as yet had no mission there—he requested to go to India as a missionary. But within months of becoming a Jesuit he became ill with a lingering malady attributed to the Roman climate, and the physician suggested he return north, perhaps to his homeland to recover.

Thomas went to Lyons, arriving there about December 1579, to see if the air there would help, but his health became worse. While in that French city he met the despicable Mr. Sledd, an Englishman in the service of his government, who sniffed out English priests before they returned home. Under the pretense of being a fervent practicing Catholic, Sledd took advantage of Thomas's friendship and learned that the latter was looking forward to ordination and to going to England to work among persecuted Catholics. Sledd accompanied Thomas on his way to the English College in Rheims (April 1580), but as they approached Paris Sledd left him so that he could report to the English ambassador living in the capital. Sledd gave his superior a detailed description of Thomas as well as the news that he would soon be crossing the Channel for England.

Thomas was ordained to the priesthood at Soissons, France, on May 28, 1580, and on June 5 set out, with other companions, for England, arriving there in the middle of the month (June 16–18). Because of Sledd's description, Dover port authorities were awaiting his arrival. Fr. Cottam was immediately recognized and arrested. A lawyer, using the name Havard, and a frequent traveler from France to London, was pressed into service to deliver him to Lord Cobham, a London magistrate. The lawyer, whose true name was Humphrey Ely, was a Catholic and a law professor at the University of Douai. When he revealed his identity to Fr. Cottam, he told him that he had no intention of handing him over to the queen's men, but that when they arrive in London they would separate and each go his own way. Fr. Cottam was rather disturbed in conscience about this deceit and thought of turning himself in to Lord Cobham, but acquaintances of his talked him out of it. When he learned that Ely was under investigation because he had not delivered the priest to the magistrate, Fr. Cottam voluntarily placed himself in Cobham's hands to save Ely further trouble.

The charge brought against him was the fact that he was a Catholic priest, and in a preliminary interrogation he made it clear that he would not change his religion even to save his life; hence, he was sent to Marshalsea Prison in London. On October 4, 1581, he was transferred to the Tower, where he underwent fierce torture. On November 20, together with Fr. Edmund Campion, he was condemned for high treason and sentenced to be hanged, drawn, and quartered. Now that there were Jesuits in England, Fr. Cottam wrote to the mission's superior asking for readmittance into the Society, which was readily granted him.

Fr. Campion's execution was carried out on December 1, 1581; Fr. Cottam languished in the Tower for another six months. On May 30, 1582, together with three diocesan priests, Frs. William Filby, Luke Kirby, and Laurence Richardson, he was dragged to Tyburn. The executioners kept Fr. Cottam for last, and as he saw each of his companions hanged, their hearts and intestines torn out, and limbs hacked off, he said to each, "William, pray for me"; "Luke, pray for me"; "Laurence, pray for me." When it was his turn the officials attempted to induce him to ask the queen's mercy, saying that she was a forgiving monarch and was eager to bestow favors upon him. To this he retorted: "I will not swerve a jot from my faith for any thing, yea, if I had ten thousand lives, I would rather lose them all than forsake the Catholic faith in any point." Unable to get him to deny his religion, they placed him on a cart and rolled him beneath the gallows. Once in position he asked the Catholics present to pray with him, and aloud he said the Our Father and as he was half-way through the Hail Mary the executioner had the cart pulled from under him. His hanging body was cut down, then disembowelled and quartered, but to keep the bystanders from taking relics, the bodies of the four martyrs were cast into vats of boiling water.

Fr. Thomas Cottam and the three diocesan priests, who died with him, were beatified by Pope Leo XIII on December 9, 1886. His memorial is on December 1, the day when the Society remembers all its English and Welsh martyrs.

Prayer

Almighty, eternal God, you chose from the people of England and Wales Blessed Thomas Cottam and his companions to be made like Christ, who died to save the world. Listen to their prayers; strengthen your Church by the same faith and love that strengthened them, and bless it always with your gift of unity. We ask this through our Lord Jesus Christ, your Son, who lives and reigns with you and the Holy Spirit, one God, for ever and ever.

June 6

S. G. Sebastian Vieira 1574–1634

Martyr of Japan

Fr. Sebastian Vieira made his fourth and final trip to Japan in 1632, where he was martyred for preaching Christ to the Japanese. He had just returned to Macao after a visit to Europe and was again eager to be with his Christian converts. He took passage to Manila, where he bribed a Chinese captain to take him on his junk to Japan. Though disguised as a Chinese sailor, Fr. Vieira spent the first ten days of the voyage hiding in the ship's hold. There was not enough light to read and the air was particularly unbearable because of the stench coming from the deerskin cargo. While in hiding he learned that a Dominican and two Franciscan missionaries were also on board; they too had bribed the captain to take them to Japan.

When the missionaries' presence became known to the sailors, the latter insisted that the captain either return to Manila or drop them on the first island they should see. So certain were they that the missionaries would bring them bad luck that they wanted to be rid of them as soon as possible. The missionaries, now that they were discovered, came on deck and heard the sailors and passengers discussing whether they should be deposited on the island of Formosa (now Taiwan), which they were soon to pass. Among the passengers Fr. Vieira recognized one of his early converts, now an apostate, and spoke to him about their former friendship. He finally induced the man to convince the sailors to allow the missionaries to remain on board.

Then a storm arose suddenly. While the sailors attributed it to the missionaries' presence, the apostate Christians aboard attributed it to their denial of Christianity. Thinking that death was imminent, the apostates asked to go to confession and promised, should they survive the storm, not to inform the Japanese authorities of the missionaries' coming to the country. The storm passed and the

P. Sebastianus Vieira Lusitanus, cum quinq. Socÿs Iaponibus Soc. IESV,
triduano Scrobis tormento, et Subiecto igne pro Fide Christi neca.
tus, in Iaponia Iendi. 6 Iunÿ A. 1634.

C. Screta d.

Melch: Küsell

S. G. Sebastian Vieira and Companions

remaining days were tranquil. As the junk was about to enter port and receive the harbor officials to check incoming passengers, the missionaries again went into hiding. Fr. Vieira hid in a water tank, where he almost died for lack of air; but when all was safe, the missionaries entered Japan unnoticed.

On touching Japanese soil, Fr. Vieira knelt down and kissed it saying: "This will be my resting place for eternity. This is the house of God and the gate of heaven." Not only did he expect to be martyred, but he was also prepared for it.

Fr. Sebastian Vieira was born in Castro d'Airo, in northern Portugal in 1574 (or perhaps 1571). He entered the Society on February 3, 1591, and made his studies for the priesthood at Évora. In 1602, together with other zealous missionaries, he left Lisbon for India. From there he went to Macao on the Chinese coast and served for a year as master of novices to young Jesuits. His first visit to Japan took place about 1604. Some time after 1606 he was in Macao as procurator of the Japanese province. In 1609 he was once again doing missionary work in Japan.

In February 1614, Shogun Iyeyasu issued his decree banishing all foreign missionaries from Japan and ordering them to proceed to Nagasaki to await deportation. For months the missionaries waited for ships to arrive, and finally in early November the exiles were taken to Macao or to Manila. Fr. Vieira was taken to Manila, but in August 1615 he was back in Japan working with the Christians in Omura. He remained there until 1619 when superiors called him to Macao, where he was again province procurator and attended the assembly of Jesuits known as a provincial congregation, December 14 to 23, 1623. One purpose of the meeting was to elect a delegate to go to Rome and report to the Jesuit general on the state of the mission, informing him of the mission's strong points and where it needed reinforcements, both in terms of money and manpower. When Fr. Vieira was chosen to go, he left Macao in February 1624 on a trip that would not bring him back to that port for another seven years. The sea voyage to Europe took more than six months and when he arrived in Portugal he visited Jesuit houses as well as his family.

He reached Rome in 1627 and there he spoke with the general, Fr. Muzio Vitelleschi, and had an audience with Pope Urban VIII. The pope was especially interested in Christianity's growth in Japan, and to His Holiness the missionary described the glories of the Japanese church as well as its tragedies. Conversions were numerous and the example of the martyrs was a powerful lesson to everyone, but there was also a dark side to report for there were apostasies as well. As the pope imparted his blessing, he said: "Go my son, and strengthen the faith in Japan, and do not spare yourself. If I hear that the executioner's sword has shed your blood in so holy a cause, I myself will inscribe your name in the list of the blessed."

Together with a number of new recruits for the mission, Fr. Vieira set out from Europe, and after a trip that lasted almost a year, he returned to Macao to report on his Roman visit. Shortly afterwards he made plans for his fourth trip to Japan. On his return there in 1632, he was appointed to two important positions: he was vice-provincial for the Jesuits, which meant he would oversee the Society's missionary operation, and he was also the bishop's vicar, which meant he would supervise the Church's growth in Japan. To fulfill both offices he was forced to do extensive traveling, much of it in disguise and at night.

Once it was learned that the "Roman priest," for this is the name the Japanese gave him after his visit to the Eternal City, had reentered the country, the governor of Nagasaki placed a price of fifteen hundred gold pieces on his head. Such a high reward enticed spies and apostates to seek him out, but for twenty months he eluded them. Toward the end of 1633, when he was on a boat off the Osaka shore, he was unexpectedly apprehended and taken to a prison in Omura. The young emperor in Yedo (today's Tokyo), having heard of Fr. Vieira's capture, wanted to know something about his preaching and had him brought to the imperial city in early 1634. Because criminals were not allowed in the emperor's august presence, the missionary was interrogated by court officials and his answers were then carried to the throne. The emperor had shown some interest in the Catholic faith so Fr. Vieira wrote a short summary of the faith, in Japanese, which the emperor read. At one point he turned to those near him and said: "If what the Christian bonze says about the soul's immortality is true, then how miserable we are. What should we do?" Sensing that the emperor was leaning towards Fr. Vieira's teaching, the emperor's uncle reminded him that he was obliged to uphold the national religion and that the law must take its course. In the end, Fr. Vieira, with seven other prisoners, was condemned to suffer the torture of the pit.

The pit was probably the most inhumane of all Japanese tortures. The victim was tightly bound around the body, as high as his breast, with one arm free so that, if he should decide, he could signal to the executioners his readiness to apostatize. The victim was then suspended head downward from a gallowslike structure into a pit, which contained excreta and other filth. The blood rushed to the victim's head, but to prevent too great a congestion there, the victim's forehead and temples were slightly slashed so that the pressure could be relieved by the slow seepage of blood. Death usually came within two or three days. Among Fr. Vieira's companions were five servant-catechists, apprehended with him off Osaka, and a Franciscan priest, Fr. Aloysius Gomez, and his catechist. All died within two days, but Fr. Vieira was still alive on the third day, and since he showed no willingness to apostatize, nor were there any signs that he would soon die, the impatient executioners built a fire around him and burned him to death.

Fr. Sebastian Vieira's martyrdom took place on June 6, 1634. His cause, and that of his companions, was opened in Macao and Japan in 1901.

Bl. James Berthieu 1838–1896

Martyr of Madagascar

Fr. James Berthieu was martyred on the island of Madagascar, off Africa's east coast, in 1896. He was a Frenchman, born on November 27, 1838, on a small farm in Monlogis, Polminhac, in the diocese of Saint-Flour. As a youth he studied at the minor seminary at Pleaux, then moved to the major seminary in Saint-Flour in October 1859, and was ordained to the priesthood on May 21, 1864. His assignment within the diocese was to a country parish in Roannes-Saint-Mary, where he remained for nine years until he decided to enter the Society of Jesus. With his bishop's permission, the thirty-five-year-old priest entered the Jesuit novitiate at Pau on October 31, 1873.

Because he had been a priest for some time, Fr. Berthieu's noviceship training was different from that of the other novices, who ordinarily were fifteen years his junior. After a year at Pau he moved to Vals, near Le Puy, and spent the year reviewing theology. Before finishing his second year of noviceship, he was appointed to the Madagascar mission, and together with a missionary companion left Marseilles on September 26, 1875. The ship made a stop at Naples, then passed through the Mediterranean into the Red Sea, and when it entered the Indian Ocean it headed for Réunion, an island east of Madagascar. When the ship docked at Saint-Denis, the two missionaries made their way to the Jesuit residence, where the superior assigned Fr. Berthieu to the island of Sainte-Marie. Before leaving for his post, he made his religious vows on November 13, 1875.

Fr. Berthieu arrived on Sainte-Marie on December 14, and immediately threw himself into his missionary work. He catechized children, dispensed the sacraments, heard confessions, and tended the sick. Two other Jesuits were on the island with him, but one was old and the other infirm, hence, the burdens of the mission were his. For four years he relished the work and the peace at that mission, but these were soon disrupted by France's decree expelling the Jesuits. In March 1880 the French government closed the Society's schools and forced the Jesuits into exile. The Madagascar missionaries did not escape the effects of that decree, and by the end of October 1881, Fr. Berthieu too had to leave Sainte-Marie. He went to Tamatave on Madagascar Island, and from there to Tananarive (now Antananarivo), the capital, then to Ambohimandroso, near Fianarantsoa in the south, where he began working among the Betsileo people. Less than two years later this missionary work also came to a halt. The Malagasy declared war on the French and in May 1883 they curtailed the religious activity of the French priests in the country. Fr. Berthieu left his mission in mid-June and, after walking some 200 miles, arrived on July 10 at Tamatave, where he met his fellow Jesuits.

Since it was impossible to engage in any priestly ministry, Fr. Berthieu turned to gardening and his efforts supplied fresh vegetables for the table.

The French soldiers on the island were without chaplains so several Jesuits, Fr. Berthieu among them, went to minister to them in the north. At the end of 1885 a treaty was signed and when peace returned, Fr. Berthieu in 1886 reopened the mission at Ambositra. Then in December 1891 he went to evangelize the Merina people in the district of Andrainarivo (today's Anjozorofady), a short distance north of Tananarive.

His new mission covered a large area. He had eighteen stations to visit and he was often on the road traveling from one station to another. His ministry was again interrupted by a Malagasy rebellion against the French in 1895. He had to leave his mission in October and this time he went to Réunion. As soon as the war ended, he was back at his station, but the treaty did not last long and in May 1896 another rebellion broke out among the Menalamba people. When the fighting came within a few hours' walk from the mission at Ambatomainty, the French colonel, concerned about the people's safety, ordered them on May 25 to move a short distance outside the village. Fr. Berthieu went with his people and camped with them in the fields. He described his view of the situation in these words: "This is above all a persecution of the Catholic faith mixed with a certain desire for independence. The devil is directing the entire operation." Non-Catholic missionaries had been, for some time, inciting non-Christians to resist the missionaries on the island. Fr. Berthieu and his people took to the road; they carried their belongings and endured the hardships of living outdoors day and night.

On June 6 Fr. Berthieu received word that it would be safer for his group to move into the capital. Thus on June 7, he celebrated Mass at 4:00 A.M. and afterwards the refugees started their march to Tananarive. On their way they were attacked by the Menalamba tribe and all were forced to scatter, seeking safety in nearby villages. Fr. Berthieu and several of his faithful found shelter in Ambohibemasoandro, a village that was predominantly non-Catholic, but since hospitality was sacred among the people, the refugees were made welcome. The following morning, June 8, the Menalamba came to the village and arrested the missionary. After maltreating him, striking him with clubs and wounding him, they stripped him of his cassock and forced him to follow them in the cold rain to the village where their chief resided. When the prisoner arrived at Ambiatibé, he was shivering from the cold and his undershirt was heavily blood-stained. Aware of the priest's influence among the Catholic population, the chief tried to get him to apostatize, but without success. Finally he said: "Renounce your villainous religion and stop deceiving these people. We will then accept you as our leader and counselor and will not kill you." To this promise of freedom the missionary replied: "My child, I cannot agree to that. I prefer to die." By this simple statement Fr. Berthieu chose martyrdom. Obeying the chief's next order, several of his men fell upon the missionary with clubs, and one of them struck him on the head, bringing him to the ground. After the assassins had done their work, they took the body and threw it into the river, never to be recovered.

Fr. James Berthieu died on June 8, 1896, at age fifty-eight. He was beatified by Pope Paul VI on October 17, 1965, and his Jesuit brethren celebrate his memorial on February 4.

Prayer

O God, you nourished your Church by the blood of your martyr Blessed James Berthieu on the island of Madagascar; we beg you to grant that by his intercession the rich seed of Christianity might everywhere flourish. We ask this through our Lord Jesus Christ, your Son, who lives and reigns with you and the Holy Spirit, one God, for ever and ever.

June 9

Bl. Joseph de Anchieta 1534–1597

Joseph de Anchieta, Brazil's most famous missionary and a founder of the cities of São Paulo and Rio de Janeiro, was born on March 19, 1534, at San Cristobál de la Laguna on Tenerife, in the Canary Islands. He attended the Jesuit college at Coimbra, Portugal, and after a year of study entered the Jesuit novitiate on May 1, 1551. Two years later—when only nineteen—he was sent to the missions in Brazil. During his noviceship his health had failed and he had suffered a dislocation of the spine, which caused him pain for the remainder of his life. Since Brazil's climate was considered mild, his superiors sent him to the mission to regain his health. His health never improved, but he did become the "Apostle of Brazil."

With six other Jesuits Joseph landed at Bahia on July 13, 1553, and immediately went to São Vicente, where he had his first contact with the Tupi Indians living on the outskirts of the settlement. He was adept at languages and within a short time learned Tupi-Guaraní, the language commonly spoken among the native population. His interest in the language was not merely academic; if he wanted to Christianize these people he must first speak their tongue. In January 1554 he accompanied his superior, Fr. Manuel de Nóbrega, to the small village of Piratininga, where they hoped to establish a mission and a school. They arrived on January 24, and on the following day Fr. Nóbrega celebrated Mass. Since it was the feast of St. Paul, they named the mission São Paulo. It was from this mission that today's great metropolis developed. Joseph's assignment was to teach Latin to those studying for the priesthood and to teach grammar and to give catechetical instruction to the Tupi and Portuguese children.

For the next two decades he remained in the São Paulo district, carrying on his missionary labors, dividing his time between natives and settlers. He became proficient in the Tupi tongue and completed a Tupi grammar in 1555, which was then used by the Portuguese settlers and missionaries. Later on he compiled a Tupi dictionary.

His only excursions from the mission were with his superior, whom he often served as interpreter. In 1563 he went with Fr. Nóbrega to negotiate peace between the Portuguese and the Tamoyo, a tribe that frequently molested the São Vicente mission and threatened that of São Paulo. The Tamoyo were supplied with arms by the Huguenots, who were attempting to establish a French settlement with a view to ousting the Portuguese. The negotiations lasted longer than expected, and until a truce was finally agreed upon Joseph was detained at Iperoig as a hostage of the Tamoyo. During those three months of loneliness and frustration, he occupied himself by composing an heroic poem in honor of the Blessed Virgin Mary. Without paper, pen, or ink, he wrote his Latin verses in the seashore's wet sand and then committed them to memory. When he again reached São Vicente, he set his poem down on paper—it had 4,172 lines.

It was in June 1566, when he was thirty-two years old, that he was ordained a priest in the Bahia cathedral. Prior to this time no bishop was available. In the following year Fr. Anchieta went with Fr. Nóbrega to found the settlement now known as Rio de Janeiro, and was appointed superior of the São Paulo and São Vicente missions. Though administrative duties were now added to his teaching and preaching, he never lost an interest in the native population. He succeeded in converting the Maramomis tribe. It was during this period that he began to write dramas for his students to perform. These plays were written in different languages: Latin, Portuguese, and Tupi. The plots were taken from the Bible and the Catholic faith and served as vehicles of instruction and edification. Because these were the first dramas written in Brazil, Fr. Anchieta is accorded the honor of being called the "Father of Brazilian National Literature." In 1577 he was appointed provincial and had a territory of some fifteen hundred miles of coastline to visit. Most of the visitations were done by small boat, but inland trips had to be done on foot. His back had always caused him trouble and as he grew older he developed a hunchback, which made riding a horse quite painful.

He was twice near death, and since his health was on a steady decline, he asked to be relieved of his duties as provincial. In 1587 he was placed in charge of the mission at Espírito Santo, where he gave ten more years to the missions, spending some of his time writing poetry and dramas. He regularly went into the wilderness to search out natives to convert and to invite them to live in villages.

Throughout his forty-four years in Brazil, Fr. Anchieta's one principle of action was: "Nothing is too arduous that has for its purpose the honor of God and the salvation of souls." Having worn himself out in the service of his Lord, he was taken in 1595 to Reritiba (today's Anchieta), and there on June 9, 1597, at age sixty-three, the indefatigable missionary rendered his soul to God. His body was then taken to Espírito Santo and buried in the Jesuit chapel.

Pope John Paul II beatified Fr. Joseph de Anchieta on June 22, 1980; his memorial is liturgically celebrated on June 9.

Prayer

Lord, pour out upon us your Holy Spirit as you did upon Blessed Joseph de Anchieta, your priest, so that like him we may become all things to all, and as faithful servants of your Word seek to gain all for your kingdom and so unite them in the love of your Son, who lives and reigns with you and the Holy Spirit, one God, for ever and ever.

June 10

Bl. Joseph Imbert ca. 1720–1794
Bl. John Nicholas Cordier 1710–1794
Martyrs of the Rochefort Prison Ships

At the time of their martyrdom, Fr. Joseph Imbert was a septuagenarian and Fr. John Nicholas Cordier an octogenarian. Both had lived through the harsh vicissitudes that led to the French Revolution and to the frightful days of the Reign of Terror, of which they were victims.

Joseph Imbert was born in Marseilles, France, about 1720. He entered the Jesuit novitiate in Avignon in 1748 and pronounced his first vows on June 29, 1750. After ordination in 1754 he taught at colleges in Chalon-sur-Saône, Besançon, and Grenoble. He was stationed in this last city when the Society was suppressed in France in 1762. Fr. Imbert then joined the diocese of Moulins, and when he refused to accept the 1790 Civil Constitution of the Clergy and take the heretical oath to support it, he was forced to relinquish his parish. While many priests left to go abroad, he remained in Moulins and continued his ministry in secret.

With the expulsion of the bishop, Fr. Imbert was appointed vicar-apostolic of the diocese, and since he was now its highest ranking official he was more than ever the object of the revolutionaries' hatred. In due time he was arrested and incarcerated in Moulins. A prison document dated July 4, 1793, indicates that he had been detained in the city's *maison commune* since June 9. In early 1794 he and twenty-four priests of the diocese, who had been imprisoned with him, began a journey that was to end in deportation. They were taken southwestward to Limoges, and from there to Saintes, about twenty miles from Rochefort, the designated port of embarkation. The Moulins prisoners remained at Saintes for several months and while there Fr. Imbert set new lyrics to Rouget de Lisle's patriotic hymn, *La Marseillaise*. The new lyrics were not designed to glorify revolution but, in view of the priests' imminent deportation, to kindle their apostolic spirit and to look upon their exile as an opportunity to carry Christ's message to others. The song was frequently sung by the prisoners and came to be known as *The Priests' Marseillaise*.

From Saintes the priests were transferred to Rochefort, one of the ports selected for transporting the refractory priests to Africa. Of these ports, Rochefort drew the greatest number of priest-deportees. On arriving from various French cities, the deportees were detained in hospitals, former convents and monasteries, and on two small ships, *La Borée* and *Nourrice*, then anchored in midstream of the Charente River and in use as hospitals for the galleys. Fr. Imbert was placed on the former. Then on April 11 the priest-prisoners in Rochefort began to be transferred to the *Deux-Associés*, anchored in the roadstead of the Ile d'Aix, a fortified island off the main coast from the mouth of the Charente. Fr. Imbert boarded on April 13. Climbing the ladder was no easy task for the elderly priests; whenever they paused to catch their breath a sailor pushed them upward. Once on deck they were searched and all objects of devotion, such as prayer books and breviaries, were confiscated. In early May the captain of the *Deux-Associés* gave notice that he then had more than 400 priests on board and there was no room for more. Thus another ship, the *Washington*, was called into service and it was on this vessel that Fr. Cordier was placed.

John Nicholas Cordier was born on December 3, 1710, near Souilly, in the Duchy of Lorraine, and entered the novitiate in Nancy on September 28, 1728. After philosophical studies at the University of Pont-à-Mousson, he taught at colleges in Dijon, Auxerre, and Autun. He returned to Pont-à-Mousson for theology and after receiving his doctorate taught philosophy at Strasbourg and some time later theology at Pont-à-Mousson. In 1757 he was transferred to Rheims, where he was prefect of studies, and then in 1761 became superior of the residence in Saint-Mihiel, in the diocese of Verdun. Subsequent to the Society's suppression in Lorraine in 1786, he remained in Saint-Mihiel and was chaplain to a convent of nuns until 1790, when the government suppressed all religious orders in France. Thereafter he resided with Canon Georges-François Steinhoff in Verdun. Despite his advanced age, Fr. Cordier was arrested on October 28, 1793, charged with being a refractory priest and ordered to be deported. He was imprisoned in Bar, the county seat. He remained there for nearly six months and on April 15, 1794, though he could only walk with a cane and this with great difficulty, he formed part of the convoy of priest-prisoners on their way to Rochefort for eventual deportation. Fr. Cordier boarded the *Washington* on June 19.

The *Deux-Associés* and the *Washington* never set sail because the English navy had successfully blockaded the French coast. Both ships had to remain at anchor off Ile d'Aix in the Charente estuary. Conditions on both vessels (former slave ships traveling between Africa and South America) were horribly harsh. The deportees were crowded underdeck, where the air was fetid and asphyxiating and without sanitation facilities. The ceiling was too low for anyone to stand erect, and when it was time to sleep, one's arms touched those of the neighbor. At night the hatchways were padlocked—if there were an emergency, there would be no exit. In the morning a barrel of burning tar was lowered into the underdeck to fumigate the prisoners prior to their coming on deck. The area marked out for them on deck was so limited that they had to stand all day, and so cramped together were they that they had difficulty in eating. Their spare meals, served but once a day, consisted of boiled beans, wormy black bread, and dried meat seasoned with rancid oil. Drinking water was of a dark color. As a consequence many came down with respiratory problems and serious illnesses, such as scurvy and typhus. It was not unusual for two or three to die on any given night. The bodies were then taken by their fellow priests, under guard, to nearby Ile d'Aix and there buried in the sand. Prayers for the dead were forbidden. Fr. Imbert, in weakened condition at the time of boarding, was among the first to fall ill, most probably of typhus, and after being on board less than two months died on June 9, 1794. He was one of the 226 victims buried on that island.

Because of protests on the part of the island's inhabitants, both vessels then moved further up the Charente and anchored off the sparsely populated Ile Madame. Due to the summer's heat, the number of those falling ill increased, with the result that a temporary hospital of marquees was erected on Ile Madame. Those transferred to the island thought themselves fortunate; they heard birds singing, saw butterflies amid the flowers, and had fresh air to breathe. Fr. Cordier, after he became ill, was taken to this makeshift island hospital and there died on September 30. He was one of the 254 victims buried in that island's sand.

With Robespierre's fall in late July of that year, the revolution was in its final weeks. In early 1795 those who survived the ordeal of the Rochefort prison ships—a total of 285—returned home. Of the 822 priests (diocesan and religious) and seven Christian Brothers condemned to deportation, 547 had died within a ten-month period, and of this number 64 (for whom there was sufficient testimony concerning the manner in which they accepted their suffering and death) were beatified by Pope John Paul II on October 1, 1995. The members of the Society liturgically commemorate their brothers Bl. Joseph Imbert and Bl. John Nicholas Cordier on January 19.

Prayer

Lord God, you honored our brothers Blessed Joseph Imbert and John Nicholas Cordier by making them one with your son, Jesus, in giving their lives for your glory. Hear their prayers, and gather into perfect unity all who believe in him. We ask this through our Lord Jesus Christ, your Son, who lives and reigns with you and the Holy Spirit, one God, for ever and ever.

Ven. Apollinaris de Almeida 1587–1638
Ven. Hyacinth Franceschi 1598–1638
Ven. Francis Rodrigues 1603–1638

Martyrs of Ethiopia

Among the Society's martyrs of Ethiopia are Bp. Apollinaris de Almeida, Fr. Hyacinth Franceschi, and Fr. Francis Rodrigues. Bp. Almeida was born in Lisbon, Portugal, on July 22, 1587, and studied with the Jesuits at St. Anthony's College in that same city. When he entered the Society on November 5, 1601, he was but a youth of fourteen. He made his Jesuit studies in Évora and Coimbra, and then taught philosophy at St. Anthony's in Lisbon, and later Scripture at Évora's university. In 1624 King Philip III of Portugal named him bishop of Nicaea and coadjutor with right of succession to Afonso Mendes, patriarch of Ethiopia. Fr. Almeida twice wrote to the king asking him to reconsider the appointment; he not only felt himself unworthy of the honor but as a Jesuit he had to refuse ecclesiastical dignities. That he finally acquiesced was only because of a royal command.

Bp. Almeida was consecrated in Évora in early 1628 and set out for India in April, but because of contrary winds the ship was forced to return to Lisbon. He again sailed in the following year and arrived in Goa on October 21, 1629. He then left for Ethiopia on November 18 and after stopping at several ports, because of bad weather, reached Massawa, an island off Ethiopia's northern coast, on July 25, 1630. From there he made his way to Fremona, the mission's center, where he arrived on August 20, 1630. He spent his first few months gathering information on the life and virtues of Patriarch Andrew de Oviedo, who had died there in 1577 and likewise investigated the death of Fr. Abraham de Georgiis, martyred at Massawa in 1595.

By way of official letters from the Portuguese king and the viceroy of India, Bp. Almeida was, on December 16, 1630, formally introduced to Negus (Emperor) Susenyos and immediately thereafter entered upon his ministry in Dancaz, the capital. The negus had been converted to the Catholic faith in 1622 by Fr. Pedro Paez, and the Jesuit mission thence prospered. The negus gave the Jesuits land and residences and also built them a seminary to educate native clergy. Conversion of the negus, however, caused unrest in the land. Aware that his acceptance of Catholicism was the principal cause of the country's internal difficulties, Susenyos abdicated his throne in July 1632 in favor of his son, Fasilidas, and allowed the nation to revert to its former belief that Christ had but one nature. This turnabout on the part of the negus meant the eventual demise of the Jesuit mission in Ethiopia. After the death of Susenyos in September 1632, Fasilidas re-possessed the houses and properties that his father had given the Jesuits and in 1633 ordered the missionaries to assemble at their headquarters in Fremona.

When the Jesuits received word in 1634 that Fasilidas had now ordered their expulsion, Bp. Almeida and six missionaries went underground. The others returned to India. The bishop and Fr. Hyacinth Franceschi found safety with a certain Cafla Mariam, an Ethiopian statesman, who was likewise a Catholic. Fr. Franceschi, who had been in Ethiopia since 1625, was an Italian, born in Florence in 1598, and had entered the Society in Rome on October 16, 1614. He had long desired to be a missionary and, thus, was sent to study in Coimbra. He left Lisbon in 1618 for Goa, where he completed his Jesuit formation. When he arrived in Ethiopia, he set about learning Amharic, that country's spoken language, and when he gained some fluency he did pastoral work in the provinces of Tigre, Dambea, and Begameder. His labors resulted in many conversions, a large number of them coming from the educated class. In 1630 he moved to Fremona and there continued his ministry.

When Bp. Almeida's and Fr. Franceschi's presence began to cause difficulties for their host, they moved into the desert of Defalo, close to the Red Sea, and hid in the thick underbrush. For four months they suffered hunger and heat, until they were rescued by a Portuguese, whom Fr. Francis Rodrigues had sent in search of them. While Fr. Franceschi went to reside with a neighboring landowner, Bp. Almeida joined Fr. Rodrigues on the estate of a Joanes Akay, governor of a coastal province and a friend of the Portuguese.

Fr. Rodrigues was born in 1603 in Carnide, a suburb of Lisbon, and as a youth had been a student of Bp. Almeida. He entered the Jesuit novitiate at Coimbra on November 18, 1618, left Portugal for the missions in 1625, and arrived in Ethiopia in 1628. He spent most of his ministry in and around Dancaz and had been put in charge of constructing the new Catholic cathedral.

From their refuge with Akay in Tigre, Bp. Almeida and Fr. Rodrigues freely ministered to the Catholics of that region and the bishop was also able to investigate the deaths of Fr. Gaspar Pais and John Pereira, whose martyrdoms had occurred in 1635. While both these Jesuits were apostolically active, Fr. Franceschi had been virtually reduced to a prisoner by his host. He lived in a tiny hut, was permitted to leave it only at night, was given little to eat, and could see no one. He tolerated this harsh solitude for a year and when unable to endure it any longer, he joined his two Jesuit brothers at the Akay estate.

When Fasilidas learned that Akay was giving shelter to the missionaries, he offered him a pardon in exchange for the prisoners. Acting either out of fear for his life or believing that the emperor would permit the missionaries to leave the country, Akay delivered them into the emperor's hands. Fasilidas then had them taken to an island in Lake Tana and imprisoned in a monastery, that island's only building. After the three Jesuits had been in chains for a year, the negus yielded to the schismatic monks' entreaties and permitted the prisoners to be executed. They were led to Oinadega in Dambea, and on a day when a fair was in progress they were hanged from a tall tree. The people attending the fair joined in throwing stones at the suspended bodies.

The martyrdom of these three occurred in the first half of June 1638; it is impossible to give a more precise date. Patriarch Mendes, writing to Rome about the martyrdom noted that it took place between the 9th and the 15th of June, 1638. The cause of these three, joined to that of five other Jesuits martyred in Ethiopia, was introduced in Rome in 1902.

June 16

S. G. Edward Billotet and 5 Companions 1812–1860

Martyrs of Lebanon

During June 1860 a fanatical Muslim sect in Lebanon, the Druses, set about massacring Maronite Christians. So fierce was this persecution that after three weeks some 7,750 Christians were slain, 560 churches destroyed, 360 villages burned, 42 convents razed, and 28 schools in ruins. The city that suffered the most was Zahle, because of its concentration of Catholics, and among the many who died in Zahle were the Jesuit martyrs, Fr. Edward Billotet and companions.

Fr. Billotet was a Frenchman born in Villefrancon on May 3, 1812. He studied at the minor seminary of Luxeuil, then at the major seminary at Besançon, and was ordained a diocesan priest in 1836. For a time he served as a professor at the minor seminary in Marnay and then parish priest at Rioz. When Fr. Billotet was thirty years old, he entered the Jesuit novitiate at Avignon on February 1, 1843, and after vows in 1845 was assigned to Lalouvesc to give parish missions. Since he had earlier requested to go to the foreign missions, he was finally assigned to Lebanon and arrived in Beirut on December 27, 1846.

Fr. Billotet's first years in Lebanon were spent teaching French, while he also studied Arabic. In 1848 he was made minister at the Beirut residence and then on November 25, 1850, was named superior of the entire Lebanese-Syrian mission. As superior he increased the number of schools—with funds supplied by the Propagation of the Faith—and in 1853 started an Arabic press for disseminating Catholic literature. He served a total of eight years as mission superior and afterwards, in February 1859, went to the Jesuit residence and church at Zahle. Because the church had sometime previously received a gift of a vineyard outside the city, Muslim officials tried to force Fr. Billotet to pay taxes. However, he was a French citizen and therefore not subject to the sultan's taxation.

Bristling because the revenue from the vineyard went to support a Christian school and a Catholic church, the Muslim leaders continued to harass Fr. Billotet and tried to force him to leave the city. But he would not leave. On one occasion in 1859 Turkish soldiers broke into the church during services. Fr. Billotet openly reproached them for not honoring the hours of prayer as they were obliged to do. To manifest their disdain, the intruders beat him and dragged him to prison, where he spent the night. Since harassment continued, he knew that they would not desist until they had taken his life.

The Druses' hostility broke out on April 17, 1860, with the burning of churches and the murder of Christians. Nothing as yet happened at Zahle, but the Jesuits there knew that the time would come. The mission superior had suggested that they seek safety elsewhere, but Fr. Billotet would not abandon his people, not at a time when they needed him most. On Sunday, June 17, the day before Zahle fell, he preached what was his last sermon; his theme was the Christian's need to be prepared to meet God.

The attack on Zahle came on June 18. That morning the city was surrounded by Muslim forces, and when the Christians saw them on the encircling hills, they sought refuge in their church. At a given signal the Muslims rushed down and in a very short time Zahle was captured. At the time Fr. Billotet was with his people praying before the Blessed Sacrament, but when he heard the shouts and screams, he went to see what was happening. Br. Habib Maksoud replaced him at the altar and read aloud the prayers in preparation for death, stopping intermittently to encourage the people. Br. Maksoud never finished the prayers, for the Druses rushed into the church and one of their number struck the tabernacle with a saber, knocking the consecrated hosts onto the floor. Another, seeing the black-robed brother standing at the altar, shot him in the chest and watched as he fell to the ground. They then proceeded to massacre the faithful within the church.

Fr. Billotet, together with Brs. Ferdinand Bonacina and Elias Younès and four school teachers, returned to the church. Unable to enter, they took shelter in a room above the choir. Their plan was to remain there until dark and then leave under cover of the night. But that plan was not to be put into effect. When the noise and cries in the streets subsided, Br. Bonacina left his hiding place and went to a nearby room to look out the window. A quick glance revealed that several Druses were still guarding the Jesuit residence. One of them, seeing him in the window, ordered him to come down and promised him freedom if he brought money with him. The brother answered that he had no money and, furthermore, he knew that if he were to go down he would be killed. At that instant he was shot in the left shoulder. Bleeding badly and thinking that he was dying, he went to where the others were to seek Fr. Billotet's absolution.

The Druses thereupon made their way into the upper part of the church building, found them, and forced all seven onto a terrace, where they again shot Fr. Bonacina. As Fr. Billotet raised his eyes to heaven and thanked God that he could offer him this sacrifice, several bullets struck him in the breast. The same happened to Br. Younès. Of the four lay persons with the Jesuits, two were killed and two were set free. Of the two who died, one was the fifteen-year-old Cherfân Habeiche, a postulant. Thus, four Jesuits and a postulant died at Zahle on June 18, 1860.

The fifth Jesuit martyr of this group died at Deir-el-Qamar. After the Zahle massacre the Jesuits at Deir-el-Qamar expected the same thing to happen there, hence, they all left the residence except Br. Haïdar Habeiche, who chose to remain and look after the school. The Druses came to the city on June 21 and their leader convinced the townspeople to lay down their arms to save their lives. Poorly equipped for fighting well-armed Muslims, the people capitulated. With everyone unarmed, the Muslims began the brutal massacre. Br. Habeiche went among the people, exhorting them to recall Christ's death and offering them his crucifix to kiss. While he was thus preparing the Christians for death, the Druses overpowered him and in seconds his blood mixed with that of the others.

Some time after these terrible events the bodies of these Jesuits were found under the rubble in Zahle and in Deir-el-Qamar and were properly buried. When the church of the Sacred Heart was rebuilt in Zahle, the bodies were interred before the main altar.

Br. Ferdinand Bonacina was born in Gavassetto near Reggio Emilia, Italy, on April 7, 1804, and entered the Jesuit novitiate in Rome on October 10, 1826. He was multi-talented; he was a first-rate carpenter and mason as well as a practicing architect. He was sent to the Syrian mission in 1840 and was placed in charge of construction. He built the Jesuit residence at Beirut, the seminary-college at Ghazir, churches in Bikfaya and Zahle, and a seminary for the Maronites. The church in Zahle was still being built so he returned there during Lent 1860 to continue working on the building. When he faced his murderers, he said: "Don't you remember me, I built a cotton mill for you." "Yes, we do," they replied, "but now you are our enemy because you are a Christian."

Br. Haïdar (Alphonsus) Habeiche was born in Ghazir on May 31, 1815. As a young man seeking adventure, he went to Egypt and when he ran out of money he earned his living by performing menial tasks. Only when he reached the bottom did he reproach himself for having wasted his life. He then turned himself around and began to live a devout Christian life. He came under the influence of a Maronite priest in Alexandria, a relative of his, who exhorted him to return home and become a monk. Back in Ghazir he attended daily Mass at the Jesuit church and in time asked to enter the Society. For his postulancy he lived with the Jesuits at Ghazir and served as the school's porter. He entered the novitiate on June 20, 1852, and when he took his vows, he also took the name of Alphonsus after St. Alphonsus Rodríguez, who had been a porter at the Jesuit college in Palma. Most of Br. Habeiche's Jesuit life was spent at Ghazir, except for one year at Zahle as catechist. At the beginning of 1860 he was sent to Deir-el-Qamar to teach at the Jesuit school and it was there that he was martyred on June 21, 1860.

Br. Habib Maksoud was born in Zahle on September 27, 1810, and was of the Melchite rite. As a prosperous young merchant he helped the Jesuits construct their school at Moallaqa and taught there without reimbursement. He entered the Society on December 24, 1847, the first novice from the Near East since the Society's restoration in 1814. He taught calligraphy and catechism to the students, was church sacristan and school treasurer, and was in charge of the Jesuit community's temporal needs.

Br. Elias Younès was a Lebanese, born in the district of Metn about 1830, and was of the Maronite rite. He was educated by the Jesuits and thought of entering the Society, but decided first to become a catechist and a teacher in the Jesuit school. He was finally received into the Society on October 30, 1856, and continued as catechist and teacher. After his vows he spent a short period in Sayda and then went to Moallaqa, a suburb of Zahle, where he was in charge of the school. When persecution seemed imminent, Fr. Billotet asked him to come to Zahle, thinking it would be safer there.

Cherfân Habeiche was born in Ghazir in 1844 of an illustrious Lebanese family. A year or so before his martyrdom, he requested to enter the Society as a brother, but could not be accepted because of his youth. The Jesuits, nevertheless, kept him at the school, where he taught in the lower grades and was sacristan. At the time of his death he was a postulant, wore the habit, and had made a vow of chastity. When the persecution began his father had sent him a horse for him to return home, but he declined the offer and chose to remain with the Jesuits.

The canonical investigation into the martyrdom of these Jesuits opened in 1932.

June 17

Bl. Modeste Andlauer 1847–1900
Bl. Rémy Isoré 1852–1900
Martyrs of the Boxer Rebellion

China's treaty with France in 1858 permitted the reentry of Catholic missionaries into China, and by the end of the century the Chinese church was once more flourishing there. Converts were numbered in the thousands every year and the building of Catholic churches was on the increase, but the peace in which the Chinese Christians lived with their non-Christian neighbors was soon to come to an end. Ever since the time of the signing of the treaty, there were some who were hostile to Catholics. Because the latter did not participate in the public festivals honoring China's deities, this was viewed by some as an unpardonable offense. By rejecting the official religion of Confucianism, the Catholic Church, they argued, had proven itself an enemy of the country. Along with this anti-Catholic bias there was an anti-foreign prejudice directed against the missionaries, who were frequently accused of seducing the Chinese from their ancestral faith. With the coup d'état of 1898, when the Dowager Empress Ci Xi imprisoned her nephew, the young Emperor Guangxu, the Boxers found an opportunity to persecute the Chinese Catholics.

The Boxers were a quasi-religious movement known in China as Yihe tuan, and the English gave them this name because of their strenuous gymnastic training. The Boxers especially hated Catholics and consequently they initiated a systematic campaign to destroy them. Though the Dowager Empress did not officially approve the Boxers, nevertheless, they were in tune with her desire to rid the nation of unwanted foreigners. It is estimated that during the Boxer uprising approximately 30,000 Catholics were put to death.

Fr. Rémy Isoré and Fr. Modeste Andlauer were the first Jesuits to die at the hands of these infamous Boxers. Fr. Isoré was born in Bambecque, France, on January 22, 1852, and studied for the diocesan priesthood. He completed his studies at the major seminary at Cambrai, but before being ordained he taught for a time and then decided to become a Jesuit. He entered the Jesuit novitiate at Saint-Acheul on November 20, 1875. He continued his ecclesiastical studies in France, was sent to China in 1882, completed his Jesuit training and was ordained on July 31, 1886.

When the Boxer rebellion began, Fr. Isoré, an austere and energetic missionary, was stationed in Weixian, in the Zhili district of Tianjin. In need of rest, he went to the Jesuit house at Xianxian to be with his religious brethren, but on June 17, 1900, news arrived that the Boxers were active near Weixian. Not wishing to leave his Christians alone at so critical a time, Fr. Isoré decided to return to his mission. He started his trip home on the morning of the 18th, and about midday he was at Wuyi, where Fr. Modeste Andlauer had his mission. Since he noticed that Boxers were already in the village—he saw their insignia outside the gate— he stopped to visit with his fellow Jesuit. The Boxers had come there to free some of their companions who had been captured the previous winter, but when they learned that a missionary was stationed in the village, they delayed their departure.

Fr. Andlauer was four years older than Fr. Isoré. He was born in Rosheim, Alsace, on May 22, 1847, entered the Society at Saint-Acheul on October 8, 1872, and was ordained to the priesthood in France on September 22, 1877. He too arrived in China in 1882. Now that the Boxers were in the village, both Jesuits knew that their prayers for martyrdom would soon be answered, and rather than retiring for the night they spent it in prayer.

The following afternoon, June 19, hearing the sharp knock of swords on the residence door, the two priests went into the adjoining chapel and secured the door behind them. They first heard the crash of the outside door and seconds later the chapel door was violently thrown open and the Boxers rushed toward the kneeling priests. One after the other, the attackers jabbed the priests with their lances, and the blood of martyrs flowed at the foot of God's altar. On the following day the murderers exposed the heads of the priests on the village gate, to indicate to the Christians what awaited them if they did not return to their ancestral religion.

Fr. Modeste Andlauer and Fr. Rémy Isoré were beatified by Pope Pius XII on April 17, 1955, together with two other Jesuits, Fr. Leo Mangin and Fr. Paul Denn, and fifty-two Chinese lay persons. The memorial of these Jesuit Boxer martyrs is celebrated on February 4.

Prayer

O God, you have used the blood of martyrs to render the Church fruitful. In answer to the prayers of Blessed Modeste Andlauer, Blessed Rémy Isoré, and their fellow martyrs, let there flower an unstinting harvest of Christians and allow us to share the glory of your saints. We ask you this through our Lord Jesus Christ, your Son, who lives and reigns with you and the Holy Spirit, one God, for ever and ever.

June 18

Bl. Thomas Whitbread 1618–1679

Bl. John Fenwick 1628–1679

Martyrs of England

Frs. Thomas Whitbread and John Fenwick, together with the three Jesuits whose biographies appear under June 19, were the innocent victims of the calumnious plot hatched by the infamous Titus Oates.

Fr. Whitbread, born in 1618, was a native of Essex. He was educated at home until it was time for him to cross the Channel, about 1630, to attend the Jesuit college at Saint-Omer in Flanders. On September 7, 1635, when he was eighteen, he entered the English Jesuit novitiate at Watten, also in Flanders. He continued his studies abroad, was ordained in 1645, and in 1647 returned to England, where he was known as Harcourt, and where he enjoyed a fruitful apostolate of more than thirty years.

After Fr. Whitbread had been superior of the Jesuits in the Suffolk district, he became superior of those working in Lincolnshire and, finally, in early 1678, he was appointed provincial of the English Jesuits. That year he made a tour of the seminaries operated by them on the Continent. In June he visited the college at Saint-Omer and there met the disreputable Titus Oates. Oates had once been an Anglican minister but had been deposed because of his irregular life. He then allegedly converted to the Catholic faith, attended the English College in Valladolid, Spain, and was subsequently expelled in October 1677. Now he was at Saint-Omer, undoubtedly attempting to infiltrate the Jesuits. When Fr. Whitbread arrived in mid-June, Oates, who was about twenty-eight years old, asked to enter the Society of Jesus. Knowing Oates' variegated past, the provincial not only declined to accept him but had him expelled (June 23, 1678) from the college for bizarre and unsavory behavior.

When Oates returned to London that June, he joined forces with a certain Israel Tonge, who believed that the Jesuits were always plotting against the king. Oates, rebuffed by the Jesuits, now sought revenge on them, and with Tonge concocted a detailed plot in which the Jesuits, in April 1678, were supposed to have planned the king's assassination, the overthrow of the government, the disestablishment of the Protestant religion, and the reestablishment of the Catholic Church. The contrived plot was brought to the attention of Charles II in mid-August, but the king remained unconvinced that the Jesuits would so plot against him. Oates elaborated his plot further, and on September 27 swore to its truth before the king's Privy Council, thereby setting into motion a series of imprisonments and martyrdoms.

In the dead of night, on September 28, Oates and a band of armed soldiers from parliament arrested Frs. John Fenwick and William Ireland. Early the next morning, before dawn, Oates and his men arrested Frs. Whitbread and Edward Mico—but both were seriously ill since their return to England, for they had contracted the plague while in Antwerp. The Spanish ambassador, under whose protection the Jesuits lived on Wild Street in Covent Garden, used his influence to ensure that the sick Jesuits were not moved from the residence. Instead, soldiers were posted to guard both bedridden men. Frs. Fenwick and Ireland, on the other hand, were taken to Newgate Prison. Sometime in December, when Fr. Whitbread's health permitted him to stand trial he joined his fellow Jesuits in prison, but Fr. Mico by this time had died as a result of the brutal treatment given him.

Fr. Fenwick's family name was Caldwell and he was born in 1628 in Durham. His parents were Protestants and he was raised in the established religion. While growing into manhood he studied the religious differences in his country, and when he became convinced of the truth of the Catholic faith, embraced it. Unable to talk their son out of his new religion, the parents evicted him from their home. Alone in the world, John traveled to the Jesuit college in Saint-Omer (about 1654), where he set himself to serious study and when he was twenty-eight entered the Jesuit novitiate at Watten on September 28, 1656. He did his philosophical and theological studies at Liège, was ordained in 1664, and then returned to the college in Saint-Omer as college procurator, staying there until 1673 or 1674, when he went on the English mission. He was stationed in London and served as the college procurator in the home country. Fr. Fenwick was arrested with Fr. Ireland on September 28 and was imprisoned at Newgate. The chains that bound him were so tight that they ate into his flesh and for a time the prison officials thought that one of his legs would have to be amputated. But since his trial was soon to take place and death was sure to be his sentence, they gave up on the idea.

Frs. Whitbread and Fenwick, together with Fr. Ireland, had their first trial on December 17, 1678, at Old Bailey. During it Oates testified that he had seen the three priests at the Jesuit conference in April, when the plot against the king was supposed to have been planned. The testimony of the second witness, a certain William Bedloe, did not corroborate the testimony of Oates entirely, for according to Bedloe he only had it on hearsay that Frs. Whitbread and Fenwick were present. Since this was insufficient evidence against both priests and since the jury, as a consequence, would have to acquit them, the court, eager to have Fr. Whitbread convicted—as provincial he was considered the plot's mastermind—suspended their trial to a later date. This was an unheard-of procedure, that a trial should be suspended after witnesses had been heard.

After Frs. Whitbread and Fenwick returned to prison, three more Jesuits, Frs. William Harcourt, John Gavan, and Anthony Turner, were apprehended in 1679. As a result of further false evidence that had been provided by a certain Stephen Dugdale, a convicted embezzler, the court brought the five priests to trial on June 13, 1679. The prosecution repeated the charge that the Jesuits had plotted the king's assassination during their meeting at the White Horse Tavern on April 24, 1678. Oates again claimed that he was present at the meeting. Bedloe, changing his former testimony, now agreed with Oates. The defense produced sixteen witnesses from Saint-Omer testifying that Oates had been at the college in April 1678, and could not have been at the conference. The Jesuits did indeed hold a meeting, April 24–26, 1678; it was not at any tavern, but was held in the palace of St. James, where Fr. Claude La Colombière was chaplain to the duchess of York. The meeting was the usual triennial business meeting to elect a delegate to go to Rome and report to the Jesuit general on the status of the English mission. Oates had most probably heard of the meeting while at Saint-Omer. Though the lying character of Oates was made clear and it was proven that he could not have been present at the meeting, nevertheless, the court instructed the jury to believe the witnesses for the prosecution, rather than those brought from the Continent. The jury returned the verdict of guilty, and the five priests were condemned to die in the manner reserved for treason, that is, to be hanged, drawn, and quartered.

The execution took place on Friday, June 20, at Tyburn. It was demanded of those about to be executed to make a public announcement of their innocence or guilt; Fr. Whitbread on this occasion said: "I do declare to you here present and to the whole world, that I go out of the world as innocent and as free from any guilt of these things laid to my charge in this matter, as I came into the world from my mother's womb. . . . As for those who have most falsely accused me . . . I do heartily forgive them, and beg of God to grant them his holy grace, that they may repent of their unjust proceedings against me."

When it was time for Fr. Fenwick to speak he said: "I do therefore declare before God that I am innocent of what is laid to my charge, of plotting the king's death, and endeavoring to subvert the government and bring in a foreign power. . . . If the judge and jury did anything amiss, I pardon them with all my soul. . . . I am very willing to and ready to suffer this death. I pray God pardon me my sins and save my soul."

The other three Jesuits being executed with them likewise spoke. When they had all concluded, the group spent some time in private prayer, standing beneath the gallows with nooses about their necks, waiting for the cart to be drawn from under them. Unexpectedly a rider crying "A pardon, a pardon!" rode on to the scene. The sheriff read the document announcing that the king was granting the five priests their lives on condition that they acknowledge their part in the plot and reveal all they knew about it. The martyrs thanked the king for his inclination to mercy, but since there never was a plot they could not acknowledge any guilt. They again asserted their innocence and said they could not accept the pardon if it meant they had to lie. After recollecting themselves once more, the cart was pulled from under them and all five victims of the hatred of Oates were permitted to hang until dead. The bodies were then cut down and quartered. Friends of the martyred Jesuits claimed the butchered bodies and buried them in the churchyard of St. Giles-in-the-Fields.

Frs. Thomas Whitbread and John Fenwick, together with their three Jesuit companions were beatified by Pope Pius XI on December 15, 1929, and their memorial is celebrated on December 1.

Prayer

Almighty, eternal God, you chose from the people of England and Wales Blessed Thomas Whitbread and Blessed John Fenwick and their companions to be made like Christ, who died to save the world. Listen to their prayers; strengthen your Church by the same faith and love that strengthened them, and bless it always with your gift of unity. We ask this through our Lord Jesus Christ, your Son, who lives and reigns with you and the Holy Spirit, one God, for ever and ever.

Bl. William Harcourt 1610–1679

Bl. John Gavan 1640–1679

Bl. Anthony Turner 1628–1679

Martyrs of England

These three Jesuits were martyred on June 20, 1679, together with Frs. Thomas Whitbread and John Fenwick. They were charged with the same fabricated crime of plotting to assassinate King Charles II.

Fr. William Harcourt's true name was Barrow, but on the English mission he was known as Harcourt and as Waring. He was born in Lancashire about 1610, and as a youth attended the Jesuit college in Saint-Omer, Flanders. Then at age twenty-two he entered the English novitiate at Watten on October 12, 1632. He completed his theological studies in Flanders, was ordained there in 1641, and in 1644 returned to England and was assigned to work in the London district. From 1671 to 1677 he served as procurator of the English Province and in 1678 became superior of the London Jesuits. When the alleged Jesuit plot against the king was revealed in September 1678, he avoided capture, though he was diligently sought. Because all Jesuits were under suspicion, he tried to persuade them to leave London and go elsewhere, but when he himself was urged to go to the Continent, he declined, saying that it was his duty to remain with those confined in prison. To avoid capture he changed his residence almost daily and used many disguises. Unfortunately, he was betrayed by a female servant at one of the houses where he lodged. Since he was always reserved and kind in his demeanor, the servant concluded that he must be a Jesuit and betrayed him to the local officials, who came and arrested him on May 7, 1679. At the time of Fr. Harcourt's imprisonment in the Newgate, he was nearly seventy years old and had completed thirty-five years on the English mission.

Fr. John Gavan was a native of London and was born in 1640. He went to study in Saint-Omer, perhaps in 1660 or earlier, and because of his youth, innocence, and candor, his fellow students affectionately called him "Angel." He entered the Jesuits at Watten on September 7, 1660, at age twenty, pursued his philosophical studies at Liège and his theology in Rome. He was ordained in 1670 and returned to England in 1671. For eight years he worked in Staffordshire, with Wolverhampton as the center of his activity, and since he was an accomplished preacher and tireless laborer in the Lord's vineyard, he made many converts to the faith. So successful was he that Wolverhampton became known as "Little Rome." When news of the Oates plot became known, Fr. Gavan's name was mentioned in Stephen Dugdale's testimony, and as a result a reward of 50 pounds was offered for his capture. Priest-hunters immediately went into earnest search of him, and because he was too well known to remain in his district, he planned to make his way to London and from there to cross over into Belgium. Disguised as a servant he started on his journey, reached London, and remained a few days in the city, sleeping in the imperial ambassador's stables. He was discovered there and arrested on January 23, 1679. At first he was incarcerated at the Gatehouse Prison, but when it was time to go to trial he was moved to Newgate.

Fr. Anthony Turner was born in Little Dalby in Leicestershire in 1628, the son of a Protestant minister. He attended the University of Cambridge, where he and his brother Edward converted to Catholicism, following their mother's example. When their father died, the two brothers went to Rome and enrolled at the English College on October 27, 1650, intending to study for the priesthood. Anthony was then twenty-two years old. In April 1653 he left Rome to make his way to Watten in Flanders, where he entered the novitiate of the English Jesuits on June 21. He studied theology at Liège, and was ordained on April 12, 1659. In 1661 he returned to England and exercised his priestly ministry for eighteen years in the Worcestershire area. Since he himself had been raised a Protestant, he was especially eager to enter into discussion with and convert those of the established religion. He longed to suffer for the Catholic faith, even if it meant martyrdom. His chance came when the Oates plot became public in September 1678. Hearing that several of his Jesuit brethren were imprisoned, he desired to share their captivity, but his superior urged him to leave the country. Fr. Turner went to London in January 1679 hoping to find a fellow Jesuit who could give him the money to cross the Channel. His search, unfortunately, was fruitless. He then decided to give his last few pennies to the first youngster he should meet and without a cent in his pockets went to the nearest justice's office to give himself up as a priest and a Jesuit, though his name never came up in the testimony of Oates nor was he the object of any special search. Nevertheless, on his own admission he was put into the Gatehouse Prison and then moved to Newgate for his trial. His brother Edward followed him into the Society in 1657, and died at Newgate Prison in 1681.

During the trial on June 13, 1679, in Old Bailey, Fr. Gavan acted as spokesman for himself and his four Jesuit brethren and adequately answered the lying testimonies of Oates, Bedloe, and Dugdale. Nevertheless, truth was ignored and lies were believed; following the judge's instructions, the jury found the five Jesuits guilty of high treason.

The remarks of Frs. Whitbread and Fenwick, as they awaited execution, have been noted elsewhere (see June 18). When it was Fr. Harcourt's turn to speak, he said: "I do here declare, in the presence of Almighty God, the whole court of heaven, and this numerous assembly, that as I hope by the merits and passion of my Lord and sweet Savior, Jesus Christ, for eternal bliss, I am as innocent as the child unborn of anything laid to my charge and for which I am here to die. . . . I forgive all that have contrived my death and humbly beg pardon of Almighty God for them, and I ask pardon of all the world. I pray God bless His Majesty and grant him a prosperous reign."

Fr. Gavan spoke in similar manner. "In this hour I do solemnly swear, protest, and vow, by all that is sacred in heaven and on earth, and as I hope to see the face of God in glory, that I am as innocent as the child unborn of those treasonable crimes which Mr. Oates and Mr. Dugdale have sworn against me in my trial, and for which sentence of death was pronounced against me the day after my trial. . . . I am contented to undergo an ignominious death for the love of you, my dear Jesus, seeing you have been pleased to undergo an ignominious death for the love of me."

Fr. Turner then looked upon the bystanders and remarked: "I am bound in conscience to do myself that justice as to declare upon oath my innocence from the horrid crime of treason with which I am falsely accused. . . . I am as free from the treason I am accused of as the child that is unborn, and being innocent I never accused myself in confession of anything that I am charged with. I die a Roman Catholic and humbly beg the prayers of such for my happy passage into a better life. . . . God in his mercy forgive all those which have falsely accused me, or have had any hand in my death. I forgive them from the bottom of my heart as I hope myself for forgiveness at the hands of God."

Upon recollecting themselves and refusing the king's pardon, Frs. Harcourt, Gavan, and Turner, together with Frs. Whitbread and Fenwick, were hanged until they were dead. Though their bodies were quartered, their Catholic friends were permitted to take these relics and bury them in the churchyard of St. Giles-in-the-Fields. Thus on June 20, 1679, five Jesuits died heroic deaths for which Pope Pius XI beatified them on December 15, 1929. The Society of Jesus celebrates their memorial on December 1, when all Jesuit martyrs of England and Wales are commemorated.

Prayer

Almighty, eternal God, you chose from the people of England and Wales Blessed William Harcourt, John Gavan, Anthony Turner, and their companions to be made like Christ, who died to save the world. Listen to their prayers; strengthen your Church by the same faith and love that strengthened them, and bless it always with your gift of unity. We ask this through our Lord Jesus Christ, your Son, who lives and reigns with you and the Holy Spirit, one God, for ever and ever.

June 20

Bl. Francis Pacheco and 8 Companions 1566–1626

Martyrs of Japan

Of the Jesuits who met martyrdom during the Great Persecution in Japan between the years 1617 and 1632, the most experienced was Fr. Francis Pacheco.

When apprehended, he was provincial superior of the Jesuits and apostolic administrator of the diocese. With his capture, the government felt it was in the final stages of annihilating the Jesuits and the Catholic Church.

Fr. Pacheco was born in Ponte di Lima, near Braga, Portugal, in 1566. As a youth he heard about the exploits of the missionaries in Japan and wished to imitate them, and while studying at the Jesuit school in Lisbon, he annually witnessed the missionaries' departure. This confirmed him in his desire and thus he entered the Society in December 1585. His request to go to the missions was not granted until 1592, when he left for the East. His first stop was Goa, India, where he continued his studies, then to Macao, where he completed them and was ordained. He subsequently lectured in theology there until 1604, when he finally went to Japan.

During his four years in central Japan, he worked in Osaka and in the capital, Miyako (today's Kyoto). In 1608 he was appointed to head the Jesuit college in Macao. Having fulfilled that position, he sailed again in 1612 for Japan and became vicar general to Bp. Luis de Cerqueira. He served in Nagasaki until he was expelled by the shogun's decree of 1614, which banished all foreign missionaries and forbade the Japanese Christians to practice their religion. Fr. Pacheco's exile in Macao was not long, for in the following year, June 1615, he secretly returned, disguised as a merchant, and took up missionary work at Takaku and the islands of Amakusa and Kani. During those years of fierce persecution he sadly saw thousands of Christians give up their religion under governmental pressure and through fear of torture. But he also witnessed the marvelous deaths of his brother Jesuits and hundreds of Christians, who remained steadfast in their faith, though it meant beheading or death by slow fire. He knew that the longer he remained in Japan the closer was his martyrdom.

Fr. Pacheco had been the apostolic administrator of the diocese since the bishop's death in 1614 and in October 1621 he was appointed the Jesuits' provincial superior. Up to the time of his appointment, the provincial had resided in Nagasaki, but Fr. Pacheco moved the residence to the seaport of Kuchinotsu in Arima, which afforded greater security and permitted easier and better contact with the Jesuits in Japan.

In 1625 Shogun Iyemitsu intensified the search for Jesuit missionaries by adding more spies to his force. It was one of Fr. Pacheco's former hosts, however, that betrayed him. An apostate, seeking reward money and hoping to gain favor with the district governor, revealed where Fr. Pacheco was staying. On December 18, 1625, the house was surrounded by some 200 soldiers. There was no escape. The soldiers found the priest and his two catechists, Paul Kinsuke and Peter Kinsei, inside; and in the house next door they discovered Br. Gaspar Sadamatsu and another catechist, John Kisaku. The Jesuits, the catechists, their hosts and families were all arrested and taken to Shimabara and placed in a dungeon, where they had to endure the winter's cold and dampness. Within a few days after their arrival, Fr. John Baptist Zola and his catechist, Vincent Kaun, both of whom had been captured on December 22, 1625, were added to their number.

P. Franciſcus Paciecus Luſit: P. Balthaſar de Torres Hiſp: P. Ioan:
nes Zola Ital, cum 6 Coadiutoribus Iaponijs Soc: IESV, lento igne
vivi pro Chriſto exuſti Nangaſacki in Iaponia 20 Iuny. A 1626.

M A

Bl. Francis Pacheco and Companions

While in prison Fr. Pacheco admitted the four catechists into the Society and transformed his group of prisoners, including the lay persons, into a quasi-religious community with set times for rising, prayer, and meditation. Though everyone suffered from lack of food and all were without privacy and decent sanitation, they still added penance to their daily living, fasting several days a week. In this manner they hoped to prepare and strengthen themselves for the martyrdom they knew was certain to come. Their greatest burden during the six months of imprisonment was their inability to celebrate Mass and recite the breviary. Even their rosaries had been taken from them.

On June 17, 1626, the district governor, having returned from visiting the shogun, carried with him the latter's order that the prisoners were to be put to death. The governor sent word to Shimabara for the prisoners to be brought to Nagasaki on June 20, and sent the same order to Omura. The two prisoners at Omura were the Jesuit Fr. Balthasar de Torres and his catechist, Michael Tozo. They had been captured on March 20, 1626, in a small village near Nagasaki, and during their imprisonment Fr. Torres received Michael into the Society.

The prisoners from Shimabara—seven Jesuits and nine Christians, among whom was the family that had given Fr. Pacheco hospitality in Kuchinotsu—were led to Nagasaki escorted by fifty soldiers. The prisoners from Omura were escorted by thirty soldiers. Both groups met on June 20 on Martyrs' Hill outside the city, where the execution was to take place. The Jesuits rejoiced in seeing each other and embraced for the last time. The first to die were the Jesuits. The governor kept the lay Christians aside, hoping some would apostatize and, contrary to Japanese custom, ordered an abundant amount of wood to be placed at the stakes so as not to prolong the victims' suffering. A slow death, he said, was for criminals, not for those who die for a cause in which they believe. The fires were set and within fifteen minutes all nine Jesuits, with prayers on their lips, returned their souls to God in heaven.

Watching the martyrs die only strengthened the other condemned Christians. Since their faith remained unshaken, they were taken to a prison in Nagasaki, and determined to die for Christ they were martyred on July 12.

Fr. Pacheco and his eight Jesuit companions, together with the nine Christians who died three weeks later, were included among the 205 martyrs beatified by Pope Pius IX on May 7, 1867. The memorial of these Jesuit martyrs is celebrated by their religious brethren on February 4.

Fr. Pacheco's companions in death were the following:

John Kisaku was born in Kuchinotsu, Japan, about 1605, and was with Br. Sadamatsu when the soldiers came to arrest Fr. Pacheco. The soldiers did not realize that John was a catechist and they asked Br. Sadamatsu: "What does that young fellow do here?" Hoping to save the twenty-one-year-old catechist, the brother answered: "He does housework here." But not wanting to miss being martyred, John approached the soldiers and said: "I've been with the fathers for a long time and I do not intend to leave them now." He asked to be bound with the others and, thus, was taken with them to Shimabara and died with them in Nagasaki. He became a Jesuit while in prison.

Peter Kinsei was born in Hachirao, Japan, about 1588. He studied at the seminary in Arima and worked as a catechist with the Jesuit missionaries. From 1618 he worked with Fr. Pacheco and was captured with him in December 1625. While in prison he was accepted into the Society and died with his brother Jesuits on June 20, 1626.

Br. Gaspar Sadamatsu was born in Hasami, Japan, about 1565. He was educated by the Jesuits and entered the Society as a brother on October 31, 1582. Because he was able to write Japanese, he became the provincial's assistant. He went into exile in 1614, but returned with Fr. Pacheco in 1615 and remained with him for the next eleven years. He was arrested on December 18, 1625, and after imprisonment with Fr. Pacheco was martyred with him on June 20 of the following year.

Paul Kinsuke was born in Urada, Japan, about 1581. At one time he had been catechist for Fr. Jerome De Angelis and later for Fr. Peter Navarro. After Fr. Navarro's death he became associated with Fr. Pacheco and was arrested with him. He fulfilled his desire of becoming a Jesuit by entering the Society while in prison at Shimabara.

Fr. John Baptist Zola was an Italian, born in Brescia on November 1, 1575, and entered the Society on October 15, 1593. He was a missionary in India from 1602 to 1606, and then crossed to Japan. He established a mission at Takaku and from there he visited the nearby islands, carrying on his priestly ministry for twenty years. When persecution broke out he ingeniously found ways of visiting his imprisoned Jesuit brethren. He was captured with his catechist, Vincent Kaun, on December 22, 1625, and was imprisoned in Shimabara with Fr. Pacheco and died with him in Nagasaki on June 20, 1626.

Vincent Kaun was a Korean, born of a noble family, probably in 1579. During the Korean war he was taken prisoner, transported to Japan and given to the Jesuits to be educated. He was baptized at age thirteen and spent the next four years at the Jesuit seminary in Arima. He became a catechist and was appointed with Fr. Zola to found a mission in Korea. For some unknown reason, only Kaun left for Peking (today's Beijing) in 1612, thinking that he would be able to penetrate the up-to-now closed Korea. He walked as far as Peking and stayed there several years trying to reenter his homeland, but without success. While there he learned to speak and write Chinese. He returned to Japan and became Fr. Zola's catechist. He was especially valuable in missionary work, not only with the Japanese, but also with the Chinese and Koreans. He was arrested with Fr. Zola and imprisoned at Shimabara. When the governor of Arima heard that Kaun was accomplished in Chinese calligraphy, he asked him to be his secretary, but when Kaun refused the governor ordered him to be tortured, hoping he would not only give up his faith but also accept his offer to be his secretary. When the torture did not succeed, the governor gave up. Kaun recuperated in prison, was accepted as a member of the Society, and died with Fr. Zola and seven other Jesuits on June 20, 1626.

Fr. Balthasar de Torres was born in Granada, Spain, on December 14, 1563. He became a Jesuit on September 23, 1579, at age sixteen, and seven years later was sent to Goa, India. He completed his studies in Macao and after ordination, taught theology in the seminary. He arrived in Japan on August 13, 1600, and spent the next twenty-five years as a missionary, working zealously among Japanese Christians. Rather than leave the country when the edict of 1614 was published, he went into hiding and continued his apostolic ministry in secret. He was captured on March 20, 1626, with his catechist, Michael Tozo, in a small village near Nagasaki, and both were sent to prison in Omura. Fr. Torres died a martyr's death in Nagasaki on June 20, 1626.

Michael Tozo was born in Chijiwa, Japan, about 1588, and from his youth had worked with the Jesuits as a catechist. He first worked with Fr. Jerome De Angelis, then with Fr. Sebastian Kimura, and finally with Fr. Torres. He was captured with Fr. Torres on March 20, 1626, and was imprisoned with him at Omura. He was accepted into the Society in Omura, and died by fire with the other Jesuits on June 20, 1626.

Prayer

Almighty God, grant that this remembrance of your martyrs, Blessed Francis Pacheco and companions, may bring us joy. May we who depend upon their prayers glory in their entry into heaven. We ask this through our Lord Jesus Christ, your Son, who lives and reigns with you and the Holy Spirit, one God, for ever and ever.

June 21

St. Aloysius Gonzaga 1568–1591

Aloysius Gonzaga, the eldest son of the marquis of Castiglione, was born on March 9, 1568. Since he was heir to the family title, the marquis proudly took him, though Aloysius was only four years old, on training expeditions to introduce him early to the art of arms. On these occasions the young lad wore a suit of armor and walked at his father's side reviewing the troops. But playing soldier had to be set aside when he came down with malaria; frequent bouts of fever made it impossible for him to continue such games. It was at age seven, so Aloysius says, that he was converted from the courtly way of life to the interior life. He now began to pray and enjoyed reciting the Psalms. When his father returned from a two-year visit to Spain in 1576, he found his eight-year-old son with the self-possession of a grownup and viewed him as a worthy heir of Castiglione. Since Aloysius was the eldest son, his future was determined, but while the father thought of the son following in his footsteps, the son was thinking of following in the footsteps of someone else.

In 1577 Aloysius and his brother Rudolph were sent to Florence to the court of their father's friend, the Grand Duke Francesco de' Medici, where they were to learn the customs of princes. The Medici court was one of Italy's most magnificent, but at the same time it was one in which intrigue and deceit abounded, where daggers and poisons were the solutions to problems, and where lust and sin were made inviting. Enveloped in such a mundane atmosphere, the sensitive Aloysius withdrew within himself and refused to participate in the games and empty show of the Florentines. This was, he felt, the only way that he could avoid sin. So repelled was he by this manner of life that one day in 1578, while visiting the church of Our Lady of the Annunciation, he made a firm determination never to offend God by sin.

From Florence Aloysius was sent to Mantua in November 1579, where he lived with the duke, his relative. There he came upon a book with brief lives of the saints and continued to recite the Psalms. It was from this daily recitation of the Psalter that the thought of the priesthood first came to him. He returned to Castiglione in 1580 and in the family library he found a copy of the *Summary of Christian Doctrine* by Peter Canisius, which, in the Italian edition, also included daily meditations. Aloysius used these for his prayer. In July of that year Castiglione was host to Cardinal Charles Borromeo of Milan who was visiting the parishes of his suffragan sees. He met the twelve-year-old Aloysius and during their conversation the saintly cardinal learned that the youth had not as yet made his First Communion, so he prepared him for it and on July 22 gave the youth Holy Communion. Aloysius thereafter looked forward to weekly Communion, daily Communion was not then the custom. Moreover, Aloysius fasted three days a week, meditated morning and evening, and attended daily Mass, whenever possible.

In 1581, as Maria of Austria, the widow of Emperor Maximilian II and daughter of Charles V, was passing through Italy on her return to Spain, the Gonzaga family joined her in her journey. Aloysius arrived with the empress in Madrid on March 7, 1582, and became a page attending the duke of Asturias, the heir apparent, and later was made a knight of the Order of St. James. By this time he was convinced that the princely life was not for him. He had a Jesuit confessor in Madrid and thought more and more about becoming a Jesuit. This desire was confirmed on August 15, 1583, while he prayed before an image of our Lady in the Jesuit church. He interiorly felt that this was what God was asking of him, and on leaving the church he visited his confessor to make known his decision, but the confessor informed him that he now had to get his father's permission.

On hearing that his eldest son and heir wanted to set aside his family heritage for the walls of a monastery, the marquis became enraged. Father and son were equally firm in their decisions and an unhappy strain was placed on their relationship. Hoping to change his son's thinking, the father took the family back to Castiglione in 1584 and sent Aloysius and his brother on a tour of the courts of

Italy. After so pleasurable a journey, surely Aloysius would abandon his thoughts of the religious life. When he returned from his tour, however, he had not changed his determination. He finally wore out his father, who granted his consent, and in early November 1585 Aloysius renounced his inheritance in favor of his brother Rudolph, left for Rome, and presented himself to Fr. General Claudio Acquaviva. He entered the novitiate of Sant'Andrea on November 25, 1585.

Aloysius was only seventeen-and-a-half years old, but he was mature because of his background and commitment. He found noviceship life less demanding than the life he had imposed upon himself at home. Under his director's guidance he could no longer continue the penances he had been accustomed to, nor could he fast as frequently as he had in the past. The maxim that led him to the novitiate remained with him throughout his years: "I am a piece of twisted iron; I entered religion to be untwisted straight." Aloysius gave himself totally to the process of becoming a Jesuit. Before completing his two years of noviceship, he enrolled at the Roman College to complete the philosophical studies he had begun while in Madrid. He pronounced his three vows of religion on November 25, 1587, and received minor orders in early 1588. His studies were now in theology and he proved an excellent student with a penetrating mind. In 1589 he returned to Castiglione for an extended period to negotiate peace between his brother Rudolph and the duke of Mantua. When he had succeeded in this, he returned to Rome in May 1590.

In the beginning of the following year, there were famine and plagues in Italy, and Aloysius in Rome begged alms for and worked with the plague-stricken. Those he found dying in the street, he carried to a hospital, washed and fed them, and prepared them to receive the sacraments. One evening, when he returned home after helping at a hospital, he told his spiritual director, Fr. Robert Bellarmine: "I believe my days are few. I feel such an extraordinary desire to work and serve God . . . that I cannot believe that God would have given it to me, if he did not mean to take me at once." So many of the young Jesuit students were becoming infected by the plague that the superior forbade Aloysius to return to the hospital. When he had made another request to serve the sick, permission was granted, but only to help at Our Lady of Consolation hospital, where contagious diseases were not admitted. Aloysius went there and while performing various chores about the place, he lifted a man out of his sick bed and tended to him. But the man was infected. Aloysius caught the plague and he himself was put to bed on March 3, 1591.

For a while Aloysius grew worse but then rallied. Though the infection passed, it left him in so weakened a condition that he never did recover. Fever and a cough set in and for weeks he lingered, wasting away. He had been told in prayer that he would die on the octave of *Corpus Christi*, but when that day arrived, June 21, 1591, he appeared better than he had on the previous days. He asked to receive Viaticum but the superior was disinclined to bring it; he did not think Aloysius was near death. That evening Aloysius again asked for Viaticum, and to keep the patient calm and undisturbed it was arranged for him to receive it. Two priests remained with him that evening. A little after ten o'clock, the pain from the sores on his side became unbearable, so he asked to be raised a bit. When the two Jesuits came to his side, they noticed a change in his face. The young Aloysius was dying. His eyes were fixed on the crucifix in his hands and as he tried to pronounce the name of Jesus he went to his Lord.

Aloysius Gonzaga was twenty-three years old and was buried in the church of the Annunciation, attached to the Roman College. Later, after the church of St. Ignatius was built, his remains were moved there. He was beatified by Pope Paul V on October 19, 1605, and was canonized with St. Stanislaus Kostka by Pope Benedict XIII on December 31, 1726. His memorial is celebrated on June 21.

Prayer

Lord God, help us to be like our brother, Saint Aloysius, who gave up honor and riches to serve you. Keep us untouched by the spirit of this world, so that we may seek your glory in all things. We ask this through our Lord Jesus Christ, your Son, who lives and reigns with you and the Holy Spirit, one God, for ever and ever.

June 22

Bl. Thomas Woodhouse 1535–1573

Martyr of England

Of the many Jesuit saints and blessed martyred in England and Wales between 1573 and 1679, Fr. Thomas Woodhouse was the first to shed his blood for Christ. Very little is known about his life prior to his imprisonment under Elizabeth I. He was born perhaps in 1535 and was ordained a priest probably in 1558, during the final year of the reign of the Catholic queen, Mary Tudor. With the accession of Elizabeth on November 17, 1558, and the imposition of a non-Catholic prayer book, together with the 1559 decree declaring the queen supreme in matters of religion, Fr. Woodhouse found that he could no longer accept the Elizabethan religious reforms and still remain a Catholic. Therefore, he resigned his pastorate in Lincolnshire in 1560 and took a position as tutor to the children of a wealthy family in Wales. The difference of religion between him and his employer caused him once more to resign his post.

Despite the laws against the Catholic Mass, Fr. Woodhouse continued to celebrate it, whenever opportunity arose. On May 14, 1561, while celebrating

Mass, he was arrested and imprisoned in London's Fleet Prison. He spent the next twelve years of his life there but because the prison officials were somewhat less than strict, Fr. Woodhouse was able to celebrate Mass in his cell and began an apostolate among the inmates, which brought some back to the Church. He also engaged in a unique ministry of his own devising; he wrote short essays urging his fellow countrymen to adhere to the true faith, then tied the essays to a stone, and when he saw a suitable individual pass his cell, he gently threw the stone out the window.

Sometime in 1572 or thereabout, he wrote a letter to the Jesuit provincial in Paris—as yet there was no Jesuit mission in England—requesting to enter the Society of Jesus. When he received a favorable reply, he permitted his enthusiasm to get the better of him and somewhat recklessly wrote a letter on November 19, 1572, to William Cecil, Elizabeth's treasurer, asking him to persuade the queen to submit to the pope. Though the pope had excommunicated her in 1570, it was done justly, Fr. Woodhouse wrote, because of the queen's "great disobedience." Rather than accede to the priest's request, Cecil ordered his case to come to trial. It took place in the Guildhall on June 16, 1573, and during it Fr. Woodhouse continually refused to acknowledge the judges' authority and contested the competence of a secular tribunal to try a priest on a religious matter. Nevertheless, because he was a priest and had spoken unfavorably of the queen, he was found guilty of high treason and received the usual sentence of traitors— to be hanged, drawn, and quartered. Three days after his trial he was taken to Tyburn and there he endured death for Christ and his Church.

Fr. Thomas Woodhouse was the second priest, but the first Jesuit, to be executed in England on religious grounds. He was beatified by Pope Leo XIII on December 9, 1886, and his memorial is celebrated on December 1, when the Society also commemorates its other English and Welsh martyrs.

Prayer

Almighty, eternal God, you chose from the people of England and Wales Blessed Thomas Woodhouse and his companions to be made like Christ, who died to save the world. Listen to their prayers; strengthen your Church by the same faith and love that strengthened them, and bless it always with your gift of unity. We ask this through our Lord Jesus Christ, your Son, who lives and reigns with you and the Holy Spirit, one God, for ever and ever.

St. Thomas Garnet 1575–1608

Martyr of England

Thomas Garnet was born in Southwark, London, in 1575, of parents known for their loyalty to the Catholic Church. He attended the grammar school at Horsham and in his early teens was page to Lord William Howard. Because every English institution of higher learning became Protestant during Elizabeth I's reign, Thomas went to the Continent in 1593 to attend the newly opened Jesuit college at Saint-Omer. From there he left in January 1595 for the English seminary at Valladolid, Spain, but did not arrive until fourteen months later, in March 1596. When the ship carrying him and five other seminarians left Calais, it met such a severe storm in the Channel that it had to seek refuge on the English coast. The ship was boarded by the English navy and the six young Englishmen were taken into custody. In London the government tried to get them to conform to Elizabeth's religion, but they refused. After months of abusive treatment and detention in various prisons, they managed to escape and eventually make their way to Valladolid. Andrew White, a fellow student of Thomas at Valladolid, became a Jesuit later, went to America with Lord Baltimore's expedition, and founded the Maryland mission. Upon completion of his own theological studies, Thomas was ordained in 1599 and left in July for his native land.

When Fr. Garnet landed on English soil, his uncle, Fr. Henry Garnet, was superior of the Jesuits in England and had been exercising his priestly ministry there since 1586. He was in charge of the entire network of priests working secretly among the Catholics, who refused to recognize the supremacy of the queen in religious matters. Fr. Thomas labored in and around Warwickshire for six years and inspired by his uncle's heroic work and the martyrdom of several Jesuits, requested to enter the Society and was accepted on September 29, 1604. His ministry, however, came to an end with the discovery of the Gunpowder Plot. Some Catholics planned to blow up the Houses of Parliament together with the king on November 5, 1605. Because the government tried to connect Fr. Henry with the plot, he had to go into hiding. At that time Fr. Thomas was residing with Thomas Rookwood, who, unfortunately, was implicated in the plot. During the government's search for Rookwood, it found Fr. Thomas, who was first put in London's Gatehouse Prison and then in the Tower. Because he was Fr. Henry's nephew, his interrogators hoped to force information from him to build a case against the uncle. Threats of torture and of the rack did not intimidate him, and after proving himself innocent of any knowledge of the plot he was sent back to prison. Seven months later, when the government decided to empty the prisons of the less threatening priests to make room for others, Fr. Thomas and forty-six other priests were put on a boat on July 10, 1606, and were informed that their lives would be forfeited if ever they were to return to England. They were then shipped off to Flanders, where they were safely deposited.

Fr. Thomas made his way to the English Jesuit novitiate at Louvain and remained there for a year. He pronounced his vows as a Jesuit on July 2, 1607, and in September of that year returned to England. Within six weeks of his arrival, he was betrayed by an apostate priest named Rouse and was again imprisoned in London's Gatehouse. During his questioning he neither admitted nor denied that he was a priest, nor would he take the oath of supremacy recognizing James I as his spiritual leader. Since there was no progress in these early interrogations, he was transferred to Newgate Prison and not long afterwards came to trial on June 19, 1608, at the Old Bailey. He was indicted for being a priest, whose orders derived from Rome, and for having returned to England, contrary to the law of the land. The only testimony brought forth to show that he was a priest was the word of witnesses, who claimed that they had seen a letter of his signed, "Thomas Garnet, Priest." On this evidence he was found guilty of high treason and condemned to the gallows, a sentence he received with joy.

On June 23 he was taken from his cell and dragged to Tyburn for execution. He mounted the cart and kissed the gallows, the instrument of his going to heaven. He turned to the people standing near him and told them that, indeed, he was a priest and a Jesuit, and that he had spent his years in England working to bring sheep back to Christ's fold. He said that he never had any treasonable designs against the king or the kingdom. Crossing his hands on his breast, he said: "This is the happiest day of my life." He then prayed to God not to lay his death against those who betrayed, arrested, or condemned him. He then recited the Our Father, Hail Mary, and the Creed, and as he was beginning the Come, Holy Spirit, the cart was drawn from under him and he was left hanging until dead. He was thirty-three years old.

Fr. Thomas Garnet was beatified by Pope Pius XI on December 15, 1929, and canonized by Pope Paul VI on October 25, 1970. His memorial is celebrated on December 1, together with his Jesuit brothers, who were martyred in England and Wales.

Prayer

Almighty, eternal God, you chose from the people of England and Wales Saint Thomas Garnet and his companions to be made like Christ, who died to save the world. Listen to their prayers; strengthen your Church by the same faith and love that strengthened them, and bless it always with your gift of unity. We ask this through our Lord Jesus Christ, your Son, who lives and reigns with you and the Holy Spirit, one God, for ever and ever.

Ven. Andrew de Oviedo 1517–1577

Bishop Andrew de Oviedo was patriarch of Ethiopia and spent twenty difficult years on that mission. If judged solely from a human point of view, those were years of complete failure; if judged supernaturally, they were the years of his sanctification.

Andrew was born in Illescas, Spain, about 1517, and graduated from the University of Alcalá. He then went to Rome, where he offered himself as a candidate for the Society. Accepted by Fr. Ignatius on June 19, 1541, Fr. Oviedo did further studies in Paris, Louvain, and Coimbra. In 1545 he was appointed rector of the Jesuit college in Gandía, Spain—newly established by Francis Borgia, fourth duke of Gandía—and arrived there in November of that year. In March 1546, when the duke's wife, Leonor, was dying, Fr. Oviedo assisted her in her last moments and in the following May he led the duke through the Spiritual Exercises. Upon the duke's decision to enter the Society, Fr. Oviedo directed him through the noviceship and received his vows on February 1, 1548. Called to Rome in 1550, and after participating in the discussions on the Society's Constitutions, Fr. Oviedo was named in 1551 rector of the new college in Naples.

Portugal had been interested in Ethiopia since the beginning of the sixteenth century, and midway through the century King John III expressed hopes of bringing the Abyssinian Christians into the Catholic Church. He thus entered into correspondence with Negus (Emperor) Claudius (Galawdewos), who, it seems, led the king to believe that he was disposed toward Catholicism. King John then asked the Society to supply the missionaries for this new harvest. Of the several appointed, three were named bishops: Fr. John Nunes Barreto was named patriarch of Ethiopia, Fr. Oviedo became bishop of Hierapolis, and Fr. Melchior Carneiro, bishop of Nicaea. Frs. Oviedo and Carneiro were also named coadjutors to the patriarch, with right of succession. Frs. Barreto and Oviedo were consecrated in Évora, Portugal, on May 5, 1555, the first Jesuits to become bishops. On the following March 15, 1556, they sailed for Goa, India, where they arrived on September 13.

Before Patriarch Barreto could enter Ethiopia, he first had to ascertain the religious climate of the country and be assured of the feelings of the negus toward Catholicism and the missionaries. Thus Bp. Oviedo and five Jesuits went as an advance guard. They left Goa on February 16, 1557, and landed at Arquico on the Tigre coast on March 17. To his great disappointment the bishop soon learned that the negus was not interested in Catholicism, had no intention of being converted, and would never relinquish his schismatic belief that Christ had one and not two natures. Unable to make headway with the negus, Bp.

Oviedo occupied himself by ministering to the small number of Portuguese Catholics living in the capital. He always retained the hope that the country would one day be converted to Catholicism.

In 1559 Claudius, having died in battle, was succeeded by his brother Minas, who was not as tolerant. When informed that Bp. Oviedo had converted several prominent individuals to Catholicism, Minas forbade the bishop to preach and proselytize. The three years of the reign of Minas were difficult, but Bp. Oviedo did not succumb to discouragement. Sarsa Dengel succeeded his father in February 1563. Because the bishop was still unable to preach and freely exercise his ministry, he moved to Maigoga, a small village between Aduwa and Aksum, where some 100 Portuguese families had settled around the church of St. George. Bp. Oviedo renamed the village Fremona, after St. Frumentius, who first converted the Abyssinians in the fourth century.

Patriarch Barreto had died in India on December 22, 1562, without ever touching Ethiopian soil, and with his death Bp. Oviedo became patriarch. He may have had a splendid title, but his fourteen years in Fremona were spent in extreme poverty. So poor was he that he lived in a thatched hut and grew his own food supply in his garden. When Fr. Borgia, now the general of the order, learned of his old friend's indigence, he wrote expressing his admiration of him and of his suffering for the faith. It was also clear to King Sebastian of Portugal and to Pope Pius V that there would be no fruit coming from the Ethiopian mission, and so both wrote (1566) to the patriarch offering him the opportunity of going to Japan or China and exercising his episcopacy there. This was not an order from the pope so Bp. Oviedo wrote to His Holiness on June 15, 1567, asking to remain where he was for two reasons: (1) the waters around Ethiopia were infested with Turkish ships and no one could escape capture, and (2) though he might not accomplish much in Fremona, nevertheless, the five or six hundred Catholic families scattered throughout the country have a pastor in him. Without him, they would have no priest. Thus the patriarch remained and continued his lonely, destitute life.

Very little is known about Bp. Oviedo's years in Fremona, but some authors, perhaps in a desire to stress the somber conditions under which he lived, describe him as tearing blank pages from his breviary to write to the king and cutting off the margins of other pages to write to the pope. In the quiet of Fremona, however, he did write a book, *On the Primacy of the Roman Church and the Errors of the Abyssinians.*

Bp. Oviedo's missionary life was filled with privation and hardship—he wore himself out in serving Christ and his flock. He died at Fremona, on a date not known for certain, but presumed to be between June 29 and July 9, 1577; the more probable date seems to be June 29. He was buried in St. George's church. His cause was introduced in Rome on June 8, 1630.

July

St. Bernardino Realino 1530–1616

Bernardino Realino was a successful lawyer who renounced his career to enter religion, and spent most of his Jesuit life as a humble parish priest. He was born in Carpi, near Modena, Italy, on December 1, 1530, and attended the Modena Academy, where he did exceptionally well in Greek and Latin. In 1548 he transferred to the University of Bologna and took courses in philosophy and medicine, but in 1551, his third year, he changed to law, thinking that a legal career would offer greater advancement and richer rewards.

Bernardino received his law degree in June 1556 and through his father's connection with Cardinal Cristoforo Madruzzo, governor of Milan, Bernardino became, at twenty-six, mayor of Felizzano, a position that included judge as well. When his term was over, the people asked that he be reappointed because they found him an honest judge and one who attended daily Mass. He was next put in charge of tax collections in Alessandria and then became mayor of Cassine. When he returned to Milan in 1562, his reputation as a competent magistrate preceded him, and the marquis of Pescara took him into his employ, making him mayor of Castelleone.

Bernardino was now in his thirty-second year and in a letter to his brother he revealed how unlike other city officials he was. He wrote: "I have no desire for the honors of this world, but solely for the glory of God and the salvation of my soul." He always saw himself as an instrument of Divine Providence and thought nothing of giving his entire salary to the poor. In 1564 the marquis named him superintendent of his estates in the Kingdom of Naples and Bernardino arrived in the capital city toward the end of June or the beginning of July. He was not, however, to remain long in the employ of the marquis, for it was in Naples that he became acquainted with the Jesuits.

One August afternoon as Bernardino was walking through the city, he noticed two Jesuit novices pass by. He was attracted by what they represented and asked someone who the clerics were. Hearing that they were Jesuits, he sought further information about the Order from one of his acquaintances and learned that the Society had only recently come to Naples. He then went to the Jesuit church and heard a sermon that moved him deeply. Three days later, wanting to make a general confession, he went to visit the Jesuit preacher who, recognizing Bernardino's religious inclinations, asked him first to meditate on certain themes for eight days and then to return. This Bernardino did and during the days of peace that filled his soul after his confession, he had a vision of our Lady, who commanded him to enter the Society. Thereupon, he left the service of the marquis for the service of Christ. He presented himself to the Jesuit provincial in Naples, was accepted, and entered the novitiate on October 13, 1564.

Bernardino's humility made him see himself as only capable of performing menial tasks, so he asked to be a brother, but his superiors instructed him to go on to the priesthood. After pronouncing his three vows of religion in October 1566, he was unexpectedly told to prepare for ordination, which he received on May 24, 1567. Though Fr. Realino had been a Jesuit for only three years, Fr. General Francis Borgia appointed him master of novices in Naples. Whatever he may have lacked in formal ecclesiastical training—he was still studying theology—his great prudence and sound judgment made up for it. Now as a priest, he began the work that was to occupy him for the remainder of his life. He preached and catechized, visited slaves on the galleys in the Naples harbor, and sat long hours in the confessional. The direction of souls was Fr. Realino's special charism.

In 1574 he was appointed to go to Lecce in Apulia, to investigate the possibility of establishing a Jesuit house and college in that city. The Lecceans were so jubilant about the Jesuits coming to their city that they offered the newly arrived priests a residence and started building them a church. Fr. Realino's coming to Lecce was the beginning of a forty-two-year period during which he exercised a pastoral apostolate, preaching in the Jesuit church and cathedral, hearing confessions, counselling clergy, visiting the sick and those in prison, and giving conferences in convents and monasteries. When the new church was completed the people then set to work on the Jesuit college, which opened in September 1583.

Fr. Realino and Lecce were inseparable. He had several times received orders from his provincial and the general to move to Naples or to Rome, but every time he was about to leave the city he was either mysteriously overcome by a high fever that required a period of rest, or else there were such severe thunderstorms that he could not leave. After several such non-human interventions kept him in Lecce, his superiors concluded that it was God's will for him to remain there and never again did they seek to transfer him.

Fr. Realino's work hardly changed from week to week. He gave himself generously to all who sought his counsel, and the lines leading to his confessional grew ever longer. Princes and prelates stood among the simple folk to await their turn to speak with "the holy old man," as he was referred to by the Lecceans. In 1583 he began a sodality for diocesan priests with a view to fostering priestly virtues and to providing them with instruction in moral theology so they could become better confessors. He was so frequently consulted in times of personal need that the people became convinced that it was his intercession with God that occasioned the many cures and miracles that were worked in Lecce.

Fr. Realino's final illness began on June 11, 1616, when a fever and an extreme weakness overcame him. He lingered on, losing his speech, but he remained conscious. On June 29 he received Viaticum and was anointed. When the city learned that he was dying, crowds gathered outside the Jesuit college. Only men were permitted to enter the cloistered residence. They knelt, kissed Fr. Realino's hand and devoutly touched religious objects to his body. Until the bishop of Lecce came on July 1, the Jesuits had succeeded in keeping the people from stripping the room of "relics." But when the bishop himself cut out a portion of the bedclothes, there was no holding back and soon the dying priest had hardly enough to cover him.

The mayor and several city magistrates also arrived, but this was an official visit—they carried a document with them, which they wanted to read to Fr. Realino. The document was the city's request that Fr. Realino be Lecce's defender and protector in heaven. When the document was read, the dying priest could only utter a sigh, which was interpreted as consent. The mayor, however, later doubted whether that sigh was actually consent and since this was a most important matter to the city, he and his delegation returned on July 2. This time Fr. Realino bowed his head and murmured a word that no one could understand, but the mayor took the nod as consent and, thus, even before the eighty-six-year-old priest had died, he had contracted to become Lecce's heavenly patron. That afternoon the Jesuits began the prayers for the dying, and about 4:00 P.M., while Fr. Realino kept his eyes on the crucifix, his speech returned for a moment and his final words were: "O Madonna, mia santissima" (O Lady, my most holy Lady).

Fr. Bernardino Realino was beatified by Pope Leo XIII on September 27, 1895, and was canonized by Pope Pius XII on June 22, 1947. St. Bernardino Realino's memorial is celebrated on July 2.

Prayer

Lord God, hear the prayer of Saint Bernardino Realino and give us the spirit of humility and charity with which you filled him, when you made him a perfect instrument of your loving kindness. We ask this through our Lord Jesus Christ, your Son, who lives and reigns with you, and the Holy Spirit, one God, for ever and ever.

Bl. John Cornelius 1557–1594

Martyr of England

John Cornelius, whose true name was John Conor O'Mahony, was born of Irish parents in Bodmin, Cornwall, about 1557. His middle name, when latinized, became Cornelius. His father was in the service of Sir John Arundell of Lanherne, who took great interest in young John. He arranged for the youth to attend Exeter College, Oxford, whence he was expelled on August 3, 1578, for "popery," that is, for maintaining Catholic beliefs. He then went to the English College in Rheims, France, arriving in September 1579, and on the following April 1, went to the English College in Rome. So outstanding was his scholastic achievement that he delivered the college's Christmas address before Pope Gregory XIII on the feast of St. Stephen, December 26, 1581. He completed his theological studies in Rome, was ordained there in 1583, and returned to England in September of that year.

Upon the return of Fr. Cornelius he made Sir John's residence in London the center of his operations. He helped confirm Sir John in his faith, who had recently been attending Protestant services to avoid losing his wealth and property. Fr. Cornelius also brought his own mother back to the Church and found a place for her in the Arundell household. So known was he for his zeal that government spies had tried to apprehend him for years.

One of the priest's longstanding desires was to become a Jesuit. While studying in Rome he had come to know them and had resolved that when time permitted he would enter the Society. His years on the English mission only strengthened that desire and, thus, he wrote to the Jesuit general in Rome and sought admission. The custom then was that all English candidates for the Society went to Flanders for their novitiate, and since Fr. Cornelius could not leave his flock without a priest, his formal entry had to be delayed. He, nevertheless, kept in contact with Fr. Henry Garnet, the superior of the English Jesuits, and placed himself under his direction. Fr. Garnet then wrote to Rome seeking permission for Fr. Cornelius to make his novitiate on his native soil, but before a favorable answer arrived Divine Providence intervened.

After Sir John's death in 1591, Lady Arundell moved the family to Chideock Castle in Dorset; Fr. Cornelius went with them and continued his ministry in Dorsetshire. While at Chideock he was betrayed by William Holmes, a servant, whom Fr. Cornelius had previously reprimanded for annoying one of Lady Arundell's maids. When the officers arrived to make the arrest on Easter Sunday, March 31, 1594, Fr. Cornelius was already out of the house, hiding in the woods. Two Sundays later, on April 14, the priest-hunters returned, and after a five-hour search they found him in a concealed priest-hole. When apprehended, the sheriff said to him, "I'm glad that I finally have you in my hands," to which he replied,

"And I, more so, for having been captured." When asked whether he was a Jesuit, he answered that he was among those who liked them. Three laymen—Thomas Bosgrave, a nephew of Lady Arundell, John Carey, and Patrick Salmon, house servants—were also taken prisoner.

The arresting officer, George Trenchard, took the four prisoners to his residence to await orders from London because Fr. Cornelius would be considered a good catch. In the ensuing two weeks, the priest discussed religion with members of Trenchard's household, and it is reported that he converted Trenchard's sister-in-law. The four prisoners were taken to Marshalsea Prison in London, and there Fr. Cornelius was interrogated by members of the Privy Council. He was tortured on the rack to reveal the names of Catholic households that had given him hospitality and the names of those who had attended his services. But Fr. Cornelius revealed nothing. Aware that his time was fast coming to an end, and lacking any definite word about beginning his noviceship as a Jesuit, he, on his own, pronounced the vows of the Society before three witnesses, two laymen and a Jesuit, and instructed each of them to make this fact known to the Jesuit superior in England.

The trial was set to take place in the city of capture and the four prisoners were returned to Dorchester. On July 2, 1594, Fr. Cornelius was condemned to the gallows, to be hanged and quartered, because he was a priest, had celebrated Mass, and had reconciled Protestants to the Catholic Church. His three lay companions were condemned merely to be hanged, for theirs was not a crime of high treason, but a felony, for having aided and assisted a priest. In the two days left to them, the prisoners prepared themselves for death, and on the afternoon of July 4, they were led to the scaffold. John Carey was the first of the group to die, then Patrick Salmon, then Thomas Bosgrave. When it was the turn of Fr. Cornelius, he approached the gallows and knelt at the foot of the ladder, prayed a while, then kissed the ground and the feet of his three companions, whose bodies still hung from the beam. He turned to the scaffold and said: "O good cross, so long desired." Once up the ladder, he prayed for his persecutors and the queen, and though forbidden to speak further, he did reveal to the bystanders that he was a Jesuit. Then kissing the noose held out by the hangman, he placed it around his neck, and thereupon he was pushed from the ladder. His body was subsequently quartered.

Fr. John Cornelius and his three companions in death were beatified by Pope Pius XI on December 15, 1929, and his memorial is celebrated on December 1, together with the other Jesuit martyrs of England and Wales.

Prayer

Almighty, eternal God, you chose from the people of England and Wales Blessed John Cornelius and his companions to be made like Christ, who died to save the world. Listen to their prayers; strengthen your Church by the same faith and love that strengthened them, and bless it always with your gift of unity. We ask this through our Lord Jesus Christ, your Son, who lives and reigns with you and the Holy Spirit, one God, for ever and ever.

St. Anthony Daniel 1601–1648

Martyr of North America

Anthony Daniel was born in Dieppe, France, on May 27, 1601. While studying law he decided to become a Jesuit and entered the novitiate at Rouen on October 1, 1621. After vows he taught in Rouen, and while he was there the missionaries in New France (today's Canada) sent a native youth to study at the college. Hearing stories from the Huron lad about missionary work in New France, a desire grew within Anthony to join in the conversion of the Huron. He then did theology at Clermont College in Paris, was ordained in 1631, and was sent to teach at the college at Eu. It was there that he met Fr. John de Brébeuf, recently exiled from New France.

In the spring of 1632 Fr. Daniel and Fr. Ambrose Davost crossed the Atlantic to minister to the settlers at the fort on Cape Breton Island. The following year the two priests were needed in Quebec, where they arrived in June, and once there they devoted their time to learning the Huron language from Fr. Brébeuf, who had since returned to the mission. On July 7, 1634, Fr. Daniel embarked on his first trip to Huronia; Fr. Brébeuf was also returning there. The Hurons, who had come to trade furs at Three Rivers, were still sick with fever from the epidemic that had recently swept through their territory. They were a cheerless group and took the two missionaries only because of the gifts the priests had offered them. On their way the canoes carrying the missionaries became separated. And at some distance from their destination, the testy natives carrying Fr. Daniel rudely deposited him and his baggage on the shore of Allumette Island. Fortunately, he was rescued by a chief of the Bear Clan and eventually made his way to Taendeuiata where Fr. Brébeuf had arrived several days before.

Fr. Daniel began his apostolic work in early 1635. He and Fr. Brébeuf invited the children to their cabin, and while the veteran missionary gave the catechetical instruction, Fr. Daniel, who had a way with children, taught them their prayers and the commandments of God by setting the lesson to music. Such was his success with children that when the superior of the mission decided to start a school for Huron boys in Quebec, Fr. Daniel was appointed its director. The missionaries in Huronia appealed to the parents to permit their sons to attend this school. A dozen boys were to make the trip, but at the time of their departure, only three could leave their wailing mothers behind. The school opened in the autumn of 1636 with only five students. The enterprise failed, and in the summer of 1638 Fr. Daniel was back in Huronia.

On his return Fr. Daniel's assignment was the village of Ossossané. After a year he was directed, in November 1639, to establish a new mission at Cahiagué. When he arrived at his new post, a smallpox epidemic was in progress and the priest went from cabin to cabin nursing the sick. As the contagion spread the people superstitiously attributed it to his presence, but the missionary bravely addressed them in council and explained that the epidemic had started prior to his coming, and if he were the cause he would not have tried to cure them. He thus won their confidence and by the following spring he had about 140 adult converts. He remained at Cahiagué for the next eight years and transformed it into a flourishing Christian village.

In 1647 Fr. Daniel moved on to Teanaustayé. He also enjoyed great success in that village, but by this time the Iroquois threat was increasing and the village, unfortunately, was near the route that the Iroquois usually followed. Toward the end of June 1648, he went to mission headquarters at Sainte-Marie to make his annual retreat, and then returned to Teanaustayé on July 2. On July 4, as soon as he had finished celebrating Mass, the fearful cry "Iroquois, Iroquois," was heard throughout the village. The children and squaws went for cover and the braves for their weapons. Fr. Daniel rushed to the cabins of the sick and dying to baptize as many as he could, telling them: "Brother, today we shall be in heaven." Because the invaders had the greater number, the relatively few Hurons could not possibly defend their village and so they ran to the church thinking that would be the best place in which to die. Fr. Daniel joined them, and when the Iroquois came he fearlessly faced them and forbade them to enter. Though at first amazed at the priest's courage and valor, they responded by raining upon him a shower of arrows and directing a bullet into his heart. As soon as he fell to the ground the assassins stripped his body and further violated it. When the chapel was fully ablaze, they tossed it into the flames and, thus, Fr. Anthony Daniel, at age forty-seven, gave his life for his sheep and his shepherd. When his Jesuit brethren came to look for the missionary's body, they could not find a trace.

With seven others, who were also martyred in North America, Fr. Anthony Daniel was beatified by Pope Pius XI on June 21, 1925, and canonized by him on June 29, 1930. St. Anthony Daniel's memorial is celebrated on October 19 with the other North American Martyrs.

Prayer

Father, you consecrated the first beginnings of the faith in North America by the preaching and martyrdom of Saint Anthony Daniel and his companions. By the help of their prayers may the Christian faith continue to grow throughout the world. We ask this through our Lord Jesus Christ, your Son, who lives and reigns with you and the Holy Spirit, one God, for ever and ever.

July 15

Bl. Ignatius de Azevedo and 39 Companions 1526–1570

Martyrs of Brazil

These forty martyrs, Fr. Ignatius de Azevedo and his new recruits for the Brazil mission, met their death off the Canary Islands at the hands of French Huguenot corsairs.

Fr. Azevedo was born in Oporto, Portugal, in 1526, and entered the Society at Coimbra on December 28, 1548. He was ordained in 1553 and was sent to Lisbon to establish St. Anthony's College, and then in 1560 went to Braga to found St. Paul's College. He traveled to Rome in 1565 as procurator for India and Brazil, and there Fr. General Francis Borgia appointed him visitor to Brazil, where he was to evaluate the missionaries' work and to ascertain how they could best be helped. He arrived in Bahia on August 24, 1566, and spent the next two years traversing the country, visiting the Jesuit houses, schools, and missions. He then returned to Europe and made his report to Fr. Borgia in 1569. He was happy to relate that the missionaries had had great success in the number of baptisms administered and in the number of catechumens under instruction. He described the works they were involved in, the schools they had opened, and the number of students attending. There was only one difficulty—the shortage of men. Fr. Borgia thus instructed Fr. Azevedo to visit the Spanish and Portuguese provinces of the Society and recruit volunteers for the Brazil mission. Fr. Azevedo was also, at the same time, appointed its provincial. The response to his visit to the Iberian peninsula was phenomenal. He gathered some seventy Jesuit volunteers, of whom a few were priests, most were scholastics and brothers and, of these, many were novices still in their first training.

Because the group was so diverse, Fr. Azevedo gathered them at Val de Rosal, near Lisbon, and for five months prepared them for life on the mission. Seven ships and a caravel left Lisbon on June 5, 1570, for the Madeira Islands, off the coast of Africa. Fr. Azevedo was aboard the *Santiago* with forty-three Jesuits; the others were distributed on two other ships, most, however, were aboard the galleon carrying Brazil's new governor Dom Luis de Vasconcelos. For the missionaries on the *Santiago*, there were scheduled times for Mass, prayer, reading, study, and so forth. The sailors also attended Fr. Azevedo's instructions to the Jesuits and participated at Mass when it was celebrated on deck. As a result of the favorable weather, the flotilla arrived at Madeira on June 12. The ships remained in port until the end of the month.

The next stop was to be the Canary Islands, but since there were rumors that the sea was infested with French corsairs, Dom Luis de Vasconcelos thought it better not to sail. The *Santiago's* captain, however, decided to take the chance, because

Qvadraginta Socij IESU, Duce P. Ignatio Azevedio, pro Catholica
fide à Calvinistis in itinere Brasilico, mari demersi A. 1570. 15. Iulij.
C. Screta del.   Melch. Küsell f.

Bl. Ignatius de Azevedo and Companions

he was carrying a heavy cargo for the island of La Palma. Notified of the captain's decision, Fr. Azevedo informed his group of the danger involved—they might outsmart the pirates but, on the other hand, they might not, which meant that they could be taken captive and even killed. Most of the Jesuits on the *Santiago* agreed to continue their journey, except the four who transferred to another ship. On June 29 the missionaries gathered on shore to sing a High Mass and receive Communion. As Fr. Azevedo took leave of his friend, Fr. Peter Dias, who was in charge of the Jesuits on the governor's galleon, Fr. Dias burst into tears, not knowing whether the two would meet again. The *Santiago* left port on June 30.

It was perfect weather with calm seas for seven days, but as the vessel approached La Palma Island a contrary wind came up and the captain decided to enter the bay at Tazacorte. There Fr. Azevedo ran into an old friend, a Dutchman, with whom he had gone to school in Oporto. After a few days in Tazacorte, the missionaries were eager to get to Santa Cruz de La Palma on the island's eastern coast and continue their passage to Brazil. The Dutchman offered to take them overland since it would be quicker than by sea, especially with the unfavorable winds. Fr. Azevedo at first accepted his offer, but the following day, after celebrating Mass, he changed his plans and decided to go by sea. To his fellow Jesuits he said: "I was resolved to go by land because of the danger from the French, but I have now decided to go by sea, and I feel in the Lord, that this is what we ought to do. If the French should capture us, what harm can they do? The most they can do is to send us quickly to heaven." Thus Fr. Azevedo and his thirty-nine companions set sail and two days later, as they were heading toward Santa Cruz de la Palma, the lookout announced sails on the horizon. The crew at first thought these might be the ships they had left at Madeira, but when the vessels came closer the sailors recognized them for what they were, French ships under the command of Jacques Sourie, a French Huguenot pirate.

Sourie's ships were fast and they easily caught up with the *Santiago* before it had a chance to turn into the harbor. One ship came alongside and three pirates jumped aboard, but before others could follow, the ships moved apart. The three pirates were quickly slain. Fr. Azevedo took the painting of our Lady, which he had received from Pope Pius V when in Rome in 1569, and set it next to the main mast and there he and his companions began to pray. Since some sailors had to relinquish their maritime tasks to fight the oncoming pirates, several of the missionaries filled in for them while the rest were sent below deck. The other pirates succeeded in boarding the ship and they soon outnumbered the sailors of the *Santiago*. When the Huguenots saw Fr. Azevedo holding the painting of our Lady, their hatred led them directly toward him and as they approached, he said: "You are my witnesses that I am dying for the Catholic faith and the Holy Roman Church." At that moment a corsair slashed his head with a sword and two others pierced him through. The pirates then picked up his body, with the painting still in its hands, and hurled it overboard.

They next went after whomever they saw in a black cassock; some they wounded and then killed, others they stripped naked, cut off their arms and threw them into the sea to drown. Within a short time the Huguenots had total command of the vessel. When some went below deck to see what they could plunder, they found the rest of the Jesuits in prayer. The pirates killed some, the rest they brought on deck.

Now that the ship was completely under their control, the pirates asked Sourie what he wanted done with the remaining missionaries. He answered: "The fathers were on their way to spread false doctrine in Brazil, throw them into the sea." First choosing those who appeared older, thinking them priests, the corsairs wounded them and then cast them overboard, but the younger ones they simply hurled into the sea, one after the other.

One of those cast into the sea is only identified as John; he was the nephew of the *Santiago*'s captain. Earlier in the voyage he expressed a desire to become a Jesuit, and during the confusion on board, he put on a cassock that had been stripped from one of the martyrs, and mixed with the other Jesuits. Thus, he too was thrown overboard. All these martyrs died on July 15, 1570.

There was one, Simon da Costa, who met his death on the following day. He had no cassock, having been a Jesuit for only a few weeks, and therefore went unobserved among the sailors. But when the *Santiago*'s crew was interrogated on the 16th, he revealed that he too was a missionary. Forthwith, Sourie ordered him beheaded and his body hurled into the sea.

Of the Jesuits on board the *Santiago,* only John Sánchez was spared. He was denied martyrdom because the pirates needed a cook and they pressed him into service. Sánchez remained on the *Santiago* until it docked at La Rochelle, France, the pirates' home port and a Huguenot stronghold. There he escaped and made his way to Portugal, where he told his fellow Jesuits the sad events that had taken place on July 15 and 16, 1570.

On May 11, 1854, Pope Pius IX confirmed the cult paid these forty martyrs of Brazil, and declared them among the blessed in heaven. Their brother Jesuits celebrate their memorial on January 19.

Fr. Ignatius de Azevedo's 39 Companions:

1   *James de Andrade* (priest), Portuguese, born in Pedrógão Grande, about 1531, entered June 7, 1558; wounded and thrown overboard alive.
2   *Francis Álvares* (brother), Portuguese, native of Covilhã, born about 1539, entered December 21, 1564; thrown alive into the sea.
3   *Gaspar Álvares* (brother), Portuguese, native of Oporto; wounded and thrown alive into the sea.
4   *Manuel Álvares* (brother), Portuguese, native of Estremoz, born about 1536, entered February 12, 1559; harshly mistreated and thrown alive into the sea.
5   *Alphonsus de Baena* (brother), Spaniard, born about 1539 in Villatobas (Toledo), entered 1568; wounded and thrown alive into the sea.
6   *Álvaro Borralho (Mendes)* (scholastic), Portuguese, native of Elvas; thrown alive into the sea.
7   *Mark Caldeira* (novice brother), Portuguese, native of Vila da Feira, born about 1547, entered October 2, 1569; thrown alive into the sea.

8   *Bento de Castro* (scholastic), Portuguese, born about 1543 in Vila de Chacim (Trás-os-Montes), entered August 20, 1561; the first to be wounded and thrown into the sea.

9   *Anthony Correia* (novice scholastic), Portuguese, born about 1553 in Oporto, entered June 1, 1569; wounded and thrown alive into the sea.

10   *Louis Correia* (scholastic), Portuguese, born in Évora; thrown alive into the sea.

11   *Simon da Costa* (novice brother), Portuguese, born in Oporto in 1570; beheaded on July 16, body then thrown into sea.

12   *Alexis Delgado* (novice scholastic), Portuguese, native of Elvas; wounded and thrown alive into the sea.

13   *Nicholas Dinis* (novice scholastic), Portuguese, born in Bragança about 1553, became a Jesuit in 1570; thrown alive into the sea.

14   *Gregory Escribano* (brother), Spaniard, native of Logroño; thrown alive into the sea.

15   *Anthony Fernandes* (novice brother), Portuguese, born in Montemór-o-Novo about 1552, became a Jesuit in January 1570; after being stabbed several times, was thrown alive into the sea.

16   *Dominic Fernandes* (novice brother), Portuguese, born about 1551, native of Vila de Borba, entered September 25, 1569; wounded and thrown alive into the sea.

17   *John Fernandes* [I] (novice scholastic), Portuguese, native of Braga, born about 1547, entered June 5, 1569; thrown alive into the sea.

18   *John Fernandes* [II] (scholastic), Portuguese, born about 1551 in Lisbon, entered April 5, 1568; thrown alive into the sea.

19   *Manuel Fernandes* (scholastic), Portuguese, born in Celorico da Beira; thrown alive into the sea.

20   *Peter Fontoura* (brother), Portuguese, born in Braga; wounded and thrown alive into the sea.

21   *Andrew Gonçalves* (scholastic), Portuguese, born in Viana de Alvito (Alentejo); wounded and thrown alive into the sea.

22   *Gonçalo Henriques* (deacon, scholastic), Portuguese, native of Oporto; thrown alive into the sea.

23   *Simon Lopes* (scholastic), Portuguese, born in Ourém; thrown alive into the sea.

24   *Francis de Magalhães* (novice scholastic), Portuguese, born in Vila de Alcácer do Sal, about 1549, became a Jesuit December 27, 1568; thrown alive into the sea.

25   *John de Mayorga* (novice brother), Spaniard, born about 1533, in Saint Jean Pied de Port in Gascogny, which was then part of Old Navarre, and entered in 1568; thrown alive into the sea.

26   *James (Pires) Mimoso* (scholastic), Portuguese, born in Nisa (Portalegre); killed by lance wound, then thrown into the sea.

27   *Peter Nunes* (scholastic), Portuguese, born in Vila da Fronteira (Alentejo); thrown alive into the sea.

28   *Manuel Pacheco* (scholastic), Portuguese, native of Ceuta, North Africa; thrown alive into the sea.

29   *Francis Pérez Godoy* (novice scholastic), Spaniard, born about 1540 in Torrijos (Toledo), became a Jesuit April 15, 1569; wounded and thrown alive into the sea.

30   *Bras Ribeiro* (novice brother), Portuguese, native of Braga, born about 1546, entered December 1569; beheaded, then thrown into the sea.

31   *Louis Rodrigues* (novice scholastic), Portuguese, born in Évora, about 1554, entered January 15, 1570; wounded and thrown alive into the sea.

32   *Manuel Rodrigues* (scholastic), Portuguese, native of Alcochete; thrown alive into the sea.

33   *Ferdinand Sánchez* (scholastic), Spaniard, born in Old Castile; wounded and thrown into the sea.

34   *John de San Martín* (novice scholastic), Spaniard, native of Yuncos (Toledo), born about 1550, and entered February 8, 1570; wounded and thrown alive into the sea.

35   *Anthony Soares* (scholastic), Portuguese, native of Vila de Trancoso, became a Jesuit June 5, 1565; severely wounded and thrown into the sea.

36   *Amaro Vaz* (novice brother), Portuguese, born about 1554 in Bemfazer, near Oporto, entered November 1, 1569; wounded and thrown alive into the sea.

37   *John de Zafra* (novice brother), Spaniard, born in Jerez de Badajoz, entered February 8, 1570; thrown alive into the sea.

38   *Stephen Zuraire* (brother), Spaniard, native of Zudaire; thrown alive into the sea.

39   *John* (candidate); Portuguese, nephew of the ship's captain, born Entre Douro e Minho; thrown alive into the sea.

Prayer

Father, we celebrate the memory of Blessed Ignatius de Azevedo and companions, who died for their faithful witness to Christ. Give us the strength to follow their example, loyal and faithful to the end. We ask this through our Lord Jesus Christ your Son, who lives and reigns with you and the Holy Spirit, one God, for ever and ever.

July 18

S. G. Jacques Sevin 1882–1951

Fr. Jacques Sevin, founder of France's Catholic Boy Scouts, was born in Lille, France, on December 7, 1882. Most of his youth was spent in Tourcoing, Belgium, where he attended the school of the Franciscan Sisters of Our Lady of the Angels and then Sacred Heart College. In 1892 he transferred to Providence College in Amiens, his father's alma mater, and remained there until early 1899, when he was forced to interrupt his studies because of continual headaches. His father then sent him to England for six months, and on his return he resumed his education in Lille.

Jacques thought of being a priest as early as 1895, but it was in 1898, while making a retreat, that he had his first thoughts about becoming a Jesuit. He continued his English studies at Lille's Catholic University and in May 1900, during another retreat, confirmed his earlier thinking. He subsequently entered the Jesuit novitiate at Saint-Acheul, near Amiens, on September 3, 1900. In the following September, as a result of a recent governmental decree, the French Jesuit students had to go into exile. They found a home in Arlon, the novitiate of the Belgian Province, and there they continued their noviceship training. Jacques pronounced his first vows there on September 5, 1902, and shortly afterwards moved to Antoing also in Belgium to pursue his classical course. In 1904 he was sent to teach English at St. John Berchmans College in Florennes, where he was also in charge of the students' theater. After three years of regency, he returned to studies, this time philosophy (1907–1910) at Gemert, Netherlands, and then theology (1911–1915) at Enghien, Belgium.

During his years in theology, Jacques kept up with events in England and after 1908 closely followed the growth of its Boy Scout movement and studied the writings of Lieut. Gen. Robert Baden-Powell, the British army officer who founded the movement in 1907. In 1913, after two articles unfavorable of the movement appeared in the Jesuit periodical *Études,* Jacques asked to spend that summer in England investigating the movement at first hand. While attending a scout rally in London on September 20, he met Baden-Powell and right then and there resolved to establish a Catholic branch of the Boys Scouts in France.

Shortly after ordination at Enghien on August 2, 1914, Fr. Sevin was sent by his provincial to visit Cardinal Francis Bourne of Westminster to negotiate with the British government the possibility of accepting religious from Alsace-Lorraine, who had been uprooted from their monasteries because of war. When the German army occupied Brussels, Fr. Sevin immediately left England for France and asked to serve as a military chaplain, but his provincial told him to return to Belgium and await further word. No further word arrived and so he completed his theological course and made his tertianship.

In August of 1916 Fr. Sevin was assigned to teach at the Jesuit school in Mouscron on the Belgian border, but the college was closed by the Germans eight days after his arrival. Whatever free time he now had he spent in writing a book about scouting. The movement had spread beyond Baden-Powell's expectations. Within one year of its founding there were 100,000 scouts in Great Britain and by 1911 there we 500,000 throughout the world. Though there were opposing voices to the movement in France, Fr. Sevin nevertheless was convinced that it was needed and that it could be the vehicle for imbuing French youth with Catholic principles. On February 13, 1918, he formed his first troop in Mouscron, but this was an underground group and the boys were without uniforms. Such anonymity helped keep the young members from being deported to Germany.

In September 1919, Fr. Sevin, now back again in his native France, was sent to teach at Metz, but within a few months he fell ill and was ordered by his physician to seek a rest cure in northern Italy. On his way he visited Paris and there the National Association of Scouts of France was formed and Fr. Sevin was asked to write the statutes of the new organization. On his return home he was named General Commissary and Secretary General of the organization. Then in 1921 Baden-Powell, acknowledging the priest's role in establishing the Boy Scout movement in France, awarded him the Silver Fox, the movement's highest honor.

In November 1921, Fr. Sevin was transferred to Lille, where he remained until 1939. His book *Le Scoutisme* appeared in the following year and although this was an *apologia* explaining the need for Catholic Boy Scouts, it also set the direction of the entire French scout movement. In 1923 he established a "school-camp" at Chamarande for the training of scout leaders. Then in February 1924, because of opposition from some of the French clergy, Fr. Sevin had to resign his position as Commissary General. It was alleged that his training of French youths as scouts would turn young men from thinking about the priesthood. On the other hand, there were those who claimed that the movement was geared to attract the youth toward Protestantism. These voices were finally silenced when Pope Pius XI approved the movement in 1926.

From 1923 to 1932 Fr. Sevin spent his summers training leaders at Chamarande; he was in charge of their religious and moral formation. In the following year he was unexpectedly relieved of all duties officially connected with the movement. He remained in Lille, however, and occupied himself in giving conferences and exhortations to priests and religious, and retreats to seminarians, laity, as well as to scout troops throughout France.

During these years Fr. Sevin envisaged a religious congregation of sisters to work with young girls. This dream was to become a reality. While giving a retreat at Anjou in 1935, he met Jacqueline Brière, the head of a Girl Scout troop in Saumur. With her he made preliminary plans for the founding of the Congregation of the Holy Cross of Jerusalem, but because of World War II these plans had to be temporarily set aside. The congregation was finally established on January 15, 1944, when the first priory was formed at Issy-Les-Moulineaux; its first members were four former Girl Scout mistresses.

Fr. Sevin remained in close touch with his congregation, and when his term as superior of the residence in Troyes ended in 1946, he was transferred to Paris. By this time his congregation had moved its priory to Chantilly, a short distance from Paris. He prepared its constitutions, which were approved in 1949, the year that the congregation moved to its permanent home in Boran-sur-Oise.

In March 1950 Fr. Sevin was informed by his major superiors that he would have to relinquish his role over his congregation and pass it on to another. The rules of the Society of Jesus do not permit its members to be in charge of congregations of sisters. His answer to the provincial was: "A Jesuit does not have two responses to make when given the decision of his superior. Very Reverend Father General and you can count on my absolute obedience. I have very much desired to inculcate this same spirit in my daughters."

In September of that same year, Fr. Sevin celebrated his fiftieth year as a Jesuit. He had not long to live. In February 1951, as he was on his way to Boran, he fell ill and it was at the priory in Boran that he spent his last months. In his final hours, his last words to his daughters were: "Be saints all of you! Nothing else counts." Awaiting death to take him home, Fr. Sevin clasped his crucifix in his hands—the same that he had received on the morning of his first vows—and kept repeating: "My companion, my companion. This is my companion." Fr. Jacques Sevin died on July 19, and was buried on the priory grounds at Boran. His cause is presently under consideration.

July 19

S. G. Raymond Artigues 1902–1936

Martyr of the Spanish Civil War

Fr. Raymond Artigues Sirvent was the first priest to be martyred in the diocese of Lérida during the Spanish Civil War. At the time of his death he was a candidate for the Society, but had not yet entered the novitiate. He was born in Lérida on December 29, 1902, and in 1915 began his studies for the priesthood at the local diocesan seminary. He was ordained on June 11, 1927, and for three years was assistant pastor at Almenar. Then in December 1930 he was transferred to a parish in Alguaire, where he labored until his death.

During his years as a parish priest, Fr. Artigues was especially known for his promotion of the Enthronement of the Sacred Heart of Jesus and his work with Catholic Action groups. Through his catechetical instructions to the young, he exercised a great influence on their lives, and it was precisely because of this influence that Lérida's atheistic revolutionary forces singled him out as one of its main targets.

Fr. Artigues first thought of becoming a Jesuit in 1934. When he approached his bishop, who was also to die a martyr two weeks after Fr. Artigues, for permission to transfer from the diocese to the Society, the bishop expressed his reluctance to let him go. This reluctance was not rooted in any ill will toward the Jesuits; the bishop, in fact, had high regard for them and even praised Fr. Artigues for his desire to join the Society. But Spain at the time was suffering from internal political problems, and the Church was suffering from the country's increasingly powerful anti-Catholic movement. Because the diocese was severely shorthanded, the bishop asked Fr. Artigues to remain in his parish a little longer. He obeyed, but his thoughts were often on the Jesuits. When he heard that his younger brother was to enter the Society, the desire of Fr. Artigues increased, and so he went to visit the Jesuit provincial on July 18, 1935, to place the problem before him. The result of the meeting was that the provincial accepted him as a candidate for the Society that same day, but asked him to remain in his parish, where he was badly needed. He was told that he would make his noviceship when peace returned to the Church, but in the meantime he was officially accepted. This brought him consolation but he was never to see the novitiate.

From July 6 to July 11, 1936, Fr. Artigues made his annual retreat, and when it was over, he wrote to his Jesuit brother that he was content to remain where he was because that was where God wanted him to be. Then on July 18 civil war broke out. On the 19th Mr. Manuel Cambray, a neighbor who lived near his rectory, sent word that the priest was welcome to stay with him and that he would probably enjoy greater safety there. At 9:30 that evening Fr. Artigues went to the Cambray residence, passing through the back gardens. They spent hours talking about Spain's critical situation; the priest felt that the country was in for a most distressing period. When he was about to leave, his host convinced him not to go out alone at that late hour and that he should spend the night with him. The next morning a servant, who came to awaken the priest so that he could celebrate Mass in the church, mentioned that all through the night he had heard patrols passing by. As Fr. Artigues was leaving the house, Mr. Cambray invited him to return again that night and said that the back door would be open.

Sometime after eleven Fr. Artigues was alone in the rectory when he heard unusually loud banging on the front door. He hurriedly left through the back, and as he was going through the gardens on his way to the Cambray house he was captured. Some dozen or so men surrounded him; others set the church ablaze. As he was being taken to their headquarters, one of the group gave him three terrible blows on the head and he immediately fell to the ground. Three others, with pistols in their hands, stood over the prostrate priest and shot him several times. About 6:00 A.M. the following day, he was buried in a common grave with others who had been killed during the previous night's disturbance.

The body of Fr. Raymond Artigues was discovered and identified in October 1940, and properly interred in another part of the cemetery. The diocesan investigation into his martyrdom was begun in Lérida in March 1953.

July 20

Bl. Leo Ignatius Mangin 1857–1900

Bl. Paul Denn 1847–1900

Martyrs of the Boxer Rebellion

Fr. Leo Ignatius Mangin and Fr. Paul Denn received their palms of martyrdom during the Boxer Rebellion of 1898–1900. The Boxers, a secret Chinese society, were given that name by the English because the members extolled physical prowess and engaged in energetic gymnastic exercises. Enemies of the Christian faith and of foreign missionaries, they began their persecution of Catholics in 1898, and as their audacity grew so did the number of martyred Chinese, a number estimated to be 30,000. On July 20, 1900, an entire village in the Zhili district of Tianjin was massacred because the Catholic villagers remained steadfast in their profession of the faith.

Fr. Mangin was born at Verny, near Metz, France, on July 30, 1857. He first studied with the Christian Brothers and then attended colleges in Metz and Amiens. He entered the Society at Saint-Acheul on November 5, 1875, studied philosophy at Louvain, taught for a time in Liège, and in 1882 went to the China mission. During the next four years, while studying theology and Chinese, a companion of his was the martyr Rémy Isoré, with whom he was ordained on July 31, 1886.

Fr. Mangin had filled various positions during his years as a missionary and in 1900 he was stationed at Zhujiahe, a town that originally had 400 inhabitants. Because of Boxer attacks in the surrounding area, that number within a very short time increased by incoming refugees to almost 3,000. Knowing that the Boxers would one day come to his village, Fr. Mangin wisely fortified it as best he could and laid in a supply of provisions. As superior of that district, he asked Fr. Denn, then stationed in Gucheng, to come to Zhujiahe.

Paul Denn was born on April 1, 1847, in Lille, France, and before his entrance into the Society at Amiens on July 6, 1872, he had worked as a bank clerk to support his widowed mother. He had thought of becoming a foreign missionary, but circumstances at home kept him from fulfilling that desire. Nevertheless, he did become an active lay apostle among his fellow workers and a member of the St. Vincent de Paul Society. It was only when he was twenty-five that he was able to leave home for the Jesuit novitiate. Shortly after his entrance he went to China and was ordained there on December 19, 1880.

The Boxers made their first attack on Zhujiahe on July 15, 1900, but the villagers were prepared and successfully repulsed them. The following day the villagers again bravely defended their citadel. On the 17th, however, 2,000 soldiers of the imperial army, on its way to Peking (now Beijing), joined the Boxers. When Fr. Mangin climbed the chapel roof to learn the strength of the attackers, he saw that his people were now badly outnumbered and knew that their defenses could not possibly hold. Nevertheless, they would defend themselves as best they could. That evening some people secretly left the village, but the priests, who had been encouraged to depart so that they could continue their work elsewhere, chose to remain with their flock.

By the 18th their defense became disorganized and by the 20th the Boxers managed to construct towers that enabled them to scale the barricade and enter the village. With hope waning, Fr. Mangin gathered the women and children into the chapel, and there he and Fr. Denn sat, facing the congregation, and led them in prayer. As the shouts and the sounds of gunfire became louder and closer, some of the women began to panic, but Fr. Mangin calmed them with the words: "Just a few minutes more and we will all be in heaven." Unable to withstand the onslaught of this final attack, the few surviving men staggered into the chapel and everyone waited for the end to come.

About 9:00 A.M. the Boxers broke down the church doors and saw a congregation on its knees and two bearded Jesuits at the altar. Meeting no resistance the Boxers first offered to spare anyone who would forsake the faith; only a frightened few did so. Then the massacre began. With the first rounds of gunfire, Fr. Denn intoned the Confiteor and Fr. Mangin pronounced the words of absolution. Both priests were among the first to fall to the chapel floor. With the priests dead, some brutish Boxers began shooting indiscriminately into the congregation, while others slashed at their victims with swords. They finally set fire to the roof and the chapel was soon filled with smoke. A few people escaped through the windows, uttering words of apostasy, but the vast majority of the Zhujiahe Catholics remained at the altar of holocaust.

The bones of the martyrs remained in the place of sacrifice until 1901, when they were collected and placed in fifty-seven coffins and were later buried in the new church erected on the same site. The death toll on that July 20, 1900, was 1,370 Catholics.

On April 17, 1955, Pope Pius XII beatified Fr. Leo Mangin and Fr. Paul Denn, together with Fr. Modeste Andlauer and Fr. Rémy Isoré, and fifty-two Chinese Catholics, chosen from the great number of Boxer martyrs.

Prayer

O God, you have used the blood of martyrs to render the Church fruitful. In answer to the prayers of Blessed Leo Mangin, Blessed Paul Denn, and their fellow martyrs, let there flower an unstinting harvest of Christians and allow us to share the glory of your saints. We ask you this through our Lord Jesus Christ, your Son, who lives and reigns with you and the Holy Spirit, one God, for ever and ever.

July 21

S. G. John Baptist Reus 1868–1947

Fr. John Baptist Reus was a German, who went to Brazil as a missionary in 1900 and spent the next forty-seven years of his life in the country of his adoption. When he died in 1947 everyone acknowledged his holiness, but only a few were aware of the extraordinary mystical graces that God had granted him during his life.

John Baptist was born on July 10, 1868, in Pottenstein, Bavaria, the eighth of eleven children. He attended the elementary school in his hometown, and for his secondary studies went, in 1880, to Bamberg, where he remained until 1889. Though his thoughts were on the priesthood, he had first to fulfill his military service, thus he entered the army on October 1, 1889, and was assigned to the infantry. After his year's duty, he was discharged on October 1, 1890, and on the 28th of that month he entered Bamberg's diocesan seminary.

John Baptist had an uncle who was a Jesuit and in time he too thought of becoming one. He visited the provincial of the Southern German province in September 1892, but since he was less than a year from ordination, the provincial suggested that he first be ordained and then enter. The ordination took place in the Bamberg cathedral on July 30, 1893, and the new priest celebrated his first Mass in his hometown on the following day. His bishop had asked him to serve a year in the diocese and appointed him to the parish in Neuhaus an der Pegnitz. Then on October 16, 1894, Fr. Reus entered the Jesuit novitiate in Blijenbeek, the Netherlands, since German Jesuits were forbidden to have houses of study in their country because of Bismarck's *Kulturkampf*. After two years of novitiate, Fr. Reus moved to the scholasticate in Valkenburg, also in the Netherlands, where he reviewed his philosophy and theology.

In early 1900 Fr. Reus expressed his interest in and willingness to go to the missions in India, but the provincial, considering the needs of the different missions, assigned him in May to the province's mission in Brazil. Together with four other Jesuit missionaries, Fr. Reus sailed from Hamburg on August 5, 1900, and docked in Rio Grande on September 15. He was first stationed at the Jesuit college in Rio Grande City, where he taught and was prefect of discipline until November 30, 1905, when he became superior of the community. In 1912 he went to Anchieta College in Porto Alegre and then in 1913 he became pastor of the Jesuit parish in São Leopoldo. When the Jesuits took over the diocesan seminary in São Leopoldo, he became spiritual father to the seminarians and taught them liturgy from 1914 until 1944.

Fr. Reus began to receive mystical graces shortly after his ordination and they became more frequent as he grew older. These spiritual experiences are known only because he faithfully kept a diary, which his superior had commanded him to write in 1934. From these sources we learn that twelve years after his arrival in Brazil, he received the stigmata which, though it never became visible, remained with him for the remainder of his life and caused him pain and prolonged suffering. During his prayer on September 4, 1912, very much like St. Francis of Assisi, he told our Lord that he wanted to love him with a seraphic love and asked that that love's flame so cleanse his heart that it could become his tabernacle. This prayer was soon answered. On September 6, our Lady and St. Joseph visited him during prayer, then that night he awakened several times and each time he felt our Lord's presence in the room. The following morning, September 7, while at prayer, he perceived our Lord gazing upon him and suddenly he felt himself filled with so overwhelming a love that his entire body was on fire and that he himself was being lifted upwards. An enormous flame descended and pierced his heart; then five rays of light were aimed at five parts of his body—the very places where our Lord had carried his wounds. When this happened, he cried out: "No, my Love, no." He tried to close his hands and pull back his feet so that the rays could not touch him, but he found that that was useless.

Mystical graces, such as visions and ecstasies, were of common occurrence in his priestly life at São Leopoldo, but neither his students nor his Jesuit brethren were ever aware of what God was accomplishing in him. As he grew older his age began to show. He left the seminary in 1942 to become spiritual father for the young Jesuit philosophers and theologians studying at Colégio Cristo Rei, but continued to teach his liturgy course at the seminary for two more years.

In 1947 Fr. Reus began to slow down and on June 10 he celebrated his last Mass. That date also marks the last entry in his diary, where he notes that during that morning's Mass he experienced the usual three ecstasies, that is, at the consecration, then before and after Communion. The love of Fr. Reus for the Mass was such that he called it "the most beautiful hour of the day." During the remaining few weeks of his life the asthma that had afflicted him subsided, but on July 11 he became so critically ill that everyone thought it was the end. Fr. Reus requested absolution and shortly thereafter sat up in bed and with ecstatic joy announced that our Lady had just come into the room. The rector, who was at his side the entire time, told him that our Lady had surely come to take him to his eternal home, and later as the rector recited the prayers for the dying, Fr. Reus interrupted him saying, "The Holy Family is now here." To everyone's surprise the crisis passed and Fr. Reus felt better, but he knew he was soon to die and prepared himself for it. He received Holy Communion every day, but refused all medicine, took only water to drink and very little nourishment. In his final days his speech became difficult. On July 20 he felt somewhat better and spoke a few words, but on the 21st he grew weaker by the hour. When the infirmarian brought him milk at 4:00 P.M., he noticed that Fr. Reus had lost his speech so he immediately went to notify the rector. In the few moments before the rector arrived, Fr. Reus peacefully and lovingly returned his priestly soul to his master.

The cause of Fr. John Baptist Reus is now under consideration in Rome.

July 22

St. Philip Evans 1645–1679

Martyr of Wales

Fr. Philip Evans, a prisoner in Cardiff Castle, was permitted to exercise within the castle's walls and on July 21, 1679, while engaged in a tennis match, he was informed that his execution was set for the following day and that he was to return to his cell. Elated at hearing the news, he asked if he could first finish the match. His euphoria was such that when he returned to his cell he took up his harp and sang praise and thanksgiving to God for allowing him to be one of his martyrs.

Philip was born in Gwent, Wales, in 1645. After studying at the English College at Saint-Omer in Flanders, at age twenty he entered the Jesuit novitiate at Watten, also in Flanders, on September 7, 1665. He made his philosophical and theological studies at Liège, and after ordination in 1675 went on the English mission and was assigned to South Wales. Fr. Evans had only four years of missionary activity in his beloved homeland, but during this relatively short period he became known for his zeal and charity. He feared no danger when it involved God's glory and the neighbor's salvation.

With the renewal of the persecution of Catholics, occasioned by the Oates plot of September 1678, whereby the Jesuits were falsely accused of planning to assassinate King Charles II, Fr. Evans was especially hunted. Besides the usual reward of fifty pounds offered by the government for the arrest of a Jesuit, the local Welsh magistrate, John Arnold, a staunch Calvinist, offered an additional two hundred pounds for the arrest of Fr. Evans. Though he had been encouraged to leave Wales until the storm passed, the priest preferred to risk his life for his sheep, and on December 2, several constables appeared at the Sker residence of Christopher Turberville in Glamorgan to arrest him. Turberville was the patron of Fr. Evans and he, in turn, was his chaplain. Not finding the priest at home, the constables were about to depart when Fr. Evans unexpectedly entered the house and was arrested. He refused to take the oaths of allegiance and supremacy, which recognized the king as supreme in all religious matters, and was committed to the jail in Cardiff Castle.

Fr. Evans spent his first three weeks in solitude in an underground cell, but at the end of December was brought up to the regular prison and joined Fr. John Lloyd, a diocesan priest, who had been captured in November. The two priests became companions, in prison and in martyrdom.

Five months passed before they were brought to trial on May 3, 1679. The delay was caused by the prosecution's inability to find witnesses to testify that Fr. Evans and Fr. Lloyd were priests. Eventually the government succeeded in finding a woman and her daughter, who testified that they had attended Masses said by Fr. Evans, heard him preach, and received Communion from him. Since their testimony was true, Fr. Evans did not speak out against them. Other witnesses appeared against Fr. Lloyd, and finally both priests were found guilty of high treason and were sentenced to be hanged, drawn, and quartered. On hearing the sentence, Fr. Evans bowed his head and thanked the judge and jury and returned to his cell, where he picked up his harp and played for himself and his fellow prisoners.

The execution was deferred for some weeks and finally on July 21, while playing tennis, Fr. Evans was notified that the execution was to take place the following day. When this news was made known outside the castle, many Welsh Catholics came to see the priests for the last time. Rather than allowing the people to express their sorrow, the priests encouraged them to remain steadfast and have patience in their sufferings. At 9:00 A.M. the following morning, July 22, the sheriff took both priests to Gallows Field, outside Cardiff, and when they arrived they fell to their knees and kissed the instrument that was to take them to heaven.

Since Fr. Evans was the first to die, he was also the first to speak: "I need not tell you why we are brought here to suffer; our sentence of condemnation is a sufficient witness that it was not for a plot or any other crime, but for being priests; consequently, I do die for religion and conscience's sake. . . . Sure if a man ever speaks truth, it must be at the hour of death, therefore, I hope nobody will doubt of what I say. If I have or had any enemies in the world, which I do not know that ever I had any in my life, I do heartily forgive them for anything done or said against me; and if I have offended anybody, I am heartily sorry for it and ask forgiveness. I pray God bless and prosper the king. I beg the prayers of all, and in particular of the Catholics here present."

He then said a few prayers in silence and mounted the ladder and from that higher position he spoke again: "This is the best pulpit a man can have to preach in, therefore, I can not forbear to tell you again that I die for God and religion's sake." He turned to Fr. Lloyd and said: "Adieu, though for a little time, for we shall shortly meet again. Pray for me all; and I shall return it, when it please God that I shall enjoy the beatific vision." Then in a loud voice, imitating our Lord on his cross, he said: "Into your hands, O Lord, I commend my spirit," and at that moment the executioner pushed him from the ladder. The ladder, unfortunately, went over with him, and because his body did not fall properly his agony was prolonged.

At the time of martyrdom, Fr. Evans was thirty-four years old and had been a Jesuit for fourteen years. He and Fr. Lloyd were beatified by Pope Pius XI on December 15, 1929, and canonized by Pope Paul VI on October 25, 1970. The Jesuits celebrate the memorial of Fr. Evans on December 1.

Prayer

Almighty, eternal God, you chose from the people of England and Wales Saint Philip Evans and his companions to be made like Christ, who died to save the world. Listen to their prayers; strengthen your Church by the same faith and love that strengthened them, and bless it always with your gift of unity. We ask this through our Lord Jesus Christ, your Son, who lives and reigns with you and the Holy Spirit, one God, for ever and ever.

July 24

S. G. Braulio Martínez 1852–1936

S. G. Lawrence Isla 1865–1936

Martyrs of the Spanish Civil War

Among the Jesuit martyrs of the Spanish Civil War are the eighty-four-year-old Fr. Braulio Martínez Simón and the seventy-one-year-old Br. Lawrence Isla Sanz. Fr. Martínez was born in Murchante, Navarre, on March 26, 1852, and by the time he entered the Jesuits on December 25, 1887, he had been a diocesan priest for several years. He made his noviceship at Veruela and then went to Tortosa to review his theology from 1889 to 1891. After serving in two Jesuit parishes, he taught canon law at the diocesan seminary in Tarragona from 1898 to 1900, and then moved to the seminary in Tortosa to teach moral theology from 1901 to 1906. He returned to Tarragona in 1906 and resumed teaching canon law. He lived there until his martyrdom thirty years later. Because Fr. Martínez had taught the priests of the diocese for three decades, he was well known among them and greatly beloved by them. When he retired from teaching he still kept in close contact with them.

Br. Isla was born in Olvega on August 10, 1865, and entered the Jesuit novitiate at Saragossa on October 10, 1890. After his vows he remained in Saragossa doing various jobs about the novitiate: helping in the garden, kitchen, laundry, and so forth. He moved to the college in Tortosa in 1900, and there he met Fr. Martínez, who arrived the following year. In 1907 Br. Isla went to the residence in Valencia and then in 1914 to the Jesuit house in Tarragona. Fr. Martínez and Br. Isla lived together for some twenty-five years; they knew each other well, and as Fr. Martínez grew older Br. Isla insisted on looking after him. When the Jesuits were suppressed in Spain in 1932, and the Tarragona community dispersed, Fr. Martínez and Br. Isla were separated; the latter went to live in a small residence with other Jesuits, while Fr. Martínez went to live in the seminary where he had taught.

Civil war broke out in Spain on July 18, 1936, and on July 21 the Catholic churches in Tarragona were set afire. From his seminary window Fr. Martínez saw the flames reach high into the sky. The following morning, July 22, the director of the seminary, fearing that the school would soon be under attack, suggested to Fr. Martínez that he leave by the orchard and go to the Balart villa. Mr. José Balart was a friend of the seminary and had offered the priests the use of his summer house. Fr. Martínez had often gone there on his afternoon walks and had worked in its garden. On the mornings of July 23 and 24, Fr. Martínez went to the nearby convent of the Little Sisters of the Poor to celebrate Mass. Though he was offered shelter in the convent, he thought the villa safe enough, and Br. Isla had come to live with him to make sure that all went well with him. On July 24 the Jesuits received word from their superior that because of the great danger to priests, they were not to leave their refuges. Fr. Martínez and Br. Isla obeyed this order, and when July 25 came, the feast of St. James, Spain's patron, they did not go out to celebrate Mass. A sister came from the convent that morning to urge them to leave because word was going around town that the revolutionaries were searching all villas for priests and religious. To her suggestion Fr. Martínez simply remarked: "I'm an old man; what can they do to me? They will not kill me. I'm staying right here." Since Fr. Martínez never harmed anyone, he never expected anyone to harm him. But unknown to him the Popular Front, consumed by hatred for the Catholic religion, sought revenge on all priests, and were hunting them as animals in the wilderness.

When it was time for their noon meal, Fr. Martínez and Br. Isla decided to prepare and eat it under the delightful trees next to the villa. While busy with their preparations, they heard loud noises at the villa's front gate, the sounds of someone trying to break it down. Shortly afterwards a half-dozen militiamen came running down the road toward the house shooting their rifles and pistols. With the intruders coming toward them, the two Jesuits decided to run. Fr. Martínez went to the left, Br. Isla to the right; thus, the soldiers divided into two groups to follow their prey. Br. Isla headed for a grove of pine trees with the soldiers shooting after him. They struck him several times. He was bleeding and his blood stained the ground. When the hunters caught up with him, they kept firing their bullets into his wounded body and did not stop until the body ceased moving. Fr. Martínez managed to get over the villa wall into a neighbor's property and through a gate in their wall, entered the open fields. Being eighty-four years old he was no match for the young soldiers, who soon caught him and led him back to the villa for questioning. When the questions came to an end they told him that he could leave, but he said: "No, you will kill me. Don't kill me; but, I forgive you for you do not know what you are doing."

As Fr. Martínez uttered these words, one of the militiamen standing a short distance away took aim and fired a bullet through the priest's heart. The bodies of both Jesuits were taken inside the villa, covered with a cloth, and placed under guard. Later that afternoon Mr. Balart came to identify the bodies and sadly recognized his friends. Fr. Martínez had a single wound in his chest and looked as if he were asleep, but Br. Isla's body was riddled with wounds. Mr. Balart requested the bodies of both Jesuits and placed them in his family vault in the cemetery.

The official diocesan investigation into the martyrdom of Fr. Braulio Martínez and Br. Lawrence Isla began in Tarragona in November 1950.

July 25

Bl. Rudolph Acquaviva 1550–1583

Martyr of Salsette

Fr. Rudolph Acquaviva and his four Jesuit companions met martyrdom in India's Salsette peninsula. Rudolph, the son of the duke of Atri, was born on October 25, 1550, in the family castle in Italy's Abruzzi region. His illustrious family was related to many of the noble houses of Italy. As a child he saw his mother visit hospitals and feed the poor, and he too followed her example. He was generous in almsgiving, even to the point of giving away the clothes he was wearing. When his father's brother, Claudio, relinquished his position of papal chamberlain to enter the Society of Jesus in 1567, the duke obtained the position for his seventeen-year-old Rudolph. Father and son subsequently went to Rome, and while the father negotiated the son's entry into Pope Pius V's court, the son was at the Jesuit house pleading with his uncle to intercede with his father to grant him permission to become a Jesuit, as well. The duke would not hear of it; Rudolph was still immature and inexperienced. It took the son two months to convince his father that his was not a hasty decision but one based on prayer and reflection. The duke finally gave his consent and on April 2, 1568, Rudolph entered the Roman novitiate of Sant'Andrea.

In 1569, after completing his first year of noviceship, Rudolph was sent to Macerata to begin his studies in the humanities and in 1571 he returned to Rome to do philosophy and then theology at the Roman College. In November 1577, since he had been accepted for the missions in India, he left Rome for Lisbon, Portugal, where he was ordained to the priesthood in early 1578. He set sail for Goa on March 24.

When Fr. Acquaviva arrived in Goa on September 13, 1578, he was assigned to teach philosophy to seminarians at St. Paul's College, an appointment he held until the end of 1579, when he was selected to go to Fatehpur Sikri, the court of Akbar the Great Mogul. Akbar had an unquenchable thirst for knowledge and truth. His territory included Moslems and Hindus, and because the religious beliefs of both were sometimes at odds with each other, he conceived the idea of uniting them into one and, thus, bring peace and harmony to his subjects. With this end in view he held weekly religious discussions at court. When he came upon several Christians and observed their practice of justice and morality, he decided to include Christian theologians in these discussions. Thus, he sent emissaries to the Jesuit college in Goa to ask for two priests to come to his court with their religious books to instruct him in the Christian faith.

Fr. Acquaviva was one of the two chosen to take Christianity to the mogul's court. The Goanese Jesuits, naturally, had great hopes that this would bring about the mogul's conversion and eventually that of India. Fr. Acquaviva and his party arrived at Fatehpur Sikri, twenty miles southwest of Agra, on February 28, 1580, and were given a warm welcome and comfortable lodgings in the royal palace. When Fr. Acquaviva presented Akbar with a seven-volume copy of the Bible, the mogul showed it the greatest of reverence; he kissed each volume and then placed it on his head. Fr. Acquaviva held his discussions on Saturday evenings and Akbar appeared not only interested in Christianity, but seemed to grow more and more convinced of its truth. The disputations went on week after week, month after month, and though Akbar acknowledged the superiority of Christ over Mohammed, he would not take the necessary step of giving up his harem and his sensual way of living. After three years of working for India's conversion, Fr. Acquaviva sadly admitted that Akbar would never be converted. In early 1583, while remaining on friendly terms with the mogul, the Jesuits left Fatehpur Sikri for Goa, where they arrived in early May.

P. Rudolphus Aquauiua Italus Ducis Atriæ filius Soc: IESU. cum qua
tuor Socijs profide Christi in India crudeliter enectus. A. 1583. 15 Iuly.
C. Screta del.   Melchior Küsel.

Bl. Rudolph Acquaviva and Companions

Within days of his return to his Jesuit brethren, Fr. Acquaviva was made superior of the mission in Salsette, a peninsula directly south of Goa. The inhabitants of Salsette were mostly Hindus and fanatically against Christianity. The peninsula had become Portuguese territory in 1550 and the first missionaries, who had gone there in 1560, had very little success. The Salsette Hindus remembered the several Portuguese punitive expeditions that destroyed their shrines and temples and, hence, they remained openly hostile to all who would attempt to abolish their religious practices.

The peninsula had about twenty-five mission churches and chapels served by twelve Jesuits. When Fr. Acquaviva came to the mission in July 1583, the missionaries gathered at Verna to lay plans for converting the peninsula's non-Christians. They organized a large baptismal service of more than 100 converts for August 5 and encouraged the new Christians to invite their non-Christian friends to instructions. Fr. Acquaviva also agreed to visit each mission and reminded the missionaries that the viceroy wanted a church or a chapel in each of the peninsula's sixty-six villages so the people could grow accustomed to the presence of the Christian cross and to Catholic ceremonies. Finally, it was decided that the visitation would begin with the southernmost village of Cuncolim.

The night before going to Cuncolim, Frs. Acquaviva, Alphonsus Pacheco and Peter Berno, and Br. Francis Aranha, met at Fr. Anthony Francisco's mission at Orlim, the station nearest to Cuncolim. On the morning of July 25, 1583, the five missionaries set out for Cuncolim, whose inhabitants had been previously notified of the Jesuit superior's forthcoming visit. On the outskirts of the village, they were met by one of the chiefs who expressed his regret that the villagers were unable to meet them because the village was then suffering from some internal discord and, perhaps, later in the day they would come to greet the visitors. The Jesuits heard the shouts and noise coming from the village but were not aware that these were shouts filled with hatred against them. As the day went on the noise increased, and since the villagers never appeared, Fr. Acquaviva decided it would be better to do what they had come to do and then leave without entering the village. Thus the missionaries marked out an area for a future chapel and two of the Christians who had come with them made a cross from two pieces of wood and erected it on the spot. There were spies, however, watching the missionaries' every action, and these immediately sent word to the villagers that a Christian cross had been raised on the spot where they had once had a temple. Thereupon hundreds of villagers shouting "Kill, kill!" rushed upon them, and before the missionaries and Christians had time to escape, they were surrounded. After the chief sorcerer learned who the group's superior was, he gave the signal. As a Hindu approached Fr. Acquaviva, the missionary said: "With all my heart, I give my soul and body to God." With a scimitar's single slash, the attacker cut the back of the priest's thighs and brought him to the ground. To show his readiness for martyrdom, Fr. Acquaviva opened the collar of his cassock and exposed the left side of his neck. At that moment someone struck him twice, trying to decapitate him. The third blow hit his shoulder and his arm was nearly cut off. It was an arrow in the breast that finally released his noble soul to God. His final words were: "Forgive them, Lord. Francis Xavier, pray to God for me. Lord Jesus, receive my spirit." He was thirty-three years old.

Now that the Hindu villagers had seen the blood of the first martyr, they would not be satisfied until all five were dead. Successively they attacked Br. Aranha and Fr. Berno, then Frs. Pacheco and Francisco. Fr. Rudolph Acquaviva, with his four companions, was beatified by Pope Leo XIII on April 2, 1893. The memorial of these martyrs is celebrated on February 4.

Prayer

Lord, may the holy offering of your martyrs, Blessed Rudolph Acquaviva and companions, dispose you to hear our prayers. With their help may we offer ourselves as they did, a living sacrifice, pleasing to you in the service of your holy name. We ask this through Jesus Christ, your Son, our Lord, who lives and reigns with you and the Holy Spirit, one God, for ever and ever.

July 26

Bl. Peter Berno 1552–1583

Bl. Francis Aranha 1551–1583

Martyrs of Salsette

Fr. Peter Berno and Br. Francis Aranha are among the five Jesuit martyrs of Salsette, India. Peter was born in Ascona, on the shores of Lago Maggiore, Switzerland, probably in 1552, where his father was a fruit merchant. Peter began his studies for the priesthood in his own diocese, but when his father moved to Rome to improve his finances, Peter went with him and secured a position at the German College, where he was also able to continue his studies. On July 2, 1577, he entered the Jesuit novitiate of Sant'Andrea in Rome, and four months later was assigned to the missions in India. He left Rome in November with Rudolph Acquaviva, but while the latter went directly to Goa, Peter remained in Lisbon, Portugal, to complete his noviceship training. He subsequently left Lisbon on April 4, 1579, arrived in Goa on October 18, and was ordained sometime in early 1580. He had learned enough Konkani to hear confessions and preach, and was therefore sent to the Margão mission in the

Salsette peninsula. Because Fr. Berno had a lively and cheerful disposition, the Marguans were easily won over by him. It has been estimated that during his three years at the mission he converted more people to Christianity than did all the other Salsette missionaries combined. When the Portuguese sent their 1582 punitive expedition against the inhabitants of Cuncolim, Fr. Berno was with it and helped destroy Hindu shrines and temples. His presence on that occasion was not forgotten.

When Fr. Acquaviva, the mission's new superior, came to the peninsula in July 1583, he gathered the Jesuits for a conference at Verna to discuss how best to convert the non-Christians. It was at that meeting that the superior decided to visit each mission and to erect a small chapel and a cross in each of the peninsula's sixty-six villages. Fr. Berno accompanied Fr. Acquaviva on his visit to Cuncolim, and with them were Br. Francis Aranha, and Frs. Alphonsus Pacheco and Anthony Francisco.

Br. Aranha was probably born in Braga, Portugal, about 1551. Perhaps in 1568 or earlier, he traveled to Goa, where his uncle, Gaspar de Leão Pereira, had been Goa's first archbishop. He entered the Society as a brother on November 1, 1571, and for a time was stationed at the Jesuit college in Cochin and then at St. Paul's in Goa. About 1577 he was assigned to the Salsette mission, where he was chiefly occupied in building churches and chapels. He always looked forward to the time when he could build one at Cuncolim, the center of the peninsula's opposition to Christianity.

The group of five Jesuits and about fifty Christians set out for Cuncolim on July 25, but they were informed that they could not enter the village because of internal problems among the villagers. They were thus asked to remain outside until someone should come for them. No one came, and since the cries from the village became more frightening, the missionaries hurriedly marked out an area for a future chapel. Unfortunately, the place they chose had been the very spot where a Hindu shrine had been, one which the Portuguese had destroyed. Then when the Christians erected a cross, the anger of the villagers boiled over and they rushed out shrieking after the missionaries. The first to fall was Fr. Acquaviva. They next struck down Br. Aranha with a sabre cut to his neck and a lance through his side. When he fell to the ground, the murderers went next to Fr. Berno, who was especially despised because of his share in destroying their temples. In addition, he had also desecrated a sacred ant hill and had killed a sacred cow. His assailants drove an iron spike into one of his eyes and then struck off his right ear. When his body collapsed, they fell upon it and mutilated it savagely. Certain that he was dead, they next turned to Frs. Pacheco and Francisco, and martyred them as well. Now that five Jesuits were lying in their own blood, the murderers fell upon the Christians who had accompanied the fathers and slaughtered a dozen of them and wounded many others.

After this despicable deed, the idolaters took some of the martyrs' blood to their shrine and smeared it on the idol as a sacrificial offering. They then returned to the site of the martyrdom to dispose of the bodies. But when they arrived, they found not five but only four bodies in black cassocks. An old woman told them that she had seen someone in black dragging himself into the woods. There they discovered an exhausted and bleeding Br. Aranha. Since he was still alive, they renewed their vengeance and struck him with knives, stakes, and lances. When these blows did not kill him, he was dragged before the idol, forced to stand up, and was ordered to bow his head before the idol. With remarkable strength the dying brother said: "I am neither stupid enough nor cowardly enough to adore a lump of wood or stone, rather than the true God." With that final expression of faith an axe struck his head. Now dead, his assailants propped up his body next to the idol and made it the target of their arrows.

Fr. Peter Berno and Br. Francis Aranha, together with Frs. Rudolph Acquaviva, Alphonsus Pacheco and Anthony Francisco, were beatified by Pope Leo XIII on April 2, 1893. Their memorial is celebrated on February 4.

Prayer

Lord, may the holy offering of your martyrs, Blessed Peter Berno, Blessed Francis Aranha, and companions, dispose you to hear our prayers. With their help may we offer ourselves as they did, a living sacrifice, pleasing to you in the service of your holy name. We ask this through Jesus Christ, your Son, our Lord, who lives and reigns with you and the Holy Spirit, one God, for ever and ever.

July 27

Bl. Alphonsus Pacheco 1549–1583
Bl. Anthony Francisco 1550–1583

Martyrs of Salsette

The last of the five martyrs of Salsette were Frs. Alphonsus Pacheco and Anthony Francisco. The family of Alphonsus was one of the old families of Castile. He was born in Minaya (Albacete), Spain, about 1549, and attended the Jesuit college at Belmonte. On September 8, 1567, he entered the Jesuit novitiate at Villarejo de Fuentes and then studied at Alcalá. His desire was to go to the Japanese mission and during his years of study he made this request of his provincial, but was refused on the basis that he could do more good in Europe. In 1574, however, Fr. Alessandro Valignano came to Alcalá seeking volunteers for the Far East missions. Alphonsus took advantage of the visitor's presence and told him of his desire to imitate Francis Xavier and that the missions had been refused him. Though Fr. Valignano could not change the provincial's decision, he kept the young man in mind. He gathered forty recruits and twelve of them were from Toledo, the home province of Alphonsus. When the group was in Lisbon, Portugal, making final preparations for sailing, one of the twelve from Toledo, a brother, suddenly fell ill. Fr. Valignano immediately wrote to the Toledo provincial requesting a replacement for the sick brother and mentioned Alphonsus Pacheco as a possibility. Interpreting this as God's choice, the provincial withdrew his prohibition and instructed Alphonsus to go to India.

After his arrival in Goa in September 1574, Alphonsus was ordained and made assistant to the rector at St. Paul's College. He held this position for three years, then was made assistant to the provincial. In 1579 he returned to Europe to oversee affairs dealing with the Goanese mission and returned in October 1581 with thirteen new missionaries. Among this number was Anthony Francisco. On his return to Goa, Fr. Pacheco became superior of the Salsette mission until Fr. Acquaviva relieved him in July 1583.

Anthony Francisco was a Portuguese born in Coimbra about 1550 and attended that city's famous university. The death of Fr. Ignatius de Azevedo and his companions in 1570 so impressed the young man that he entered the Society on September 7, 1571, in order to go to the missions. He arrived in Goa with Fr. Pacheco in 1581, continued his theological studies at St. Paul's College, and was ordained in 1582. Fr. Francisco was then assigned to the Moluccas, but because the ship on which he was traveling was wrecked shortly after leaving Goa, he returned and was appointed to the mission at Orlim on the Salsette peninsula. His active missionary career lasted only a few months.

When Fr. Acquaviva arrived on the peninsula to take over as mission superior, Fr. Pacheco served as his guide and introduced him to several of the missions. After the conference of Jesuits at Verna, the superior, together with Frs. Pacheco and Berno, and Br. Aranha, spent the night of July 24 at Fr. Francisco's mission at Orlim. The next morning, after they had celebrated Mass, the group headed southward for Cuncolim to begin the visitation of all the peninsula's villages. (The events leading up to their arrival at Cuncolim and subsequent to it are narrated under July 25.)

The hostile villagers of Cuncolim first martyred Frs. Acquaviva and Berno, and Br. Aranha. When Fr. Pacheco saw them massacring his companions, he boldly faced the assailants and said: "Strike me, it is I who have destroyed your idols." At that moment a lance pierced his breast. Extending his arms in the form of a cross and raising his eyes, he prayed: "Lord, you were pierced with a lance for me. I ask you to pardon those who have wounded me and to send them other missionaries to lead them to heaven." Because he had a prayer on his lips, they sent another lance through his throat. He died saying the name "Jesus."

The last to fall was Fr. Francisco; his head was split open and his body riddled with arrows. After him the villagers killed about a dozen of the Christians who had accompanied the missionaries. All five Jesuits were between thirty and thirty-five years of age. Days after the bodies of the missionaries had been thrown into a well, they were recovered and taken to the mission at Rachol and later to Goa.

Frs. Alphonsus Pacheco and Anthony Francisco and their three Jesuit brothers were beatified by Pope Leo XIII on April 2, 1893; the memorial of these five martyrs of Salsette is celebrated on February 4.

Prayer

Lord, may the holy offering of your martyrs, Blessed Alphonsus Pacheco and Blessed Anthony Francisco, and companions, dispose you to hear our prayers. With their help may we offer ourselves as they did, a living sacrifice, pleasing to you in the service of your holy name. We ask this through Jesus Christ, your Son, our Lord, who lives and reigns with you and the Holy Spirit, one God, for ever and ever.

July 28

S. G. Anthony Repiso Martínez 1856–1929

Fr. Anthony Repiso spent his entire priestly life as a humble and modest parish worker. He was born on February 8, 1856, in Venta de Córdoba, a small town twenty-five miles from Mexico City, on the main road to Pueblo. He was the fifth and youngest child—an only son—of his father's first marriage. Because of the parents' desire to give their children a good education, the Repiso family moved to Mexico City.

When Anthony was fourteen (1870) he entered the diocesan minor seminary in Mexico City. His father opposed his son's desire to become a priest; his mother had died in 1868. The father had hoped that his son would one day succeed him in his position as a farm manager and carry on the family name. But Anthony would not change his mind. He started seminary life as a day student; after morning classes he returned home for the noon meal and then back to school until 5:00 P.M. In 1873, when he was about to begin his study of philosophy, the family moved to Iztacalco (now part of Mexico City), a greater distance from the seminary. Without public transportation, the youth walked the couple of miles to and from school each day. To arrive on time for morning class, he left home before 6:00, remained there for lunch and returned home at 8:00 in the evening. When it was time to begin theology (1876), he was given a scholarship and boarded at the seminary and returned home only during vacations.

Anthony's years of study in preparation for the priesthood finally came to an end and on March 20, 1881, he was ordained. He celebrated his first Mass on March 25 in Iztacalco, and on the following day received his pastoral assignment, assistant at Our Lady of Guadalupe parish in Villa de Guadalupe. This was the first of five parishes in which he served prior to becoming a Jesuit; the last was in Xochimilco, just south of Mexico City, famous for its floating gardens. Here he founded a parish school (as he had done a few years before at St. Andrew's parish in Villa Victoria) as well as a boarding school for the daughters of the ranchers living on the outskirts of Mexico City.

Fr. Repiso served the archdiocese for twelve years; none of the parishes were wealthy. If they were, he would not have fitted in. With the archbishop's knowledge and approval, he requested admission into the Society of Jesus. When this was granted, he left his Xochimilco parish on August 2, 1893, and on the 14th entered the novitiate at San Simón, near Zamora, in the state of Michoacán. At the time of his entrance he was thirty-seven years old and an experienced pastoral worker; nevertheless, he blended in perfectly with the younger novices and had no difficulty in sharing their humble chores about the house. Two years later he pronounced his first vows and was given the next two years, also at San Simón, to brush up on his reading in moral theology.

In 1897 Fr. Repiso was assigned to the Jesuit residence in Oaxaca. There he came to know several young girls who wanted to enter religion, but were unable because of their families' low economic status. He also saw that many youngsters were being left at home while their parents were at work. The idea came to him on November 15, 1898, that perhaps a new religious congregation could care for and educate these youngsters. The matter was brought before the Jesuit provincial, and with his blessing Fr. Repiso went ahead with his plans. The congregation known as Sisters of the Divine Shepherd formally came into being on January 14, 1900. Fr. Repiso wrote its rule, based on that of the Society and imbued it with Ignatian spirituality. But two years after founding and guiding the young congregation, his superiors thought it better to distance him from it and, consequently, he was transferred in 1902 to Puebla.

While in Oaxaca, however, Fr. Repiso was granted his request to have a share in our Lord's Passion. When one of his young sodalists, who had become gravely ill, was on the point of death, he sat next to her bed and told her: "Daughter, when you arrive in heaven, tell our Lord to send me something so that I may imitate him in his Passion." The young girl died and sometime later a pimple appeared on his left shoulder. In time it increased in size until the open wound covered a good portion of the left side of his back. Years later (1924) when a physician suggested that he would be able to take care of it, the priest merely responded that since the Lord had granted it to him in answer to his own request, he couldn't possibly now ask the Lord to relieve him of it.

Fr. Repiso's transfer to Puebla was only for a year. He was not tied down to any given parish but traveled the diocese giving missions. He returned to the novitiate at San Simón in 1903 to make his tertianship. Then in early 1904 he was assigned to Chihuahua, where the bishop had given the Society a house and asked the Jesuits to care for the local shrine of Our Lady of Guadalupe. Both were run down and in need of repairs. Fr. Repiso worked first on the house so that he could move in, and then on the shrine. When he arrived there attendance at Sunday Mass numbered fifteen, but by the time a year had passed, he had a thousand on Communion Sundays. In a year's time he was again transferred.

His new assignment was in Nonoava in Sierra Tarahumara. During his fifteen years there, he concentrated on his flock's spiritual growth. He promoted the Spiritual Exercises and the Apostleship of Prayer, and established sodalities for the girls, from which many vocations came. His next three years (1920–1923) were spent as pastor in Tepotzotlán, not far from Mexico City. This parish covered a vast area and had a few mission stations, to which he traveled by horse on Sundays so that his people could assist at Mass.

In 1923 he was appointed superior of the residence in León. With the election in 1924 of the rabid anti-Catholic Plutarco Elías Calles as president of the country, a systematic persecution of the Church began. On January 4, 1926, the president limited the number of priests that could minister in a given area, and on July 31 a new penal code against the Catholic Church went into effect. The Mexican bishops' response to the government's excessive restrictions on the Church's freedom was to suspend all Church services in the country. Religious communities were subsequently dissolved by the state and priests had to live in private homes. Though they risked their lives, they continued, as best they could, to minister to the faithful in secret. When the churches reopened in June 1929, Fr. Repiso's health no longer permitted him to be active. In addition to the large cancerous wound on his back, which was a source of constant pain, he also suffered from a hernia and hemorrhoids. He fell gravely ill in July, and on Saturday, July 27, at 10:45 P.M., after reciting the Ignatian prayer *Take and Receive*, Fr. Repiso died in the Lord. His cause is presently under consideration.

S. G. Emmanuel Peypoch 1870–1936

Martyr of the Spanish Civil War

Fr. Emmanuel Peypoch Sala was born on December 2, 1870, at Estany, near Barcelona, Spain, and entered the Society of Jesus on July 30, 1888, at Veruela. He completed his noviceship, pronounced his vows, and began his study of philosophy at Saragossa. In 1893 he went to Tortosa to finish his course in philosophy and then spent a year in Valencia teaching Greek and history. In 1896 he went to the Philippines and taught at the Ateneo de Manila for the next four years, and in 1901 returned to Spain for a year before going to St. Louis University, Missouri, for his theological studies in 1902. Fr. Peypoch was ordained in St. Louis in 1905, and did tertianship at Florissant, Missouri. By 1907 he was back in Manila where he taught for another sixteen years. Only because of poor health did he return to Spain and in 1926 he was assigned to the retreat house in Manresa, where he gave retreats and parish missions.

When the news broke on July 18, 1936, that Spain was in civil war, Fr. Peypoch was giving a retreat to fellow Jesuits in Manresa. He informed his retreatants of what was happening and asked their prayers for the country. The retreat ended on the morning of the 21st—the day that the revolutionaries set fire to churches and convents—and because priests were now being hunted, Fr. Peypoch asked several families in Manresa to take one or two Jesuits into their homes until they could safely return to their residences.

Fr. Peypoch went to the apartment where he lived and where his sodality had an oratory and held its meetings. On the morning of July 22, several members of the Revolutionary Committee appeared at Fr. Peypoch's flat to search it. After an hour of questioning, the police took him to headquarters where the interrogation continued. He readily admitted that he was a Jesuit and a priest, that he taught languages, and that his principal work was preaching. He returned to his flat at 4:00 P.M. and told the sodalists, who anxiously awaited him, that he returned because "I am not worthy to appear before my Creator." He also added that, as he was leaving headquarters, he was quietly advised to leave Manresa and go into hiding.

With the help of his sodalists, he dismantled the oratory, hid the church furnishings as best he could, and went to take shelter with the Vers family, whose son was a sodalist. As long as he was with them he was unable to celebrate Mass, but on the 25th, the feast of Spain's patron, St. James, he gathered the family together, and for a half hour they prayed, recited the rosary, and read from a spiritual book.

Not wishing to endanger his hosts any longer, Fr. Peypoch decided to seek refuge in Artés, his mother's native area. On the morning of the 28th he put on his jacket, placed his crucifix in his pocket, and bade his friends goodbye. He avoided the main roads and traveled mostly through fields. He spent that night in a vineyard. Before dawn on the 29th he was again on his way. As he approached Puente de Cabrianes, he was unfortunately recognized by a woman, who passed the word on to the communist revolutionaries.

Fr. Peypoch was headed toward the inn "Les Tàpies," whose owner was a friend of his, and on his way there he stopped at a farm to ask for something to eat. Not knowing who the man was the people refused him food but offered him a glass of water. By this time Fr. Peypoch was being followed—an easy task because of his footprints in the soil. At 8:15 A.M. he knocked on the back door of "Les Tàpies" and his friend received him joyfully. The priest told the innkeeper that he thought he was being followed; nevertheless, the friend was not alarmed and offered his guest something to eat. Instead of eating, Fr. Peypoch, who was weary from walking and climbing over vines in the fields, asked to rest. Just as he was about to lie down the revolutionaries surrounded the inn and knocked on the door. The innkeeper was surprised to see the militiamen and when asked if a man had just arrived at the inn, he could not deny what the soldiers already knew. They entered the inn and ordered the priest to go with them, forcing him to walk backwards with his hands in the air. They took him to a spot in the woods about five minutes away, and there they shot him in the head and body. It was 9:00 A.M., July 29. The murderers then robbed the body of its money and returned to the inn, where they ordered a hearty breakfast and paid for it with the martyred priest's pesetas. When they had their fill, they demanded a mule of the innkeeper, and with it they took the priest's body to the edge of the Calders road and there dumped it. On the following day the innkeeper received permission from the municipal authorities in Calders to take his friend's body, which he then laid to rest in a private vault in the Viladecavalls Cemetery.

The diocesan investigation into the martyrdom of Fr. Emmanuel Peypoch began in Vich in November 1950 and the cause is under consideration.

July 31

St. Ignatius of Loyola 1491–1556

Founder of the Society of Jesus

It was in early June 1521 that soldiers carried the wounded Iñigo de Loyola to his ancestral home to recuperate from wounds received in battle. Since 1517 he had been in the service of the duke of Nájera, viceroy of Navarre, and under the duke's leadership he had participated in several skirmishes without injury to himself. But when the French troops stormed the fortress at Pamplona on May 20, 1521, a stray cannon shot broke one of his legs and wounded the other. When the party arrived at Loyola castle, Iñigo was feverish—the wound in his leg refused to heal—and to add to his discomfort he learned that the broken leg had to be reset, a procedure to be performed without anesthesia. Instead of improving, he grew worse and by the end of June his physician advised him to prepare for death. Then, unexpectedly, on the morning of June 29, the feast of Sts. Peter and Paul, he felt better and within days he was out of danger. The wound healed and the bones in the broken leg mended; but unfortunately, one leg was shorter than the other and an unsightly bone protruded below the knee. As long as this condition remained he could not wear the hose and the close-fitting boots that were then in fashion, and thinking more of his appearance than of the pain he would have to endure, Iñigo ordered the surgeon to saw off the offending bone and to lengthen his leg by systematic stretching.

For days Iñigo remained in bed and quietly submitted to the stretching. During his days of recovery, boredom set in and he asked for some novels of chivalry, his favorite reading, but there were none such in the Loyola castle. Instead, he was given the only two books in the house: *Life of Christ* by Ludolph, a Carthusian monk, and *Flos sanctorum,* a collection of lives of the saints. Iñigo set about reading them, and as it happened, this was the most important reading he would ever do.

Iñigo de Loyola was born in 1491 in the family castle in Azpeitia, in the Basque province of Guipúzcoa, Spain. He was the youngest of the thirteen children of Beltrán de Loyola and Marina Saénz de Licona, and was given the name Iñigo after the saintly Benedictine Abbot of Oña. About 1506 he went to serve as page to Juan Velázquez de Cuéllar, King Ferdinand's Minister of Finance, and when the Velázquez household visited the royal court, so did Iñigo. After about eleven years with Velázquez, he entered the service of the duke of Nájera, and his injury at Pamplona was God's way of telling Iñigo that he wanted him in the service of his Son, the eternal King.

During convalescence, Iñigo reflected on what he had read and went on to question his former way of life. He asked himself: "Why cannot I walk the same paths as did the saints?" The more he reflected, the more convinced he grew that he needed to do penance and, thus, he resolved to go on pilgrimage to Jerusalem. One evening, perhaps the end of August or early September 1521, our Lady with the Child Jesus appeared to him in his room. This was the night of his transformation; he now determined to follow the path of the saints. As he continued to read his books, he continued to reflect; and the more he reflected, the more did God become the center of his life.

By February 1522 Iñigo's right leg was sufficiently healed for him to put his plan into action. Without informing his family that he was on his way to Jerusalem, he set out for Barcelona. At one of his stops, before arriving at Our

S. IGNATIUS De LOYOLA
SOCIETATIS JESU FUNDATOR.

St. Ignatius of Loyola

Lady's shrine at Montserrat, he bought himself a pilgrim's staff and a pair of sandals, and had a long tunic made from rough cloth. He arrived at Montserrat on March 21, found a confessor, and made a general confession in writing that took him three days to prepare. On the 24th, the eve of our Lady's Annunciation, he gave his robes to a beggar and clothed himself in his sackcloth tunic. He was doing everything according to plan. That night he went to our Lady's altar, and imitating the rites of chivalry, spent the evening in a vigil of arms, kneeling and standing the whole night through. He left early on the 25th and headed for Barcelona, but on the way he stopped at Manresa, a town on the banks of the Cardoner, where he intended to spend but a few days. The few days, however, turned into ten months, for it was there that God began to train him in the spiritual life. Iñigo spent several hours of each day in prayer and spent a like number helping at a nearby hospice. At Manresa he became familiar with other spiritual books, among them the *Imitation of Christ,* a book which he always esteemed and recommended to others.

After living in Manresa for almost a year, it was time for him to go to Barcelona and secure passage for Italy and then on to Jerusalem. He left Manresa at the end of February 1523, sailed from Barcelona in mid-March and reached Gaeta, Italy, five days later. Iñigo arrived in Rome on Palm Sunday, March 29. During his stay in the Eternal City, he received Pope Hadrian VI's permission for the Jerusalem pilgrimage, and by mid-April he was on his way to Venice. He set sail for the Holy Land on July 14.

Iñigo, a pilgrim among pilgrims, first saw Jerusalem on September 4. He prayed in the Garden of Olives, in the Holy Sepulcher, and on the Mount of the Ascension, and also visited Bethlehem. Ludolph's *Life of Christ* now became vibrantly alive, so much so that he chose to remain in the Holy Land, but the Franciscan superior, custodian of the Holy Places, strongly dissuaded him. He sadly rejoined his companions, left the Holy Land on September 23, and after three months of harsh weather and a few vessel changes, landed in Venice in mid-January 1524.

Iñigo, now thirty-three years old, had to chart his future anew. His only desire was to help souls, so he determined to study for the priesthood. He returned to Barcelona in March 1524 and began his study of Latin. When not with his books, he spent his time in prayer, penance, and begging. During the summer of 1526 he moved to Alcalá de Henares, ready to begin his university studies. In Alcalá he gathered students and grownups about him, spoke to them about prayer and explained to them the meaning of the gospels, St. Paul, the commandments, and so on. This good work, however, was not acceptable to all; some began to remark: "How can this Iñigo, who is neither university trained nor a priest, instruct others about God?" His preaching was thus brought to the attention of the Inquisition and in April 1527 he was put in prison, but after forty-two days of detention was released. Though no one had difficulty with his doctrine, he was, nevertheless, ordered to change his pilgrim's garb to that of a layman or student and to stop teaching in public.

Unable to tell others about God in Alcalá, Iñigo went to Salamanca, where he hoped to attend its university. He arrived, perhaps in July 1527, and immediately went into the streets to preach. Within two weeks of his coming, the Dominicans in the city suspected him of heresy and had him put in prison. He explained to his examiners how he discoursed about the Trinity and the Eucharist, and in the end they found no fault with his teaching. After twenty-two days of confinement, he was released and told that he could teach children but he had to refrain from speaking on more complicated theological matters. Feeling unwelcome in Salamanca, he decided to go to Paris, where he arrived on February 2, 1528.

During Iñigo's seven years in the French capital, he reviewed his Latin at the Collège de Montaigu (1528–1529), studied philosophy at Sainte-Barbe (1529–1533) and theology with the Dominicans at Saint-Jacques (1533–1535). To support himself during these years of study, he spent two months each summer begging alms from the Spanish merchants in Flanders. He once made a trip to London (1531), where he collected enough money to last him the year through.

When Iñigo began his studies at Sainte-Barbe, he shared a room with Peter Favre and Francis Xavier. He explained to them how he intended to spend his life for the salvation of souls, and Favre, having the same aspirations, became his first recruit. Xavier still had dreams of worldly success and thus it took time before Iñigo won him over. Among their friends at the university, there were others who also desired to consecrate themselves to God in the service of souls. From these men Iñigo recruited James Laínez, Alphonsus Salmerón, Nicholas Bobadilla, and Simon Rodrigues; when he felt they were ready, he directed each of them through the Exercises.

At the beginning of August 1534, these seven companions decided to make private vows of chastity, poverty (to be practiced when they had completed their studies), and to go to Jerusalem and work for the conversion of the infidels. If unable to remain in the Holy Land, or if the trip there should prove impossible, they would then go to Rome and place themselves at the disposal of the pope. The date chosen for these vows was the feast of our Lady's Assumption, August 15. Early that morning the seven met in the crypt of the chapel of Saint-Denis in the Montmartre section of Paris, and since Favre was the only priest among them—he had been ordained earlier that year—he was the celebrant. Before receiving Holy Communion, each of the seven pronounced his vows. This service joined them together in a closer companionship, but as yet they had no thought of forming a religious congregation.

When Iñigo received his master's degree in March 1535, the university latinized his name to "Ignatius," and thenceforth he also began to use that form of his name. While in Paris, Ignatius was often troubled with stomach pains. So poor was his health in 1535 that he had to interrupt his stay there and return home, where his native air, so his physician thought, would cure him. Before leaving the French capital, Ignatius placed Favre in charge of the group and planned for everyone to meet in Venice in the spring of 1537, by which time they all would have completed their theological studies. Ignatius set out for Spain in early April and was in his native Azpeitia by the end of the month. Choosing not to live with his relatives in the family castle, he lodged at the Hospital of the Magdalene and supported himself by begging. He did in Azpeitia what he had done in other cities—he gathered the children and taught them about God and arranged to speak to the adults three times a week. When the adult sessions proved popular, he made this a daily explanation of the faith. Feeling better by the end of July, he bade farewell to his family and friends and set out for Venice.

Ignatius arrived in Venice for his second time at the end of December 1535, and because he would have to wait more than a year before his companions joined him, he applied himself to studying theology, giving the Spiritual Exercises, and to assisting in a hospital. Favre, in the meantime, added three members to their Paris group: Claude Le Jay, Paschase Broët, and John Cordure. Because war had broken out between France and Spain, and Paris was rife with anti-Spanish feelings, the group departed Paris for Venice two months ahead of schedule. They left on November 15, 1536, and after several close brushes with French soldiers, arrived at their destination on January 8, 1537.

Since they had to wait for the pilgrim ship to arrive—and it was not due in port until sometime during the summer—they volunteered their services at two hospitals, where they washed patients, made beds, and swept floors.

In preparation for their Jerusalem trip, Ignatius sent his men to Rome in March to seek papal permission for their pilgrimage and to request ordination for the non-priests among them. The group met Pope Paul III on April 3, Easter Tuesday, and impressed by these university trained men, the pope not only granted permission for their pilgrimage and ordination, but also gave them money toward their passage to Jerusalem. At the same time he informed them that tensions were growing in the Mediterranean and that they might never reach their goal. On their return to Venice, they went back to their volunteer work at the hospitals. On June 24, 1537, Ignatius and five others were ordained and all postponed celebrating their first Masses until they had time to prepare themselves better.

During the summer it became increasingly clear that, with the Turks in the Adriatic, it was unlikely that the pilgrim ship would reach Venice, so the pilgrims changed their plans. They broke up into groups of two and three and went to several northern Italian cities to spend forty days in prayer. On July 25 Fr. Ignatius, together with Favre and Laínez, went to Vicenza and found shelter in the ruins of an abandoned monastery outside the city walls. These days were as spiritually rich for Fr. Ignatius as those in Manresa, for God granted him innumerable interior consolations and spiritual visions. When the forty days were over, he again postponed his Mass. He never revealed his reason, but it is most probably because he still hoped to celebrate it in the land where Jesus himself had lived. In September he called his companions to Vicenza to discuss future plans, the outcome of which was that he was to go to Rome and offer the group's services to the pope, while the others were to go to various university centers, such as Padua, Siena, and Bologna, and there begin their preaching apostolate. One final item was determined: if anyone should ask them who they were, they would answer the "Company of Jesus." They called themselves *Compañía de Jesús*, but when that was rendered into Latin it became *Societas Jesu*, and when this is translated into English it becomes *Society of Jesus*.

Together with Favre and Laínez, Fr. Ignatius set out for Rome in November 1537, and when still a few miles outside the city, they visited a small chapel at La Storta, where Fr. Ignatius had a vision of God the Father in which he told him: "I will be favorable to you in Rome." He was comforted to know that God would show him his favor, but he did not know whether he would meet success or persecution. The three pilgrims had their audience with Pope Paul III and placed themselves and their companions at his disposal. Aware that these were Paris-trained theologians, the pope accepted their offer and immediately appointed Favre and Laínez to teach Scripture and theology at Rome's Sapienza University. Fr. Ignatius was left to carry out his own particular apostolate of preaching and helping souls.

A full year after his arrival in Rome, Fr. Ignatius chose to offer his first Mass. On Christmas eve, 1538, he and his companions went to the church of St. Mary Major and there in the Chapel of the Manger, where the Bethlehem relic was preserved, he celebrated the Mass.

The work of the companions prospered in Rome as it did in other Italian cities. Because God had manifested his will by keeping them in Italy, they now abandoned plans for the Holy Land and Fr. Ignatius asked his men to come to Rome during Lent 1539, to discuss whether they should remain as they are, or form a stable group. Up to this time they never thought of founding a new religious congregation. With the Jerusalem pilgrimage no longer a possibility, they had to think about the future. These first Jesuits discussed the matter for several weeks and their unanimous decision was to form a new order, if this met with the pope's approval. They saw themselves as a group dedicated to the salvation of souls, living in community under obedience to their head, and through him obedience to the pope. They regarded themselves as teachers of Christian doctrine, ready to travel wherever the pope should wish to send them.

By summer 1539, Fr. Ignatius had composed a summary description of what the order was to be—its goals and the means of attaining them—and this he submitted to the pope for approval. In September Pope Paul sent his verbal approval; the written bull of approbation, *Regimini militantis ecclesiae,* was not issued until September 27, 1540. With its publication the Society of Jesus was canonically established.

Now that the Society had papal approval, a superior had to be elected and its constitutions written. Fr. Ignatius, therefore, convened his men in Rome during Lent 1541; those unable to attend were to send in their choice for superior. Three were unable to come: Favre was in Germany, while Rodrigues and Xavier were in Portugal, waiting to board ship to go to the missions in the East Indies. When the ballots were read on April 8, each was a vote for Fr. Ignatius. His own ballot showed that he voted for "the one whom the majority would elect." Faced with the unanimous decision of his confreres, he was reluctant to accept the office and asked them to reconsider their votes after a few more days of prayer. The second ballot, on April 13, confirmed the earlier one, but he still hesitated and asked for a few days in which to pray and seek the counsel of his Franciscan confessor. The advice he received was that he had to accept the office of general because this was the evident will of Almighty God. Conforming his will to that of Divine Providence, Fr. Ignatius and his five companions, on April 22, Friday of Easter week, set out to visit Rome's seven pilgrim churches. When they arrived at St. Paul Outside-the-Walls, they made their confessions to one another, and as Fr. Ignatius celebrated Mass in our Lady's chapel, these Jesuits, at the moment of Communion, pronounced their vows in the newly formed Society of Jesus.

Fr. Ignatius had fifteen years in which to form and guide the Society. Besides overseeing its growth and development, he wrote its Constitutions, preached in Rome's churches, and taught Christian doctrine to children. He interviewed candidates for the Society and directed them through the Exercises. He also carried on an extensive correspondence, not only dealing with the Society's affairs but also guiding many in the spiritual life. The Society did not limit its activity to Rome; it soon had houses in the major Italian cities, as well as in Spain, Portugal, France, Germany, and the Low Countries. From these contacts a stream of candidates for the Society made its way to Rome; among them was the scholarly Peter Canisius and the saintly Francis Borgia. As Jesuit influence increased in these cities, colleges were opened and so rapid was the Society's growth that by 1556, the year when Fr. Ignatius died, it totalled 1,000 members in 76 houses in 12 provinces that included Brazil, Japan, and India. All this in the span of fifteen years.

Fr. Ignatius was also attuned to the needs of Rome. He established the House of St. Martha for former prostitutes and a home for young girls who were in danger of being exploited. He founded an orphanage and had a house built for Moslems and Jews who had expressed a desire to become Christians. He started the Roman College in 1551 and to help counteract the influence of the Reformation in Germany, he founded a college in Rome for German seminarians (1552). In addition, the pope appointed Jesuits to attend the various colloquies with Lutheran theologians in Germany, and later chose Jesuits as his theologians at the Council of Trent.

Ever since his Paris days, Fr. Ignatius had suffered from stomach ailments; these were especially troublesome during the last ten years of his life. As his work increased, especially his concern about the Society's Constitutions, his health declined. In 1554 he spent the months of June and July in bed. The following winter he found new strength, but by April 1556 he was failing again. The summer was oppressive and since he was not getting better, his physician recommended that he go to the villa on the Aventine, which he did on July 2. The air there, however, did not cure him and so he returned to the residence in Rome's center on July 24. So intense was the heat that summer that several of the community were ill with fever. When the physician arrived to examine them, he also checked on Fr. Ignatius. But the founder was neither better nor worse; he had survived similar bouts in the past and the physician was sure he would survive this one. Fr. Ignatius, however, thought differently.

On Thursday, July 30, he called his secretary Juan de Polanco to his bedside and asked him to go and request the pope's blessing for him and to recommend the Society to his good will. Though he was hinting that death was imminent, Polanco put more trust in the physician's statement that he would recover. And so he told the founder that several letters had to be written and sent to Spain that day so he would go to the Vatican the following day. Fr. Ignatius intimated that he would prefer Polanco to go that afternoon; nevertheless, he told him, "Do as you wish." Polanco returned to his letters. Later, when he was with Fr. Ignatius for the evening meal, they chatted as usual, and sure that he had made the right decision, Polanco went peacefully to bed.

After midnight Fr. Ignatius had a turn for the worse and when the infirmarian checked on him at daybreak, it was clear that he was in his last moments. The brother hurriedly called several priests to the founder's room, and Polanco rushed off to the Vatican. But before he returned, Fr. Ignatius had given his soul to God. The news of his death brought many to the Jesuit residence, and when the body was made ready for visitors there was a long line of priests and prelates, of Rome's nobility and of Rome's poor, all coming to kiss the venerable hands of the founder of the Society of Jesus. On Saturday evening, August 1, he was buried in the church of Our Lady of the Way, and when that church was replaced by the church of the Gesù, his remains were interred there in 1587.

Ignatius of Loyola was beatified on July 27, 1609, and on the 31st of that month, in the Gesù's chapel of Our Lady of the Way, Fr. General Claudio Acquaviva offered the first Mass honoring the new blessed. Ignatius was then canonized by Pope Gregory XV on March 12, 1622, together with Francis Xavier. Jesuits celebrate the feast of their founder on July 31, the day when he left this world for heaven.

Prayer

Lord, in your providence you guided Saint Ignatius to found the Society of Jesus. Enrich it, we pray, with gifts of heart, mind and spirit. Make us all one with you in holiness and love, so that we may know your will and obey it as your faithful servants. We ask this through our Lord Jesus Christ your Son, who lives and reigns with you and the Holy Spirit, one God, for ever and ever.

August

August 2

Bl. Peter Favre 1506–1546

Peter Favre was Fr. Ignatius' first recruit. He was born on April 13, 1506, in the village of Villaret, Savoy. As a youth he shepherded his father's flock on the high pastures of the Alps and had no other education than what one receives at home. He was endowed, however, with an extraordinary memory; he could hear a sermon in the morning and then repeat it verbatim in the afternoon for his friends. He longed to go to school, but his family was too poor, and years later he wrote in his Memorial that in his sadness at not being able to study, he wept himself to sleep every night.

Peter's parents heard his weeping and finally acquiesced to his wishes and sent him in 1516 to a small school operated by the parish priest seven miles away. The ten-year-old quickly learned to read and write and the following year went to La Roche, a dozen miles away, where he remained until he went to the University of Paris in 1525.

Peter arrived in the French capital about October of that year and resided at the College of Sainte-Barbe, where his roommate was Francis Xavier. Francis had just come from Navarre and was the same age as Peter. Both gave themselves to their studies, beginning with philosophy and advancing to theology. In October 1529, they accepted another roommate, Ignatius of Loyola, who had been in Paris for over a year, and of whom it was said that whoever came into contact with him invariably changed for the better.

Ignatius had difficulties with Greek so Peter tutored him in Aristotle. While Peter served as Ignatius' guide in academic matters, Ignatius served as Peter's guide in spiritual matters. Now in his mid-twenties, Peter was still undecided about his future. Should he be a lawyer? A teacher? A priest? A monk? It was while living in Paris that he learned of Ignatius' plan to follow Christ. This was what Peter needed to give direction to his life. Under Ignatius' influence he

P. Petr. Faber, Allobrox, Villareti, ortu Pastoritio
nat. prim. S. Ignatij Soci. Missionib. et laborib. Apo-
stolicis per Germaniam, Hispaniam, Lusitaniam.
notissimus. Angelorum cultui addictissimus.
Obijt Romæ. 1 Aug. 1546.

Bl. Peter Favre

decided to become a priest, and shortly before his ordination Ignatius led him through the Spiritual Exercises for a period of thirty days.

While Ignatius was working with Peter he was also working on Francis and several other students. By the time Peter was ordained, May 30, 1534, Ignatius had gathered about him six like-minded individuals willing to vow themselves to follow Christ in poverty and chastity, and to go to Jerusalem to work for the conversion of the Turks. On August 15, 1534, the feast of our Lady's assumption, Ignatius and his six companions met in the crypt of the Chapel of Saint-Denis on Montmartre, and while Fr. Favre celebrated Mass—he was the only priest among them—each pronounced his vows. Their departure for Venice and the Holy Land was planned for January 1537; meantime, they had to complete their theological studies at the university. If the journey to the Holy Land proved impossible, then they would go to Rome and place themselves at the disposal of the pope.

When Ignatius returned to Spain for a period of convalescence, Fr. Favre was left in charge of the group. They left Paris in November 1536 and arrived in Venice in January of the following year to find that Ignatius had arrived before them. While waiting for the sailing season to the Holy Land to open, they worked in two of the city's hospitals. In March Ignatius sent Fr. Favre and the others to Rome to request Pope Paul III's approval of their proposed journey. Though His Holiness readily granted their request, he at the same time informed them that it was unlikely that the group would get there, because war with the Turks seemed imminent. Fr. Favre and companions returned to Venice; since the pope's fears proved correct, he and Ignatius directed their steps toward Rome in November to offer their services to the pope. The pope responded by appointing Fr. Favre to Rome's Sapienza University, where he lectured on theology and Scripture until May 1539.

In the summer of 1539 the pope appointed Frs. Favre and James Laínez, another of the first Jesuits, to assist Cardinal Ennio Filonardi in preaching reform in Parma, where the clergy, over the years, had become lax and the faithful neglectful of their religion. The two Jesuits preached on scriptural topics, morality, and the Christian life with conspicuous results. After a year of this missionary preaching, the majority of the Parmesans were again attending church, but Fr. Favre was quick to acknowledge that this success was not due to their eloquence, but to God working through the Spiritual Exercises.

Fr. Favre's stay in Parma lasted only a year. In the summer of 1540 he was instructed to accompany Dr. Pedro Ortiz, Emperor Charles V's representative to the religious colloquy to be held between Catholics and Protestants at Worms in Germany. They arrived in Worms in late October, and though it was a Lutheran city Fr. Favre set about preaching, hearing confessions, and giving the Exercises. The colloquy was late in starting and when it did begin on January 14, 1541, it lasted only four days, for the emperor then transferred it to Ratisbon (today's Regensburg). Fr. Favre moved to Ratisbon in February and spent the next six months working among the Catholic faithful there. He was not directly involved in the theological discussions, but he followed them closely and sent letters to Fr. Ignatius describing the events taking place in the city. Fr. Favre had more requests from priests, prelates, and princes to make the Spiritual Exercises than he himself could handle, and he wrote Fr. Ignatius that there was enough work in Ratisbon for ten more Jesuits. The colloquy's momentum, unfortunately, began to slow down and when it came time to discuss the Eucharist and Christ's real presence, a point bitterly disputed among the participants, the colloquy collapsed and the emperor's fond hope of unifying the Catholics and Protestants met a sad end.

Now that Fr. Favre and Dr. Ortiz were free, they made their way to Spain to establish Jesuit contacts in that country. As soon as they arrived in Madrid in November 1541, Fr. Favre began giving missions and sermons as well as conferences and retreats to the clergy. He explained the purpose of the Society to the Spanish prelates and prepared the way for Jesuits to come to Spain. After a short two months, he received notice in January 1542 that Pope Paul had appointed him assistant to Cardinal Giovanni Morone, papal nuncio to Germany, and he once more had to cross Europe on foot. Arriving at Spires, Germany, in April, he followed his usual method of activity: sermons, confessions, retreats. He also lectured on the Psalms at the University of Mainz, and it was while he was there that a young theological student from Cologne came to visit him, requesting to know more about the Society. The student was Peter Canisius, who went through the Exercises under Fr. Favre's guidance and then became a Jesuit.

In July 1544 Fr. Favre was assigned to Portugal at the request of King John III, who wanted him to pursue establishing the Society in that country. Fr. Favre spent the next two years in Portugal and Spain. Then in the spring of 1546, Pope Paul appointed him one of the papal theologians at the ecumenical council being held at Trent. Fr. Favre again had to set about traveling, but his health was greatly weakened from the frequent bouts of fever that he had suffered over the past years. He wanted to visit Fr. Ignatius before going to Trent in northern Italy so he sailed from Barcelona and made his way to Rome, arriving on July 17. He had not seen Ignatius for seven years and their greeting was as warm as the Italian sun above them. Before Fr. Favre had a chance to set out for Trent, the fever again attacked him. Though only forty years old, he knew that his end was coming and waited for it peacefully. On July 31 he made his confession, and on the morning of August 1 he heard Mass and received the last sacraments. That afternoon, while in the company of Fr. Ignatius, the gentle Fr. Favre went to God in the company of the angels to whom he was singularly devoted. Fr. Favre was buried in the church of Our Lady of the Way in Rome, but when the church of the Gesù was being erected in 1569 on the site of the former church, Fr. Favre's remains and those of other early Jesuits were reinterred.

On September 5, 1872, Pope Pius IX, acknowledging the cult that had been paid to Peter Favre in his native Savoy, confirmed it by apostolic decree and declared that he was among the blessed in heaven. Bl. Peter Favre's memorial is celebrated on August 2.

Prayer

Father, Lord of heaven and earth, you revealed yourself to Blessed Peter Favre, your humble servant, in prayer and in the service of his neighbor. Grant that we may find you and love you in everything and in every person. We ask this through our Lord Jesus Christ, your Son, who lives and reigns with you and the Holy Spirit, one God, for ever and ever.

August 3

Ven. Brian Cansfield 1582–1645

Brian Cansfield was born in Roberts Hall, Tatham, in Lancashire, England, probably in 1582. His early education was in the local school and his upbringing was Protestant. His brothers, however, were Catholic, and they continually encouraged him to adopt their faith. Finally, at sixteen, Brian went to the English College at Saint-Omer in Flanders, and there in 1598 became a Catholic. After three years at Saint-Omer he transferred to the English College in Rome, enrolling there on October 15, 1601. Three years later, having decided to enter the Society, he returned to Flanders and became a Jesuit in November 1604. He completed his theological education and was ordained. His desire to return to England and work for his persecuted Church was eventually fulfilled in 1618.

In England Fr. Cansfield made use of the names Christopher Benson and Barton, and labored in Lancashire, Lincolnshire, Devonshire, and Yorkshire. During his more than twenty-five years on the English mission, he converted many Protestants to the faith and strengthened that of countless Catholics. Like all priests on the mission, he knew that arrest could come at any time, nonetheless, he never curtailed his activity. When Fr. Cansfield's arrest did take place, it was a case of mistaken identity, and the treatment he received at the hands of his captors was the cause of his death.

Sometime in 1645, the wife of a certain judge in Yorkshire became reconciled to the Church through the efforts of an unidentified Jesuit. When the judge learned that his wife had given up Protestantism for Catholicism, he became so enraged that he ordered the priest-hunters to search throughout Yorkshire until the priest who had converted his wife was apprehended. He swore that he would not rest until that priest was hanged and quartered. The priest-hunters set out on their task. During their hunt they unexpectedly came upon Fr. Cansfield celebrating Mass and seized him at the altar. While being taken to the judge, his captors struck him and abused him, all of which he bore with patience. When he was brought before the judge, the latter's joy was overflowing—he finally had the priest in his hands—and he immediately committed him to the prison in York Castle.

The officials in the prison judged that the beating that Fr. Cansfield had already endured was not enough, so they continued to abuse him. In time, the mistake was recognized that Fr. Cansfield was not the priest who had reconciled the wife, therefore the judge withdrew the charges against him and allowed him to go free. When Fr. Cansfield emerged from prison he was a broken man. His health at the time of his arrest was not robust and the various beatings he suffered, insufficient food, and the dampness of his cell all contributed to weakening his health beyond repair. He may have been given his freedom, but the results of the judge's hatred for the Catholic faith remained with him.

Fr. Cansfield went to reside with his Jesuit brethren hoping to recover but he never did rally and on August 3, 1645 (some sources give 1643), a few days after his release, he died. He was about sixty-three years old and had been a Jesuit for forty-one years. Pope Leo XIII declared him Venerable in 1886.

August 14

S. G. Joachim Valentí 1884–1936
S. G. Louis Boguñá 1893–1936
S. G. Joseph Vergés 1898–1936

Martyrs of the Spanish Civil War

During the week of July 13, 1936, thousands of sodalists from the diocese of Gerona gathered at our Lady's sanctuary in that episcopal city to participate in a convention. Fr. Joseph Vergés de Trías, moderator of the largest sodality in Gerona, was one of the priests promoting the gathering. Fr. Louis Boguñá Porta, director of a sodality in Barcelona, came to Gerona on July 16 to attend the final days of the meeting. On July 18, before the convention ended, civil war erupted.

Churches and convents were set afire and priests had to seek refuge with friends. These two Jesuits were offered shelter by Mrs. Bassols, a widow, who lived with her two sisters.

Fr. Vergés was the youngest of the three Jesuits martyred in Gerona. He was born in Barcelona on January 10, 1898, and entered the Society at Gandía on October 11, 1916. After humanistic studies at Saragossa, he taught for three years (1921–1924) at the College of St. Dominic in Orihuela, then did philosophy (1924–1927) and theology (1927–1931) at Sarriá, where he was ordained in 1930. In 1932, shortly after completing his Jesuit formation, the Society was suppressed in Spain and, thus, he moved to Gerona to exercise his ministry there in secret.

Fr. Boguñá, on the other hand, was born near Barcelona, at San Andrés de Palomar, on April 14, 1893, and joined the Jesuits on August 17, 1909, at Gandía. He did his early studies at Gandía and Sargossa, and in 1916 went to Tortosa for philosophy. From 1919 to 1923 he taught mathematics and French at the Jesuit school in Saragossa, and from 1923 to 1927 did his theological studies at Sarriá, where he was ordained in 1926. After tertianship he was assigned to the College of the Sacred Heart in Barcelona and, among other things, directed the sodality at the Torras y Bages Academy.

While staying at the Bassols residence, Frs. Vergés and Boguñá were fortunate enough to be able to celebrate Mass every day. With the city's churches destroyed, they also daily went out to distribute Communion to the faithful who were now unable to attend Mass. They learned where the religious sisters, whose convents had been burned, were staying, and visited them to encourage them. They also kept in contact with other Jesuits hiding in the city. Because of their frequent coming and going, they knew that they could easily be spotted and reported, so they decided to change their residence; but before they were able to accomplish this, revolutionary forces intervened.

Fr. Boguñá went to the city's tax building almost daily and his frequent visits were noted by a guard on duty. Knowing that the visitor did not work in the building, the guard reflected on these numerous trips and concluded that since the head of the tax office, who was a fervent Catholic, was ill, the visitor must be a priest, bringing him Communion. Thus the Jesuits at the Bassols residence were betrayed.

Frs. Vergés and Boguñá were not the only priests to whom Mrs. Bassols had offered hospitality. A diocesan priest, Fr. John Guix, who had been in charge of Sacred Heart Church, the former Jesuit parish in the city, was with them, and on August 13, another Jesuit, Fr. Joachim Valentí de Martí joined them. Fr. Valentí had known the Bassols family from an earlier sojourn in Gerona, and when he arrived he did not expect to find two other Jesuits there. He was born in Tarragona on October 17, 1884, and entered the Society on April 9, 1904, in Saragossa. He studied philosophy (1910–1913) at Tortosa, taught (1913–1916) at the Jesuit school in Sarriá, remained there for theology (1916–1920), and was ordained in 1919. His next assignment was to teach Latin at the College of St.

Joseph in Valencia from 1921 to 1928, and from there he went to the Jesuit church in Gerona, where he was a parish priest. In 1932, at the time of the Society's suppression in Spain, he spent three months living with the Bassols family, and then went to Barcelona to carry on his ministry among working people.

Dressed as a laborer, Fr. Valentí arrived at the Bassols home at 9:00 P.M., on August 13. He had come to Gerona on the 11th to secure a working permit from the trade union office; this would allow him to mingle freely with the workers and to continue his ministry undiscovered. He said he could not stay long; as soon as the permit was granted, he would leave because there were many in Barcelona who depended upon him. The four priests and the three ladies had their evening meal and afterwards Fr. Boguñá listened to the radio, while Fr. Vergés enjoyed a game of Parcheesi with the three sisters, and Fr. Valentí played solitaire. Eventually everyone retired.

That evening armed militiamen surrounded the Bassols residence and at 11:00 P.M. the group's leader, accompanied by a few soldiers and the guard from the tax building, knocked loudly at the door of the Bassols home. A neighbor came out to tell them that it was useless to knock because the three old ladies who lived there would never hear the knocking. To this one of the men replied: "And some priests are living here too." The ladies at first did not dare open the door, but as the knocking grew louder and louder, Mrs. Bassols finally acquiesced. The leader explained to her that he was searching for some soldiers who might be hiding in the house. But the lady assured him that there were none there. Pointing to a hat on the rack, the intruder asked: "To whom does that man's hat belong?" Again she repeated that there were no soldiers in the house. At that moment Fr. Vergés came down the stairs and behind him was Fr. Valentí. Then Frs. Guix and Boguñá appeared. While the priests were being searched, the leader ordered the entire house as well as the garden and a nearby orange grove to be gone over. For three hours the priests and ladies were kept in a parlor and when the search was completed, the militiamen led the priests out of the house. Fr. Valentí turned to Mrs. Bassols and said: "if we do not see each other again here, then in heaven."

The prisoners were driven a short distance outside Gerona, until they reached the crossroads leading to Can Veray and there, while the victims' backs were turned, they were killed by machine gun fire. Two bodies fell at the side of the road and two fell next to the railroad tracks. It was 2:30 A.M., August 14. The bodies of the four martyrs were buried on the 15th in the cemetery at Celrá; their remains were recovered in 1939 and taken to Gerona. The diocesan investigation into the martyrdom of Frs. Joachim Valentí, Louis Boguñá, Joseph Vergés, and the diocesan priest John Guix, opened in Gerona on September 26, 1951.

August 17

S. G. Charles Odescalchi 1786–1841

Fr. Charles Odescalchi, after serving the Roman Church for fifteen years as a cardinal, resigned his rank and exchanged his robes for the Jesuits' simple cassock. He was born in the family's palace in Rome on March 5, 1786, and because his father was a prince of the Roman Empire and duke of Sirmium, the future of Charles promised to be bright. He was educated at home, but because he had no inclination toward politics or world affairs, he chose to become a priest and was ordained on December 31, 1808.

During the following year, Fr. Joseph Pignatelli came to Rome with his small group of Jesuits expelled from the Kingdom of Naples, and after Fr. Odescalchi became acquainted with them, he thought of entering the Society. Finally, after Pope Pius VII had restored the Society on August 7, 1814—after forty-one years of suppression—and was again permitted to accept novices, Fr. Odescalchi was among the first to apply and was scheduled to enter the Roman novitiate of Sant'Andrea on November 12, 1814. His younger sister Vittoria, however, when she learned of her brother's plans, was convinced that she could not live without him near her, and so she used her influence with Pius to intercede in her behalf. Obedient to the pope's wishes, Fr. Odescalchi postponed his entrance until Vittoria's future was assured.

Vittoria married three years later and her brother again made plans to enter the Society, but this time it was Pope Pius himself who did not want to lose him. To ensure that Fr. Odescalchi would always be at his side when needed, the pope named him to the Sacred Rota. Disappointed that Fr. Odescalchi was unable to enter the Society as he had desired, the Jesuit provincial in Rome sent him a letter notifying him of his acceptance by the Society when "certain difficulties shall have been overcome." This letter brought Fr. Odescalchi a certain amount of consolation and at the same time strengthened his hope that someday he would be able to fulfill this desire of his. These "certain difficulties," however, were to increase, and it would be twenty years before he would be able to call himself a Jesuit.

In 1819 Pope Pius sent Fr. Odescalchi to Vienna as papal legate, and on his return he became the pope's adviser in naming bishops to vacant sees throughout the world. During the ensuing months the pope's appreciation of his person and administrative ability so increased that on March 10, 1823, the pope named him a cardinal at age thirty-seven and on the 25th of the month he was consecrated archbishop of Ferrara. Since the Pope's health now began to deteriorate, Cardinal Odescalchi remained in Rome and attended Pius until his death on July 20. With Leo XII's election on September 28, 1823, Cardinal

Odescalchi went to Ferrara, but within three years Pope Leo asked him to return to Rome as prefect of the Congregation of Bishops and Regulars.

Cardinal Odescalchi fulfilled his duties as head of this congregation not only under Leo, but also under Pius VIII and Gregory XVI. Then in 1834 Pope Gregory appointed him his vicar for the diocese of Rome. The cardinal was now forty-seven years old and in his innermost being he still desired to be a Jesuit. Pope Gregory felt that the Church had first claim on the cardinal's outstanding talents, however, and the cardinal remained in Rome. When the city was ravaged by a plague in 1837, the cardinal organized medical services so well that every part of the city was visited and helped. He likewise established houses to care for the children made orphans as a result of the plague. So thorough and heroic was his leadership during those tragic months that Rome never forgot his extraordinary love and concern for its citizens.

In the spring of 1838, after the plague had subsided and the city returned to its normal rhythm, the cardinal again approached the pope and asked to resign his cardinilatial office. Pope Gregory was especially reluctant to lose so valuable a coworker; nevertheless, he left the decision to a committee of four cardinals. The committee weighed Cardinal Odescalchi's request to resign against his success as the pope's vicar in Rome, his prudence and wisdom as papal adviser, and the love that the Roman clergy and faithful had for him. In the end the committee felt that it had to deny the cardinal's request for the good of the Church.

The summer of 1838, however, brought a change in Cardinal Odescalchi's health and Pope Gregory advised him to leave Rome for a much-needed rest. Before leaving the city, the cardinal penned another letter to the pope (October 23, 1838) asking that his resignation be accepted. Perhaps thinking that he could no longer go against the divine motions in his friend's soul, the pope accepted the resignation on October 31. On November 3, Fr. Odescalchi wrote to Fr. John Roothaan, the Jesuit general in Rome, and informed him of the pope's acceptance of his resignation and to affirm that he was prepared to enter the Society.

Fr. Odescalchi entered the Jesuit novitiate in Verona on December 6, 1838. During his years as a Jesuit he chose not to exercise his episcopal powers and preferred to be called "Father." He pronounced his three religious vows on February 2, 1840, and for the remaining eighteen months of his life was spiritual father to young Jesuits at the seminary in Modena. During this period he was in great demand for parish missions and retreats to clergy and seminarians. Fr. Odescalchi waited twenty-four years to be numbered among the sons of St. Ignatius, but when that time finally came, God gave him only three years to live the life he so long desired to live. He died in Modena on August 17, 1841, at age fifty-five.

Fr. Charles Odescalchi was revered during life and after death, and because of the many graces attributed to his intercession before God, his cause was initiated.

August 18

Bl. Albert Hurtado Cruchaga 1901–1952

Throughout South America the name of Fr. Albert Hurtado Cruchaga is associated with *El Hogar de Cristo,* a Catholic charity that provides the homeless with a place to live. Albert was born in Viña del Mar, Chile, on January 22, 1901, and though his parents may have been of old aristocratic families, they were without wealth and lived on a small estate. Albert's father died when Albert was four, and his mother had to sell the farm for far less than it was worth in order to pay off the family's heavy debts. She and her two sons then went to live with relatives. From an early age Albert knew what it was to be poor and remembered how frequently the family had to move. When a scholarship had been offered him, he attended the Jesuit school in Santiago.

Though only in his early teens, Albert grew concerned about the people who lived in the slum districts and, thus, he spent each Sunday afternoon helping them. When he graduated from St. Ignatius school in 1917, he thought of becoming a Jesuit, but his spiritual director, knowing the family's financial condition, suggested that he postpone his entrance until his mother and younger brother were better situated. Albert secured a job during the afternoons and evenings to help support the family and at the same time earned enough to begin the study of law at the Catholic University. The poor always remained close to Albert, and though he was doing double duty—working and studying—he continued to spend his Sunday afternoons with them. In 1920 he interrupted his studies to enter military service and after his discharge returned to the university, where he graduated in August 1923. On the 14th of that month, he entered the Jesuit novitiate at Chillán; he was twenty-two years old.

After eighteen months at Chillán, Albert went, at the beginning of 1925, to Córdoba in Argentina to finish his novitiate training and there he pronounced his first religious vows on August 15, 1925. He began his study of the humanities and in 1927 went to Spain for philosophy. By 1931 he had completed his first year of theology, but because the Society had been dissolved in Spain in 1932, he went first to Ireland for several months, and then to Louvain, where he finished his studies for the priesthood. He was ordained in Belgium on August 24, 1933, did his final year of Jesuit training at Drongen, and returned to Chile in January 1936.

On Fr. Hurtado's return to Santiago, he taught religion at St. Ignatius and gave adult classes in pedagogy at the Catholic University. He was also in charge of the school's sodality and involved its members in apostolic works, especially teaching catechism in the villages. Retreat work was also important to him. No matter how crowded his schedule, he managed to fit retreats into it. When the number of those requesting retreats grew, he built a retreat house next to the Jesuit novitiate and these retreats, in turn, resulted in vocations to the priesthood, diocesan and religious.

In 1941, when a former fellow student of his at the university, who had also been a former army companion, became auxiliary bishop of Santiago, Fr. Hurtado was asked to become director of *Catholic Action*, first in the archdiocese and then on the national level. He kept the position until the end of 1944, when Providence led him to another important work. During a women's retreat he was giving in October 1944, he asked his audience to think of the many poor people in their city—men, women, youths, children, who were without a roof over their heads and were forced to spend the nights outdoors, in the rain and cold of winter. This remark so moved his audience that the women responded by offering him donations for the poor. This was the beginning of *El Hogar de Cristo*. With the generous benefactions he received, Fr. Hurtado opened a hospice for youth and then one for women and children in Santiago. *Hogar* means hearth or home, and thus the homeless poor were made welcome into Christ's home. The hospices increased in number and they not only offered shelter for the night, but also helped rehabilitate people and taught them skills and true Christian values. Fr. Hurtado visited the United States (1945–1946) and while residing with the Jesuit community at Georgetown University, pursued courses in sociology at the Catholic University of America. While in the States he also studied the operation and management of Fr. Flanagan's Boys Town with the idea of adapting it to his own country. His last six years were devoted to the spread of these hospices, which were established in many Chilean cities, and today are found throughout South America. Between the years 1947 and 1950, Fr. Hurtado also wrote three books: *On Unions, Social Humanism,* and *The Christian Social Order.* In 1951 he started a monthly periodical called, *Mensaje* ("Message"), devoted to explaining the Church's social teaching.

Though by the end of 1951 Fr. Hurtado was only fifty years old, his health began to fail. By the following May he was quite ill and his physician thought some rest at the seashore would help him. But at the end of May the priest returned to Santiago, where it was finally discovered that he had pancreatic cancer. During his suffering the pain increased almost daily and he was heard to say, "I am content, O Lord, I am content." He lingered until August 18, 1952, when, as his Jesuit brethren surrounded his bed recommending him to God, this apostle of the poor returned his soul to its Maker. When his body was taken to St. Ignatius church, his many friends crowded the building to see their father for the last time. The funeral took place on the 20th with so large a crowd that many had to remain outside.

Fr. Albert Hurtado is vividly remembered for his charity and Christ-like love of the poor. He was beatified by Pope John Paul II on October 16, 1994, and his fellow Jesuits liturgically celebrate his memorial on August 18.

Prayer

God our Father in Blessed Albert Hurtado, priest, you have given us a magnifi-
cent sign of your love. Through his intercession grant that, always faithful to
your will, we may love all with the sentiments of your Son and thus ceaselessly
promote your kingdom of justice, love, and peace. We ask this through our Lord
Jesus Christ, your Son, who lives and reigns with you and the Holy Spirit, one
God, for ever and ever.

August 19

S. G. Thomas Sitjar and 10 Companions 1866–1936

Martyrs of the Spanish Civil War

These eleven Jesuits, seven priests and four brothers, were martyred in Gandía
and Valencia, Spain, between August 19 and December 29, 1936. The first to
die was Fr. Thomas Sitjar Fortiá, rector of the Gandía novitiate. When the Spanish revolutionary government suppressed the Society in 1932, the novices left
Gandía to continue their studies in other countries, but the Jesuits who remained moved into small apartments in the city. Though the community was
dispersed, Fr. Sitjar remained its superior.

He was born on March 21, 1866, in Gerona, and entered the Jesuit novitiate at Veruela on July 21, 1880. After completing his philosophy at the scholasticate in Tortosa, he spent eight years (1889–1897) teaching philosophy at the
diocesan seminary in Montevideo, Uruguay. He returned to Tortosa for theology
and was ordained in 1900. From 1902 to 1921 he taught metaphysics to young
Jesuits at Tortosa and later at Sarriá. In October 1923 he became superior of the
residence in Tarragona and in February 1929 was appointed rector in Gandía.

During the years following the Society's suppression, the ministry of the
Spanish Jesuits was greatly curtailed, but it had not come to an end. That end
came in July 1936 when civil war broke out. Fr. Sitjar was, at the time, living in
a small apartment with Br. Peter Gelabert, and though many friends had asked
him to move in with them, he always refused, saying: "If they kill us, then it will
be God's will."

On July 25, shortly after 10:30 P.M., a week after civil war had erupted, a
terrible banging was heard on Fr. Sitjar's door. He answered it, but only after Br.

Gelabert had escaped through a window. Fr. Sitjar was taken into custody. Because he had a bad leg and could not walk as quickly as his captors would have liked, they pushed and beat him and tried to rip his cassock off him. That night he was taken to a school that had been converted into a prison, and by noon of the following day Br. Gelabert, Fr. Constantine Carbonell, and Br. Raymond Grimaltos joined him.

Though under guard, the four Jesuits were able to have visitors and friends who supplied them with mattresses for sleeping and food for meals. On August 17 and 18 they were taken before their accusers, who asked them about their political views and party affiliation, to which Fr. Sitjar merely answered: "We belong to God's party." The prisoners were taken back to their cell, where they peacefully awaited the inevitable. Shortly after midnight on August 19, Fr. Sitjar was told that he was being set free, but rather than giving him his freedom, his captors took him and two other gentlemen to the Albaida road near Palma de Gandía and executed them beneath an olive tree. When the bullet pierced his heart, the seventy-year-old priest had a rosary in his hand. It was close to 3:00 A.M.

Fr. Sitjar's three Jesuit prison companions died four days later. About midnight on August 23, Fr. Carbonell, Brs. Gelabert and Grimaltos, and ten others were told to get ready for their trip to Valencia. They knew they were going to their death and hence they asked Fr. Carbonell for absolution. When the soldiers arrived they took the prisoners to an olive grove outside Gandía on the road to Valencia. Fr. Carbonell raised his arms to heaven in prayer, while Brs. Gelabert and Grimaltos fell to their knees. When the officer in charge gave the signal three more Jesuits were given to God. Fr. Carbonell was seventy years old, Br. Grimaltos was seventy-five, and Br. Gelabert forty-nine.

The next Jesuit to be martyred was Br. Joseph Tarrats. Since the time of the Society's suppression in Spain, he had been living with Br. Vincent Sales and Fr. Paul Bori in a building adjacent to a home for the aged operated by the Little Sisters, and where several old Jesuits were living in retirement. The two brothers helped the sisters and everything was relatively peaceful until civil war erupted. When the home's chaplain had to leave, Fr. Bori assumed his duties. The home went undisturbed for a month, but then on August 24, 1936, the communists took the home over and introduced their own staff. They set guards at all the doors and transformed the chapel into a dining area. During this period of occupation, Fr. Bori, though no longer able to celebrate Mass, continued his visits to the sick and aged, while Br. Tarrats worked in the infirmary and Br. Sales in the garden. All this time they kept their Jesuit identity to themselves. Br. Tarrats, unfortunately, was denounced on September 28, and he and three others of the infirmary staff were taken that day to a place on the outskirts of Valencia called Rambleta, where they were executed. The following day, September 29, Fr. Bori and Br. Sales were likewise taken from the home and driven to a secluded place near a cemetery. There they offered their final sacrifices to God. Br. Tarrats was fifty-eight years old, Fr. Bori was seventy-two, and Br. Sales fifty-five.

Fr. Darius Hernández was also martyred on September 29, 1936. He had been superior of the Jesuit residence in Valencia since September 1928, and was well known in the city. During August and the first weeks of September 1936, he changed his residence frequently and with the false identification card he carried, he was able to get about the city and do some priestly work. As the days passed the danger grew; he was finally arrested on September 13 and imprisoned. He remained there until September 29 when at 8:30 P.M. he was taken to the outskirts of Valencia, to an area known as Picadero de Paterna and was executed.

The next Jesuit to be martyred was Fr. Narcissus Basté. He had lived in the Jesuit residence in Valencia for almost thirty years, and when the community had to disperse, he moved into a small apartment, where he was able to celebrate Mass daily and where other Jesuits also came to celebrate. The communists, in the beginning, respected him because of what he had done over the years in promoting workers' causes. He was arrested several times. The first was on August 17; among the officers interrogating him was one who had some years before benefitted from the priest's advice and, thus, he used his influence on his comrades to have Fr. Basté released, supposedly in view of the priest's seventy years. His second arrest came on September 6, and again he was released because of age, but with the warning: "Father, be careful and do not go out. This time you are dealing with us, next time you may be dealing with others." Finally, the priest was apprehended on October 15 by communist soldiers, who killed him that same day.

Fr. Alfred Simón died on November 29, 1936. He had been rector of the College of St. Joseph in Valencia, and because he was known in the city he had no difficulty in finding families willing to take him in after the revolution had begun. Though he frequently changed his residence, he was, nevertheless, arrested on a few occasions and released either because of a friend's influence or because a friend had bought his freedom. He was finally arrested in late November and on the 29th of the month was taken out and martyred.

The last of these eleven Jesuits to die was Fr. John Baptist Ferreres. He had been professor of moral theology and canon law at the Jesuit scholasticate and was famous throughout Spain for his writings. When the revolution broke out he was living in Barcelona and had been arrested in mid-August but was released because of his age. He was seventy-five years old, frail and weak. Given a safe-conduct pass to go to his hometown of Ollería, near Valencia, he arrived there on August 12. A few days later he was questioned by communist forces and all his religious articles were taken from him. At the end of August he was taken to Valencia and imprisoned with hundreds of others, but soon had to be taken to the prison infirmary, which he was never to leave. He immediately made friends among the sick and because he had been a professor everyone had questions to ask of him. In addition, the prisoners gathered around him each evening to recite the rosary. While in the infirmary Fr. Ferreres suffered a stroke, and because he was unable to move, bed sores developed. Due to the lack of proper medical care and sanitary conditions, his condition grew worse. During his illness he longed to receive Holy Communion, so one of the priests in prison arranged for Communion to be smuggled in. After he received the Sacrament, Fr. Ferreres said: "I'm so happy, now I can die." He died several days later on December 29, 1936.

Fr. Sitjar's companions:

Fr. Constantine Carbonell Sempere was born on April 12, 1866, at Alcoy, near Alicante, and entered the Jesuits on November 22, 1886. After his philosophical studies, he taught at the college in Orihuela (1893–1898), did theology at Tortosa and Gandía, and was ordained in 1901. In 1906 he was appointed minister of the community at the Gandía novitiate, and in January 1920 became superior of the minor seminary in Tortosa. In September 1922 he was appointed superior of the Jesuit residence in Alicante, and in 1926 returned to Gandía as minister of the community and Fr. Sitjar's assistant. He lived with Br. Grimaltos only a few doors from Fr. Sitjar's apartment. At about 5:00 A.M., on the morning of July 26, as both were on their way to Fr. Sitjar's to celebrate Mass, they were told by a lady who lived in the building that Fr. Sitjar and Br. Gelabert were not there. Later that morning Fr. Carbonell and Br. Grimaltos were arrested and taken to the school where Fr. Sitjar was held. They remained there until August 23, 1936, when they and Br. Gelabert were martyred.

Br. Raymond Grimaltos Monllor was born in Puebla Larga, in the province of Valencia, on March 3, 1861, and entered the Jesuits on June 1, 1890, at age twenty-nine. During his entire Jesuit life he was a gardener. He arrived at Gandía in 1917. He was arrested with Fr. Carbonell and was martyred with him on August 23, 1936.

Br. Peter Gelabert Amer was born at Manacor on the island of Majorca, on March 29, 1887, and entered the Society at Gandía on February 9, 1907. In 1911 he returned to Majorca and thirteen years later was again in Spain. He worked for a while at Veruela, but in 1930 was assigned to the Gandía novitiate. When the novitiate was closed in 1932, he lived with and looked after the aging Fr. Sitjar. Though he escaped on the night of July 25, he was captured the following day when the house in which he found refuge was searched. He spent a month in prison and died with Fr. Carbonell and Br. Grimaltos on August 23, 1936.

Br. Joseph Tarrats Comaposada was born in Manresa on August 29, 1878, and entered the Society on August 28, 1895. During his early years as a Jesuit he was a tailor at the scholasticate in Tortosa, and then in 1910 became infirmarian at the Jesuit residence in Valencia. He was arrested while working at the home for the aged and won his martyrdom on September 28, 1936.

Fr. Paul Bori Puig was born on November 12, 1864, at Vilet de Maldá, in the province of Tarragona, and had been a diocesan priest before becoming a Jesuit on September 7, 1891. He taught for a time and did parish work, and then in 1918 became minister and then house treasurer at the novitiate in Gandía, where he stayed until the community had to disperse. When the communists took over the home for the aged, his ministry was reduced to visiting the sick and hearing clandestine confessions. When he was taken from the home with Br. Sales on September 29, he asked the soldiers: "Which of you are going to kill me?" When they indicated which ones, the priest said: "In the name of that God for whom you are about to kill me and in whom you do not believe, I forgive you." He then gave them his blessing. Their response was gunfire.

Br. Vincent Sales Genovés was born in Valencia on October 15, 1881, and entered the novitiate on October 9, 1915, at age thirty-four. He spent his entire Jesuit life at Gandía. He had been at the home for the aged in Valencia with Br. Tarrats and was led to martyrdom with Fr. Bori on September 29, 1936.

Fr. Darius Hernández Morató was born in Buñol, in Valencia province, on October 25, 1880, and entered the Society on September 28, 1896. He did philosophy and theology at Tortosa and was ordained in 1912. He taught rhetoric at the college in Saragossa, then worked in parishes in Valencia and Barcelona, and in September 1928 was appointed rector of the most prominent Jesuit house in Valencia. When he died on September 29, 1936, he was fifty-six years old.

Fr. Narcissus Basté Basté was born at San Andrés de Palomar, near Barcelona, on December 16, 1866, and entered the Society on April 29, 1890. He was ordained in 1899 and went to the Valencia residence in 1902, and for the remainder of his life worked in its parish with labor groups and sodalists. He was arrested on October 15, 1936, and his martyrdom occurred the same day.

Fr. Alfred Simón Colomina was born in Valencia on March 8, 1877, and entered the Jesuits on December 18, 1895. After ordination in 1909, he was dean at the College of St. Joseph in Valencia, and then in 1913 became the school's rector. He left there in 1916 to become rector of the scholasticate in Sarriá, outside Barcelona. In 1921 he was rector of the Jesuit residence in Barcelona and in 1927 returned to St. Joseph's in Valencia, again as rector. After several arrests and several weeks in prison, the fifty-nine-year-old Fr. Simón was again apprehended toward the end of November and shed his blood on November 29, 1936.

Fr. John Baptist Ferreres Boluda was born in Ollería, in the province of Valencia, on November 28, 1861, and entered the Society on June 30, 1888. Because of his earlier training at the diocesan seminary, he was ordained in 1890 and taught theology in several of the province's schools. In 1899 he went to the scholasticate in Tortosa and began teaching moral theology and canon law. The texts he wrote in both these fields became standard texts in Spain. After sixteen years in Tortosa he moved to Sarriá and for another dozen years continued his teaching and writing. When civil war broke out, his health was already on the decline, and his arrest and imprisonment in Valencia hastened his death, which took place on December 29, 1936.

The investigation into the martyrdoms of Fr. Thomas Sitjar and his ten Jesuit companions opened in Valencia on May 3, 1956.

August 23

S. G. **Martin Santaella** 1873–1936

S. G. **Alphonsus Payán** 1877–1936

S.G. **Emmanuel Luque** 1856–1936

Martyrs of the Spanish Civil War

During the early months of the Spanish Civil War, three Jesuit priests died the death of martyrs at Almería on Spain's southern coast. Fr. Martin Santaella Gutiérrez had been a diocesan priest prior to his entrance into the Society. He was born in Montefrío, in the province of Granada, on February 3, 1873; after studying at the diocesan seminary and ordination, he was appointed pastor at Algarinejo. He was forty-four years old when he chose to become a Jesuit and began his noviceship in Granada on June 28, 1917. After his two-year period of probation he spent a year in private study and then in 1920 was assigned to give parish missions. For fifteen years he traveled throughout Andalusia and wherever he preached the people remembered him as being affable and as having great compassion toward the poor and needy. In 1935, when he was sixty-two years old, he gave up his role as an itinerant preacher to become vice-superior at the Jesuit residence in Almería.

When Spain's civil war broke out in July 1936, Fr. Santaella refused to seek personal safety and go into hiding; he remained at the apartment and carried on his ministry as best he could. He was arrested at home on the morning of July 23, and after interrogation was detained in various prisons, and finally taken to the ship *Astoy-Mendi,* a floating prison in the Almería harbor. Despite the ship's crowded conditions, lack of ventilation, and great heat in the hold, he went among the prisoners to encourage them and to hear the confessions of those who so desired. Prisoners were periodically taken from the hold, presumably to be executed. On August 27 a soldier descended to the prisoners and set about choosing some to go to work in the coal bunkers of the *Jaime I,* a warship anchored in the harbor. While everyone was concerned that he would be called, Fr. Santaella thought it a good time to visit a sick priest in another part of the hold. His Jesuit companions tried to dissuade him from going, but he disregarded them. As he was making his way to the priest, the soldier noticed him moving about and called out: "That fat priest over there, let him go too!"

When the prisoners arrived on board the *Jaime I* they were paired off and each pair was assigned to one of the men in charge of the bunkers. Their job was without purpose; to shovel coal from one side to the other, and vice versa. If they relaxed in their effort, the guard was there with a rubber rod to strike them on head and shoulders. The bunkers had a small air opening leading to the outside and as long as the guards were there, the vents remained open. After the prisoners had toiled for four hours, the guards left and the vents were closed. The chute openings in the bunkers' roofs were then opened and in poured coal dust in such amounts that, though the electric lights remained on, the prisoners could see nothing. After fifteen minutes of breathing in the noisome dust, the prisoners were ordered out. To get to the exits they had to follow the sound of the guards' voices, and when they emerged, they were cudgeled and taken on deck. A witness said that the sixty-three-year-old Fr. Santaella had to be given artificial respiration, but never revived. It was also commonly believed that his body had then been thrown into one of the ship's furnaces. In any case Fr. Santaella never left the *Jaime I*.

The two other Jesuits who also died in Almería were Frs. Alphonsus Payán Pérez and Emmanuel Luque Fontanilla. Fr. Payán was born at Gines, in the province of Seville, on February 20, 1877, and entered the Granada novitiate on November 6, 1895. After studying philosophy at Granada and theology at Murcia, he taught at the Jesuit schools in Chamartín and Villafranca. In 1925 he took up residence at the Jesuit parish in Granada, where, as an outstanding preacher, he was known for his ability to communicate the truths of the faith in a way that the faithful could easily understand. During the days before the establishment of the Spanish Republic, Fr. Payán was arrested on two occasions for speaking out against the dictatorship, but charges were never proven and he was released both times. In July 1936 he went to Almería to preach a novena in honor of our Lady and was there when civil war broke out. Though a hiding place was offered him, he chose to remain in the residence with Fr. Luque, then in his eightieth year.

Fr. Emmanuel Luque Fontanilla was born in Marchena, in the province of Seville, on December 28, 1856, and entered the Society at Murcia on September 11, 1887. After studies at Oña, he went to teach Spanish history and geography at Villafranca, and then in 1896 became spiritual father at the seminary in Granada. In 1906 he moved to Murcia, where he was made superior, and then in 1909 went to work in the Jesuit parish in Granada. He arrived in Almería in 1913 and continued a pastoral ministry. Fr. Luque spent a total of twenty-three years in Almería and during that time he gained a great following among the people, who loved him for his great concern for the poor. The clergy appreciated him and many made him their confessor, as did the bishop himself. When hostilities broke out in Almería, the aged Fr. Luque thought it useless to seek safety; he himself was waiting to go to God. He thus placidly remained at the Jesuit residence.

Toward the end of July the communist soldiers came to the residence and arrested Frs. Luque and Payán and for several days held them in a convent, which had been turned into a prison. Then on August 27 they were taken to the *Astoy-Mendi* in the harbor. Together with these two Jesuits were two bishops, thirty-eight priests, and fifty lay people. On the night of August 31 the prisoners were notified that some of them were to be transferred to a prison in the city. The announcement was properly interpreted to mean that some had been chosen for execution. Among those whose names were read out were Frs. Payán and Luque. When the latter's name was called out, one of the prisoners remarked: "If Fr. Luque is not safe here, then none of us are." Even some of the communist soldiers were surprised that the old priest had been picked, for everyone in Almería knew that he was politically harmless.

The bodies of both Jesuits were discovered in 1941, together with others, in a deep abandoned well at Taberna, outside the city. They were then taken to Almería and interred in the Jesuit church. The diocesan process investigating the martyrdoms of Frs. Martin Santaella, Alphonsus Payán, and Emmanuel Luque opened in Almería on January 18, 1956.

August 24

S. G. Andrew Carrió 1876–1936

Martyr of the Spanish Civil War

Fr. Andrew Carrió Bertrán spent twenty-five years of his Jesuit life at the College of St. Dominic in Orihuela in southeastern Spain; five years as a scholastic and twenty as a priest. Since his second arrival there in 1912, he was in charge of the spiritual development of the young men attending the school. When the Society was suppressed in Spain in 1932, the Jesuits were forced to disperse. The younger Jesuits went to continue their studies in other countries, while the older ones remained, but moved into small residences to continue their ministry among the people. Fr. Carrió and a few others rented a house near Calle Mayor and used it as their center of operation.

Andrew Carrió was born in Sallent, near Barcelona, on November 30, 1876. He entered the Jesuit novitiate outside Saragossa on September 10, 1891, and after noviceship remained there for his classical studies and a year of philosophy. Rather than continuing his philosophy, he was sent in 1897 to Orihuela to be prefect of students for five years, and then in 1902 went to Tortosa to complete his philosophical course. In 1904 he went to Buenos Aires, Argentina, and worked at the Jesuit school there until 1908, when he returned to Spain to begin theology at Tortosa. He was ordained in 1931 and after tertianship in Manresa, Fr. Carrió returned to Orihuela in 1912 and remained there until his death.

While the Jesuits were living in their residence near Calle Mayor, some revolutionaries, on the night of April 2, 1936, threw a bomb into the house. It caused little damage but Fr. Carrió interpreted this as a warning. Then one night, toward the end of April, he heard some individuals pass by outside and a voice saying: "Those Jesuits have to be killed." On May 1 the revolutionary party held a demonstration on Calle Mayor, uncomfortably close to the Jesuit residence. Realizing that they were no longer safe at that address the priests secretly left that night for different parts of the city. Fr. Carrió went to another Jesuit house and stayed with his religious brethren until the middle of July.

On July 23, a few days after civil war had broken out, Fr. Carrió went to live with a certain Mr. Emile Salar. As long as he remained with the Salar family, the priest was able to celebrate Mass daily and to administer the sacraments to all who asked for them. On several occasions he succeeded in visiting other Jesuits in the city to learn what was happening to his brethren. The peace and safety he enjoyed in the Salar household, however, came to an abrupt end on August 12, when the mayor of Orihuela issued an ordinance decreeing that all religious, male and female, not born in Orihuela had to leave the city within forty-eight hours. Fr. Carrió came from the north so he had to seek refuge elsewhere. A friend of his, Mr. José Meseguer of Alquerías, took him to his country estate and had him stay with a widow who lived on the property. On August 21 Mr. Meseguer returned to take Fr. Carrió to another refuge, an inn in Alcázares, whose owner he knew. They had to be especially careful because the priest was without a traveling pass. The driver of the bus going to Alcázares happened to know Mr. Meseguer and therefore asked no questions of Fr. Carrió. Both passengers arrived at the inn, where the priest registered as Mr. Andrews, who had come to benefit from the local baths.

Fr. Carrió was intent on getting to Alicante and Mr. Meseguer promised to get him the required pass, which was issued on August 25. Early the following day Mr. Meseguer set out for the Alcázares inn. He went directly to the baths and when he inquired of the manager about Mr. Andrews, he was told that he had left the previous day. Then a woman standing nearby added: "Yes, and they killed him." Unable to ask further questions without arousing suspicion, Mr. Meseguer wondered whether Fr. Carrió had left on his own or been apprehended. Thus he went to the clerk at the main desk and asked if Mr. Andrews had paid his bill before leaving and learned that he had. Whatever made Fr. Carrió leave for Alicante without his pass remains unknown.

On the morning of August 25, Fr. Carrió had departed the inn at Alcázares and walked to the bus stop to board the bus going to Alicante. That bus stop was, unfortunately, located next to the communists' local office. When the communists saw him waiting for the bus they suspected he was a priest, as they later said, "because of the goodness in his face." After Fr. Carrió had boarded the bus, the soldiers telephoned to the next stop and informed the revolutionaries at San Javier to apprehend him when the bus arrived. Thus Fr. Carrió was detained and he readily admitted that he was a Jesuit, thus pronouncing his own sentence of death.

Fr. Carrió spent that day in a cell beneath a staircase, and when he asked for food that evening, they offered him two raw eggs in a cup and told him: "For the trip you're going to take, this is enough." Before dawn the next day, August 26, they took the prisoner to the road going from San Javier to Sucina, and there they shot him. Later that morning a road worker, making his usual rounds, discovered the body and testified that the face was unrecognizable, that the arms were crossed on the breast, and that the man had died from gunshot wounds. He also found a rosary hidden in the man's sock, about seventy-five pesetas in a pocket, and the wallet identified him as Andrew Carrió. The town of Sucina then claimed the body and buried it in the local cemetery.

The investigation into Fr. Carrió's martyrdom began in Orihuela in March 1954.

August 25

Bl. Michael Carvalho 1579–1624

Martyr of Japan

Ever since Michael Carvalho was a Jesuit novice in Coimbra, Portugal, he longed to go on the Japanese mission. When he finally arrived in the East, he met one frustrating delay after another. His own impatience got the better of him, and when he did begin his missionary work, it was immediately cut short and he was cast into prison. Fr. Carvalho's brief missionary career was without significant accomplishment, but God does not measure a martyr's worth by what he achieves. He measures it by the love in the martyr's heart.

Fr. Carvalho was born in Braga, Portugal, about 1579, and in 1597, when he was eighteen, he entered the Society and in 1602 he left for India. Having arrived at Goa, he completed his studies at St. Paul's College and was ordained. He was now prepared and eager to go to Japan, but he was asked to teach theology at the Goa seminary. He would have preferred to be a missionary, but the classroom was the will of his superior and, therefore, the will of God. During the ten years of teaching theology he continued to nurture his interest in Japan and finally he received his heart's desire. In early 1619 he left Goa, suffered shipwreck off Malacca, and after a year still unable to get passage to Japan, boarded a vessel that took him to the coastal harbor of Anam. From there he walked to Macao, then sailed to Manila, and took passage for Nagasaki.

Disguised as a Portuguese soldier, Fr. Carvalho landed at Nagasaki on August 21, 1621. At the time of his arrival, the Great Persecution against the Catholics was in force; all missionaries were in hiding and exercised their priesthood only in secret. Fr. Carvalho went to the small island of Amakusa off Nagasaki, once a Christian stronghold and now a relatively safe place, where an inexperienced missionary could learn the Japanese language. After two years of study he gained a degree of fluency, but his eagerness to go out and preach God's word and his enthusiasm for confronting the non-Christians with the truths of Christianity imprudently led him to go before the district's non-Christian governor. He introduced himself as a priest and Jesuit, and informed the governor that he had come to preach Christ's Gospel and to convert the people. The governor, surprised at the missionary's brashness, and perhaps admiring his audacity, ordered him taken outside his jurisdiction, so as not to be forced to hand him over to the punishment reserved for those spreading a proscribed religion.

Fr. Carvalho found himself on the island of Kyushu in unknown surroundings, but Providence arranged that two Christians, who had known him in Amakusa, recognized him and led him to the Jesuit provincial in Nagasaki. Fr. Francis Pacheco, the provincial, commented on the priest's imprudence in needlessly endangering himself and suggested that if he wanted to begin his missionary apostolate, he could go to Omura, for the Christians there had requested a priest to visit them and hear confessions. The task in Omura completed, the missionary was returning to Nagasaki on July 22, 1623, when a spy noticed him, and suspecting him to be a priest, delivered him to the police. Thus Fr. Carvalho's apostolate ended shortly after it had begun. He was taken to a prison in Omura, where his companions were a Dominican, two Franciscan priests, and a catechist. The prison was an enclosure made of stakes and without roof or walls. It permitted the heat and the cold, the wind and the rain to beat upon the prisoners. Their food was but a few handfuls of rice and a saucer of water in the morning and evening. They were unable to wash or change clothing and were without sanitation. In a letter that Fr. Carvalho wrote to another Jesuit, he noted: "We are all feeble and infirm in body, but we are sustained and consoled in spirit for God grants his favors in proportion to our sufferings."

Fr. Carvalho spent thirteen months in the enclosure and finally on August 24, 1624, word arrived from Nagasaki that the five prisoners were to be executed by slow fire. The next morning they were taken to the shore where they boarded a boat that took them to Hokonohara, near Shimabara. There the prisoners, with ropes about their necks, walked to the stakes awaiting them. Each held a crucifix in his hand, with eyes fixed on the figure of our Lord, and each sang psalms to God. Fr. Carvalho was the first to be fastened, and while the others were being tied to their stakes, he spoke to the onlookers. "You must understand that we are Christians and that we die of our free and voluntary accord for the faith of Christ our Lord." Because the execution was by slow fire, the wood around the stake was so arranged that it would not all go up in flames at once. The wood was lit, then there was great heat and finally the martyrs' clothes began to burn. The martyrdom lasted almost two hours and Fr. Carvalho and his companions returned their souls to the God who had made them. The longing that he had in his heart was now satisfied.

On May 7, 1867, Pope Pius IX beatified 205 Japanese martyrs, among them were the five who died near Shimabara on August 25, 1624. Fr. Michael Carvalho's memorial is celebrated by his Jesuit brethren on February 4.

Prayer

Almighty God, grant that this remembrance of your martyr, Blessed Michael Carvalho, may bring us joy. May we who depend upon his prayers glory in his entry into heaven. We ask this through our Lord Jesus Christ, your Son, who lives and reigns with you and the Holy Spirit, one God, for ever and ever.

August 26

Ven. Aloysius Mary Solari 1795–1829

Aloysius Solari was born on May 13, 1795, in Chiavari, in northern Italy; his baptismal name was Augustine. When he was eleven his father sent him to a Savona school operated by the Vincentians, in the hopes that his son would give up his love for amusement and settle down. After his father's death in 1807 there was a remarkable change in the youth; he now applied himself to his studies, received good grades, and developed a piety that was noted by his teachers. As he grew into adolescence, he felt more and more drawn to the priesthood, and when the Society of Jesus was restored on August 7, 1814, after having been suppressed for forty-one years, the youth decided that he should become a Jesuit.

His widowed mother vigorously opposed the idea; he was her only son and she knew not how she could manage without him. Because of his mother's pleas, he temporarily set aside his thoughts of the Jesuits, but never did he smother the desire within him. He then attended the University of Genoa and began his study of philosophy. The following year, however, he returned home and began his theological instruction under an Augustinian priest, a certain Fr. Piaggio. In his spare time the young man taught catechism to the local children and visited hospitals, the poor, and those in prison.

After he received minor orders, he again brought up the subject of the Jesuits to his mother, and again he received the same firm negative reply. Now, more than ever, he prayed to St. Aloysius Gonzaga to make it possible for him to enter the Society. A week after he had been ordained a deacon, he felt he could wait no longer, so he secretly left home and on September 27, 1817, presented himself at the Jesuit novitiate in Chieri. But the Jesuits would not accept him without his mother's consent. His mother finally agreed, and in gratitude to St. Aloysius for gaining this favor for him, he changed his name to Aloysius Mary. He entered the novitiate on October 2, 1817, and two years later on October 3, 1819, pronounced his three vows as a Jesuit. After completing his noviceship he taught rhetoric to upper classmen at the Jesuit school in Turin, but then in January 1820, because of poor health, was given the less demanding task of teaching grammar to younger boys.

In 1821 Aloysius went to Rome to complete his training, and there he was chosen to be among the first Jesuits to go to Naples to reopen the Jesuit college, after it had been closed for many years. While teaching his classes he also completed his theological studies and was ordained a priest in 1824, at age twenty-nine.

In December of that same year the young priest was sent to Benevento to teach in the newly-opened college and to assist in its parish. Fr. Solari became a powerful preacher and every Friday preached on the Sacred Heart of Jesus, a devotion he cultivated from the time of his entrance into the Society. His students in Benevento viewed him as an exemplary priest and many chose him as their confessor. In his own private life he was so given to penance and mortification that his superiors had to restrain him. In his desire for martyrdom he volunteered for the foreign missions, but before he could go to foreign lands, his death came to him.

Fr. Solari spent only five years in Benevento. Amid his fruitful labors, he became suddenly ill in early August 1829, presumably from scarlet fever, which rapidly carried him to his death on August 27. He was thirty-four years old and had been a Jesuit for twelve years.

Fr. Aloysius Solari's cause was introduced in Rome on December 12, 1906.

St. David Lewis 1616–1679

Martyr of Wales

Throughout his thirty-one years as a missionary in South Wales, Fr. David Lewis was commonly known as Mr. Charles Baker, but to the faithful to whom he ministered, he was *Tad y Tlodion,* "Father of the poor."

David Lewis was a Welshman, native of Abergevenny, Gwent, born in 1616. His father was a Protestant, his mother a Catholic, and of the nine children born into the Lewis family, David, the youngest, was the only one brought up Protestant. As a child he attended the Royal Grammar School where his father was headmaster, and then went to London to study law at the Middle Temple (1632). He made a long visit to Paris (about 1635) with a fellow student, the son of Viscount Savage, and there he became a Catholic. He returned to Abergevenny and lived with his parents and came to know his maternal uncle, John Pritchard, a Jesuit priest ministering in South Wales. Upon the death of his parents, the result of an epidemic, David left England in August 1638, and in the following November enrolled at the English College in Rome. He was ordained to the priesthood in the Eternal City on July 20, 1642, and entered the Jesuit Roman novitiate on April 19, 1645.

Fr. Lewis was sent to work in Wales in 1646, but after a year he was recalled to Rome to serve as spiritual director for the seminarians at the English College. In 1648 he returned to his homeland and made his headquarters at Cwm, a small village on the Hereford-Gwent border, where the Jesuits maintained a residence named after St. Francis Xavier. For the next three decades he worked tirelessly in the apostolate, showing special interest and care toward the poor and needy, and was twice superior of that district.

Because of the plot fabricated by Titus Oates alleging that the Jesuits were intent on Charles II's murder and the reestablishment of the Catholic faith in the land, anti-Catholic hatred ran high and the Jesuits were forced to leave their residence at Cwm to seek safety as each could find it. Fr. Lewis went to live in a small cottage in Llantarnam village, and there he was arrested, betrayed by an apostate couple. William James had once worked for nearly four years at the Jesuit residence in Cwm. Now that the Jesuits were hunted, William and his wife Dorothy, eager to earn the fifty pounds offered by the government for the capture of a Jesuit and the two hundred pounds offered by the Welsh magistrate John Arnold, a rabid Calvinist, decided to betray Fr. Lewis. The couple learned where the priest was living and passed the information on to Arnold. Before daybreak on Sunday, November 17, 1678, as Fr. Lewis was about to celebrate Mass, six soldiers burst into his cottage, apprehended the priest, and took him to Llanfoist, where Arnold and magistrates awaited them. With the Jesuit now in his hands, Arnold led him triumphantly to Abergevenny for interrogation. William and Dorothy James were there, and the husband testified that, while a servant at Cwm, he many times assisted at a Mass of Fr. Lewis. In view of this testimony, the Jesuit was committed to Monmouth Jail and charged with being a Catholic priest. For two months he lived in calm solitude and then on January 13, 1679, he was transferred to the prison at Usk. He was taken back to Monmouth for his trial on March 29, 1679, at which time several witnesses testified that they had attended his Masses and had seen him administering the sacraments. Though Fr. Lewis offered a defense, it was a foregone conclusion that the jury would bring in a verdict of guilty. This it did, and Fr. Lewis was sentenced to die as a traitor.

The execution of Fr. Lewis was not to take place immediately. He was then sent in May to London, where he underwent further interrogation. His examiners on this occasion were Oates, the mastermind behind the infamous plot, and his henchmen William Bedloe and Stephen Dugdale. After a long and detailed scrutiny they found that they could not lay any charge against the priest, and thus he returned to Usk, where he remained for another three months.

Finally, on August 27, 1679, Fr. Lewis was dragged to the gallows outside Usk to be executed. The speech he made on that occasion was so powerful that it was later published. He began: "I believe you are here met not only to see a fellow native die, but also with expectation to hear a dying fellow native speak. . . . I speak not as a murderer, thief, or such like malefactor, but as a Christian, and therefore am not ashamed." He then went on to assert his innocence with regard to any plot against the king and the kingdom, and to state that his examiners in London found nothing with which to charge him. He continued: "My religion is the Roman Catholic; in it I have lived above these forty years; in it I now die, and so fixedly die, that if all the good things in this world were offered me to renounce, all should not move me one hair's breadth from my Roman Catholic faith. A Roman Catholic I am; a Roman Catholic priest I am; a Roman Catholic priest of that religious order called the Society of Jesus I am, and I bless God who first called me. . . . Please now to observe, I was condemned for reading Mass, hearing confessions, administering the sacraments, and therefore dying for this I die for religion." He ended by telling his bystanders to be firm in their faith.

The oratory of Fr. Lewis so roused the people that the executioner feared the crowd would stone him if he went ahead with the hanging, and so he left the scene. A blacksmith was bribed to take his place and the execution proceeded. Fr. Lewis recollected himself in private prayer, and as he said the words: "Sweet Jesus, receive my soul," he was hanged and remained hanging until dead. His body was then taken down and his friends buried it in the churchyard of St. Mary's Priory in Usk.

Fr. David Lewis was sixty-three years old at the time of his death. He was beatified by Pope Pius XI on December 15, 1929, and canonized by Pope Paul VI on October 25, 1970. His memorial is celebrated on December 1.

Prayer

Almighty, eternal God, you chose from the people of England and Wales Saint David Lewis and his companions to be made like Christ, who died to save the world. Listen to their prayers; strengthen your Church by the same faith and love that strengthened them, and bless it always with your gift of unity. We ask this through our Lord Jesus Christ, your Son, who lives and reigns with you and the Holy Spirit, one God, for ever and ever.

August 28

St. Edmund Arrowsmith 1585–1628

Martyr of England

Edmund Arrowsmith was born in Haydock, in the parish of Winwick, south Lancashire, in 1585. His baptismal name was Brian. His parents were Catholics and because they had harbored priests in their home and had refused to attend Protestant services, they were persecuted for their steadfastness to the Catholic faith. When Brian's father died, an old priest in the neighborhood took the boy into his service and undertook his education. The youth attended the local grammar school and recited the first half of our Lady's office as he walked the mile to class and the other half on his return home. In December 1605, because all schools of higher education were Protestant, the twenty-year-old Brian went to the Continent to attend the English College at Douai. Shortly after his arrival, he was confirmed and adopted the name Edmund, after his father's brother, a priest at Douai. His studies were interrupted for a time because of poor health, but he was eventually ordained to the priesthood at Arras in December 1612, and in June 1613 he was sent on the English mission.

Fr. Arrowsmith's area of apostolic activity was in Lancashire, where he spent fifteen years. He is described as being undistinguished in appearance, but of great sincerity in nature, of great sweetness in conversation, and of indefatigable energy in fulfilling his priestly duties. He was somewhat outspoken and an early biographer wrote that he "often wished him merrily to carry salt in his pocket to season his actions, lest too much zeal without discretion might bring him too soon into danger." About ten years after Fr. Arrowsmith's return to England, he was arrested for the first time (probably in 1622) and imprisoned in

Lancaster Castle. During his time there he boldly argued religious questions with the Protestant Bishop of Chester, John Bridgeman. This incarceration, however, was not of long duration, for when the Prince of Wales became interested in the Infanta Maria, King James I, hoping to give the impression that he was friendly toward Catholics and thus promote his son's suit for the hand of the Spanish princess, magnanimously granted pardon to all Catholic priests in England's prisons.

Ever since he made the Spiritual Exercises under a Jesuit at Douai, Fr. Arrowsmith thought of entering the Society of Jesus. He finally did so on July 21, 1623, at Clerkenwell, London. He then spent two months in spiritual retreat and returned to Lancashire for the remaining five years of his life. During the summer of 1628 he was again apprehended, this time betrayed by a young man whom he had attempted to help. The young man was involved in an incestuous marriage and Fr. Arrowsmith tried to lead him back to virtue, but the gentleman took offense at the priest's advice and betrayed him to the local Justice of the Peace. Warned of the danger, Fr. Arrowsmith hurriedly rode off to Blackburn, but the priest-hunters overtook him on the road, caught him at Brindle Moss and committed him to the jail in Lancaster Castle under suspicion of being a priest. During his trial on August 26, he neither admitted nor denied his priesthood; he felt it was the court's duty to prove the charge rather than that he should condemn himself. When asked if he were a priest, he simply replied: "Would that I were worthy of being a priest." Though no proof was introduced against him, the jury still found him guilty of being a priest, a Jesuit, and of seducing others to the Catholic faith. This was viewed as high treason and he was condemned to death. On hearing his sentence, he fell to his knees, bowed his head, and said: "Thanks be to God!"

He was then taken back to prison, but was now placed in a small dark hole, where he was barely able to sit in a cramped position. He remained there for two days, preparing for his journey to heaven. On Thursday morning, August 28, he was informed that sentence was to be carried out that day. Shortly before noon he was dragged to the place of execution, less than a mile outside Lancaster. Upon his arrival, a Protestant minister attempted to get him to plead the king's mercy, but to this he answered that the only mercy he looked forward to was the mercy of heaven. As he approached the ladder leading to the gallows, he prayed for a time and was heard to say: "I freely offer Thee my death, O sweet Jesus, in satisfaction for my sins, and I wish this little blood of mine may be a sacrifice for them." He then kissed the ladder and went up and from that higher position he asked the Catholics present to pray with him. He prayed for the king and the kingdom, forgave his persecutors, and asked forgiveness of all whom he may have offended. Then he said: "Be witnesses with me that I die a constant Roman Catholic and for Jesus Christ's sake; let not my death be a hindrance to your well-doing and going forward in the Catholic religion, but rather an encouragement therein." He then pulled the cap over his head, fixed himself in prayer, and as he spoke the words, "O good Jesus!" the executioner pushed him from the ladder. He remained hanging until dead, and when cut down his body was disembowelled and quartered; the portions were then exposed on the walls of Lancaster Castle. He was forty-three years old, had spent fifteen years on the English mission and had been a Jesuit for five years.

Fr. Edmund Arrowsmith was beatified by Pope Pius XI on December 15, 1929, and canonized by Pope Paul VI on October 25, 1970. His memorial is celebrated on December 1, together with his Jesuit brethren who had given their lives for the faith in England and Wales.

Prayer

Almighty, eternal God, you chose from the people of England and Wales Saint Edmund Arrowsmith and his companions to be made like Christ, who died to save the world. Listen to their prayers; strengthen your Church by the same faith and love that strengthened them, and bless it always with your gift of unity. We ask this through our Lord Jesus Christ, your Son, who lives and reigns with you and the Holy Spirit, one God, for ever and ever.

August 31

S. G. Joseph Picco 1867–1946

Fr. Joseph Picco never held any important position in the Society; he was always someone's assistant. But it was his simplicity and humility that attracted countless people to seek him out as an adviser and confessor. He was born on July 4, 1867, at Nole Canavese, near Turin, in northern Italy, the third of ten children. He received his early education from his uncle, the parish priest, and in 1878 enrolled in the apostolic school of Canon Ortalda in Turin. In 1880, when he was thirteen, he transferred to the Salesian school at Lanzo, where he often served St. John Bosco's Mass. After finishing at Lanzo, he entered the archdiocesan seminary at Chieri in October 1883, where, after two years of study, he made a retreat at the Jesuit retreat house, Casa di Sant' Antonio, located near the seminary. When he completed the Spiritual Exercises of St. Ignatius his mind was made up to be a Jesuit, and he entered the novitiate at Chieri on September 22, 1885. Seven years later his younger brother Julius followed him into the Society. Julius once asked him why he had become a Jesuit rather than a Salesian because he had been educated by Salesians and had known Don Bosco. Joseph's answer was: "That was not my way."

Joseph pronounced his vows on November 13, 1887, and remained at Chieri for another two years studying the humanities. From 1889 to 1891 he taught at Turin's Social Institute and at St. Thomas College in Cuneo. While there he came down with pleurisy and its effects remained with him for the rest of his life. In October 1891 he returned to Chieri to begin his study of philosophy. Attracted to the Alaskan missions, he requested to go there in 1893, but his health was so poor that this was out of the question. In 1894 he returned to Turin's Social Institute and in October 1896 he was back at Chieri for his studies in theology.

Joseph always had great concern and love for the sick and he showed this concern during his student days. In November 1898, Fr. Romuald Fumagalli, in the last stages of cancer, arrived at Casa di Sant' Antonio to await death. He needed much care and with the infirmarian already overworked, Joseph volunteered to care for him. For seven months when he was not in class, he was at the priest's side, nursing him, bathing him, caring for him. Fr. Fumagalli died on July 5, 1899, and Joseph now looked forward to ordination scheduled for July 31. But Providence intervened. As a result of sacrificing himself for the dying priest, his own health broke, his ordination was postponed, and he was sent to Monaco to recuperate. It was only on April 8, 1901, that he was ordained to the priesthood.

During the years from 1901 to 1912, Fr. Picco fulfilled a variety of duties. He was confessor at the major seminary in Turin, and in 1904 went to the Jesuit parish in Genoa; from there he moved to the retreat house at Quarto al Mare. In 1909 he was spiritual father at Cuneo, and then in early 1912 he was made assistant pastor at San Remo. In October 1912 he was appointed assistant director of the retreat house in Gozzano, near Novara, and there he spent the remainder of his life. Besides giving the Spiritual Exercises he preached missions and novenas in the villages and taught catechism each Sunday to the children. He promoted the League of Perseverance and served as confessor to several communities of nuns and to the clergy. He was especially fond of the Forty Hours devotion and was particularly devoted to our Lord in the Blessed Sacrament. So highly did he honor the priesthood that in 1901 he had offered himself as a victim for priests who were unfaithful in their calling. He repeated this offering each day of his life. During World War I, when St. Thomas College moved from Cuneo to Gozzano as a result of the government taking over the school as a military hospital, Fr. Picco was sent to Cuneo as chaplain to the soldiers. His years at Gozzano were many and fruitful; his work was simple and without distinction in the eyes of men, but in the eyes of God it was a perfect offering.

Fr. Picco's health was always fragile and he often suffered from pulmonary trouble. The medical profession at that time obviously had no wonder drugs; the only remedy for his condition was to spend the summers in the mountains. In 1902 Fr. Picco went to Crissolo to regain his strength, which he continued to do almost every succeeding summer until 1945. But he was not one to lounge about doing nothing. He immediately threw himself into the local apostolate, hearing the confessions of the summer pilgrims who came to the shrine of St. Chiaffredo. He sought out the sick and the poor and brought them Communion and consolation. He taught catechism in the surrounding hamlets and initiated the daily recitation of the evening rosary. Over a period of forty-three years, Fr. Picco made his summer home at Crissolo, where the people loved him as much as he loved them.

As the years progressed, Fr. Picco slowed down but he did not stop. It was not until April 11, 1946, that he had the first intimation that death was approaching. On that date he was returning from taking Communion to a sick parishioner when he suffered an attack of pleurisy and was forced to go to bed. Good Friday was coming and he hoped to die on that day, but the physician's skill kept him alive; in fact he rallied so that when Pentecost came he was able to resume saying Mass. He celebrated his seventy-ninth birthday on July 4, and though his movements were slow and difficult, he was able to get around and continued to offer Mass. On August 6 an acquaintance noticed that he was now walking about and asked him whether he was getting better. Fr. Picco simply answered that he was not, but then added: "Do you know when I am going to die? I will die on the feast of St. Raymond Nonnatus, that is on August 31." Fr. Picco continued to speak in this manner throughout the month and when his brother Julius visited him on August 30, Fr. Picco asked him to take his Mass the following morning, but Julius never attached any importance to that request. Early on Saturday August 31, Julius went to the sacristy for Mass, but when he did not find his brother there, he went to his room and looked in. The light was on and Fr. Picco was prostrate on the floor. When the physician arrived to certify the death, he uttered words that were in everyone's mind: "We are not standing before the body of a man, but before the relics of a saint."

Fr. Picco's body was taken to the small chapel in the retreat house that same day. Lines of people came to see him for the last time, to touch him, and to request his intercession in heaven. He was buried on Monday, September 2. Fr. Joseph Picco's cause was introduced in Rome on December 10, 1973.

September

September 2

Bl. James Bonnaud 1740–1792

Bl. William Delfaud and 12 Companions 1733–1792

Martyrs of the French Revolution

In 1926 Pope Pius XI beatified 191 Frenchmen: 2 archbishops, 1 bishop, 176 priests, 6 seminarians, 5 laymen and 1 brother, all of whom were massacred in the early days of September 1792 during the French Revolution's first Reign of Terror. Of this number twenty-three were Jesuits. The story of these martyrs is part of the history of that revolution, which began with the storming of the Bastille on July 14, 1789. In its origins the French Revolution intended to right the wrongs the people suffered under an aristocratic rule, but little by little, the leaders of the revolution transformed it into a rabid anti-Catholic persecution. Prior to the revolution, French liberals had succeeded in 1762 in having the Jesuits suppressed in France, their schools closed, and the Jesuits either forced into exile or other ministries. Later in 1773, Pope Clement XIV, unable to withstand the pressure from various European governments, yielded to the French liberals' demands and suppressed the Society of Jesus throughout the world. The twenty-three blessed commemorated here on September 2 and 3 are sometimes called ex-Jesuits because their martyrdom took place during the years of the Society's suppression. Nevertheless, because they always remained Jesuits in desire and intention, Pope Pius XI honored them as Jesuits in the brief announcing their beatification.

The anti-Catholic character of the French Revolution can be seen by the decrees it enacted. On November 2, 1789, the National Constituent Assembly placed all ecclesiastical property at the disposal of the nation, and on February 13, 1790, it suppressed monastic vows, forbade religious orders to accept new members, and declared that monks and nuns were free to leave their monasteries. After the assembly had dealt with the religious orders, it turned its attention to the diocesan clergy and on July 12, 1790, enacted its infamous Civil Constitution of the Clergy. By this decree the assembly intended to constitute a national church in France, totally independent of the pope, and ordered that bishops and priests, now servants of the state, were to be elected by the people in the same way that civil magistrates were elected.

The assembly went still further on November 27, 1790, when it decreed that all clergy were to take an oath to support this Civil Constitution. The clergy recognized the constitution's anti-Catholic and anti-papal tenor, but some felt that they could take the oath with reservations, while others were of another opinion. Though the penalty for refusing to take the oath was loss of citizenship and priests were liable to prosecution as disturbers of the peace, nevertheless, when it came time for the oath to be taken in January 1791, only one-third of the parish clergy and only three of France's forty-four bishops took it. Those who refused the oath, that is, the nonjuring clergy, unfortunately, had to relinquish their parishes in favor of the "constitutional" clergy. Of the nonjuring priests, some left France for neighboring countries and others went to Paris, where it was possible to live in anonymity and secretly minister to the Catholics who chose to remain faithful to the Church. Many of these priests, unable to officiate in public, took positions as chaplains in the many convents of Paris.

Being divided, the French clergy turned to the pope for guidance and direction. Pope Pius VI, who had a higher opinion of King Louis XVI than anyone else at the time, confidently felt that the French monarch would satisfactorily solve his country's problems and, hence, delayed any pronouncement. But the King's weakness was made clear in December 1790 when he confirmed the clergy's obligation to take the oath to support the Civil Constitution. The pope, now realizing the gravity of the situation in France, issued two briefs in 1791, one dated March 10 and the other April 13, in which he condemned the Constitution as being based on heretical principles. He also denied that ecclesiastical power depends on civil authority or that the election of pastors in the Church belongs to the people. When the condemnation by Pius was made known in France, many priests who had previously taken the oath now retracted; and those who had not taken it were encouraged in their struggle against the government's anti-Catholicism. In October 1791 the Legislative Assembly succeeded the Constituent Assembly and among its enactments it repeated the decree that nonjurors were to take the oath; they would otherwise be suspect of rebellion against the country. The nonjuring clergy, however, remained at peace in their decision to be faithful to the Church.

While France was suffering its revolution, new difficulties arose from its neighbors. Both Prussia and Austria viewed the French Revolution as a threat; therefore, in order to protect themselves and their monarchical governments, they invaded France. War was declared on April 10, 1792, and the days of Louis as an ineffective ruler were numbered. On August 9, 1792, a mob of rebels, filled with revolutionary and egalitarian ideals, overthrew the king and cast the royal family into prison. The following day the assembly announced the official dissolution of the monarchy and in its place established a commune. This was the beginning of the Reign of Terror. Between August 15 and August 31 the assembly passed laws almost daily against the nonjuring clergy and on the 26th it decreed their deportation to South America. After the commune took over the city, revolutionaries roamed through Paris searching for and arresting all the nonjuring priests they could find. Because the prisons were already crowded with political prisoners, the commune turned several Paris seminaries and monasteries into improvised prisons for priests.

Though the assembly talked of deporting the nonjuring clergy, their fate was determined by the commune's more radical members who directed a certain Commissar Stanislas Maillard to see to the clergymen's dispatch. Maillard was instructed to keep the cries of the dying to a minimum and to take enough brooms with him to sweep away the blood. On the morning of September 2, 1792, news arrived that the Prussians had taken Verdun, a city 150 miles from the capital, and the frightened Parisians thought Paris would be next. That fact and a rumor that the prisoners were plotting an uprising convinced the revolutionaries that Sunday, September 2, was a good time to carry out their plan.

That afternoon Commissar Maillard and his men initiated the massacre by going to the Abbey of Saint-Germain-des-Prés, where they forced their way into the building. They called the prisoners before them, and as each priest refused to take the oath to support the Civil Constitution, he was condemned on the spot and struck down with a sabre. Twenty-one of the blessed died at the abbey that day, but there were no Jesuits among them. Finishing his task about 3:30 P.M., Maillard suggested that with nothing more to do at the abbey, they could go to the Carmelites, where more than a hundred priests were imprisoned in the monastery chapel.

Maillard's group, now augmented by blood-thirsty bandits and cutthroats, forced open the gates of the monastery garden. At that hour of the afternoon a number of priest-prisoners were taking their exercise. The invading murderers jumped upon them and butchered and clubbed them to death. Most priests were still locked in the chapel. Maillard, in a desire to give his massacre the semblance of a trial, set up a table outside the chapel door and called the priests out two at a time. Standing before the commissar, each priest was asked to take the oath. When he refused he was thrown against the chapel steps and became the target of slashing sabres and jabbing bayonets, of swinging clubs and well-aimed guns. When the bodies were removed, two more priests were called forth, and so the proceedings went on until ninety-five priests were martyred. Of this number fourteen were Jesuits; their names and brief descriptions are below.

Fr. James Julius Bonnaud was born on October 27, 1740, in the West Indies, in the city of Cap Français, today's Cap Haitien, Haiti. He was taken to France as a child (about 1753), and was educated at the Jesuit school in La Flèche. He entered the Society on December 20, 1758, and after his early formation, taught for two years at Quimper, Brittany. When the Jesuits were expelled from France in 1762, he entered the seminary of Saint-Firmin and then went to Flanders (1764), where he earned degrees in theology and canon law. On his return to France, he joined the diocese of Paris. He authored several scholarly works and in 1788 was transferred to Lyons, where the archbishop made him his vicar general. Fr. Bonnaud wrote the archbishop's 1789 Lenten pastoral letter and in it he warned the faithful of an imminent persecution against all institutions, political, civil, and religious. Fr. Bonnaud then moved to Paris (1791) and continued to write tracts and booklets against the revolutionaries and their anti-papal Civil Constitution. Because he staunchly defended the rights of the Church and spoke out against the revolution and its ideals, the revolutionaries were especially eager to silence him. Finally arrested sometime after August 10, 1792, he was among those imprisoned in the Carmelite monastery and there he died for Christ on September 2.

Fr. William Anthony Delfaud was born on April 5, 1733, at L'Estang-de-Lol, near Daglan, in today's diocese of Sarlat. He entered the Jesuits on October 21, 1752, at Toulouse. After his early years of study, he taught for a time at Mauriac, Montpellier, and Cahors, and then went to Tournon for theology (1761). Still a student for the priesthood when the French Jesuits were suppressed in 1762, he returned to his home diocese to complete his courses and was ordained in 1764. He remained at the Sarlat seminary as professor until 1770. When his uncle retired as archpriest of Daglan, Fr. Delfaud succeeded him, and when the diocesan clergy sought someone to represent them at the States General at Versailles, Fr. Delfaud was elected (1789). In Paris he saw the growing strength of the anti-Catholic movement and in 1790 wrote a public letter to his parishioners, *The Friend of Peace, or a Letter by a Curate, Member of the National Assembly, to His Parishioners on the Troubles that Afflict His Province.* In January 1791 Fr. Delfaud refused to take the oath to support the Civil Constitution and together with Fr. Claude Laporte published, in that same year, their reasons, *A Statement to Their Electors, with Some Observations on Public Order and on Religion so Necessary for Its Reestablishment.* In this statement both priests attested their willingness to shed their blood for religion's sake. Because of his firm and unrelenting opposition to the revolution, Fr. Delfaud was especially singled out and was finally arrested sometime after August 10, 1792, while at the Eudists, a congregation founded by St. John Eudes. He was held at the Carmelite monastery and a few hours before his martyrdom on September 2, he sent this message to friends: "Tell them that I have never felt better nor happier."

Fr. Francis Balmain was born at Luzy in the present diocese of Nevers, on May 25, 1733, and entered the Jesuits on July 20, 1753. After his years of early training, he taught at Rheims, Autun, and Chaumont, then went to Pont-à-Mousson for theology and was ordained in 1764. Because the duke of Lorraine had refused to allow the Society to be suppressed in his territory, the Jesuits there continued their schools under his protection, and Fr. Balmain remained at Pont-à-Mousson teaching theology. After the duke's death, however, the Lorraine parlement voted in 1768 to suppress the Jesuits and Fr. Balmain returned to Luzy, where he resided for a few years. He then went to Paris and in March 1778 became chaplain for the Daughters of the Cross. Sometime after August 10, 1792, he was arrested at the house of the Eudists, where he had been living, and was taken to the Carmelite monastery and there martyred.

Fr. *Charles Bérauld du Pérou* was born in Meursac, in the diocese of La Rochelle, on November 17, 1737, and entered the Jesuits in Paris on September 19, 1753. He made his studies at the Jesuit college of Louis le Grand in Paris and then taught at La Flèche. When the Society was suppressed in Paris (1762), he entered the seminary of Saint-Firmin and then in 1765 went to Pont-à-Mousson in Lorraine, where the Jesuits still maintained their schools. When the duke of Lorraine died in 1766 and the Lorraine parlement voted to suppress the Society of Jesus two years later, he may have entered the Eudists in Paris. Over the years he exercised various offices in their houses, and it was at their residence in Paris that he was arrested sometime after August 10, 1792. He was taken with other priests to the Carmelite monastery and martyred on September 2.

Fr. *Claude Cayx-Dumas* was born on November 6, 1724, at Martel, near Cahors, in southern France. He entered the Society on October 8, 1744, at Toulouse, and after noviceship and philosophy taught for several years. After theology and ordination he taught at Clermont College and then in Carcassonne. When the Society was suppressed in Paris (1762), he devoted himself to apostolic works, which he exercised for a period of twenty-five years, eighteen of which were spent in the diocese of Paris. In 1790 he became chaplain to the Ursuline Sisters of Saint-Cloud in Versailles. Now in his late sixties, he retired to the St. Francis de Sales Home for priests at Issy, outside Paris, and was arrested there on August 15, 1792, together with two other Jesuits, Frs. Claude Gagnières des Granges and Francis Vareilhe-Duteil. They were taken to the Carmelite monastery in Paris and were martyred on September 2.

Fr. *John Charton de Millou* was born in Lyons on October 17, 1736, and entered the Society in the same city on September 7, 1751. After noviceship and philosophy, he taught at Embrun, Bourg-en-Bresse, and Roanne. He began his theology in 1761, but when the Society was suppressed the following year he finished his course in a diocesan seminary and was ordained. In 1767 the archbishop of Paris appointed him chaplain to the Sisters of the Most Blessed Sacrament. He was a well known preacher in Paris and an excellent spiritual director. Through these special gifts of his he helped bring many into the Church, but this success also made him the special prey of his persecutors. For greater security in his ministry, he changed his name to de Millou, but this did not save him from the hands of his captors. He was arrested in August 1792 and detained in the Carmelite monastery, where he was martyred.

Fr. *James Friteyre-Durvé* was born on April 18, 1726, at Marsac, in the Auvergne, and entered the Society at Toulouse on August 30, 1742. He taught in various schools, then did his theological studies at Tournon and was ordained in 1755. At the forced dispersion of the Society in France in 1762, he worked for a time in his home diocese and then went to Paris, where he became a renowned preacher. In 1775 he preached a series of Lenten sermons at the royal court and in 1777 preached another series at Notre Dame cathedral. In recognition of his accomplishments Louis XVI granted him a pension and made him a canon at Saint-Denis. He relinquished this office in 1784 in order to live a community life with the Eudists, but when the revolution came with its persecution of the Church, he initiated a new ministry. Dressed as a street merchant, carrying his wares on his back, he went through Paris visiting the houses of Catholics, especially of those who were sick and dying. He frequently changed his residence to escape the notice of the revolutionaries; nevertheless, he was arrested toward the end of August 1792, and when he refused to subscribe to the Civil Constitution, was imprisoned in the Carmelite monastery. He was one of the first to be martyred there, walking in the monastery garden, when Maillard and his men broke down the garden gate and clubbed them to death.

Fr. Claude Gagnières des Granges was born in Chambéry, Savoy, on May 23, 1722, and joined the Society at Toulouse on September 12, 1740. He was ordained in Paris in 1753 and was so successful a teacher that one of his students had said of him: "He was a man who had read everything and forgot nothing." His activity during the years between the Society's suppression in France (1762) and his martyrdom in 1792 is lost to history. It is known that in 1787, or thereabouts, he was residing at the St. Francis de Sales Home at Issy, a hospice for retired priests. He was arrested there on August 15, 1792, and taken to the Carmelite monastery, where he was martyred.

Fr. Claude Laporte was born at Brest, Brittany, on December 6, 1734. He entered the Society in Paris on September 24, 1753, and taught between the years 1756 and 1762. Not yet ordained when the Paris parlement suppressed the Jesuits in 1762, he enrolled in a diocesan seminary and was probably ordained in Brest in September 1763. From 1766 to 1769 he was director of an artisan's sodality in Brittany, and from 1776 to 1786 was chaplain at the Brest Naval College. From there he was assistant pastor at Saint-Louis parish, and after he refused to take the demanded oath, he left Brest for Paris, where he was arrested on August 17, 1792, imprisoned and later martyred.

Fr. Mathurin Le Bous de Villeneuve (de la Villecrohaine) was born in Rennes on December 19, 1731. He entered the Jesuits in Paris on September 27, 1751, and after the Society's suppression in France (1762), became chaplain to the Benedictine Sisters on rue Bellechasse in Paris. He was arrested in the latter part of August 1792 and incarcerated in the Carmelite monastery, where he was clubbed to death on September 2.

Fr. Charles Le Gué was born at Rennes on October 6, 1724. On December 28, 1741, he entered the Society in Paris, and after the usual Jesuit training, taught during the years 1745 to 1750. From 1752 to 1761 he was at the college of Louis le Grand, first as a student of theology and then, after ordination, as a prefect of students. In 1762 when the French Jesuits were suppressed and their schools closed, he took to preaching. He preached the annual series of Advent and Lenten sermons in Parisian churches and in 1783 gave the Lenten series before the royal court in Versailles. Felt called to live in community, he joined (February 2, 1791) Fr. Peter Joseph de Clorivière and four other like-minded priests in founding the Society of the Sacred Heart of Jesus, a congregation in imitation of the suppressed Society of Jesus. After August 10, 1792, he was arrested in Paris for his refusal to support the Civil Constitution and was held in the Carmelite monastery, where he met his martyrdom on September 2.

Fr. Vincent Le Rousseau de Rosancoat was born at Chateauneuf, in the diocese of Quimper, Brittany, on July 3, 1726. He studied at the Jesuit college in Quimper and at seventeen entered the Society in Paris on October 11, 1743. He did philosophy and theology at Louis le Grand in Paris and was ordained. From 1754 to 1762 he taught philosophy at Nevers, and after the suppression of the French Jesuits in 1762, returned to his hometown to continue his priestly ministry. From 1775 to 1780 he was chaplain to a convent of Ursuline Sisters at Carhaix in Normandy, and from 1780 he was in Paris as chaplain to the Sisters of the Visitation on rue du Bac. In late August 1792 the revolutionaries came to the convent seeking another priest, but finding Fr. Le Rousseau, they arrested him and placed him in the Carmelite monastery, where he was butchered on September 2.

Fr. Loup Thomas-Bonnotte was born on September 13, 1719, at Entrains in the present diocese of Nevers and entered the Jesuits in Nancy, on September 7, 1734. He followed the regular course of studies in the Society, was ordained, and entered on a successful career in the classroom, teaching Scripture, literature, and mathematics. With the French government's closing of the Jesuit schools in 1762, he returned to his home diocese and there carried on his priestly ministry until 1772, when he went to Paris and became chaplain to the Ursuline Sisters on rue Saint-Jacques. He was arrested in the latter part of August 1792 for refusing to take the oath and was taken to the Carmelite monastery and martyred there. He was the oldest of the twenty-three Jesuit martyrs of the French Revolution.

Fr. Francis Vareilhe-Duteil was born at Felletin, in the diocese of Limoges, on June 15, 1734, and joined the Society at Fontenay on November 22, 1751. He did his philosophy at Bordeaux and taught at Poitiers, where he also did his theology. When the French Jesuits were suppressed and expelled in 1762, he became a canon in a parish in Nancy. During the summer of 1792, however, he went for a period of rest to the St. Francis de Sales Home for retired priests in Issy, and there on Wednesday, August 15, 1792, he was arrested with ten other priests for having refused to take the required oath. That evening he was imprisoned in the chapel of the Carmelite monastery and was martyred on September 2.

These fourteen Jesuits and the nine who are listed under September 3, were beatified by Pope Pius XI on October 17, 1926, and Jesuits liturgically celebrate their memorial on January 19.

Prayer

Lord, it was for the defense of the rights of your Church that your holy martyrs, Blessed James Bonnaud, William Delfaud and companions gave their lives, strengthened by the Spirit's own courage. Hear our prayer and make us always love your Church as her loyal and devoted children. We ask this through our Lord Jesus Christ, your son, who lives and reigns with you and the Holy Spirit, one God, for ever and ever.

September 3

Bl. Alexander Lanfant and 8 Companions 1726–1792

Martyrs of the French Revolution

After the dreadful massacre of the nonjuring priests at the Abbey of Saint-Germain-des-Prés and the Carmelite monastery, the Parisian rabble had still not satisfied its thirst for martyrs' blood. During the early hours of September 3, 1792, the mob advanced to the improvised prison in the Vincentian seminary of Saint-Firmin, where some ninety priests were imprisoned. At 5:30 A.M. the still blood-stained assassins invaded the seminary and ordered the priests on to the street, where the crowd greeted them with "Death! Death!" If the assassins hoped that this demonstration of the crowd would frighten the priests into accepting the Civil Constitution they were soon proven wrong. The priests were ordered to return within the seminary and each appeared before a hastily set-up tribunal. Within an hour or so seventy-two priests died because they chose to be faithful to their religion and their Church. Some priests were butchered, others beheaded, and still others thrown out the windows to be clubbed to death by the waiting crowd. The bodies of the victims were stripped, mutilated, and piled on a carriage to be carted away. Of those who died at Saint-Firmin, seven were Jesuits.

The massacre was still not over, for during the early hours of September 4 the mob advanced to La Force, a prison for political and aristocratic undesirables, where a few nonjuring priests were also detained. The mob formed itself into two lines in front of the prison and demanded that the prisoners be brought forward so that justice could be carried out. When the prisoners did appear they were forced to walk between the lines of ruffians and endure the blows, strokes, and jabs of brutish men. The priests were expected to recite the oath supporting the Civil Constitution, but since they refused they were killed on the spot. Their bodies were then torn to pieces and thrown outside onto the street. Among those who died at La Force, three are numbered among the blessed, and of these three one was a Jesuit, Fr. Francis Le Livec.

During this madness of early September it is estimated that some 1,400 individuals were executed, 217 of whom were priests. Because there was in some cases insufficient evidence, not all were beatified on October 17, 1926. Of these blessed, twenty-three were Jesuits and the Society celebrates their memorial on January 19.

The Jesuit blessed who died between September 3 and 5 are:

Fr. Alexander Charles Lanfant was born in Lyons on September 9, 1726, and entered the Society in Avignon on September 7, 1741. After his Jesuit training and ordination, he taught at Aix, Besançon, and Marseilles. When the Society was suppressed in Paris in 1762, he went to Lorraine, where he continued his ministry under the protection of the duke, who had refused to suppress the Society in his territory. When the duke died in 1766 and the Lorraine parlement voted the Society's suppression (1768), Fr. Lanfant went to Vienna, where for three years he was preacher at the court of Empress Maria Theresa. He returned to Paris and became preacher at the court of Louis XVI, and from 1789 to 1791 served as the king's confessor. Because he was thought to have had too great an influence on the French monarch, the revolutionaries were particularly eager to arrest him. He was finally apprehended during the night of August 29–30, 1792, while staying at a certain bookbinder's residence, and then imprisoned at the Abbey of Saint-Germain-des-Prés. Some days prior to the arrest, a priest, who had supported the Civil Constitution, went to visit the bookbinder on business and recognized Fr. Lanfant, but had nothing to do with the latter's arrest. When this "constitutional" priest heard that the mob was on its way to massacre the prisoners at Saint-Germain, he went to his friends among the city magistrates and secured an order that Fr. Lanfant was not to be touched, but was to be moved to a safe place. Thus, without ever knowing the reason, he escaped being martyred on September 2. The following afternoon he was set free, once more through the efforts of the same priest. As Fr. Lanfant was walking away from the prison some people recognized him and began to cry out for his death, but police officers, who had kept him in view since he had left the prison, came between him and the crowd, and to save him from the mob's wrath returned him to the prison. On September 5 when the prison gates were opened and the revolutionaries entered, they recognized Fr. Lanfant; their hatred was so overpowering that they rushed toward him and dragged him out on to the street and killed him.

Fr. René Andrieux was born in Rennes, northern France, on February 16, 1742. He was first educated at the Jesuit school in his native city and entered the Society in Paris on September 27, 1761, just one year before the liberals in the French parlement voted the Society's suppression. Intent on becoming a priest, he transferred to a seminary in Laon operated by a group of priests known as the Community of St. Nicholas du Chardonnet. He joined this group and in 1776 became director of its seminary. In 1786 he was elected superior general of the congregation. When in January 1791 the government ordered all clergy to subscribe to the Civil Constitution, Fr. Andrieux and his priests resolutely refused. It was at his seminary that he and other members of his congregation were arrested on August 13, 1792, and imprisoned in the seminary of Saint-Firmin, where they met their death on September 3. Of the twenty-three Jesuits martyred during the French Revolution, Fr. Andrieux was the youngest.

Fr. John Benoît-Vourlat was born in southern France in Lyons, on March 26, 1731, and entered the Jesuits on September 7, 1746, in the city of his birth. After his years of study and ordination in the Society, he taught literature and philosophy at Lyons, Marseilles, and Besançon. He became known for his special ability in directing souls, and sometime after the suppression of the French Jesuits (1762), he went to Paris, where he became chaplain to the Sisters of Perpetual Adoration of the Blessed Sacrament. Advancing in age, he took up residence in the house of the Eudists, where he was arrested on August 30, 1792, and imprisoned at Saint-Firmin. He was beheaded on September 3.

Fr. Peter Guérin du Rocher was born at Sainte-Honorine-la Guillaume, in the diocese of Séez, on March 1, 1731. He studied at the Jesuit school at Caen and entered the Society in Paris on September 10, 1745. He did his philosophical and theological studies at Louis le Grand in Paris, was ordained in 1760, then taught philosophy at Bourges until the French Jesuits were suppressed (1762). In 1764 he left France and went to Italy, then Germany, and settled for a while in Poland, where he taught canon law and became interested in Oriental languages. As a result of his studies he published *The True History of Fabled Times* (Paris, 1777), in which he maintained that the narrations found in the books of the Pentateuch were not derived entirely from Egyptian legends, as the French Encyclopedists held, but were based on true events that had been somewhat transfigured in the telling. Having achieved renown for his scholarship, the archbishop of Paris named him director of a house of new converts in Paris and Queen Marie-Antoinette chose him as her confessor. Now much too influential a priest for the revolutionaries to ignore, they arrested him on August 13, 1792, together with his Jesuit brother Robert. They were taken to Saint-Firmin, where they were martyred on September 3.

Fr. Robert Guérin du Rocher was born at Repas, in the diocese of Séez, on October 23, 1736, and entered the Jesuits in Paris on September 25, 1752, six years after his brother Peter. After his early studies in the Society, he went in 1757 to teach at Nevers and then in 1762 taught literature at Eu. Still unordained when the Jesuits were suppressed in 1762, he traveled to Asia Minor, apparently, to work in the Near East mission. It is not known where or when he finished his theology and was ordained, but he was pastor in Salonika (then under Turkish rule), between the years 1769 and 1773. He was eventually expelled by the Turks, it seems, because of the conversions he had made, and returned to Paris, where he was spiritual director for the Sisters of the Visitation on rue du Bac. In 1782 he was chaplain at the Salpétrière, a Paris home for the aged. In France he published his *Letter of an Apostolic Missionary and Curate in the Levant to the Archbishop of Paris on the Present State of Religion among the Greeks*. In 1790 he went to live with his brother Peter, the director of a house for new converts in Paris, and there he was arrested on August 13, 1792, and taken to Saint-Firmin, where he died a martyr's death on September 3.

Fr. Elias Herque du Roule was born in Lyons on May 31, 1741, and entered the Society in the same city on September 7, 1758. Very little is known about him except that he taught at Marseilles between 1761 and 1762, and at Dôle until 1765, and that he studied theology at Avignon. He was arrested on August 13, 1792, while engaged as chaplain at a foundling home in Paris, imprisoned at Saint-Firmin, and beheaded on September 3.

Fr. John Seconds was born in Rodez on September 3, 1734, and entered the Jesuits on November 6, 1750, at Toulouse. He followed the regular course of training in the Society and was ordained to the priesthood in the same year that the French parlement decreed the suppression of the Jesuits (1762). He became associated with the hospital of Our Lady of Mercy in Paris and was likewise engaged in preaching. Between the years 1780 and 1786 he had preached several times before the king. He was arrested at the hospital on August 10, 1792, for his refusal to submit to the demands of the Civil Constitution, was imprisoned at Saint-Firmin, and was martyred on September 3.

Fr. Nicholas Verron was born on November 7, 1740, at Quimperlé, in Brittany, and joined the Jesuits on September 15, 1757, in Paris. After ordination he was assigned to teach at Louis le Grand in Paris. What he did immediately after the Society was suppressed in 1762 is not known, but he was in the Netherlands between 1774 and 1778, and in 1779 was in Paris, where he served as chaplain to the Sisters of St. Aura. On August 10, 1792, the nuns were forced from their convent by the revolutionaries and Fr. Verron kept in touch with the dispersed congregation until he himself was arrested on August 18. He was incarcerated at Saint-Firmin and martyred on September 3.

Fr. Francis Le Livec was born at Quimper in Brittany, on May 5, 1726, and entered the Jesuits in Paris on September 29, 1741. After he pronounced his vows, he studied philosophy at Louis le Grand in Paris, and then taught for a period of five years at Amiens. He did his theological studies at Rouen and after ordination was placed in charge of the sodality in that city. He was then transferred to Brittany, where he taught philosophy at Vannes and was made treasurer of the Jesuit school at Brest. With the suppression of the French Jesuits (1762), he went to northern Italy and Germany, where he taught French, physics, and mathematics, but after some years returned to France, where he became chaplain in a hospital in Tours, and later moved to Paris to become chaplain to the Daughters of Calvary. He was arrested sometime after August 10, 1792, and was taken to La Force prison where he was beheaded on September 4.

Prayer

Lord, it was for the defense of the rights of your Church that your holy martyrs, Blessed Alexander Lanfant and companions gave their lives, strengthened by the Spirit's own courage. Hear our prayer and make us always love your Church as her loyal and devoted children. We ask this through our Lord Jesus Christ, your Son, who lives and reigns with you and the Holy Spirit, one God, for ever and ever.

September 4

Bl. Anthony Ishida 1570–1632

Martyr of Japan

Of the 205 Japanese martyrs beatified in 1867, Fr. Anthony Ishida and his five non-Jesuit companions were the last to die. The Great Persecution, begun in 1614 with Shogun Iyeyasu's decree proscribing the Christian faith and ordering the banishment of all missionaries, continued for ten years after Fr. Ishida's death. During those ten years there were more martyrs and among them some forty Jesuits.

Fr. Anthony Ishida was born in 1570, in Shimabara, of Catholic parents whose Portuguese name was Pinto. He attended the Jesuit seminary at Arima and for a time worked with the Jesuits as a catechist. He entered the Society as a novice in January 1589. Anthony was a student of theology when Taikosama Hideyoshi ordered the execution of twenty-six martyrs on Nagasaki's holy hill, among whom were the Jesuits Paul Miki and his two companions. With persecution in the air, Anthony went into hiding. When peace returned with the Taikosama's death in 1598, he continued his studies and was probably ordained in 1612, or perhaps earlier. Fr. Ishida was conversant with the teachings of Buddhism and was frequently asked to partake in religious disputes with Buddhist bonzes. Invariably he won the debates and became so formidable an opponent that the bonzes pleaded illness rather than face him. He was an eloquent preacher, one of the best apologists the Japanese Church had at the time, and his fame spread throughout southern Japan.

With Iyeyasu's decree of 1614 Fr. Ishida went underground, as did two dozen other Jesuits, and clandestinely he practiced his ministry in and around Hiroshima, moving about in disguise, always risking his life for his sheep. In 1616 he was imprisoned for almost three years, but when the daimyo who had imprisoned him died in 1619, he was set free by the new daimyo. He then went to Nagasaki and resumed his undercover ministry for another ten years.

Fr. Ishida's labors came to an end with his arrest on November 14, 1629, after he had attended a sick Christian in Nagasaki. He was taken before Takenaka Uneme, governor of Nagasaki, who had recently renewed efforts to extirpate Christianity. The governor treated his prisoner with respect and courtesy and asked him to debate several distinguished bonzes who, finally, withdrew from the dispute. Uneme was more impressed by Fr. Ishida's manner of exposition than by the content of the debate and considered setting him free. But he feared that if he did so, it would be reported to the shogun. Hence Fr. Ishida was cast into prison in Omura on December 10, 1629, and there he met five others awaiting martyrdom: three Augustinian priests, one Japanese priest, and a Franciscan tertiary.

Fr. Ishida remained in prison for two years until November 1631, when Uneme again tried to get him to deny his faith. The governor arranged a disputation with the Confucian scholar, Saito Gonnai, and throughout the two-day discussion Fr. Ishida would neither join the Buddhist sect nor deny Christianity. When told his conversion was the will of the shogun, he replied: "The will of the shogun cannot prevail over the will of God, the universal Lord." Unable to get him to apostatize, Uneme resorted to torture. Some distance from Omura at Unzen, there is an extinct volcano with pools of scalding sulphurous waters known as "the mouths of hell." Today it is a health spa, but many a martyr had died there. In December 1631 Fr. Ishida and companions were taken to Unzen, stripped of their clothing, and one at a time immersed in the boiling water until their flesh began to blister. They were then taken out and an attending physician applied a medical treatment. The torture was repeated six times a day for thirty-three days, at the end of which their bodies were open wounds of rotting flesh. Through the strength that God gives martyrs, Fr. Ishida and companions steadfastly remained loyal to God. Acknowledging defeat, the soldiers supervising the torture returned the prisoners to Nagasaki in early January 1632.

The news of Fr. Ishida's and his companions' victory over torture spread through the Nagasaki district and many Japanese Christians were strengthened in their faith. For eight more months they lingered in a Nagasaki prison until Uneme decided he had had enough. On the morning of September 3, all five prisoners were secretly taken to Martyrs' Hill, outside the city, to die by slow fire. At the hill the prisoners saw the stakes and wood awaiting them. They embraced each other, and still refusing to apostatize they were fastened to the stakes. They prayed aloud and called upon God to give them the strength to persevere to the end. That grace was granted them, and when the fire had burned itself out the executioners took the martyrs' ashes and cast them into the sea.

Fr. Anthony Ishida and his five companions were among the 205 martyrs beatified by Pope Pius IX on May 7, 1867. Fr. Ishida is liturgically commemorated in the Society on February 4.

Prayer

Almighty God, grant that this remembrance of your martyr, Blessed Anthony Ishida, may bring us joy. May we who depend upon his prayers glory in his entry into heaven. We ask this through our Lord Jesus Christ, your Son, who lives and reigns with you and the Holy Spirit, one God, for ever and ever.

Bl. Thomas Tsuji 1570–1627

Martyr of Japan

Fr. Thomas Tsuji stood before his judge and when asked who he was, whence he came, and what he was doing, he responded: "For many years the people of Nagasaki have seen Thomas Tsuji, a religious of the Society of Jesus, and have heard him preach the Christian message. I am he, and I am prepared to uphold with my life and to testify with my blood to the truths that I have faithfully taught." Because Christianity had been proscribed in Japan since 1614 and missionaries were forbidden to preach the Christian faith, Fr. Tsuji was found guilty and sent to a prison in Omura.

Fr. Tsuji was born of a noble Japanese family in Sonogi, near Omura, about 1570. His early education was with the Jesuits in Arima. He entered the Society in January 1589 and was ordained a priest in Nagasaki sometime before 1613. He was an excellent preacher and his fame spread throughout southern Japan. Because he was outspoken in his condemnation of the scandalous conduct of some of the Christian Japanese in the city, he was transferred to Hakata and was exercising his priestly ministry there when the edict of 1614 ordered the banishment of all Catholic priests. Obeying the order, as did eighty other Jesuits, Fr. Tsuji went to Macao and remained there for four years. In August 1618, disguised as a merchant, he returned to his native land and secretly resumed his apostolic work. Unlike the European Jesuits who had to stay indoors during the day and minister only in the dark of night, Fr. Tsuji worked day and night, achieving great success. He went about his missionary work in disguise; sometimes he appeared as a prosperous Japanese gentleman, and at other times as an artisan, but his favorite disguise was the humble wood seller who could knock at the doors of Christian homes without being noticed.

As the persecution against Christians grew in intensity and his own workload increased every day, Fr. Tsuji found his energy waning. His brother Jesuits were being martyred and he wondered whether he could match their heroic example. Doubting himself, but not his faith, he yielded to uncertainty and depression. Finding it difficult to continue living up to the ideals that the Society demanded of its men, he was released from his religious vows in late 1619.

Within a short time after his departure from the Society, he requested to be readmitted. Immediate readmission was impossible, but the Jesuit superiors kindly permitted him to go through a period of probation. This lasted six years, during which time he showed himself a more zealous missionary by exposing himself to countless dangers in order to help other Christians. He was readmitted into the Society in 1626 and was assigned to continue his work in Nagasaki, where he was captured.

Fr. Tsuji had been living with a devout Christian, Louis Maki, and his son John. On the morning of July 21, 1626, just moments after he had celebrated Mass, which the Makis attended, the house was unexpectedly invaded by soldiers and the three were taken prisoner. Fr. Tsuji appeared before the district governor, admitted that he was a Jesuit priest, and was ordered to a prison in Omura. Louis and John Maki were likewise committed to prison on the charges of collaborating with a priest and offering him hospitality.

While in prison Fr. Tsuji had to endure the visits from members of his family, who endlessly asked him to think of them and not bring shame upon them. They insisted that he give up the Christian religion and come and live with them. But he replied: "What you ask me to do is wrong, and even if you offered me a thousand Japans, or the whole world, I could not do it."

After thirteen months of incarceration the three prisoners were taken in September 1627 to Nagasaki to receive sentence. On September 7 they were led outside the city to the hill made holy by many martyrs and there they were tied to stakes. Fr. Tsuji turned to his companions, comforted them, and urged them to think of Christ's passion. When the fire was set to the faggots about the stakes, he blessed his companions, raised his eyes to heaven and prayed silently. When the flames began to twirl and wrap themselves about his body, he chanted the psalm: *Praise the Lord, All You Nations.* Many witnesses have attested that a few moments prior to his death his breast burst open and from it there issued a flame that rose upwards and upwards until it was lost from sight. The sacrifice offered by Fr. Tsuji and his companions was found to be most pleasing.

Pope Pius IX beatified Fr. Tsuji and his two companions together with other Japanese martyrs on May 7, 1867. Jesuits commemorate Fr. Tsuji's heroic sacrifice on February 4, the day when the Society liturgically celebrates the memory of its brethren who were martyred during Japan's Great Persecution.

Prayer

Almighty God, grant that this remembrance of your martyr, Blessed Thomas Tsuji, may bring us joy. May we who depend upon his prayers glory in his entry in heaven. We ask this through our Lord Jesus Christ, your Son, who lives and reigns with you and the Holy Spirit, one God, for ever and ever.

September 6

Ralph Corby's parents were converts to the Catholic faith. Because Catholicism was being persecuted in their native county of Durham, England, they moved to Ireland, where they entered the service of the Earl of Kildare and held positions at Maynooth Castle. It was there on March 25, 1598, that Ralph was born. When the child was five the family returned to County Durham. In 1613 the family moved to Saint-Omer in Flanders, where Ralph and his two brothers started classes at the English College. After six years studying humanities at Saint-Omer, Ralph enrolled in 1619 at the English College in Seville, Spain, and in 1621 transferred to the college in Valladolid. After ordination to the priesthood in 1625, he returned to Flanders and entered the Society of Jesus at Watten, that same year. He did further studies in Liège, and finally ended his Jesuit formation in Ghent. In 1631 or 1632 he was sent on the English mission.

Fr. Corby was not the only member of his family to enter religion. His two brothers, who studied with him at Saint-Omer, became Jesuit priests, his third brother died as he was preparing to enter the Jesuit novitiate, and his two sisters became Benedictine nuns in Brussels. When there were no more children in the Corby household, the father became a Jesuit brother at age seventy; the mother a Benedictine nun in Ghent, who lived to be a hundred.

Fr. Corby's priestly ministry focused on County Durham where there were few priests in the area. Consequently, he had to travel much, no matter the season of the year. He generally covered the distances on foot, but when he was forced to travel on horseback because of poor health, he felt he had to offer an excuse for this luxury. Though unable to preach in public, he made up for it through his private instructions. He spent twelve years in the county confirming Catholics in their faith and administering the sacraments to them. His Catholics called him their "dearest Father" and "the apostle."

Fr. Corby was arrested on the morning of July 8, 1644, while celebrating Mass at Hamsterly Hall, near Newcastle. He was about to read the Epistle when Puritan soldiers broke into the house. The priest-hunters, thus, had abundant proof of his priesthood, so that when he was taken to Sunderland for a preliminary examination he readily signed a confession admitting that he was a priest. The following day he was put on a ship headed for London; his companion in chains was Fr. John Duckett, a diocesan priest, who had been apprehended on July 2. The two priests became close friends and were to be companions in imprisonment and in death as well.

In London both priests were ordered to Newgate Prison to await trial, and while they were there, negotiations began for an exchange of prisoners. A certain Scottish colonel, captured during the Thirty Years' War, was being held in Germany by the emperor and the government was trying to negotiate his release. The emperor's representative in London suggested Fr. Corby in exchange for the Scottish colonel. But when the plan was made known to Fr. Corby, he felt he had to decline and suggested that Fr. Duckett be the one to enjoy freedom: he was the younger, had better health, and could accomplish much more for the Church. But Fr. Duckett also declined. The prisoners preferred martyrdom to freedom. Their trial took place on September 4 in Old Bailey; both had previously confessed that they were priests, hence the trial was a mere formality. Both were found guilty of high treason and sentenced to death.

Frs. Corby and Duckett returned to their cells and during the intervening days they had many visitors. Several ambassadors came to see Fr. Corby, among whom were those of France, Spain, and Bavaria. To the ambassador of France he gave a medal and a rosary for the queen and promised to remember her, her family, and her nation in Paradise. On the morning of September 7 the priests celebrated their last Masses and about 10:00 A.M. they were called from their cells to make their way to Tyburn. Both appeared in cassocks, thus professing that they were being executed for being priests. When they arrived at the place of execution, they kissed the gallows and stepped on to the cart that was placed in position beneath. Fr. Duckett permitted his companion to be his spokesman. Fr. Corby briefly told the bystanders that they were priests and that their crime was priesthood. The two priests then embraced each other, and as they recollected themselves in prayer, the cart was slowly drawn from under them. They were left to hang until dead. Their bodies were subsequently disembowelled and quartered, but to prevent the people from taking relics, the sheriff in charge of the execution ordered the bodies and robes to be burned.

Fr. Ralph Corby was forty-six years old and was a Jesuit for fourteen years. He and Fr. Duckett were beatified by Pope Pius XI on December 15, 1929, and the Jesuits celebrate Fr. Corby's memorial on December 1, the day when they commemorate all the Jesuit martyrs of England and Wales.

Prayer

Almighty, eternal God, you chose from the people of England and Wales Blessed Ralph Corby and his companions to be made like Christ, who died to save the world. Listen to their prayers; strengthen your Church by the same faith and love that strengthened them, and bless it always with your gift of unity. We ask this through our Lord Jesus Christ, your Son, who lives and reigns with you and the Holy Spirit, one God, for ever and ever.

St. Melchior Grodziecki 1584–1619

St. Stephan Pongrácz 1582–1619

Martyrs of Košice

Frs. Melchior Grodziecki and Stephan Pongrácz met during the first stage of their Jesuit training, but neither foresaw that they would be martyred together for God and his Church.

Stephan was born in Alvincz Castle in Transylvania, probably in 1582. He entered the Society at Brno, Moravia, on July 8, 1602, and then studied at Prague in Bohemia, and at Graz in Austria. After ordination to the priesthood in 1615, he was stationed at the Jesuit college at Humenné. In early 1619 he was sent to Košice, which was then in Hungary but is in today's Slovakia.

Melchior was born in the family castle in Grodiec, near Cieszyn in Silesia, Poland, about 1584. He attended the Jesuit college in Vienna and entered the novitiate at Brno on May 22, 1603, where he met his future companion in martyrdom. After studies in Prague, Melchior was ordained in 1614 and worked in Prague until moving to Košice.

In the early part of the seventeenth century, Košice was a stronghold of Hungarian Calvinists and the few Catholics who lived in the city and its outlying districts had been without a priest for some time. The king's deputy in the city, Andrew Dóczy, asked for two Jesuits to care for the religious needs of these neglected Catholics and, thus, Frs. Pongrácz and Grodziecki arrived in Košice. The former was a Hungarian who worked among his own people, while the latter, a Pole, worked among those who spoke a Slavic tongue and among Germans. So grateful was Dóczy for their coming that he housed them in his official residence. As their missionary work among the Catholics prospered, Calvinist hatred increased.

Gabriel Bethlen, Calvinist prince of Transylvania, taking advantage of Hungary's involvement in the Thirty Years' War, attempted to expand his territory by appropriating some of the king's lands. When Frs. Pongrácz and Grodziecki heard the news that Bethlen's Protestant army, under the command of Georg I Rákóczi, was marching toward Košice, they left the small towns where they had been carrying on their apostolate and returned to the city to be with the Catholics. They were joined by the diocesan priest Mark Križevčanin, who was then administrator of the nearby Széplak Abbey. Fr. Križevčanin had been educated by the Jesuits in Vienna and Rome, and knew Frs. Pongrácz and Grodziecki. Hearing of the approach of Rákóczi's army, he too went to Košice.

Rákóczi gained control of the city on September 5, 1619. When he learned from the Calvinist minister that there were three priests in Košice, he sent a

P. Melchior Grodecius Silesius et P. Stephanus Pongratz Hungarus Societatis IESV, odio Fidei Catholicæ crudelissimè necati a Calvinistis in Hungaria A. 1019 7 bris Septembris

St. Melchior Grodziecki and St. Stephan Pongrácz

guard to arrest them. The priests were confined to their residence and all food and drink was forbidden them. On the night of September 6 they heard each other's confessions and spent the night in prayer, knowing that the inevitable was soon to come. Before the sun rose on September 7, the peace of their room was shattered by soldiers who, under orders of their commander, tried to get them to apostatize and accept Calvinism. When the priests repeatedly refused, the soldiers lost patience and beat them until the three lay prostrate. The soldiers then chose Fr. Križevčanin to be their first victim. They stripped him of his cassock, stabbed him many times, crushed his fingers, rubbed flaming torches into his sides until his ribs were visible, and when he fainted, they beheaded him.

They next vented their savagery on Fr. Pongrácz, repeating the tortures they had inflicted on Fr. Križevčanin, but also twisted a rope about his skull so tightly that it was almost crushed. They then cut off his nose and ears, tied his hands behind him, suspended him from a beam in the room, and barbarously carved his body. Leaving Fr. Pongrácz in his agony, they next turned to Fr. Grodziecki, who suffered tortures similar to those of Fr. Križevčanin, even to being beheaded. The soldiers gave two further blows to Fr. Pongrácz's head and then cast the three bodies outside into a ditch carrying foul water to the sewer. Fr. Pongrácz, however, was not dead; he remained alive for another twenty hours and received his martyr's crown toward evening on September 8. The city's Protestant leader forbade the burial of the martyrs. It was six months after their deaths that a devout countess received permission to bury them.

Frs. Stephen Pongrácz and Melchior Grodziecki, together with Canon Mark Križevčanin, were canonized by Pope John Paul II on July 2, 1995. Their memorial is liturgically celebrated by the Society on this day.

Prayer

O God, you gave to your people in the holy martyrs of Košice, Stephan, Melchior, and Mark, fearless shepherds and vigorous defenders of the faith. By their intercession grant also to us help in our troubles and an ever greater constancy in faith. We ask this through our Lord Jesus Christ, your Son, who lives and reigns with you and the Holy Spirit, one God, for ever and ever.

S. G. Richard Tena 1877–1936

Martyr of the Spanish Civil War

Fr. Richard Tena was martyred when he was fifty-nine years old, and when it was time for him to die he manifested extraordinary courage. He was born at Azuaga, in the province of Badajoz, near the Portuguese border, on December 28, 1877. He entered the Jesuit novitiate in Granada on August 3, 1894, and remained there for his early studies. He spent a year teaching in Málaga (1902–1903), then returned to Granada for further studies, and later taught at Cádiz. Richard's health failed and he was forced to postpone his theology until 1914, when he went to Loyola. He was ordained in 1917 and his first assignment after years of study was working in the Jesuit parish in Badajoz. Fr. Tena later went to Madrid and when his health allowed, he engaged in parish duties and taught catechism.

As he grew older his physical condition deteriorated. He was slightly bent over and often had to sit down to rest. Even when he went out for fresh air, he always carried a folding chair under his arm in case he needed it. After hearing afternoon confessions, he regularly went to the nearby park, chose a cool spot, and read from the book he carried with him. Such was the peaceful and uneventful life he lived until 1932, when the Spanish Republic decreed the suppression of the Society of Jesus. Too infirm to go into exile as younger Jesuits did, Fr. Tena went to his hometown and lived with his sister. He spent his time praying, reading, and preparing to go to heaven. Never did he imagine the manner of death that was to be his.

When civil war broke out in Spain in July 1936, the revolutionaries in Azuaga at first left the old priest alone, but then on September 6 they subjected him to a long interrogation. Because he was a Jesuit they ridiculed and insulted him, but he remained calm throughout. Now that he was in the hands of the revolution, he expected death and tried to make himself ready for what was to come. When the interrogation was over and after the soldiers had left his sister's house, Fr. Tena quietly sat down and read his breviary. He went to bed late that night waiting for the revolutionaries to return at any moment. They came back the following morning at 7:30 and took the ailing priest to prison. The neighbors who witnessed Fr. Tena's arrest noted how happy he was.

Within hours Fr. Tena was assigned to mop the prison floors, and because he was not as fast or as agile as the jailers would have him, they abused him. They then subjected him to further questioning and demanded of him: "Say there is no God." Repeatedly they ordered: "Say there is no God." Though weary from the maltreatment he had earlier received, Fr. Tena slowly rose from where he was sitting and with full composure faced his adversaries and began to speak about God. Striking him, someone shouted: "Deny God." Fr. Tena would not deny the God who had created him and loved him. Placing a pistol next to the priest's breast, a revolutionary again shouted: "Deny God." In answer to this order the prisoner serenely and solemnly began to recite the Creed: "I believe in God the Father Almighty, and in Jesus Christ his only Son . . ." The brute holding the pistol was so visibly moved by the priest's courage that he threw the weapon on the floor and said: "I'm not going to kill this man." Fr. Tena's tormentors then left him alone for a time.

A few hours before dawn on September 8, he was taken from the prison and forced to walk to the cemetery. He could hardly walk on his own and had to be helped. His body was broken, but his spirit remained unimpaired. Once inside the cemetery the revolutionaries again demanded his apostasy, commanding him: "Blaspheme God." Fr. Tena responded: "I am a priest. You may be able to take temporal life from me, but you cannot take from me my soul or eternal life." Fr. Tena then crossed his arms on his breast, raised his face to heaven, and with a voice that carried through the dark cemetery, he cried out: "Long live Christ the King!" As he uttered these words he was shot and his body was then buried in a common grave. Three years after his martyrdom, his remains were recovered and interred in another part of the cemetery.

The investigation into Fr. Richard Tena's martyrdom began in November 1948 and the study of his cause continues.

September 9

St. Peter Claver 1580–1654

On June 26, 1580, in the small village of Verdú, Catalonia, Spain, the youngest of the four children of Peter Claver, a well-to-do country farmer, was born and baptized in the local church and named after his father. Almost nothing is known about young Peter's early years except that at age thirteen he had already decided to become a priest. At sixteen he went to Barcelona to study at the university and while there, he came into contact with the Jesuits who operated Belén College. Peter now wanted to be a Jesuit and soon presented himself to the Jesuit provincial. He was accepted and began his noviceship in Tarragona on August 7, 1602. Two years later, on August 8, 1604, he took the three vows that bound him to the Society of Jesus.

With noviceship at an end, it was time for Peter to begin his philosophical studies and, thus, he was sent to the college of Montesión in Palma, on the island of Majorca. He looked forward to this change because he had already heard about Montesión's doorkeeper, Br. Alphonsus Rodríguez, who was known for his holiness and excellence as a spiritual guide. Shortly after Peter's arrival in Palma on November 11, 1605, as a twenty-five-year-old scholastic, he got to know the seventy-two-year-old brother and a spiritual friendship grew between them. Almost daily Peter and Alphonsus met somewhere in the college or on the grounds to have spiritual talks. Alphonsus sensed Peter's desire to do something great for God and so he spoke to him about the harvest to be gathered in the New World and of the heroic work of the missionaries there. He then said: "Peter, why do you not go, you too, and gather souls for Christ." The young scholastic took the aged brother's suggestion seriously, prayed over it, and then requested his provincial's permission to go to the New World.

Before Peter could receive a reply, he was sent in 1608 to Barcelona to begin his studies in theology. These were interrupted by a letter from his provincial on January 23, 1610, instructing him to go immediately to Seville and prepare his departure for the New World. On April 15, the future saint of the slave trade, together with three Jesuit priests, left Spain on a new adventure. The ship docked at Cartagena in the Caribbean (in present-day Colombia) in June or July 1610, and Peter made his way to the Jesuit college in Bogotá to finish his theological studies. In November 1615, having completed the course, he returned to Cartagena to begin work among the slaves that were being brought into the country. Little did he know that he was to spend the remainder of his life working among the world's most unfortunate creatures. Finally, on March 19, 1616, now thirty-six years old, Peter was ordained a priest, the first Jesuit to be ordained in Cartagena.

Cartagena played an important role in the slave trade. It was a prosperous port with an excellent harbor and was one of the two Spanish-American ports designated to receive slaves from West Africa. It is estimated that during Fr. Claver's years there about 10,000 slaves passed through the port annually. As soon as news arrived that a slave ship was coming into port, the word was passed on to Fr. Claver. He then went through the city begging for fruits, biscuits, or sweets so that he had something to offer the arriving slaves.

When the ship docked, the black cargo was usually in a piteous condition. The passage sometimes lasted months and the slaves spent their days and nights chained to one another. When the weather was especially fine and the sea calm, they were permitted on deck, but they spent the greater part of the voyage in the dark, windowless bowels of the ship. The hard floor served as their bed. Their food was just enough to keep them in reasonable condition so as not to hinder future sale. Sanitary conditions were lacking and disease often broke out. It was a successful voyage if only a third of the cargo had died during passage.

Fr. Claver was always at the dock awaiting the ship. He had his baskets of food on one side and his interpreter on the other. When he boarded the vessel, the slaves saw that his was not a cruel face but one of kindness, that he came not to maltreat, but to bring peace. The interpreters—the priest had several of them for the different African languages—had once been slaves themselves and had come to Cartagena in the same way as the wretches before them so they were able to gain their confidence. Fr. Claver offered each slave a fruit or a biscuit and embraced each in charity. After visiting those on deck, he went below to minister to the sick.

The holds where the slaves were kept were hot and reeked with stench, so much so that when one of the crew had to descend to them he could only endure the foul place for ten or fifteen minutes at most. But Fr. Claver did not recoil, he stayed below until his task was completed. He first looked after the dying; to these he briefly spoke about God and baptized them. Then he went to those ill from disease or wounded by the lash; he cleansed their wounds, applied ointment and bandages, and offered them brandy to revive their spirits. Only after he had seen each one did the priest return home.

Within a couple days of the ship's arrival, the slaves were taken ashore and housed in sheds built near the docks. Fr. Claver was there to help transfer, and if need be, carry the sick to their new quarters. Once they were ashore he visited them daily. He shared with them the food he carried in his basket, looked after the sick, then sought out the healthy who were not yet baptized. These he gathered together and through his interpreter instructed them in the faith. Fr. Claver had no time to waste; no one knew when the slaves would be sold and taken to other cities. To meet this exigency, the priest's instruction was necessarily brief and he conferred baptism sooner than was the custom. So numerous were these baptisms that shortly before his death, in response to a Jesuit brother's question about how many baptisms he had performed in Cartagena, he quietly answered, "a little over 300,000."

Fr. Claver did not know what it was to take a day off. During the periods when there were no slave ships in port, or slaves in the sheds, he visited two hospitals, one for general cases and the other for lepers. He also visited the Dutch and English prisoners, incarcerated after the Spanish had captured the islands of St. Christopher and St. Catherine. For thirty-five years Fr. Claver showed boundless compassion for abandoned people. He made himself the slave of slaves and gave up his body to a singular martyrdom. He remembered the words of Br. Alphonsus: "Look for God in all men and serve them as images of him." Wonderfully did he put those words into practice.

In 1650 the plague swept through Cartagena and its surrounding districts, and Fr. Claver went to work among those afflicted. Eventually, he himself became one of its victims. Because his own Jesuit community had been greatly reduced by the plague and the remaining priests were occupied with the sick in the city, the Jesuits hired a former slave to care for him. The last four years of Fr. Claver's life were years of helpless dependence. The priest was unable to celebrate Mass or hear confessions, and rarely was he able to get out of bed or go outdoors. Rather than caring for his patient, the hired man abused and mistreated him, answering the saint's charity with cruelty. He ate the more appetizing portion of his food and fed him the leftovers. He likewise refused to bathe him and care for his needs.

Through all this Fr. Claver never complained and, hence, no one knew of it. The priest was convinced that this was what he deserved.

When the Cartagenians, slave and free, heard the news that Fr. Claver had been anointed, they flocked to his room to see him for the last time. So great was their number that a witness said that people went in and out of his room as if it were a church. In their desire for mementoes of the holy man they stripped the room of everything except the bed clothes. On the night of September 7, 1654, Fr. Claver fell into unconsciousness and between one and two of the following morning, the feast of the Nativity of Our Lady, he, who styled himself the "slave of black slaves for all time," was finally liberated into the hands of his Master.

Fr. Peter Claver was beatified by Pope Pius IX on July 16, 1850, and canonized by Pope Leo XIII on January 15, 1888, together with his mentor Alphonsus Rodríguez, who had urged him to go to the New World to become a saint. St. Peter Claver's memorial is celebrated on September 9.

Prayer

Lord God, you called Saint Peter Claver to be the servant of slaves and a heroic example of patient charity. Grant through his prayers that we may seek what belongs to Christ, and love our neighbor, not in word only but in our whole lives. We ask this through our Lord Jesus Christ, your Son, who lives and reigns with you and the Holy Spirit, one God, for ever and ever.

September 10

Bl. Francis Gárate 1857–1929

On the outskirts of Azpeitia, Spain, near the ancestral home of St. Ignatius of Loyola, Francis Gárate, the second of seven children, was born on February 3, 1857. His early life was spent in an atmosphere of faith and piety—daily Mass in the Loyola basilica, and Sunday Mass in the parish church in Azpeitia. In 1871 at age fourteen, he left home to begin working at the recently opened Jesuit school in Orduña, and after three years entered the Society as a brother. Two of his brothers followed his example and became Jesuit brothers as well.

Because the Jesuits had been expelled from Spain during the 1868 revolution, Francis went to southern France, where the Spanish Jesuits maintained a novitiate in exile. On the morning of January 16, 1874, three youths and two adults left Azpeitia on their walk to France. The youths were Francis and two friends, all three were entering the Jesuits; the adults were the fathers of Francis and one of the other boys. The Carlist War was still being waged in northern Spain so the fathers wisely took the boys through the mountains and kept them clear of all areas where soldiers might be quartered. The group arrived in Poyanne, France, the following day, when Francis immediately began his postulancy. He became a novice on February 2. After two years of noviceship, he pronounced his vows of poverty, chastity, and obedience on February 2, 1876, and remained at Poyanne for another year, carrying out the various tasks assigned him.

In October 1877 Br. Francis was appointed infirmarian at the college in La Guardia, a city in the extreme west of Spain, near the Atlantic Ocean and Portuguese border. Two smaller institutions were associated with the college and he served as infirmarian for these as well, having some 200 young boys under his care. His deep interest in the sick and his limitless kindness toward them escaped no one's notice. These qualities, however, were especially appreciated by the students under his care. He thought it nothing to remain all night at a sick student's bedside and then do a full day's work the following day. After ten years as infirmarian the strain on his health began to show. In March 1888 he was transferred to the University of Deusto in Bilbao, in northern Spain, to take up the position of doorkeeper.

At Deusto, Br. Francis chose the poorest room in the house; to him it was the perfect room, since it was near the porter's lodge. He was courteous to all who visited him. To students he gave encouragement and advice and at times helped them copy their class notes; to those troubled he offered consolation; to the hungry he gave food and saw that the poor were clothed. As for himself, he was abstemious in food and considered the clothing others left behind good enough for him. His forty-one years at Deusto were years of prayer, mortification, and continuously living in the presence of God. Like his patron, St. Alphonsus Rodríguez, whose picture hung in his simple room, Br. Francis prayed while he worked and worked while he prayed. Practically never was he without a rosary in hand.

When Br. Francis was seventy-two years old his health began to fail. On September 8, 1929, the feast of our Lady's nativity, he had his first sharp abdominal pains. The infirmarian suggested that he go to bed, and he agreed, but after he had finished several chores. It was evening when he finally settled in at the infirmary. That night, knowing that he was soon to die, he requested Viaticum, and because his discomfort was so great, the rector summoned the community's physician. He arrived about midnight and finding an obstruction in the urethra, performed a minor surgical intervention; the patient found temporary relief, but he was not to recover. Early in the morning Br. Francis asked to be anointed, and as it approached 7:00 A.M, the feast of St. Peter Claver, he yielded his soul to God.

The esteem in which Br. Francis Gárate was held in life was made manifest at the time of his death. Countless former students came to have a final glimpse of him, whom they had happily numbered among their friends. They made sure their rosaries and crucifixes touched his coffin. Br. Francis was beat-ified by Pope John Paul II on October 6, 1985, and his brother Jesuits celebrate his memorial on September 10.

Prayer

God, rewarder of the faithful, who has given us in Blessed Francis Gárate an outstanding example of enduring fidelity in your service, grant that following in his footsteps, we may open our hearts to Christ and serve him in the poor. We ask this through our Lord Jesus Christ, your Son, who lives and reigns with you and the Holy Spirit, one God, for ever and ever.

September 11

Bl. Charles Spinola 1564–1622

Bl. Sebastian Kimura and 8 Companions 1565–1622

Martyrs of Japan

When Fr. Charles Spinola arrived in Japan in 1602, the Japanese Christians were enjoying a period of great peace under Shogun Iyeyasu, but as long as the shogun remained a non-Christian there was no assurance that the peace would continue. The peace, in fact, came to an end in 1614 when he proscribed Christianity.

Fr. Charles Spinola, the son of the Italian Count of Tassarolo, was born in 1564, in Madrid, Spain, where his father was tutor to prince Rudolph, the em-peror's son. After early studies in Spain, Charles went to Nola, Italy (1572), and there attended the Jesuit school, while living with his uncle Philip Spinola, Bishop of Nola. When the news of the martyrdom in India of Rudolph Acqua-viva reached Italy (1583), Charles was so moved by this heroic example of love of God that he determined it would be his supreme happiness to die for Christ and the faith. Thus he chose to enter the Society and became a Jesuit at the Nola novitiate on December 23, 1584. Charles went to Naples for his study of phi-losophy and there pronounced his three vows on December 25, 1586. Since his health was not the best, he was sent to complete his philosophy at Brera College in Milan and remained there for theology as well. He was ordained in Milan in 1594, and though he had asked to go on the foreign missions he was sent, in-stead, to give parish missions in Cremona.

P Carolus Spinola ex Marchionib, Italiæ. P. Sebaſtianus Kimura primus è Ia͡ponibus Sacerdos, cum 7. alijs Soc. IESV, lento igne pro Christi fide exuſti. Nangasachi in Iaponia 10 Septemb. A 1622
c s i   M X E

Bl. Charles Spinola, Bl. Sebastian Kimura, and Companions

Fr. Spinola finally received his long-awaited letter appointing him to the missions, and together with the Sicilian Jesuit, Jerome De Angelis, sailed from Genoa in early 1596. This was but the beginning of a long journey filled with many unfortunate incidents. The vessel struck a rock and was forced to return to Genoa. He and his companion then got passage on another ship and landed in Barcelona. In order to be in Lisbon in time to catch the spring sailing for India, they crossed Spain and Portugal on foot. They then set sail for Japan on April 10, 1596. By mid-June the ship crossed the Tropic of Capricorn and as it was heading for the Cape of Good Hope a violent storm shattered its rudder. Since the substitute rudder could not last through a return trip to Lisbon or the distance to India, the captain decided to try for a port in Brazil. On July 16 they sailed into Bahia and spent the next five months waiting for the ship to be repaired. On December 12 they again started on their way, but in March 1597 another storm enveloped them and the ship sprang a leak. All hands were kept busy at the pumps; the ship was left to the mercy of the winds, which took it back across the Atlantic. On March 25 the weary passengers entered the harbor of Puerto Rico.

After another five months the ship was still not ready to go to sea, so the missionaries got passage on another vessel and on August 21, 1597, eight ships left Puerto Rico for Lisbon. Two days out a storm dispersed the group and the ship carrying the missionaries made its solitary way toward its destination. On October 17, off the Azores, it encountered an English pirate ship that took them to Yarmouth, England. Both missionaries finally left England in early January 1598 on a German ship and a week later arrived in Lisbon, the port from which they had departed two years previously. They remained in Lisbon for a year and at the end of March 1599 again set sail for the Indies. They arrived in Malacca, Malaya, in July 1600, and from there they went to Macao on the China coast. It was not until July 1602 that Frs. Spinola and De Angelis set foot in Nagasaki, Japan—six years after they had begun their journey.

Fr. Spinola immediately went to the seminary in Arima to study Japanese and when sufficiently fluent, he took a parish at Arie where he remained for two years. From Arie he went to the capital Miyako (today's Kyoto), where he was minister at the Jesuit college and taught mathematics and astronomy, two subjects that especially interested the Japanese. Seven years later (1611) he was transferred to Nagasaki, was named procurator of the province—in charge of all its temporal needs—and remained in this post until his capture.

By 1612 the number of Christians in Japan reached two million and the non-Christian leaders interpreted this rapid growth as a national threat. They succeeded in poisoning the mind of Shogun Iyeyasu into believing that the missionaries were preparing the nation for a takeover by Spain. Dutch and English traders, who were never friendly toward Spain or Catholicism, agreed that this was the missionaries' intention, thus hoping to gain all of the Japanese trade once the Spaniards and Portuguese were expelled. The result of these lies was Iyeyasu's edict of 1614 banishing all foreign missionaries and forbidding the Japanese Christians to harbor priests or to practice their religion. This was the beginning of the Great Persecution. About one hundred Jesuits complied with the order and left Japan, but a score remained and among them was Fr. Spinola.

For four years he eluded the priest-hunters. He changed his name to Joseph of the Cross, and since he could not sufficiently disguise the fact that he was European, he ventured out only when dark. Then during the night of December 13, 1618, he, Br. Ambrose Fernandes, and their catechist, John Chugoku, were arrested in the house of a Portuguese Christian.

The three were led away with ropes around their necks and taken to the prison in Suzuta, near Omura, a dozen miles from Nagasaki. The prison was an enclosure made of stakes, similar to a bird cage, as Fr. Spinola had described it in one of his letters, with neither walls nor roof. The prison faced the sea so that during summer the prisoners suffered the heat of the sun, and in winter they had to endure cold rain, icy snow, and whipping winds. They never washed or changed clothes. Food was minimal, a few handfuls of rice. The enclosure was only twenty-four square yards, yet at one time it held up to three dozen prisoners. There was no room to stretch; the prisoners had to squat and lean upon each other. The Nagasaki Christians bribed the guards and, consequently, food was smuggled into the prison as well as writing materials and what was needed for Mass. After the first few months, Fr. Spinola celebrated Mass every day for his fellow prisoners.

After thirteen months of imprisonment, Br. Ambrose Fernandes, much weakened by the ordeal, died on January 7, 1620. Sometime after his death, perhaps in the autumn of that year, four more prisoners were added to their number. They were Anthony Kyuni, Gonzalo Fusai, Peter Sampo, and Michael Shumpo, who for some time, and of their own accord, had been living a quasi-religious life near Nagasaki. They had all been active catechists with the Jesuits prior to the 1614 edict, and all had gone into exile to Macao or Manila. They returned to Japan (1616–1617) and built a hermitage for themselves on the outskirts of Nagasaki, where they lived a life of prayer and penance, imitating a Jesuit noviceship. Because they visited the sick, encouraged the persecuted Christians, and taught catechumens, they were mistaken for priests and were arrested. When they refused to desist from preaching the Christian faith, they were imprisoned in the former Jesuit novitiate of All Saints, now confiscated by the government. After eighteen months of detention and still unwilling to relinquish their catechetical work, they were sent to the prison at Suzuta and enclosed with Fr. Spinola. For two years they remained under his spiritual direction and, with the permission of the Jesuit provincial, Fr. Spinola accepted the four of them as novices into the Society.

In the summer of 1621 another Jesuit was added to their number. This was Fr. Sebastian Kimura, the first Japanese to be ordained a priest. He was born in Hirado in 1565 of Christian parents and was the cousin of Br. Leonard Kimura. He first studied with the Jesuits in Hirado and then attended their seminary in Arima. In 1582 he joined the Jesuits and for a time served as a catechist in Miyako. He then went to Macao for theology and returned to Japan, where he was ordained in Nagasaki in September 1601.

Fr. Kimura was an eloquent preacher, and when the Jesuits were forced to go undercover in 1614 he became adept at disguising himself. At times he appeared as a soldier or a merchant, a coolie or a physician. Because of these various disguises he was able to visit many Christian homes and prisons to administer the sacraments. His activity was especially noted by the police and he was among those particularly sought out. In June 1621 he received word from his provincial to leave Nagasaki until the pressure lessened, but before he had a chance to depart, he and his catechist, Thomas Akahoshi, and an assistant at the Jesuit residence, Louis Kawara, were betrayed by a Korean servant. They were arrested on June 30 and sent to Suzuta to be imprisoned with Fr. Spinola and the other Christians. Since Fr. Spinola was conducting a novitiate in the prison, Kawara and Akahoshi asked to join the novices, as did John Chugoku.

In September 1622 the prisoners received word that they were to be taken to Nagasaki. They felt certain that martyrdom would soon be theirs. Before leaving the enclosure, Fr. Spinola accepted the vows of his seven novices. On September 9 the twenty-four prisoners at Suzuta—each with a rope around his neck, and the Jesuits wearing cassocks that had been smuggled in for this occasion—were led to Nagasaki with an escort of 400 soldiers. When the Christians arrived at Martyrs' Hill, they waited for another group of thirty-three prisoners from the city. When the two groups met, they embraced. Fr. Spinola recognized Isabel Fernandez among them, the wife of Dominic Jorjes, who had been Fr. Spinola's host, and her four-year-old son Ignatius, whom he had baptized and named after the founder of the Jesuits. The religious in the group were condemned to death by slow fire, the others were to be beheaded. Of the Jesuits only John Chugoku was beheaded—there were not enough stakes.

When fastened to his stake, Fr. Spinola intoned the psalm, *Praise the Lord, All You Nations,* and the martyrs joined in a song of thanksgiving to God for having been chosen to give this particular witness of their love. The fires were lit, but the wood was so arranged as to prolong the victims' suffering. Because Fr. Spinola was greatly weakened after four years of imprisonment, he was the first of the group to die, within a half hour after the fires began. Fr. Kimura was the last to die, having endured his martyrdom for three hours, during which time he remained immobile with arms outstretched in the form of a cross.

Nine Jesuits died on Martyrs' Hill on September 10, 1622, but when Pope Pius IX beatified the 205 Japanese martyrs on May 7, 1867, Br. Ambrose Fernandes, who had died in prison, was also included among them. The liturgical memorial of these Jesuit martyrs is celebrated by their brethren on February 4.

The following are brief biographical sketches of Br. Fernandes and the seven novices who entered the Society during their imprisonment at Suzuta.

Br. Ambrose Fernandes was born in Sisto, in the diocese of Oporto, Portugal, in August 1551, and went to India in 1571 to make his fortune. He first served in the Portuguese army in Salsette, India, and then worked for various wealthy merchants in Goa and Macao. While on a business trip to Japan the vessel on which he was traveling met a frightful storm. After concluding his master's business he requested to enter the Society and, thus, was able to fulfill an old desire as well as the vow he had made during the rough voyage to Japan. He entered the novitiate in Nagasaki as a brother in January 1579. He spent his Jesuit life in that city doing missionary work, seeing to the temporal needs of his community, and acting as interpreter when needed. When the missionaries were expelled from Japan in 1614 he went undercover. He was arrested with Fr. Spinola on the night of December 13, 1618, and later taken to the enclosure at Suzuta. After thirteen months of harsh imprisonment he died on the morning of January 7, 1620. He was sixty-nine years old.

John Chugoku was born in Yamaguchi, Japan, about 1573. As a young man he entered the service of an influential knight and joined him in the invasion of Korea. After John had returned home, his wife abandoned him, about 1600, and so he went to Arima, where he came into contact with Jesuit priests. He became a Christian, worked with the Jesuits, and accompanied them on their missionary journeys. He was arrested with Fr. Spinola and Br. Fernandes on the night of December 13, 1618, and while imprisoned at Suzuta, made his noviceship under Fr. Spinola's direction and pronounced his religious vows days before being beheaded on September 10, 1622.

Anthony Kyuni was born of a noble family in Mikawa, Japan, about 1572. He was married but it is unclear whether his wife had died or whether it was with her permission that he went to Nagasaki and began studies at the seminary. He became a catechist and also worked in the printery operated by the Jesuits and in their infirmary. During the missionaries' exile, he too went to Macao in 1614. He returned to Nagasaki in 1617, determined to dedicate himself to God and to live the life of a hermit. He chose a secluded spot on the mountain between Nagasaki and the village of Himi, and there erected a simple hut for himself and his future companions. He and companions were arrested in 1619 and imprisoned in the former Jesuit novitiate in Nagasaki. During the winter of 1620 they were transferred to the prison in Suzuta where they began their noviceship training under Fr. Spinola.

Michael Shumpo was born of a Christian family in Owari, Japan, in 1589. He studied with the Jesuits in Miyako, entered the seminary in Arima in 1602, became a catechist, and later was sacristan of the church in Miyako. After three years of exile in Macao he returned to Japan in 1617, desiring to join Anthony Kyuni in the hermitage outside Nagasaki. Suspected of being priests, he and his companions were arrested in late 1619 and detained in the old Jesuit novitiate of All Saints. During the winter of 1620 they were taken to the prison in Suzuta where they requested to enter the Society and began their noviceship under Fr. Spinola.

Gonzalo Fusai was born in Okayama, Japan, about 1580. He was of a noble family and for several years lived at the court of the daimyo of Bizen-Mimasaka. He accompanied his lord during the campaign in Korea but later left him to go to Nagasaki, where he became a Christian and a catechist. When he returned from exile in Macao in 1617, he joined his friends, Anthony Kyuni and Michael

Shumpo in the hermitage near Nagasaki. He was arrested and imprisoned with them, and with them entered the Society, while at Suzuta. He pronounced his religious vows prior to his martyrdom.

Peter Sampo was born in Oshu, Japan, about 1580. He left home to seek a better income and emigrated to central Japan, where he entered the service of a great lord. He then moved to Hiroshima where he became a Christian, and later served the daimyo of Hoki. When his master died he moved to Nagasaki, shaved his head, and built a small straw house for himself next to the Jesuit novitiate. Taking the advice of a Jesuit, he gave up his solitary life and became a catechist and went with the missionaries into exile in 1614. He returned to Nagasaki in 1616 and secretly continued work as a catechist, until he joined Anthony Kyuni's group of hermits on the mountain between Nagasaki and Himi. He was apprehended with them, and with them suffered imprisonment and martyrdom.

Louis Kawara was born in Arima, Japan, in 1583. As a young man he had served in the court of Michael, prince of Arima, and when the prince turned apostate, he wanted Louis to do the same. Rather than offend his master, Louis pretended to abandon the faith, though he continued to live a Christian life. When Michael learned of this pretense of Louis, he expelled him from court and confiscated his property. Louis then went with his family to Nagasaki and lived in abject poverty. After his wife and children had died, he built a little house for himself in an out-of-the-way place and lived as an ascetic. Christians visited him and listened to his exhortations. Mistaken for a priest because his facial features were similar to those of a European, he was twice arrested, but then freed. He was arrested a third time on June 30, 1621, with Fr. Kimura and both were sent to the Suzuta enclosure. Moved by the example of those who had been admitted into the Society, he too requested to become a Jesuit. He was accepted, and when martyrdom was near, he pronounced his religious vows.

Thomas Akahoshi was born at Higo, Japan, about 1565, of a noble family. He served the daimyo of Higo and after his wife had died, went to Nagasaki and became a catechist with the Jesuits. He went into exile with them in 1614 but returned to Japan and worked with Fr. Kimura, with whom he was arrested. He was imprisoned at Suzuta and there entered the Society and pronounced his vows before being burned alive.

Prayer

Almighty God, grant that this remembrance of your holy martyrs, Blessed Charles Spinola, Blessed Sebastian Kimura, and their companions, may bring us joy. May we who depend on their prayers glory in their entry into heaven. We ask this through our Lord Jesus Christ, your Son, who lives and reigns with you and the Holy Spirit, one God, for ever and ever.

September 12

S. G. Emmanuel González 1889–1936

S. G. Joseph Sánchez and 2 Companions 1891–1936

Martyrs of the Spanish Civil War

When the Spanish Civil War broke out in July 1936, the Jesuit residence in Ciudad Real had only four Jesuits, but because it was a center of intense apostolic work, the atheistic revolutionary party tried to silence the Jesuits by imprisoning them. Frs. Emmanuel González Hernández and Joseph Sánchez Oliva lived there and had been friends for most of their lives—they had been students together and had often been stationed in the same religious house. There were also two Jesuit brothers with them, Dominic Ibarlucea Oregui and Anthony Sanchiz Martínez, both of whom were younger than the priests.

Fr. González was born at Baños de Montemayor, in the province of Cáceres, on October 17, 1889, and entered the Jesuit novitiate at Granada on December 27, 1903, when he was fourteen. He remained at Granada for his studies in the humanities and philosophy, and then from 1913 to 1917 taught grammar at the Jesuit school in Ciudad Real. For theology he went to Sarriá, near Barcelona, and was ordained on July 26, 1920. He returned to Ciudad Real in 1924 to teach geography and history at the minor seminary. From 1926 to 1927 he was assistant to the master of novices at Aranjuez, after which he returned to Ciudad Real to become spiritual director of young seminarians.

Fr. Sánchez, who was born on November 10, 1891, at Molina de Segura, in Murcia province, was also fourteen years old when he entered the Granada novitiate on December 7, 1905. He left Granada in 1913 to go to Oña for philosophy and in 1916 was teaching at Ciudad Real. In 1920 he went to Sarriá for theology and was ordained on July 30, 1922. After studies he spent the years 1925 to 1927 at the minor seminary in Puerto de Santa Maria, and in 1927 moved to Ciudad Real to become rector of the Jesuit community and of the minor seminary in that city.

Frs. González and Sánchez were different types, but they wonderfully complemented each other and together they had great success with the young seminarians. The former was serious, but patient and understanding; the latter always had a smile and was filled with enthusiasm.

Br. Ibarlucea arrived at Ciudad Real in 1929 to be the seminary's infirmarian. He was born in Marquina, in the province of Vizcaya, on October 6, 1906, and entered the Society at Aranjuez on January 8, 1925. Br. Sanchiz came to Ciudad Real in 1931 as cook. He was born on December 13, 1906, in Villar de Cañas, in Cuenca province, and joined the Jesuits on July 2, 1926, also at Aranjuez.

When the Society was suppressed in Spain in 1932, the Jesuits abandoned their large residence in Ciudad Real, and although some left the city, these four moved into a small residence and quietly continued their apostolic work. When civil war broke out on July 18, 1936, Fr. Sánchez was giving a retreat to a group of sisters in the city and Fr. González was making his own retreat at Daimiel. Because of the turmoil which was then dividing the nation, Fr. Sánchez interrupted the retreat he was conducting on July 22 and returned to the residence, where both brothers were waiting. On August 18 two policemen came to ask Fr. Sánchez to accompany them to City Hall, where they questioned him on the whereabouts of Fr. González, what name he was using, and where the arms were hidden. But to all these questions Fr. Sánchez could give no answer. Dissatisfied with the priest's performance, the police thereupon placed him in the city jail and went to arrest the two brothers.

When Fr. González concluded his retreat in Daimiel, he surmised that the revolutionaries would soon be looking for him, so rather than return to Ciudad Real he remained in Daimiel with friends, changing residence every two or three days. The police finally tracked him down on August 19, as he was counseling a young seminarian. That night he was taken to the jail in Ciudad Real, where he joined his three Jesuit brethren.

Because his hearing had become greatly impaired over the past years, Fr. González spent his time in prayer—always with a rosary in his hand—and seldom spoke because there was very little that he heard. Fr. Sánchez, on the other hand, exuded optimism, and his words were filled with hope as he tried to encourage the other prisoners. After a time both priests were brought before a tribunal of judges, who tried to implicate them in the nationalist movement, that is, the party fighting the communists. To all the charges of conspiracy, Fr. Sánchez merely replied that their apostolate was among the working class people and their task was to preach Christ and his gospel. Because the judges had no success, they turned to insults and ridicule and finally accused the priests of inciting the people against the government. Fr. Sánchez calmly responded: "Just take a look at the crime you are about to commit. I am not saying this just to save myself; no, my greatest desire is to die a martyr for Christ, but do not commit this sin. Nevertheless, I am happy that the workers for whom I have labored so long will now open the gates of heaven for me. Long live Christ the King!"

On September 5 Frs. González and Sánchez were taken from the city jail to the provincial prison, where they found the two brothers, who had been taken there some days previously. Late on September 7, under cover of darkness, nine men were taken from the prison, among them Fr. González and Br. Ibarlucea. At about 1:30 in the morning of September 8 the nine prisoners were taken by truck to the Las Casas cemetery, where they were lined up and shot one by one. The execution lasted three-fourths of an hour and not a single cry or murmur was heard from the victims. The next morning the nine bodies were buried in a common grave.

Twenty-four hours later the scene was repeated, but this time eighteen prisoners were taken and Fr. Sánchez and Br. Sanchiz were among them. As they were leaving the prison the priest encouraged the brother, saying: "Come, let us go. Christ is calling us." When the truck arrived at the Carrión cemetery it was the morning of September 9; the moon was shining overhead. Again the victims were lined up and shot one by one. The bodies of these martyrs were recovered and it was found that Fr. González' head had been separated from his body and that Fr. Sánchez had a medal of our Lady and the crucifix, which he wore about his neck, between his lips.

The official diocesan investigation into the martyrdom of Frs. Emmanuel González and Joseph Sánchez, and Brs. Dominic Ibarlucea and Anthony Sanchiz began in Ciudad Real in November 1947.

September 13

Ven. Peter Dias and 11 Companions 1517–1571

Martyrs of Brazil

When Fr. Ignatius de Azevedo (see July 15) visited Portugal seeking volunteers for the Brazil mission, Fr. Peter Dias was one of the priests who chose to join him. Fr. Dias was born in Arruda dos Vinhos, near Lisbon, Portugal, in 1517, and entered the Society on March 28, 1548. After ordination he was procurator at the Jesuit college in Coimbra, where he also taught moral theology.

As the flotilla of ships left Lisbon on June 5, 1570, the seventy some Jesuit missionaries were aboard three different vessels. Fr. Azevedo had more than forty Jesuits on one, Fr. Dias was in charge of some twenty aboard the vessel carrying Dom Luis de Vasconcelos, the new governor, on his way to Brazil, and Fr. Francis de Castro was with the others on a third ship. When the flotilla stopped at Funchal on the island of Madeira, off the African coast, all the ships stayed behind except the *Santiago,* which carried Fr. Azevedo and his group. The ship's captain was eager to do some trading in the Canary Islands. Within sight of Santa Cruz de la Palma, Fr. Azevedo's ship was attacked by Huguenot pirates and he and thirty-nine Jesuits were martyred.

When the story of their martyrdom reached Madeira, Fr. Dias wrote a letter (August 17, 1570) to the Portuguese provincial informing him of the event. As soon as the seas were free of corsairs the ships left Funchal for Brazil, and after some weeks crossing the Atlantic, they were all but in sight of Brazil when a violent storm overtook them. Its winds buffeted the vessels, tore the sails, and tossed the ships wherever they willed. Several of the ships were lost at sea, but the two carrying the missionaries survived the gale. The battered hulk of the ship on which Fr. Dias was traveling was now many miles off course, but found a haven in the small port of Santiago, Cuba, while the vessel carrying Fr. Castro was blown toward Santo Domingo. The ship of Fr. Dias had to be abandoned and the passengers and crew made the long trek over the island to Havana, where in late July or early August 1571, they secured passage on board a vessel returning to Europe. When they arrived in Angra, in the Azores, they found that Fr. Castro and his missionary companions had preceded them there.

The governor was not one to collapse in adversity nor was Fr. Dias, so preparations were immediately made to sail for Brazil a second time. Because some of his companions had become ill, Fr. Dias had them return to Portugal; he only kept thirteen with him. Now outfitted, the ship set sail for Brazil on September 6, 1571. After six days at sea, they met five pirate ships in the vicinity of the Canary Islands. Four were French under the command of Jean Capdeville, the other was an English marauder. Capdeville was a French Huguenot, who had served as Jacques Sourie's lieutenant, when the latter's crew martyred Fr. Azevedo and his fellow Jesuits in the same waters fourteen months previously.

The ship of Dom Luis boldly faced the enemy and with a salvo brought down the mast of the leading Huguenot vessel and killed about twenty men. The ships were five against one; Dom Luis had no chance of surviving this encounter. When his ship was surrounded, he and the crew fought valiantly; the governor was the first who fell victim to the corsairs. During the fighting, Fr. Dias, Fr. Castro, and a few scholastics went among the wounded, bandaging their wounds and carrying them to safety. The ship was soon overrun by pirates brandishing swords. Their eyes quickly picked out the black cassocks of the Jesuits; they hacked Fr. Castro to pieces and then dealt countless blows to Fr. Dias. With the two priests there also died a scholastic and two novices. This was September 13, 1571.

The remaining nine Jesuits were kept below deck until the following day and then brought up in groups of three. They were subjected to torture and indignity and then thrown alive into the sea. Of the nine, seven drowned, the other two, Sebastian Lopes and James Fernandes, both strong swimmers, stayed afloat and were eventually rescued by one of the pirate ships. When they reached France a few weeks later, the two surviving Jesuits, together with the others taken from the Portuguese vessel, were given their freedom. The Jesuits then made their way to Portugal, where they narrated the story to which they had been sad witnesses.

The 11 companions of Fr. Peter Dias:

1   *Ferdinand Álvares* (brother), Portuguese, native of Viseu, born in 1534, entered May 28, 1560; thrown alive into the sea, September 14.

2   *John Álvares* (scholastic), Portuguese, native of Estreito (Oleiros), born about 1545, entered November 1, 1564; thrown alive into the sea, September 14.

3   *Michael Aragonéz* (scholastic), Spaniard, native of Guisona (Catalonia), born 1543, entered August 1567; wounded and thrown alive into the sea, September 13.

4   *James de Carvalho* (brother), Portuguese, native of Tondela (Viseu); thrown alive into the sea, September 14.

5   *Francis de Castro* (priest), Spaniard, born in Montemolin (Andalusia), about 1535, entered August 19, 1560; killed, then thrown into the sea, September 13.

6   *Peter Dias* (scholastic), Portuguese, born in Bouzela (Viseu), about 1541; thrown alive into the sea, September 14.

7   *Alphonsus Fernandes* (scholastic), Portuguese, native of Viana do Alentejo, born about 1548; thrown alive into the sea, September 14.

8   *Peter Fernandes* (brother), Portuguese, born about 1544, thrown alive into the sea, September 14.

9   *Gaspar Góes* (scholastic), Portuguese, native of Portel, born about 1546; killed and body thrown into the sea, September 13.

10   *Andrew Paes* (scholastic), Portuguese, born in Oporto, about 1549; thrown alive into the sea, September 14.

11   *Francis Paulo* (brother), Portuguese; thrown alive into the sea, September 13.

September 14

S. G. Francis Mary Galluzzi 1671–1731

Francis Mary Galluzzi was born in Florence, Italy, on January 9, 1671, and after attending the Jesuit school of San Giovannino in his native city, entered the Roman novitiate of Sant'Andrea on May 24, 1688. Two years later, on May 25, 1690, he pronounced his three vows of religion and began his study of the humanities, with the resolution: "I will show more interest in the advancement of piety than in letters; I will seek the honor of God more than that of the world; I will consider the judgment of angels more than that of men." He later taught Latin at Loreto (1697–1698) and at the Roman College (1698–1700) and afterwards began his theological studies in Rome and was ordained in 1703. On completing his Jesuit training, he taught philosophy for a year (1705–1706) at the college in Prato.

Fr. Galluzzi always had a humble opinion of himself and of his talents. While going through the Society's course of studies, he deemed himself unfit for the priesthood and asked to be a brother, but his superiors thought otherwise. Now that he was a priest, he asked to go on the missions, either to a little parish in some outlying area or to work among non-believers in the New World. Again his superiors thought otherwise. Rather than to some out-of-the-way village, he was sent to the center of Rome (1706), where he carried on a fruitful apostolate at the Oratory of St. Francis Xavier. At that time it was more commonly known as the Oratory of Fr. Gravita, who founded it in the early part of the century. It is adjacent to the church of St. Ignatius and today it is known as Caravita. Fr. Galluzzi made himself fully available to Rome's faithful and that small oratory soon became one of the city's busiest churches. He heard confessions, taught catechism, preached sermons, visited hospitals and prisons, directed priests and religious in the spiritual life, and gave retreats and missions in the city and suburbs.

In 1713 he was transferred to the Roman College to be chaplain and student counselor. Though he resided only three years at the college, his influence was felt for years afterward. Many were the vocations he sent to the different religious orders, so that several religious communities wrote him expressing their gratitude for the youths he had directed to them. In 1716 Fr. Galluzzi returned to his apostolate at the oratory, but retained ties with the Roman College and continued to be spiritual father to many of its students.

In addition to his many and varied activities, Fr. Galluzzi found time to write three dozen books and pamphlets on saints and holy Jesuits, meditation manuals, and novenas. When Fr. Anthony Baldinucci died in 1717, he wrote his biography; it was a friend writing about a friend. He also promoted Aloysius Gonzaga's canonization and then published a biography of the saint after the canonization in 1726. Because the hours of the day were insufficient for Fr. Galluzzi to do all that he wanted to do, he limited himself to only a few hours of sleep each night, and to save time, so it is said, he ate but one meal a day.

As age and weakness began to set in, he was taken to his confessional at the oratory, still making himself available to his many penitents. On August 19, 1731, he fell seriously ill and was forced to take to his bed. Unable to go to his penitents, they came to him, those of high estate as well as Rome's priests and seminarians. So esteemed was he for his holiness that the then superior general of the Society, Fr. Michelangelo Tamburini, came to kiss his hands and asked to be remembered in his prayers. Pope Clement XII said of Fr. Galluzzi that he had never known a priest who burned with so much zeal for the glory of God and the salvation of souls.

Fr. Francis Galluzzi died on September 7, 1731. He was sixty years of age and had spent forty-three in the Society of Jesus. He was interred in the church of St. Ignatius in Rome, and his cause for beatification was begun in 1917.

September 15

Bl. Camillus Costanzo 1571–1622

Bl. Augustine Ota 1572–1622

Martyrs of Japan

The black-robed Jesuit walked resolutely to the stake that awaited him. As his executioners fastened him and prepared the wood, he spoke to the people who had come to witness the execution: "I am Camillus Costanzo, an Italian and a member of the Society of Jesus. I am to be burned alive for having preached the Gospel of Christ and God's law. We Christians do not fear those who can kill the body but cannot kill the soul. Life here below may be filled with privations and hardships, but it will come to an end and will be followed by the dawn of eternal life, which knows no setting."

Fr. Costanzo was born at Bovalino, in Calabria, southern Italy, in 1571. As a young man he served under Prince Albert during the siege of Ostend, and when he returned to Italy he began law studies in Naples, but later set them aside and entered the Naples province of the Society on September 8, 1591. After completing his Jesuit training and ordination in 1602, he was assigned to the Chinese mission and left Italy in March 1603. He arrived in Macao in March 1604, but because he seems to have failed to comply with certain Portuguese regulations, he was refused entry. After a year of waiting he turned toward Japan and landed at Nagasaki on August 18, 1605.

Within a year Fr. Costanzo was speaking Japanese and was working among the Christians in and about the city of Sakai. God blessed his efforts by granting him 800 converts. When the decree banishing all foreign missionaries from Japan was promulgated in 1614, Fr. Costanzo went to Macao and for six years studied Buddhist texts, and wrote, in Japanese, a dozen pamphlets refuting the claims of the Buddhist religion and two treatises explaining the Catholic faith. By the end of 1621 he was eager to return to Japan, and though the priests in Macao had begged him to remain, he felt he had to go. Disguised as a soldier he embarked for Nagasaki, but when the vessel docked the captain tried to detain him. The captain had penetrated the disguise and wanted to notify the district governor that he had a priest on board. At the same time two Christians who had known the priest in Sakai recognized him and got him safely ashore. Fr. Costanzo chose Hirado Island in western Japan as his mission area and there he met the Japanese Augustine Ota, whom he made his missionary companion.

Augustine Ota was born about 1572 on Ojika, one of the islands in the Goto group. His family was non-Christian and he had studied with Buddhist bonzes in a local temple. But in 1585 during his stay in Ota, he was converted by the Jesuits and at his baptism took the name Augustine. Because he had first-hand knowledge of Buddhism, he was especially valuable to the missionaries in their evangelization of Japan. After his wife died, and since he had no children, he spent all his time and effort in spreading Christianity. Though the persecution was in full vigor, he, nevertheless, went about converting his compatriots to Christianity.

It was during this period of his life that he met Fr. Costanzo. Augustine joined the priest as a catechist and together they visited the islands off the western shore of Japan as well as a part of the mainland. Their active association lasted only four months for on April 24, 1622, they were both arrested.

A Christian woman living in Ikitsuki was intent on converting her pagan husband and learning that Fr. Costanzo was on the island, convinced her husband to hear him preach. The husband only feigned interest, for when he learned the priest's whereabouts he passed the information on to the local governor. The police traced the priest to the island of Uku and both he and Augustine were arrested and sent to the prison at Ikinoshima. With certain death approaching, Augustine wrote to the Jesuit provincial in Japan requesting admission into the Society. When the affirmative reply arrived, Fr. Costanzo accepted Augustine as a novice and the day before his death Augustine pronounced his three vows. After four months in prison, Br. Augustine Ota was beheaded on August 10, 1622, and his body was thrown into the sea.

Fr. Costanzo had another month to live. He was transferred to Tabira, which faces Hirado and the sea of Japan. There on September 15 he was bound to a stake, and while the executioners prepared the wood, he preached to the people telling them who he was and why he was being executed. He then exhorted the Christians to live courageously and invited the non-Christians to embrace the Catholic faith. The wood was set on fire, and when the smoke cleared and the flames began to twirl about his body, the bystanders saw that his eyes were fixed on heaven. They then heard him singing the psalm, *Praise the Lord, All You Nations,* and when he had concluded this he began to sing *Sanctus, Sanctus, Sanctus,* and having repeated it a few times he bowed his head in death.

Fr. Camillus Costanzo and Br. Augustine Ota were included among the Jesuits beatified by Pope Pius IX on May 7, 1867, and their offering of themselves to God is remembered by their brother Jesuits on February 4.

Prayer

Almighty God, grant that this remembrance of your holy martyrs, Blessed Camillus Costanzo and Blessed Augustine Ota, may bring us joy. May we who depend on their prayers glory in their entry in heaven. We ask this through our Lord Jesus Christ, your Son, who lives and reigns with you and the Holy Spirit, one God, for ever and ever.

St. Robert Bellarmine 1542–1621

Fr. Robert Bellarmine was an eminent scholar, the greatest theologian of his age, and an intrepid defender of the Church. When Pope Clement VIII named him a cardinal, he remarked: "We elect this man because he has not his equal for learning in the Church of God."

Robert was born on October 4, 1542, in central Italy, in the small city of Montepulciano, and was the nephew, on his mother's side, of Pope Marcellus II. He attended the local grammar school until 1557 when the Jesuits opened a school in his native city. When Robert expressed his desire to become a Jesuit, his father was at first opposed, but then relented and wrote to the general in Rome, Fr. James Laínez, to accept his son into the Society and requested that the boy remain at home for another year to test the sincerity of his vocation. In an uncommon gesture, Fr. Laínez agreed to the father's plan and arranged that the year at home would count as Robert's novitiate. When the year was up, the youth left for Rome on September 16, 1560, and on his arrival in the Eternal City went directly to the general's residence, where he pronounced his religious vows.

After two weeks at the motherhouse, Robert moved to the Roman College to begin his study of philosophy. In 1563 he went to Florence to teach and in the following year to Mondovì in Piedmont. Though still unordained and looking more like eighteen than twenty-two, he frequently preached in the city's cathedral. In 1567 he went to the University of Padua for theology, where he preached every Sunday. From Padua he transferred, in May 1569, to the university in Louvain, and though still engaged in studies, he found time to preach Latin sermons to the university community. Robert was ordained on March 25, 1570, and that same year, when the Jesuits opened their own theologate in Louvain, he was appointed its first professor of theology. Fr. Bellarmine spent seven years at that university center and during that time became familiar with the writings of the Reformers, especially those of Martin Luther and John Calvin, whose teachings were rapidly becoming widespread in northern Europe. Thus, he taught his theological course with a view to answering the Reformers' objections against the Roman Church.

Fr. Bellarmine was called to Rome in 1576 to the chair of "controversial theology" at the Roman College. Controversial theology treated those theological disputes that were then dividing the Christian Church, together with an extended explanation of the Roman Church's position. His eleven years of teaching were years of academic success. His lectures attracted students and his scholarship led the pope to name him to the papal commissions on revising the Vulgate (Latin) Bible and in preparing a new edition of the Septuagint (Greek) Bible. In 1586 he

J. Kilian sc.

P. Robert, Bellarmin, S.J. Ital, Monte-Politian g, S.R.E. Cardinalis, Marcelli IIth Pont: Nepos, Eccle- fiæ Catholicæ Athleta, Hærefum Expugnator, zelô Apoftolicò, et vitæ, fanctimoniâ confpicuus, Obyt Romæ 17 Sept: A°1621. Ætatis 80.
109.

St. Robert Bellarmine

published the first volume of his *Controversies,* based on his Roman lectures. The *Controversies* is Fr. Bellarmine's most important work. It appeared in three volumes (vol. 2 was published in 1588, and vol. 3 in 1593) and later went through some twenty editions and was read by Catholics and Protestants alike.

In 1588 Fr. Bellarmine was relieved of his obligation to teach and was given time to prepare the remaining volume of his masterwork for publication. Though he did not lecture, he still maintained contact with the Jesuit students at the college, among whom was Aloysius Gonzaga. He was their spiritual director. On December 28, 1592, he became rector of the college and had 220 Jesuits under him. Then on November 24, 1594, he was appointed provincial of the Naples province. So conscientious was he in fulfilling this office that, during the two years he was provincial, he twice visited the houses under his jurisdiction. Then in February 1597, when the Jesuit cardinal, Francis Toledo, theological adviser to Pope Clement VIII, died, the Holy Father turned to Fr. Bellarmine and asked him to assume the role his brother Jesuit had so ably filled.

In Rome, in 1598, he published his *Catechism,* which enjoyed a wide audience and was translated into sixty-two languages and was still in use in the middle of the nineteenth century. Because the pope was greatly dependent upon Fr. Bellarmine, rumor spread through the city that he would soon be a cardinal. Though he and Fr. General Claudio Acquaviva had done all they could to avoid this development, nevertheless, they bowed in obedience to the pope when he, on March 3, 1599, named Fr. Bellarmine a cardinal of the Roman Church. As a cardinal he now had to be surrounded by servants and gentlemen-in-waiting, and had to have carriages to transport him wherever he went. In his personal life, however, he still lived very simply for he never relinquished being a Jesuit. Whenever the month's account showed a surplus of funds, these he distributed among Rome's poor.

To Cardinal Bellarmine's surprise, in 1602 the Holy Father named him Archbishop of Capua. On April 21 he was ordained bishop and within a week was in his diocese, some nineteen miles north of Naples. He took his pastoral appointment seriously. Each Sunday he preached in his cathedral and during the week visited one of his parishes. He regularly recited the Divine Office with the cathedral canons and by his exhortations renewed the spiritual fervor of several monasteries and convents. On the death of Pope Clement he participated in the conclave that elected Leo XI on April 1, 1605. Leo lived only a month and Cardinal Bellarmine found himself, in the second conclave, one of the leading candidates for the chair of Peter; thus he prayed: "From the papacy, deliver me, O Lord!" Paul V was elected on May 16 and the new pope asked Cardinal Bellarmine to remain in Rome, where he was named to several congregations, among them those of the Holy Office, Rites, and Propagation of the Faith.

The Jesuit training that Cardinal Bellarmine had received never left him, and even as a cardinal he made an annual eight-day retreat. He later extended it to an annual thirty-day retreat, and during those weeks of quiet prayer, he wrote ascetical works, for example, *On the Ascent of the Mind to God* (1614), *The Eternal Happiness of the Saints* (1615), and *The Art of Dying Well* (1620).

As the cardinal passed into his seventy-seventh year, he felt himself slowing down; he suffered much, especially since his legs had become swollen. Realizing that he had not many more years left, he longed to return to the Roman novitiate of Sant'Andrea and live the simple life he once knew. He requested Paul V's permission to retire, but was told that neither the Church nor the pope could do without him. After Paul V's death in January 1621 and the election of Gregory XV, he again asked permission to retire, but it was again denied him because his presence was deemed necessary to the new pontiff. Obedient as always, the cardinal stayed on.

Finally, because advanced age and loss of hearing were beginning to show themselves more clearly, Gregory XV permitted Cardinal Bellarmine to move to the Jesuit novitiate. He arrived on August 25, 1621, and three days later was taken by a violent fever, from which he never recovered. The pope came to visit him, as did many cardinals and bishops, each asking the dying cardinal to remember him in heaven. In order to have a remembrance of their holy colleague, many cardinals and bishops placed their skullcaps on his head and their crosses on his breast. These they kept as mementoes of one whom they highly esteemed and greatly loved. Cardinal Bellarmine grew steadily worse and on the morning of September 17, between six and seven o'clock, after he had concluded his prayers, his voice began to fail and he softly repeated: "Jesus, Jesus, Jesus!" With the name of his Savior on his lips the saintly scholar went to heaven.

Ten years prior to his death, Cardinal Bellarmine had asked to be buried at the feet of Blessed Aloysius Gonzaga, but the simple funeral he had requested was transformed by order of the pope into a funeral befitting one whose service to the Church had been outstanding. The cardinal's body was first buried in our Lady's chapel in Rome's Gesù church, and then in 1923 it was transferred to the church of St. Ignatius, where it now reposes.

Cardinal Robert Bellarmine was beatified by Pope Pius XI on May 13, 1923, canonized by the same pontiff on June 29, 1930, and declared a Doctor of the Universal Church on September 17, 1931. His memorial is celebrated on September 17.

Prayer

Lord our God, creator of the world, your power and godhead are seen in the things you have made. As we give you glory for the wisdom and teaching of Saint Robert Bellarmine, we ask that mankind may be obedient to the faith revealed to us in our Lord Jesus Christ, your Son, who lives and reigns with you and the Holy Spirit, one God, for ever and ever.

September 24

S. G. Ignatius de Velasco and 6 Companions 1890–1936

Martyrs of the Spanish Civil War

These seven Jesuits, five priests and two brothers, were martyred in Madrid by communist revolutionary forces between August 7 and December 4, 1936.

Fr. Ignatius de Velasco y Nieto was born on July 19, 1890, at Las Arenas, in the Spanish province of Vizcaya, and studied to be a mining engineer. While living in Madrid he came to know Fr. Joseph Mary Rubio and frequently accompanied him on his visits to the poor. It was this association with Fr. Rubio that set the young man to think about the Society of Jesus and eventually led him to leave school and enter the novitiate. He did not stay very long; his father was in poor health and Ignatius had to return home. He finished his studies in engineering and then, when he was twenty-seven, entered the novitiate once more, at Granada, on November 12, 1917. After completing his noviceship, he spent the years 1920 to 1922 doing classical studies and the years from 1922 to 1925 in philosophy. He then went to Chamartín College in Madrid to teach mathematics (1925–1927), and finally to Oña for theology (1927). Ignatius found his theological course somewhat difficult; he was older than his fellow Jesuits and had a poor memory. At one time he thought of becoming a brother, but through perseverance in studies he passed his examinations and was ordained in 1930. He finished theology in 1931 and went to Portugal for tertianship. The Society had been suppressed in Spain in early 1932 so he taught mathematics at the Jesuit college in Liège, Belgium, for two years.

Now that he was a priest, his interests began to change. It was no longer engineering and mathematics that attracted him, it was the poor. He remembered their great number in Madrid, those who lived in misery and without sufficient food and, thus, he asked permission of his superiors to set engineering aside and to continue the apostolate begun by Fr. Rubio many years before. Permission was granted and Fr. Velasco left Belgium in 1934 to return to Madrid, where he set himself to helping the unfortunate. He lived as poorly as they did and never had a peseta in his pocket. This apostolate was terminated, however, in July 1936 by the outbreak of war between Spain's communist and nationalist movements.

Now that the country was involved in civil war and priests were vigorously hunted by communist revolutionaries, Fr. Velasco's Jesuit community had to disperse. He went to live with his sister. A cousin of theirs was recently jailed and when Fr. Velasco's sister returned from visiting him on September 20, she related how contented the prisoners were; the priests in prison celebrated Mass daily and everyone had the opportunity to receive Communion. Their cousin compared it to being in the catacombs during early Christian times. Fr. Velasco's spirit brightened and he remarked that he would not mind being in prison, for there he could do much good for others. He also added: "And if they kill me, so much the better. I will go to heaven without passing through purgatory." At this statement his mother began to cry. He turned to her saying: "Don't cry, mother. If they kill me I will die as a priest, as a Jesuit; I will be a martyr and I will go to heaven. I became a Jesuit in order to die for Christ. For this I left you and my career. So, don't cry."

Fr. Velasco's desire was soon fulfilled. The very next day, September 21, at 10:00 A.M., several militiamen came to the house and took the entire family to their station. The soldiers informed them that they were looking for a certain individual and as soon as they found him everyone else would be free. When they arrived at the station the men were placed in one room and the women in another. When Fr. Velasco was interrogated, knowing well that he was the object of their search, he openly admitted that he was a Jesuit priest. They then asked him why his identification card described him as an engineer and he simply said that he was also an engineer.

Fr. Velasco was detained at the station for two days and then on September 23, about 11:45 P.M., a rough voice shouted into the room where the men were kept, "Ignatius de Velasco." Each man knew what that meant. The priest gave a goodbye embrace to everyone and left with the soldiers. They took him to the road that led to Andalusia and there the forty-six-year-old Fr. Velasco was martyred. It was about 1:00 A.M., September 24. That same day his body was identified and buried.

Several weeks before Fr. Velasco's death, Brs. Ignatius Elduayen y Larrañaga and Pascual Ruiz Ramírez died at the hands of revolutionaries. Br. Elduayen was born on March 9, 1884, at Azcoitia, in Guipúzcoa province, and entered the Jesuits at Granada on July 30, 1903. He came to Madrid in 1917 to work at Chamartín College and then in 1931 was assigned to the Gregorian University in Rome. He returned to Madrid in 1935 and lived at the Christopher Columbus Academy (the former Chamartín College), and was in charge of the school's lay workers. Br. Ruiz, who was born on February 14, 1901, in Ciudad Real, entered the Society in Granada on June 14, 1917. He was a tailor at the Granada scholasticate for three years and then spent seven years at the College of St. Callistus in La Paz, Bolivia. Upon his return to Madrid he too was stationed at the academy.

At 9:00 A.M. on August 7, 1936, the academy was invaded by communist soldiers who arrested the two Jesuit brothers and five lay workers. A search of the house yielded a chalice used at Mass. This was sufficient evidence to make an arrest and the seven were taken to the soldiers' station for questioning. Br. Elduayen was separated from the others and while he was being interrogated Br. Ruiz suggested to the others that they make an act of contrition. They then recited the rosary. All through the day they waited, not knowing what was to happen, and finally at 9:30 in the evening, they were taken from their rooms and led outside. Brs. Elduayen and Ruiz and one of the lay workers were put in one car, and the four others in another. Both cars headed for the Pozuelo road, but before the second car arrived gunshots were heard—Brs. Elduayen and Ruiz, and Felix, the worker who accompanied them, had been killed. The other four workers were also shot, but only one, whose name was Nicholas, was killed, the other three were wounded and survived the incident. At the time of their martyrdom, Br. Elduayen was fifty-two years old and Br. Ruiz thirty-five.

Fr. Jesús Ballesta Tejero probably died on August 8, 1936, a day after the two martyrs above. He was born on January 1, 1903, at Vera da Moncayo, in the province of Saragossa, and entered the Jesuit novitiate at Veruela on January 5, 1918. He did his philosophy and theology at Sarriá, near Barcelona, and was ordained in 1932. After ordination he spent a year in the Netherlands and another in Belgium, and when he returned to Spain in 1934 he went to Madrid. Fr. Ballesta was especially interested in workers' movements, and since the province had recently initiated a labor institute in Madrid, he went there to be part of it. When the revolution broke out in July, the priests had to disperse, but Fr. Ballesta's identity card indicated that he was a priest so he could not easily leave the building or go onto the street. While his fellow Jesuits left for other residences, Fr. Ballesta merely went to live with a family on another floor, and from there he continued his ministry, as best he could, until he was betrayed by a worker.

On August 8 communist revolutionaries forced their way into the apartment building and shouted: "There's a priest hiding here." Hearing the disturbance below, Fr. Ballesta left his apartment and went up to that of the Sisters of Charity. Someone below, however, directed the soldiers to look upstairs. When the communists knocked at the sisters' door and entered they immediately saw Fr. Ballesta. "Are you the traitor?" they asked. To this he replied: "A traitor, no, but a priest. Whom do you want?" They told him they were looking for a priest. He responded: "I am the one. My name is Jesús; I am thirty-three years old, and I am ready to die for him who first died for me." He was then taken from the apartment and nothing more was heard of him. No one knew whether he was in prison or had been killed. Finally, in January 1940 a photo of a body was found, with a note identifying it as that of Fr. Ballesta; it bore the date August 9, 1936. The priest was probably martyred the day he was arrested, August 8, and the body was probably discovered the following morning and photographed by city officials.

Fr. John Gómez Hellín met his martyrdom on October 2, 1936. Born in Alguazas in Murcia province on September 15, 1899, he began his noviceship at Granada on June 14, 1917. After his study of philosophy he spent three years (1923–1926) teaching history and Spanish at the College of the Sacred Heart in Sucre, Bolivia. He returned to Spain for theology and was ordained in 1929. Since 1932, the year of the suppression of the Jesuits in Spain, Fr. Gómez carried on his priestly ministry at Didaskalion, a boys' school in Madrid. When civil war broke out, he and another Jesuit went to live with the latter's relatives. For two months Fr. Gómez lived in peace, but on September 20 the house was searched. Because he carried a card identifying him as a teacher, nothing was done to him, but ten days later the communists returned and asked if he was a Jesuit. When he admitted that he was, they responded, "That's enough," and took him away. They detained him for two days, then in the early hours of October 2, 1936, he was martyred on the road leading to Vicálvaro.

The oldest of these seven Madrid martyrs was Fr. Joseph Alegre Jiménez. He was born at Cartagena in Murcia province on November 1, 1865, and entered the Society on October 7, 1881. After his years of study and training, he spent most of his priestly life at Chamartín College in Madrid. When the Jesuits had to disperse because of the suppression, Fr. Alegre went to live with a Jesuit brother next to the convent of the Sisters of Mary Reparatrice, whose chaplain he was. They had their first search on August 10, but no one was arrested. Eight days later there was another, and Fr. Alegre was taken to communist headquarters, where he readily declared: "It does not matter to me if you shoot me, but I am telling you that I am a Jesuit." Since he was in his seventy-first year, the revolutionaries told him to go home and stay out of trouble. On August 22 he moved in with the Gallego family and remained there for almost three months. On November 7 the Gallego residence was searched and all the men, including Fr. Alegre, were taken to the Hieronymite monastery, which had recently been converted into a prison. He was there during the nationalist movement's heavy bombardment of Madrid on November 9. In retaliation for the damage done to their planes, the communists began executing prisoners. Early in the morning of November 10, as dawn was about the break, they took Fr. Alegre from his cell and made him a martyr. As the priest was leaving the prison one of the guards asked what was Fr. Alegre's crime. The answer was: "He's a Jesuit!"

The last of these martyrs was Fr. Emmanuel de la Cerda y de las Bárcenas. He was born in Madrid, December 5, 1900, and entered the novitiate at Granada on October 6, 1926. Throughout his years of Jesuit training he was especially interested in natural history and spent three years (1925–1928) in La Paz, Bolivia, continuing his studies in that field. He returned to Spain to do his theology at Oña and in 1931 was ordained. He was teaching in Madrid when civil war broke out and he went to stay with his parents. Listed as a student on his identity card, he had no trouble going about the city administering the sacraments to all who desired them. However, one day in mid-September 1936, after visiting someone who was dying, he was unexpectedly apprehended and taken to Model Prison. Even in prison he continued his priestly work of preaching, catechizing, and hearing confessions. In November he was transferred to the Porlier Prison and there continued the same apostolic work. Then very early on the morning of December 4 his name was suddenly called out. He was being summoned to martyrdom. He went to the other priest in the cell with him and asked for absolution. After embracing everyone, he was taken by his jailers to be executed.

The cause of Fr. Ignatius de Velasco and his six Jesuit companions was opened in Madrid on September 28, 1945.

St. René Goupil 1608–1642

Martyr of North America

René Goupil was the first of the eight canonized North American Martyrs to die for the faith. He was born in Saint-Martin du Bois, in the diocese of Angers, France, on May 13, 1608. Though he had been trained as a surgeon and enjoyed a successful career, he set this aside to enter the Society in Paris on March 26, 1639. After a few months, however, he had to leave the novitiate because of deafness. He then offered himself to the Society as a *donné,* that is, a lay assistant who would share in the work of the missionaries, bind himself by promise to obey the Jesuit superior, work without salary and live a celibate life.

He was accepted for the Huron mission and when he arrived in New France in 1640 he was assigned to the hospital in Quebec to care for the French settlers and the Algonquin Indians at their reduction in nearby Sillery. Though obedient to his assignment, he wished he were more involved in the conversion of the native peoples.

René's chance to go among them came when Fr. Isaac Jogues arrived in Quebec in 1642 seeking assistants for the Huron mission. Fr. Jogues was eager to take René with him—the frontier always had need of people experienced in medicine. The missionary explained what life would be like and what hardships and privations were to be expected; René was willing to face all these dangers.

On August 2, just a day's journey up the St. Lawrence the flotilla carrying Fr. Jogues, René, and the Hurons, was unexpectedly ambushed by some seventy Mohawks, on the warpath against the French. The Mohawks had the greater number and the missionaries and Hurons were taken captive. The captors beat the missionaries and savagely bit out their fingernails and ground their forefingers with their teeth until they were formless masses. After this barbarity the prisoners were again placed in the canoes to continue the journey.

Fr. Jogues and René were in the same canoe and a few days after their capture René spoke about how he wanted to be a Jesuit and consecrate himself to God's service. With their future now uncertain, he asked Fr. Jogues if he could pronounce the vows of the Society as a brother. As the canoe slipped quietly through the placid waters, René, remembering the vow formula he once memorized as a novice, pronounced his vows of poverty, chastity, and obedience. He was now a Jesuit.

As the canoes came nearer their destination the Mohawks met a group of their nation coming toward them. To entertain themselves both groups went ashore and forced the prisoners to run the gauntlet. The Mohawks formed two rows and the captives had to run naked up a hill, passing between the rows while being beaten on head, back, neck, and shoulders. When this brutality was over, they made their way to their village, Ossernenon (today's Auriesville, N.Y.), on the Mohawk River.

The group arrived on August 14 and when they landed the prisoners once again had to run the gauntlet. The Mohawks unmercifully beat René on the face and head so that his features were so swollen and bloodied that only the whites of his eyes were distinguishable. When he collapsed under the blows, they kicked him aside so as not to hinder the others behind him. The missionaries were then exposed on a platform for the entire village to jeer at, and braves jabbed sharp instruments into their already wounded flesh. After enduring these tortures, they were taken to a longhouse, placed on the ground and tied to stakes, while children dropped hot coals upon them. When this torturous introduction to Ossernenon was over, René and Fr. Jogues were given as slaves to the chief who had captured them. They lived out their slavery as beasts of burden, performing any and every task, no matter how degrading.

René always enjoyed children and took every opportunity to talk and play with them. On one occasion, while playing with the four-year-old son of a dead Mohawk warrior, he took the child's hand into his own and guided it in making the sign of the cross. Unknown to René, the child's grandfather was watching, and having once been told by the non-Catholic Dutch that that sign was an invocation of evil spirits, he rushed madly to René, kicked him aside and seized his grandson. When Fr. Jogues heard of the incident, he went to find René. Together they went into the nearby forest, where they frequently went to pray, and prepared themselves for death. On their return to the village, as they were reciting the rosary, two braves approached them. One was the boy's uncle, who commanded them to return to the village with Fr. Jogues walking first. Fr. Jogues heard a slight noise and turned around to see the uncle whip a blanket from his shoulders, raise his tomahawk and dash it upon René's head. He knelt beside his dead companion and waited for his blow to come, but he was ordered to his cabin. The date was September 29, 1642.

Very early the next morning, Fr. Jogues went in search of René's body and found it in a ravine, in shallow water. It was stripped naked and the village dogs had already begun to gnaw at it. He took it into deeper water and temporarily covered it with stones, intending to return to give it proper burial. The next day the body was no longer where he had placed it and he presumed the force of the water had taken it away. But several months later he learned from a friendly Mohawk that children had discovered the body and had played with it somewhere along the stream. He continued his search and finally found some bones with a skull crushed in, and these he buried.

At a later date, Fr. Jogues wrote of René's death to his superior: "He deserves the name of martyr not only because he has been murdered by the enemies of God and his Church, while laboring in ardent charity for his neighbor, but most of all because he was killed for being at prayer and especially for making the sign of the cross."

Together with Fr. Isaac Jogues and six other Jesuits martyred in North America, René Goupil was beatified by Pope Pius XI on June 21, 1925, and canonized by him on June 29, 1930. St. René Goupil's memorial is celebrated with the other North American Martyrs on October 19.

Prayer

Father, you consecrated the first beginnings of the faith in North America by the martyrdom of Saint René Goupil and his companions. By the help of their prayers may the Christian faith continue to grow throughout the world. We ask this through our Lord Jesus Christ, your Son, who lives and reigns with you and the Holy Spirit, one God, for ever and ever.

October

S. G. Francis Rodrigues da Cruz 1859–1948

Fr. Francis Rodrigues da Cruz was eighty-one years old when he became a Jesuit. He had wanted to do this for sixty years, but it was only eight years before his death that he succeeded.

He was born in Alcochete, near Lisbon, Portugal, on July 29, 1859, the fourth of six children. His father was in the lumber business and the family lived in a house the father had built on the outskirts of town, overlooking the Tagus River. When Francis was nine he and his brother went to Lisbon to continue their education at the Industrial Institute and then at the Lycée. Though Francis in his early youth thought about becoming a priest, the year 1875 was his year of decision for he then enrolled at the University of Coimbra and began courses leading to the priesthood. He earned his degree in theology before he was twenty-one, and since he was too young to be ordained, he taught philosophy at the seminary at Santarém. When it was time for ordination his health was rather poor and he doubted that he could go through so long a ceremony. Nevertheless, he was ordained on June 3, 1882, and continued at Santarém until 1886, when his health became so poor that he was forced to relinquish his teaching schedule and go to Braga, where he directed a school for orphan boys interested in entering the seminary. Within eight years he also had to give that up for health reasons.

Fr. Cruz returned to Lisbon and became spiritual director of the students at the minor seminary, and as his health improved he took on other tasks. When the seminary moved from Lisbon in 1905, Fr. Cruz remained in the city and for the next forty-three years labored tirelessly in that Portuguese capital. For most of this time he lived at the Reparation Convent and devoted his time to helping the poor and visiting prisons and the sick. His special joy, however, was in helping his fellow priests when they needed someone to substitute for them or just an extra hand. He frequently gave novenas and preached the Forty Hours in neighboring parishes, and when the archbishop made an official visit to a parish, he usually preceded him, giving a triduum to prepare the people for the General Communion at the time of the visit. So often had he given these tridua in preparation for the archbishop's visit that his fellow priests humorously dubbed him "the precursor."

Fr. Cruz was in Vila Nova de Ourem in 1913 to preach at a First Communion Mass. This was a few years before our Lady's apparitions made Fatima famous. There lived in the parish a young girl named Lucia dos Santos, who knew her catechism exceptionally well, but because she was under the required seven years of age, her name did not appear on the list of communicants. With tears in her eyes she approached Fr. Cruz and told him the cause of her sadness. Sensing the child's tremendous desire to receive Holy Communion, Fr. Cruz quizzed her on her understanding of the faith and then prevailed upon the pastor to permit the child to receive with the others.

Four years later Lucia was one of the three children to whom our Lady appeared, and because the parish priest was convinced at the time that Lucia and the other two children were being deceived by the devil, he asked Fr. Cruz to question them and set them straight. After talking to them (June or July 1917), Fr. Cruz told them: "Be assured, have no fear; it was not a devil who appeared to you but the Holy Virgin."

Fr. Cruz's most important apostolate was, perhaps, in the confessional. The lines outside his box were always long, not only with women and children, but also with laborers and soldiers, business men and government officials. All who went to Fr. Cruz for confession found a holy, humble, and kind confessor. In 1925 the cardinal thought of making him a canon in the cathedral chapter and wrote to him about the appointment. But Fr. Cruz responded saying that he felt that he was called by God to minister to the wretched and the afflicted and in this manner he could best give praise and glory to God. The cardinal acquiesced to Fr. Cruz's desire, but some time later appointed him director of the Apostolic Union, an association of diocesan priests seeking to deepen their spiritual life.

Though Fr. Cruz was always active among the diocesan clergy, he was at heart a Jesuit. When studying at the University of Coimbra, he became acquainted with the Society, and in his last year, 1880, he made an eight-day retreat under a Jesuit's direction and thought of entering the Society. His health, unfortunately, was not sufficiently robust to take on more years of study and the rigors of community life. A few years after ordination, in 1886, he vowed to enter the Society, whenever his health would permit him to do so. He identified himself with the Jesuits and their work, and when they were expelled from Portugal in 1910, he wanted to go into exile with them, but the Jesuit provincial pointed out to him that by remaining in Portugal he could continue to do good for the Church.

When the Jesuits returned from exile he regularly visited them, but since his physical condition always remained uncertain there seemed no possibility of his ever becoming a Jesuit. In 1929, however, the Jesuit general, Fr. Wlodzimierz Ledóchowski, obtained an indult from Pope Pius XI granting the seventy-year-old Fr. Cruz permission to take Jesuit vows on his deathbed. From that time onward Fr. Cruz carried a copy of the vow formula with him. But as the years passed the aging priest began to worry that his might be a sudden death and, hence, he would never be able to pronounce the vows. Once again in 1940, the Holy Father granted an indult authorizing the eighty-one-year-old priest to take vows as a Jesuit without making noviceship and permitting him to live with friends, who had been caring for him for the past several years. Fr. Cruz chose December 3, 1940, as his vow day; it was the feast of his patron, St. Francis Xavier. His desire at long last was fulfilled.

Fr. Cruz continued his apostolate of hearing confessions and counselling the clergy, but he was now under obedience to a Jesuit superior. In December 1947 he had to give up celebrating Mass because of his health, but he attended and received Communion daily. On September 30, 1948, he visited his superior to discuss plans for his annual retreat, and before leaving the residence he requested to go to confession. The next morning, October 1, he received Communion in his room, but after his thanksgiving he collapsed, and within a few minutes the eighty-nine-year-old Fr. Cruz gave his soul to his Savior.

The funeral of Fr. Cruz was held in the Lisbon cathedral and Cardinal Emanuele Gonçalves Cerejeira, Patriarch of Lisbon, ordered that it be the same as for a patriarch. The church was filled with Fr. Cruz's friends: priests, diocesan and Jesuit, sisters whom he had directed, penitents whom he had counselled, and the poor whom he had assisted. They were all there to thank him for his Christ-like love and kindness. During his sermon, the cardinal said: "The holy Fr. Cruz will remain one of the purest glories of our patriarchate. The clergy of Lisbon will always venerate him as a striking example of an apostolic worker, of a priest totally consecrated to the glory of God and the salvation of souls. In him they will find a model and an advocate." Within three years the cardinal began the diocesan investigation into Fr. Cruz's life and holiness. His cause is presently being studied.

October 2

Ven. John Beyzym 1850–1912

Fr. John Beyzym left Poland in 1898 and spent the last fourteen years of his life as a samaritan caring for abandoned lepers in Madagascar. He was born on May 15, 1850, at the family estate in Beyzymy Wielkie in Poland's Wolyn region. He was the eldest of five children and his early education took place at home. During the January 1863 uprising the family lost its estates and was forced to separate; John's mother took the children and went to live with her sister in the Podole region, while John's father, who was sought by the cossacks, left Russian-occupied Poland and crossed into Austrian held Galicia.

John then did his secondary studies in Kiev (now in Ukraine) and when he completed them in 1872, he thought about becoming a diocesan priest. He visited his father in Porudnie—he had not seen him for eight years—and told him of his desire. During their conversation, it seems, John's father suggested that he think of the Jesuits, and on December 10, 1872, father and son travelled to the Jesuit novitiate at Stara Wieś, near Brzozowa in Galicia. John was accepted as a novice the following day.

John had his first contact with suffering humanity during his noviceship; a cholera epidemic broke out in the neighborhood and he and a few other novices were permitted to accompany the priests and brothers as they visited the stricken in the villages. After his studies at Stara Wieś, John was sent in 1878 to Ternopol as a student prefect, and the following year he went to Cracow for his theological studies. He was ordained on July 26, 1881, and returned to Ternopol to teach French and Russian. In 1887 he was transferred to Chirov, where he taught and was also in charge of the school's infirmary.

As early as 1879, Fr. Beyzym had requested to work among lepers, and over the years this desire had never left him. When he was in his late forties he wrote to the Jesuit general, Fr. Luis Martín, expressing this longing of his: "I well know what leprosy is and what I ought to expect; but this does not frighten me, rather, it attracts me." After an exchange of letters, the general assigned him to the leprosarium in Mangalore, India, but because Fr. Beyzym knew no English, India was out of the question. He did know French and thus he was reassigned to Madagascar, where several French Jesuits worked with lepers.

Fr. Beyzym sailed from Marseilles on November 10, 1898, passed through Suez, then the length of the Red Sea, into the Indian Ocean, and finally docked at Majunga on Madagascar's west coast. He then made his way to Tananarive (now Antananarivo), capital of the island. French Jesuits had been in Madagascar since the middle of the nineteenth century, but only a few worked at the island's two hospices for lepers; the larger hospice was at Ambahivuraka, near Tananarive, and the smaller at Marana, near Fianarantsoa in the south.

When Fr. Beyzym arrived in Ambahivuraka, there were about 150 sick men, women, and children living totally abandoned in a desert area. He found them living in huts better suited for animals than for humans, and without medical care; their bodies were covered with sores and many were without hands or feet. Death was frequent, not because of the disease but because of hunger.

The first thing that Fr. Beyzym did was unheard of in the Madagascar mission. Unlike others, he went and lived among the lepers. He put his earlier infirmary training to immediate use; he treated their wounds as best he could without medicine, and saw that the wounds were clean and properly bandaged. He repaired their huts, prepared their food, and saw that they had water for bathing. The government ration of rice was hardly enough to keep them alive so he went into the city and begged food and clothing for them and regularly shared his own modest ration of rice with them. They were materially poor, but they were likewise spiritually poor, and so while caring for their wounds he also cared for their souls. He brought God to them as well as the sacraments.

Fr. Beyzym was not long in Ambahivuraka before he realized that a hospital was needed, with a doctor and nursing sisters. He suggested this to the superior of the Jesuit mission, but there were no funds for such an ambitious project. This idea would not leave him and he was determined that his people should have a hospital so that they might live in hope. To fulfill his dream he would need 150,000 francs, and though civil authorities granted permission for a hospital they doubted that he could collect that much money. Confidently placing his project into the hands of Our Lady of Częstochowa, Fr. Beyzym began writing letters to Catholic missionary organizations and magazines in Poland. In his letters he described the misery of the disease, the plight of his people, and explained their needs. His letters were published and the response they received was extraordinary. Donations arrived from various missionary groups, but mostly from the Polish people, at home and elsewhere, who themselves had very little to spare. His hospital could now become a reality.

For the site of the hospital Fr. Beyzym chose Marana, near Fianarantsoa, where there was water and the land was more suitable for agriculture. Construction began in 1903. He himself designed the hospital for 200 patients, with separate buildings for men and women, together with pharmacy, dispensary, and living quarters for missionaries and sisters. There was also a large chapel. Because there were fewer sick at Marana than at Ambahivuraka, he was able to supervise the entire building program and was often seen using a shovel or pushing a wheelbarrow. What time he had free, he sculpted decorations for the chapel's interior.

After several years in Marana, Fr. Beyzym enjoyed a most unexpected surprise. The sick at Ambahivuraka, that is, the ambulatory, traversed the 180 miles—a month's journey over mountains and through deep valleys—to Marana so that they could again be with the Polish samaritan, who had shown them love. The missionary welcomed and embraced each one of them.

The hospital, named after Our Lady of Częstochowa, opened on August 16, 1916, and was staffed by the Sisters of St. Joseph of Cluny. The sick now wore uniforms and were expected to observe the sanitary and moral rules of the hospital. They formed a large family and also attended church services in common.

As the hospital was nearing completion Fr. Beyzym heard of the distressing situation in which Polish deportees were living on the Russian island of Sakhalin, north of Japan. With the hospital now a reality, he wanted to help his fellow countrymen, but that desire was never to be fulfilled. Weakened by his labors and worn out by penances and an austere life, he contracted a fever which never left him. He died two months later, October 2, 1912, surrounded by those whom he loved.

On December 21, 1992, the decree acknowledging Fr. Beyzym's exercise of extraordinary virtue was promulgated.

October 3

St. Francis Borgia 1510–1572

Fr. Francis Borgia was the Society's third superior general, and it was during his term of office that the first Jesuit missionaries came to Florida, the earliest Jesuit mission on American soil.

Francis was the oldest son of the third duke of Gandía and was born in the family palace in the ancient kingdom of Valencia on October 28, 1510. His great grandfather on his father's side was Pope Alexander VI, and his mother's grandfather was King Ferdinand the Catholic. In his early years Francis was trained, as were all young nobles, to ride, hunt, fence, and dance. When his mother died in 1520, he went to live with his uncle the archbishop of Saragossa. There he studied the humanities and music, and in 1522 was appointed page to his youthful cousin Catherine, Emperor Charles V's sister, who was then companion to her mother Queen Juana "the mad," at Tordesillas. Upon Catherine's marriage to John III of Portugal in 1525, Francis returned to Saragossa and began his study of philosophy.

In response to the invitation of Emperor Charles, Francis returned to court in 1528 and in summer 1529 married Leonor de Castro of Portugal, Empress Isabella's first lady-in-waiting. Francis and Leonor were greatly beloved by Charles and Isabella, who bestowed on them many honors. Francis was made Marquis of Llombai in 1530, though he was only twenty years old, and was placed in charge of the imperial household. For the next ten years the Borgias, with their eight children, lived happily and in great familiarity with Charles and Isabella, until May 1, 1539, when Isabella unexpectedly died. The empress was to be buried in the royal chapel in Granada and Francis, with bishops and other nobles, escorted the body to that southern city. The cortege arrived on May 16 and on the following day, after Mass had been celebrated and prior to placing the body in the tomb, the coffin was opened for official recognition of the body.

S. Francisc, Borgia, S.I. Generalis III. è Regio Hispan. sangvine
Dux Gandiæ, etc. In funere Augustæ Isabellæ aulam mundi exoso vivé
re et servire Deo statuit, Societatem complex, verbo et opere salutē
proximi, etiam Romæ in peste, cordi suo sumpsit. Alias pro Viri Nobi,
lis obstinati anima, adusq, sangvineu Crucifixi profluviu, licet fru,
stra, mira egit, à Pio V. ad Reges in Legationē mis, in negotio con,
tra Turcas, optimo succelsu. Ioāne da Austria contra Turcas Victore.
Obyt Romæ 1572   23.

S. FRANCISCUS BORGIA.

St. Francis Borgia

Francis saw not the once beautiful face of the thirty-six-year-old queen, but a face beyond recognition. He exclaimed: "Never again, never again, will I serve a master who can die on me." Francis now understood the tragic transitoriness of human life and material possessions. He always regarded this date as the day of his conversion, for he now dedicated himself to a more perfect life, one given to prayer and penance.

On his return from the sad mission to Granada, Francis was appointed Viceroy of Catalonia, in June 1539. Then upon his father's death, January 8, 1543, he became the fourth duke of Gandía and returned to the family palace to undertake the administration of his estates. After his wife Leonor died on March 27, 1546, he considered spending the remainder of his life in God's service. Francis had become acquainted with the Jesuits, knew Fr. Peter Favre, and in November 1545 had founded a Jesuit college in Gandía. In May 1546 the duke, now a widower, made a retreat under Fr. Andrew de Oviedo, rector of the college, and on June 2 vowed to become a Jesuit as soon as he could arrange his temporal affairs. When Fr. Favre left Gandía for Rome, the duke asked him to inform Fr. Ignatius of his resolve. In writing to the duke, Fr. Ignatius praised him for his decision, accepted him into the Society, recommended that he tell no one of his intention for the present, that he arrange marriages and positions for his eight children, and begin his study of theology. But, at the same time, he was to continue living as befit his noble rank. On February 1, 1548, Francis pronounced his vows as a Jesuit and on August 20, 1550, earned a doctorate in theology from the university he had founded.

Though 1550 was a Holy Year and Francis did want to make a pilgrimage to Rome, his main purpose for going there was to see Fr. Ignatius and arrange for his public entrance into the Society. He set out from Gandía on August 30 with his son, Juan, servants, and several Jesuits. He was not to see his beloved Gandía again. Arriving in Rome on October 23 he declined Pope Julius III's offer to use the Borgia apartments in the Vatican and lived at the Jesuit residence with Fr. Ignatius instead. In Rome Francis played the role of pilgrim and tourist, visiting shrines and monuments, but within the Jesuit community he lived as a Jesuit and even served at table. In early February 1551, he left for Spain and went directly to the Basque region of Guipúzcoa, thinking he would be unknown there. He arrived at Oñate in April, and a month later his cousin, the emperor, accepted his resignation of his title and his passing it on to his son Carlos. Immediately after reading the emperor's letter, Francis donned the Jesuit cassock. He was ordained a priest on May 23 and celebrated his first Mass on August 1 in the tiny oratory in Fr. Ignatius' ancestral home at Loyola.

Fr. Borgia spent the next three years performing the duties of an ordinary parish priest, living an uneventful life, preaching and caring for his parishioners. This peaceful existence was interrupted when Fr. Ignatius asked him in February 1552 to visit Portugal and pacify certain individuals who had become disturbed because Fr. Simon Rodrigues had been removed as provincial in December 1551. Fr. Borgia got as far as Salamanca when, on April 23, he learned that the trip was no longer necessary. He returned to Oñate and continued his pastoral work. In 1554 he was named Commissary General in Spain, a position that placed him over the Spanish and Portuguese provincials. In this capacity he founded some twenty colleges and Spain's first novitiate at Simancas. When the first general congregation convened on June 19, 1558, almost two years after Fr. Ignatius died, Fr. Borgia did not attend, but sent two missives to the assembled fathers.

In 1561 Pope Pius IV called Fr. Borgia to Rome. When Fr. James Laínez, who succeeded Fr. Ignatius as general, left to attend the last session of the Council of Trent, Fr. Borgia was chosen vicar general. When Fr. Laínez returned in January 1564, Fr. Borgia became assistant for Spain and Portugal, and when the general died on January 19, 1565, he was elected on July 2 of that same year to succeed him as the order's third superior general.

Fr. Borgia's generalate lasted seven years and was spent in revising the Society's rules, overseeing its expansion, promoting missions in India, North and South America, and in reading and writing countless letters. It was he who began the Gesù church in Rome as well as the novitiate of Sant'Andrea. He was very friendly with Pope Pius V, and when His Holiness asked him to accompany Cardinal Michele Bonelli on the latter's mission to secure Spain's help against the Turks, Fr. Borgia could not decline. This trip, however, hastened his death. Fr. Borgia left Rome on June 30, 1571, and by the end of August was in Barcelona, where he had once been viceroy. Everyone wanted to see "the holy duke," and the welcome he received overpowered the humble Jesuit. He did not know that he had become a living legend among the Spaniards. He and the cardinal were in Valencia in September, and though he was only thirty miles from Gandía, which he had left twenty-one years previously, he would not return to it. Hence, his children and grandchildren came to visit him.

When the mission in Spain was over in December 1571, the cardinal thought of returning to Rome by sea to avoid travelling overland during the cold winter months. These plans were changed when the cardinal received word from the pope to go to France. The winter of 1571–1572 was unusually cold, and the thin, weary, and wasted Fr. Borgia felt it most acutely, so that travelling now became torture for his pain-racked body. It was only when they heard the news that Pius V was dying that the cardinal's entourage turned and headed for Rome. The cardinal was in great haste to arrive before the pope's death so he went on ahead. Fr. Borgia was now suffering from fever and pleurisy. Crossing the Alps in a litter was slow and dangerous, and when they reached Turin, he was forced to spend several weeks at rest. Feeling somewhat better during the summer, he made his way to Ferrara to visit his relatives, the d'Este family, and there he learned that the pope had died on May 1, 1572. The fever returned and again the general was constrained to remain longer than he had intended. Finally on September 3 he left Ferrara, eager to arrive in Rome, so that he could die there.

His prayer was answered, for when he arrived in the city at the end of September he was immediately put to bed. Hearing the news that Fr. General had returned, many visitors came to see him, so many that he eventually had to ask them: "Leave me, for now I have only time for God." Three days later, during the night of September 30, the sixty-one-year-old Fr. General, in peace and serenity, exchanged his human life for a better life.

Fr. Francis Borgia was beatified by Pope Urban VIII on November 23, 1624, and was canonized by Pope Clement X on April 12, 1671. In 1617 his body was taken to Madrid and venerated at the Professed House until 1931, when revolutionaries destroyed the residence. The charred remains were collected and are now in the Jesuit church on Calle Serrano. Fr. Francis Borgia's memorial is celebrated in the Society on October 3.

Prayer

Lord our God, you called Saint Francis Borgia from a royal palace to be your servant. Grant through his prayers that all who have died to sin and renounced the world may live for you alone. We ask this through our Lord Jesus Christ, your Son, who lives and reigns with you and the Holy Spirit, one God, for ever and ever.

October 4

S. G. Salvador Garcidueñas 1856–1927

Salvador Garcidueñas was a Mexican, born at Santa Clara del Cobre (today's Villa Escalante), in the state of Michoacán, on August 6, 1856. The Garcidueñas family had six children. the parents, who set great value on a good education, moved to Morelia, the state capital, and there Salvador attended elementary and secondary school. When he was twenty he thought of following his older brother, Nicanor, who was then at the diocesan seminary but, in the end, chose to prepare for a career in law. The thought of being a priest, however, never left him, and after he received his law degree in 1879 at age twenty-four he entered Morelia's major seminary.

Salvador remained at the seminary only a few months, for in early 1880 he decided to become a Jesuit, though there were no Jesuits at the time in Morelia. Since its restoration in 1814, the Society had a difficult time reestablishing itself in Mexico, principally because of the anticlerical governments which forbade religious orders to establish houses or monasteries. During the period that Salvador chose to enter the Society there were only forty-eight Jesuits in the entire country; of this number twenty-nine were priests, and most of these were foreign born. It is not known how he came to know about the Society. Nevertheless, determined that he wanted to be a son of St. Ignatius, Salvador went to Tepotzotlán, near Mexico City, to visit the superior of the Mexican Jesuits. He was accepted as a candidate and on April 27, 1880, arrived at the novitiate in San Simón, not far from Zamora and not many miles from his birthplace.

The novitiate was small, about a half dozen novices lived in a converted ranch house. Salvador pronounced his vows in April 1882 and in 1883 went to study philosophy at Puebla. He began teaching there in 1885 and in 1888 was sent to Oña in Spain for theology, and there he was ordained on July 27, 1890.

Upon the return of Fr. Garcidueñas to his native land, he was assigned, during the summer of 1891, to the shrine of Our Lady of the Angels in Mexico City's Los Angeles district. There he spent the remaining thirty-six years of his life. When he arrived in Los Angeles it had its fights and murders, its robberies and bloodshed; but within ten years the quarter was calm and peaceful. The police, who now rarely had to visit the district, attributed the peace to the influence of Fr. Garcidueñas. The priest, however, ascribed the calm to our Lady, to whose care he had confided the people of his district.

Fr. Garcidueñas had the wonderful charism of dealing with people. He touched their hearts and was like a parent to them, but especially to those who were sick. These he visited, cared for, and comforted. His greatest gift was in handling children. Since the government had closed the Catholic schools and failed to open public schools, the children ran wild through the streets. He gathered them about him and patiently endured their constant tugging at his cassock. Whether he played games with them or took them on trips to visit other parts of Mexico City, or to pray at some shrine, his concern was always to tell them about God. He regularly held catechism classes for them and realizing the children's need to learn secular subjects as well he took the matter into his own hands. He established a school with free instruction for the children and paid the teachers by begging alms.

The influence of Fr. Garcidueñas was likewise felt among the adults in his district and in the city. He was an excellent director of souls and a good confessor, to judge from the number of people who sought him out. Among his many penitents he numbered the archbishop of Mexico City, and whenever his people saw him dressed in his best, they said: "He's on his way to see the archbishop."

The peace and quiet in which Fr. Garcidueñas lived and worked was shattered with the coming of Venustiano Carranza as president (1915–1920). Under Carranza the Church was persecuted. The priests who had been with Fr. Garcidueñas at the shrine had to leave and he alone remained, caring for the shrine as best he could. For a time the government turned the church into barracks, but he remained nearby to assist his people. Then his priests returned and by 1921 everything was again in full operation. But another persecution came with President Plutarco Elías Calles (1924–1928), who wanted to stifle the voice of the Church and bring it under his control. In June 1926 Calles issued a decree ordering the banishment of all foreign priests and bishops and the imprisonment of the Mexican clergy. This "Calles' Law" was to go into effect on July 31. As their response to this unjust decree, the Mexican hierarchy ordered the suspension of all ecclesiastical services in Mexican churches. The churches would remain open, but there would be no public services. On July 30, the day before the suspension was to take effect, Fr. Garcidueñas held a special service at the shrine and with tears in his eyes he consecrated the Los Angeles district to our Lady asking her protection over his people.

After the service the priests quietly disbanded, each going to his prearranged hiding place, but Fr. Garcidueñas remained. Though public services were forbidden, he continued to give the sacraments secretly and carried Holy Communion to the sick. On Sundays the people continued to gather in the church to pray, and though there could be no Mass, a member of the congregation led the people in reciting the Mass prayers. At the same time Fr. Garcidueñas, in a room adjacent to the shrine, celebrated Mass in unison with those prayers. As for sermons, he wrote them out and they were read to the congregation.

During this difficult time, when the spiritual work of Fr. Garcidueñas was greatly curtailed, a cancer developed on his shoulder that soon caused him much pain. August 6, 1927, was his seventy-first birthday and several of his friends came to his residence to celebrate the day with him. He was about to tell them that this would be the last time that they would so get together, but his eyes filled and he could not continue. Nor could he tell them that he had cancer. Within days after this gathering, he began to fail and it became more difficult for him to get around. By October 2 he was confined to his bed and received the anointing of the sick. The following day he grew worse and on his lips were frequently heard the words of the Psalmist: "The Lord of mercies has filled me with his good gifts." On October 4, about 4:30 in the morning he received Viaticum and shortly thereafter died.

In those days of persecution, there could be no funeral service. After his death the priests, who had gathered at his bedside, celebrated their Masses in a private chapel, then prepared the body and placed it in a parlor of the residence for Fr. Garcidueñas's friends to visit for the last time. His remains now lie buried at the foot of the altar at the shrine of Our Lady of the Angels, where he spent his entire priestly life. Every Catholic in the Los Angeles district looked upon this priest as a saint. Many have attributed cures to his intercession and some have testified that they had seen him raised in the air while at prayer. Because of this reputation for holiness, the cause of Fr. Salvador Garcidueñas is under study.

October 6

Bl. Diego Aloysius de San Vitores 1627–1672

Martyr of the Marianas

Fr. Diego Aloysius de San Vitores, the "Apostle of the Marianas," died a martyr's death on the island of Guam. He was born of noble parents in Burgos, Spain, on November 12, 1627. While attending the Imperial College in Madrid, he resolved in 1638 to enter the Society of Jesus, but since he was little more than eleven, the Jesuit provincial could not possibly accept him. His parents, furthermore, wanted him to follow a political career and not be hidden away in a monastery. Determined that the Society was to be his life he prayed ceaselessly, and our Lady, to whom he was especially devoted, brought it about that his parents finally granted their permission. Diego arrived at the novitiate at Villarejo de Fuentes on July 30, 1640, and after completing his noviceship went to Huete to continue his study of the humanities for a year. He then moved on to Alcalá de Henares for his courses in philosophy and theology and was ordained on December 23, 1651.

The one desire of Fr. San Vitores was to be a missionary in China or Japan. Rather than being sent to a foreign land, his superiors assigned him first to teach grammar at Oropesa and then to be tutor in theology to the young Jesuits studying in Madrid. In 1655 he was transferred to Alcalá de Henares to teach philosophy. Shortly after his arrival, he became involved with our Lady's sodality and had the sodalists visiting hospitals, comforting the sick, making beds, and sweeping floors. Whatever time Fr. San Vitores had to spare, he spent it giving parish missions in the suburbs. Only toward the end of 1659 did the Jesuit general, Fr. Goswin Nickel, assign him to the missions; not to China, or Japan, but to the Philippines.

Fr. San Vitores set sail from Cádiz, Spain, on May 15, 1660, and landed at Veracruz, Mexico, on July 28. He traveled to Mexico City, and unable to get immediate passage to the Philippines he busied himself with missions and street preaching, as he had done in Alcalá. After eighteen months of patient waiting, he and thirteen other Jesuits left Acapulco on April 5, 1662, and arrived in the Philippines on July 10. Fr. San Vitores spent the next three months studying Tagalog, the country's language, and once he was sufficiently fluent he became master of novices and dean at Manila's university. Academic duties, however, did not keep him from pastoral work. During his five years in the Philippines, he not only worked in Manila, but also did missionary work in the interior of Luzon and on the island of Mindoro.

During his stay in the Philippines, the thoughts of Fr. San Vitores were often on the Ladrones, a group of islands about 900 miles northeast of the Philippines. On his way to Manila the ship carrying him had stopped there to pick up supplies, and while it was in port he went ashore and tried to converse with the natives. In this he was unsuccessful, but he did learn that they knew nothing of Christianity. Thus, on July 18, 1664, he wrote to King Philip IV of Spain describing the harvest that was waiting in the Ladrones and ended by encouraging the king to open a mission there. The king not only approved the mission but also asked Fr. San Vitores to head it.

Before he could set foot in the Ladrones, Fr. San Vitores first had to visit the viceroy in Mexico City. Thus, he left Manila on August 7, 1667, landed at Acapulco in January 1668 and went directly to meet the viceroy. Having received the royal authorization to initiate the new mission and the royal subsidy to defray the cost of opening it, he left Acapulco on March 23, 1668, and landed on the island of Guam on June 16.

The Ladrones form an archipelago in Micronesia. In 1668 they became the Las Marianas after Queen Mariana of Austria, who continued to sponsor the mission after Philip IV's death in 1665. At the time of the Jesuit missionaries' arrival in Guam, they were warmly greeted, thanks to a shipwrecked Spaniard who had been living there since 1638. Because the Spaniard was friendly with the island's several chiefs, he had paved the way for the missionaries' welcome. Fr. San Vitores chose Guam's principal town as his headquarters and named it St. Ignatius de Agadña. Among his first converts was the town's chief, Quipuha, and with the chief's protection, the mission prospered. The missionaries imitated the simple life of the native Chamorros—they walked barefoot, wore a garb made of matted fibers, and ate frugal meals. They also abstained from eating fish and often slept on the ground. After their first six months, the missionaries counted 13,000 natives who had been baptized (of which 6,000 were on Guam alone), and 20,000 under instruction.

Besides his missionary work on Guam, Fr. San Vitores also evangelized the large islands of Saipan and Tinian; other missionaries visited the remaining islands in the archipelago. In January 1670 his companion Fr. Luis de Medina was martyred in Saipan, the first Jesuit to die in the Marianas. Fr. San Vitores also thought of martyrdom; he prayed for it, and knew that it would one day be his.

On April 1, 1672, the missionary set out with his companion Pedro Calonsor in search of a servant, whom he hoped to save from a dissolute life. Early in the morning of April 2, they came to Tumon, where they expected to find the fugitive servant. As they entered the village, they heard the cries of a new-born child coming from the hut of a Christian friend, Matapang. The priest entered and asked the father whether he wanted the child baptized, but Matapang, who was one of the mission's first converts and whose life the missionary had once saved, immediately snapped back and threatened the priest. Surprised at Matapang's strange reaction, the priest left the hut to pursue his search. Matapang also left, but to find his friend Hirao and ask his help in killing the priest.

After the servant had been found, Fr. San Vitores and Calonsor returned to Matapang's hut. He was not there so they baptized the child and then went to the edge of the village to await Matapang's return. It was about nine in the morning when Matapang and Hirao appeared, and without a word of warning Matapang sent a spear into Calonsor's chest. When the missionary saw his companion fall at his feet, his hand automatically grabbed hold of the crucifix about his neck. He then fell on his knees and readied himself for what was to come. Raising his eyes and looking into those of his friend, he said: "Matapang, may God have mercy on you." At that moment Hirao struck the priest with a cutlass, splitting his head down to the neck. Both men then stripped the bodies, tied them together, dragged their burden to the sea and loaded it on to a canoe. When they were a short distance from shore, they threw the bodies into the water. Fr. Diego Aloysius de San Vitores died on April 2, 1672. He was beatified by Pope John Paul II on October 6, 1985, and his memorial is celebrated by his Jesuit brethren on October 6.

Prayer

O God, who, by the service and the martyrdom of your priest Blessed Diego Aloysius de San Vitores revealed the light of the Gospel and the love of Christ to unbelievers, grant by his intercession that we, too, may be made witnesses to the truth of the Gospel and to the message of love. We ask this through our Lord Jesus Christ, your Son, who lives and reigns with you and the Holy Spirit, one God, for ever and ever.

October 7

S. G. Emile Martínez 1893–1934
S. G. John Baptist Arconada 1890–1934
Martyrs of Spain

Fr. Emile Martínez and Br. John Baptist Arconada died in the socialist uprising in Asturias during Spain's Second Republic. Toward the end of September 1934, Fr. Martínez and Br. Arconada left their residence in Gijón to go to Carrión de los Condes, where Fr. Martínez was to give a retreat and in which Br. Arconada was to participate. The retreat ended on October 2, and at the request of the priests at the retreat house Fr. Martínez and Br. Arconada stayed on an extra day. Since Fr. Martínez had to be back in Gijón for the morning of October 5, a First Friday, both Jesuits left Carrión de los Condes on October 4, made their way to Palencia, and there caught the express train for Gijón. They boarded the train at 4:00 P.M., and were scheduled to arrive at 10:00 that night, but neither of them was to see Gijón again.

Emile Martínez was born in Ahedo de las Pueblas, in the province of Burgos, on May 28, 1893. When the Martínez family moved to Tudela de Navarra, Emile attended a private school and then the Jesuit College of St. Francis Xavier, where he graduated in 1912. That autumn he matriculated in the diocesan seminary, but on April 3, 1913, he entered the Jesuit novitiate at Carrión de los Condes. he pronounced his vows there and after a year studying humanities went, in 1916, to Burgos to study rhetoric, then to Oña for philosophy (1918–1921). For regency (1921–1924) he taught at the colleges in Gijón and Valladolid, then returned to Oña for theology (1924–1927). While at Oña he manifested his singular talent for dealing with young boys; he regularly gathered them about him to teach them catechism and to speak to them of God and Christian living. He was ordained on July 30, 1927, and for his final year of theology went to the French scholasticate at Fourvière, near Lyons, in southern France.

Fr. Martínez did at Fourvière what he had done at Oña. In the vicinity of Lyons there was a colony of some 4,000 Spaniards who had come to France looking for work. Because they knew no French, they were in effect cut off from their religion. Fr. Martínez brought them together, acted as their chaplain, baptized their children, and performed marriages. After a year in France, he returned to Spain for tertianship and in 1930 was assigned to the college at Gijón.

Br. Arconada was living at Gijón when Fr. Martínez arrived. He had been born at Carrión de los Condes on February 15, 1890, and entered the Society at Loyola on July 5, 1908. His early years as a Jesuit were spent as infirmarian in various colleges—Burgos, Orduña, Bilbao, Salamanca, Valladolid. Then in 1929 he was transferred to the College of the Immaculate Conception in Gijón and was assigned to supervise students.

The train that was to take Fr. Martínez and Br. Arconada to Gijón on October 4 met its first delay at Linares at 8:00 P.M. The passengers surmised that there must have been a derailment somewhere ahead or that the engine had lost its power. They were unaware that a socialist uprising was in the making. The train eventually moved on, but met one delay after another. When it finally arrived at the station in Ujo at 5:30 A.M. on October 5, nine hours behind schedule, the stark reality of the uprising hit them. Revolutionary soldiers commandeered the engine, boarded the train, searched the cars for arms, and forced the passengers to detrain. Once off the train the passengers were searched and then released.

Fr. Martínez and Br. Arconada returned to the train to decide what they should do, when the latter remembered that the Muñiz family of Ujo once had sons attending the college at Gijón. The resourceful brother left the train, made his way to the city, and succeeded in finding the residence of Dennis Muñiz, who, upon hearing that the two Jesuits were stranded, immediately opened his house to them. Br. Arconada returned to the train for Fr. Martínez and together they made their way to their refuge, arriving there at 5:00 P.M. They had not eaten all that day and Mrs. Muñiz kindly served them and talked Fr. Martínez into giving up the cassock he was wearing in exchange for some of her sons' clothes. The Jesuits remained with the Muñiz family until the morning of October 7. Unwilling that their presence cause trouble for the Muñiz household, the two Jesuits decided to risk crossing the mountains to reach Oviedo some fifteen miles away. They made good time and as they approached the town of Santullano, thinking it was still untouched by revolutionaries, they descended the mountain to take the main road to Oviedo. No sooner were they on the road, near the bridge entering Santullano, than they were unexpectedly stopped. They explained to the soldiers that their train had been halted at Ujo—they even produced their train tickets—and thus were on their way to Oviedo. From their general behavior the soldiers suspected they were priests and decided to take them to headquarters in Mieres. When brought before the socialist commander, they admitted that they were Jesuits. The commander then remarked: "We have no room for any more arrests. Take them and do with them what you like." Led from the magistrate's hall under guard and with several individuals tagging behind them, the group walked toward the outskirts of Mieres heading for Santullano. When the group stopped to rest on benches near a wall, bystanders unashamedly shouted out: "Kill them now! don't let them celebrate any more Masses." After a short respite, the group returned to the road and arrived at Santullano about 3:00 P.M. The two religious were again the object of insults, and when they heard their fellow Spaniards blaspheme God, they openly confessed their faith in him. At Santullano's City Hall they were sentenced to death, and as the sentence was announced, the people shouted: "Kill them! If they believe in God, let God perform a miracle for them."

Fr. Martínez and Br. Arconada remained at City Hall until ten that night, October 7, 1934. They then were taken out into the dark, loaded onto a truck, and transported to an abandoned mine tunnel between Santullano and Mieres. When the truck stopped the martyrs were told: "This is the end of the line for you." Bravely the two Jesuits positioned themselves in front of the tunnel, embraced each other, and together in a loud voice said: "Long live Christ the King!" Before the echo of that act of faith had died, both Jesuits were shot in the breast. The soldiers then crushed Fr. Martínez's head and beat that of Br. Arconada. The bodies of both martyrs were taken to a cemetery, where some forty other bodies were waiting, and were buried in a common grave. Two weeks later the grave was opened and the bodies of the two Jesuits were identified and properly interred in another place in the cemetery.

The official investigation into the martyrdom of Fr. Emile Martínez and Br. John Baptist Arconada was initiated in Oviedo in 1952.

October 11

S.G. John Baptist Messari 1673–1723

S.G. Francis Mary Bucherelli 1686–1723

Martyrs of Vietnam

The Jesuit mission in Tonkin (now the northern portion of Vietnam) dates from 1624, with the arrival of Fr. Alexandre de Rhodes (1591–1660). So extraordinary was his success that by 1658 the mission numbered some 300,000 Catholics. During the mission's first century, despite sporadic general persecutions (1659, 1695, 1712), conversions increased. It was during the 1721 persecution, however, that the Society had its first Vietnam martyrs, Frs. John Baptist Messari and Francis Mary Bucherelli.

With the coming of this persecution, churches were closed or destroyed and the missionaries were forced to go underground in order to minister to their flocks. Months of harsh living, continually eluding police and spies, without proper food and rest, all these began to take their toll on the missionaries' health. Thus the Jesuit superior in China ordered Frs. Messari and Bucherelli to go to Macao, where they would be safe; they would then be able to return another day. Toward the end of 1722 both priests made their way as far north as Lofeu, near the Chinese border, but because police were in the region they and their three catechists hid in a wooded area. There they were apprehended.

John Baptist Messari was born in Gorizia, now part of Italy, on August 12, 1673. He entered the Society in 1701 in Vienna, after having been ordained to the diocesan clergy. He sailed for the Indies in 1706, was in Macao the following year, and did missionary work in China's southern provinces. He first went to Tonkin in 1712, but his work came to an end when he was accused before the regional governor, a Chinese apostate Christian, of pouring "death waters" on the heads of dying children. He was condemned to death, but when a bonze warned the governor that he would lose favor with the king of Cochin China, at whose court the Jesuit Juan Arnedo enjoyed great favor, the sentence was suspended and the missionary was set free on condition that he leave the territory. Fr. Messari thus went to Macao in 1714. But he was back in Tonkin in 1715, and in a letter he wrote that year, he described his mission field as being vast and that he had some 14,000 Christians under his care. His labors until the 1721 persecution were fruitful and conversions were plentiful.

Francis Mary Bucherelli was born in Tuscany, in the city of Empoli, on May 21, 1686. He studied with the Jesuits in Florence, and when he entered the Society in Rome in 1700 it was with the intention of one day going to the foreign missions. He made his studies at the Roman College, and while a student of theology he received word of his appointment to India and was given but two days to prepare for the voyage. He left Rome at the end of 1713 and stopped off in Siena to visit his younger brother, Luigi, also a Jesuit. He subsequently sailed from Lisbon, Portugal, in 1714, and after arrival in Goa, India, completed his theological course and was ordained. He went to the Tonkin mission in 1716. After a year he wrote his brother Luigi describing his manner of life. He lived on a boat, which served him both as home and church. In that fashion he traveled throughout his mission ministering to the faithful. With the coming of persecution, mission stations were destroyed, Christians were arrested, and all his travel and apostolic work had to be done at night. On receipt of his superior's order to go to Macao, he met Fr. Messari and they travelled together until they and their catechists were apprehended near Lofeu.

Now in the hands of police, they had chains placed on their feet and were taken to the Tonkinese capital, Ketcho (today's Hanoi). Led before a tribunal of mandarins, the priests were interrogated and then they and the catechists were ordered to tread upon a crucifix. Rather than doing what they were told, they knelt down and kissed it. Thus the two Jesuits were found guilty of preaching a religion forbidden in that kingdom and the catechists for following its ways and assisting in its spread. Additional chains were put on them and they were ordered to prison, where each was placed in a cage-like alcove, under continual guard. After six months of living on sparse rations (a cup of rice per day), in a cell that restricted movement, under the hot sun, and suffering from weakness and maltreatment, both priests became seriously ill. Fr. Messari died on June 15 or 23, 1723, as a result of a severe case of dysentery.

Having lost one of the prisoners and fearing the king, the mandarin in charge expended special care on Fr. Bucherelli and had a physician come to assist him. He remained in prison for another four months and during that period other Tonkinese Christians were brought in. On the morning of October 11, 1723, under pretext that the king had decided to send the priest and the nine Christians (five were catechists) to China, they were led to the royal palace. On arriving there a mandarin appeared and read out their sentences. To Fr. Bucherelli, he said: "You foreigner, because you have preached your religion, which is prohibited in this realm, His Highness has condemned you to be beheaded." He then addressed the Christians: "Because you have followed Christ's teaching, His Highness orders you to be beheaded and that your heads be fixed on posts for three days." They then changed their clothing for the white robes of the condemned and began their long, slow walk to the place of execution.

On the way Fr. Bucherelli spoke to his Christians: "Brothers, be courageous, we will shortly see each other in heaven." One of the catechists then intoned the Litany of Our Lady, and after that other hymns, so that the rest of the journey was taken up with sacred songs. At the place of martyrdom their chains were removed and each went to a waist-high post placed in the ground. They knelt down and with their backs to the post they were tightly bound. At a signal the executioners standing at each post raised and swung their sabres. Within seconds ten martyrs went to God. The Christians who witnessed these deaths claimed the bodies. They buried Fr. Bucherelli's body separately but placed those of their nine brethren in a common grave.

October 12

S. G. James Rem 1546–1618

Fr. James Rem is known throughout Bavaria, Germany, for his untiring zeal in promoting devotion to our Lady. He was born in Bregenz (Austria) in June 1546, and when he enrolled at the Jesuit-operated college in Dillingen in 1564, that was his first contact with the Jesuits. After two years under their tutelage, he asked to be admitted into the Society and was sent to Rome for his noviceship in August 1566. He entered the Roman novitiate on September 20, 1566, and among his fellow novices were Stanislaus Kostka and Rudolph Acquaviva. After vows in September 1568, he returned to Germany to complete his studies at Dillingen and was ordained in Augsburg on May 16, 1573. He celebrated his first Mass in Dillingen on May 21 and afterwards began his ministry among the students there.

Fr. Rem's love of our Lady was such that he had to tell others about her wonders, so that they too could love her as he did. With this in mind, he established the first Sodality of Our Lady in southern Germany on November 18, 1574. He had become familiar with it while in Rome, where the first sodality had been formed in 1563. For his sodality he did not seek large numbers at first, but looked for young men who took their Catholic faith seriously and were willing to lead fervent Christian lives, dedicated to our Lady. He was sure the numbers would come later. In 1585 he left Dillingen for Munich, where he also began a sodality. In the following year, 1586, he was transferred to Ingolstadt and there he remained until his death in 1618. For thirty years his work at Ingolstadt did not change; he had charge of the boarding students. He also established a sodality for them, which grew and developed over the years. In 1595 Fr. Rem took his best sodalists and formed the *Colloquium Marianum*, a group of young men of high ideals, whose goal was holiness. Fr. Rem wrote the rules for the group. These were later approved by Pope Paul V in 1612.

In Fr. Rem's meditating on our Lady's titles in the Litany of Loretto, he was hard put to decide which title best expressed Mary's virtues and privileges.

He was inclined to choose *Mater admirabilis,* "Mother most admirable," but at the same time he wished he knew what our Lady herself preferred. Then on April 6, 1604, while singing the litany with his sodalists, our Lady appeared to him as they sang the words *Mater admirabilis, ora pro nobis,* to let him know that this was the title under which she wanted him and his sodalists to invoke her. In remembrance of this event it became customary among Ingolstadt sodalists to repeat that invocation three times when reciting or singing the litany.

Fr. Rem's influence on his sodalists was long lasting. After they left school they kept in touch with him and many of them chose to become priests and religious as a result of his good example and religious dedication. Fr. Rem's life was directed to praising our Lord and our Lady, and to exhorting his sodalists to do the same. On several occasions our Lord and our Lady appeared to him during prayer; nor was it rare for him to enter into ecstasy when celebrating Mass. His sodalists knew him to utter prophecies that they had seen come true, and to know when sodalists in other cities had departed this life.

Fr. Rem's health began to fail in 1618, he grew progressively weaker and on October 9 he took a turn for the worse and was anointed. Then on Friday, October 12, at 4:00 in the afternoon he entered eternal life. Fr. Rem was seventy-two years old and had been a Jesuit for fifty-two years. His cause has only recently been opened and is undergoing the usual investigation.

October 13

Ven. Paul Anthony Capelloni 1776–1857

Paul Anthony Capelloni was a Roman, born on February 21, 1776. He attended the Roman College, operated at the time by diocesan priests because the Society of Jesus had been suppressed in 1773. Many of the teachers, however, were former Jesuits. Paul then attended Lucarini College in Trevi and in 1794 returned to Rome to enter the Capranica, a distinguished seminary. He remained there until 1798, when the seminary was forced to close by the French, who were then occupying the city. He subsequently continued his study of theology with the Dominicans and was ordained a priest in 1801. After ordination he became tutor to the two sons of Marquis Angelo Vitelleschi, and also did pastoral work at Rome's Gesù church, which was now staffed by former Jesuits. Because of Fr. Capelloni's oratorical skills, he soon became a favorite in the Gesù pulpit; his sermons were popular as were his Three Hours devotions on Good Friday.

Since Fr. Capelloni had refused to take the oath of loyalty to Napoleon I in 1811, he was forced to leave Rome. He went to Rieti and resided with the Vitelleschi family for the next three years. These were not idle years; he kept himself busy with pastoral work and carried it out with the same energy as he had done when he was in Rome. After Pius VII had restored the Society of Jesus on August 7, 1814, Fr. Capelloni returned to Rome and entered the Jesuit novitiate of Sant'Andrea on November 30, 1814. He was thirty-eight years old and one of the first Italians to enter the restored Society.

Toward the end of 1815, after a year of noviceship, he was sent to Ferentino as pastor of the Jesuit church. He labored there until November 1821 where his preaching also bore much fruit, not only among the Ferentini but also in the surrounding towns and villages, where he often gave missions. When his parishioners heard that he was being transferred to Naples, they tried to prevent his leaving. Thus he had to slip away secretly.

In Naples Fr. Capelloni reopened the Jesuit church known as Gesù Nuovo. The church had been closed since 1806, the year when Fr. Joseph Pignatelli and his fellow Jesuits were expelled from Naples by the French. As the new pastor Fr. Capelloni had much work ahead of him. He gradually brought back the former parishioners and restored all liturgical functions. He celebrated the First Fridays of the month with special care and fostered devotion to our Lady, under her title of the Immaculate Conception. While fulfilling his pastoral duties, he also served as chaplain for the soldiers lodged in the city and at times filled in as chaplain to the royal court. Bl. Francis Jerome, beatified in 1806, had been a priest at the Gesù Nuovo and had been involved in pastoral work similar to that of Fr. Capelloni. It was only natural for the latter to take the former as his special patron and promote his cause toward canonization. Among the pastor's first projects was to have the relics of Bl. Francis brought back to Naples. They had been taken to Rome in 1806 to keep them from being violated by the occupying French forces. Then with the canonization on May 26, 1839, Fr. Capelloni arranged an eight-day celebration in Naples, ending with St. Francis Jerome being named the city's patron. Fr. Capelloni's love for the Neapolitans was boundless. When a cholera epidemic hit the city in 1836 and 1837, he doubled his efforts in visiting and helping the stricken.

In March 1848 revolutionaries attacked the Jesuit college and residence; Fr. Capelloni and fellow Jesuits were kept under house arrest for little more than a day and then shipped off to Malta as exiles. Their exile lasted little more than a year; by mid-1849 Fr. Capelloni returned to Naples, to his parish, pulpit, and ministry.

After a phenomenally fruitful thirty-five years in Naples, Fr. Capelloni, following a short illness, died on the night of October 13–14, 1857. He was buried in the church, where he had been pastor. In recognition of his life of charity, humility, and holiness, his cause was introduced in Rome on June 23, 1909.

October 14

St. John Ogilvie 1579–1615

Martyr of Scotland

After an absence of twenty-two years, Fr. John Ogilvie returned to his native Scotland in 1613 to begin a missionary career that lasted only eleven months and ended in martyrdom. He was born in Drum-na-Keith, Banffshire, in 1579, and because his father had conformed to the state-established religion, young John was brought up a Calvinist. Sometime in 1591 or 1592 he left Scotland to tour and study in France, Germany, and Italy. Then in 1596 he decided to become a Catholic and went to Louvain, and while at the Scots College he was reconciled to the Catholic Church. When the school closed because of lack of funds, he went, in June 1598, to Regensburg and attended the college of the Scottish Benedictines. But after six months he transferred in December to the Jesuit college at Olomouc. There he determined to become a Jesuit and joined the Austrian province and entered its novitiate at Brno in Moravia on November 5, 1599. After he pronounced his first vows of religion on December 26, 1601, he began his three-year course of philosophy at Graz, then taught for a time in Vienna, and returned to Olomouc to do his theological studies. In 1610 he was sent to France and was ordained in Paris toward the end of that year.

Fr. Ogilvie was quite eager to return to Scotland to work among his coreligionists. Since Scotland was then much too dangerous a place for missionaries, his superiors assigned him to Rouen, France, and only in May 1613 did he receive the word he so anxiously awaited. In November he arrived on the shores of Leith, Scotland, disguised as a horse dealer with the name John Watson. He immediately made his way to Banffshire, the district where he spent his youth, and remained there for a few weeks. He then moved to Edinburgh to begin his ministry and soon added Renfrewshire and Glasgow to his area of activity. He had considerable success in reconciling people to the faith. He frequently traveled between Edinburgh and Glasgow and on October 3, 1614, he returned to Glasgow in order to receive five individuals into the Church on the following day. One of these was Adam Boyd, his future betrayer.

When Fr. Ogilvie arrived in Glasgow, Boyd informed the Protestant archbishop, John Spottiswoode, of the priest's presence and both planned how best to apprehend him. On October 4, as Fr. Ogilvie waited at a designated spot in the market square to be taken to where the service was to be held, the archbishop's men surrounded him and asked him to go with them to a nearby house, where the archbishop was awaiting him. When the priest and archbishop met, the latter angrily struck the priest on the face and said: "You are overbold to say your Masses in a reformed city." To this Fr. Ogilvie only replied: "You act like a hangman and not a bishop in striking me." After the archbishop's men had expressed their anti-Catholic hatred by covering him with blows, they took him to the prison in the bishop's castle. The following day he underwent his first examination under the archbishop's leadership, but showed his interrogators that he was not to be bullied or forced into acknowledging the king's supremacy in religious matters.

After the interrogation he was put into a dark, stench-filled cell, where his feet were weighted down and where he was tortured, not to any extreme degree, but only to overcome his obduracy and make him more willing to cooperate at the time of the next examination. The second interrogation took place on December 12. Fr. Ogilvie was taken from Glasgow to Edinburgh and appeared before a council appointed by King James I. Again he withstood its questioning and since he manifested no signs of breaking, his captors devised a torment whereby for the next eight days and nine nights he was to go without sleep. To guarantee that he would have no rest, a guard stayed with him at all times. Whenever the prisoner showed signs of sleep, the guard jabbed him with pins or daggers. This torture lasted until the morning of December 21 when he was given the remainder of the day to prepare for his third interrogation scheduled for the 22nd. Though the prisoner was physically worn out and mentally tired, he still refused to divulge the names of the Catholics who had befriended him and those who had attended his services. Unable to gain any information from him, he was returned to Glasgow on December 24 to await the king's pleasure.

During his stay in the Glasgow prison, Fr. Ogilvie began writing the story of his arrest and imprisonment, and through the kindness of those who had come to visit other prisoners, he managed to have it smuggled out, sheet by sheet, and sent to his Jesuit superior. His fourth interrogation came on January 18, 1615, when he was asked to respond to a series of questions posed by the king himself. The questions dealt with religious supremacy and were so worded that the prisoner's answers would either condemn him or be his renunciation of Catholicism. In answer to the royal queries, Fr. Ogilvie unashamedly and unambiguously answered that the pope—he alone and not the king—was supreme in religious matters and that the pope had power not only to excommunicate the king but also to depose him. These answers were then sent to the king in London. Fr. Ogilvie well knew that his responses meant his death. When he returned to his cell that day, he began his preparation for heaven.

Toward the end of February James I read Fr. Ogilvie's responses and then sent orders to Glasgow that the priest's trial was to take place on March 10. If he did not change his opinions he was to suffer death. At 11:00 A.M. of that fateful day Fr. Ogilvie faced his judges at the Tolbooth in Glasgow's square. The charges against him were no longer those of Archbishop Spottiswoode, that he had celebrated Mass and converted Protestants to the Catholic faith, but his denial of the king's spiritual jurisdiction, his upholding of the pope's spiritual primacy, and his condemnation of the oaths of supremacy and allegiance. Two hours after his trial had begun the jury found him guilty of high treason and he was sentenced to be hanged and quartered that afternoon.

While the judges and jury were at lunch, Fr. Ogilvie remained at the Tolbooth and there he knelt and prayed. Three hours later the sheriff came to escort him to the public square for execution. Clutching his rosary in his hand, the priest followed. He mounted the steps of the platform and went to the scaffold and kissed it, and then spent some time in prayer. The hangman then tied his hands. As the prisoner climbed the ladder, he recited several invocations from the Litany of the Saints, and when he finally said, "Lord, have mercy on me. Lord, receive my soul," the executioner pushed him from the ladder. He did not die immediately, but continued to hang in agony. The hangman then grasped his legs and sharply tugged him downward, making his death less painful. Fr. Ogilvie's body was cut down, but contrary to the sentence, it was not quartered. It was later buried outside the city in a place reserved for criminals.

Fr. John Ogilvie, the only canonized Scottish martyr from the time of the Reformation, was thirty-six years old when he gave his life for Christ. He was beatified by Pope Pius XI on December 22, 1929, and canonized by Pope Paul VI on October 17, 1976. The Jesuits celebrate his memorial on October 14.

Prayer

Lord God, you revealed the power of the Holy Spirit in the life of your martyr, Saint John Ogilvie. Through his example and prayers give us strength to serve the Church under the banner of the Cross, and to carry out in every land the work entrusted to us by the successor of Saint Peter. We ask this through our Lord Jesus Christ, your Son, who lives and reigns with you and the Holy Spirit, one God, for ever and ever.

October 19

St. Isaac Jogues 1607–1646

St. John de La Lande ?–1646

Martyrs of North America

The slender, wiry Black Robe watched as the ship slowly made its way to its berth. From his position on deck he easily picked out the French inhabitants of

Quebec, for he himself was a Frenchman. But waiting with them he saw the strange natives of that new land; they were half-naked, with bodies painted in bright colors and whose facial features were unfamiliar to him. In these strangers he recognized the reason why he had come to New France. The missionary was Fr. Isaac Jogues.

Isaac was born in Orléans, France, on January 10, 1607. At seventeen he entered the Jesuit novitiate in Rouen, did his philosophical studies at La Flèche and theology at Clermont College in Paris. He was ordained in January 1636, celebrated his first Mass on February 10, and on April 8 was on his way to the Jesuit mission in New France, where he arrived on July 2. He wrote his mother of the joy he experienced when he first glimpsed the natives waiting on shore—it was so great that he thought he was entering Paradise. His joy may have been great, indeed, but he was not entering an earthly Paradise. Fr. Jogues came to New France to be martyred.

The new missionary was assigned to the Huron mission. He went to Three Rivers, south of Quebec, to await a flotilla of Hurons, who were due to arrive and with whom he would travel on their return journey. On August 24, 1636, he set out on his first mission. The trek to Huronia was 900 miles, most of it was by water routes, but at times the Indians had to carry the canoes and supplies over many miles to avoid the numerous cascades. After nineteen days of exhausting travel they arrived at Ihonatiria on September 11. It was during this trip that the Indians, unable to pronounce the name of Fr. Jogues, called him "Ondessonk" or "Bird of Prey."

In Huronia, Fr. Jogues met his hero, Fr. John de Brébeuf. He set about learning the Huron language and practiced it by instructing the Indians in the faith. When a smallpox epidemic broke out in the settlement and the local medicine men were unable to dispel it, the Indians attributed the contagion to the presence of the Black Robes among them. Like the missionaries before him, Fr. Jogues learned to live with the constant threat of death; no one knew when some brave would take it upon himself to apply a tomahawk to their heads. But the epidemic, fortunately, passed. When Ihonatiria was abandoned, Fr. Jogues went to Teanaustayé and from there to Sainte-Marie.

The village of Sainte-Marie was a thriving enterprise. The missionaries had instructed the Indians how to cultivate the land, tend the crops, and care for fowl, swine, and cattle. It was so prosperous a village that when a group of Chippewas came to Sainte-Marie and saw how it flourished, they invited the Black Robes to establish a mission among them. Fr. Jogues visited them in September 1641 and found the Chippewas peaceful and eager to hear about God. On his return he urged his superior to send them missionaries, but the number of Jesuits in New France was small. The mission was committed for the present to evangelizing the Hurons, and only after they had been converted would they be able to go to the western tribes.

Fr. Jogues spent that winter and the spring of 1642 at Sainte-Marie preparing his neophytes for baptism, which was solemnly administered on Holy Saturday. One of the 120 adult converts was Ahtsistari, the tribe's greatest war chief. Understandably, the Jesuits felt that Christianity was beginning to take root. Though he was happy and successful at Sainte-Marie, Fr. Jogues, nevertheless, longed for a greater harvest, the conversion of the entire Huron nation, even if it meant more suffering on his part. One day, while at prayer, he expressed his desire to undergo any hardship whether of body, mind, or soul, so that the faith could be implanted in the souls of these people. After he had made his prayer, deep within his soul he heard the words: "Be it done to you as you asked. Be comforted! Be of strong heart!" Fr. Jogues then knew that God had accepted the sacrifice of himself and that this was a prophecy of what was to come.

In June he accompanied a group of Hurons to Three Rivers for supplies. The Iroquois were again at war with the French and he understood the dangers before him. The group arrived without incident on July 17, 1642, and Fr. Jogues went on to Quebec to see his fellow Jesuits and to request missionaries for the Huron mission. Because there were no priests available, the superior suggested René Goupil. René was not a Jesuit, but a *donné*, a lay assistant who promised to work with the missionaries without recompense other than food and clothing. He likewise promised to be obedient to the Jesuit superior and to live a life of celibacy. Since René was a surgeon, he would be invaluable on the mission.

On the return to Sainte-Marie, one day out of Three Rivers, August 2, the party noticed footprints on the shore and soon heard the shrill cry of war whoops and a volley of shots. About seventy Mohawks had caught sight of the flotilla and swooped down upon them. In the exchange a Frenchman was injured. When Fr. Jogues tried to care for him the Mohawks beat him, bit out his fingernails, and chewed his forefingers. René was likewise the victim of Mohawk barbarity. With three Frenchmen and twenty Hurons as prisoners, the Mohawks made their way through the St. Lawrence, into the Richelieu River, through Lake Champlain and into Lake George heading for their village of Ossernenon. While Fr. Jogues and René were making this fateful trip, René spoke to his companion about his desire to be a Jesuit brother and asked if the priest would accept his vows there and then. Fr. Jogues could not refuse such an earnest request.

Before arriving at their destination, the Mohawks met some of their own nation and to display their prisoners and to engage in torture both groups took to shore. The prisoners were forced to strip and run up a rocky hill between two rows of Indians, who beat them on head, neck, back, and shoulders as they passed. Fr. Jogues was the last in line receiving the greatest fury. When this torture came to an end, the prisoners and captors continued on their way by water. On August 14, the flotilla finally arrived at Ossernenon (today's Auriesville, N.Y.), on the bank of the Mohawk River. The prisoners again had to endure the pain of running the gauntlet. Fr. Jogues and René were then exposed on a platform where village braves took turns stabbing them. To add to the pain of Fr. Jogues, a squaw cut off his left thumb with a jagged shell. The men were then led to a longhouse and tied to the ground so that children could drop hot coals on their naked bodies.

After three days of torture, Fr. Jogues and René were given as personal slaves to the chief who had captured them. Within weeks of his capture, René, because he had made the sign of the cross on a child, was tomahawked to death by a brave on September 29, 1642. Seeing his companion fall to the ground Fr. Jogues knelt by the body with lowered head and awaited his blow, but it never came.

Fr. Jogues lived out his months of slavery carrying out degrading types of work and suffering everyone's contempt. To his captors he was no more than a beast of burden, but to the captive Christian Hurons, he was still their priest and to these he continued to bring the consolations of the faith. For his own moments of prayer, he walked into the forest at the settlement's edge and there prayed to God in private. The forest was his chapel.

In September 1643 he accompanied several Mohawks on a trading trip to the Dutch settlement of Fort Orange (Albany). The Dutch had heard of his capture and torture and had made attempts to ransom him, but without success. Now that he was with them they pressed him to escape, but the missionary thought of his Christian Hurons who would be without a priest. If he were to return to Ossernenon, death was sure to be his, sooner or later. Fr. Jogues eventually saw the wisdom of the plan and hid himself in one of the Dutch ships. He endured six weeks of concealment until the Indians' anger subsided and the Dutch were able to take him to New Amsterdam (New York). On November 5, 1643, he was given free passage to Europe.

Fr. Jogues disembarked at Cornwall in England and secured passage across the Channel. It was Christmas eve. On Christmas morning he landed in Brittany, his first touch on French soil in seven years. He looked for a church to attend Mass, went to confession, and stood with the peasants heartily singing the season's carols. When he received Communion after so many months, he realized that he now had been liberated. From there he went to the Jesuit residence at Rennes and when his brethren learned that it was Fr. Jogues who was visiting them, they received him as they would a hero. The French, who had heard of his capture and torture, were especially interested in the mission in New France and now that he was with them, it was as if a martyr had returned to life. The sole regret of Fr. Jogues regret was his inability to celebrate Mass because of his mutilated hands. He was missing his left thumb and the index finger on his left hand was nothing but a stub, while on his right hand the thumb and index finger were atrociously disfigured. With such mangled hands he was unable to hold the host correctly but his brethren requested a dispensation of Pope Urban VIII, who most willingly granted it with the memorable words: "It would be shameful that a martyr of Christ be not allowed to drink the blood of Christ."

Fr. Jogues stayed in France briefly; he yearned to return to his mission. In April 1644 he visited his mother in Orléans and in early May was at sea again heading for New France. He arrived in June and in July he attended the peace conference at Three Rivers between the French and the Indians representing the Iroquois federation. The conference lasted several months and peace terms were finally hammered out, but before a final settlement could be made the conference needed the approval of the Mohawks as well. Fr. Jogues was chosen as envoy to obtain their consent. Together with two Algonquins and four Mohawks, he left for Ossernenon on May 16, 1646. As the peace party passed through Lake George, Fr. Jogues recalled that it was the eve of the feast of Corpus Christi, and so he named that body of water "Lake of the Blessed Sacrament," a name which lasted for over a hundred years until it was changed to honor England's King George II.

The embassy stopped at Fort Orange, where Fr. Jogues met his Dutch friends and repaid the ransom they had given the Indians at the time of his escape. By June 5 the embassy arrived at Ossernenon. The Mohawks were amazed that their former slave now came to them as the ambassador of the powerful French nation. Fr. Jogues, now dressed as a Frenchman and not in his black robe, offered them the gifts of the French government and explained the terms of the treaty which they accepted. Before departing the village, he visited the few Christian Huron prisoners remaining there, heard confessions, and baptized some elderly Mohawks.

Fr. Jogues returned to Quebec on July 3 and thinking that the Mohawks would accept him as a missionary now that peace had been agreed upon, asked permission of his superior to return to them. He was told to remain at Three Rivers, but if some exceptional opportunity should arise for him to go there, then he could do so. That opportunity came in September when the Hurons were about to send an embassy to the Mohawks, at their invitation, to arrange the details of the treaty. The Hurons asked Fr. Jogues to lead them and he saw this as the opportunity God was offering him. In a letter to France, penned shortly before he left, he wrote: "I shall go, but I shall not return. It will be a happiness for me, if God will be pleased to complete the sacrifice there where he began it."

On his return to the Mohawks, Fr. Jogues was accompanied by John de La Lande and several Hurons. In answer to his request for an assistant, the superior offered him the young *donné*. John was an experienced woodsman, intelligent, and brave. He was born in Dieppe and came to New France as a settler sometime before 1642. There he offered himself to the Jesuits as a *donné*, desiring to devote his life to the service of God and to work with the missionaries. Upon hearing that Fr. Jogues wanted a companion, he volunteered for the task. The veteran missionary spoke to the young man with great frankness, describing the hardships and rigors of missionary life, of suffering, and he even hinted that there might be captivity, torture, and death. But the missionary's description of possible privations could not undo John's determination. He took the missionary's mutilated hands into his own and professed his desire to share his future with him, even if it meant martyrdom.

The small party left Quebec on September 24, 1646, and not many days into their trip they learned that the Mohawks were again on the warpath. This so frightened the Hurons in the party that all but one returned to Three Rivers, leaving the two missionaries and one Indian to make the trip alone. While Fr. Jogues and his companions were paddling their way to Ossernenon, the natives of that village had whipped themselves into a fury against him. On his earlier visit as ambassador, he had left behind a black chest in the care of a friendly Mohawk. To assure the superstitious Indians that there were no evil charms within, he opened it and showed that it only contained vestments, books, and beads. Now that their corn crop had failed and because an epidemic had struck the village, the Indians regarded the chest as the cause of their misfortunes. A party of death-seeking Mohawks took to the waterways in search of any Frenchman to kill. To their astonishment, and only a short distance from their settlement, they unexpectedly came upon Fr. Jogues and his party. When the Mohawks recognized him as the hated Ondessonk, they shrieked in jubilation, seized the three of them, and forced them to strip and undergo a beating. They then dragged the prisoners to their village. Before an onlooking crowd the captors proceeded to cut strips of flesh from the neck and arms of Fr. Jogues. The date of Fr. Jogues' return was October 17.

The Wolf and Turtle Clans at Ossernenon were friendly toward the Black Robes and desired peace with the French, but the war-like Bear Clan breathed blood and death. Somehow the Wolf Clan managed to get the prisoners placed under its protection. On the following day, October 18, while Fr. Jogues was still recovering from the previous day's torture, an Indian brave came to invite him to a feast at the chief's lodge. Fr. Jogues rightly feared treachery, but at the same time he could not refuse without giving offense. He was taken to the lodge and just as he was entering it an Indian, concealed within, struck him on the head with a tomahawk and dragged his body through the village. Ondessonk was now dead.

When John was told the news of the death of Fr. Jogues, he was advised to remain within the lodge and under no circumstances to leave it. Now that the priest was dead the blood-seeking Mohawks sought to vent their wrath on him. They tried to entice him from the lodge, but without success. He spent his time thinking of Fr. Jogues and how he was in heaven with God. He wondered about his body lying somewhere in the village and thought it would be possible under cover of darkness to find it and recover some of the articles that he had with him. Then, if he were ever released, he would take these relics to the Jesuits in Quebec. In the silent darkness he decided to leave the safety of his lodge. Unknown to him, some Indians spent a watchful night at his door and as soon as he put out his head, a tomahawk crashed down upon it. It was the early morning of October 19. When day arrived the bodies of Fr. Jogues and John de La Lande were thrown into the Mohawk River and their heads were exposed on the palisades enclosing the Mohawk village.

Fr. Isaac Jogues and John de La Lande, together with René Goupil, Frs. John de Brébeuf, Gabriel Lalemant, Charles Garnier, Anthony Daniel, and Noel Chabanel, were beatified by Pope Pius XI on June 21, 1925, and canonized by him on June 29, 1930. The memorial of these eight North American Martyrs is celebrated on October 19.

Prayer

Father, you consecrated the first beginnings of the faith in North America by the preaching and martyrdom of Saint Isaac Jogues, Saint John de La Lande, and their companions. By the help of their prayers may the Christian faith continue to grow throughout the world. We ask this through our Lord Jesus Christ, your Son, who lives and reigns with you and the Holy Spirit, one God, for ever and ever.

October 21

Ven. Aloysius La Nuza 1591–1656

For thirty years Fr. Aloysius La Nuza traveled Sicily's cities, towns, and villages, preaching sermons and missions. So effective was he that the people called him their "Apostle." Aloysius was born in Licata, Sicily, in 1591, the son of a Spanish officer. His early youth was spent in Spain, but on his return to Sicily, he enrolled at the Jesuit school in Palermo. After a time he thought of becoming a Jesuit, and over a period of three years he several times applied to enter the Society, but each time the provincial told him that his health was too frail to withstand the rigors of religious life. Finally, at age eighteen, he was accepted and entered the novitiate at Messina on February 16, 1609. Two years later, February 17, 1611, he pronounced his vows of poverty, chastity, and obedience. After the usual years of studying the humanities in Caltanisetta, philosophy in Messina, and teaching in Trapani, Aloysius returned to Palermo for his theological studies and was ordained in 1623. His first assignment as a young priest was to teach rhetoric to young Jesuit scholastics and then in 1626 he was assigned to give parish missions.

Fr. La Nuza's priestly ministry was totally devoted to preaching God's word. For three decades he gave the annual Advent and Lenten series of sermons, and outside these seasonal periods, he was an itinerant parish missioner. He crisscrossed Sicily and went to the mainland to preach in Calabria. He visited the off shore islands of Lipari and Pantelleria, and went as far as Malta. The size of the city or town where he was preaching did not matter to him, nor the type of audience that was his. His only concern was to bring God's word to the people, whether they be city or country folk. His style was simple and his delivery sincere, at times emotional and fiery, but never uninteresting. Beneath his words and delivery his audience perceived a man of great faith and deep prayer, of mortification and dedication to God.

Besides sermons and hours of hearing confessions during the time of a mission, Fr. La Nuza regularly visited the prisons and the sick in their homes and in hospitals. He took the time to solve family disputes and was ready to reconcile feuding parties. If a ship should dock while he was in the city, he went aboard to minister to the galley slaves. Whenever Fr. La Nuza saw someone in need of consolation or encouragement, he was there to help them.

If constant traveling is not easy in our own century, it was certainly much less so in the seventeenth. The many years of being on the road, in all seasons and in all kinds of weather, began to have their effect on Fr. La Nuza. It was at Carini, near Palermo, that the missioner's health broke. He had arrived on October 9, 1656, and began the mission the following day. During the first days he noticed the absence of the local farmers, but realized that it was impossible for them to be there; they had to be in the fields. So he decided, if they were unable to come to him, he would go to them.

On Saturday, after the fifth day of the mission and before Sunday's General Communion, he went out to the farms, and as the workers were coming in from the fields, he gathered them about him and preached to them. So energetic was his sermon that afternoon that he began to perspire profusely. Evening came with its cool breezes and after walking back to the parish, he went directly into the courtyard, where he spent the next few hours hearing confessions. The cool night air kept blowing upon him, but he would not leave until all had a chance to be absolved. He felt himself growing feverish, but he convinced himself that that would pass with a good night's sleep. The following day he attempted to preach, but was unable, and eventually had to go to bed. The physician diagnosed pneumonia. Because he would receive better care in nearby Palermo, he was taken to the Jesuit residence on October 18. But Fr. La Nuza was not to recover. A day or so before his death on October 21, he asked that a statue of our Lady be placed near him. He said he wanted to keep his eyes on his heavenly mother.

As soon as the church bells tolled the sad news of Fr. La Nuza's death, crowds of friends gathered outside the Jesuit residence. While he lived among them, the people attributed many miraculous cures to him, even raising a dead person to life and now that he was in heaven, they were eager to touch his body and whisper their petitions to him. Fr. Aloysius La Nuza's cause was introduced in Rome on February 17, 1713, and on March 25, 1847, the decree declaring his exercise of heroic virtue was promulgated.

Bl. Dominic Collins ca. 1566–1602

Martyr of Ireland

Dominic Collins was born about 1566 in the seaport town of Youghal, in County Cork, Ireland. The family was well established and well respected; his father and a brother were at one time mayors of Youghal.

At the time of Dominic's birth, Elizabeth I was queen of England and Ireland and, hence, Irish Catholics periodically suffered persecution. In 1560 the Irish Parliament established Anglicanism as the official religion of the land. In the same year it passed the Act of Supremacy, which recognized Elizabeth as supreme head of the Church of Ireland, and the Act of Uniformity, which required all church services to follow the Book of Common Prayer. In some areas as in Youghal and the surrounding region, these laws were not fully enforced; the government first had to gain control in secular matters before it could regulate religious affairs.

In 1577, when Dominic was going on eleven, two Jesuits came to Youghal to open a school. The lad may have attended it; it is known that he had studied Latin as a youth. The school, however, lasted only a few years; it was a victim of the government's attempt (February 1580) to take the town from the earl of Desmond, Catholic hereditary overlord of Youghal.

When twenty, Dominic went to the Continent because there were no careers open to young Catholic men in Ireland. After landing at Les Sables-d'Olonne on France's western shore, he made his way to Nantes in Brittany and for three years (1586–1589) worked as a servant in various inns. Sufficiently fluent in French and having earned enough money to outfit himself, he enlisted in the army of Philip Emmanuel de Vaudemont, duke of Mercoeur, who, as a member of the Catholic League, was fighting against the Huguenots in Brittany.

Dominic's nine-year military career in France was successful; he attained the rank of captain of cavalry. After he had successfully recovered the land and castle at Lapena from the Huguenots, the duke made him its military governor, and when Henry of Navarre, recently become king of France, offered him 2,000 ducats for the castle, Dominic refused. Later, however, when he saw that the Catholic League was coming apart and that Henry had declared war on Spain, he handed the castle over to the Spanish general, Don Juan del Aguila, who then furnished him with letters of recommendation to be presented to King Philip II of Spain. Dominic made his way to Philip's court and the king, upon reading the letters, granted him a monthly pension of twenty-five crowns.

Now in the service of Spain, Dominic was assigned to the garrison stationed at La Coruña, on the Bay of Biscay. During Lent 1598, he met the Irish Jesuit Thomas White, who had come from the Irish College in Salamanca to hear the confessions of his countrymen serving in the Spanish navy. In their conversations Dominic told the priest of his desire to do something more with his life, because neither the world nor the military interested him any longer. Dominic thought of becoming a Jesuit so Fr. White introduced him to the Jesuit superiors in that area. Though Dominic was thirty-two years old, the provincial thought it wise to delay entrance, perhaps to test the strength of his vocation.

On December 8, 1598, Dominic finally entered the Jesuit novitiate in Santiago de Compostela as a brother and after the usual noviceship training pronounced his first vows on February 4, 1601. Seven months later, much to his surprise, he was assigned as companion and assistant to Fr. James Archer, who was about to sail as chaplain of the Spanish expedition that King Philip III was sending to assist the Catholics in Ireland. Fr. Archer, an Irish Jesuit, had long been known to English authorities because of his close contacts with Irish Catholic leaders and his frequent trips to Spain.

The expedition set sail from Belem, near Lisbon, on September 3, 1601; the two Jesuits, however, were not traveling on the same vessel. Because of a storm, the fleet was scattered; Fr. Archer reached Kinsale, Ireland, on September 23, but the ship in which Br. Collins was sailing was forced to return to La Coruña and only much later did he land at Castlehaven, some thirty miles west of Kinsale. He immediately began his search for Fr. Archer, whom he found on February 1, 1602, at nearby Castle Gortnacloghy, whither the priest had gone after the fall of Kinsale. Both Jesuits then proceeded to Dunboy Castle, which the Irish had recently regained. With the landing on June 6 of huge English forces, Fr. Archer left for Spain hoping to persuade the king to send reinforcements.

The English army attacked Dunboy Castle and after days of heavy bombardment the castle towers began to topple. On June 17 the remaining seventy-seven defenders were forced to retire into the castle's cellars. That evening, it seems, there was talk of a promise that their lives would be spared if they surrendered. A contemporary account relates that Br. Collins emerged and gave himself up. Apparently, he was to act as intermediary for the defenders. The assault, however, continued on July 18 and except for Br. Collins and two others, all not killed in action were executed in the castle courtyard. That evening, Br. Collins was taken to a prison in Cork and within days of his imprisonment various offers were placed before him. His life would be spared if he volunteered information and undertook some service to merit the queen's favor. Since he understood the offer to mean that he was to divulge information about Catholics, renounce his vocation as a Jesuit, and join the established Church, he flatly refused. He was then offered an honorable position in the government's military; this too he rejected. Protestant ministers visited him and tried to get him to apostatize by offering ecclesiastical preferment. Nor were they successful. The most painful was when relatives came, urging and pleading with him to renounce the faith to save his life and to preserve the family from the disgrace of having one of its members executed as a criminal. When he insisted that he would not and could not give up his faith, the relatives, in turn, suggested that he could remain a Catholic in heart, while outwardly conforming to the new religion. They too met with refusal.

On July 9 Br. Collins was interrogated at length and condemned to death. He was detained in Cork Prison until October 31 when he was taken to Youghal, his hometown, and hanged. Eyewitness accounts record that he wore his Jesuit cassock and that he cheerfully climbed the ladder. When he reached the top, he addressed the bystanders, telling them that he had come to Ireland to preach the Catholic faith. To an English captain standing nearby, he said that he would most willingly undergo not one but a thousand such deaths for the same cause. He remained hanging for three or four hours and when the rope snapped his body fell to the ground in a kneeling position. It was then stripped of its clothing and left naked. Under cover of night Catholics came and buried the body in a nearby place.

Br. Collins, together with sixteen other martyrs, who died in Ireland between the years 1579 and 1654, was beatified by Pope John Paul II on September 27, 1992. His Jesuit brethren celebrate his memorial on October 30.

Prayer

In troubled times, O Lord, you gave us as a pattern of constancy Blessed Dominic Collins and his companion martyrs, who for the joy that was set before them, endured the cross, rejecting its shame. Grant, by their prayers, that faithfully following your commandments we may bring forth fruits of unity and peace. We ask this through our Lord Jesus Christ, your Son, who lives and reigns with you and the Holy Spirit, one God, for ever and ever.

October 31

St. Alphonsus Rodríguez 1533–1617

Alphonsus Rodríguez, the second son of eleven children, was born in Segovia, Spain, July 25, 1533. His father was a successful wool and cloth merchant and the family was comfortably established. When Fr. Peter Favre, one of St. Ignatius' first companions, came to Segovia to preach, the Rodríguez family offered him the hospitality of its home. This was the first contact Alphonsus had with a Jesuit, and while Fr. Favre lived with them, he prepared the young boy for his First Communion.

When Alphonsus was almost twelve, his father sent him to the Jesuit college at Alcalá, but the youth never completed his studies because of his father's sudden death. When Alphonsus returned home, he helped his mother operate the family business and in time took over its management completely. When he was about twenty-seven years old, he married Maria Suárez and the young couple had three children; Gaspar, Alphonsus, and Maria. Their happy life together did not last long. In quick succession his son Gaspar died, then his daughter Maria; shortly, thereafter, his wife, and finally the young Alphonsus.

Not only was Alphonsus now without family, but his cloth business began to decline due to the heavy taxes levied on exporting wool products. The business went from bad to worse and, finally, he had to give it up altogether. The young widower viewed himself a failure, and filled with internal anxiety and distress, he sought spiritual direction from the Jesuits, who had recently arrived in Segovia. It was through the inconsolable death of his wife and family that God chose to lead Alphonsus to an extraordinarily intimate union with himself. Alphonsus spent these sad and lonely years in prayer and penance seeking to do God's will and there gradually grew in him the desire to give himself to God as a Jesuit. He presented himself as an applicant for the priesthood, but the response he received was disheartening. He was told that he was too old—he was about thirty-five years of age—that he lacked the necessary education to pursue the studies leading to the priesthood, and that his health was not sufficiently vigorous to endure the hard life of the Society.

Alphonsus may have been disappointed but he was not vanquished. He went in 1568 to Valencia, where his spiritual father had been transferred, and there he returned to the classroom to complete his studies so that he could eventually become a priest. After two years of further education he once more applied for entrance into the Society, and if he could not be accepted as a priest, he would be happy to be a brother. But the fathers who examined him in Valencia came to the same conclusion as those in Segovia. The age and health of Alphonsus were against him. Though the examiners cast negative votes, Fr. Provincial overrode their decision and granted Alphonsus permission to enter. He is supposed to have said that if Alphonsus were not fitted to be a priest or a brother, he could, nevertheless, enter to become a saint.

On January 31, 1571, at age thirty-seven, Alphonsus entered the Jesuit novitiate and after six months was instructed to go to the college of Montesión in Palma on the island of Majorca, off the Spanish coast, to complete his noviceship training. Br. Alphonsus arrived in August and remained there for the next forty-six years of his life. He pronounced the three vows of religion on April 5, 1573, and took on various positions at the college until 1579, when he was made the college's doorkeeper. As doorkeeper his duty was to receive the visitors who came to the college, search out the fathers or students who were wanted in the parlors, deliver messages, run errands, console the sick at heart who, having no one to turn to, came to him, give advice to the troubled, and distribute alms to the needy. In his memoirs he tells us that each time the bell rang he looked at the door and envisioned that it was God who was standing outside seeking admittance. On his way to the door, he would say: "I'm coming, Lord!" Every visitor that came to Montesión was greeted with the same happy smile with which he would have greeted God. For fifteen years Br. Alphonsus was in charge of that porter's lodge—a position without glory and challenge, repetitious and monotonous, but one demanding humility and holiness. When he was sixty-one, and because his health was on the decline, his superiors made his labors easier by relieving him of the long hours at the door and allowed him to act as assistant to the new porter. Now that his work was less, Br. Alphonsus had more time for prayer.

No student came to Montesión who did not feel the presence and influence of Br. Alphonsus. they came to him for advice and encouragement and asked his prayers, which he most willingly said for them and their needs. When occasion offered, he spoke to them of devotion to our Lady—the rosary was almost always in his hand—and for many he copied the entire Little Office of the Blessed Virgin for their private recitation. His interest in the students never lessened, and in 1605, when he was seventy-two, the young Peter Claver came to the college. Peter was aflame with a desire to do something for God, but because of his youth, he knew not how to accomplish it. Peter approached Br. Alphonsus; they became friends and often met on the college grounds to discuss prayer and the pursuit of holiness. It was Br. Alphonsus who urged Peter to go to the South American missions. Peter followed his mentor's advice and it was in Cartagena, Colombia, that he labored heroically among the slaves brought from Africa.

The quality and depth of the prayer life of Br. Alphonsus was known to only a few during his lifetime. He was always appreciated for his charity, kindness, obedience, and holiness, but it was only after his death, when his memoirs and spiritual notes were discovered, that it was learned how the humble brother was favored by God with remarkable mystical graces, ecstasies, and visions of our Lord, our Lady, and the saints.

As Br. Alphonsus reached his eighties, he became more and more feeble, quite thin, and rather bent over. He could no longer assist at the porter's lodge and in 1615 he was confined to his bed only to rise now and then to attend Mass. In his last months his memory began to fail, he was not even able to remember his favorite prayers. He now had to be satisfied with the names "Jesus" and "Mary." When it became clear that he was about to die, the community at Montesión gathered in his room to commend his soul to God. When his Jesuit brethren had concluded their prayers, Br. Alphonsus opened his eyes wide and looked upon all who surrounded him, he then lowered them to the crucifix in his thin hands, kissed it, and said, "Jesus!" With the name of his Savior on his lips, Br. Alphonsus went to God. The date was October 31, 1617.

Br. Alphonsus Rodríguez was beatified by Pope Leo XII on May 20, 1825, and canonized by Pope Leo XIII on January 15, 1888. His memorial is celebrated in the Society on October 31.

Prayer

Lord our God, in Saint Alphonsus, our brother, you have shown us the way of fidelity that leads to joy and peace. May we remain watchful and attentive as companions of Jesus, who became the servant of all, and now lives and reigns with you and the Holy Spirit, one God, for ever and ever.

November

November 1

Bl. Peter Paul Navarro 1560–1622

Bl. Peter Onizuka 1604–1622

Bl. Dennis Fujishima 1584–1622

Martyrs of Japan

Fr. Peter Paul Navarro was born in Basilicata, southern Italy, in the small town of Laino, in December 1560. When eighteen he entered (1579) the Jesuits in Nola and during his novitiate asked to be sent to the Japanese mission. His request was honored and by 1584 he was studying in Goa, India, and was ordained there in 1585. Shortly afterwards he was on his way to Japan, where he arrived in August 1586.

Fr. Navarro landed on the island of Hirado in western Japan, and after spending a year in language study, served in mission posts in Shikoku and Honshu. He knew that if he wanted to be successful in evangelizing the Japanese he himself must become one of them. Thus he became fluent in speaking and writing the language, adopted the Japanese form of dress, ate their food in their style, and used their type of furniture. By this he intended to show that the Japanese need not relinquish their customs and cultural traditions to become Christians.

When Fr. Navarro was expelled from his missions because of a local persecution against Christians, he went to northern Kyushu to the kingdom of Bungo, where much of his missionary activity became centered. In 1614 when Shogun Iyeyasu's edict expelling all foreign missionaries from Japan was published, he was one of the two dozen Jesuits who went underground rather than leave the country as eighty others had to. For the next seven years he concentrated his efforts in the province of Shimabara in western Kyushu. During this time he went about in disguise, assuming a variety of roles. At times he was a

P. Petrus Nauarrus Italus, Dionysius Fugixima, et Petrus Oni-
zuccha Iapones Soc: IESV. vivi pro Fide lento igne consumti
Ximabaræ in Iaponia 1 Novemb: A. 1622.
C. S. d.
                                                          M. K. :

Bl. Peter Paul Navarro, Bl. Peter Onizuka, and Bl. Dennis Fujishima beggar or wood seller, sometimes a farmer or a tradesman. These disguises were essential for him to enter Christian homes, and there to administer the sacraments, and celebrate Mass. Fr. Navarro was aware that he was being hunted by the police, and to evade capture he spent his days in hiding and did his moving about only at night. During this period he wrote in Japanese, *An Apology of the Christian Faith against the Calumnies of the Pagans.*

During his final years in Shimabara Fr. Navarro was ably assisted by two catechists, Peter Onizuka and Dennis Fujishima. Peter was in his teens, having been born about 1604, in Hachirao, Japan. He had been in contact with missionaries since his childhood. His father was a steadfast Christian who not only helped fugitive priests but also housed them. Dennis, on the other hand, was approaching forty and had been born in Aitsu, about 1584. He was of a noble family and became a Christian while still young. He had been married, but his wife had left him, apostatized, and started a new life for herself. Dennis had been accompanying Fr. Navarro on his missionary journeys since 1615.

Sometime in late December 1621, after Christmas, Fr. Navarro, his two catechists, and their servant, Clement Yuemon, were apprehended by priesthunters and delivered into the hands of the *daimyo* of Arima. Fr. Navarro was found guilty of being a missionary and his companions were guilty of collaborating with a missionary in spreading the proscribed Christian religion. Though the daimyo was pagan, he held the missionaries in esteem and saw to it that they were treated with respect. He had them taken to Shimabara and detained in a house owned by a Christian and where they were cared for by Christians as well. In addition, he allowed Fr. Navarro to celebrate Mass, and he himself frequently came to converse with him. When the daimyo offered the prisoners freedom if they would give up Christianity, he learned that they preferred torture and death to denying the faith. Because the daimyo did not want to see them die, he planned to transfer them secretly to Macao and set them free, but orders came from the shogun on October 27, 1622, that the prisoners were to die by slow fire. The *daimyo* reluctantly informed his prisoners of the news on October 28 and Fr. Navarro, happy that his prayers had been answered wrote a letter to his Jesuit friend, Fr. John Baptist Zola, saying: "I give infinite thanks to the Lord and I ask you to thank him with me. I also ask your prayers for perseverance until my final breath."

When November 1, the day of execution, arrived, Fr. Navarro celebrated the Mass of All Saints and the two catechists, Peter and Dennis, who had asked to enter the Society, pronounced their Jesuit vows during that final Mass. As he awaited the executioners, Fr. Navarro took time to write a last note to Fr. Matthew de Couros: "For many years I have prayed for this great grace from God, but always with some fear that I would not be heard because of my many sins. The Father of mercies now gives me this long-desired grace. May he be blessed forever!" When it was afternoon the four prisoners, escorted by some fifty soldiers and a large crowd of Christians, made their way to the place of execution. On their way the priest chanted the Litany of Our Lady and his companions joyfully sang the responses.

As they approached the shore the martyrs saw the standing stakes erected on a piece of land projecting into the bay, awaiting them. The *daimyo* had instructed the soldiers to arrange the wood around the stakes so as not to prolong the prisoners' suffering. Thus, in flames, the three Jesuits, Frs. Peter Paul Navarro, Peter Onizuka, and Dennis Fujishima, and their faithful servant Clement Yuemon, gave final heroic witness of their great love for God.

With 201 others, these four martyrs were beatified by Pope Pius IX on May 7, 1867, and their memorial is liturgically celebrated by their Jesuit brethren on February 4.

Prayer

Almighty God, grant that this remembrance of your martyrs, Blessed Peter Paul Navarro and companions, may bring us joy. May we who depend on their prayers glory in their entry in heaven. We ask this through our Lord Jesus Christ, your Son, who lives and reigns with you and the Holy Spirit, one God, for ever and ever.

November 3

Bl. Rupert Mayer 1876–1945

Rupert Mayer was born in Stuttgart, Germany, on January 23, 1876. After finishing his secondary education in Ravensburg in 1894, he told his father of his desire to become a Jesuit, but his father asked him to be ordained first, and if he should continue in his desire then he could enter the Society. The son accepted his father's proposal and pursued university studies in philosophy at Fribourg, Switzerland (1894–1895), and Munich (1895–1896), and theological studies at Tübingen (1896–1898). Only for his final year did he go to the seminary at Rottenburg. Rupert was ordained on May 2, 1899, and celebrated his first Mass on May 4.

Fr. Mayer served as an assistant pastor in Spaichingen for a year and then entered the Jesuit novitiate at Feldkirch, Austria, on October 1, 1900. After noviceship he moved to Valkenburg, in the Netherlands, for further studies. From 1906 to 1911 he traveled through Germany, Switzerland, and the Netherlands, preaching missions in parishes large and small, but his characteristic apostolate began when he was transferred to Munich in 1912.

At the time of his arrival in Munich the city was filled with people coming from farms and small towns, all seeking housing and employment. The migrants put a great strain on the city and Fr. Mayer involved himself in their plight. He searched out jobs and homes for many and collected food and clothing for the poor. Since the city was becoming "pagan," he spent his best efforts in seeing that the migrants preserved their faith.

Germany was soon involved in World War I and Fr. Mayer volunteered his services in August 1914. He was first assigned to a camp hospital, but was later made Field Captain and traveled with his men to France, Poland, and Romania, where he was in the front line of battle. His courage became a legend among his soldiers; he was with them in their trenches, and when they were dying he stayed with them until the end. His courage was infectious and his presence gave the men hope. It was nothing for him on a Sunday to officiate at eight services. In December 1915 he was awarded the *Iron Cross* for bravery—a rare honor for a chaplain. But his army career came to a swift end when his left leg was shattered on December 30, 1916, and had to be amputated. On January 6, 1917, he left the field of battle to begin his convalescence.

Fr. Mayer was back in Munich and found its citizens suffering from the war's aftermath. He again went among his people and aided them in any way he could. In 1921 he was appointed director of the men's sodality and within nine years the membership grew to over 7,000. The men came from fifty-three different parishes, and when he wanted to speak to each group, it sometimes meant seventy talks in a given month. For the convenience of travelers he introduced Sunday Masses (1925) at the main railroad terminal and he himself celebrated the first two, beginning at 3:10 A.M. His apostolate extended to the entire city; if Munich were a single parish, then its pastor would have been Fr. Mayer.

Postwar Munich saw the rise of communist and socialist movements, and from the beginning Fr. Mayer kept close watch on them. He attended their meetings and shared the platform with their speakers, not to praise them but to point out where they were wrong and to indicate the evils to which they were leading their audiences. He witnessed the rise of Adolf Hitler and while others were unable to discern the falsehoods Hitler was propagating, he bravely spoke out against them, always stressing Catholic principles. For Fr. Mayer a Catholic could not be a National Socialist, and so it was inevitable that conflict should arise between him and the Nazi movement. His opposition was not just political, it was a religious response, for he knew he was dealing with evil and he heroically tried to prevent his people from rushing headlong into destruction.

In January 1933 Hitler became chancellor of the German Reich and began to show his true colors. He made a move to close church-affiliated schools and started a campaign to defame the religious orders in Germany. Fr. Mayer spoke out against this persecution from the pulpit in St. Michael's in downtown

Munich and because he was a powerful influence in the city, the Nazis could not tolerate such a force to oppose them. On May 16, 1937, the Gestapo ordered him to stop speaking in public. He obeyed this order, but continued to preach in church. Within two weeks he was arrested on June 5 and sent to Stadelheim Prison; his trial was not until July 22, when he was given a suspended sentence. His superiors asked him to remain silent and he acquiesced, until the Nazis took advantage of his silence to defame him in public. To exonerate himself, his superiors permitted him to return to the pulpit. On January 5, 1938, he was again arrested and served his suspended sentence in Landsberg Prison. In May, because of a general amnesty, he returned to Munich and restricted his work to small discussion groups.

The Nazis were still fearful of the now sixty-three-year-old Fr. Mayer. So he was arrested once more on November 3, 1939; the pretext was his supposed cooperation with a royalist movement. He was sent in late December to the Oranienburg-Sachsenhausen concentration camp near Berlin. He spent seven months there, but by August 1940 his health began to deteriorate so rapidly that camp officials feared he might die. Not wanting him to become a martyr, they sent him to the Benedictine Abbey at Ettal, in the Bavarian Alps. While living in solitary confinement, he spent his time in prayer, waiting for the disposition of Divine Providence. Then on May 6, 1945, American soldiers entered Ettal and freed the prisoners. Fr. Mayer was back in Munich on May 11 and immediately resumed his apostolic work in St. Michael's church.

The years in prison and confinement showed in the aging priest. On November 1, 1945, the feast of All Saints, Fr. Mayer was celebrating the 8:00 A. M. Mass in St. Michael's and after reading the gospel he began his sermon. His topic was the saints in heaven and the Christian's duty to imitate them to gain Paradise. But in the middle of the sermon, while his thoughts were on heaven, his heart stopped, and the sixty-nine-year-old Fr. Mayer collapsed and died shortly afterwards. He was buried in the Jesuit cemetery at Pullach, outside Munich. On May 23, 1948, his remains were brought back to the city and interred in the crypt of the Bürgersaal, the church next to St. Michael's, where the men's sodality regularly met.

Fr. Rupert Mayer was beatified by Pope John Paul II in Munich on November 3, 1987, and his memorial is liturgically kept in the Society on November 3.

Prayer

Loving Father, you made the blessed priest Rupert Mayer a steadfast confessor of the faith and a selfless helper of the poor; through his intercession, raise up in the Church new, exemplary heralds of the gospel and give us all a heart open to the needs of others. We ask this through our Lord Jesus Christ, who lives and reigns with you, in the unity of the Holy Spirit, one God, for ever and ever.

November 4

S. G. **Francis Audí** 1872–1936

S. G. **John Rovira** 1877–1936

S. G. **Joseph Llatje** 1893–1936

Martyrs of the Spanish Civil War

Among the Jesuit Servants of God who died during the Spanish Civil War, three died at Tortosa: namely, Frs. Francis Audí Cid and John Rovira Orlandis, and Br. Joseph Llatje Blanch.

Fr. Audí was superior of the Jesuit retreat house in Tortosa, when he and Fr. Rovira were martyred. He had been born in Roquetas, near Tortosa, on February 8, 1872, and entered the Jesuit novitiate outside Saragossa on September 1, 1893. After finishing his classical studies and philosophy, he taught at St. Joseph's College in Valencia, then went to Tortosa for theology and was ordained in 1906. After tertianship he was assigned in 1908 to the college in Orihuela, where he taught psychology. He moved in 1917 to the retreat house in Tortosa and became superior of the community in 1919. He transferred to Huesca in 1924 to be superior of the retreat house, and in September 1927 returned to Tortosa, again as superior.

Fr. Rovira came to the Tortosa retreat house in 1927. His native city was Palma in Majorca, where he had been born on October 4, 1877. He entered the novitiate near Saragossa on November 25, 1895. He spent the years from 1902 to 1904 in Madrid doing graduate studies and then went to Tortosa in 1906 for theology. He was ordained in 1909. He spent three years (1911–1914) in Rome studying for an advanced degree in Sacred Scripture and on his return to his homeland he taught Old Testament at the Jesuit theologate in Sarriá (1915–1927).

Frs. Audí and Rovira had been living in the same community since 1927. When the community was forced to disperse in 1932, as a result of the Society's suppression in Spain, both priests remained together. Then when civil war broke out in mid-July 1936, they separated, each finding refuge with friends. In the early hours of July 31, 1936, Fr. Audí made his way to the farmhouse of his brother Thomas. On August 3 Fr. Rovira joined him and for three months the priests lived on the farmhouse's upper floor. The shutters were always closed; the priests rarely went downstairs where the family of Thomas lived, and they never went outside. Through all this Fr. Audí kept his spirits high, but Fr. Rovira was of a different temperament; he was always worried, sometimes on the verge of panic, and spent most of his time alone in his room. He once thought of going to Majorca, but Fr. Audí talked him out of the plan, for he was sure to be captured and killed.

Communist soldiers unexpectedly came to the farmhouse on November 3 intending to search it. They claimed a radio was illegally hidden inside. As soon as Fr. Audí heard what was happening downstairs, he made his way into the orchard, but Fr. Rovira kept to his room. In checking the house the soldiers found the priest and took him downstairs and searched him. They then pushed him outside and forced him and Thomas Audí to walk to headquarters. By the time they arrived Fr. Rovira was exhausted. Only with great difficulty did he manage the stairs leading into the building, and when the department chief saw him, the chief angrily remarked: "This is not Fr. Audí!"

The soldiers again went to the farmhouse about midday, but Fr. Audí was not there. Early that afternoon he did return, and quietly waited for the soldiers to appear. They came before 3:00 P.M. and took him to headquarters. Now that both priests were in their hands, they were beaten, brutally kicked, and trampled upon. When they refused to blaspheme and deny God, the kicks became more frequent. About 10:00 that evening both Jesuits were taken from their cells and led outside to a quiet roadside, where they were martyred. Without knowing what had happened to the two priests, Thomas Audí was released the following day.

On November 4, as soon as dawn came, the son and son-in-law of Thomas walked along the road going to Valencia to see what they could find. Half way between Tortosa and Santa Bárbara, they found the bodies of both priests in a ditch. Each had his hands tied behind his back. Fr. Audí had suffered several blows to his head and many bruises over his body, but it was gunshots that killed him. Fr. Rovira had received worse treatment at the hands of the revolutionaries; his skull was smashed open and his face badly bruised as was his body. Later that day, when the Audí family attempted to have the bodies buried together, city officials refused the request. They, however, permitted Fr. Audí's body to be placed in the family plot, but Fr. Rovira's was placed in an unmarked grave.

The third Jesuit to die in Tortosa, but two months earlier, was Br. Joseph Llatje. He had been born on August 17, 1893, also in Roquetas, and entered the Society at Gandía on February 2, 1909. He was the tailor at the Tortosa scholasticate for six years (1912–1918), and when he went to St. Dominic's in Orihuela, he was in charge of the laundry room (1918–1925). He then moved to Lérida, and when that community had to disperse because of the decree of suppression, he went to Barcelona.

At the time civil war erupted, Br. Llatje was planning to go to Tortosa to visit his ailing father. Traveling while war was in progress was somewhat dangerous; his friends tried to dissuade him, but if he felt he had to go, they advised him not to wear his religious habit. His friends' entreaties went unheeded. Br. Llatje took the night train from Barcelona on July 28. When it stopped at Tortosa at 4:00 A.M. the following morning, the communists detained him to question him. He claimed that he was merely on his way to see his sick father so two guards accompanied him. Satisfied that the father was ill and that the brother was speaking the truth, they instructed him: "Don't leave the house and nothing will happen to you." Br. Llatje thus spent the month of August with his family. When his sister expressed her fears, he simply responded: "If they kill us, what of it, we will be martyrs."

On September 5 Br. Llatje's freedom came to an end. At 9:30 that evening, after everyone had gone to bed and he alone was still awake, a half-dozen armed men came to the house and asked him to accompany them to headquarters, where they wanted him to make a declaration. Assured that it would only take a few minutes, he did not bother to notify his family that he was going. As the group departed his sister-in-law, from an upstairs window, saw that they had handcuffed him and put him in a car. She then heard it go off and a short time later she heard three shots; then a car drove through town at great speed.

Early the next morning, Mr. Llatje instructed another son to walk along the road and see what happened the previous night. Less then a mile away he found his brother stretched on the ground, dead from gunshot wounds. The body was then taken to the cemetery and buried.

The diocesan investigation into the martyrdoms of Frs. Francis Audí and John Rovira, and Br. Joseph Llatje was officially opened in Tortosa on November 25, 1950.

November 5

All Saints and Blessed of the Society of Jesus

Today's feast is something of a family celebration, when Jesuits joyfully remember their brothers who have been canonized and beatified. Besides the Society's 44 saints and 140 blessed, there are other Jesuits, whose love of God and humble lives have been wonderfully rewarded by God by taking them unto himself in heaven. We may not be able to give the names of these Jesuits, nor their number, but we do rejoice with them for they have achieved the goal that each of us still strives to attain.

Today's feast tells us that holiness is our goal in life. When St. Ignatius chose to describe the purpose of the Jesuit order, he used these words: "The end of this Society is to devote itself with God's grace not only to the salvation and perfection of the members' own souls, but also with the same grace to labor strenuously in giving aid toward the salvation and perfection of the souls of their fellowmen" (*General Examen,* 1, 2). The ultimate goal of a Jesuit, then, is to become holy and to strive to make those with whom he comes into contact holy as well. It matters not what type of work the Jesuit may be engaged in: he could be a university professor teaching biology or a parish priest dispensing sacraments; he could be operating a soup kitchen for the city's poor or be in a foreign land telling others about God and Christ. Whatever he does, he does for the salvation of others and for his own salvation as well. By teaching others to love God, the Jesuit himself learns to love God more, and by trying to get others to advance in holiness, he too advances in holiness.

The Jesuits who have achieved heaven prove that holiness is within reach and that St. Ignatius did not ask his sons to aspire to something impossible. During the months he spent in the cave on the banks of the Cardoner in Manresa, St. Ignatius experienced God's extraordinary graces and came to see how the *Spiritual Exercises,* which he was then writing, could be a valid way of achieving holiness. Whenever a candidate presented himself for the Society, the founder insisted that he first go through the Exercises to learn what God was asking of him. And for the past four hundred and fifty years, the Exercises has been the Society's main instrument in arousing holiness in others. Many of the Jesuits whose biographies appear in this volume spent a good part of their priestly ministry preaching the Exercises in cathedral cities and tiny villages. St. John Francis Regis preached them in southern France and Bl. Anthony Baldinucci did the same in central Italy; Ven. Aloysius La Nuza preached them throughout Sicily and Ven. Philip Jeningen carried them throughout southern Germany. The saints, blessed, and others, whom we devoutly remember today, were all nurtured on St. Ignatius' *Spiritual Exercises.*

Individuals do not become holy on their own; God is the source of all holiness. As we praise our Jesuits in heaven today, we likewise praise God for all he has done in and through his saints. If the saints achieved anything during their lifetime, it was God who accomplished it. Though St. Francis Xavier poured water on innumerable heads in India, it was God who made them Christians. Though St. John de Brébeuf exhibited unbelievable courage during torture, it was God who supported and granted him the strength to give valiant witness to the faith. Saints ascribe everything to God and nothing to themselves.

To be holy one must first be humble, and St. Ignatius wanted to instill this humility in his sons, when he wrote that the candidates seeking entrance into the Society be told

> to how great a degree it helps and profits one in the spiritual life to abhor in its totality and not in part whatever the world loves and embraces, and to accept and desire with all possible energy whatever Christ our Lord has loved and embraced. Just as the men of the world who follow the world love and seek with such great diligence honors, fame, and esteem for a great name on earth, as the world

teaches them, so those who are progressing in the spiritual life and truly following Christ our Lord love and intensely desire everything opposite. That is to say, they desire to clothe themselves with the same clothing and uniform of their Lord because of the love and reverence which he deserves, to such an extent that where there would be no offense to his Divine Majesty, and no imputation of sin to the neighbor, they would wish to suffer injuries, false accusations, and affronts, and to be held and esteemed as fools (but without their giving any occasion for this), because of their desire to resemble and imitate in some manner our Creator and Lord Jesus Christ, by putting on his clothing and uniform, since it was for our spiritual profit that he clothed himself as he did. For he gave us an example that in all things possible to us we might seek, through the aid of his grace, to imitate and follow him, since he is the way which leads men to life *(General Examen,* 4, 44).

The humility St. Ignatius asks of his followers is the humility that Christ possessed and which the saints and blessed of the Society eminently manifested in their lives.

It is sometimes suggested that the saints are really inimitable; for who of us can imitate the courage of St. Andrew Bobola or the extraordinary patience of St. Alphonsus Rodríguez? Perhaps we seek to imitate the wrong things! We can indeed imitate the saints in their humility, seeking to be clothed with the clothing and uniform of our Lord and to be treated as fools as he had been treated. Once we achieve humility, God will the take over and grant courage to his martyrs and patience to his confessors.

Today's feast is, therefore, a feast to encourage all of us, who are still working our way to salvation. Holiness is possible to us; and because our saints and blessed are in the presence of the Blessed Trinity, these brothers of ours become our intercessors asking God for the graces, strength, and perseverance we need to fulfill our vocation.

When the bishops of the Church assembled in Rome for the Second Vatican Council, they spoke of our call to holiness and encouraged us to pray to our saints in heaven.

It is most fitting, therefore, that we love these friends and co-heirs of Jesus Christ who are also our brothers and outstanding benefactors, and that we give due thanks to God for them, "humbly invoking them, and having recourse to their prayers, their aid and help in obtaining from God through his Son, Jesus Christ, our Lord, our Redeemer and Savior, the benefits we need." Every authentic witness of love, indeed, offered by us to those who are in heaven tends to and terminates in Christ, "the crown of all the saints," and through him in God who is wonderful in his saints and is glorified in them *(Lumen gentium,* 50).

Prayer

Lord God, Father of our Lord Jesus Christ, you call us to your service though you know how weak we are. Help us to be good soldiers of Christ under the banner of his cross. Bring to perfection the work you have begun in Saint Ignatius and so many of his followers, now acclaimed as saints and blessed. We ask this through our Lord Jesus Christ, your Son, who lives and reigns with you and the Holy Spirit, one God, for ever and ever.

November 6

S. G. James de Mesquita and 4 Companions 1553–1614

When the recently converted Japanese princes sent four noble envoys to Europe to visit the kings of Portugal and Spain and to offer the pope their obedience, it was Fr. James de Mesquita who led the delegation on that extended trip. Fr. Alexander Valignano had first been appointed to guide the youthful envoys, each about fourteen or fifteen years old, with Fr. Mesquita as interpreter. The group left Nagasaki on February 20, 1582, but during the voyage to Tuticorin, India, Fr. Mesquita fell ill with fever. When the ship docked, he was sent ashore to recuperate while the others proceeded to Goa to await his arrival. When his health returned Fr. Mesquita walked from Tuticorin to Goa and arrived in October 1583, only to learn that Fr. Valignano had been appointed provincial of India and was now unable to make the journey to Europe. Hence Fr. Mesquita was placed in charge of the group. After long delays in various ports the group arrived in Lisbon, Portugal, on August 10, 1584, thirty months after it had left Japan.

Wherever these four noble youths visited they were greeted as royalty. When they met the king of Portugal it was as if four heads of state had come to Lisbon. Throughout these and subsequent official visits, Fr. Mesquita was at the youths' sides, serving as their interpreter. When they arrived in Spain, they spent several days with Philip II at the Escorial and then sailed from Alicante for Livorno. Passing through Pisa, Florence, and Siena, they were sumptuously feted; they finally entered the Eternal City on March 22, 1585. They lodged at the Jesuit residence, where Fr. General Claudio Acquaviva welcomed them.

Rome celebrated the envoys' official entry on March 23. Surrounded by cardinals and bishops, knights and cavalry, the four youths, dressed in their ceremonial robes, presented a magnificent pageant for the Romans. Amid the pealing of church bells and the sound of trumpets, the entourage made its way to the Vatican to meet the ailing Pope Gregory XIII. Seeing the first fruits of Christian Japan before him, the pontiff embraced each warmly and with tears in his eyes affectionately greeted them. Since Pope Gregory died eighteen days later, on April 10, the nobles remained in Rome for the election of the next pope, Sixtus V, whose coronation they attended. They left the city on June 3, 1585, going first to Bologna and then to Venice, where Tintoretto painted their portraits. They made their way back to Lisbon, where Philip II, at his own expense, had fitted out a vessel for their return journey. They set sail on April 12, 1586, and reached Goa on May 29, 1587.

Fr. Valignano joined the group at Goa for the trip to Japan, but now he was envoy for the Portuguese viceroy in India and was on his way to visit Toyotomi Hideyoshi, ruler of Japan, to express Portugal's gratitude for all he had done for the Catholic Church. But when the ship docked at Macao in July 1588, the priests learned that Hideyoshi, since July 1587, had turned against the Catholic Church, had banished all missionaries, and had initiated a persecution.

Since Hideyoshi was no longer favorable toward Christianity as he once had been, Fr. Valignano, rather than going directly to Japan, wrote to him from Macao requesting an audience. Hideyoshi agreed. The four nobles with Frs. Valignano and Mesquita and full entourage arrived in Nagasaki on July 21, 1590. But it wasn't until March 3, 1591, that they had their meeting. Though unable to get Hideyoshi to rescind the decree of banishment, it would not be enforced with full vigor as long as the missionaries refrained from meddling in Japanese politics. He likewise permitted some Jesuits to remain in Nagasaki to care for the Portuguese community.

Fr. Mesquita thus made Nagasaki the center of his apostolate. As a Portuguese, having been born in Mesão Frio in 1553, he became superior of the Jesuits in Nagasaki and was rector of the Portuguese church and college from 1598 to 1611. By Hideyoshi's decree, the church was only to be used by the European community, thus the Jesuits ministered to the Japanese Christians in their homes. On his return from Europe Fr. Mesquita brought a printing press with him and in 1591 began printing Catholic books. In July of that same year the four nobles who had visited Europe all entered the Society, and one of them, Julian Nakaura, later died a martyr's death on October 26, 1633.

The missionaries' work came to a unexpected halt in early 1614, when Shogun Iyeyasu decreed the banishment of all missionaries and the closing of all Christian churches. He ordered the missionaries to proceed to Nagasaki for deportation. Of the eighty Jesuits in Japan, sixty-two went to Nagasaki and eighteen went into hiding to continue ministering to the Japanese Christians. When the missionaries arrived in Nagasaki, there were no ships in port; then in June one did arrive, but it was not scheduled to leave for several months. So the missionaries lived in cramped quarters and without proper food. Impatient that he could not get the missionaries out of the country soon enough, Iyeyasu ordered them on October 27 to gather at the port and wait on shore for ships to arrive. There, open to the elements, the missionaries built straw huts to keep from the sun. It was at this time, while on shore and within view of Nagasaki, that Fr. Mesquita became ill. He was sixty-one years old and physically worn out after the ordeal of the last several months. He did not want to leave his beloved Japan and prayed that the Lord would take him before ships arrived. That prayer was heard, for he died on November 4, 1614, and three days later junks came into port to take his Jesuit brothers into exile.

Fr. James de Mesquita's cause was opened in Macao in 1901 and with him, in that cause, are the following Jesuits.

Fr. Anthony Francis de Critana was a Spaniard, born in the small village of Almodóvar del Campo, in the diocese of Toledo, about 1548. When he entered the Society at the Jesuit college in Alcalá de Henares in 1569, he was twenty-one years old and had already earned a doctorate in philosophy from the University of Alcalá. After ordination he was minister at the residence in Toledo for seven years. He then left Lisbon on April 10, 1584, and arrived in Hirado, Japan, in August 1586. Fr. Critana was originally scheduled to work in the province of Bungo, but because that province was at war with Satsuma, he was reassigned to Yamaguchi. From 1598 to 1614 he was prefect of the church at All Saints College in Nagasaki. Due to Tokugawa Iyeyasu's decree of 1614 expelling all missionaries, he joined his Jesuit brethren on the shore awaiting the arrival of ships to take them into exile. With his fellow Jesuits he boarded one of them on November 7, but because he was physically burned out as a result of his earlier suffering and the privations on board the junk, he fell ill and died on November 24, 1614. They were about ninety miles from Manila. In response to the Jesuits' request, the Portuguese captain did not bury the body at sea, but placed the sealed coffin on a small sloop, and when they arrived in the Philippines, the body was buried in the Mariveles area and later taken to the church attached to St. Ignatius College in Manila.

Fr. Gaspar de Crasto was born in Braga, Portugal, about 1560 and entered the Society at Coimbra in 1580 as a brother. For a time he served as infirmarian at the college. When Pope Sixtus V named Fr. Sebastian de Morais first bishop of Japan in 1588, the new bishop asked Br. Crasto to accompany him. During the long voyage to India, he put his knowledge of medicine to use by caring for sick passengers and crew. Unfortunately, the bishop himself fell ill and died at Mozambique. Br. Crasto continued his trip to Goa. In 1591 Fr. Peter Martins was named to succeed Bp. Morais, and as he was about to leave for Macao, he asked Br. Crasto to go along with him. Perceiving that the brother could become an excellent missionary, the bishop began teaching him Latin and moral theology, and in 1596 ordained him in Macao. That year both of them set sail for Japan and arrived in Nagasaki on August 14, 1596. Fr. Crasto immediately set about his missionary work. At the time of the 1614 decree banishing all missionaries, he remained behind for a time, but then left Japan in 1615 for Macao.

By 1620 he was again in Japan carrying out his priestly ministry. When he heard that Fr. Francis Pacheco, the Jesuit provincial, had been captured in December 1625 and that the area was full of spies searching for priests, Fr. Crasto, already in his sixty-fifth year, went into hiding. Because he had to endure the winter months in a cave, without fire and sufficient food, his health broke and he became seriously ill. When his Christians found him they carried him to a protected spot in the woods of Takaku, but the missionary's health was beyond repair. He died amid the peaceful trees on May 7, 1626, and it was there that his Christians buried him.

Fr. John Baptist de Baeza was born in Ubeda, Spain, in 1558. Before his entrance into the Society in 1579, he studied both civil and canon law at the University of Salamanca. After ordination as a Jesuit he left for India in 1586. The vessel he was traveling on made routine stops at Mozambique, Goa, and Macao, so he took advantage of the delays to go ashore and preach to the people. He arrived in Nagasaki on July 21, 1590, and began his apostolic work in the kingdom of Higo. It is said that after a period of three years he had performed 70,000 baptisms, not counting those of infants. Like St. Francis Xavier, who had also evangelized Japan, Fr. Baeza had his Christians support his weary arms so that he could continue baptizing. From Higo he moved to Shimabara to be vicar general to Bp. Luis Cerqueira, who succeeded Bp. Peter Martins in 1598.

After being expelled from Shimabara in 1612, Fr. Baeza returned to his work up north. But two years later when Iyeyasu's decree was issued he went to Nagasaki. He, however, did not go into exile; he went into hiding and for almost twelve years lived with Michael Nakashima in Nagasaki. When asked how he managed to elude his persecutors for so long a time, he only replied that God saw to it that he had not yet been apprehended.

Toward the end of his life Fr. Baeza was stricken with paralysis. Unable to move about as he would like, his Christians carried him from house to house in a basket. He had often thought of death and was sure that it would be by the sword, or fire, or perhaps on a cross, but it was only as he grew older that he realized that God was asking of him a slow martyrdom, through pain and suffering. Because his physical condition was so poor, plans were in progress to have him go to China, but before they matured, he died on May 7, 1626.

Fr. Matthew de Couros was born in Lisbon, Portugal, about 1568 and entered the Society on December 22, 1583. Having requested to go to the missions, he left Lisbon in April 1586 on the same vessel that took Fr. Mesquita and the four Japanese nobles back to Goa. He did some of his studies in India and Macao and on July 21, 1590, left for Nagasaki, where he completed them. In March 1596 he returned to Macao, but on August 14 of that year he was again in Japan. Fr. Couros labored first in Arima and was among the exiles that left Nagasaki in November 1614, but his stay in Macao was short, for he was back in Japan in August 1615. He was provincial of Japan from July 1617 to October 1621, when Fr. Francis Pacheco succeeded him. Then when Fr. Pacheco was captured in

December 1625, Fr. Couros once more assumed responsibility for the mission and was vice-provincial until 1630, when he again became provincial.

Most of the ministry of Fr. Couros in Japan had to be done at night so that he would not fall into the hands of spies. If he had to venture forth during the day, he always did so in some disguise. As provincial he did much traveling and this made him more vulnerable, but through God's beneficent protection he was never apprehended during the many years he worked in Japan. He often had to seek refuge in strange hiding places, but perhaps the most distressing of them all was the pit. In one of his letters dated 1626, he describes such a refuge. One of his hosts had a pit or a subterranean cavity built for him—large enough so that he, his catechist, and servant could live in it. There was no light, and most of the time they lived in darkness except when they were eating, or when he was reciting the breviary, or when his duty as provincial required him to write letters. The men did not leave the pit, and the food provided was poor and meager because his host could not buy large amounts without causing suspicion. After Fr. Couros left one pit, where he had spent a total of thirty-five days, he went to another.

After years of privation and suffering, Fr. Couros's body was unable to endure much more. One day, as he was traveling between Miyako (today's Kyoto), and Hasami, he became ill and could no longer continue his travels. Seeing a leper nearby, he asked him to take him to his hut to rest, thus, hoping to regain some strength. The leper gladly took him in and offered him whatever he could, but the sixty-five-year-old priest was not to get better and after several days of intense suffering he died, most probably on October 29, 1633.

November 7

Bl. Anthony Baldinucci 1665–1717

Anthony Baldinucci was born in Florence, Italy, on June 19, 1665, and at age eleven began his studies at the Jesuit school known as San Giovannino. When his older brother Philip entered the Dominicans, Anthony thought of following him into the same order. Because of his delicate health his father suggested that he forget the Dominicans and try to learn God's will for himself and he recommended that Anthony make the Spiritual Exercises under a Jesuit's direction. The outcome of this retreat was that he chose to follow St. Ignatius and entered the Roman novitiate of Sant'Andrea on April 21, 1681.

Anthony's next sixteen years were spent in Jesuit training. He pronounced his three vows of religion on April 22, 1683, and began his study of the humanities at the Roman College in 1684. In 1687 he taught at Terni and in 1690 at Rome. He had now been in the Society for nine years and on three occasions had requested to go to the foreign missions—India, China, or Japan—but each request was denied due to his uncertain health. In God's wisdom Anthony was to become a missionary, not in any foreign country but in his own native land. During his years of theology in Rome he frequently spent Sunday afternoons in the public squares encouraging those who gathered round to hear him, to attend the missions then being held in the local Roman parishes. Little did he realize that such missions would one day be his chief work. He was ordained on October 28, 1695, and spent another two years completing his Jesuit training.

In 1697 Fr. Baldinucci was assigned as an assistant at the Jesuit parish in Frascati, about a dozen miles south of Rome; part of his assignment was to spend four months of the year giving missions in the surrounding cities, towns, and villages. For twenty years his apostolate was principally missions and retreat work, with headquarters either at Frascati or Viterbo, a city north of Rome. During these years his routine did not vary much. He walked barefoot to his mission assignment, no matter what the weather, carrying his bag with notes and personal belongings over his back, with a pilgrim's staff in his hand. When asked why he insisted on walking barefoot, he replied: "That God may be moved by my sufferings to touch the hearts of my hearers." His missions lasted from eight to fourteen days, depending on the needs of the parish and his sermons were always based on the meditations in St. Ignatius' *Spiritual Exercises.*

During a mission Fr. Baldinucci regularly held a penitential procession to help prepare the parishioners for confession, and at the mission's end there was a General Communion service, when everyone would receive the Eucharist. The time he did not spend in the pulpit he spent in the confessional, or teaching catechism to children, or visiting the sick. When the mission came to an end, he had a bonfire built outside the church in which playing cards, dice, worldly books, and songs were fed to the flames. On one such occasion he counted 240 daggers and small arms and 21 pistols laid at his feet. When it was time to move on, he led the parishioners in procession to the next village, praying all the while that the succeeding parish receive the graces the previous parish had been granted.

Fr. Baldinucci's preaching was simple and vivid, at times dramatic, but always effective. From his diary we know that between 1697 and 1717 he visited thirty dioceses and gave 448 missions—an average of twenty-two missions a year. As a man of deep prayer and extraordinary penance, the people readily perceived his holiness, and many claimed to have witnessed his miracles.

On October 18, 1717, when he arrived at Pofi to begin another mission, his health was far from what it should have been, and then on the 26th it broke completely so that he had to be put to bed. Toward October's end there was a temporary improvement, and while some looked forward to his recovery he himself knew that death was approaching. On November 5 he received Viaticum and the last anointing. On the following day he grew more feeble and in the afternoon his speech became difficult, but those near his bed could still make out his constant prayer: "Jesus and Mary, my hope." About 4:00 P.M., convulsions began and these remained with him through the night and the following morning. At 11:00 A.M., on November 7, this indefatigable fifty-two-year-old home missioner, after spending thirty-five years as a Jesuit and twenty as an active preacher in the Italian countryside, returned his soul to the Lord.

Fr. Anthony Baldinucci was beatified by Pope Leo XIII on March 25, 1893, and his memorial is liturgically celebrated on July 2.

Prayer

O God, in addition to the great humility and austerity of life for which Blessed Anthony Baldinucci was known, you inspired him with a great zeal for the salvation of men. Through his merits and prayers, grant that we may be freed from selfish desires and love you in and above all things. We ask this through our Lord Jesus Christ, your Son, who lives and reigns with you and the Holy Spirit, one God, for ever and ever.

November 12

Bl. Gaius 1572–1624

Martyr of Japan

Gaius was the first Korean to be admitted into the Society. He was born in 1572 and while still a youth his parents offered him to a Buddhist monastery, where he began life as a monk. After some time, however, he became dissatisfied with the Buddhist teaching about God, and so left the community and went to live as a hermit in the mountains, far from the sea. Amid this silence he prayed and meditated. Living in close contact with nature, he grew more and more convinced that there must be but one Lord of the universe, more powerful than the idols to which he had been praying. One night in 1592, when he was twenty years old, he had a dream in which an aged man told him that during that same year he would cross the sea and after enduring many hardships all his desires would be fulfilled. Since he had neither the intention nor the desire to make a sea voyage he discounted the dream.

That year Japan invaded Korea and many Koreans, including Gaius, were captured and handed over as slaves to Japanese lords. As the ship carrying him approached the Japanese island of Tsushima, it suffered shipwreck, but Gaius and others successfully reached shore. From there he was taken to Miyako (today's Kyoto), and upon arrival his master encouraged him to learn a trade so that he could make a way for himself in the world. Gaius answered that he had already chosen his way of life, and the best thing for him would be to enter a Buddhist monastery.

Using his influence the master got Gaius admitted into the monastery attached to Miyako's chief temple and released him from all obligations as a slave. Gaius, however, never achieved peace of soul because his doubts about Buddhist teachings returned. He contacted his former master, who, in turn, put him in touch with a Christian relative of his. Gaius then secretly attended catechism instructions at the Jesuit church and decided to become a Christian. With the head bonze's permission, he departed the Buddhist monastery.

After baptism in Miyako Gaius asked to work with the missionaries and share their apostolic labors. His offer was accepted for the Jesuits were aware how valuable Gaius could be in instructing the Koreans living in Japan after the war. He thus became a catechist and worked first in Osaka, then in Sakai, and finally in Kanazawa.

When foreign missionaries were expelled from Japan by Shogun Tokugawa Iyeyasu in 1614, Gaius, not among the catechists going into exile and unwilling to remain behind, attached himself as a servant to Takayama Ukon, a former government official, now a Christian, also going into exile. He lived with Takayama in Manila until the latter's death in February 1615. By the following August Gaius was on his way back to Japan with two other Jesuits.

As a Korean Gaius had no difficulty getting through the tight immigration controls at Nagasaki's harbor. In the city he lodged with another Korean Christian and made contact with the Jesuits and other priests in hiding. Being free, he immediately resumed missionary work: instructing Christians and non-Christians, baptizing children and converts, visiting the sick and the imprisoned, and burying the dead. He worked secretly and amid danger until 1623, when he was arrested on a visit to a Spanish Franciscan priest in a Nagasaki prison. Not long after his arrest, the governor of the city offered Gaius his freedom if he ceased his apostolic labors, but he answered that he feared neither prison, torture, nor death itself. Thereupon the governor condemned him to be burned alive, but shortly afterwards changed his mind and sent him back to prison.

Gaius remained in prison for more than a year and half and while there he requested admission into the Society, saying that since "he was a son of the Society, he would so like to die in it." Permission was granted, but before the good news of his acceptance reached him, martyrdom intervened. On November 15, 1624, the governor signed the execution order and that same day Gaius was taken to Nagasaki's Hill of Martyrs, and there embraced martyrdom by being burned alive. Gaius was among the 205 martyrs beatified by Pius IX on May 7, 1867. His Jesuit brethren celebrate his feast on February 4.

Prayer

Almighty God, grant that this remembrance of your martyr, Blessed Gaius, may bring us joy. May we who depend upon his prayers glory in his entry into heaven. We ask this through our Lord Jesus Christ, your Son, who lives and reigns with you and the Holy Spirit, one God, for ever and ever.

November 13

St. Stanislaus Kostka 1550–1568

Stanislaus Kostka was only eighteen years old when he died and had been a Jesuit novice for less than a year. He was a Polish noble by birth, born sometime in the middle months of 1550, at the family estate of Rostków, in Mazovia, Poland. His father was castellan of Zakroczym and a senator of the realm. Though Stanislaus had been born into a distinguished family and was destined for public life, his parents carefully educated him in the Catholic faith and kept him from all luxury and self-indulgence.

In 1564, when Stanislaus was fourteen, his father enrolled him and his older brother Paul in the recently opened Jesuit college in Vienna, a school especially favored by the nobility. During their first seven months the brothers boarded at the residence adjoining the college. When Emperor Maximilian II reclaimed that building, the boarders had to take lodging elsewhere. Thus, in March 1565 Paul, who always had an eye for comfort, rented rooms in the house of Senator Kimberker and there the Kostka brothers resided while attending school.

Stanislaus followed courses in the humanities and was a member of the St. Barbara Sodality. Being of a serious and quiet nature, he avoided all unnecessary contact with visitors, applied himself to his studies, dressed plainly for a noble, and spent so much time in prayer that Paul derisively nicknamed him "the Jesuit." Being that they were now in the senator's house and no longer under the direct supervision of the Jesuits, Paul interpreted the natural meekness and humility of Stanislaus as a reproach to his own worldly and carefree way of life. The result was that he began to harass his younger brother. Whatever Stanislaus did was either an offense or an irritation, and Paul retaliated by abusing him physically and verbally. Paul's unjust treatment lasted eighteen months, but rather than break the resolves of Stanislaus it only confirmed them. In fact, Paul's actions strengthened his brother in the practice of virtue and in his desire to become a Jesuit.

In mid-December 1565 Stanislaus unexpectedly fell ill with an undiagnosed sickness and it was thought that he would not recover. Due to the gravity of the illness, Stanislaus requested to receive Viaticum, but Paul kept putting him off, telling him that his sickness was not that threatening. The real reason for this delay was that Senator Kimberker was a staunch Lutheran and would not allow a priest to enter his house with the Blessed Sacrament. Realizing that Paul was not going to call the priest, Stanislaus prayed to St. Barbara, patroness of his sodality, to intercede with God so that he could receive Communion before he should die. This humble prayer was answered in a remarkable fashion, for the saint and two angels appeared to Stanislaus in his room and brought Communion to the sick youth. When the consolation of this visit passed, our Lady, carrying the Christ Child in her arms, then came to visit Stanislaus, and in her maternal way placed the Child in his arms and indicated that he was to enter the Society of Jesus. After these extraordinary favors, the youth recovered and resumed his classes at the college.

Stanislaus approached the Jesuit provincial in Vienna about entering the Society, and though the provincial would have liked to admit him, he informed Stanislaus that he first must have his parents' consent. The young man knew that his parents would never allow him to become a Jesuit. He thus took his predicament to another Jesuit who suggested that he go to Augsburg, Germany, and request admission of the German provincial, Fr. Peter Canisius. Nothing could now deter the resolute Stanislaus. He quietly left Vienna on the morning of August 10, 1567, and once outside the city donned the simple garb of a pilgrim and headed for Augsburg. Angered by his brother's successful escape, Paul set out after him. Though he caught up with his younger brother, he did not recognize him in his pilgrim dress, passed him by, and presumed that Stanislaus had taken another road.

Stanislaus walked the 450 miles to Augsburg only to find that Fr. Canisius was in Dillingen, another day's journey. When the determined Stanislaus found the provincial, he knelt at his feet and offered him the letter of introduction that a Viennese Jesuit had written for him. Stanislaus opened his heart to Fr. Canisius, who immediately sensed his sincerity and agreed to admit him. Since the young man felt that he was still too near to Poland and that his father's political influence could reach into Germany, the provincial arranged for him to accompany two Jesuits who were soon to leave for Rome. Until the day of departure, Stanislaus served table at the Dillingen school and attended to the needs of the noble youths studying there. In late September he and his two companions set out on their long walk over the Alps to Rome, where they arrived on October 25.

The three travel-worn Jesuits found their way to the residence of their general, Fr. Francis Borgia, and Stanislaus handed him the letter of introduction which Fr. Canisius had written. With reference to Stanislaus, Fr. Borgia read: "He is a Polish noble and his name is Stanislaus. He is an excellent, intelligent young man. . . . On his arrival here he was so eager to carry out his long-standing ambition—some years ago he committed himself unreservedly to the Society, though not yet admitted to it. . . . He was very eager to be sent to Rome to be as far away as possible from any harassment by his family. He also wished to advance as much as he could in the path of holiness. . . . We expect great things of him." The new novice spent approximately three months at the Jesuit residence of the Gesù, then a month in early 1568 at the Roman College, and the remaining months at the novitiate of Sant'Andrea. His noviceship lasted only ten months, but during that time his prayer was purified and his union with God grew more intense.

In early August 1568 Stanislaus had a premonition that he would die on August 15. On August 10 he was taken ill with a fever, but his case did not seem to be especially serious. When on August 14 he told the brother infirmarian, who cared for him, that he was going to die on the following day, the brother let the remark pass because Stanislaus did not seem to be critically ill. But that afternoon the patient took a sudden turn for the worse and appeared to have lost all strength. The brother then arranged for Viaticum to be brought to him and with his fellow novices in the room, Stanislaus received his Lord for the last time. He was anointed and then chatted cheerfully with his brethren before they retired for the night. After they departed Stanislaus spent his time in prayer and repeated the words of the Psalmist: "My heart is ready, O God, my heart is ready!" He asked to be placed on the floor, where he remained until the following morning. At about 3:00 A.M. he stopped his prayers and with his face illumined by great joy indicated to the priests in the room that our Lady was approaching with her court of angels and saints to take him to heaven. Thus the eighteen-year-old Stanislaus gave his soul to God. It was August 15, 1568, the feast of our Lady's assumption. He was buried in the Jesuit church attached to the novitiate, but his remains now lie beneath the altar dedicated to him in the new church of Sant'Andrea al Quirinale in Rome.

Stanislaus Kostka was beatified in 1605, only thirty-six years after his death, and the first member of the Society of Jesus to receive this honor. He was canonized by Pope Benedict XIII on December 31, 1726. His memorial is celebrated on November 13.

Prayer

Lord our God, you looked on Saint Stanislaus Kostka with love as he consecrated his youth to you with such generosity of heart. Renew us in spirit so that we may be eager and joyful as we walk the way of your commandments. Help us to fill our days with good works and so redeem the shortness of this life. We ask this through our Lord Jesus Christ, your Son, who lives and reigns with you and the Holy Spirit, one God, for ever and ever.

St. Joseph Pignatelli 1737–1811

Fr. Joseph Pignatelli is the link that connects the Society of Jesus from the time of its suppression to that of its restoration. He was born on December 27, 1737, of a princely family; both his father, who was Italian, and his mother, who was Spanish, were of noble descent, and the birth took place in the family palace in Saragossa, Spain. When Joseph's mother died in 1743, his father moved with the younger children to Naples. But within four years the father too was dead. At age twelve Joseph returned to Saragossa with his younger brother Nicholas to attend the Jesuit school, and by special privilege he resided in the Jesuit community. Living among the Jesuits confirmed him in his vocation and on May 8, 1753, he entered the novitiate at Tarragona and two years later pronounced his religious vows. He spent the following year in classical studies at Manresa—the city where St. Ignatius of Loyola spent ten months after his conversion and began writing his *Spiritual Exercises*. The following three years were spent at Calatayud studying philosophy and the next four back in Saragossa doing theology.

Fr. Pignatelli's ordination to the priesthood took place the week before Christmas 1762. He was then assigned to teach grammar to young boys at the school, where he himself had studied, and to assist in its parish. For four-and-a-half years this Spanish grandee humbly taught his classes, visited the local prisons, and ministered to condemned convicts as they went their way to execution. This apostolate, however, was soon to come to an end.

The enemies of the Society of Jesus had been at work in Spain, as they had been in France and Portugal, and on April 3, 1767, King Charles III, without making known his reasons, expelled the Jesuits from his kingdom and confiscated their property. With one royal stroke of the pen 5,000 Spanish Jesuits were made homeless. Because Fr. Pignatelli was of the nobility, he was given the opportunity to remain in Spain, but he chose exile with his fellow Jesuits. With great foresight the elderly rector at Saragossa delegated his authority to the young priest to exercise while they were in exile. When the Saragossan Jesuits arrived in Tarragona, they met other Jesuits waiting to board ship. Among them was the provincial, who likewise delegated his authority to Fr. Pignatelli, thus making him acting provincial over some 600 Jesuits. After three long months at sea and after having been refused entry at the port of Civitavecchia on Italy's western shore and at that of Bastia on the island of Corsica, the thirteen ships carrying the Spanish Jesuit exiles made a short stop at Ajaccio, permitting them to live ashore and be cared for by their brethren, who operated a college in that city. After three weeks they were again on board and were taken in August 1767 to Bonifacio on Corsica's southern tip. Through Fr. Pignatelli's ingenuity, there they converted abandoned residences into Jesuit housing. When France acquired the island from Genoa in September 1768, the Jesuits were once more herded onto ships and taken to Genoa; from there they made their way on foot to Ferrara in the Papal States. The 300 miles to Ferrara were difficult; some Jesuits were old, some in bad health, and all were worn out and exhausted.

Through the kindness of Fr. Pignatelli's cousin and future cardinal, Msgr. Francis Pignatelli, the exiles found a welcome. Fr. Pignatelli did not know how long he and his Jesuits would enjoy the peace of Ferrara, for he was aware that the princes of Europe were pressuring the pope to suppress the Society. Clement XIII heroically withstood that pressure, but his successor, not of the same caliber, crumbled beneath it. On July 21, 1773, by his brief *Dominus ac Redemptor noster* Clement XIV decreed the dissolution of the Society of Jesus. This meant that Fr. Pignatelli and 23,000 others were no longer Jesuits; they were no longer bound by their vows. Those who were priests remained priests but those who were not, reverted to the lay state. When he heard this decree read to him, Fr. Pignatelli was saddened in heart. This was but another opportunity for him to abandon himself to Providence.

Fr. Pignatelli then moved to Bologna and continued, as best he could, to live the life of a Jesuit, and for the next twenty-four years (1773–1797) he kept in contact with his dispersed brethren. In all this darkness there was a light still shining, for Catherine the Great of Russia had forbidden the promulgation of the papal brief of suppression in her territories, and so the Jesuits in White Russia (today's Belarus) continued an uninterrupted existence. Fr. Pignatelli heard about them and wrote to their superior requesting readmission. In the meantime, Ferdinand, duke of Parma, wished he again had Jesuits in his territory and thus he too entered into negotiations with those of White Russia. Consequently, in 1793 three Jesuits came to his duchy to open a house of the Society. Fr. Pignatelli associated himself with this group and on July 6, 1797, when he was sixty years old, he again promised God poverty, chastity, and obedience, just as he had done in Spain in 1755. Inasmuch as he was known for his humility, charity, and prayerfulness, Fr. Pignatelli was made master of novices in 1799 at Colorno— the only Jesuit novitiate in western Europe at that time. And on May 7, 1803, the superior in Russia appointed him provincial of Italy. When the duchy of Parma was occupied by French troops in 1804, the Jesuits were expelled, but happily they found hospitality in Naples because Pius VII had, by special brief of July 30, 1804, restored the Society in the Kingdom of the Two Sicilies. Many former Jesuits now came to them to be readmitted and all were again active in the Jesuit apostolate.

Fr. Pignatelli's stay in Naples lasted less than two years, for Napoleon's brother, Joseph Bonaparte, overran the country and the fifty or so non-Neapolitan Jesuits had to leave the kingdom. They headed for Rome where Pius VII welcomed them and offered them the old Roman College building for their residence until they found something more suitable. They eventually found a home at St. Pantaleon's near the Roman Coliseum and there they set up regular community life. Within months of their arrival in the Eternal City, the Jesuits had a novitiate in Orvieto and were teaching in six diocesan seminaries.

When Fr. Pignatelli came to Rome he was in his seventieth year and had been in exile for forty years. He still cherished the hope that the Society would be officially restored throughout the world during his lifetime. But now his health was weakening and he doubted he would live to see that day. Age and infirmity began to manifest themselves, and during his last two years he suffered from hemorrhages, most probably due to stomach ulcers. In his final six months the hemorrhages became more frequent and brought on greater pain. In October 1811 he was confined to bed. On the evening of November 15, while his community was recommending his soul to God, Fr. Pignatelli peacefully died in the Lord. Three years after his death, Pius VII, on August 7, 1814, restored the entire Society. Fr. Pignatelli's dearest hope was finally realized.

Fr. Joseph Pignatelli was beatified by Pius XI on May 21, 1933, and canonized by Pius XII on June 12, 1954. His memorial is celebrated on November 14.

Prayer

Lord God, in a time of trial you gave Saint Joseph Pignatelli courage and strength to unite his scattered companions. May we always receive support from our brothers and remain faithful to our vocation in the midst of every change. We ask this through our Lord Jesus Christ, your Son, who lives and reigns with you and the Holy Spirit, one God, for ever and ever.

November 15

St. Roch González 1576–1628

Martyr of River Plate

Roch González de Santa Cruz, an intrepid missionary, was one of the main architects of the Jesuit reductions in Paraguay along the River Plate. It was through his industry that many of them became economically successful settlements.

Roch was born in the capital city of Asunción in 1576, a descendant of early Spanish colonists. Desiring to become a priest, he studied Latin with the bishop, and when the Jesuits opened a school in the capital in 1587 he continued his training with them. He was ordained a priest on March 25, 1599, and his first assignment was evangelizing the Indians near Asunción. His success led the bishop to recall him to the city and name him pastor of the cathedral. In 1609 rumors circulated that the bishop, who was then residing in Buenos Aires, was planning to make him his vicar general. Though this brought joy to others' hearts, Fr. González was distressed. He was not looking for honors or preferment, and to avoid them he requested to become a Jesuit and entered the Society on May 9, 1609.

Not far from Asunción there lived on the banks of the Paraguay and Pilcomayo rivers the Guaycurú. It was to these people that Fr. González was sent in 1609 while still a novice. He was to bring them to Christianity and at the same time civilize them so that the Spaniards could safely pass through Guaycurú territory on a shortcut to Peru. By the following year he saw good results from his efforts. His preaching prospered, he was becoming fluent in the Guaraní tongue, and though only a few Guaycurú asked for baptism, hundreds had been pacified. They formerly came to the capital to terrorize the citizenry, now they came to walk the streets and sleep peacefully in town. He likewise taught them how to plow, sow, tend the land, and harvest crops. After two years among them, he was transferred in 1611 to the reduction of St. Ignatius and, thereafter, that settlement also flourished. He laid out the public square, supervised the construction of houses for the Indians, founded a school, and built a church. He also taught them the essentials of farming and introduced the raising of cattle and sheep. The primary goal of Fr. González was always evangelization; he continually preached to them and gave them catechism instruction. Because the Indians were especially attracted by color, music, and display, he made good use of these when he planned public celebrations of Mass or when he had processions through the reduction's streets, on such feasts as Corpus Christi.

Fr. González spent a successful four years at St. Ignatius. His next twelve years of missionary activity were devoted to the founding of a series of reductions in what is today known as southern Brazil, Paraguay, Uruguay, and northeastern Argentina. In 1615 he began establishing settlements along the Paraná River and on March 25 he raised a cross in an area he had marked out to be the public square. He then set about constructing houses and a chapel. This became Itapuá, or Our Lady of the Incarnation. He saw quick results from his preaching, for by June he had his first baptisms. When Fr. González was among his Indians, he lived as they lived and ate what they ate. When famine hit the settlement he endured it with the same resolution that they did; and when an epidemic struck he served them as nurse bringing them back to health. He succeeded as a missionary because he was multi-talented: while being pastor of souls, he was likewise architect and mason, farmer and physician.

In 1619 a *cacique,* or chief, from the depths of the jungles of Uruguay came to the settlement at Incarnation, and when he saw what Fr. González had done there, he asked him to come among his people. Uruguay was still unchartered and Fr. González was the first Jesuit to enter that territory. He founded the town of Concepción in 1620 in honor of Our Lady's Immaculate Conception, and later founded Candeleria. On August 15, 1628, together with the recently ordained Fr. John del Castillo, he founded the reduction of the Assumption at Iyuí, a village of 400 Indians. After a few days he left Fr. Castillo in charge and went to Itapuá, where he met Fr. Alphonsus Rodríguez and took him with him to establish a new mission at Caaró.

The two Jesuits arrived at their new station on November 1 and named it All Saints. They first erected a cross in the center of the village and within a few days baptized three children. The local witch doctor, Nezú, did not appreciate the influence the missionaries were beginning to have over his people, nor did he like the doctrine they were preaching because he had several wives. Jealous of their success, Nezú, in conference with his subordinates, decided to kill the missionaries in his area. On the morning of November 15, after he had finished celebrating Mass, Fr. González left the chapel and noticed some Indians setting up a bell. As he bent down to attach the clapper, one of Nezú's henchmen rushed at him and with a quick blow of an ax split the priest's skull. The martyr fell dead at the assassin's feet. When Fr. Rodríguez heard the noise, he came out of the chapel and the murderers immediately struck him down. They then cast the priests' bodies into the chapel and set it afire.

News of the missionaries' deaths reached the neighboring reduction of Candeleria, and on November 17 Fr. Peter Romero came to All Saints, found the bodies of the martyrs and took them to his reduction. They were later transferred to the reduction of the Immaculate Conception.

Frs. Roch González, Alphonsus Rodríguez, and John del Castillo were canonized by Pope John Paul II on May 16, 1988. Their memorial is celebrated on November 16.

Prayer

Lord, you called your martyrs, Saints Roch González, Alphonsus Rodríguez, and John del Castillo, to go out from their own country to sow the seed of your word in distant lands. May it yield a hundredfold in a harvest of justice and peace. We ask this through our Lord Jesus Christ, your Son, who lives and reigns with you and the Holy Spirit, one God for ever and ever.

November 16

St. Alphonsus Rodríguez 1598–1628

Martyr of River Plate

Fr. Alphonsus Rodríguez accompanied Fr. Roch González on his last mission among the Indians in South America. Fr. González was an experienced missionary and had lived among the Indians since 1609. The young Fr. Rodríguez knew he had much to learn from the veteran. He was happy to be associated with so great a missionary, but this mission was to last only fifteen days, for both were to be martyred.

Alphonsus was born in Zamora, Spain, on March 10, 1598. He entered the Jesuit novitiate at Villagarcía on March 25, 1614, and in 1616 was assigned to the missions in Spanish America. He left Spain in November, arrived in Buenos Aires, and then went to Córdoba for his studies in philosophy and theology prior to ordination. A companion of his on the trip from Spain was Fr. John del Castillo. Fr. Rodríguez was ordained in 1624, and then went to the reduction in Paraguay along the River Plate. He is known to have been in Itapuá in 1627 and it was there that Fr. González met him in 1628, when the young missionary asked to accompany him on his next assignment. Fr. González was glad to have a young priest with him as he headed for Caaró.

The two Jesuits arrived on November 1, named the site All Saints, and immediately set about erecting the cross at whose base they would preach. Because the missionaries were making noticeable progress among these Indians, the local witch doctor Nezú, seeing that his influence was waning, decided it would only be by the priests' death that he could regain control over his people. Hence he determined to kill the missionaries in his territory. On the morning of November 15, Fr. Rodríguez went into the woods to fell a tree that was to serve as a pole on which to hang the chapel bell. He and several Indians were carrying the tree into the village when Fr. González emerged from the chapel after having celebrated Mass. Fr. Rodríguez then went in to offer his Mass, but before he began he heard unusual noises and came out to investigate. He did not see his companion's massacred body near the bell, and by the time he could ask "What's happening?" two of Nezú's men attacked him and struck him on the head as he fell to the ground. He was only thirty years old. The attackers then threw both bodies into the church and proceeded to destroy the altar and smash the chalice. The chalice was made of metal and the murderers attached the shining broken pieces about their necks to form a necklace. They then collected the priests' books and vestments, piled them near the altar, and set everything aflame.

Fr. Peter Romero, the missionary at the reduction next to Candeleria, came to All Saints on November 17 to claim the bodies of the two Jesuits and transported them to his settlement. Later they were taken to the reduction of the Immaculate Conception.

Frs. Alphonsus Rodríguez and Roch González, together with Fr. John del Castillo, were canonized by Pope John Paul II on May 16, 1988. Their memorial is celebrated on November 16.

Prayer

Lord, you called your martyrs, Saints Alphonsus Rodríguez, Roch González, and John del Castillo to go out from their own country to sow the seed of your word in distant lands. May it yield fruit a hundredfold in a harvest of justice and peace. We ask this through our Lord Jesus Christ, your Son, who lives and reigns with you and the Holy Spirit, one God, for ever and ever.

November 17

St. John del Castillo 1596–1628

Martyr of River Plate

John del Castillo was the third Jesuit to die a martyr's death in the Jesuit reductions of South America. He was born in Belmonte (Toledo), Spain, on September 14, 1596, and at first decided on a career in law. He attended the University of Alcalá, but during his first year realized he had a vocation to be a Jesuit, so he entered the novitiate in Madrid on March 21, 1614. In November 1616 he was on his way to the South American missions and one of his companions on this journey was Alphonsus Rodríguez. The ship docked at Buenos Aires and the young scholastics then made their way to Córdoba for their studies in preparation for ordination. John was ordained in 1625 and was at the reduction of the Incarnation at Itapuá in 1628, when Fr. Roch González visited it. Fr. González then took him that August as his associate to Iyuí, which he named Assumption because it was founded on August 15. Fr. González left Fr. Castillo in charge of the settlement and then went on to found that of All Saints at Caaró.

Unknown to Fr. Castillo, the hatred and jealousy of the witch doctor Nezú, in whose territory Iyuí was located, led him to convince his subordinates that all the missionaries had to die. On November 15 they murdered Frs. González and Rodríguez at All Saints. After they had done their deed, they reported to Nezú how successfully they had carried out his orders. On November 17 Nezú indicated

that the next victim was to be Fr. Castillo at Iyuí. Nezú's men entered the reduction of the Assumption in mid-afternoon and found Fr. Castillo reading his breviary. When asked what he was doing, he politely answered that he was praying.
He knew nothing of the murder of his companions at All Saints and, hence, had
no reason to suspect these newcomers to the settlement. The visitors surrounded
him, attacked and beat him, and forced him to go into the woods, where they
stripped him of his clothing, tied his hands and then struck blow after blow until
he was dead. His body was set on fire and the assassins then went to rob his
dwelling and the chapel. They took the Mass vestments and vessels for Nezú to
wear and use. Fr. Castillo's body was recovered and taken to the reduction of the
Immaculate Conception, where it was interred together with his fellow martyrs,
Frs. González and Rodríguez.

Fr. John del Castillo, with the two Jesuits who had died at All Saints, was
canonized by Pope John Paul II on May 16, 1988. Their memorial is celebrated
on November 16.

Prayer

*Lord, you called your martyrs, Saints John del Castillo, Roch González and
Alphonsus Rodríguez to go out from their own country to sow the seed of your
word in distant lands. May it yield a hundredfold in a harvest of justice and
peace. We ask this through our Lord Jesus Christ, your Son, who lives and reigns
with you and the Holy Spirit, one God, for ever and ever.*

November 18

Bl. Leonard Kimura 1575–1619

Martyr of Japan

The Kimura family was a distinguished Catholic family of old Japan. When Fr.
Francis Xavier visited the island of Hirado off Japan's western shore in October
1550, the first person to receive the waters of baptism from that missionary was
Leonard's grandfather. It was also the grandfather who offered hospitality to the
saint. Leonard's parents moved to Nagasaki, then becoming a Christian center,
and it was there that Leonard was born in 1575. He attended the Jesuit school
and for fourteen years served as a lay catechist, traveling with the Jesuit priests

on their missionary trips. In November 1602, when he was twenty-seven years old, he became a Jesuit brother and served the community as cook, tailor, and painter. Later he again took up his catechetical career and joined the missionaries on their apostolic journeys.

Rather than leave Japan as so many Jesuits were forced to do when the decree of 1614 banished all missionaries, Br. Kimura stayed behind. For the next two years he worked alone and lived the life of a fugitive, careful not to leave any trace that could lead to his arrest. In December 1616, however, while in Nagasaki, he was captured with a small group of Christians. Since he was dressed as a Japanese gentleman, his captors did not know that they had caught a Jesuit in their net. At his trial the judge offered him the usual 200 pieces of silver if he would reveal the whereabouts of a Jesuit priest, but Br. Kimura honestly answered: "I know one Jesuit; he is a brother and not a priest." The judge then offered the accustomed 100 silver pieces for information concerning this brother, to which Br. Kimura calmly replied: "I am the brother." Because of this admission, he was sent to prison.

In prison Br. Kimura found four companions, all laymen and all arrested for harboring priests. One of these was his own brother-in-law, Andrew Tokuan, and one was the Portuguese Dominic Jorjes, who had for some years given hospitality to Fr. Charles Spinola. The other two were the Korean Cosmas Taquea and the Japanese John Xoum. Their imprisonment lasted almost three years, and Br. Kimura, catechist as he was, set about instructing the jailers and non-Christian prisoners in the fundamentals of the Catholic faith. During this time he made ninety-six converts and transformed the prison into a Christian community, with fixed times for prayer and meditation.

Sometime about the middle of November 1619, the five prisoners were brought before Governor Gonroku, who asked why Br. Kimura had remained in Japan after the emperor had forbidden it under pain of death. He replied: "I remained so that I could teach you about the true God and preach his law, and as long as I live I will never stop doing it." Gonroku's answer was: "Death by slow fire."

On the morning of November 18, the five prisoners were led to the hill of execution near Nagasaki. On his way Br. Kimura kept his lips moving in prayer for himself and his companions, asking our Lord and our Lady to come to their assistance in these their final moments. The martyrs were fastened to stakes and after the wood caught fire and the flames began to rise, Br. Kimura's voice filled the air preaching the glory of the Catholic faith, for which he and his companions were offering themselves as burnt sacrifices.

A contemporary who attended the execution recorded that about 20,000 people were present—some filled the shoreline and many others were offshore in boats—to witness the event. Perhaps the non-Christians attended out of curiosity, but the Christians were present to see their brethren go to heaven. Never did they see five men die so joyfully.

On November 29, eleven days after Br. Kimura's martyrdom, his blood brother Anthony, a layman, was also martyred on that hill. Later, on September 10, 1622, his sister Mary, whose husband had died with Br. Kimura, and his Jesuit cousin Sebastian Kimura were also martyred there. The Kimura family boasts five members in the ranks of the blessed.

Br. Leonard Kimura was one of the thirty-four Jesuits who died during the Great Persecution and who were beatified by Pope Pius IX on May 7, 1867. The Society celebrates the memorial of these blessed martyrs on February 4.

Prayer

Almighty God, grant that this remembrance of your holy martyr, Blessed Leonard Kimura, may bring us joy. May we who depend upon his prayers glory in his entry into heaven. We ask this through our Lord Jesus Christ, your Son, who lives and reigns with you and the Holy Spirit, one God, for ever and ever.

November 19

S. G. Joseph Mark Figueroa 1865–1942

The only extraordinary thing in Br. Joseph Figueroa's life was that he had been porter for fifty-four years at the Jesuit College of the Immaculate Conception, Santa Fe, Argentina. Other than this his life was ordinary and simple. He was born on October 7, 1865, in the tiny village of Tinajo, on the island of Lanzarote, Canary Islands. His father was a farmer, but because farming on the island was difficult and he wanted to offer his children a better future, he took his family to Uruguay and set up a farm near Santa Lucia outside Montevideo. Joseph spent his youth helping his father on the farm, and to prepare him one day to manage it, his father sent him to school—a total of four months. Joseph learned to read, write, and do basic arithmetic, just enough to handle the finances involved in operating the family farm.

The pastor of the parish that the Figueroa family attended noted Joseph's regularity in attending Mass and in receiving the sacraments. He likewise observed that the young man was serious-minded and manifested a sound piety. One day he inquired of the youth whether he was interested in the religious life. This manner of thinking fit with Joseph's own, and so the pastor arranged for him to meet the Jesuit rector of the Montevideo seminary. Convinced that Joseph had a vocation, the rector then introduced him to the provincial superior, who eventually accepted him as a brother. Joseph left home on January 30, 1886, and began his postulancy at the college in Montevideo. He spent his time getting to know the Jesuit life and doing household tasks. When his six months were up, he went to Córdoba, Argentina, and began his noviceship on August 15, 1886.

On May 29, 1888, Br. Figueroa was transferred to Santa Fe and for a time helped the infirmarian and the house buyer. He pronounced his religious vows on August 15, and in the following year became assistant to the college porter, a position he took over in 1891 and kept until his death.

During his fifty-four years of service in the college and Jesuit community, Br. Figueroa witnessed many changes, the college continually grew in number of students and in physical size. He knew every student that passed through the school and after graduation many kept in contact with him. The diocesan seminary was part of the college until 1906, when Santa Fe, having become a diocese, separated the seminary from the college. While the seminarians were at the college, Br. Figueroa showed them special respect—they were future priests—and to help them foster their spiritual life and to aid them in their studies, he acted as a clearinghouse for them, ordering periodicals as well as devotional and theological books from abroad. After the seminarians became priests they continued to make use of his service.

Br. Figueroa's early years at the college were not too busy, so for a time he continued to help the buyer and took care of the garden, cultivating flowers to be placed before our Lady's statue. As the college grew, his work in the porter's office increased. Telephones were installed and this meant more messages and more running around in search of people. Throughout his years in the porter's lodge, students noted that no matter what hour of the day it was, Br. Figueroa was always patient and cheerful, making visitors feel that they were the only ones who mattered.

Br. Figueroa enjoyed good health until 1940 when he began to suffer from heart trouble. In the beginning of 1942, there was a noticeable decline, he now became tired and frequently had to rest. But after a few minutes of repose, he was back at his job. During the middle of June he caught pneumonia and everyone expected this to be the end, but he recovered and by August he was again at his post. Thus he continued until November 19, 1942, when the heart that gave so much to others, now gave itself totally to God.

Br. Figueroa's acquaintances numbered in the tens of thousands. When his death was reported in the city, everyone felt that they had lost someone especially close to them. By the archbishop's order all the churches in Santa Fe tolled their bells and the city magistrate ordered the funeral cortege to follow the same route as for a high-ranking government official.

Br. Figueroa, it seems, never received extraordinary graces from God; there were no visions nor ecstasies in his life. His holiness was born from a sincere humility, a deep piety, and a profound love of God. Shortly after his death the diocese of Santa Fe urged the promotion of his cause, and it is presently under study.

S. G. Hernando de Santarén and 7 Companions 1567–1616

Martyrs of Mexico

In the early seventeenth century eight Jesuits were martyred by the Tepehuan, living in northwestern Mexico, in what is now the state of Durango. Some of these had been converted to Christianity by Fr. Jerome Ramírez, who had come among them in 1596 and who, by 1597, had established three villages, Santiago Papasquiaro, Santa Catalina, and Guanaceví. Over the years the number of converts grew as did the villages. The missionaries devoted themselves to teaching the native population the fundamentals of the Catholic faith as well as how to cultivate the land, grow crops, and build homes. The village government, however, always remained in the hands of the Indians themselves. All was peaceful in the villages and in their contacts with the Spanish colonies until 1616, when an Indian rebellion erupted.

The Tepehuan revolt had religious and political elements. Though the Indians had been converted, some could not totally withdraw themselves from the influence of their medicine men, one of whom, Quautlatas, an apostate convert, seems to have been the revolt's leader. Since the power of Quautlatas had diminished with the coming of the missionaries, he saw them as his chief opponents. Thus he appealed to the nationalist spirit of the Tepehuan and urged them to cast out the foreigners—missionaries and Spaniards alike—so that the tribe could again be free. This idea proved appealing to many.

The rebel plan was to attack the village of San Ignacio del Zape on November 21, 1616, the feast of the Presentation of Our Lady, when the missionaries would all be present for the blessing of a new statue of our Lady. Many Spaniards would also be there, and since it was a religious festival, they would, for the most part, be unarmed. The rebellious Indians were, thus, sure to have a quick and easy victory. The proposed plan, however, never saw fruition for the uprising was unexpectedly ignited a few days earlier.

The first of the eight Jesuits to die was Fr. Hernando de Tovar, one of the two native Mexicans in this group of martyrs. He was born in the Spanish colony of San Miguel de Culiacán in western Mexico in 1581, and as a youth had come into contact with Jesuits, many of whom had stayed at his parents' home when they visited the city. In 1594 Fr. Hernando de Santarén (see below) lived with the Tovar family for several months, and young Hernando helped care for the missionary during the latter's illness. Neither foresaw that twenty-two years later they would be martyred for the same cause.

Hernando entered the Jesuit novitiate at Puebla on August 10, 1598. He made his studies in Mexico City and was probably ordained in 1608. Though an exceptional preacher, he preferred to minister to native peoples and, thus, was sent to the Parras mission, where he labored for seven years. Shortly before the rebellion, he visited Culiacán and on his return stopped at the Tepehuan mission of Santa Catalina. That same evening, November 15, 1616, a muleteer, leading a train of mules heavily-ladened with clothing and merchandise for a nearby wealthy mining district, also stopped to spend the night in the village.

On the following morning the rebel Indians, consumed with greed for the muleteer's cargo, decided to advance the outbreak of the uprising by robbing and killing him. And when they saw that Fr. Tovar was about to return to his mission, the insurgents feigned friendship by offering grain to his mule. Without warning one of them gave the missionary a blow on the head, which knocked him to the ground. As he was lying helpless, another thrust a lance into his breast. Between November 16 and 20, eight Jesuits died for their faith.

The next two to be martyred were Frs. Bernard de Cisneros and Diego de Orozco. Cisneros was born in 1582 in Carrión de los Condes, near Palencia, Spain, and entered the novitiate at Villagarcía on March 21, 1600. After three years of study he was sent to Mexico in 1605 and there completed his preparation for the priesthood. By 1610 he was at Santiago Papasquiaro working among the Tepehuan.

Fr. Orozco was assigned to the same village in 1615 and had but one year of missionary life before being martyred. He was born in 1588 in Plasencia de Estremadura, Spain, and entered the novitiate at Villagarcía on March 19, 1603. He accompanied Fr. Cisneros to Mexico in 1605, did his studies in Mexico City, and was ordained in 1614. The following year he was sent to Santiago Papasquiaro as assistant to Fr. Cisneros.

Both missionaries had heard rumors of a possible uprising. When Fr. Cisneros brought this to the attention of the Papasquiaro chief, the latter and three aides went on November 15 to seek out the rebels and negotiate peace. Unfortunately, they were brutally murdered. When this news reached the village, together with word that some 200 Indians were marching toward them, the villagers took refuge in their church—the only sturdy building in the compound. From November 16 to 18 the insurgents tried to force their way into the church, but without success. On the 18th their number grew to 500; the reinforcements were those who had attacked Santa Catalina two days previously. With so large a force besieging the church, Fr. Cisneros decided to sue for peace. As he opened the church door, he met with a shower of arrows that wounded him.

Eventually, making the claim that they too were Christians, the rebels proposed peace and asked those in the church to lay down their arms and come out. Relying on the supposed Christianity of the attackers, those within emerged in solemn procession together with the Blessed Sacrament. The rebels at first showed reverence for the Sacrament, but this was merely hypocrisy on their part, for when everyone was clearly in the open they fell upon their innocent victims. An attacker grabbed the Blessed Sacrament from the hands of Fr. Cisneros and trampled the hosts to the ground; another pierced him with a lance, and a third finished him with a blow to the head. Fr. Orozco received an arrow in his chest and his body was cut in two with an ax.

The two missionaries, Frs. John del Valle and Louis de Alavés, stationed at Zape, were also martyred on November 18. Fr. Valle was born in Vitoria (Vizcaya), Spain, on October 22, 1575, entered the Society at Villagarcía on April 21, 1591, and sailed for Mexico in 1593. He did his studies in Mexico City and was ordained in 1602. Two years later he went to work among the Tepehuan, where he labored for twelve years. Fr. Alavés came to Zape in 1615. He had been born in Tequisistlán (Oaxaca), Mexico, on January 29, 1589, and entered the Jesuit novitiate at Tepotzotlán on May 21, 1607. After ordination in 1614 he was assigned to assist Fr. Valle at Zape. Fr. Valle had invited other Jesuit missionaries and many Spaniards to come for the November 21 feast. It was to be a great festival, and therefore many Indians were already in the village preparing for that special day. On the morning of November 18, some of the insurgents, who had taken part in the massacre at Santa Catalina on the 16th, took the villagers of Zape by surprise. They arrived at the moment when both priests entered the church to celebrate Mass. Hoping to talk peace to them, Frs. Valle and Alavés came out of the church, the former carried a statue of our Lady and the latter one of our Lord. But before they were more than a few paces outside, both were brought down and murdered. The rebels then went on to massacre the Zape Christians.

On the following day, November 19, two more Jesuits were killed, Frs. John Fonte and Jerome de Moranta. Fr. Fonte was born in Villa de Tarraza, near Barcelona, Spain, on August 20, 1574, and became a Jesuit at Saragossa on April 7, 1593. He was ordained in Barcelona and in 1599 went to Mexico, assigned to the Tepehuan mission. He mastered their language and prepared a dictionary, grammar, and a catechism for the use of other missionaries. When the rebellion began, he was at Ocatlán; his companion of ten years was Fr. Jerome de Moranta, who had been born in Palma, Majorca, in 1574, and had entered the Society in 1595. He arrived in Mexico in 1605. Since both missionaries intended to be present at Zape for the festivities on November 21, they left their mission on the 19th, and not far from their station they unexpectedly encountered the rebels, who shot arrows into their hearts and clubbed them to death.

The last of the martyrs was Fr. Hernando de Santarén. He was the oldest of the eight and the most experienced; he had spent twenty-two years ministering to the native peoples of Mexico. He was born at Huete (Cuenca), Spain, in February 1567, and entered the Society at Villarejo de Fuentes in October 1582. He was in Mexico by October 1588 and there completed his theological studies and was ordained on March 19, 1593. During his two decades on the mission, he had been stationed in various villages and had evangelized several different tribes. His first assignment was in 1594 to Mocorito, but when his health failed he went to Culiacán, where he resided with Fr. Hernando de Tovar's family until able to resume work. In 1595 he worked among the Guazave in northern Sinaloa and then in 1597 with the Indians at the Topia mines. He likewise worked among the tribes in southern Sinaloa and for a period was superior of the Sinaloan mission.

The Nebones, natives living in northern Mexico, had for some time requested a priest to evangelize them. Because Fr. Santarén was the best equipped missionary in that part of Mexico and had great facility with languages, his superior assigned him to this new mission. On his way there he planned to stop at Zape and join in the festivities. On November 20, only a day's journey from Zape, he came upon a village that was totally deserted. He entered the church and found the altar in ruins; he rang the church bell, but no one came. He had not as yet heard of the uprising and the massacres in the several villages. He mounted his mule and cautiously took the road to Santiago Papasquiaro. On the road he met a band of rebel Indians who surrounded him. Amid shouts of joy they knocked him from his mule and with a club, struck his head so that his brains spewed forth on the ground. They then stripped his body and threw it into the river.

With the insurrection and the martyrdom of these missionaries, the Jesuit Tepehuan mission came to an end. The cause of these eight Jesuits is presently under study.

November 23

Bl. Michael Pro 1891–1927

Martyr of Mexico

Fr. Michael Augustine Pro Juárez died for Christ the King. He was born on January 13, 1891, in Guadalupe de Zacatecas, Mexico, the son of a mining engineer. His early education was, for the most part, by private tutors. At fifteen he went to work in his father's office in the Division of Mines and remained there until he was twenty. When his second sister entered the convent in February 1911, Michael was so moved by her leaving for the religious life that he asked himself: "Why shouldn't I do the same thing?" So on August 10 he presented himself at the Jesuit novitiate at El Llano in Michoacán. When he entered the novitiate he had not yet completed his secondary education and studies, in the beginning, were difficult for him. If his memory could not get him through, he said, then he would compensate by working for greater perfection of soul. His fellow

Jesuits referred to him as "the brother who is convinced that God wants him to be a saint." Michael was not wrong in that conviction. He pronounced his vows on August 15, 1913, and remained at El Llano for further studies.

The political atmosphere in Mexico was rapidly changing and the country was being harassed by the rebellious General Venustiano Carranza and the bandit Pancho Villa, who directed their attacks against the Catholic Church and the clergy. They sacked church buildings and subjected priests and religious to torture and mutilation. Word of these events came to the novitiate and Michael foresaw further persecution. On August 5, 1914, a group of Carranza's men ransacked the novitiate's main house and burned the library. Knowing that this was but the beginning, the rector bought street clothing for his seminarians and sadly informed them that they would have to disperse, leaving each to his own ingenuity to cross into the United States. The seminarians left on August 15 and Michael with two companions went to Texas, where they had a short stopover before going on to California. A building at Los Gatos had been offered to the exiled seminarians by the Jesuits of the California province, and Michael arrived there on October 9. He spent a year at Los Gatos and in 1915 was sent to Granada, Spain, for his studies in philosophy. In 1920 he was assigned to teach in Nicaragua and after two years returned to Spain for theology. In 1924 he went to Enghien, Belgium, to complete his theological course and to study sociology. He was interested in the worker movements and knew that this training would be valuable to him on his return to Mexico. He was ordained on August 30, 1925, at age thirty-four. While he was in Belgium the persecution of the Mexican Church worsened—the president was now Plutarco Elías Calles, a rabid anti-Catholic.

Fr. Pro left Europe for his homeland in June 1926 and entered Mexico without difficulty. He was in Mexico City by early July, and at the end of that month the government suppressed all public worship and closed the churches. Every Catholic priest was now a hunted criminal. Though the government had issued its orders, the faithful Mexicans still sought out their priests to receive the sacraments. Fr. Pro continued his priestly duties in secret; he established stations in different parts of the city and visited them once a week to preach, hear confessions, celebrate Mass, and distribute Communion. At times he had up to 300 Communions at each station and the number tripled on First Fridays. His family had moved to Mexico City so he usually lived with them, but he also had three or four other residences in different parts of the city. In his labors for the church Fr. Pro was helped by his two brothers, Humbert and Robert, who were active in printing and distributing literature for the Religious Defense League. Ever since his return home, Fr. Pro lived without fear and for a whole year he prayed that he might be accepted by God as a sacrifice for the faith in his country. If he were arrested, he would consider his prayer answered.

Fr. Pro carried on his clandestine priestly work from July 1926 to November 1927. On Sunday, November 13, there was an assassination attempt on the life of General Alvaro Obregón; the bomb exploded but the general was only slightly injured. Neither Fr. Pro nor his brothers were involved in the plot, but the car used in the attempt had previously been owned by one of them—it had been sold just days before the attempt had been made. The brothers surmised that the police would be looking for them so they decided to make their way to the United States.

On Thursday, November 17, the night before Fr. Pro was to bid goodby to his brothers, he secured a room for them and himself from a faithful Catholic woman. Before dawn of the following day the house was surrounded and soldiers arrested the three Pro brothers. Fr. Pro encouraged his brothers: "From here on we are offering our lives for the cause of religion in Mexico. Let all three of us do it together that God may accept our sacrifice." They were taken to the police station, interrogated, and detained in a dark cell in the station's bowels. When the news broke that Fr. Pro had been arrested for the bombing, the mastermind behind the plot, Luis Segura, surrendered to the police, and though Calles had the criminal in custody, he still wanted to make an example of Fr. Pro. On November 22 he invited his associates to be present at a special execution the following day.

On the morning of November 23, 1927, a group of soldiers escorted Fr. Pro to the prison yard. He had no inkling that he was about to be executed until he entered the yard and saw it filled with spectators. He clasped his little crucifix in his right hand and gripped his rosary in his left. When asked if he had a final wish, he requested a few moments for prayer. He refused the blindfold offered him, and when he saw the rifles pointing at him, his face turned into a smile for he knew that God was accepting his sacrifice. As he stood in front of the bullet-chipped wall, he stretched out his arms in the form of a cross, and when the order to shoot was given, he reverently said: "Viva Cristo Rey!—Long Live Christ the King!" It was 10:38 A.M. Humbert was then brought out and executed. Robert was to be the third, but he was spared at the last minute. Two others were also executed that morning, one of them was Luis Segura.

Fr. Pro's father claimed the bodies of his two sons and that night held a wake in his house. Thousands of workers as well as soldiers came to see the martyr for the last time. The following day Fr. Pro was buried in the Jesuit crypt in the Dolores Cemetery and his brother Humbert was laid nearby.

Fr. Michael Pro was beatified by Pope John Paul II on September 25, 1988.

Prayer

God our Father, you gave your servant Michael Augustine Pro the grace to seek ardently your greater glory and the salvation of your people. Grant that, through his intercession and following his example, we may serve you and glorify you by performing our daily duties with fidelity and joy and effectively helping our neighbor. We ask this through our Lord Jesus Christ, your Son, who lives and reigns with you and the Holy Spirit, one God, for ever and ever.

Ven. Edward Mico 1628–1678

Edward Mico was born in Essex about 1628 of Catholic parents. While still young he enrolled (perhaps in 1643) at the English College in Saint-Omer, Flanders, and from there, at age nineteen, went to the English College in Rome, arriving on October 27, 1647. During his stay there he became acquainted with the Jesuits and eventually requested permission of the Jesuit general to enter the Society. He interrupted his course in philosophy and left Rome on March 28, 1650; he went north to the English novitiate at Watten, Flanders, and formally entered the Society on June 15, 1650. After two years of noviceship training, he went to Liège to complete his philosophical studies and do his theology. He was ordained on March 31, 1657, and for a time taught at Saint-Omer. He may have gone to the English mission as early as 1661. He carried on his priestly ministry in Hampshire, Wiltshire, Dorset, and Sussex and for the last six years of his life (1672–1278) was assistant to three successive provincials.

When Fr. Thomas Whitbread, the English provincial, went to visit the English Jesuit seminaries in Belgium in 1678, Fr. Mico accompanied him. Upon their return to London in late summer, both men were taken ill with a severe fever, the result of the plague they had contracted while in Antwerp. Their condition was such that at times it was expected they would die. It was at this time that the fabricated plot of Titus Oates was revealed. When Oates was authorized to arrest those whom he had accused of masterminding the plot, he immediately set out to apprehend the Jesuit provincial and, thus, before dawn on September 29, 1678, he and a group of armed soldiers went to the Jesuit residence on Wild Street. Upon forcing their way in, they found Frs. Whitbread and Mico ill in bed, and were informed that both were too sick to be moved. The residence was next to that of the Spanish ambassador, Count Egmont, and it enjoyed the ambassador's protection. Fr. Mico was also the ambassador's chaplain. When the soldiers insisted on taking the ill Jesuits to prison, the count appeared and invoking his authority threatened the intruders and reminded them that his property was immune from such searches. Constrained to yield to the ambassador's demands, Oates left a half-dozen soldiers to guard each of the bedridden Jesuits. Since the soldiers were unable to take Fr. Mico with them, as a departing gesture they struck him several times with their muskets and plundered his room looking for incriminating letters.

Some seventeenth- and eighteenth-century accounts of Fr. Mico's death narrate that a few weeks after his arrest, when his health permitted, he was taken to Newgate Prison and that he died there on December 3, 1678, before his case was tried. However, in 1930, a researcher found an entry (dated November 25, 1678) in the Privy Council Register stating that Fr. Mico, who had not been committed to prison by reason of illness, had died in his lodgings on Wild Street. The entry likewise indicates that the coroner was to ascertain that the body was indeed that of Fr. Mico. Because there are no additional entries in the register referring to Fr. Mico, it can be presumed that the coroner found that Fr. Mico had indeed died in his lodgings. In addition, the burial register at St. Giles-in-the-Fields, in whose parish Wild Street was situated, records that an "Edward Micoe" was buried on November 26, 1678. The probable date now given for his death is November 24.

Fr. Edward Mico was declared Venerable by Pope Leo XIII in 1886 and at that time was thought to have died in prison. Because he had been apprehended and kept under house arrest with soldiers guarding him day and night, he equivalently died in prison.

November 26

St. John Berchmans 1599–1621

Extraordinary accomplishments are not required for holiness. It was John Berchmans' ordinary deeds done extraordinarily well that brought him to sanctity. John was born in Diest, Belgium, on March 13, 1599, and in his early years he imbibed the piety that pervaded his parents' home. At age nine he attended the local school and lived in the rectory of Notre Dame parish with several other boys interested in the priesthood. The pastor instructed them in prayer and in serving Mass, and helped with their studies. When John completed his third year, his father withdrew him from the school and suggested he learn a trade in order to help the family's finances. John's disappointment was immediately perceived; leaving school meant he could never become a priest. What was certain was that his father could no longer afford his education. Aware of the problem in the Berchmans' home, the pastor of the Diest Béguinage offered to take John into his house as a servant and pay for his education in return. In 1612 John then went to Mechlin to serve in the household of Canon Froymont. His duties were to serve table, run errands, and care for some of the boarders who attended the cathedral school as John did. It was difficult to work after spending a full day in class, but since he wanted to be a priest, John was willing to embrace the means no matter how toilsome they were. In 1615, when the Society opened its college in Mechlin, John transferred there, met the Jesuits, and chose to join them rather than follow the diocesan priesthood.

John's decision to be a Jesuit was a disappointment to his father, since the family needed the help he could give it as a diocesan priest. His father, however, consented, and John entered the Jesuit novitiate in Mechlin on September 24, 1616. As a novice he performed all the prescribed duties with joy and exactness. He learned how to control himself and not yield to instinct. He also made it a rule always to impose some penance on himself when at table. Nothing was too small or humiliating for him—everything was the will of God. Then in December 1616, his mother died, and following her death his father gave up the shoemaker shop, entered the diocesan seminary and was ordained a priest in April 1618.

After John pronounced his three vows of religion on September 25, 1618, he went to Antwerp to begin philosophy. He was there only three weeks when he was informed that he was to go to Rome for studies. He looked forward to visiting his father before leaving for Rome, but his father had died before John had a chance to get to Mechlin. John arrived in Rome on December 31 and lived at the Roman College. He was as faithful to his religious duties and studies there as he had been in the noviceship. He enjoyed his three years of philosophy and did so well that when he concluded the course in 1621, he was asked to defend the entire course of philosophy in a public disputation. He had studied hard for his final exam, with the result that his health suffered, and in preparing for the public disputation held on July 8, he became weaker. He hoped he would regain his strength after it was over, but since there was to be a disputation at the Greek College on August 6 and he was the best of the Jesuit students, he was asked to represent the Roman College.

John's health was greatly debilitated by the strain of study. The day after the event at the Greek College he had his first attack of dysentery; then a fever set in which he could not shake. When the superior saw how pale and weak John had become, he directed him to go to the infirmary. The illness grew worse; his lungs became inflamed and each day he became more feeble. When members of the community visited him, he spoke of Paradise as if he were soon to be there. Seeing how his patient was quickly slipping away, the brother infirmarian suggested he receive Communion on the following morning, though it was not a Sunday.

The next morning the Jesuit community came in procession bringing Viaticum to its dying brother. After receiving his Lord, John asked to be anointed. Everyone was in tears; John alone was calm. Now that he was preparing to go to his Lord, he asked for his crucifix, rosary, and rule book and said: "These are the three things most dear to me; with them I willingly die." The next day he endured a stream of Jesuits and classmates coming to see him for the last time. Fr. General likewise paid him a visit. John's last night on earth was spent in prayer. The following morning, August 13, when the Jesuit community heard the tolling bell at 8:30, they knew that John was in Paradise.

It was the simplicity of John's life that made him attractive. His rector wrote: "What we universally admired in him was that in all the virtues he showed himself perfect and that, with the help of divine grace, to which he responded his utmost, he performed all his actions with all the perfection that can be imagined." The Jesuits in Rome were convinced that John was a saint, and within a year after his death they began gathering data to be used for his beatification. Pope Pius IX beatified him on May 9, 1865, and Pope Leo XIII canonized him on January 15, 1888. The memorial of St. John Berchmans is celebrated on November 26.

Prayer

Lord our God, you invite us always to give you our love, and you are pleased with a cheerful giver. Give us a youthful spirit to be like St. John Berchmans, always eager to seek you and to do your will. We ask this through our Lord Jesus Christ, your Son, who lives and reigns with you and the Holy Spirit, one God for ever and ever.

November 28

S. G. Bartholomew Arbona and 10 Companions 1862–1936

Martyrs of the Spanish Civil War

These eleven Jesuits, martyred during the Spanish Civil War, met their deaths in or near Barcelona between July 21, 1936, and March 16, 1937. The oldest was Fr. Bartholomew Arbona Estades, who had been born on December 20, 1862, at Sóller, on the island of Majorca. He entered the Jesuit novitiate at Veruela, near Saragossa, on December 6, 1879. He did his classical studies at Veruela, philosophy at Tortosa (1884–1887), then taught Greek at St. Ignatius' College in Manresa (1887–1891), returned to Tortosa for theology (1891–1895), and was ordained in 1894. He subsequently was minister or assistant to the rector at the Veruela novitiate for seven years (1898–1904), and later rector of St. Dominic's College in Orihuela (1906–1909). In 1909 he began teaching moral theology at the diocesan seminary in Tortosa and continued for the next sixteen years. After leaving the classroom he spent some time at the Jesuit residences in Barcelona, Alicante, and Palma, and after the Society had been suppressed in Spain in

1932, he returned to Barcelona. Because the large Jesuit houses were closed, Fr. Arbona lived with several Jesuits in a small residence until the outbreak of civil war in July 1936, when each had to seek refuge for himself.

Like all Spanish Jesuits of the time, Fr. Arbona, in order to avoid arrest by the communists, frequently changed residence, sometimes spending only a few days in a place. Though he had to change residences, he did not go into hiding. For three months he carried on an apostolate of administering the sacraments to the people of Barcelona and to those in the suburbs of Sarriá and Pedralbes. He said Mass in different houses on different days; he preached, heard confessions, and distributed Holy Communion to the faithful. Since he wore the uniform of a messenger service, his visits to these houses went unsuspected. He likewise used to walk through Barcelona's parks, and though he gave the appearance of one carrying on a conversation with a friend, he was actually hearing a penitent's confession. He did the same when he walked the crowded city streets or when he visited a bank or public building. Whenever someone urged him to exercise more caution, he simply responded: "Why? I've been praying for martyrdom for forty years." And when a friend offered him the opportunity to go to France, he refused, saying: "This is our hour! Christ's soldiers do not flee, they stand and fight." Because churches had been burned and Catholics were unable to attend Mass, Fr. Arbona frequently gave his people consecrated hosts in a folded paper, so that they could take Holy Communion themselves at home. It is said that he often distributed more than a thousand hosts a week in this way. This practice was frowned upon by some priests, and when the bishop asked him to discontinue it, he immediately submitted to the bishop's request. This happened in early November when the seventy-four-year-old Fr. Arbona had but a few more weeks to live. Unable to continue his usual apostolate, he now sat in the park, fed the pigeons, and waited for people to approach him for confession.

Fr. Arbona's arrest early in the morning of November 25, 1936, was totally unexpected. His host had withdrawn his savings from various Barcelona banks and several revolutionaries, aware of these withdrawals, came to his house a little after midnight to rob it. They forced the owner to hand over the money and while searching the house they came upon Fr. Arbona sleeping in his room. They ordered him out of bed, and as one of the men helped the priest put on his jacket, he slipped his hand into a pocket and withdrew a piece of paper with a host inside. "Oh, you are a priest!" he exclaimed. To this Fr. Arbona answered: "Yes, you have said it." That was enough. They took him to their local station, where he was interrogated and toward evening they transferred him to the San Elías Prison, a former Poor Clare convent.

When the prisoners at San Elías heard that a priest had been brought in, they all asked to go to confession. Fr. Arbona was in prison for three days, and then on the morning of November 29 the prisoners noticed that he was gone. Sometime during the previous night he had been taken away and in the early hours of that morning was executed. After forty years Fr. Arbona's prayer was answered.

Of Fr. Arbona's ten Jesuit companions, eight met death before he did. When civil war was only a few days old, four were arrested on July 21, 1936, at St. Joseph's Retreat House in the Bonanova section of Barcelona. Fr. Joseph Romá and Br. Philip Iriondo were stationed at the retreat house. The former provincial Fr. Joseph Murall, was visiting the house at the time and on the morning of July 21, Fr. Felix Cots came to see how his brethren were faring. Fr. Cots arrived a little before 9:00 A.M., and within minutes the house was surrounded by some twenty armed men, who had come looking for concealed weapons. They found none, but they arrested the four Jesuits and took them to their local headquarters. While the two cars with the Jesuits were parked outside, a group of young men surrounded the cars and urged the soldiers to kill the prisoners because they were priests. Five minutes later the cars drove off to the area known as San Ginés dels Agudells, where the prisoners were told to get out and walk along the road toward a small hill. As the four walked to their execution, Fr. Murall spoke for the group: "We die for Jesus Christ. We harbor no evil against you, rather, we forgive you with all our hearts." The soldiers then shot their prisoners and left the bodies for others to find. Fr. Murall, however, was only wounded, and after he discovered that his three Jesuit brethren were dead, he slowly crawled away and found refuge with a nearby Catholic family.

The next two Jesuits to die were Fr. Francis Xavier Tena and Br. Joseph Sampol. After the Jesuit schools had been closed in Spain, Fr. Tena lived with Br. Sampol and two other priests, but when the communities had to disperse in July 1936 with the coming of the revolution, Br. Sampol continued to care for the seventy-three-year-old Fr. Tena. He saw to it that the priest had a safe place to stay and about mid-August helped him move into a residence in the Pedralbes area, where two religious sisters were also staying. The sisters told Fr. Tena that the apartment was not altogether safe—but no place in Spain was then safe for a priest. In an effort to allay their fears, he said: "What could happen to us? Martyrdom? Then let it be as God wants it to be!" On Saturday, August 22, he left the apartment to buy cuff links and a pencil, and as he passed the concierge he noted that she took particular interest in him. His fears were well founded, for that evening the woman reported him to the police.

Not long after midnight—it was now Sunday, August 23—about a half-dozen policemen came to the apartment in response to the concierge's report. The sister who answered the door affirmed that she saw no one who could be called "suspicious." The police forced their way in and searching the apartment found Fr. Tena in his room conversing with a friend. Looking about the room one of the soldiers found a copy of the New Testament and shouted: "So, you are a priest!" That book was reason enough to take Fr. Tena and his visitor to prison. After Fr. Tena had been led away, no one knew where he had been taken or what had happened to him. On Monday, the following day, Br. Sampol went to the morgue at Barcelona's Hospital Clinic to see if the priest had been killed the previous night, but did not find the body there.

Br. Sampol's arrest came on August 26, when the apartment where he was staying was searched. He was martyred early the next day. His body was identified at the morgue on the day after his death by one of the sisters who had given him refuge. Fr. Tena's death seems to have occurred on August 26, the day before that of Br. Sampol, but this only became known after the revolution had ended and photographs of cadavers had been discovered, including one of Fr. Tena, which carried the date August 26, 1936.

Fr. Michael Mendoza was superior of the Jesuit infirmary on the outskirts of Tarrasa. When the government decreed the Society's suppression in 1932, he moved the sick Jesuits into the diocesan seminary and then in April 1936 moved them to a residence in Sarriá. When the revolution began in July, they all had to disperse and Fr. Mendoza went to live with the Delás family in Barcelona. Sometime in early August the police came to the Delás apartment, in response to a report that two priests were living there. Besides Fr. Mendoza, the diocesan priest Fr. Joseph Colomar was there. The police arrested both priests as well as Mr. Delás. Fr. Mendoza was interrogated at the local station, and when the revolutionaries put in a call to central headquarters to learn what should be done with the prisoners, Fr. Mendoza expected death. To their surprise headquarters ordered their release. They never learned the reason but suspected that because Mr. Delás was a native of Colombia, the communists most probably did not want to create problems with a foreign country. Fr. Mendoza continued to live with the Delás family for another month, but then on the morning of September 1, 1936, the police returned and arrested him. All that day Mr. and Mrs. Delás heard nothing of him, and the following day they went to the hospital's morgue to see whether they could find his body. When they found it, the face was covered with blood. He had received three wounds in the face and one in the head. Mr. Delás formally identified it and learned that it had arrived at the morgue at 11:00 P.M. on September 1, having been found in a Barcelona square. Fr. Mendoza had no fear of martyrdom and had once told his host: "It is only a matter of two minutes and there is another martyr in heaven." He was forty-seven years old.

The next to die was Fr. Joseph Muñoz, the youngest of these eleven martyrs. He had just finished tertianship in the Netherlands and arrived in Barcelona two days before the revolution erupted. he went undercover and clandestinely worked among the people of Barcelona. Sometime in early October a friend of his, who cared for an Englishman's house, while the latter was away, offered Fr. Muñoz its use. It was ideal he thought; everyone knew it was empty. Before the Englishman had left for his vacation, however, he had an argument with one of his servants and fired him. That servant, now seeking revenge, notified the revolutionaries that the house was empty and that it would be easy to strip it of its valuables. Thus, on October 12 the soldiers came and while going through the house they found Fr. Muñoz in the back room. Looking about the room they noticed a crucifix on a night table and a breviary next to it. Taking this as proof he was a priest, they beat him and took him to the station, where he admitted that he was a Jesuit priest. His friends only knew of his martyrdom when a lady went to the morgue on the morning of October 15 to see if she could find her husband's body. There she unexpectedly came upon that of Fr. Muñoz. She made formal identification of it and learned that the priest had been killed that morning and that the body was brought in at 8:00 A.M. She noticed that he had two gunshot wounds in his head and three in his abdomen.

Five days after Fr. Muñoz's martyrdom, Fr. Demetrius Zurbitu died. He had been working in Saragossa but had come to Barcelona to give the Sisters of Mary Immaculate their annual retreat. The retreat ended on July 19 and because civil war had broken out the day before, he was caught in Barcelona. He found shelter with two friends, Ignatius and Paco Berenguer. The French consul in Barcelona had arranged for him to escape into France, but he would not leave Spain as long as he knew that Catholics were being persecuted. He lived in relative quiet until the night of October 19, 1936, when several soldiers came looking for Ignatius Berenguer. It was 8:30 P.M. and Fr. Zurbitu was at home alone. The patrol searched the apartment and found a tiny black case containing hosts as well as a breviary in Fr. Zurbitu's room. They realized that they had caught a priest, but rather than taking him directly to the station they waited for Ignatius to return. When he did not come, they took Fr. Zurbitu with them. It was 1:30 A.M. on October 20. Later that day the priest was taken to the Moncada Cemetery along with several others and executed.

When Fr. James Noguera died, he had been a Jesuit for twelve years. He had just completed his theological studies in the Netherlands and returned to Barcelona in September 1935. He was making his annual retreat under Fr. Emmanuel Peypoch in Manresa, when civil war began. He returned to Barcelona on July 25 and was taken in by the Oliver family, whose son John was also a Jesuit. Fr. Noguera spent six months with this family. Because the photograph on his identity card showed that he was a priest, he was unable to leave the house, hence most of his priestly ministry had to be done from the apartment. On the morning of February 7, 1937, two Jesuit brothers came to tell him that they would soon get him a card showing that he was a physician, because Fr. Noguera had been trained as a physician before becoming a Jesuit, and that within days he would be able to get about the city. As the brothers were leaving the building, a patrol of five soldiers stopped them and asked where they had been. They indicated the apartment and the soldiers took them up with them. When the soldiers asked Fr. Noguera for his papers, he knew this was the end. The patrol took Fr. Noguera to the San Elías Prison and kept him there until the morning of February 14. That night the city had suffered a severe bombardment by the nationalist forces and in retaliation Fr. Noguera, with thirty-two others, was taken to the Moncada Cemetery and executed. Witnesses affirmed that when it came time for the priest to be shot, he said in a loud voice: "Long live Christ the King!"

The last of these martyrs was Br. Constantine March. With the coming of the revolution he went to live with his older brother. His brother's house had been searched twice and he doubted that he would survive a third search, thus, he kept moving about. His eventual capture was somewhat of an accident. Beneath the apartment where he lived, an elderly Cuban lady, with a friend of hers, listened to the Radio Mass transmitted from Florence, Italy, every Sunday morning. The friend's servant denounced the Cuban lady to the police and on Sunday morning, February 21, 1937, a patrol came to confiscate the radio. At the last minute the group decided to check several other apartments in the same building. Br. March was at home, and when he produced his identity card showing that he was a businessman from Orihuela, the patrol was about to leave. But when the men saw a crucifix in the apartment, and when they asked if he were a priest, Br. March said no, but admitted to being a Jesuit brother. Thereupon he was taken to San Elías Prison and kept there until March 16. Early that morning sixteen names were read out—most of them priests—and Br. March was among them. All were taken to the Moncada cemetery and executed.

Fr. Bartholomew Arbona's companions:

Fr. Felix Cots Oliveras was born in Manresa on February 1, 1895, and entered the Society at Gandía on August 26, 1909. Between his years of philosophy (1916–1919) and theology (1923–1927), he spent four years teaching at the College of the Immaculate Conception in Santa Fe, Argentina. He was ordained in 1926 and after tertianship taught ethics in Barcelona and was appointed rector of the business school in that same city in 1930. After the Society's suppression he remained superior of a group of dispersed Jesuits, and when civil war erupted he visited the retreat house to see if his brethren needed help. He was arrested there on July 21, 1936, and was martyred that day with Fr. Romá, and Br. Iriondo. Fr. Cots was forty-one years old.

Fr. Joseph Romá Carreres had been a priest prior to his entrance into the Society. He was born at Castell de Castells, in Alicante province, on December 1, 1885, and entered the novitiate at Gandía on November 27, 1911, when he was twenty-six years old. After noviceship he spent a few years privately studying philosophy and theology, and then in 1918 went on the Philippine mission. He spent a year in Australia learning English, and for most of his fifteen years in the Philippines he was procurator of the mission and was assigned to the cathedral in Zamboanga. Fr. Romá returned to Spain shortly before civil war broke out and was engaged in giving retreats. He was arrested at the retreat house on July 21, 1936, and martyred the same day. He was fifty-one years old.

Br. Philip Iriondo Amundarain was born in Baliarráin, in the province of Guipúzcoa, on May 26, 1869. He entered the novitiate at Veruela on September 8, 1894. After noviceship he went to the house of studies at Gandía and there served the community for twenty-two years. His next assignments were in Huesca, Saragossa, and Palma. He was at the theologate in Sarriá when the suppression came and eventually he moved to St. Joseph's Retreat House, where he was arrested with three other Jesuits on July 21, 1936, and martyred that very day. He was sixty-seven years old.

Fr. Francis Xavier Tena Colom was born in Villafranca del Cid, in the province of Castellón, on March 9, 1863, and entered the Jesuits at Veruela on June 12, 1880. He studied philosophy in Tortosa (1884–1887), taught philosophy at St. Dominic's College in Orihuela (1887–1892), returned to Tortosa for theology (1892–1896), and was ordained in 1895. He became rector of St. Dominic's in Orihuela in 1899, then in 1904 became assistant to the provincial and in 1913 was appointed superior of the Philippine mission. He returned to Spain in 1921 and became superior (1922) of the minor seminary in Tortosa. After his term as superior, he taught moral theology at the diocesan seminary in the same city. Because of ill health he went to Barcelona; it was there that he was arrested and died a martyr on August 26, 1936.

Br. Joseph Sampol Escalas was thirty-seven years old when he was martyred and had been a Jesuit for thirteen years. He was born in Salinas de Santanyí in Majorca on October 11, 1899, and entered the Jesuits at Gandía on May 10, 1923. After noviceship he served as cook in Veruela and Sarriá, then served the community at St. Dominic's in Orihuela. When the Society was suppressed, he was sent to Argentina for a few years. He returned to Spain just months before the revolution erupted, was arrested on August 26, 1936, and was martyred on August 27.

Fr. Michael Mendoza Reig was a diocesan priest before entering the Jesuits at Gandía on September 29, 1916. He was born in Barcelona on June 21, 1889. After noviceship he taught moral theology at the diocesan seminary in Barcelona and continued teaching until 1926, when he became spiritual director of the seminarians in Valencia. At the time of the religious upheaval in Spain, Fr. Mendoza was caring for the infirm Jesuits in Tarrasa. He was arrested in Barcelona on September 1, 1936, and was martyred the same day.

Fr. Joseph Muñoz Albiol was born on November 12, 1904, at La Galera, in the province of Tarragona, and entered the Society at Gandía on January 2, 1920. He did his classical studies at Veruela (1922–1925), philosophy at Sarriá (1925–1928), and taught at Saragossa (1928–1931), but because of the Society's suppression he went to the Netherlands for theology, was ordained there in 1934, and in July 1936 left to return to Spain. His ministry in his native country lasted only three months. He was martyred on October 15, 1936, at age thirty-one.

Fr. Demetrius Zurbitu Recalde was born on December 22, 1866, at Betelu in Navarre and entered the Jesuits at Veruela on July 20, 1901, when he was thirty-four. He did his early studies at Veruela and philosophy at Tortosa (1907–1910), taught two years at Gandía and three at Veruela, then went to Sarriá for theology (1915–1919), and was ordained in 1918. He spent a year in Rome studying Scripture and in 1921 returned to Barcelona to direct several sodalities associated with the college. He spent three years in Madrid (1926–1929) as an editor of the religious journal *Razón y Fe* and in 1929 was assigned to Saragossa. He was arrested in Barcelona on October 19, 1936, and was martyred the following day. He was sixty-nine years old.

Fr. *James Noguera Baró* was born at Vilanova de Alpicat, in Lérida province, on September 14, 1901, and entered the Gandía novitiate on December 7, 1924. Because of his previous medical training as a physician, he spent only two years doing classical studies (1926–1928) and two of philosophy (1928–1930). After he began his study of theology, he had to go to the Netherlands to complete the course and was ordained there in 1933. He returned to Barcelona in September 1935, was arrested on February 7, 1937, and was martyred on February 14. He was thirty-five years old.

Br. *Constantine March Battles* was born at Manresa on March 10, 1877, and entered the novitiate at Veruela on August 30, 1892. As a brother he served the communities in Veruela and Tortosa, then in 1918 went to the college in Saragossa, where he remained for six years, until be moved to St. Dominic's College in Orihuela in 1924. At the time of the Society's suppression, he went to Rome to work at the Society's headquarters and returned to Barcelona in 1934. In Barcelona he was secretary-treasurer of the Ramon Lull Academy at Sarriá and taught penmanship to students. He was arrested on February 21, 1937, and was martyred on March 16. At the time of his death he was sixty years old.

The cause of Fr. Bartholomew Arbona and his ten Jesuit companions was officially opened in Barcelona on November 20, 1950.

November 29

Ven. Bernard Francis de Hoyos 1711–1735

The life of Bernard Hoyos was remarkably short. He died when he was only twenty-four, but in that brief period he accomplished so much in promoting devotion to the Sacred Heart of Jesus that he is recognized as Spain's earliest "Apostle of the Sacred Heart."

Bernard was born on August 21, 1711, in Torrelobatón, near Valladolid. In 1721 he attended the Jesuit school in Medina del Campo and in 1722 enrolled at their school in Villagarcía. The Jesuit novitiate was next door, and having received his widowed mother's reluctant permission he applied for admission. The Jesuits had no choice but to reject his application—the youth was only fourteen and looked as if he were ten, and his health was fragile. The determined Bernard stayed on at the school, praying all the while that one day he would enter the Society. Eventually, his prayer was answered and, though he had not yet reached his fifteenth birthday, he entered the Jesuit novitiate on July 11, 1726. Within a few months after entrance, God granted him many extraordinary graces and favors. These mystical experiences in which Christ, our Lady, and the saints appeared to him continued throughout his short life. Besides these periods of ecstasy and joy, there were also times of abandonment and darkness of soul that prepared and purified him for still greater favors.

Bernard pronounced his vows of poverty, chastity, and obedience on July 12, 1728, and in the following October went to Medina del Campo to begin his study of philosophy. Then in September 1731 he went to St. Ambrose College in Valladolid for theology. Bernard's extraordinary graces never interfered with his studies, and few people knew that he had been so blessed by God. Exteriorly he lived the typical life of a Jesuit scholastic, whose time is almost totally given to his studies.

A remarkable change came about in Bernard's life in May 1773. A Jesuit friend from Bilbao asked him to translate that portion of Fr. Joseph de Gallifet's book, *On Devotion to the Most Sacred Heart of Jesus,* that dealt with the institution of the feast of *Corpus Christi.* The friend needed this material for a sermon he was then preparing. Bernard withdrew the book from the library and began reading it on May 3. It proved so inspiring, he later wrote to his spiritual director, that he felt an extraordinary and irresistible impulse to go and pray before the Blessed Sacrament and to offer himself to help spread the devotion to Jesus' Sacred Heart. The following day, as Bernard's desire took deeper root, our Lord appeared to him telling him that he had chosen him to be the one to propagate the Sacred Heart devotion in Spain. On succeeding days our Lord continued to appear and to reveal to him the treasures of his heart, as he had previously done to Sister Margaret Mary Alacoque. Bernard was still in studies and so he indicated to our Lord that he felt helpless to take on such a mission, but Jesus gave him the assurance that he would be his guide.

From then on Bernard's total concern was the diffusion of this devotion. He asked priests who were assigned to give parish missions, also to preach on Christ's Sacred Heart. He introduced the Sodality of the Sacred Heart into Spain and was instrumental in establishing it in other cities. He wrote to king and bishops, requesting them to petition the Holy See to extend the Office of the Sacred Heart to Spain. And through the generosity of a benefactor, he had a book on the Sacred Heart published, *The Hidden Treasure,* written by his spiritual father at his request. He then sent copies to members of Spain's royal family, nobility, and to all bishops and higher ecclesiastics. In his zeal to promote the devotion still further, he ordered from Rome thousands of holy cards portraying the Sacred Heart and distributed them among the faithful. He then secured copies of the plates and had the cards printed in Spain. Running parallel with this intense activity, Bernard continued his studies. When time came for his class to be ordained, Bernard was under the required canonical age of twenty-four; a dispensation was obtained and he was ordained on January 2, 1735.

In September 1735, Fr. Hoyos began his tertianship, also in Valladolid. This period of training, similar to a third year of novitiate, is intended to revive the interior life of the young priest, who has spent the last several years of his life in concentrated study. Though the interior life of Fr. Hoyos needed no resuscitation, he, nevertheless, looked forward to the opportunity of another thirty-day retreat. On November 16, shortly after finishing the retreat, he contracted typhoid. One of his frequent prayers during his illness was: "Oh, how good it is to dwell in the Heart of Jesus." Even in moments of delirium, he spoke of the Sacred Heart. His condition grew steadily worse and on November 29 he was anointed, responding to the prayers himself. Then his eyes closed and with a smile on his face he gave his soul to his one and only love.

Fr. Bernard de Hoyos had been a priest for less than a year and never had the opportunity to preach a mission on the Sacred Heart of Jesus. Nevertheless, he exercised an apostolate so important and widespread that he is now acknowledged as Spain's first "Apostle of the Sacred Heart." The cause of Fr. Hoyos was introduced in Rome on February 11, 1914, and on January 12, 1996, the decree proclaiming his exercise of heroic virtues was promulgated.

December

December 1

St. Edmund Campion 1540–1581

Martyr of England

On the morning of June 25, 1580, a jewelry merchant named Mr. Edmonds landed at Dover, England, after crossing the Channel from France. Port authorities were on the watch for disguised Catholic priests entering England and were somewhat suspicious of Mr. Edmonds. But after checking his identification and asking him questions, they were finally satisfied and permitted him to enter the country. Unknown to them, however, the merchant was Fr. Edmund Campion, a Jesuit, who was to become the most famous of the English martyrs.

Edmund Campion was born in London on January 25, 1540, of Catholic parents who later turned Protestant. His early education was at Christ-Church Hospital, Newgate Street, where on August 3, 1553, he read an address welcoming Queen Mary Tudor to London. Next he attended St. John's College, Oxford. He became an important personage at the university and a lecturer with a great following among the students, who willingly called themselves "Campionites." When the school's founder, Sir Thomas White died in 1564, Edmund delivered the funeral oration; and on the occasion of Queen Elizabeth's visit to Oxford on September 3, 1566, the twenty-six-year-old Edmund gave a memorable speech of welcome in Latin. So strong was the impression he made upon Her Majesty and Lords Cecil and Leicester that they tried to recruit him for the queen's service.

Edmund most probably took the Oath of Supremacy, acknowledging the queen's sovereignty in matters of religion, in 1564, the year he received his degree. By 1568 he was a deacon in the Established Church, but his ordination became a source of disquiet to him. In pursuing his studies toward priestly ordination, he read the writings of the Church Fathers and through his reading became convinced that the Catholic Church had the true faith. Unable to live as a Catholic in England he decided to go to Dublin, setting out sometime after August 1, 1569. He stayed in Ireland until May 1571 when, because of growing anti-Catholic feeling in the Irish capital, he returned briefly to England. In June he left for the recently founded English College at Douai, a seminary on the Continent that trained priests for England.

Edmund's first action in Douai was probably to become officially reconciled with the Roman Church. Then he devoted himself to his studies. On January 21, 1573, he earned his degree, and not long afterward, set out for Rome intent on becoming a Jesuit. He entered the Eternal City in February or March, applied for entrance into the Society of Jesus, and was accepted in April. Since there was neither an English province nor an English Mission, he was assigned to the Austrian province and went to Prague and Brno for his novitiate. After he pronounced his vows, he taught at Prague, was ordained there, and expected to spend the rest of his life there. He wrote and directed plays for his students and was acknowledged as the foremost orator in Prague.

In 1579 the Jesuit general in Rome decided to open a mission in England and Fr. Campion was one of the first to be assigned to it. He left Prague on March 25, 1580, and arrived in Rome on April 5. On April 18 he, Fr. Robert Persons, and Br. Ralph Emerson left Rome for England. Stopping off at Saint-Omer in Flanders, they joined others who were also on their way to England. But the news of their imminent departure was picked up by Elizabeth's spies in France and the English ports of entry were notified of their impending arrival. The priests separated when they reached the French coast. Fr. Persons left for England in mid-June and Fr. Campion and Br. Emerson followed him nine days later, on the night of June 24, and arrived on their native soil the following morning.

Fr. Campion had been away from England for eight years. He went directly to London where he remained for a brief period. While there he wrote a manifesto of his mission which has come to be known as "Campion's Brag." In it he declared that his coming to England had a religious and not a political purpose. The statement was intended to be used, in the event of his capture, to offset the government's expected claim that he was on a purely political mission. So powerful was this manifesto that, unknown to him, it was widely distributed to help encourage Catholics to remain firm in their faith.

Fr. Campion exercised his priestly ministry in Berkshire, Oxfordshire, Lancashire, and Yorkshire, staying at Catholic homes one or two nights or visiting households where Catholics were employed. He usually arrived during the day, preached and heard confessions during the evening, then celebrated Mass and distributed Communion the following morning and shortly thereafter was again on his way. In the middle of May 1851 he returned to London to have his little book *Rationes decem* ("Ten Reasons") published; it was addressed to the academic world and gave ten arguments showing the falsity of Protestantism and the truth of the Catholic religion. The book was ready for distribution by June 27, and a good number of the 400 copies printed were left on the benches of Oxford

P. Edmundus Campianus, et P. Alexander Briantus. Angli S. I pro
Fide suspensi et secti Londini in Anglia A: 1581. 1. Decembris.

C. S. d.   M D

St. Edmund Campion and St. Alexander Briant

University's Church of St. Mary for everyone to pick up and read. Since Fr. Campion's name was still well known at Oxford, the book was eagerly read.

In July he left London to renew his rounds, and on his way to Norfolk he visited the Yate family at Lyford Grange in Berkshire and left early the following morning. When the Yate's Catholic neighbors learned that Fr. Campion had been there, they pressed Mrs. Yate into inviting him back again; everyone was eager to hear the famous preacher. Mrs. Yate sent word to Fr. Campion; he returned and planned to spend the weekend at the Grange and leave on Sunday. Two other priests were also at the Grange. On Sunday, July 16, about fifty Catholics gathered to attend Mass and hear Fr. Campion's sermon. A certain George Eliot, a professional priest-hunter, who pretended to be a fervent Catholic, was also in the congregation. Knowing that the family was staunchly Catholic, he took it upon himself to visit the house on the chance that a priest might be celebrating Mass there. And through the good graces of someone in the kitchen, he had been admitted to the service. Rather than remain for something to eat after the Mass, Eliot hurriedly left to notify the local magistrate to have the house searched. A search party arrived but all they found were a few concealed priest-holes but no priests. Eliot would not give up and had the guards spend the night outside, listening to every noise. During the night the mistress of the Grange asked Fr. Campion to speak to her household, which he did. When the group was disbanding someone accidentally stumbled, and the noise raised an alarm among the guards. The house was again searched, more carefully this time, and the priests were discovered.

Fr. Campion and his two priest companions were taken to the Tower in London on July 22, where Fr. Campion was put in the room known as "little ease," a cell where a grown man could neither stand upright nor lie down flat. After three days he was taken to Leicester House, where he again met Queen Elizabeth and the Earl of Leicester. The queen, it appears, had requested the meeting to give Fr. Campion an opportunity to abjure his Catholic faith and enter the Protestant ministry. It was suggested that there were no limits to the heights he could reach in the Established Church. Since he would not apostatize, he was returned to his prison cell and five days later was tortured on the rack. Since his *Rationes decem* requested a meeting with Anglican divines, four such conferences were held, but Fr. Campion was given neither books nor time to prepare for the meetings. Though the first was held shortly after he had been racked, he, nevertheless, ably upheld the truth of the Catholic faith.

With no winner emerging from these disputations, it was determined that Fr. Campion had to be executed, and the government sought a charge that carried more weight than the fact that he was merely a Catholic priest. On November 14, 1581, he was led to Westminster Hall, where he and seven other priests heard the charges against them—that at Rome and at Rheims they had formed a conspiracy against the life of the queen, had exhorted foreigners to invade the country, and had entered England with the intention of stirring up rebellion to support the invading force. The trial was set for November 20. When Fr. Campion was asked at the trial to raise his hand to take an oath, he was unable to do so because of his recent torture. One of the other priests came forward and raised it for him. The priest later related that he had noticed that Fr. Campion's fingers were without nails. Fr. Campion defended the priests indicted with him, asserting their loyalty to the queen in temporal matters and denying that they had entered England for political reasons. Sentence was passed that same day and all were found guilty of high treason and were condemned to be hanged, drawn, and quartered. Upon hearing the verdict, the priests joined together in singing the *Te Deum,* a hymn praising God.

Fr. Campion remained in chains for another eleven days, and on December 1, was dragged through the muddy streets of London to Tyburn. With him were Fr. Ralph Sherwin, a diocesan priest, and the Jesuit Fr. Alexander Briant. Fr. Campion was the first of the three to die, and when one of the officials asked him to confess his treason, he remarked: "I am a Catholic man and a priest; in that faith have I lived and in that faith I intend to die. If you esteem my religion treason, then I am guilty; as for other treason, I never committed any. God is my judge." In his final words he forgave those who condemned him, and as he bowed his head and folded his hands in prayer, the cart was driven from under him and he was left hanging. The executioner then cut him down and further violated his body by tearing out his heart and intestines, and hacking his body to pieces.

Fr. Edmund Campion was beatified by Pope Leo XIII on December 9, 1886, and was canonized by Pope Paul VI on October 25, 1970. His memorial is celebrated on December 1, together with the other Jesuit martyrs of England and Wales.

Prayer

Almighty, eternal God, you chose from the people of England and Wales Saint Edmund Campion and his companions to be made like Christ, who died to save the world. Listen to their prayers; strengthen your Church by the same faith and love that strengthened them, and bless it always with your gift of unity. We ask this through our Lord Jesus Christ, your Son, who lives and reigns with you and the Holy Spirit, one God, for ever and ever.

St. Alexander Briant 1556–1581

Martyr of England

Fr. Alexander Briant was the third martyr to die at Tyburn on December 1, 1581. He was dragged from the Tower with Frs. Edmund Campion and Ralph Sherwin, and saw them hanged and quartered for their religion. When his turn came he courageously mounted the cart beneath the gallows, made a public profession of his Catholic faith, and expressed joy that God had chosen him to die in the company of these two martyrs. The executioner then did his duty.

Alexander Briant, born in Somerset, England, about 1556, and began his studies in 1574 at Hart Hall, Oxford. The new religion of Elizabeth I was not to his liking so he crossed the Channel in August 1577 to attend the English College at Douai and there was reconciled to the Catholic Church. He continued his study of theology and was ordained in 1578. In August 1579 he returned to England and exercised his ministry in his native shire. But this apostolate lasted less than two years, for he was arrested by priest-hunters during their search for Fr. Robert Persons, a Jesuit who had come to England in June 1580. Fr. Briant came to London in April 1581 to visit Fr. Persons, for they had known each other for some time. Fr. Persons, before his return to the Catholic Church, had been one of Fr. Briant's teachers at Baliol College, Oxford; and since Fr. Briant's return to England he had succeeded in bringing Fr. Person's father back into the Church. Hence both priests had great esteem for each other. On April 28, having been informed by a spy as to where Fr. Persons lived, priest-hunters came to arrest him. They searched the house, but unable to find him—he was out of the city at the time—they went next door to continue their hunt and there they found Fr. Briant.

The hunters cast Fr. Briant into the Counter Prison and kept him without food and with little drink for six days, hoping to gain needed information from the famished prisoner. After the sixth day, he was transferred, May 5, to the Tower for interrogation. He was asked Fr. Person's whereabouts, and where he usually celebrated Mass, who attended it, who made their confessions to him, and so on. When Fr. Briant refused to respond to these questions, sharp needles were forced beneath his nails, and when he did not break under torture, he was placed on the rack for two days. When the rackmaster threatened to make him a foot longer, the priest laughingly defied him to do so. He then spent eight days in a dark dungeon after which be was again stretched on the rack. He narrated the details of his torture in a letter he wrote to the English Jesuits saying that when he was first placed on the rack he set his mind firmly on Christ's passion and so absorbed was he in that thought—he did not know whether it was a miracle or not—that he felt no pain during the torture, only when it was over. He said he was writing the letter to them because, just as he was about to endure his second racking, he had determined to enter the Society if ever released from prison. However, now that he had endured the torture and doubted that he would ever be set free, he was requesting to be admitted to their number. The English Jesuits accepted him upon receipt of his letter.

On November 21, 1581, the day after Fr. Campion had been tried, Fr. Briant, together with six other priests, was tried at Westminster Hall. He entered the Hall holding in his hands a small wooden cross that he himself had made, and kept looking at it during the trial. When a Protestant minister standing next to him snatched it from his hands, Fr. Briant said: "You may tear it from my hands, but you cannot tear it from my heart. I shall die for him, who first died for me." He was charged with having taken an oath against the queen's life while at Rome and at Rheims, though he had never been in Rome, and had not been in Rheims when the alleged oath was to have taken place. Nevertheless, he was found guilty of the charge and condemned to death as a traitor.

Fr. Briant's martyrdom took place on Tyburn Hill on December 1, 1581, and after he had been hanged, he was cut down while still alive so that he could also suffer disembowelment. He was then beheaded and his body quartered. He was twenty-five years old. Together with Frs. Campion and Sherwin, his companions in death, he was beatified by Pope Leo XIII on December 9, 1886, and canonized by Pope Paul VI on October 25, 1970. His memorial, together with the other Jesuits martyred in England and Wales, is celebrated on December 1.

Prayer

Almighty, eternal God, you chose from the people of England and Wales Saint Alexander Briant and his companions to be made like Christ, who died to save the world. Listen to their prayers; strengthen your Church by the same faith and love that strengthened them, and bless it always with your gift of unity. We ask this through our Lord Jesus Christ, your Son, who lives and reigns with you and the Holy Spirit, one God, for ever and ever.

December 3

St. Francis Xavier 1506–1552

Fr. Francis Xavier was the greatest missionary the Church has known since apostolic times. He was born Francisco de Jassu y Javier, on April 7, 1506, at the family castle in Navarre, Spain, the fifth and youngest child of Juan de Jassu and

Maria de Azpilcueta. His early education was at home, and in September 1525, at age nineteen, he set out for Paris, where he began university studies. He matriculated at the College of Sainte-Barbe and his roommate was the young Savoyard, Peter Favre. Both were more interested in their degrees than in their futures, but all this changed when the Basque Ignatius of Loyola moved in with them in September 1529. It was not long before Ignatius won Peter over to his way of thinking—to become a priest and work for the salvation of souls—but Francis proved more difficult. He had aspirations of worldly advancement.

Francis earned his licentiate degree in the spring of 1530 and began explaining Aristotle at the College of Dormans-Beauvais, while he continued to reside at Sainte-Barbe. It was only when Peter went to visit his family in 1533 that Ignatius, now alone with Francis, was able to break down his friend's resistance. Tradition has it that Ignatius put this question to him: "What shall it profit a man if he gain the whole world and lose his own soul?" Francis finally yielded to the grace God was offering him through his fellow Spaniard. In addition to Peter and Francis, Ignatius won four other students to his way of thinking; they now numbered seven, and all were of the same mind and heart. Ignatius' interest in the Holy Land overflowed into the others' hearts, and to express their commitment to God, the group met on August 15, 1534, in the chapel of Saint-Denis in Montmartre, to pronounce private vows of poverty, chastity, and of going to the Holy Land to convert infidels.

Francis and Ignatius began their study of theology in 1534, and then in March 1535, Ignatius had to return to his homeland because of his health. Before his departure, however, all agreed to meet in Venice, Italy, in 1537, to prepare for their journey to Jerusalem. On November 15, 1536, Francis and companions left Paris for Venice and arrived the following January. They found Ignatius waiting for them. After two months of working in Venice hospitals, the group went to Rome to request papal permission for their pilgrimage and ordination for the non-priests among them. They returned to Venice where Francis, Ignatius, and four others were ordained on June 24, 1537. Feeling insufficiently prepared to celebrate their first Masses, they dispersed to several cities. Francis and Alphonsus Salmerón went to Monselice, near Padua, and there spent forty days in prayer. When this was over, they met in Vicenza, where Fr. Francis celebrated his first Mass.

Because Venice's impending war with the Turks kept the companions from going to the Holy Land, they asked Fr. Ignatius to go to Rome and place the group at the pope's disposal, while they, in turn, would go to various university centers and begin preaching. Fr. Francis and Nicholas Bobadilla went to Bologna, and there the former began an apostolate that would only end at death.

Sick with fever, Fr. Francis arrived in Rome in April 1538, a mere shadow of his former self. His strength returned, however, and he began preaching in the French church of St. Louis. During Lent 1539 he participated in the discussions that eventually led the companions to agree to form a religious order. Before the pope officially granted his approval to the new Society, he had asked

Fr. Ignatius to respond King John III of Portugal's request by sending two Jesuits—there were only ten in all—to the newly settled Portuguese colony in India. The two chosen for the Society's first mission were Bobadilla and Simon Rodrigues. When Bobadilla fell ill, Fr. Ignatius found a substitute in Fr. Francis, the only priest then not committed to a specific task. The two missionaries left Rome on March 15, 1540, and arrived in the Portuguese capital at the end of June. Since the fleet had already sailed for the East and the next sailing would not be until the following spring, the two Jesuits spent their days preaching in the city and ministering to prisoners. When the king saw the work they were accomplishing, he asked for one to remain and open a school. Rodrigues was chosen to stay and the other was to go to India. Thus, Providence arranged for Fr. Francis Xavier to become the first Jesuit missionary.

As Fr. Francis boarded the *Santiago* in Lisbon, the king's messenger handed him a papal letter appointing him apostolic nuncio. This gave him authority over all Portuguese clergy in Goa, India. The ship sailed on April 7, 1541, his thirty-fifth birthday. After four long, tiring months at sea, the vessel reached Mozambique, where it had to await favorable winds. After six months the missionary again set sail in February 1542, this time on a smaller vessel, and touched the shores of Goa on May 6, thirteen months after he had left Lisbon.

Fr. Francis spent five months in Goa and in addition to preaching to the Portuguese, visiting prisons, and ministering to and celebrating Mass for lepers, he tried to learn Tamil. His first missionary endeavor was among the recently converted Paravas, the pearlfishers who lived on India's southeastern shore above Cape Comorin. The Paravas, some 20,000, had been converted between 1535 and 1537, but had been without a priest for years. It was the task of Fr. Francis to reinstruct them in the faith they had embraced. Unable to speak Tamil, he made use of interpreters and for two years went from village to village baptizing all he thought ready, and leaving a catechist in charge when it was time for him to move on. By the end of 1544 he was on the western shore of India at Travancore, and during the months of November and December he is supposed to have baptized 10,000 individuals. From there he went northward to Cochin and in January 1545 he heard from a traveler that the Molucca Islands were ripe for harvest. This was what the zealous missionary wanted to hear. He left Cochin for São Thomé (now part of Madras), where he visited the tomb of St. Thomas the Apostle. In September 1545 he embarked for the Portuguese city of Malacca in Malaya.

The great trading center of Malacca was only a stopping off point for him. On January 1, 1546, he set sail for the Moluccas, the famed Spice Islands, and landed at Amboina on February 14. For three months he visited the island's Christian villages, and at nearby Seran baptized over 1,000 persons. In June he set out for Ternate, an island of heathens, and then in September went to Moro, an island known for its headhunters. After this hasty reconnaissance visit, he was back at Malacca in July 1547 and arranged for two Jesuits to take his place.

At Malacca he met Anjiro, a Japanese nobleman interested in becoming a Catholic. It was through him that Fr. Francis learned about Japan. He returned to Goa, where as superior of the mission he tended to business matters, and assigned the newly arrived Jesuits to different tasks. It was not until April 15, 1549, that he, together with Anjiro and several other Jesuits, set sail for Japan, a land that had not yet heard the voice of Christianity.

They stopped at Malacca, where Fr. Francis was unable to convince any of the Portuguese captains to take him and his group to Japan—they were afraid of the uncharted waters. Thus he hired a pagan pirate and his junk. They departed on June 24, 1549, and landed on August 15 at Kagoshima in southern Japan, Anjiro's native city. Anjiro secured an audience with the local prince, who readily gave the Jesuits permission to preach Christianity. More interviews followed, but Fr. Francis could not get anywhere with the prince. The missionary's goal was to get to the emperor in order to convert him and the nation, but no one would tell him how to get to Miyako (today's Kyoto), the Imperial City. After a year in Kagoshima and after making only 100 converts, he decided he was wasting time, so the Jesuits left for Hirado, a port used by the Portuguese on the upper coast of Kyushu.

Within two months of his arrival, he made 100 converts. But because he was still eager to get to the emperor, he did not want to remain long on the island. He crossed over to the mainland and went to Yamaguchi, Japan's second largest city. He was there only a week when he began preaching in the city's streets. When he finally had his audience with the daimyo things did not go well and so he left the city in December 1550 for Sakai. When Fr. Francis and Br. John Fernandez arrived in Sakai, they visited a merchant who offered them hospitality and arranged for them to go to the Imperial City. The two Jesuits were hired as domestic servants by a prince on his way there. The princely entourage arrived in January 1551, and for the first time Catholic missionaries saw Asia's largest and most beautiful city. After trying for eleven days to get an audience with the Son of Heaven, the dispirited Jesuits returned to Hirado. They did learn, however, that the most powerful lord in Japan was not the emperor, but the daimyo of Yamaguchi! They had failed once but they would try again; this time they would not appear as poorly-clad Europeans, but as individuals worthy of the daimyo's attention.

Together with three Christian servants, Fr. Francis and Br. John sailed to the mainland, and there rented horses and a litter. Dressed in colorful, flowing, silken robes, with turbans on their heads, they ceremoniously made their way to Yamaguchi. The doors of the daimyo's palace were immediately opened for these illustrious lords, and never did the daimyo suspect that the visiting "nobles" were the same "barbarians" he had brushed away several months previously. Fr. Francis offered the daimyo priceless gifts; clocks and music boxes, mirrors and crystals, cloth and wine. After the grateful daimyo had accepted these signs of friendship, the missionary presented his credentials, letters from

King John III of Portugal and Pope Paul III. The daimyo responded affirmatively to all of the requests of Fr. Francis and authorized the priests to preach the Christian religion in the empire. At the same time he permitted the Japanese to embrace Christianity, if they chose to do so. Finally, he granted the missionaries a monastery as their residence in the city. Having established themselves as noblemen and diplomats, the Jesuits were visited by many Japanese and within six months gained 500 converts.

When Fr. Francis felt it was time to leave, he asked Fr. Cosmas de Torres to come to Yamaguchi and take over. In September 1551 Fr. Francis and Br. John left for Bungo, where they found a Portuguese vessel in the harbor. They boarded it for Malacca and India and hoped to return to Japan the following year. But seven days out from Japan the ship was caught in a typhoon and drawn into a whirlpool. When it was finally cast out, it was some thousand miles off course. On December 17 the vessel entered the Bay of Canton and dropped anchor off Sancian Island. The eyes of Fr. Francis looked toward the distant land of China, and at that moment he felt China's call. A ship happened to be waiting there for favorable winds, and when the winds came the two missionaries joined the crew and sailed for Singapore, arriving toward the end of December. Fr. Francis found a letter from Fr. Ignatius awaiting him; he was informed that in October 1549 he had been appointed provincial of the "Indies and the countries beyond." He reached India in January 1552 and found another letter telling him to return to Rome to report on the status of the mission. But Fr. Francis felt that the report could wait until he had visited China.

He left India in April 1552 and in September he again entered the Bay of Canton and landed on desolate Sancian Island. Sancian was a hideout for Chinese smugglers but it was also used by Portuguese traders. Determined to get to China, the missionary tried to entice some of the smugglers to take him there, but none wanted to take the risk. He eventually hired one of them, but after he paid him, the man disappeared. In the meantime Fr. Francis looked longingly toward China, not knowing that his missionary days were over. On November 21 he was taken ill with a fever and was confined to his leafy hut on the island's shore. His Christian Chinese servant, Antonio, faithfully cared for him in his final illness, and years later wrote an account of the saint's last days. On November 28 the missionary went into a coma but regained consciousness on December 1. Throughout his waking hours he prayed constantly, until the early morning of December 3, when he went to heaven. His body was buried on the island, and when spring came his remains were taken to Malacca, and a few years later to Goa, where they were interred in the church Bom Jesus.

Fr. Francis Xavier was beatified by Pope Paul V on October 21, 1619, and canonized by Pope Gregory XV on March 12, 1622. His feast is celebrated on December 3. In 1910 he was made patron of the Propagation of the Faith and in 1927 patron of the missions.

Prayer

Lord God of compassion and mercy, you opened a door in the East for Saint Francis Xavier, when you sent him to preach your Gospel. Send us in our day over the face of the earth, so that the joy of our Mother, the Church, may be made perfect. We ask this through our Lord Jesus Christ, your Son, who lives and reigns with you and the Holy Spirit, one God, for ever and ever.

December 4

Bl. Jerome De Angelis 1567–1623
Bl. Simon Yempo 1580–1623

Martyrs of Japan

Fr. Jerome De Angelis and Br. Simon Yempo, together with a Franciscan priest and forty-seven lay Christians, were the first martyrs during the reign of the Shogun Iyemitsu, who succeeded his father Hidetada in August 1623. Rather than end the persecution against the Christians, Iyemitsu continued the severe policies of his father and of his grandfather Iyeyasu and renewed the decree of 1614 proscribing the Christian religion and banishing all foreign missionaries.

Jerome was born in Castrogiovanni (today's Enna) in Sicily, probably in 1567. For a time he studied law in Palermo, and while a student he made the Spiritual Exercises of St. Ignatius, which resulted in his giving up law and entering (February 2, 1586) the Society in Messina. Nine years later, about to finish his course in theology, he was assigned to the Japanese mission and he immediately set out for Lisbon and the voyage to the Indies. He arrived in Genoa, where he met Fr. Charles Spinola in December 1595. Together they traveled to Lisbon, and then sailed for the Indies on April 10, 1596. They were not to arrive in Japan until six years later because of a series of unfortunate and harrowing incidents that took them back and forth across the Atlantic Ocean, episodes which are described in Fr. Spinola's biography. In January 1598, after two years of adventures, they found themselves once more in Lisbon. Before they set out a second time for Japan in March 1599, Jerome was ordained to the priesthood.

After Fr. De Angelis arrived in Nagasaki in July 1602, he was sent to Fushimi in central Japan and then to Sunpu (now Shizuoka) to establish a Jesuit residence and a center for missionary activity. Later on he was sent to Edo (today's Tokyo) to do the same. He spent his first twelve years on the mission in central Japan, but then came the deplorable edict of 1614 which was meant to bring an end to the Catholic missions. While many of his Jesuit brethren were forced into exile, to Manila or Macao, Fr. De Angelis went into hiding in Nagasaki and continued to labor among the Japanese Christians. To conceal his identity, he disguised himself as a merchant and thus, unobserved, he continued to minister to his flock.

During this period of clandestine work, Fr. De Angelis became associated with the catechist Simon Yempo. Simon was born in Nozu, Kyushu, in 1580, and as a youngster entered a Buddhist monastery. When the head bonze became a Christian in 1596, so did young Simon. Two years later, hoping to become a catechist and to work with the Jesuits, he enrolled at a Jesuit seminary. Simon was an especially valuable addition to the missionary effort; he had firsthand knowledge of Buddhism and its monastic traditions, which he referred to when explaining the truths of Catholicism to his fellow Japanese. In 1614 he went into exile with the Jesuits, but sometime later returned to his native soil and offered his talents to Fr. De Angelis.

Since the persecution of Christians was not lessening, many traveled to the northernmost part of Honshu Island, and some crossed over to Yezo Island (today's Hokkaido). As the people moved northward, so did their priest. Fr. De Angelis was the first missionary to preach Christianity in Oshu and Dewa in 1615; and in 1618, when he and Simon crossed over to Yezo, he may have been the first European to set foot on that island. They remained there until 1622. Because they were many miles from the central government, the Christian communities lived in peace and without fear. In his letters to his provincial and in those to his friends in Italy, the missionary described Yezo: the land, the weather, and especially the native inhabitants, the hairy Ainus, who were unlike the Japanese. In 1622 he was instructed to return south to Edo, where he was to be superior of the Jesuits working in that city and the surrounding district. Again he went underground and carried out his ministry during the night. It was during this second stay in Yedo that he accepted Simon Yempo as a brother in the Society.

In November 1623 a dissatisfied Christian informed the authorities as to where Fr. De Angelis and Br. Yempo were staying, but when the soldiers made their raid, both Jesuits were out of the house. The soldiers, nevertheless, arrested the owner. In the general roundup they apprehended some forty-seven Christians. When Fr. De Angelis heard this news, he decided to deliver himself so that his host could go free. Unwilling to be separated from the priest, Br. Yempo went with him and together they surrendered to the authorities. The host, unfortunately, was not released.

Fr. De Angelis and Br. Yempo were sent to two different prisons. The former preached to the jailers in his and converted all eight of them, while the latter preached to his jailers and to other pagan prisoners and converted forty of them. In early December the shogun ordered their execution by slow fire, and on December 4 fifty prisoners were taken to a plain near Yedo. The authorities kept the two Jesuits and the Franciscan Francis Galvez to the end. While the Christians were dying, Fr. De Angelis encouraged them to persevere in their love of God and reminded them that the tribulations of this world are passing, whereas the joys of heaven are eternal. As he saw each martyr bow his or her head in death, he raised his hand in absolution. Then it was time for the three religious to die. As the flames wrapped around their bodies, Fr. De Angelis turned his stake into a pulpit. In a loud voice he told the spectators that he and his companions were dying for the Christian religion and asked the Catholics among them to remain steadfast in their faith. The flames leaped higher and the three religious, standing immobile, made their last total offering to God.

Of the fifty who died at Yedo that day only the three religious were beatified by Pope Pius IX in 1867. All are worthy of being called "blessed," but because of insufficient information concerning them—many of their names are not even known—they were not included in the brief of beatification. Jesuits celebrate the memory of Fr. Jerome De Angelis and Br. Simon Yempo on February 4, the day they recall the death of all their martyrs in Japan.

Prayer

Almighty God, grant that this remembrance of your martyrs, Blessed Jerome De Angelis and Blessed Simon Yempo, may bring us joy. May we who depend upon their prayers glory in their entry into heaven. We ask this through our Lord Jesus Christ, your Son, who lives and reigns with you and the Holy Spirit, one God, for ever and ever.

December 6

S. G. Walter Ciszek 1904–1984

Fr. Walter Ciszek spent twenty-three long and difficult years behind "the Iron Curtain," in the Soviet Union—five in Soviet prisons, ten in prison camps, and eight as a common laborer.

Walter's parents immigrated to the United States during the last decade of the nineteenth century and settled in the small town of Shenandoah, Pennsylvania, amid a thriving Polish community. The son of a mine worker, Walter was born on November 4, 1904. He attended St. Casimir's parochial school but found more joy in the school's playground than in its classrooms. He decided on becoming a priest when in the eighth grade, and though his father could not conceive how this "toughy" could ever be a priest, nevertheless, he arranged for him to do his high school studies at Sts. Cyril and Methodius Seminary in Orchard Lake, Michigan. Walter then stayed on for his college work and sometime during his college years he read a life of St. Stanislaus Kostka, whose courage and determination impressed him. During his final year's annual retreat, given by a Jesuit, Walter, without seeking anyone's advice, decided to enter the Society of Jesus and wrote to the Jesuits in Warsaw, Poland, asking to be admitted. They, in turn, suggested that he contact the Jesuits in New York City.

During the 1928 summer vacation, Walter traveled to New York to see the Jesuit provincial, and though he had arrived unexpectedly, he was interviewed and told to return home and await a letter. When the letter arrived it instructed him to report to the novitiate of St. Andrew-on-Hudson, Poughkeepsie, New York, on September 7. He always did things totally on his own; he only notified his family that he was entering the Jesuits on the morning that he was leaving home. He was twenty-four years old and knew what he wanted.

Walter was older than the other novices, and after a few months the novice master came to the decision that Walter was not cut out to be a Jesuit and suggested that he return home. But Walter was determined and he talked the master into letting him remain. In early 1929 the novices were told about a letter of Pope Pius XI calling upon Jesuits to study at the new Russian Center in Rome and to prepare for missionary work in Russia. As soon as he heard the pope's appeal, Walter knew that this was for him; he wanted to volunteer at once, but the master thought he should wait until he had pronounced his first vows.

A second novitiate for the Maryland–New York province was opened in Wernersville, Pennsylvania, and Walter was among the first novices sent there. He pronounced his religious vows on September 8, 1930, and immediately afterward wrote to the Jesuit general volunteering for the Russian mission. His offer was accepted, but he was to continue his studies until notified to come to Rome.

In 1931 he moved on to Woodstock College in Maryland for his philosophical studies and while there he received his summons. He sailed for Europe during the summer of 1934, and that fall he began his theology at Rome's Gregorian University and his Russian studies at the Russicum. He was ordained in Rome on June 24, 1937.

Because conditions in Russia at the time were such that it would have been imprudent to send missionaries there, Fr. General assigned Fr. Ciszek to work among the Russian Catholics of Albertyn, Poland. He arrived in November 1938 and immediately began his pastoral work. By 1939 there were rumors of war and then on September 1, Germany invaded Poland. While the Germans entered Poland from the west, the Russians entered from the east and on October 17 they occupied Albertyn.

Since Russia had come to him, Fr. Ciszek decided to go further into the country and minister to the spiritual needs of its Catholics. With his superior's permission he made his plans and took on a new identity. He became Vladimir Lypinski, a widower, without a family. He signed up with a lumber company to work in the Urals and left Lwów on March 19, 1940. After a two-week trip in crowded boxcars, without windows and sanitation facilities, the volunteer workers arrived at Chusovoy. From April 1940 to June 1941 Fr. Ciszek worked in lumber camps, sometimes hauling and stacking lumber, sometimes serving as truck driver. The daily wage was barely enough to buy a loaf of bread. To celebrate Mass, he went into the forest where he knew he would not be disturbed.

On June 22, 1941, Germany invaded Russia and early the following morning Fr. Ciszek was arrested as a German spy and sent to prison in Perm. During his first interrogation he learned that the Russians had penetrated his disguise; they knew his true name and that he was a priest. He was then taken to Moscow, where he arrived in early September and placed in the infamous Lubianka Prison. He arranged his prison day into periods of prayer, exercise, rosary, meditation, etc., according to the strokes of the clock in the Kremlin tower. Interrogations were frequent and debilitating, but he always gave the same answer: his reason for being in Russia was spiritual and not political.

Finally, on July 26, 1942, he was convicted of being "a Vatican spy" and sentenced to fifteen years of hard labor. He remained in solitary confinement at Lubianka until June 1944, when he was temporarily transferred to Moscow's Butirka Prison. He was again at Lubianka in March 1945, and though the war had come to an end in May of that year, he was kept there until June 1946, when he was taken to begin his sentence of hard labor.

Along with other prisoners, Fr. Ciszek boarded a prison car for the two-week trip to Krasnoyarsk, some 2,500 miles east of Moscow, midway across the vast expanse of Siberia. There the prisoners boarded barges for the slow trip on the Yenesei River to Dudinka, within the Arctic Circle. There they worked twelve hours a day loading coal on to barges. When the coal was finished, they loaded logs, and when the river froze, they loaded trains with dried and canned food. Since there was another priest in the camp, Fr. Ciszek was again able to say Mass. He also heard the confessions of the other prisoners and distributed Communion among them.

In December 1946 he was transferred to the Norilsk area, about forty miles from Dudinka, and remained there until 1955. During those years he was assigned to various camps to perform a variety of jobs. He was a coal miner and a construction worker; he helped build a copper factory and worked on extending the city of Norilsk; for a time he assisted in the camp's medical center and then in a quarry. In these several prison camps Fr. Ciszek met fellow priests and together they were able to celebrate Mass. He also had the opportunity to give retreats and spiritual counsel to fellow workers.

In October 1953 Fr. Ciszek was sent to the nearby Kayerkhan mines, and in April 1955 was notified that he was to be released after serving fourteen years and nine months of his sentence. He was given three months off for good behavior. Now a free man, he walked out of the camp on the morning of April 22,

1955. He made his way to the station and took the train to Norilsk, where he contacted a priest he had known and who had been released several months previously. Through this priest and other released prisoners he found a place to live as well as a job. He also resumed his priestly activity, but not openly; a room in an apartment was converted into a chapel and it was open to all who wanted to come and pray. Within weeks he was celebrating three Masses on Sundays in different parts of the city; there were always baptisms and weddings.

During his years at Norilsk, Fr. Ciszek had several times been warned by the Secret Police about missionary activity. Since praying at home was not illegal and since he carried out his priestly work only in private homes, he was not in violation of any law, nor did he feel that he ought to stop. When the other priest in Norilsk had to leave, Fr. Ciszek was the sole priest in a city of some 120,000 inhabitants. All Norilsk was now his parish.

Because of his well-attended liturgical celebrations during Holy Week and Easter in 1958, the police ordered him to leave the city. He was to go to Krasnoyarsk and await instructions. He flew there on April 13 and registered at the hotel as instructed. On his second day in the city, he chanced upon a Lithuanian gentleman who, in conversation, told him that their priest had died and that they were looking for another one. Fr. Ciszek revealed that he was priest and volunteered his services; he soon had a Lithuanian "parish," but after two months, he was again ordered by the police to move on.

He then went south to Abakan, where he found a job as an auto mechanic and worked there until 1963. One October evening the Secret Police came to his residence and told him that he was to go to Moscow. He was met at the Moscow airport and after a few days in the capital, was again taken to the airport, where he met an official from the American consulate. Only then did he realize that he was on his way to the United States. His companion on the trip home was a young American student who had been falsely accused of espionage and had spent two years in a Soviet prison. Both were being given their freedom in exchange for two Soviet spies.

Fr. Ciszek and companion arrived in New York City on October 12, 1963. Family members and Jesuits were waiting to greet them. Once back in the United States, Fr. Ciszek was associated with the John XXIII Center for Eastern Christian Studies at Fordham University, and spent much of his time giving retreats to communities of nuns, as well as priests and seminarians. His retreats were powerful and memorable. His goodness and kindness were everywhere in evidence. He never expressed bitterness toward the Russians but always charity, and viewed his prison years as God's way of preparing him for the clandestine but fruitful priestly work he had accomplished in the prison camps and during the years after his release. He saw God's Providence in every event of his life. During his last eight years he suffered from a severe heart condition and arthritis and died on December 8, 1984. He was buried at the Jesuit novitiate in Wernersville, Pennsylvania. Fr. Ciszek's cause for beatification is now under consideration.

December 7

St. Charles Garnier 1606–1649

Martyr of North America

Fr. Charles Garnier seemed an unlikely candidate for the Jesuit missions in New France. He was born on May 25 or 26, 1606, to a wealthy Parisian gentleman. Charles had received an excellent education and entered the Jesuit novitiate in Paris on September 5, 1624, when he was eighteen. He pursued his philosophical and theological courses leading to the priesthood at Clermont College in Paris and was ordained in 1635. Fr. Garnier immediately requested to go to the Indian mission in North America, but because of his father's protest, his petition was denied. The request was repeated in 1636, the father now yielded, and the son was appointed to the Huron mission. He made his way to Dieppe and left France on April 8, 1636, traveling with other missionaries, one of whom was Fr. Isaac Jogues.

The French vessel carrying the missionaries landed in Quebec on June 11, and by July 1 Fr. Garnier was on his way to Three Rivers to meet the flotilla of Hurons coming for their annual fur-trading visit. He departed with them in mid-July and arrived at Ihonatiria in Huronia on August 13. There he was fondly greeted by Fr. John de Brébeuf, and in his first letter to his father, Fr. Garnier wrote: "there is no place on earth where I could be happier."

The new missionary spent two years learning the Huron language from the veteran Fr. Brébeuf, and after becoming fluent in it, he was assigned to the mission at Ossossané. In November 1639 he and Fr. Jogues were sent to the Petuns, whom they found to be quite hostile to Black Robes. They remembered that the Hurons had accused the missionaries of causing the epidemic that had swept through Huronia in 1636.

After spending the winter months among them, both missionaries acknowledged that the visit was a failure and hence they returned to Ossossané. Fr. Garnier, however, was not discouraged; he returned to the Petuns in the autumn of 1640 with Fr. Pierre Pijart. He felt they were now less menacing and he decided to remain. How long he worked among them is not known, but it is recorded that from 1644 to 1646 he was with the Huron Christians at Saint-Ignace. Then during the winter of 1647 he and Fr. Leonard Garreau went back to the Petuns and founded two missions. Fr. Garnier had charge of Etarita and Fr. Garreau was in charge of Ekarreniondi. Finding the Petuns more responsive than on previous visits, Fr. Garnier built a chapel at each station and within a short time he baptized 184 Indians.

The incursions of the Iroquois were becoming more frequent. They had martyred Fr. Anthony Daniel and had burned Teanaustayé in July 1648. In November 1649 the Hurons reported that the Iroquois were on the warpath against the Petuns, whose villages they swore to burn during the winter. Faced with this threat, Fr. Garnier instructed his newly arrived assistant Fr. Noel Chabanel to return to headquarters. Fr. Garnier had accomplished a great deal among the Petuns and much could still be done, but he thought it better to spare his assistant's life, if he could. Fr. Chabanel, thus, left the mission on December 5. On the 7th in mid-afternoon, while Fr. Garnier was making his customary round of the village, the fearful shouts "Iroquois, Iroquois!" were heard in Etarita. The attackers struck down men, women, and children. Fr. Garnier rushed through the village encouraging others to flee, but he himself would not. As he was about to enter a burning cabin to baptize the sick within, an Iroquois bullet penetrated his breast and another tore into his abdomen. When he fell to the ground the savage pounced on the priest, tore off his cassock, and left him to die in the cold. A short time afterward, Fr. Garnier regained consciousness and seeing a Petun brave in pain a short distance away, struggled to rise and help him. He crawled but a few feet and fell again. Once more he raised himself and advanced a few more paces toward the dying Petun, but at that moment an Iroquois warrior swooped down upon him, scalped him and plunged a tomahawk deep in his brain.

Twelve miles away at Saint-Matthias, another Petun village, Fr. Garreau saw the dark smoke rising from Etarita and knew what the sad story must be. Inexplicably, the Iroquois did not continue their madness and, thus, Saint-Matthias was spared. On December 8 Fr. Garreau and several scouts went to Etarita and found Fr. Garnier's body; they washed it in the December snow, covered it, dug a shallow grave near the chapel, and recited funeral prayers as they lowered it into its resting place. In 1650, when the missionaries were leaving Huronia to return to Quebec, they took Fr. Garnier's remains with them.

On June 21, 1925, Pope Pius XI beatified Fr. Charles Garnier together with seven other Jesuits, who had given their lives for the faith in Canada and the United States. Their canonization took place on June 29, 1930. St. Charles Garnier's memorial is celebrated with that of the other North American Martyrs on October 19.

Prayer

Father, you consecrated the first beginnings of the faith in North America by the preaching and martyrdom of Saint Charles Garnier and his companions. By the help of their prayers may the Christian faith continue to grow throughout the world. We ask this through our Lord Jesus Christ, your Son, who lives and reigns with you and the Holy Spirit, one God, for ever and ever.

St. Noel Chabanel 1613–1649

Martyr of North America

Noel Chabanel was the last of the eight canonized North American martyrs to meet death in Huronia in Canada. He was born on February 2, 1613, in Sagues, southern France, and entered the Society of Jesus at Toulouse on February 9, 1630, at age seventeen. He followed the prescribed course of studies for Jesuits and after ordination taught rhetoric for several years in the Jesuit college in Toulouse.

Fr. Chabanel arrived in Quebec on August 15, 1643, but because the Iroquois Indians were on the warpath against the French, it was impossible for him to set out for Huronia. He thus spent a year studying the Huron language at Sillery, where the veteran missionary Fr. John de Brébeuf was in charge. Finally in August 1644, together with Fr. Brébeuf, he joined the Hurons as they returned to their territory, after the annual fur-trading expedition to Three Rivers. The missionaries arrived at Sainte-Marie in Huronia on September 7.

Though Fr. Chabanel was intelligent and an excellent teacher, he made little progress in language study. He was so accustomed to the refined sounds of French that the guttural sounds of the Huron language were offensive to him. His natural sensitivity revolted at the filth of the Indians among whom he had to live, and he could not adjust to their customs; thus, he unwillingly developed a loathing for them. In France he had longed for martyrdom; but now that he was among the Indians, he wished he were elsewhere. Whenever his nature pined for France, he responded by affirming his decision to remain in Huronia, even if it meant a new crucifixion each day. Understanding Fr. Chabanel's state of mind, his superior was willing for him to return home, but he chose to remain. It was through this gloom, this dark night that enveloped his soul, that God was trying the future martyr's fidelity. This internal torture lasted for a few years and on June 20, 1647, he generously promised God: "I vow perpetual stability in this Huron mission." He knew it was God that brought him there and hence he would remain.

Fr. Chabanel traveled with Fr. Brébeuf through the Indian villages, and from the winter of 1647 on, worked among the Algonquins at Sainte-Marie. In the fall of 1649 he was sent to Etarita to assist Fr. Charles Garnier in his work among the Petuns. As he was about to leave, he told his closest friend: "This time I hope to give myself to God once and for all and to belong entirely to him." The missionary's stay with Fr. Garnier lasted only a few weeks. The threat of the Iroquois was growing and it was rumored that they intended to annihilate the Petuns and burn their villages. In view of this threat, Fr. Garnier instructed Fr. Chabanel to return to the mission's center of operation. Obedient as always, Fr. Chabanel bade Fr. Garnier goodbye on December 5. That day he visited the Petun village of Saint-Matthias at Ekarreniondi and spent the nights of the 5th and 6th with the two priests stationed there. On the 7th he walked with his Huron companions a difficult eighteen miles through thick woodland and when night came the party rested. His companions soon fell asleep, but he stayed awake and prayed. Toward midnight he heard noises in the distance and as the sounds came nearer he recognized the victory songs of the Iroquois mingled with the sad cries of their captives. Unknown to him, Etarita had been attacked that afternoon and Fr. Garnier massacred by these same Iroquois. Fr. Chabanel awakened his companions, who then decided to return to Saint-Matthias. Because the priest was so worn out from fatigue and hunger, he was unable to keep up with them. At daybreak he continued his way to headquarters, as he had been ordered. He came to a river that was much too deep to cross, so he waited patiently on shore for help. An Indian found him there and took him into his canoe. The missionary, however, never reached the other shore, for the Indian, formerly a Christian but now an apostate, robbed him of his belongings, tomahawked him, and threw his body into the river.

Two years after the missionary's death, his murderer boasted that he had rid the world of a Frenchman and after killing him, disposed of the body by dumping it into the river. He also admitted that he had done this because of his hatred for the missionaries and their faith.

Fr. Chabanel died on December 8, 1649. Though his years among the Hurons were not as adventurous as some of his companions, and his death not as excruciating, nevertheless, the Lord accepted his noble offering to remain in the missions, though his natural inclination was to be elsewhere. With his death, God's acceptance of Fr. Chabanel was made complete.

With Fr. Charles Garnier and six other Jesuits, all of whom labored among the Hurons and met martyrs' deaths, Fr. Noel Chabanel was beatified by Pope Pius XI on June 21, 1925, and canonized on June 29, 1930. His memorial, with that of the other North American martyrs, is celebrated on October 19.

Prayer

Father, you consecrated the first beginnings of the faith in North America by the preaching and martyrdom of Saint Noel Chabanel and his companions. By the help of their prayers may the Christian faith continue to grow throughout the world. We ask this through our Lord Jesus Christ, your Son, who lives and reigns with you and the Holy Spirit, one God, for ever and ever.

December 9

S. G. Louis Stephen Rabussier 1831–1897

Louis Stephen Rabussier was born in Herblay, France, on December 12, 1831, and was a student at the diocesan seminary in Versailles, when he decided to enter the Society of Jesus. He began his novitiate on September 6, 1851, at Saint-Acheul and pronounced his first vows on September 8, 1853. For the next six years he taught in Poitiers, then Paris and Metz, and in 1860 began his theological course at Laval. He was ordained on September 19, 1863, and after completing his Jesuit studies, taught Scripture and Hebrew at Laval until 1866. Because his eyesight had become impaired, he gave up teaching and devoted his time to giving the Spiritual Exercises to religious communities throughout France.

From 1867 to 1884 Fr. Rabussier made his headquarters at the Jesuit residence in Bourges, and had great influence on the spiritual growth of a dozen or so religious communities through his annual retreats and monthly conferences. The congregations that specially benefitted from his knowledge of ascetical theology were the Trappists and Benedictines (both male and female branches), as well as Carmelites, the Religious of the Sacred Heart, and the Sisters of Nevers. He was a most understanding spiritual director and is said to have had the gift of reading hearts. He guided many young candidates to the diocesan clergy and to the religious life.

In 1879, while residing in Bourges, he formed an association of apostolically minded young ladies, who sought not only their own spiritual advancement but also desired to help others in need through a variety of charitable works. These ladies called themselves Zelatrices of the Sacred Hearts and, many of them eventually entered religious congregations. The idea of the Zelatrices spread quickly, and within a few years several French dioceses had a chapter. The success that came from this endeavor, however, did not meet with everyone's approval, especially among his own Jesuit brethren.

Fr. Rabussier's opponents argued that there was no need of another pious association, when so many were already in existence, e.g., Third Orders, the sodality, Children of Mary. But unlike these, the Zelatrices did not stop at personal sanctification as their goal, they were filled with zeal and wanted to help those less fortunate than they. Afraid that Fr. Rabussier's group would reduce the membership in the then existing associations, the opposition grew to such a point that the matter had to be referred to the Jesuit general in Rome. Fr. Pieter Beckx studied the matter and then wrote to Fr. Rabussier saying that he could not condemn a work of God and one that was accomplishing so much good, but he reminded him of the Jesuit rule forbidding members of the Society to have a women's spiritual organization totally dependent upon them, and thus, for the sake of peace, he asked Fr. Rabussier to stop promoting the association and to cease being its director. Fr. Rabussier obeyed immediately, and to make it easier for him, he was transferred to Rouen in September 1884.

During his eight years in Rouen, Fr. Rabussier worked intensely, giving missions, retreats, and the annual Lenten series of sermons. In 1889 he founded a congregation dedicated to the religious education of the young. Since priests and sisters were no longer permitted to teach religion in French schools and the children were without any catechetical instruction, this new foundation was meant to fill that need. His associate in this venture was Marie-Ignace Melin, and the name of the foundation was Congregation of the Holy Family of the Sacred Heart. The first members of this new congregation came from the Zelatrices.

Though Fr. Rabussier's health began to decline in 1892, he continued giving retreats, but not as many as before. In October 1897 he moved to Poitiers and there he suffered a stroke on November 23. Within a few days the paralysis spread to other parts of the body, and soon he was unable to move his jaw or to take food. He could hardly speak. Throughout this last days he repeated the names, "Jesus, Mary, Joseph," and the prayer "Mary, mother, my true mother, show yourself a mother to me." On the morning of December 9, shortly before 7:00 A.M., while his Jesuit brothers were saying the prayers for the dying, Fr. Rabussier, nineteenth-century France's great apostle of the interior life, left this world to be with his Lord. He was sixty-six years old and had been a Jesuit for forty-seven years. The investigation into his cause began in February 1950.

December 10

S. G. Peter Mayoral 1678–1754

Fr. Peter Mayoral, one of Chile's most famous missionaries, was born in Madrid, Spain, on October 16, 1678. He attended the Jesuit college in his native city and there he entered the Society on August 15, 1697. He left Spain the following year for the mission in Chile, was in Buenos Aires by the end of August 1698, and arrived in Santiago de Chile on March 4, 1699. After completing his studies in philosophy and theology, he was ordained in Santiago on July 26, 1708.

Though Fr. Mayoral's health was never robust, he lived an active missionary life, working among the Araucanian Indians in central Chile. For two centuries this warlike nation had successfully kept the Spaniards from converting and civilizing them. When their number decreased so that they could no longer oppose the colonizing foreigners, they finally permitted the Spaniards and missionaries to come among them. Fr. Mayoral's task was immense; not only was he to evangelize them, but he had to civilize them as well. He was their pastor and teacher; their physician and carpenter. Missionary life among the Araucanians was difficult and dangerous; death was always a possibility. He likewise knew that if he wanted to succeed in converting them, he would have to live among them, in the same poverty, eat the same food, and endure the same hardships. All this he gladly did.

Fr. Mayoral labored among the Araucanians mostly in and around San Cristóbal, a village south of Concepción. The strain of missionary life eventually took its toll and the priest's health broke. His superiors sent him to the college at Buena Esperanza (today's Rere), high in the Andes. There he kept himself busy doing pastoral work, but after a time he suffered from liver problems and stones. When the attacks came, he was forced to remain in bed, but as soon as he was able to be on his feet, he was visiting the sick or hearing confessions in the church. After five years of such suffering, he died with a prayer to St. Francis Xavier on his lips. It was December 9, 1754.

During Fr. Mayoral's lifetime, he was known for his humility and practice of poverty; the people reverenced him for his holiness of life and attributed to him the gifts of prophecy and reading of hearts. He was also looked upon as a miracle worker. When, during the earthquake of 1751, the Jesuit college at Buena Esperanza was spared, while everything around it had collapsed, the people attributed this to the missionary's prayers. Shortly after his death, the bishop of Concepción began collecting data on Fr. Mayoral's life; his cause was introduced in Rome in 1910.

December 11

S. G. Hyacinth Alegre 1874–1930

Fr. Alegre's name is associated with a hospital for the sick poor in Barcelona, Spain, a reminder that it was his love for the sick that brought that hospital into existence. Hyacinth Alegre Pujals was born in Tarrasa, on the outskirts of Barcelona, on December 24, 1874, as midnight was about to strike. He spent his first sixteen years in his native city and attended its Royal College. During his student days he became interested in the Jesuits, though there were none in Tarrasa. He had read a biography of Fr. Bernard de Hoyos, the young Jesuit who did much to promote devotion to the Sacred Heart of Jesus in Spain, and Hyacinth found Jesuit life appealing. When the Jesuit priest Ildephonse Roca came to Tarrasa to preach, Hyacinth went to speak with him. Upon graduating from the Royal College in 1891, he informed his mother—his father had died in 1888—that he wanted to become a Jesuit, but when she said that she couldn't bear losing her son, he entered the diocesan seminary in Barcelona instead. After a year at the seminary, his mother finally approved his entrance into the Society, and on August 30, 1892, Hyacinth was at the novitiate in Veruela.

He spent six years at Veruela's former Cistercian monastery, now the Jesuit house of studies. After two years of novitiate, he pronounced his religious vows, spent three years studying the humanities, and one studying philosophy. In 1898 he transferred to Tortosa to complete his philosophical course and in 1900 began teaching, first in Valencia, then in Barcelona. In 1904 he returned to Tortosa for theology and was ordained on July 30, 1907.

After completing tertianship, Fr. Alegre was assigned to the College of the Sacred Heart in Barcelona, and from 1909 to 1918 he carried out his tasks with great humility, supervising the students during their hours of study, recreation, and meals. He also taught mathematics to the youngest students. In 1918 he was named moderator of the students' sodality and was placed in charge of their religious formation. As he taught the young men to pray and love God, his own prayer life and his own love of God advanced. While acting as sodality moderator, he was also assigned to teach catechism to workers and to visit the sick in Barcelona's hospitals.

During these years Fr. Alegre developed a special love for the sick, which stayed with him for the remainder of his life. He daily visited one or another hospital, and became so well known among the people of Barcelona that they called him "Apostle to the sick." If he had a preference among the sick, it was for those who were poor and lonely, those without visitors or anyone to care for them. Fr. Alegre showed them his special attention, and when they were discharged, he continued to check on their recovery and needs. His priestly heart went out to the sick poor, he conceived the idea of a special hospital where charity cases could receive proper attention and care. He was contemplating what St. Joseph Cottolengo had achieved in Turin, Italy, in 1828, when he founded his Little House of Divine Providence, a hospital for the sick and unfortunate. In time this Turin institution became known as Cottolengo after its founder. Fr. Alegre had heard of Turin's Cottolengo and desired a similar institution in Barcelona. He visited Turin in 1927 to learn how that hospital operated and on his return to Spain, he began making plans and collecting funds. The hospital was completed after his death and was named Cottolengo del Padre Alegre. In addition to the one in Barcelona there are several others in Spain, each continuing the vision that Fr. Alegre had of offering proper health care to the sick poor.

At the beginning of December 1930, Fr. Alegre discovered a tumor in his nose, but thought nothing of it. When the tumor began to swell and cause him pain, he went to the infirmarian and was subsequently confined to his room. The physician saw him on the 6th, but confident that the priest would survive began to joke with him. Fr. Alegre, however, sensed that this illness was to take him to God. During the night of December 7 to 8 the tumor grew and caused him great pain, and on the 9th he was transferred to the infirmary. When the physician visited his patient, he suggested an operation, but when the surgeon saw him on the morning of the 10th, he discovered that the tumor's poison had already gone to the priest's brain, and that any operation would be useless. Death was imminent and the news of Fr. Alegre's condition spread through Barcelona. All during the 10th, visitors came to see him, family members as well as sodalists.

That evening about 7:00, the Jesuit rector began the prayers for the dying. Fr. Alegre's religious brethren brought him a relic of St. Theresa of the Little Flower, hoping for a miraculous cure, but the patient responded: "That's for others. I want to go to heaven." By 8:00 his breathing became more difficult and forty minutes later he peacefully went to heaven.

Fr. Hyacinth Alegre was first buried among his deceased Jesuit brethren, but in 1955 his remains were moved to the chapel of Barcelona's Cottolengo del Padre Alegre. His cause is presently under study.

December 12

Bl. Thomas Holland 1600–1642

Martyr of England

When the Prince of Wales visited Madrid in 1623 to bargain for the hand of the Infanta Maria, select students from the English colleges in Spain came to the city to greet their Prince Charles. For this happy occasion the young Thomas Holland, a seminarian at St. Alban's in Valladolid, was chosen to extend a welcome by delivering a Latin oration. Little did Thomas realize that the prince he was praising in Madrid would be the king for whom he would pray as he stood beneath the gallows waiting to be executed for his Catholic faith.

Thomas Holland was born in Sutton, near Prescot, in Lancashire, in 1600, and as a youth attended the English College at Saint-Omer in Flanders for six years. In August 1621 he traveled to Spain to attend the English College in Valladolid and in 1624 returned to Flanders where he entered the Society of Jesus. He made his novitiate at Watten and did his theological studies at Liège where he was ordained. He returned to Saint-Omer to be the seminarian's spiritual director, and because his knowledge of the ascetical life was vast, the students dubbed him "Library of Piety." Fr. Holland then spent a brief period in Ghent, but because of poor health, he was, in 1635, assigned to the English mission, with the hope that his health would improve in his native air.

The transfer to England did not help his health. Because of the difficult conditions in which he had to live, it only grew worse. With many priest-hunters in London who eagerly sought to betray a priest for the reward it would earn them, Fr. Holland had to stay indoors during the day and carry on his ministry at night or in the early morning. He could not even walk in the garden of the house where he stayed. Of necessity he became a master of disguises and used the names Saunderson and Hammond as aliases. Being fluent in French, Flemish, and Spanish, he often passed himself off as a foreigner. The many hardships he had to endure resulted in a loss of appetite which, in turn, brought on poorer health. Nevertheless, during his seven years in England his wretched health never interfered with his ministry.

On October 4, 1642, as he was returning from a sick call, Fr. Holland was arrested on suspicion of being a priest. He was detained at New Prison in London for two weeks, then transferred to Newgate when it was time for his trial. While in prison he rarely used his bed for sleeping and often spent the night in prayer, but was always careful not to give the jailer any opportunity to conclude from his actions that he was a priest. His trial took place at the Old Bailey on December 7, when four witnesses claimed that he was a Catholic priest, though no proof was brought forth to confirm their testimony. When asked to swear that he was not a priest, he refused; and the jury subsequently found him guilty. He was again in court on Saturday, December 10, to receive his sentence, and on hearing that it was death, he said: "Thanks be to God." Back in his cell he invited the Catholics there to join him in singing the *Te Deum*, the great hymn of thanksgiving.

Fr. Holland had but two days to live. Visitors came and asked to have their intentions remembered and the French ambassador offered to intervene with the king, but the priest preferred martyrdom to freedom. On Sunday Capuchin friends brought him the articles necessary for Mass and, thus, he celebrated Mass in his cell that day and early Monday morning as well.

About mid-morning of the 12th, he was dragged to Tyburn for execution. When he arrived he found a crowd standing in silence, waiting for him to speak. He began: "I have been brought here to die as a traitor, a priest, and a Jesuit; but in truth none of these things has been proved." He then mounted the cart, placed the noose about his neck, and again spoke to the people, telling them that he was truly a priest and a Jesuit, and that he pardoned the judge and jury that had condemned him. He recited acts of faith, hope, charity, and contrition, and then prayed for King Charles I, the royal family, parliament, and the nation "for whose prosperity and conversion to the Catholic faith, if I had as many lives as there are hairs on my head, drops of water in the ocean, or stars in the firmament, I would most willingly sacrifice them all." These words brought cheers from the crowd. He then turned to his executioner, forgave him for what he was about to do, and gave him the few coins he still had in his pocket. He shut his eyes in prayer, looked at a priest in the crowd, and received absolution. The cart was drawn from under him and he remained hanging until dead. His body was then beheaded and quartered and exposed on London bridge. He was forty-two years old and had been a Jesuit for eighteen years.

Fr. Thomas Holland was beatified by Pope Pius XI on December 15, 1929, and his memorial is kept on December 1.

Prayer

Almighty, eternal God, you chose from the people of England and Wales Blessed Thomas Holland and his companions to be made like Christ, who died to save the world. Listen to their prayers; strengthen your Church by the same faith and love that strengthened them, and bless it always with your gift of unity. We ask this through our Lord Jesus Christ, your Son, who lives and reigns with you and the Holy Spirit, one God, for ever and ever.

December 13

Ven. Francis de Paola Tarín 1847–1910

Since the revolutionaries in Spain had forced all religious orders to leave the country, Francis Tarín secretly crossed battlefields and headed toward France in order to reach Poyanne, a city just over the French border, where the Spanish Jesuits maintained a novitiate in exile. Francis knocked on the novitiate door and he asked to become a Jesuit. His arrival was unexpected; no one there knew anything about the twenty-six-year-old gentleman. The Jesuits, nevertheless, took him in, and after a short time he was admitted as a novice of the Society on October 30, 1873.

Francis, the ninth of eleven children, was born in the village of Godelleta, near Valencia, on October 7, 1847. He first attended his village school and then that of the Piarist Fathers in Valencia. In the summer of 1866, before beginning his study of law at the University of Valencia, he made a trip to Saragossa with his father and there visited the shrine of Our Lady of the Pillar. When he went forward to kiss the pillar, as all pilgrims were doing, he sensed something within him that made him desire to lead a different and better kind of life.

In Valencia in 1869, while studying law, Francis fell ill with a lung infection that brought him near death and forced him to interrupt his studies. He returned home and spent the next few years recuperating and helping his brothers in their textile business. As he grew older, he became more and more convinced that God wanted him to be a Jesuit. So on a Sunday morning, the last day of August 1873, without telling his parents—only his confessor knew his plans—Francis quietly left Valencia and started on his journey to the novitiate in exile in southern France. He arrived at Poyanne on October 9, forty days after he had left home and after he had traveled some 550 miles, mostly on foot.

On November 1, 1875, after two years of noviceship, Francis pronounced his vows of poverty, chastity, and obedience. In 1878 he returned to Spain to continue his studies in philosophy at the reopened scholasticate in Carrión de los Condes, in the diocese of Palencia. Next he went to Oña for theology and was ordained there on July 29, 1883.

While at Oña, Fr. Tarín began an apostolate among the poor that was to characterize his future as a priest. He and a companion organized an evening school for the men and boys who lived near the theologate. Besides teaching them reading, writing and basic mathematics, they also offered their students religious instruction and enrolled them in our Lady's sodality.

In 1884 Fr. Tarín left Oña to be assistant dean at Puerto de Santa María near Cádiz. One day, in a game with the students, a player missed kicking the ball and unintentionally gave Fr. Tarín a wicked blow in his right ankle. The resulting wound never healed; it grew continually worse and in the end was one of the causes of his death.

In September 1886 he was assigned to the Jesuit residence at Talavera de la Reina. There he directed the St. Vincent de Paul Society and in the following year went to Murcia for his tertianship, where he also acted as assistant to the master of novices. His move to Madrid in the summer of 1888 was the beginning of his many years of giving parish missions. These usually lasted eight to fifteen days, depending on the size of the parish, and he gave about thirty-five of these a year. His schedule during a mission was unbelievable. The day began with a 3:30 A.M. public recitation of the rosary in church or in procession through the village streets; this was followed by songs and prayers. Then he celebrated Mass and gave a sermon until it was time to teach catechism to the children. In the afternoon he visited the sick in their homes and in the hospitals; and if a prison was nearby, he went there to preach. He returned for the evening service to deliver another sermon and then went to the confessional, where he often remained well into the night. He usually got three to four hours of rest at night and the next morning he once again began the day with the public rosary.

Because of his heavy schedule and the ulcerated wound in his leg, Fr. Tarín was in need of rest, but he would not hear of it. His provincial, therefore, appointed him superior of the Jesuit house in Seville to lessen his labors.

Fr. Tarín arrived in Seville in September 1898 and remained there until August 1904, but he could not take it easy. He started evening classes for adults, organized a home to rehabilitate homeless women, continued visits to prisons and hospitals, and gave novenas in the parishes in the suburbs. What was meant to be a relatively easy position for a worn-out priest turned into a heavy workload, and in May 1904 his health broke. His leg caused him pain and, in addition, he contracted tuberculosis and pneumonia. On August 12, 1904, he left Seville to recuperate in Madrid. He arrived so ill that no one thought he would recover. Recover he did, and by the end of the month he was at Ciudad Real ready for work. In 1906 he gave twenty-six missions, in 1907 thirty-two, and in 1908 thirty-nine.

Fr. Tarín was back in Seville in 1909 to continue his missions in the countryside. Toward the end of 1910 he was in El Coronil conducting a mission. On its fourth day, while helping to rearrange choir benches for the children, he tripped and injured his already wounded leg. It began to bleed and when the physician saw it, he urged the priest to suspend the mission and go to bed. This Fr. Tarín would not do; he insisted on continuing the mission, though he had to rest his foot on a stool while he preached.

Because he could not be talked out of giving the next scheduled mission, he boarded the train and was on his way to Seville when the ticket collector accidentally bumped his bad leg and it began to hemorrhage. With great difficulty Fr. Tarín made it to the Jesuit residence and went to his room. This was November 21, 1910. His superior came to see him and forbade him to go to the next mission. Fr. Tarín obeyed, and now that he had to remain home, he spent the time making his own retreat. When the infirmarian saw Fr. Tarín's leg, he described it as a wound from ankle to knee, black and swollen like a leather bottle full of oil. The patient made his retreat sitting in his room with leg raised; he was not improving. His temperature rose, and on December 4 he celebrated his last Mass. His physician judged the case hopeless and Fr. Tarín began to prepare for death. On December 8 he received the last sacraments and before receiving Communion he asked the community to forgive his faults, his bad example, and his lack of progress in the spiritual life. Fr. Tarín's agony lasted three days during which he often prayed: "Heart of Jesus, burning with love for us, inflame our hearts with love for you." He died on December 12, 1910.

The sixty-three-year-old parish missioner was buried in the church of the Sacred Heart in Seville and the inscription on his tomb aptly calls him "Minister of the Gospel, unwearied worker for the salvation of souls." Fr. Francis Tarín's cause was introduced in Rome on November 14, 1934, and on January 3, 1987, the decree proclaiming his exercise of heroic virtue was promulgated.

December 14

S. G. Horace Vecchi 1577–1612

S. G. Martin de Aranda 1556–1612

S. G. James de Montalbán ?–1612

Martyrs of Chile

Three Jesuits, Frs. Horace Vecchi and Martin de Aranda Valdivia and Br. James de Montalbán, were martyred by the Araucanian Indians in Elicura, Chile, in the early part of the seventeenth century. Fr. Vecchi was born in Siena, Italy, on October 24, 1577. When he was sixteen he began law studies at the University of Siena, but in 1597 went to Rome, where he entered the Society on September 9. When his novitiate was over, he studied at the Roman College and, one day, as he listened to a Peruvian missionary describe the work of his brother Jesuits among the native population, he was inspired to request permission to work in Peru. He left Spain in April 1604 and arrived in Lima in early 1605. There he completed his studies and was ordained. In 1608 he went to the Arauco district in central Chile to work with the tribes that were at peace with the Spaniards. His missionary apostolate only lasted four years; his death did not come from the pacified Indians, whom he instructed, but from others who were still uncivilized.

Fr. Martin de Aranda was born about 1556 of Spanish parents in Villarrica in Araucanian territory. He had been a cavalry officer in the service of the king of Spain and headed an expedition that had gone as far north as Quito. He helped found the city of Riobamba, and was appointed its first governor by the viceroy of Peru. Recalled to Lima to receive a reward, he made the Spiritual Exercises and decided that the only service worthy of him was the service of God. Thus on March 12, 1592, he entered the Society of Jesus. Because he knew little Latin, he entered as a brother, but when his superiors evaluated his abilities, they instructed him to study theology in preparation for the priesthood. He was ordained in 1596 and was assigned to help Fr. Michael de Urrea in his work among the Chuncho Indians in the Peruvian Andes. But before he got near his destination, Fr. Urrea had been killed. Hence, Fr. Aranda was reassigned to his native Arauco district as chaplain to the Spanish garrison stationed there. He cared for the soldiers' spiritual needs and those of the Indians who lived nearby. The soldiers had been without a priest for several years; he therefore had much work to do. Within months of his arrival he had the soldiers attending Mass and receiving monthly Communion. He continued this work until 1612, when he and Fr. Vecchi were assigned to evangelize the more difficult Araucanian tribes in the Elicura valley.

In November 1612 the governor and Fr. Louis de Valdivia traveled into the valley hoping to negotiate a peace treaty with the still non-civilized Araucanians. They were successful and on November 26 some 400 Spaniards met with Araucanian caciques for the signing ceremony. Among the chiefs was the seventy-year-old Utablame, who took pride in the fact that in the past he had fought against seventeen different governors. He made it known that he was reluctant to give up the use of arms but because the conditions of the treaty were reasonable, he was willing to extend his hand in friendship. After Utablame accepted the treaty, others did likewise; and to show their good will, the caciques requested missionaries to live among them.

Some Spaniards suggested that the mission be postponed for a time because of the known hatred of one of the caciques, Anganamón. Just a few weeks before, three of his wives, one a Spanish captive and the other two Indian, together with their daughters, had escaped and sought refuge with the Spaniards. When Anganamón requested the return of his wives and daughters, he was told that the Spanish woman, who was a Christian, and the two Indian women, who became Christians, could not now return. The cacique returned to his people, but vengeance took hold of his heart. Foreseeing that Anganamón could cause trouble, the Spaniards thought it unwise to send missionaries to their death. But the Jesuit provincial thought otherwise and, thus, he assigned Frs. Vecchi and Aranda and Br. James de Montalbán to Elicura.

Br. Montalbán was still a novice; he had been born in Mexico, had been a tailor and had served in the Spanish army in Lima and Chile. He entered the Society in October 1612, and after being a Jesuit for only two months, was sent on his first missionary endeavor.

On December 14, five days after the three missionaries had arrived at their mission in Elicura, Anganamón, with some 100 young braves, unexpectedly appeared before them and demanded his wives and daughters. When the missionaries answered that the women were now Christians and wanted to remain among the Spaniards, the chief gave the order for his braves to fall upon them. Fr. Vecchi suffered a lance wound in the throat, two axe strokes over his right ear and two in his torso. Fr. Aranda's head was smashed and his body beaten with clubs. Br. Montalbán had his head crushed and received six lance wounds in his body and an axe wound in his throat. When the Indians had finished, they left the stripped bodies for the birds and wild animals to prey upon.

The Spaniards recovered the bodies of the three Jesuits soon afterwards and took them to their garrison where Fr. Louis de Valdivia celebrated their requiem. These were the first martyrs of Chile and their cause is now under investigation.

December 17

S. G. Stephen Kaszap 1916–1935

Stephen Kaszap was a novice when he died; he had not yet reached his twentieth birthday, but had proven himself a young hero of suffering. He was born on March 25, 1916, in Székesfehérvár, Hungary, the ancient Alba Regia of the Romans. He was a stubborn child, so his mother described him, easily angered, and always insisting on his own way. Only after his parents had threatened him with the police did he go to school. After four years in an elementary school, he attended St. Stephen's, an institution operated by Cistercians. His scholastic performance during his early years was uneven, but when he entered his teens things began to change. Stephen now controlled his temper, became serious-minded, and improved in his studies so that in his final years he was among the top students of his class. During these years he kept a journal, jotting down not only ordinary events, but also his growth in the spiritual life. Passages from this diary reveal a spiritual maturity rare in one so young. With regard to his success in studies he wrote: "My work is directed by the word of God; the faithful accomplishment of my duty."

At age fifteen Stephen joined the sodality and began attending daily Mass in the church adjacent to the school. His life at St. Stephen's was not all books. He was a scout and enjoyed camping out; furthermore, he was an athlete, an exceptional gymnast. During his final year he participated in the national gymnastic competition for secondary schools held in Budapest and placed fourth. When he returned home, he carried with him four gold, three silver, and seven bronze medals. The day of his greatest athletic triumph, however, was March 17, 1934, when another competition was held in his native city. He won all prizes and was declared "champion" of Western Hungary. Stephen held success in his hands, but this was not an occasion for pride; he looked upon his performance with uncommon modesty and humility. In his journal, under the date of April 19, 1934, he asked himself: "What will make a man happy?" In his answer he rejects wealth, glory, and pleasure, and adds: "Interior joy is a tender and delicate flower which withers in hearts that are maddened by money, poisoned by honors, and hardened by pleasure. It blooms in all its beauty in noble souls that know but a single end, the loftiest, the holiest, 'Eternal God'."

Stephen had always wanted to be a priest, but he never thought about which order he would like to enter. In the spring of 1934, during the school retreat, he read Bishop Ottokár Prohászka's *Ways and Stations*. He especially wanted to read the book, because Prohászka had been Bishop of Székesfehérvár, and had only died in 1927. In one of its chapters, the bishop reflects on his happy days at the German-Hungarian College in Rome and his studies with the

Jesuits. Stephen felt that the Jesuit life would suit him and the inclination soon became a decision.

He entered the novitiate outside Budapest, on July 30, 1934. He was eighteen years old. He was robust in appearance and photographs show him a handsome young man. A good part of his novitiate days, however, were days of suffering, the result of a disease that slowly undermined his strength. He now called upon the courage, discipline, and self-control he had acquired in becoming a champion gymnast, to suffer with joy and resignation.

Sometime before Christmas 1934, Stephen's ankles became swollen, his joints ached, and he could hardly walk. Ulcers appeared on his fingers, neck, and face. Then his tonsils became inflamed and he burned with fever. His journal tells us his inner feelings: "The cross that God gives is to be borne willingly and cheerfully." "A little sickness does much more for us than ten or twenty years of health." Stephen recovered but in the following January the ulcers reappeared and the fever returned. Subsequently a series of nosebleeds plagued him until a minor surgical operation sealed the vein. Then a large red ulcerous patch appeared on his left thigh and the brother infirmarian, fearing that it might be erysipelas, immediately called the physician. The doctor lanced the ulcer and treated it for a day, but it continued to increase in size and Stephen was anointed and taken to the hospital where he underwent an operation on March 19, 1935.

He recovered somewhat and returned to the novitiate, but his tonsils again caused him distress and the ulcers reappeared. Amid this pain he had the calmness of soul to pen his spiritual testament, which begins: "Most Sacred Heart of Jesus, grant that I may renounce myself more and more; I wish to keep nothing for myself, neither my prayers nor my pains." The date was October 18, 1935. When the ulcers cleared and he felt a bit better, the physician suggested that his native air might do him good, so on November 3, Stephen returned home to be with his family. He took his Greek books with him and spent a few days studying, but on the 8th the fever again took hold of him and ulcers once more covered his body. He was taken to the hospital near home where it was confirmed that he had erysipelas. After two weeks in quarantine Stephen was discharged.

Because he seemed on the mend, the physician at home recommended that he now have his tonsils removed, and so Stephen went to the hospital in Budapest and was operated on December 4. He returned to his parents' home on the 14th, thinking that with the cause of his illness now gone, he would soon return to health. But this was not to be. That night he became chilled and fever attacked his body. The doctor examined him on the 16th and, suspecting that a tumor was growing in Stephen's throat, had him taken to the hospital that afternoon. The patient could no longer speak, nor eat; the tumor was strangling him. All night long he fought against suffocation; though tears flowed from his eyes, he kept them fixed on the crucifix in his hand. Finally, at 3:00 A.M. on the 17th, the surgeon made an opening in his larynx and inserted a tube to ease his breathing. When Stephen revived, he wrote on the bed cover with his finger "I want a priest." The sister caring for him judged that he was no longer in danger of death and so she disregarded his request. The nurses changed at 5:00 A.M., and seeing that there was a different sister at his bed, he wrote her a note. "I am unable to go to confession. I only want absolution. I cannot receive Communion, because I cannot swallow. I want Extreme Unction." The sister immediately went for the priest who lived next door to the hospital, but by the time he arrived Stephen had already lost consciousness. The priest absolved and anointed him and remained with him until he heard Stephen's final gasp. It was 6:10 A.M., December 17, 1935. In his hands Stephen clasped his crucifix and a medal of our Lady.

It was after Stephen had died that they found a note containing his final words, presumably written shortly before he became unconscious. The note was intended for his parents. "Good-bye. We shall meet on high. Do not weep. It is my birthday in heaven. God bless you."

Stephen's resignation in suffering and heroic acceptance of the Divine Will was never forgotten. Convinced that Stephen was living with God, the people of Székesfehérvár brought their petitions to him, asking his intercession with God in their behalf. Many of these petitions were answered, so the diocese, within six years of Stephen's death, initiated the canonical process investigating his life and virtues.

December 21

Ven. Thomas Bedingfeld 1617–1678

Thomas Bedingfeld, whose family name was Downes, was born in Norfolk, England, in 1617. Since it was impossible to get a Catholic education in England at the time, he went (probably in 1630) to study at the English College in Saint-Omer, Flanders. From there he moved (1636) to the English College in Valladolid, Spain, and after a year returned to Flanders, it seems, and then entered the Society on January 8, 1639. He was twenty-two years old. After novitiate at Watten, Thomas did his philosophical course at Liège, and theology at Pont-à-Mousson in Lorraine. After ordination in 1645 he returned to Watten, where he was treasurer for several years. He was then transferred to Liège to be minister of the college and then to Ghent as spiritual father and vice-rector. He spent the next six years as his province's procurator in Brussels and in 1670 returned to England.

In England he used the name Bedingfeld—his mother's name—and was assigned as chaplain and confessor to the duke of York, King Charles II's

Catholic brother. Between July and September 1678, unknown to the Jesuits in London, Titus Oates and Israel Tonge, out of hatred for the Society, fabricated a plot designed to destroy them. A packet of five forged letters was sent to Fr. Bedingfeld at Windsor Castle, where the duke of York was attending his brother at court; the letters supposedly came from the Jesuit provincial and other London Jesuits, but were actually sent by Oates and Tonge. The letters directed that the king's assassination should be carried out at the first convenient opportunity and that this information should be kept from the duke. Oates and Tonge had arranged for the packet of letters to be intercepted and thus bring this "popish plot" into broad daylight.

On September 1, 1678, Fr. Bedingfeld happened to visit the Windsor Post Office shortly after the packet arrived, and seeing that it was addressed to him, took it. The letters surprised him; they were written in an unfamiliar hand, were filled with misspellings, and certainly not from those whose names appeared on them. He judged the contents had to be false; nevertheless, he took them to the duke, who in turn, passed them on to the king, who acknowledged that he had heard about such a supposed plot but assured the duke that the letters were forgeries and that Fr. Bedingfeld had no share in the scheme. The Jesuit then took them to his provincial, Fr. Thomas Whitbread, since they supposedly came from him and other London Jesuits. Upon reading the letters Fr. Whitbread foresaw a new persecution of the Society and in this he was correct.

Though King Charles II viewed the letters as forgeries, nevertheless, he yielded to popular fury and parliamentary pressure and permitted the sixty-one-year-old Fr. Bedingfeld to be arrested and taken to Gatehouse Prison on November 3, 1678, and to be interrogated by the Privy Council. The priest's health was already poor and the foulness of the prison aggravated it further, so that before he could come to trial, at which he would most certainly have been condemned to death, he died on December 21, 1678. He was declared Venerable by Pope Leo XIII in 1886.

December 23

S. G. William Eberschweiler 1837–1921

The Eberschweiler family had seven children, and William, who was born in Püttlingen, Germany, on December 5, 1837, was the eldest of five sons. When he was still a child, his family moved to Bitburg and there William attended the parish school. For his secondary education he went in 1851 to Trier and lived in a diocesan-sponsored student residence. During his days in Trier, he received a letter from a friend who had entered the Vincentians in Paris. The letter described the joys of religious community life, and so beautifully did the friend draw the picture that William began to think about joining the Vincentians. However, during the annual retreat, given by a Jesuit, he changed his mind and now decided to become a Jesuit. William's brother Fritz was also at Trier and made the same retreat, and independent of William, he also decided to enter the Society, though up to now he had looked forward to a military career. Both brothers entered the Jesuit novitiate at Friedrichsburg, near Münster, on September 30, 1858. Fritz later came to the United States and worked as a missionary among the Indians in Montana. Two younger brothers also became Jesuits; one of them, Charles, came to the United States, and first worked among Indians, but later became spiritual director at a diocesan seminary in Columbus, Ohio, and there died.

Because William's health was somewhat fragile, he twice had to interrupt his novitiate. During his first absence from the house he spent two months at Göttendorf, but for his second he went to Feldkirch, Austria, where he helped prefect students. He finally took his three vows of religion on January 6, 1861. He spent 1862 at Münster studying the humanities and in the following year began philosophy at Aachen. In 1866 he went to Maria Laach for theology and was ordained there on September 13, 1868.

Young Fr. Eberschweiler returned to Aachen in September 1868 to direct our Lady's sodality, and in 1870 was transferred to Gorheim, near Sigmaringen. He went there to be assistant to the master of novices, but before a year had passed he was made master and remained there until December 1872, when the novitiate was closed by the *Kulturkampf,* an anti-Catholic movement originating in Prussia. The German Jesuits found refuge in France, Italy, and the Netherlands, and Fr. Eberschweiler became rector of the exiled German juniorate in Wijnandsrade, Netherlands. He served as rector until September 1876 when he became spiritual director of the young Jesuits in the same community. In 1884 he went to England as spiritual director of the theological students at Ditton Hall and after six years returned to Wijnandsrade. When the juniorate moved to nearby Exaten in 1894, Fr. Eberschweiler moved with it and remained the juniors' spiritual director until his death.

For more than forty-five years Fr. Eberschweiler was a spiritual guide to his younger Jesuit brethren. He was especially qualified for this task, for God had granted him many extraordinary graces and, thus, he was well endowed to instruct others in prayer, in the religious life, and how to advance in the love of God.

In December 1917 when he was in his eightieth year, he was hospitalized. A swelling appeared on his right hand and when it would not respond to ordinary treatment his physician diagnosed it as a growth that had to be operated on.

The operation took place but the malady somehow lingered and the hand would not heal. Since there was no improvement, the physician suggested that the top portion of the thumb be amputated. Fr. Eberschweiler, however, requested that the operation be postponed until he had a chance to make a novena to St. Francis Xavier. The novena was answered, but circuitously. On the last day of the novena, he woke up with a high fever; he had pneumonia and the amputation had to be put off. When the pneumonia passed, the surgeon postponed the operation because he had to be out of town for several days. When he returned he found the thumb so improved that the amputation was no longer necessary. The thumb remained stiff as did the fingers of the hand, but the priest was again able to celebrate Mass.

After five months in the hospital, Fr. Eberschweiler returned to his community and lived a semi-retired life. He knew that death was not far off, and on December 11, 1921, he wrote: "The Lord is near! The Lord is near! Rejoice, again I say rejoice, but in the Lord!" While celebrating Mass on the 16th he suddenly began to tremble and a great weakness came over him. Then his lungs began to fill and his worn-out body was no longer able to fend off infection. When told that his condition was serious, his calm remark was: "I am ready." He became progressively weaker and on the 22nd he was, for the most part, only able to repeat the prayers that the priest, who sat next to his bed, recited for him. But then to the priest's surprise, Fr. Eberschweiler asked him to write a letter to a priest-friend in the United States. In the letter he told his friend that for the past thirty years Jesus had personally promised him, not once, but countless times, that his death would be happy and peaceful. He now had no doubt of it and with death approaching, he looked forward to it with great calm and even desire. He also mentioned that our Lady had given him the same assurance as did her Son. He ended the letter by asking his friend to remember him in his prayers. On the following morning, December 23, with firm assurance in God's presence at his hour of death, Fr. Eberschweiler peacefully entered eternity.

He was buried on December 25 in the Jesuit cemetery in Exaten. Then in May 1958 his remains were transferred to Trier, where they were interred in the seminary church. His cause is presently in Rome undergoing the usual investigation.

December 25

Bl. Michael Nakashima 1583–1628

Martyr of Japan

Michael Nakashima was born in Machiai, in today's prefecture of Kumamoto, Japan, ca. 1583, of non-Christian parents. When he was eleven he was baptized by Fr. John Baptist de Baeza, and later on, as a young man, he took a private vow of chastity and lived a life of piety and penance. Because the Christian religion had been proscribed in Japan and the missionaries had to go underground, Michael invited Fr. Baeza to live with him in his home in Nagasaki. The priest remained in hiding there for twelve years. When Fr. Baeza died in 1626, Michael invited another priest into his home. He was aware that he was taking great risks, but it was worth it; he had the joy of frequently attending Mass. While the priests were with him he brought Christians to his house almost nightly, by circuitous routes to confuse the spies, and there they received the sacraments. Michael was once suspected of helping missionaries, but nothing came of the charge. He continued his activity, though the risk was growing greater. Sometime in 1627 he was received into the Society as a brother. In August of that year he was brought before the district governor and though nothing was proven against him, he was placed under house arrest for a year. He accepted the sentence with serenity and continued to live his penitential way of life.

It was the custom in Nagasaki that when an execution was to take place the people of the city were expected to supply the faggots for the fiery punishment. On September 3, 1628, a wood collector called at Br. Nakashima's house, but he refused to contribute, saying that he wanted no part in the unjust killing of a minister of God. His remark was passed on to the governor and shortly thereafter he was apprehended, his house confiscated, and he was sent to a prison in Shimabara. He was stripped and was beaten with clubs to get him to deny his faith. But through it all he would not deny his Lord. He told them: "Tear me to pieces and rip my soul from my body, but you will never force that detestable word of denial from my mouth."

When this form of torture did not produce the desired effect, the prison guards resorted to the loathsome water torture. Br. Nakashima was forced to lie down; he was then gagged and funnels were placed in his nostrils through which gallons of water were forced into his body. The brutes then jumped on his abdomen to force the water out. This procedure was repeated several times, but the Jesuit remained undaunted and refused to apostatize. Writing about this experience to a friend, he said: "When the pain became too intense, I invoked our Lady, the Blessed Virgin, and my pain instantly ceased."

Br. Nakashima's constancy enraged his persecutors to greater ferocity and in the middle of December they decided he should experience the scalding sulphurous waters at Unzen. The Japanese called the place "the mouths of hell." There was an extinct volcano at Unzen, whose seething waters formed several surging pools in the crater. It was to these that he was taken. His torture began on December 24, 1628. His tormentors first subjected him to a repetition of the water torture, then they dragged him into a shallow pool of the bubbling waters. They made him stand there for a time and when they took him out to place him into a deeper pool portions of his flesh fell from his feet. He was then put into a second pool and after a while he was led to a still deeper one, where the water came up to his neck. When he was finally pulled from this last pool he was unable to walk; his body was one open wound, and in places his bones were exposed. Thus they left him to spend that cold December night in the open, lying on hay that was meant to be his bed.

Early the next morning, as soon as the sun rose, the torturers were again at his side, but because Br. Nakashima was unable to stand and go into the boiling water, they devised a way of pouring the scalding fluid over his head and body. For two hours he endured this treatment and the only words that came from his lips were the names of Jesus and Mary. While the Christian world was thinking of Christ's birth on earth, Br. Nakashima was thinking of his own birth in heaven, and that morning he made his way to God.

Br. Michael Nakashima was beatified by Pope Pius IX in 1867, together with 204 other martyrs. His Jesuit brethren honor him and the other Jesuits who died in the same persecution, on February 4.

Prayer

Almighty God, grant that this remembrance of your martyr, Blessed Michael Nakashima, may bring us joy. May we who depend upon his prayers glory in his entry into heaven. We ask this through our Lord Jesus Christ, your Son, who lives and reigns with you and the Holy Spirit, one God, for ever and ever.

December 28

S. C. Olegario Corral 1871–1936

S. G. Martial Mayorga 1902–1936

Martyrs of the Spanish Civil War

Numbered among the many priests and religious martyred in Spain during that country's civil war, are the Jesuits Frs. Olegario Corral García and Martial Mayorga Paredes.

Fr. Corral was the elder of the two. He was born on September 17, 1871, at Sando, near Salamanca, and spent four years at Salamanca's diocesan seminary before entering the Society of Jesus at Loyola on June 15, 1889. He passed through the usual course of studies in the Society: humanities and philosophy, teaching at the University of Comillas, then theology and ordination. In 1907 he was appointed to teach grammar and rhetoric at Salamanca and then from 1908 to 1918 at Carrión de los Condes. From there he went to lecture in philosophy at Comillas. Whatever time he had free from class, he devoted to preaching and writing.

On August 12, 1936, revolutionaries from Santander's Popular Front forced their way into the university and took it over. Together with other Jesuits and students, Fr. Corral was taken to Santander and temporarily detained in an improvised prison. A few days later, along with three Jesuits and several seminarians and students, he moved into a Santander boarding house and kept himself busy preparing new editions of his books. During the first months of civil war he heard about the killing of priests and religious and realized that death could come to him at any moment.

At 11:00 A.M. on December 27, 1936, as Fr. Corral was walking along a Santander street, he heard the siren blare forth and he hastened to the nearest shelter. When the all-clear sounded and he was about to leave with the others, he was recognized by one of the police as being a priest. He was thus arrested and eventually taken before one of the revolutionary leaders in Santander.

His friends searched for him all that day and the next. Finally, on the evening of the 28th, after visiting several prisons and places of detention, they located him in another boarding house, but the guard on duty would not permit them to see him. When asked if Fr. Corral needed anything, the guard suggested that they could bring him food. They brought food that evening, but were never sure that the priest had tasted it. They returned the following morning with breakfast, but when they asked about Fr. Corral's condition, the guard merely told them that he was released during the night. After Fr. Corral's disappearance on August 28, no one ever heard anything more about him. It was presumed that he, like many other martyrs, had been shot and his body thrown over the steep cliffs near the lighthouse.

Fr. Mayorga was born on July 7, 1902, in Mazuecos, in the province of Palencia. Following the example of his older brother, Balthasar, he enrolled at the Comillas diocesan seminary in 1915 and studied there for six years. Rather than continue his plans to become a diocesan priest, he chose to become a Jesuit and entered the Society's novitiate at Carrión de los Condes on December 2, 1921, and there pronounced his vows in 1923. He then did his course in philosophy at Oña (1923–1926) taught for four years at Carrión de los Condes (1926–1930), and returned to Oña for his theological studies. When the Society was dissolved in Spain by government order in 1932, he went to Portugal and completed his Jesuit formation at Entre-Os-Rios. After ordination he returned to the University of Comillas in 1936 to teach biology and natural history.

Fr. Mayorga was in Spain only a few weeks when civil war erupted in July. On August 12 he was arrested with other Jesuits and with his brother Balthasar, who taught canon law at the seminary, and was taken to a makeshift prison in Santander. Through the intervention of a friend, the Mayorga brothers were released on August 15 and subsequently resided with a friend in Santander. The brothers were again arrested on October 11 and taken before a revolutionary judge, who ordered them imprisoned. On October 14 they were led from prison and on the following day shot to death on the Camargo plain. Their bodies were discovered and identified in October 1937. The investigation into the martyrdoms of Fr. Olegario Corral and Fr. Martial Mayorga opened in Santander on May 26, 1956.

December 30

S. G. John Peter Médaille 1610–1669

John was born on October 6, 1616, in Carcassone, in southern France. His was a well-to-do family, "famille de robe"; his father was the king's attorney in the Carcassone courts. Nothing is known of John's early education, but because of the family's position he may have had private tutors. When the Society opened its school in Carcassone in October 1623, John enrolled and studied with the Jesuits for three years. On September 15, 1626, he entered the novitiate in Toulouse, and after two years of learning about prayer and what a Jesuit's life should be, he pronounced his first vows.

In September 1628 John passed to the juniorate to study rhetoric, but by then Toulouse was besieged by the plague. A pestilence had hit the city in August and by the end of September it was raging more fiercely than ever. The city's health officials, having no other alternative, advised all to leave. While the Jesuit priests helped care for the afflicted, the students—juniors, philosophers, and theologians—moved in early October to a farm in Lardenne, less than three miles away. Among the theological students with John at Lardenne was John Francis Regis, whose successor as an itinerant missioner in France's mountainous Velay and Vivarais regions he would one day become. When the plague gave signs of petering out in August 1629, the community returned to Toulouse and John began his study of philosophy.

John returned to his alma mater in Carcassone to teach grammar for a couple of years before retracing his steps to Toulouse for his theological course. He was ordained in 1637 after two years of theology and was assigned to the school in Aurillac, where he directed the sodality and was minister of the Jesuit community, in charge of temporal affairs. Fr. Médaille spent a total of five years in Aurillac, but during his final year (1641–1642) he assisted Fr. Jerome Sauret in giving parish missions throughout the Saint-Flour diocese.

After a year's experience on the road as an itinerant home missioner, it was time for tertianship, which he made in Toulouse (1642–1643). Among his fellow tertians was Noel Chabanel, who shortly thereafter sailed for Quebec to work among the Huron Indians and was martyred in 1649.

The Society opened its school in Saint-Flour in 1643 and Fr. Médaille was in the group of Jesuits who inaugurated it. He was minister of the community and students' confessor. His apostolic work, however, was not limited to the confines of the school buildings, he also preached and heard confessions in various city churches and in nearby towns and villages. During his five years in Saint-Flour, he gained a reputation as a compelling preacher and discerning director of souls.

From 1650 onward Fr. Médaille was exclusively involved in traveling about giving missions in several of France's southern dioceses. The years between 1650 and 1654 were spent working out of the Jesuit residence in Aurillac, and the remaining fifteen years of his life were spent in the diocese of Clermont and adjoining dioceses. Most missions were in country places, spread out over a vast mountainous area of the Auvergne. It was difficult getting to them even in fine weather, and next to impossible when the weather was less than favorable. Fr. Médaille and his Jesuit companion usually walked from parish to parish, regardless of the climate. The length of the mission depended on the area's needs; he sometimes spent several days in a place and sometimes two weeks.

The mission's day was taken up with various tasks: there was an early morning sermon, Mass, instruction for the first communicants, catechism for the other children in the afternoon, and when the workers returned from the fields, a sermon for them in the evening. Most of the in-between hours were spent in the confessional and often late into the night. He visited the old and sick in their homes and sometimes went into the fields to instruct the shepherds. The mission always ended on Sunday with a General Communion.

During his missions Fr. Médaille had come to know some widows and young ladies who would have liked to have entered religion, but had neither the education nor the dowry to do so. Because there were many of these devout women interested in serving God and their neighbor, Fr. Médaille conceived what he called his "little design." These ladies would live in small groups of three to six; they would wear no distinctive garb, nor would there be cloister, but they would visit the sick and aged in their homes. He put this plan into effect about 1646 and wrote a rule for them. But since he was always on the road, traveling, preaching, and giving missions, these groups would need a stabilizing element.

Sometime before 1648 Fr. Médaille visited the new bishop of Le Puy, Henry de Maupas, and informed him of his "little design." The bishop was immediately enthusiastic and offered Fr. Médaille's group of ladies an old hospice near the cathedral that they might use as a residence for homeless children. The bishop officially visited the six ladies on October 15, 1650, and accepted them under his protection. Thus was born the Congregation of the Sisters of St. Joseph. While Fr. Médaille continued his itinerant missionary apostolate, the bishop kept his watchful eyes on the growing congregation. The Jesuit founder, however, never forgot his "little design." He wrote (ca. 1654) the congregation's constitutions, which are a blend of Ignatian and Salesian spirituality. The founder's particular spiritual charism is encapsulated in his *Maxims of Perfection for Souls Aspiring to High Virtue.*

Since Fr. Médaille's health had been gradually on the decline, his superior judged he needed a rest and in October 1669 assigned him to the Jesuit college at Billom as students' confessor. He was there but three months when he died on December 30. A contemporary, writing Fr. Médaille's obituary said: "He spent a good part of his life giving missions in the province, and gained such a reputation for zeal and holiness, that people often referred to him as 'the saint' and 'the apostle.' His apostolic labors likewise bore much fruit, so much so that he was beloved not only by the poor, but also by the wealthy, and was especially beloved by the bishops in whose dioceses he worked."

December 31

St. John Francis Regis 1597–1640

Fr. John Francis Regis was a crusader—his armor was his black cassock and the country to be reconquered was his own native land. He was born in Fontcouverte, in southern France, on January 31, 1597. He attended the Jesuit school in Béziers from 1611 to 1616, and in his final year decided to become a Jesuit. He entered the novitiate at Toulouse on December 7, 1616, and when he had completed his noviceship, he moved to Cahors for a year's study of the humanities, then to Tournon for philosophy. Before advancing to theology, he taught grammar at Le Puy and Auch. He went to Toulouse for his final preparation for the priesthood and while he was there a dreadful plague ravaged the city and the seminarians had to be sent into the country. John asked to assist in caring for the plague-stricken, but that was work for priests and not scholastics. Living conditions in the improvised country theologate were crowded and the seminarians shared rooms. Thus, John's roommate witnessed how, after only a few hours of sleep, he rose to spend the remainder of the night in prayer. It was John's closeness to God that prepared him to be the great apostle that he eventually became. The seminarians, in due time, returned to Toulouse and John was ordained on May 19, 1630. That summer a milder form of the plague returned, and Fr. Regis went among the sick like an angel of peace, healing bodies as well as souls. His companion in this mission became infected and died, but Fr. Regis was spared.

The first assignment of Fr. Regis after he finished his Jesuit formation was to teach at Pamiers, and on holidays he joined his fellow Jesuits in various apostolic works in the diocese. He proved an excellent missionary and, thus, was sent to Montpellier in 1632 to help the bishop recall the Catholics of that diocese to the practice of their faith. There was nothing outstanding in any of the actions of Fr. Regis during the eight years he traveled as a home missioner, but the results were extraordinary. France still suffered from the sad effects of the Wars of Religion—that civil strife between French Calvinists and Catholics. Since a good portion of southern France had been under the control of the Huguenots, the Catholics in those areas had been forced to abandon the practice of their faith. Their churches had been destroyed and their priests slain. Now that peace returned to the country, it was the task of the home missioner to rekindle the faith that had once been there.

After two years in the diocese of Montpellier, Fr. Regis went in 1634 to Viviers at the bishop's request, and then for the remaining years of his life he went from town to town, in diocese after diocese, climbing mountain after mountain to carry God's message to those who eagerly awaited it. Whether it was a town or a village, he tried to remain in the parish for several days. His sermons were simple and unadorned, but were sincere and flowed from a heart close to God. Besides preaching, he heard confessions, celebrated Mass, and catechized the children. He consoled the disturbed of heart, visited prisons, collected food and clothing for the poor, and also founded homes for former prostitutes so that they might be rehabilitated.

Sometime in mid-December 1640, Fr. Regis had an intimation that he was soon to die. He interrupted the mission he was giving at Montregard and hastened to Le Puy, his headquarters. There he told a fellow Jesuit, "I have interrupted my mission to prepare for death," and went on to say that he would spend the next three days in retreat and then make a general confession of his entire life; this confession would be his last. When his triduum of prayer was over, he was asked to remain in Le Puy for a few days more, but his answer was: "The Master does not wish it." Together with Br. Claude Bideau, his companion, he set out on December 17, reached Montregard that day, and continued the mission. The two Jesuits left Montregard on December 23 to go to Lalouvesc, the site of the next mission, which was to begin that night. On their way snow began to fall, and as darkness approached, they lost their way and wandered for hours in the woods. They eventually found a battered shack that provided them temporary shelter from the freezing cold. The next morning, the day before Christmas, they started for Lalouvesc. When they arrived at the village church, they were surprised to learn that the people had been waiting since the night before. Rather than taking a few minutes to eat and rest, Fr. Regis immediately went to the pulpit and preached. He then heard confessions and celebrated Mass. He returned to the confessional and remained there until he had to stop to celebrate the Midnight Mass. Christmas Day was spent in the confessional as was most of the 26th. It was not until 2:00 P.M. of the 26th that he was free to offer another Mass. Unable to reach the confessional after Mass because of the crowd that filled the church, he heard confessions in the sanctuary.

Above the chair where Fr. Regis was sitting there was a broken window and the cold December air blew directly upon him. Later in the afternoon, in the midst of a confession, he collapsed and had to be taken to the pastor's home. When he regained consciousness, the people again insisted on going to confession, though he was lying in bed. When he lapsed into unconsciousness a second time, it was clear that this was no mere fainting spell. The physician arrived and confirmed that pneumonia had set in and there was nothing that could be done. Fr. Regis lingered until the 31st, always in prayer with his crucifix in his hands. As the day was about to end, shortly before midnight, he opened his eyes wide and with a smile on his face told Br. Bideau, who was at his side: "Brother, I see our Lord and our Lady opening the gates of Paradise for me." Then he silently uttered: "Into your hands, O Lord, I commend my spirit." Thus he passed to God.

Fr. John Francis Regis was buried on January 2, in the church of Lalouvesc, the scene of his final mission. He was beatified by Pope Clement XI on May 8, 1716, and canonized by Pope Clement XII on June 16, 1737. His memorial is celebrated on July 2.

Prayer

Lord our God, you sent out your holy priest, Saint John Francis Regis, to bring the gospel of peace to towns and villages. In our own day call many others to work in the harvest-field of your Son, who lives and reigns with you and the Holy Spirit, one God, for ever and ever.

Appendix I

General Liturgical Calendar of the Society of Jesus

1	Solemnity of Mary, Mother of God, and of the Giving of the Holy Name of Jesus. Titular Feast of the Society of Jesus	Solemnity
19	*Bl. James Salès, priest, and William Saultemouche, religious; Bl. Ignatius de Azevedo, priest, and companions; Bl. James Bonnaud, priest, and companions; Bl. Joseph Imbert and John Nicholas Cordier, priests, martyrs*	

FEBRUARY

4	St. John de Brito, priest; Bl. Rudolph Acquaviva, priest, and companions; Bl. Francis Pacheco, Charles Spinola, priests, and companions; Bl. James Berthieu, priest; Bl. Leo Mangin, priest, and companions, martyrs	Memorial
6	St. Paul Miki, religious, and companions, martyrs	Memorial
15	St. Claude La Colombière, priest	Memorial

APRIL

22	The Blessed Virgin Mary, Mother of the Society of Jesus	Feast
27	St. Peter Canisius, priest and doctor of the Church	Memorial

MAY

4	*Bl. Joseph Rubio, priest*	
16	St. Andrew Bobola, priest and martyr	Memorial

JUNE

9	*Bl. Joseph de Anchieta, priest*	
21	St. Aloysius Gonzaga, religious	Memorial

JULY

2	St. Bernardino Realino, St. Francis Regis, St. Francis Jerome, Bl. Julian Maunoir, Bl. Anthony Baldinucci, priests	Memorial
31	St. Ignatius of Loyola, priest and founder of the Society of Jesus	Solemnity

AUGUST

| 2 | *Bl. Peter Faber, priest* | |
| 18 | *Bl. Albert Hurtado Cruchaga, priest* | |

SEPTEMBER

7	Sts. Stephan Pongrácz, Melchior Grodziecki, Jesuit priests; Mark Križevčanin, canon of Estergom, martyrs	Memorial
9	St. Peter Claver, priest	Memorial
10	*Bl. Francis Gárate, religious*	
17	St. Robert Bellarmine, bishop and doctor of the Church	Memorial

OCTOBER

3	St. Francis Borgia, priest	Memorial
6	*Bl. Diego Aloysius de San Vitores, priest and martyr*	
14	St. John Ogilvie, priest and martyr	Memorial
19	Sts. John de Brébeuf and Isaac Jogues, priests, and their companions, martyrs	Memorial
30	*Bl. Dominic Collins, religious and martyr*	
31	St. Alphonsus Rodríguez, religious	Memorial

NOVEMBER

3	*Bl. Rupert Mayer, priest*	
5	All Saints and Blessed of the Society of Jesus	Feast
13	St. Stanislaus Kostka, religious	Memorial
14	St. Joseph Pignatelli, priest	Memorial
16	Sts. Roch González, John del Castillo, and Alphonsus Rodríguez, priests and martyrs	Memorial
23	*Bl. Michael Augustine Pro, priest and martyr*	
26	St. John Berchmans, religious	Memorial

DECEMBER

| 1 | Sts. Edmund Campion and Robert Southwell, priests, and their companions, martyrs | Memorial |
| 3 | St. Francis Xavier, priest | Feast |

Appendix II

Saints of the Society of Jesus [44]
According to Date of Canonization

(B=Bishop   P=Priest   S=Scholastic   C=Brother   M=Martyr)

		Date of Death	Date of Canonization	Date under which Biography appears
P.	Ignatius of Loyola	July 31, 1556	Mar. 12, 1622	July 31
P.	Francis Xavier	Dec. 3, 1552	"	Dec. 3
P.	Francis Borgia	Sept. 30, 1572	Apr. 2, 1671	Oct. 3
S.	Stanislaus Kostka	Aug. 15, 1568	Dec. 31, 1726	Nov. 13
S.	Aloysius Gonzaga	June 21, 1591	"	June 21
P.	John Francis Regis	Dec. 31, 1640	June 16, 1737	Dec. 31
P.	Francis Jerome	May 11, 1716	May 26, 1839	May 11

Martyrs of Japan

		Date of Death	Date of Canonization	Date under which Biography appears
S. M.	Paul Miki	Feb. 5, 1597	June 8, 1862	Feb. 6
S. M.	John de Goto	"	"	"
C. M.	James Kisai	"	"	"
C.	Alphonsus Rodríguez	Oct. 31, 1617	Jan. 15, 1888	Oct. 31
S.	John Berchmans	Aug. 13, 1621	"	Nov. 26
P.	Peter Claver	Sept. 8, 1654	"	Sept. 9
P.	Peter Canisius	Dec. 21, 1597	May 21, 1925	Apr. 27
B.	Robert Bellarmine	Sept. 17, 1621	June 29, 1930	Sept. 17

Martyrs of North America

		Date of Death	Date of Canonization	Date under which Biography appears
C. M.	René Goupil	Sept. 29, 1642	June 29, 1930	Sept. 29
P. M.	Isaac Jogues	Oct. 18, 1646	"	Oct. 19
C. M.	John de La Lande	Oct. 19, 1646	"	"
P. M.	Anthony Daniel	July 4, 1648	"	July 4
P. M.	John de Brébeuf	Mar. 16, 1649	"	Mar. 16
P. M.	Gabriel Lalemant	Mar. 17, 1649	"	Mar. 17
P. M.	Charles Garnier	Dec. 7, 1649	"	Dec. 7
P. M.	Noel Chabanel	Dec. 8, 1649	"	Dec. 8
P. M.	Andrew Bobola	May 16, 1657	Apr. 17, 1938	May 16
P.	Bernardino Realino	July 2, 1616	June 22, 1947	July 2
P. M.	John de Brito	Feb. 4, 1693	"	Feb. 4
P.	Joseph Pignatelli	Nov. 15, 1811	June 12, 1954	Nov. 14

		Date of *Death*	*Date of* *Canonization*	*Date under which* *Biography appears*
Martyrs of England and Wales				
P. M.	Alexander Briant	Dec. 1, 1581	Oct. 25, 1970	Dec. 2
P. M.	Edmund Campion	"	"	Dec. 1
P. M.	Robert Southwell	Feb. 21, 1595	"	Feb. 21
P. M.	Henry Walpole	Apr. 7, 1595	"	Apr. 7
C. M.	Nicholas Owen	Mar. 2, 1606	"	Mar. 2
P. M.	Thomas Garnet	June 23, 1608	"	June 23
P. M.	Edmund Arrowsmith	Aug. 28, 1628	"	Aug. 28
P. M.	Henry Morse	Feb. 1, 1645	"	Feb. 1
P. M.	Philip Evans	July 22, 1679	"	July 22
P. M.	David Lewis	Aug. 27, 1679	"	Aug. 27
P. M.	John Ogilvie	Mar. 10, 1615	Oct. 17, 1976	Oct. 14
Martyrs of River Plate				
P. M.	Roch González	Nov. 15, 1628	May 16, 1988	Nov. 15
P. M.	Alphonsus Rodríguez	"	"	Nov. 16
P. M.	John del Castillo	Nov. 17, 1628	"	Nov. 17
P.	Claude La Colombière	Feb. 15, 1682	May 31, 1992	Feb. 15
Martyrs of Košice				
P. M.	Melchior Grodziecki	Sept. 7, 1619	July 2, 1995	Sept. 7
P. M.	Stephan Pongrácz	Sept. 8, 1619	"	"

44 Saints = 15 Confessors and 29 Martyrs
= 1 Bishop, 33 Priests, 5 Scholastics, 5 Brothers

Appendix III

Blessed of the Society of Jesus [140]
According to Date of Brief of Beatification

(B=Bishop   P=Priest   S=Scholastic   C=Brother   M=Martyr)

		Date of Death	Date of Decree of Beatification	Date under which Biography appears
Martyrs of Brazil				
P. M.	Ignatius de Azevedo	July 15, 1570	May 11, 1854	July 15
P. M.	James de Andrade	,,	,,	,,
C. M.	Francis Álvares	,,	,,	,,
C. M.	Gaspar Álvares	,,	,,	,,
C. M.	Manuel Álvares	,,	,,	,,
C. M.	Alphonsus de Baena	,,	,,	,,
S. M.	Álvaro Borralho (Mendes)	,,	,,	,,
C. M.	Mark Caldeira	,,	,,	,,
S. M.	Bento de Castro	,,	,,	,,
S. M.	Anthony Correia	,,	,,	,,
S. M.	Louis Correia	,,	,,	,,
S. M.	Alexis Delgado	,,	,,	,,
S. M.	Nicholas Dinis	,,	,,	,,
C. M.	Gregory Escribano	,,	,,	,,
C. M.	Anthony Fernandes	,,	,,	,,
C. M.	Dominic Fernandes	,,	,,	,,
S. M.	John Fernandes [I]	,,	,,	,,
S. M.	John Fernandes [II]	,,	,,	,,
S. M.	Manuel Fernandes	,,	,,	,,
C. M.	Peter Fontoura	,,	,,	,,
S. M.	Andrew Gonçalves	,,	,,	,,
S. M.	Gonçalo Henriques	,,	,,	,,
S. M.	Simon Lopes	,,	,,	,,
S. M.	Francis de Magalhães	,,	,,	,,
C. M.	John de Mayorga	,,	,,	,,
S. M.	James (Pires) Mimoso	,,	,,	,,
S. M.	Peter Nunes	,,	,,	,,
S. M.	Manuel Pacheco	,,	,,	,,
S. M.	Francis Pérez Godoy	,,	,,	,,
C. M.	Bras Ribeiro	,,	,,	,,
S. M.	Louis Rodrigues	,,	,,	,,
S. M.	Manuel Rodrigues	,,	,,	,,
S. M.	Ferdinand Sánchez	,,	,,	,,
S. M.	John de San Martín	,,	,,	,,
S. M.	Anthony Soares	,,	,,	,,

		Date of Death	Date of Decree of Beatification	Date under which Biography appears
C. M.	Amaro Vaz	"	"	"
C. M.	John de Zafra	"	"	"
C. M.	Stephen Zuraire	"	"	"
M.	John (candidate)	"	"	"
C. M.	Simon da Costa	July 16, 1570	"	"

Martyrs of Japan

		Date of Death	Date of Decree of Beatification	Date under which Biography appears
P. M.	Charles Spinola	Sept. 10, 1622	May 7, 1867	Sept. 11
P. M.	Francis Pacheco	June 20, 1626	"	June 20
P. M.	John Baptist Machado	May 22, 1617	"	May 22
C. M.	Leonard Kimura	Nov. 18, 1619	"	Nov. 18
C. M.	Ambrose Fernandes	Jan. 7, 1620	"	Sept. 11
C. M.	Augustine Ota	Aug. 10, 1622	"	Sept. 15
S. M.	Thomas Akahoshi	Sept. 10, 1622	"	Sept. 11
S. M.	Gonzalo Fusai	"	"	"
S. M.	Louis Kawara	"	"	"
P. M.	Sebastian Kimura	"	"	"
S. M.	John Chugoku	"	"	"
S. M.	Anthony Kyuni	"	"	"
S. M.	Peter Sampo	"	"	"
S. M.	Michael Shumpo	"	"	"
P. M.	Camillus Costanzo	Sept. 15, 1622	"	Sept. 15
C. M.	Dennis Fujishima	Nov. 1, 1622	"	Nov. 1
P. M.	Peter Paul Navarro	"	"	"
C. M.	Peter Onizuka	"	"	"
P. M.	Jerome De Angelis	Dec. 4, 1623	"	Dec. 4
C. M.	Simon Yempo	"	"	"
P. M.	James Carvalho	Feb. 22, 1624	"	Feb. 22
P. M.	Michael Carvalho	Aug. 25, 1624	"	Aug. 25
S. M.	Gaius	Nov. 15, 1624	"	Nov. 12
C. M.	Vincent Kaun	June 20, 1626	"	June 20
C. M.	John Kisaku	"	"	"
C. M.	Peter Kinsei	"	"	"
C. M.	Paul Kinsuke	"	"	"
C. M.	Gaspar Sadamatsu	"	"	"
P. M.	Balthasar de Torres	"	"	"
C. M.	Michael Tozo	"	"	"
P. M.	John Baptist Zola	"	"	"
P. M.	Thomas Tsuji	Sept. 7, 1627	"	Sept. 5
C. M.	Michael Nakashima	Dec. 25, 1628	"	Dec. 25
P. M.	Anthony Ishida	Sept. 3, 1632	"	Sept. 4
P.	Peter Favre	Aug. 1, 1546	Sept. 5, 1872	Aug. 2

		Date of Death	Date of Decree of Beatification	Date under which Biography appears
Martyrs of England				
P. M.	Thomas Woodhouse	June 19, 1573	Dec. 9, 1886	June 22
P. M.	John Nelson	Feb. 3, 1578	"	Feb. 3
P. M.	Thomas Cottam	May 30, 1582	"	May 30
P.	Anthony Baldinucci	Nov. 7, 1717	Mar. 25, 1893	Nov. 7
Martyrs of Salsette				
P. M.	Rudolph Acquaviva	July 25, 1583	Apr. 2, 1893	July 25
C. M.	Francis Aranha	"	"	July 26
P. M.	Peter Berno	"	"	"
P. M.	Anthony Francisco	"	"	July 27
P. M.	Alphonsus Pacheco	"	"	"
Martyrs of Aubenas				
P. M.	James Salès	Feb. 7, 1593	June 6, 1926	Jan. 19
C. M.	William Saultemouche	"	"	"
Martyrs of French Revolution				
P. M.	James Bonnaud	Sept. 2, 1792	Oct. 17, 1926	Sept. 2
P. M.	Francis Balmain	"	"	"
P. M.	Charles Bérauld du Pérou	"	"	"
P. M.	Claude Cayx-Dumas	"	"	"
P. M.	John Charton de Millou	"	"	"
P. M.	William Delfaud	"	"	"
P. M.	James Friteyre-Durvé	"	"	"
P. M.	Claude Gagnières des Granges	"	"	"
P. M.	Claude Laporte	"	"	"
P. M.	Mathurin Le Bous de Villeneuve	"	"	"
P. M.	Charles Le Gué	"	"	"
P. M.	Vincent Le Rousseau	"	"	"
P. M.	Loup Thomas-Bonnotte	"	"	"
P. M.	Francis Vareilhe-Duteil	"	"	"
P. M.	René Andrieux	Sept. 3, 1792	"	Sept. 3
P. M.	John Benoît-Vourlat	"	"	"
P. M.	Peter Guérin du Rocher	"	"	"
P. M.	Robert Guérin du Rocher	"	"	"
P. M.	Elias Herque du Roule	"	"	"
P. M.	John Seconds	"	"	"
P. M.	Nicholas Verron	"	"	"
P. M.	Francis Le Livec	Sept. 4, 1792	"	"
P. M.	Alexander Lanfant	Sept. 5, 1792	"	"

		Date of Death	Date of Decree of Beatification	Date under which Biography appears
Martyrs of England				
P. M.	John Cornelius	July 4, 1594	Dec. 15, 1929	July 3
P. M.	Francis Page	Apr. 20, 1602	"	Apr. 20
C. M.	Ralph Ashley	Apr. 7, 1606	"	Apr. 9
P. M.	Edward Oldcorne	"	"	Apr. 8
P. M.	Thomas Holland	Dec. 12, 1642	"	Dec. 12
P. M.	Ralph Corby	Sept. 7, 1644	"	Sept. 6
P. M.	Peter Wright	May 19, 1651	"	May 19
P. M.	William Ireland	Jan. 24, 1679	"	Jan. 24
P. M.	John Fenwick	June 20, 1679	"	June 18
P. M.	John Gavan	"	"	June 19
P. M.	William Harcourt	"	"	"
P. M.	Anthony Turner	"	"	"
P. M.	Thomas Whitbread	"	"	June 18
P.	Julian Maunoir	Jan. 28, 1683	May 20, 1951	Jan. 28
Martyrs of the Boxer Rebellion				
P. M.	Modeste Andlauer	June 19, 1900	Apr. 17, 1955	June 17
P. M.	Rémy Isoré	"	"	"
P. M.	Paul Denn	July 20, 1900	"	July 20
P. M.	Leo Ignatius Mangin	"	"	"
P. M.	James Berthieu	June 8, 1896	Oct. 17, 1965	June 8
P.	Joseph de Anchieta	June 9, 1597	June 22, 1980	June 9
C.	Francis Gárate	Sept. 9, 1929	Oct. 6, 1985	Sept. 10
P.	Joseph Mary Rubio	May 2, 1929	"	May 4
P. M.	Diego Aloysius de San Vitores	Apr. 2, 1672	"	Oct. 6
P.	Rupert Mayer	Nov. 1, 1945	Nov. 3, 1987	Nov. 3
Martyrs of England				
P. M.	Roger Filcock	Feb. 27, 1601	Nov. 22, 1987	Feb. 27
P. M.	Robert Middleton	Apr. 3, 1601	"	Apr. 3
P. M.	Michael Pro	Nov. 23, 1927	Sept. 25, 1988	Nov. 23
C. M.	Dominic Collins	Oct. 31, 1602	Sept. 27, 1992	Oct. 30
P.	Albert Hurtado Cruchaga	Aug. 18, 1952	Oct. 16, 1994	Aug. 18
Martyrs of the Rochefort Prison Ships				
P. M.	Joseph Imbert	June 9, 1794	Oct. 1, 1995	June 10
P. M.	John Nicholas Cordier	Sept. 30, 1794	"	"

140 Blessed = 8 Confessors, 132 Martyrs
         = 76 Priests, 30 Scholastics, 33 Brothers, 1 Candidate

Appendix IV

Venerables of the Society of Jesus [36]
According to Date of Death

(B=Bishop   P=Priest   S=Scholastic   C=Brother   M=Martyr)

		Date of Death	Date under which Biography appears
P. M.	Peter Dias [I]	Sept. 13, 1571	Sept. 13
P. M.	Francis de Castro	"	"
S. M.	Michael Aragonéz	"	"
S. M.	Gaspar Góes	"	"
C. M.	Francis Paulo	"	"
C. M.	Ferdinand Álvares	Sept. 14, 1571	"
S. M.	John Álvares	"	"
C. M.	James de Carvalho	"	"
S. M.	Peter Dias [II]	"	"
S. M.	Alphonsus Fernandes	"	"
C. M.	Peter Fernandes	"	"
S. M.	Andrew Paes	"	"
B.	Andrew de Oviedo	June 29–July 9, 1577	June 29
P. M.	Abraham de Georgiis	Apr. 30, 1595	Apr. 30
P.	Louis de La Puente	Feb. 16, 1624	Feb. 16
P. M.	Gaspar Pais	Apr. 25, 1635	Apr. 25
P. M.	John Pereira	May 2, 1635	"
B. M.	Apollinaris de Almeida	June 9–15, 1638	June 15
P. M.	Hyacinth Franceschi	"	"
P. M.	Francis Rodrigues	"	"
P. M.	Bruno Bruni	Apr. 12, 1640	Apr. 12
P. M.	Louis Cardeira	"	"
P.	Brian Cansfield	Aug. 3, 1645	Aug. 3
P.	Aloysius La Nuza	Oct. 21, 1656	Oct. 21
P.	Francis del Castillo	Apr. 11, 1673	Apr. 11
P.	Edward Mico	Nov. 24, 1678	Nov. 24
P.	Thomas Bedingfeld	Dec. 21, 1678	Dec. 21
P.	Francis Nevill	Feb. end 1679	Feb. 25
P.	Philip Jeningen	Feb. 8, 1704	Feb. 8
P.	Emmanuel Padial	Apr. 28, 1725	Apr. 28
P.	Bernard Francis de Hoyos	Nov. 29, 1735	Nov. 29
P.	Aloysius Mary Solari	Aug. 27, 1829	Aug. 26
P.	Paul Anthony Capelloni	Oct. 13, 1857	Oct. 13
P.	Francis de Paola Tarín	Dec. 12, 1910	Dec. 13
P.	Adolph Petit	May 20, 1914	May 20
P.	John Beyzym	Oct. 2, 1912	Oct. 2

36 Venerables = 16 Confessors and 20 Martyrs
            = 2 Bishops, 24 Priests, 6 Scholastics, 4 Brothers

Appendix V

Servants of God of the Society of Jesus [127]
According to Date of Death

(B=Bishop P=Priest S=Scholastic C=Brother M=Martyr)

		Date of Death	*Date under which Biography Appears*
P. M.	Anthony Criminali	May 1549	May 28
P. M.	Gonçalo da Silveira	Mar. 15, 1561	Mar. 14
S.	Francis Gaetano	Apr. 20, 1601	Apr. 19
P.	Matthew Ricci	May 11, 1610	May 12
P. M.	Horace Vecchi	Dec. 14, 1612	Dec. 14
P. M.	Martin de Aranda	"	"
C. M.	James de Montalbán	"	"
P	James de Mesquita	Nov. 4, 1614	Nov. 6
P.	Anthony de Critana	Nov. 24, 1614	"
P.	John Cardim	Feb. 18, 1615	Feb. 18
P. M.	Hernando de Tovar	Nov. 16, 1616	Nov. 20
P. M.	Louis de Alavés	Nov. 18, 1616	"
P. M.	Bernard de Cisneros	"	"
P. M.	James de Orozco	"	"
P. M.	John del Valle	"	"
P. M.	John Fonte	Nov. 19, 1616	"
P. M.	Jerome de Moranta	"	"
P. M.	Hernando de Santarén	Nov. 20, 1616	"
P.	James Rem	Oct. 12, 1618	Oct. 12
P.	Gaspar de Crasto	May 7, 1626	Nov. 6
P.	John Baptist Baeza	"	"
P.	Matthew de Couros	Oct. 29, 1633	"
P. M.	Sebastian Vieira	June 6, 1634	June 6
P.	Stephen Le Fèvre	May 10, 1657	May 10
P.	John Peter Medaille	Dec. 30, 1669	Dec. 30
P.	Peter Joseph Mary Chaumonot	Feb. 21, 1693	Feb. 20
P.	Eusebio Francisco Kino	Mar. 15, 1711	Mar. 15
P. M.	John Baptist Messari	June 25–23, 1723	Oct. 11
P. M.	Francis Mary Bucherelli	Oct. 11, 1723	"
P.	Francis Mary Galluzzi	Sept. 7, 1731	Sept. 14
P. M.	Bartholomew Álvares	Jan. 12, 1737	Jan. 12
P. M.	Emmanuel de Abreu	"	"
P. M.	Vincent da Cunha	"	"
P. M.	John Caspar Kratz	"	"
P.	Peter John Cayron	Jan. 31, 1754	Jan. 31
P.	Peter Mayoral	Dec. 9, 1754	Dec. 10
P.	Peter Joseph de Clorivière	Jan. 9, 1820	Jan. 9

		Date of Death	*Date under which Biography Appears*
B.	Charles Odescalchi	Aug. 17, 1841	Aug. 17
P.	John Philip Roothaan	May 8, 1853	May 8
P. M.	Edward Billotet	June 18, 1860	June 16
C. M.	Ferdinand Bonacina	″	″
C. M.	Habib Maksoud	″	″
C. M.	Elias Younès	″	″
M.	Cherfân Habeiche	″	″
C. M.	Haïdar Habeiche	June 21, 1860	″
P. M.	Alexis Clerc	May 24, 1871	May 25
P. M.	Leo Ducoudray	″	″
P. M.	Anatole de Bengy	May 26, 1871	May 26
P. M.	John Caubert	″	″
P. M.	Peter Olivaint	″	″
P.	Paul Ginhac	Jan. 10, 1895	Jan. 10
S.	Peter Barbarić	Apr. 15, 1897	Apr. 15
P.	Louis Stephen Rabussier	Dec. 9, 1897	Dec. 9
P.	Richard Friedl	Feb. 27, 1917	Feb. 26
P.	William Eberschweiler	Dec. 23, 1921	Dec. 23
P.	Adalbert Mary Baudiss	Apr. 25, 1926	Apr. 24
P.	Saturninus Ibarguren	Feb. 9, 1927	Feb. 9
P.	Salvador Garcidueñas	Oct. 4, 1927	Oct. 4
P.	Anthony Repiso Martínez	July 27, 1929	July 28
P.	Hyacinth Alegre	Dec. 10, 1930	Dec. 11
P.	John Sullivan	Feb. 19, 1933	Feb. 19
P.	Thomas Esteban	1934	Jan. 30
P. M.	Emile Martínez	Oct. 7, 1934	Oct. 7
C. M.	John Baptist Arconada	″	″
P.	Ignatius Arámburu	Jan. 5, 1935	Jan. 5
S.	Stephen Kaszap	Dec. 17, 1935	Dec. 17
P. M.	Raymond Artigues	July 20, 1936	July 19
P. M.	Felix Cots	July 21, 1936	Nov. 28
C. M.	Philip Iriondo	″	″
P. M.	Joseph Romá	″	″
C. M.	Lawrence Isla	July 25, 1936	July 24
P. M.	Braulio Martínez	″	″
P. M.	Emmanuel Peypoch	July 29, 1936	July 29
C. M.	Ignatius Elduayen	Aug. 7, 1936	Sept. 24
C. M.	Pascual Ruiz	″	″
P. M.	Jesús Ballesta	Aug. 8, 1936	″
P. M.	Louis Boguñá	Aug. 14, 1936	Aug. 14
P. M.	Joachim Valentí	″	″
P. M.	Joseph Vergés	″	″
P. M.	Thomas Sitjar	Aug. 19, 1936	Aug. 19
P. M.	Constantine Carbonell	Aug. 23, 1936	″
C. M.	Peter Gelabert	″	″
C. M.	Raymond Grimaltos	″	″

		Date of Death	*Date under which Biography Appears*
P. M.	Andrew Carrió	Aug. 26, 1936	Aug. 24
P. M.	Martin Santaella	"	Aug. 23
P. M.	Francis Xavier Tena	"	Nov. 28
C. M.	Joseph Sampol	Aug. 27, 1936	"
P. M.	Emmanuel Luque	Aug. 31, 1936	Aug. 23
P. M.	Alphonsus Payán	"	"
P. M.	Michael Mendoza	Sept. 1, 1936	Nov. 28
C. M.	Joseph Llatje	Sept. 5, 1936	Nov. 4
P. M.	Emmanuel González	Sept. 8, 1936	Sept. 12
C. M.	Dominic Ibarlucea	"	"
P. M.	Richard Tena	"	Sept. 8
P. M.	Joseph Sánchez	Sept. 9, 1936	Sept. 12
C. M.	Anthony Sanchiz	"	"
P. M.	Ignatius de Velasco	Sept. 24, 1936	Sept. 24
C. M.	Joseph Tarrats	Sept. 28, 1936	Aug. 19
P. M.	Paul Bori	Sept. 29, 1936	"
P. M.	Darius Hernández	"	"
C. M.	Vincent Sales	"	"
P. M.	John Gómez Hellín	Oct. 2, 1936	Sept. 24
P. M.	Narcissus Basté	Oct. 15, 1936	Aug. 19
P. M.	Martial Mayorga	"	Dec. 28
P. M.	Joseph Muñoz	"	Nov. 28
P. M.	Demetrius Zurbitu	Oct. 20, 1936	"
P. M.	Francis Audí	Nov. 3, 1936	Nov. 4
P. M.	John Rovira	"	"
P. M.	Joseph Alegre	Nov. 10, 1936	Sept. 24
P. M.	Bartholomew Arbona	Nov. 29, 1936	Nov. 28
P. M.	Alfred Simón	"	Aug. 19
P. M.	Emmanuel de La Cerda	Dec. 4, 1936	Sept. 24
P. M.	Olegario Corral	Dec. 28, 1936	Dec. 28
P. M.	John Baptist Ferreres	Dec. 29, 1936	Aug. 19
P. M.	James Noguera	Feb. 14, 1937	Nov. 8
C. M.	Constantine March	Mar. 26, 1937	"
P.	Ferdinand de Huidobro	Apr. 11, 1937	Apr. 10
C.	Joseph Mark Figueroa	Nov. 19, 1942	Nov. 19
P.	Joseph Picco	Aug. 31, 1946	Aug. 31
P.	John Baptist Reus	July 21, 1947	July 21
P.	Francis Rodrigues da Cruz	Oct. 1, 1948	Oct. 1
P.	Igino Lega	Mar. 21, 1951	Mar. 21
P.	Jacques Sevin	July 19, 1951	July 18
P.	Felix Cappello	Mar. 25, 1962	Mar. 25
P.	Emmanuel García Nieto	Apr. 13, 1974	Apr. 13
P.	Walter Ciszek	Dec. 8, 1984	Dec. 6
P.	Pedro Arrupe	Feb. 5, 1991	Feb. 5

127 Servants of God = 44 Confessors and 83 Martyrs

= 1 Bishop, 102 Priests, 3 Scholastics, 20 Brothers, 1 Candidate

Index

Bold type indicates the full biography;
other occurrences of the name follow.

Credits for Engravings:

Engravings on pp. 57, 158, 183, 203, 222, 291, 300, 364, and 417 are from Mathias Tanner, *Societas Jesu usque ad sanguinis et vitae profusionem militans* . . . (Prague, 1675). Those on the cover, frontispiece, pp. 117, 234, 242, 315, and 331 are from Tanner, *Societas Jesu apostolorum imitatrix* . . . (Prague, 1694). C. Screta was the artist and Melchior Küssel was the engraver for both volumes. Engravings were reproduced from copies in Loyola University Chicago Archives, Rare Book Collection, E. M. Cudahy Library.